Black Knights

Black Knights

ARABIC EPIC AND THE MAKING OF MEDIEVAL RACE

Rachel Schine

The University of Chicago Press CHICAGO AND LONDON

PUBLICATION OF THIS BOOK HAS BEEN AIDED
BY A GRANT FROM THE BEVINGTON FUND.

The University of Chicago Press, Chicago 60637
The University of Chicago Press, Ltd., London

Published 2024
Printed in the United States of America

33 32 31 30 29 28 27 26 25 24 1 2 3 4 5

ISBN-13: 978-0-226-83616-4 (cloth)
ISBN-13: 978-0-226-83617-1 (paper)
ISBN-13: 978-0-226-83618-8 (e-book)
DOI: https://doi.org/10.7208/chicago/9780226836188.001.0001

Publication of this book has been aided by a grant from the Bevington Fund.

Library of Congress Cataloging-in-Publication Data

Names: Schine, Rachel, author.
Title: Black knights : Arabic epic and the making of medieval race / Rachel Schine.
Other titles: Arabic epic and the making of medieval race
Description: Chicago : The University of Chicago Press, 2024. | Includes bibliographical references and index.
Identifiers: LCCN 2024009315 | ISBN 9780226836164 (cloth) | ISBN 9780226836171 (paperback) | ISBN 9780226836188 (ebook)
Subjects: LCSH: Arabic literature—750–1258—History and criticism. | Epic literature, Arabic—History and criticism. | Race in literature. | Black people in literature. | Heroes in literature.
Classification: LCC PJ7529 .S35 2024 | DDC 892.7/134—dc23/eng/20240305
LC record available at https://lccn.loc.gov/2024009315

⊗ This paper meets the requirements of ANSI/NISO Z39.48-1992 (Permanence of Paper).

Contents

Introduction * 1

Part One: Making Race

1. Origin Stories of the Black-Arab Hero * 39
2. Conceiving ʿAbd al-Wahhāb * 81
3. The (Popular) Science of Difference * 117

Part Two: Race through Time

4. The Past * 161
5. The Present * 189

Part Three: Race through Space

6. Venturing Abroad * 229
7. Returning Home * 273

Conclusion * 313

Acknowledgments 323
Appendix 327
Bibliography 331
Index 355

Introduction

> A racial imaginary is . . . the way our culture has imagined over and over again the narrative opportunities, the kinds of feelings and attributes and situations and subjects and plots and forms "available" both to characters of different races and their authors.
>
> CLAUDIA RANKINE AND BETH LOFFREDA

> The media play a part in the formation, in the constitution, of the things that they reflect. It is not that there is a world outside, "out there," which exists free of the discourses of representation. . . . The reality of race in any society is, to coin a phrase, "media-mediated."
>
> STUART HALL

> And this Black boy will be met with wondrous events and strange affairs, which we shall mention in due time, if God Almighty wills.
>
> SĪRAT DHĀT AL-HIMMA

Like his father before him—chief of the Arabian tribe of Kilāb—Junduba was born to be a hero. Like many a hero, though, he was separated from his family at birth and does not yet know his own destiny. He has trained for years under the chief of a rival tribe and is now ready to strike out on his own. One day, he rides into battle against an older woman, Shamṭā (the Gray-Haired One), and kills her in mounted combat, a feat at which many had tried and failed. Shamṭā's legion of forty soldiers look on, shocked, then approach him to do battle in her name. Junduba repels them all. Soon after, our hero delivers an impassioned address:

> "Woe to you! What a sight this is, look what you've done! Are you not men of intelligence [*rijāl aṣḥāb ʿuqūl*]? I have killed Shamṭā for your sakes, for you are lions bold [*usūd wa-shujʿān*], yet you were serving an old woman

of no power and no consequence [*ʿajūz lā qadr li-hā wa-lā shaʾn*]. I did this to her because of what she has done to [other] men—she left no general with his head intact. I did not fight you for wealth, for I haven't have taken a single share from you [*lam ākhudh minhu ʿiqāl*]." Having witnessed what he had done, when the men heard his speech, they glanced at one another and said, "He's onto something [*wallāhi al-ṣawāb alladhī qālahu*]." They repeated his words among themselves, then intoned, "By the greatest God, this prince has spoken rightly." They inclined toward him and replied, "Do as you wish, for we are slaves to you [*naḥnu lik min jumlat al-ʿabīd*]."[1]

Junduba then seals their agreement with poetry, saying:

Sons of Ḥām, come heed my words
And take the favors [*fuḍūl*] I can proffer,
Don't seek slaying me today:
With blade and shackle I'll counteroffer [*fa-yanbaghīkum ḥusāmī maʿ kubūlī*]!
Your tribe is of Ḥām, son of Nūḥ
Riders on choice horses, all
I can't stand seeing you debased,
In some anklet-wearer's thrall
Doing bidding for an evil crone,
Brought up in her husband's care
Shame on you for serving her
—Mighty lions, champions fair [*usd fuḥūl*]!
I've replaced her many subjects
With a dread day of devastation
So, Hamites, become my comrades [*ʿaṣabatī*]
Enjoy esteem [*ʿizz*] and warm reception [*qubūl*]
I'll give you her captured fortress
You'll thank me now, and soon see why! [*fa-mannaw bi-l-riḍā thumm qubūl*]
Go before me there in battle
Lances drawn, and spears held high[2]

1. *Sīrat Dhāt al-Himma*, I:18. The language of the epics is in a Middle Arabic register. Some grammatical inconsistencies are commonplace. I have transliterated the Arabic throughout pausally, except in instances where final short vowels are necessary to discern the meaning, avoid awkwardness, complete a classical construction, or indicate an attached pronoun.

2. *Sīrat Dhāt al-Himma*, I:19.

The first martial act of the first hero in the *Tale of the Princess, Possessor of Ambition*, or *Sīrat al-Amīra Dhāt al-Himma*—the longest epic in the Arabic language, a multigenerational romp that reimagines two centuries of frontier warfare between Muslim armies and the Byzantines—is one that restores the social balance of his world. Rather than being left as free radicals after Shamṭā's demise, a league of Black soldiers whom the text vacillates between referring to as "knights" (*fursān*) and "slaves" (*ʿabīd*) and whom different editions of the tale characterize irresolutely as "of [Shamṭā's] people" (*qawmihā*) or "of her army" (*jundihā*), is persuaded instead to serve another master.[3] The success of Junduba's references to procuring the men rank and station, despite their already being "champions" (*fuḥūl*), as well as his offer of a fortress and booty that they may well have taken themselves, suggests that the men regard subsuming their autonomy to an Arab general to be a protective measure: a band of Black men raiding independently will not be able to accrue social capital, and, even worse, may arouse suspicion, draw fire, or be vulnerable to exploitation.

Perhaps the men can hear the duality in Junduba's overtures to their virility, which also whisper of their precariousness. To be sure, Junduba appeals to the Black soldiers as men and foments outrage at their serving under a woman who had felled so many of their gender. But in appealing to the group as *fuḥūl*, "champions" or "stallions," Junduba also draws attention to the fact that these bound men have been kept intact; *fuḥūl* is a term used for uncastrated slaves and freedmen.[4] As with the texts' uncertainty about whether these men are mighty knights who share a sense of peoplehood with their Arab peers or an enslaved collection of troops brought together solely for that purpose, their bodies are poised between promise and threat.

Also ambivalent is Junduba's manner of addressing the men's lineage—"Children of Ḥām, son of Nūḥ." This nomenclature refers to the belief, popular at the time, that all of mankind is descended from one of Nūḥ's (Noah) three sons, and that Ḥām (Ham) in particular has fathered all Black people. Many also believe that this is because Ḥām was cursed

3. Though the above-cited edition of the *sīra* uses *qawm*, BNF MS Arabe 3840 uses *jund*. BNF MS Arabe 3840, fol. 10v.

4. This distinction may also be pertinent to why the lineal and racialized origins of Shamṭā's militia are so heavily emphasized. Shaun Marmon notes that by the Mamluk period it had largely become conventional to designate *fuḥūl* by their "(perceived) ethnicity and/or skin color," while their enslaved eunuch counterparts were primarily defined "in terms of their eunuchness." Shaun Marmon, *Eunuchs and Sacred Boundaries in Islamic Society* (Oxford: Oxford University Press, 1995), 133n103.

following an encounter with his father while the latter was naked and drunk (though in Islamic renderings, he is usually simply asleep), and his progeny were darkened and bound in eternal servitude to his siblings, Sām (Shem) and Yāfit (Japheth). Though the consequence of blackness is not mentioned in the Hebrew Bible, in which the original curse story occurs, by the medieval period the conflation between Ḥām's blackness and his slavery was embedded in Jewish, Christian, and Muslim apocrypha.[5] Junduba does not reference the curse directly, though—as in so many Arabic texts, though he subscribes to Noahic genealogy, he does not necessarily subscribe to this supposed reason for the "Hamites" becoming Black.[6] We may even read his reference to Ḥām's father, Nūḥ, as allusively plaiting the genealogies of the Black men together with that of their Arab-Muslim would-be commander, whose people descend from Sām and who venerate Nūḥ as a prophet.

Then there is the subtle paronomasia that stitches together Junduba's many references to lions (*usūd, usd,* sg. *asad*), a common term in Arabic for fighters of high acumen, and the black (*aswad*) color of the men with which *usūd* is homographic. As with their manliness and lineage, overtures to their leonine mettle draw the Black men into relation with Junduba—a powerful warrior who is said to have withstood Shamṭā's troops "with the fortitude of lions [*thibāt al-usūd*]"—while also reinforcing their difference. Even when praised, the men are not having a discourse of equals with their new leader, who we have been told from the moment of his birth resembles a moon, or a moon-chunk come to earth (*filqat al-qamr*), in beauty and perfection. Instead, Junduba gestures to their relatively disfavored identity and offers to better their lot through service to him and through conducting their raiding at his bidding. Otherwise, he will cut them down with the sword (*ḥusām*) and (re-)chain them in fetters (*kubūl*). Despite these grandiose threats, Junduba also treats this as a moment of negotiation, offering the men not only abstract abundance through their rank and station, but also an entire fortress (*ḥiṣn*) belonging to their former commander. One sees an echo here of a dynamic that Hussein Fancy has noted elsewhere of the exchange of mercenary services for lavish gifts. Rulers know that swords for hire across a cultural divide come with other costs, and "charismatic" gift-giving that enables their self-sufficiency, as

5. Genesis 9:20–27

6. Haroon Bashir notes several instances in which medieval Muslim authors affirm Noahic genealogies while rejecting the specifics of the "curse of Ḥām" narrative. Haroon Bashir, "Black Excellence and the Curse of Ham: Debating Race and Slavery in the Islamic Tradition," *ReOrient* 5 (2019): 92–116.

with a castle outpost, may reveal a desire to isolate people as much as to elevate them.[7]

Little can Junduba know that three generations later, the social balance that he has so cannily restored will tip once again, but this time because of his own descendants. To Junduba's grandson, Maẓlūm, there will be born a girl named Fāṭima. She will go by many other names as well, though, from the Fiend of the Banū Ṭayy—a rival tribe by whom she is captured in childhood—to the Possessor of Ambition (*Dhāt al-Himma*), a nom de guerre that will also become part of her epic's title, making hers the only Arabic epic named for a woman. Like Shamṭā, Fāṭima will continue to fight and oversee vast armies well into her old age, a detail her adversaries often remark upon. She does so alongside her son, ʿAbd al-Wahhāb, a Black child whose unexpected color and, indeed, whose inclinations in his very soul lead him to affiliate strongly throughout his life with the so-called sons of Ḥām that Junduba brings under his generalship.

As generations progress and these astonishing new forms of heroes arise, the ambit of *Sīrat Dhāt al-Himma*, also known as *Sīrat al-Mujāhidīn* (*The Tale of the Pious Warriors*), likewise spirals outward. The plot moves from internecine conflicts between the north Arabian tribes of Sulaym and Kilāb, each instrumental to conquering the Levant, to their joint battles against Byzantine Christians (*al-Rūm*) in Anatolia and, in particular, against a villainous Muslim judge (*qāḍī*) turned crypto-Christian spy named ʿUqba and his muscle-bound and clever Byzantine accomplice, Shūmdaris. Because of this backstory, Claudia Ott traces the text's likely origins to the twelfth century and the end of Mirdasid rule in Syria; the dynasty traced their origins to the tribe of Kilāb.[8]

Sīrat Dhāt al-Himma's cosmic conflict between Islam and Christianity persists far beyond the historic sites of seventh- to ninth-century Arab-Byzantine warfare, and the protagonists of the epic find themselves in a variety of Mediterranean islands, Persian territories and, importantly for the present study, East African environs. The text's three central heroes, ʿAbd al-Wahhāb, his mother Fāṭima, and their lifelong companion al-Baṭṭāl, typify the three central military archetypes of the work—ʿAbd al-Wahhāb is Black, Fāṭima a highborn Arab, and al-Baṭṭāl, of the rival tribe of Sulaym, is unusually pale and blonde, can pass for Byzantine, and often keeps company with servants and military slaves from the Caucasus.

7. Hussein Fancy, *The Mercenary Mediterranean: Sovereignty, Religion, and Violence in the Medieval Crown of Aragon* (Chicago: University of Chicago Press, 2016), 64–65.

8. Claudia Ott, *Metamorphosen des Epos: Sirat al-Mugahidin (Sirat al-Amira Dat al-Himma) zwischen Mündlichkeit und Schriftlichkeit* (Leiden: Universiteit Leiden, 2003).

As often happens, these identities are mutable across cultures, and in the Ottoman Turkish iteration of these tales, al-Baṭṭāl becomes Baṭṭāl Ghāzī, a Turkic warrior par excellence and the story's central protagonist.[9] Each of these figures is thus primed as a go-between across their tale's overlapping frontiers. But ʿAbd al-Wahhāb is also just one of a legion of people, raced as Black, who contribute to the Arab Muslims' success throughout the work, as intimated by the story of Junduba's mercenaries above. He is frequently linked with these other Black figures in the text not only as their leader, but also at the level of language, in a morphological partnership, with ʿAbd al-Wahhāb's name euphonous not only with his tribal epithet of Kilāb but also with the "noble blacks"[10] whom he stewards—*al-sūdān al-anjāb*. Their significance to the narrative is often embodied in the epic's extended titles, written in ornamental strings of rhyming clauses (*sajʿ*). One exemplary manuscript advertises the drama of the central heroes and villains as follows:

> The Tale of the Pious Warriors, Champions of the Oneness of God [*abṭāl al-muwaḥḥidīn*], al-Dalhamma and al-Baṭṭāl, the prince ʿAbd al-Wahhāb, the tribe of Kilāb, and the noble Blacks [*al-sūdān al-anjāb*], and what transpired between them and ʿUqba the slippery [*al-murtāb*], and Shūmdaris the deceiver [*al-kadhdhāb*], in full.[11]

In rising through the ranks to heroic prominence at the forefront of both his own tribe and of their most legendary literary account, ʿAbd al-Wahhāb also joins another league beyond the text, a cadre of Black heroes or those with Black family who are scattered throughout their own epic worlds, from ʿAntar of *Sīrat ʿAntar*—a pre-Islamic warrior poet who is raced as Black and was born to an enslaved Abyssinian mother, albeit of royal descent, and a father from the Arabian tribe of ʿAbs—to Abū Zayd al-Hilālī of *Sīrat Banī Hilāl*—born with black skin to two Arab parents due to a miracle. There is also Sayf ibn Dhī Yazan of *Sīrat Sayf b. Dhī Yazan*—a hero who is raced as Arab and white, and yet like ʿAntar was also born to

9. On the Ottoman Turkish *Baṭṭālnāmeh*, see Georgios S. Dedes, "The Battalname: An Ottoman Turkish Frontier Epic Wondertale: Introduction, Turkish Transcription, Translation and Commentary" (PhD diss., Harvard University, 1995).

10. "Blacks" is the plainest meaning of the Arabic noun *sūdān*. When not translating directly from the Arabic, I refer instead to Black people.

11. Gustav Flügel, *Die arabischen, persischen und türkischen Handschriften der Kaiserlich-Königlichen Hofbibliothek zu Wien* (Vienna: Kaiserlich-Königlichen Hofbibliothek, 1865), 18.

a pre-Islamic Yemeni Arab king and an Abyssinian noblewoman. Each figure's push and pull of difference from or conformity to their kin, inscribed upon their bodies, becomes a lightning rod affecting their social affinities and religious, legal, and genealogical standing in their tales.

This book asks: why these Black heroes? What did their blackness do within the worlds built through storytelling among Arabic-speaking Muslims in the Middle Ages? What possible futures did it conjure and delimit, what present orders did it explain, and what pasts did it help to index morally, geographically, and culturally? I am less interested in the intellectual history of Arabic epics as such than in what this corpus of thousands of pages of lore that, uniquely among Arabic prose-works of their time, extensively narrativizes the lives of legendary people raced as Black in predominantly non-Black spaces, can allow us to see if treated as part of the social-historical archive.

In the ensuing chapters, I argue alongside many others that these heroic literatures are at once entertaining and didactic. I also argue that they are particularly instructive in the potentials of racialized differences among humans. From their elaborate origin tales to the ages of pious renewal they introduce, to their sojourns in the unconquered "lands of the Blacks" (*bilād al-sūdān*) recruiting their putative brethren, Black heroes become at once biologized, worlded, and transcendent mediums for fruitful encounters with others. They powerfully exemplify a growing Muslim world's historical and emergent multiplicity, as well as its hierarchies and norms. As anchors for a range of other Black characters—valorous and villainous, intimate and exotic, and even mundane on-set extras like Shamṭā's hapless troops—these Black champions of varied pre- and early Islamic Arab expansions help weave aspirational histories of the Muslim world community, or *umma*, as always already having had the scripts and tools for admitting extremely different peoples and positioning them to its ultimate strength. In the tales, these scripts and tools are frequently outlined in what I call allegories of assimilation: cosmic and earthly forces collude to render the everyday institutions for incorporating and organizing a tangle of different human types, from slave soldiery and post-manumission clientage to tutelage and marriage, as part of an intricate grand design. This guidance can also operate in the negative, showing how to resist undesirable forms of difference that do not fit within this plan.

Already, I have used a collection of what are by no means given terms of analysis, but rather imply specific practices of reading and translating—blackness, whiteness, Arabness, racialization, and even epic. I attend to these choices below.

Race and Racialization

I am not the first person to bring together the Black figures of Arabic epics for analysis. In his foundational three-volume study, *The Arabian Epic*, published in 1995, the British Arabist Malcolm Lyons includes a section on what he terms the "racial groups" within the texts. Alongside "Blacks," he lists Jews, Kurds, Turks, and so on as groups that stand outside the texts' primary focus on Arab heroes, often of tribal renown. Concerning Black people alone, though, he writes, "of the audience to which the narrators of the cycles could appeal, a number must have been either black or of mixed race, and perhaps for this reason the ambivalence seen in the treatment of the Kurds is even more marked when it comes to the question of colour."[12]

In his labeling, Lyons appears to assume that reified ideas of race were already in place in these roughly eight-hundred-year-old texts, or that the language of race is the best language we presently have to talk about whatever category concepts there were. But in pointing to the representations' ambivalence, Lyons leaves aside the question of what these racially Black presences in Arabic epics may have meant to audience members who identified with them, or to their majority non-Black, Arab listenership and readership. Nor could Lyons have predicted the turn in recent years toward critical contemplations of racial construction in premodernity, and particularly the so-called medieval period—a term that I will use despite its status as something of a Eurocentric shibboleth. Indeed, I deploy *medieval* especially for its evocation of a pregnant, interstitial time after Late Antiquity, which intersects with Islam's rise in the seventh century, and before the Columbian Exchange. Historically, this notional era between eras has also worked to bracket off Islam's contributions to global currents. In this framing, prior to the medieval period, there arose the "form of rationalization that was unknown and could not have existed before the Greeks developed those forms of abstract and systematic thinking which we usually call philosophy" that some have speciously identified as the genesis of taxonomic, and hence racial, thought. This is followed by Greek thought's supposedly fated reclamation and mobilization by Christian Europeans during the Renaissance, after centuries of Arab-Muslim preservation.[13] The medieval period thus supplies a ground for piecing together and critiquing dominant narratives about the history of race. Furthermore, it overlaps generatively with what is

12. Malcolm Lyons, *The Arabian Epic: Heroic and Oral Story-Telling* vol. 1 (Cambridge: Cambridge University Press, 1995), 24.

13. Miriam Eliav-Feldon, Benjamin Isaac, and Joseph Zeigler, eds., *The Origins of Racism in the West* (Cambridge: Cambridge University Press, 2009), 10.

sometimes called the "classical period" of Arabic cultural production. This phrasing also has its problems: though the texts with which I am concerned trace their origins to between the seventh and fifteenth centuries, they are rarely associated with a classical linguistic register or heritage.

I do not take up the use of "race" directly in the fashion of Lyons. Rather, I analyze what I refer to as racialization in a variety of Arabic epics as well as across their intertexts, with special attention to *Sīrat al-Amīra Dhāt al-Himma*. I say "racialization," rather than "race," because, per Adam Hochman,

> We need to abandon the idea that individuals and groups simply belong to races and start thinking in terms of processes. If race is a social kind, we can turn to racial formation theory for an account of the processes through which races are created, inhabited, transformed, and destroyed.[14]

For premodern contexts, which is to say those in which we are considering race avant la lettre, it is especially valuable to speak of the process that produces what becomes known as race—henceforth, racialization—prior to or simultaneously with the social categories that process engenders. One hallmark of processes of racialization is their invisibility as such; race is what Ron Mallon refers to as a "covert construction," in that though it is a social kind, societies throughout time have fashioned race, like various other identity formations, through the language of the objective, organic, and suprahuman.[15] This is one significant way in which race contrasts with ethnicity. As I discuss further below, the social formedness and plasticity of ethnicity is often unmasked. We normatively speak of ethnicity as shared language, culture, customs, and narratives. Premodern Arab-Muslim peoples understood blackness as an epiphenomenon of creation, nature, and history. They articulated this in ways that are often familiar. There is of course no one Arabic word from the medieval period that we might directly translate as "race," but rather a semantic field of terms that have been applied in what I read as race-making: words that invoke one's roots (*ʿirq, aṣl*), one's stock (*jins, ʿunṣur*), and, most prominently for our purposes, one's lineal heritage (*nasab*) all articulate individuals' biocultural inheritance in essentialized terms that trace back to a primordial place or

14. Adam Hochman, "Racialization: A Defense of the Concept," *Racial and Ethnic Studies* 49, no. 8 (2018): 1245.

15. Ron Mallon, *The Construction of Human Kinds* (Oxford: Oxford University Press, 2016).

people of origin. Scholars have varied in how they translate each of these terms along lines similar to Robert Bartlett's discussion of translations of the Latin *gens*, with which *jins* is cognate.[16] Edmund Hayes notes a similar concern with the Persian term *nezhād*, which is "often translated both as 'lineage,' and as 'race' or 'ethnicity,'" implying a "duality of meaning," or perhaps a separability of meanings, where "no such duality is present."[17]

While I do not necessarily translate any of the foregoing as "race," I take them *en masse* as templates for dividing humans in ways that could be racialized. Often, I will refer to these divisions as reifying human, social, or social-as-natural kinds. I do so in view of an opening anecdote in the prolific ninth-century litterateur al-Jāḥiẓ's (d. 868) treatise *Fakhr al-Sūdān ʿalā-l-Bīḍān* (*The Boasts of the Blacks over the Whites*), from his teacher al-Aṣmaʿī (d. 831):

> Al-Aṣmaʿī said: "Fizr ʿAbd al-Fazāra, the one with the pierced ear [*khurba*],[18] stated, 'Among all beings, there is a tendency toward harmony [*in al-wiʾām yatatarraʿ fī jamīʿ al-ṭamsh*]. The she-goat doesn't keep the company of sheep if she doesn't find billy-goats, and the ewe flees from clawed beasts and shies from the camel.' And Abū Zayd the Grammarian (al-Naḥwī) [similarly] composed the verse, 'Were it not for harmony, one would surely perish [*law-lā al-wiʾām la-halaka al-insān*].'"[19]

Social concord, in other words, comes not from everyone getting along, but from everyone being in their proper place, which here is tantamount to staying among their own kind. Nietzsche referred to the constructive process of forgetting arbitrary individual differences when creating a

16. Robert Bartlett, "Medieval and Modern Concepts of Race and Ethnicity," *Journal of Medieval and Early Modern Studies* 31, no. 1 (2001): 39–56.

17. Edmund Hayes, "The Death of Kings: Group Identity and the Tragedy of *Nezhād* in Ferdowsi's *Shahnameh*," *Iranian Studies* 48, no. 3 (2015): 370.

18. The combination of this man's generic name that designates him as enslaved in the tribe of Fazāra and the reference to his slit or pierced ear mark him as unfree and/or foreign—with Sindī and Ḥabashī (Abyssinian) men especially noted for their pierced ears. This makes it perhaps all the more remarkable that a description of natural differences in status is voiced by him. On the use of *akhrab* or *kharbāʿ* to refer to enslaved people with pierced or slit ears, and on Sindī and Ḥabashī men figuring as examples of those with such piercings, see Ibn al-Manẓūr, *Lisān al-ʿArab* (Beirut: Dār Ṣādir, 1955–56), 1121.

19. Al-Jāḥiẓ, *Rasāʾil al-Jāḥiẓ* vol. 1, ed. ʿAbd al-Sallām Hārūn (Cairo: Maktabat al-Khanjī, 1964), 177–78.

broad kind as condensing down to the *qualitas occulta*, or "hidden quality," behind a mess of tentatively related objects or behaviors, "whereas nature is acquainted with no forms and no concepts, and likewise with no species."[20] Al-Jāḥiẓ's anecdote renders this hidden quality self-asserting and self-reinforcing—there is behavioral intuition conferred through speciated difference among animals, and humans have this, too.

Throughout this book, I show that Arabic epics, or *sīras*, produce their own logic in which "kind" asserts itself over people's lives and decisions. This is frequently done explicitly, using phrases such as "like inclines toward like," or nature toward nature (*al-jins ilā-l-jins yamīl, al-ṭabʿ yamīl ilā-l-ṭabʿ*); in a more overt and intimate expression of its biosocial implications, sometimes blood stirs toward it's like (*taḥarrak al-dam ilā-l-dam*) within a single lineage.[21] Beyond immediate family, though, by what are these shared kinds determined and delimited? Why draw the boundaries of kind, as the *sīras* do, between Black and white or between primordial lineal categories rather than, say, between hero and villain, or young and old? Indeed, such alternatives were available when considering what social harmony (*wiʾām*) might mean. Another common interpretation of al-Jāḥiẓ's aphorism was that humans would perish if they could not form groups that share common values and model themselves on one another's comportment, such that "the child emulates the adult and the ignorant emulates the learned."[22]

I contextualize the *sīras*' articulations of kind by comparing across Arabic-speaking Muslim spaces and beyond them. For example, in contrast with the connotations of more cognate terms to race like *raza* in Spanish, which Ana M. Gómez-Bravo shows was initially used to mean a defect in an object's purity as with an alloyed metal or stained gemstone, to have *nasab, ʿirq,* or *ʿunṣur* in early Arabic literature is to have strength of social standing.[23] *Nasab* is typically found paired with *ḥasab,* or inherited merit, and one who is said to exhibit these two qualities is typically a person with known lineal bona fides. According to Louise Marlow, in the early

20. Friedrich Nietzsche, "On Truth and Lying in a Non-Moral Sense," in *The Birth of Tragedy and Other Writings*, Raymond Guess and Ronald Speirs, eds. (Cambridge: Cambridge University Press, 1999), 145.

21. I explain the workings of blood in *Sīrat Dhāt al-Himma* at length in chapter 3, but for a discussion of this specific usage in the tale, see Melanie Magidow, "Epic of the Commander Dhāt al-Himma," *Medieval Feminist Forum: A Journal of Gender and Sexuality*, Subsidia Series 9, Medieval Texts in Translation 6 (2018): 20.

22. Ibn al-Manẓūr, *Lisān al-ʿArab*, 4749.

23. Ana M. Gómez-Bravo, "The Origins of 'Raza:' Racializing Difference in Early Spanish," *Interfaces: A Journal of Medieval European Literatures* 7 (2020): 80.

Islamic period this usage spurs an apologetic counternarrative, in which people claim that their *ḥasab* is their *dīn* (religious fidelity) and that their *nasab* is their Islam, effectively saying that individual righteousness can outweigh lineage while also reinforcing lineage's rhetorical importance.[24]

We might productively place these usages alongside other medieval developments. The semantic range of Arabic terms for social-as-natural kind may diverge from Gómez-Bravo's description of *raza*'s connotations in significant ways, however, it has similarities to connotations of the first appearances of the word *race* in fifteenth-century French texts studied by Charles de Miramon. *Race* became linked with ideas about heritable nobility within dynasties due to understandings of heredity that preceded its usage. According to de Miramon, though, this is contradictory. Ideas of biologically transferred merit stand "against the ideological core of nobility, which insists on individual virtue."[25] In other words, the term *race* as applied to intergenerational yet individual nobility embedded similar tensions to the pairing of *ḥasab* and *nasab*. In medieval Arabic-speaking domains the use of racialized descriptors was moreover both sustained and militated against in a discursive dynamic that Justin Stearns characterizes as moving between "genealogical thinking" on the one hand and "environmental determinism" on the other.[26] Pious urgings to not visit the status of parents upon children at all further complicated both of these concepts of externally fashioned destiny, but also show the ways in which racialized categories were linked with morality. In his twelfth-century treatise written to vindicate his Black peers, *Tanwīr al-Ghabash fī Faḍl al-Sūdān wa-l-Ḥabash* (*Illuminating the Darkness: On the Virtues of the Blacks and Abyssinians*), the jurist Ibn al-Jawzī (d. 1201) duly opens by toggling between great men who came from base forebears and base men who came from great ones, closing with a reference to Bilāl, the formerly enslaved Abyssinian man who first called Muslims to prayer:

24. Louise Marlow, "Ḥasab o Nasab," in *Encyclopaedia Iranica*, online ed., updated March 20, 2012, http://www.iranicaonline.org/articles/hasab-o-nasab; see also Editors, "Ḥasab wa-Nasab," in *Encyclopaedia of Islam*, 2nd ed., ed. Peri Bearman, Thierry Bianquis, C. Edmund Bosworth, E. J. van Donzel, and Wolfhart P. Heinrichs (Leiden: Brill Online, 2012), https://referenceworks.brillonline.com/entries/encyclopaedia-of-islam-2/hasab-wa-nasab-SIM_2751?s.num=321&s.start=320.

25. Charles de Miramon, "Noble Dogs, Noble Blood: The Invention of the Concept of Race in the Late Middle Ages," in *The Origins of Racism in the West*, ed. Miriam Eliav-Feldon, Benjamin Isaac, and Joseph Ziegler, (Cambridge: Cambridge University Press, 2009), 215.

26. Justin Stearns, "Race in the Islamicate Middle East: Reflections after Heng," *Cambridge Journal of Postcolonial Literary Inquiry* (2022): 115.

> Praise be to God who selected humankind out of all creatures, and then selected the people of piety and faith [for favor], and who made the object of His inspection people's hearts and not their bodies. He scrutinizes the purity of one's inner qualities [*ṣafā' al-asrār*] and not one's cleanness of color [*naqā' al-alwān*]. . . . He brings the living from the dead, and hence brought the Khalīl [Abraham] from Āzar, the blasphemous, and [He] brings forth the dead from the living, and so too brought Canaan from Noah, in accordance with his capacity. Abū Ṭālib worshipped idols while ʿUthmān submitted to Islam. And Abū'l-Jahl went astray while Bilāl called the *adhān*.[27]

Despite Ibn al-Jawzī's pleas, overlapping ideas of genealogy and place, human and animal, and color and culture were nonetheless assiduously chronicled by keepers of knowledge and tradition and held to be precise and predictive. They held that the world's many genealogies could be traced to Nūḥ's children, Sām, Yāfit, and Ḥām (Shem, Japheth, and Ham). These genealogies became a useful heuristic for the emerging Arabic science of mapping the known world that originated with ʿAbbasid imperialization in the ninth and tenth centuries, which in turn took many of its cues from Greco-Roman geography and humoral pathology. In this combined model, primordial peoples settled in the globe's different climes (*iqlīm*, pl. *aqālīm*), each of which produced distinct physically observable and inwardly meaningful qualities. Generations progressed—with Sām's descendants inhabiting the world's temperate, Mediterranean zones, Yāfit's in the globe's north, and Ḥām's in the globe's south—and differences of local nature produced by the climes solidified the brothers' progeny as different human types. Under the conceptualization of global lineages, words like *nasab* that in the pre-Islamic period, were used for granular, local distinctions of tribe and clan became generalized to describe all of humanity, though not in fixed ways.

In the early Islamic period when the geographical and ethnological innovations that linked Noahic, humoral, and Arabian interpretations of heredity were being made, *nasab*, one's lineage, was also gradually changing meaning in another respect, namely, it was paternalizing. Where in the pre-Islamic period, people who had a mix of male Arabian and female non-Arabian parentage were pejoratively dubbed *hajīns*, or mixed, showing that matriliny mattered, in the Islamic era *nasab* came to mean

27. Ibn al-Jawzī, *Tanwīr al-Ghabash fī Faḍl al-Sūdān wa-l-Ḥabash*, ed. Marzūq ʿAlī Ibrāhīm (Riyadh: Dār al-Sharīf, 1998), 3.

one's lineage through one's father. *Hajīn* identities, concomitantly, start to disappear. Paternal rights, though, still were mediated by womb kinships. They were not tied to blood and blood quantum as they would be elsewhere.[28]

Elizabeth Urban notes the importance of these maneuvers for sustaining caliphal legitimacy, despite the increased use of foreign concubinage, because it let leaders keep claiming what she calls "full Arabness."[29] To do this, people drew on sacred histories. Various genealogists, or *nassābun*, touted God's urging to "know one another" (Q 49:13) and to look across difference as a basis for their ongoing verificatory practices, despite the Qur'ān's warnings of genealogy's meaninglessness in the final hour (Q 23:101).[30] Caliphs themselves adduced historical foreign concubine mothers who were progenitors of contemporary Arabness, like Hājar (Hagar). A constellation of institutions arose that reified patrilineal lineage's importance and let people extend its value to others. These included the role of *umm walad*, which enabled the children of concubines to claim this paternity, and *walā'*, or being "brought close" by manumission and clientage, which let pseudo-agnates attach themselves to a male head of house. But of course, not everyone who technically had an Arab patrilineal *nasab* was racialized in the same way. Nor was there a fixed agreement across genres, times, places, and even single textual traditions, about the nuances of how these human categories and their backgrounding, nonhuman causes worked. Flexibility is part of these categories' utility. Urban's caliphs were able to successfully make their claim on full Arabness.

28. Some scholars have adduced this as a reason to avoid the term *race* altogether, as I discuss further in chapter 3. For example, on womb kinship and ideas of race, see Mana Kia, *Persianate Selves: Memories of Place and Origin before Nationalism* (Stanford, CA: Stanford University Press, 2020), 133–34.

29. Elizabeth Urban, *Conquered Populations in Early Islam: Non-Arabs, Slaves, and the Sons of Slave Mothers* (Edinburgh: Edinburgh University Press, 2020), 119. The legal reification of concubinage aided not only in constructing ideas of Arabness and ethnicity, but of marriage and wifehood as a contrasting yet overlapping condition. On the relationship between concubinage and marriage see Kecia Ali, *Marriage and Slavery in Early Islam* (Cambridge, MA: Harvard University Press, 2010).

30. The tradition of opening genealogies with God's statement that He made mankind into peoples and tribes to engender mutual knowledge originates relatively early, with Ibn Ḥazm's *Jamharat Ansāb al-ʿArab*. Ibn Ḥazm uses the verse to justify the genealogical sciences, saying, "Thus the mutual knowledge (*taʿāruf*) of people by means of their *nasab* is an objective that the Almighty had in creating us peoples and tribes, hence it must be the case that the science of *nasab* is a science of high regard (*jalīl rafīʿ*), for with it comes mutual knowledge (*taʿāruf*)"; see Ibn Ḥazm, *Jamharat ansāb al-ʿarab* (Cairo: Dār al-Maʿārif, 1948), 1–2.

In contrast, the Black heroes of the *siyar shaʿbiyya* both fall into and exploit what sociologist Neda Maghbouleh has called a "racial loophole," in which one's classification at a legal level differs from their racialization in daily life. Despite being Arab "on paper," the heroes are consistently perceived as Black, which is in turn entangled with non-Arabness in ways that generate myriad "everyday contradictions and conflicts."[31]

Blackness and Whiteness

People who are said to be Black in the *sīra*s are my primary case for thinking about racialization. I refer to blackness and its use in Arabic epics as racializing, while I refer to certain other identity groups, like Arabs or Abyssinians, as ethnicities—though, to be sure, there are many instances in which these identities are given racial meanings. Following recent work by Peter Webb, I also do not take for granted that Arabs were a self-designating collective with a sense of shared identity during Islam's earliest centuries, or that what made one Arab was ever stable.[32] And yet, seen through the nostalgic and aspirational gaze of the *sīra*s themselves, the existence of "Arabs" who know themselves as such is an eternalized fact of history.

So too with the existence of "Blacks" (*al-sūdān*), as in the "noble Blacks" of the subtitle above. Their designation obscures as much as it reveals: it blurs the lines between many discrete, self-distinguishing peoples who engaged with Arabic-speaking Muslims and the territories over which they presided throughout the Middle Ages, yet the term's use also points to the fact that some variety of structural and intellectual processes occurred to blur those lines in the first place. In other words, *black* does not operate as an ethnonym, but rather as a racialized classifier. There were many ethnicities aggregated and compressed into shifting configurations of "Blacks" by medieval Arabic speakers, from the Beja, Nubians, Ethiopians, Bantu peoples, and so on, to, in certain contexts, peoples of Southeast Asia and Indian Ocean and Oceanian islands, including Sumatrans and Javanese.[33]

31. Neda Maghbouleh, *The Limits of Whiteness: Iranian Americans and the Everyday Politics of Race* (Stanford, CA: Stanford University Press, 2017), 5.

32. Peter Webb, *Imagining the Arabs: Arab Identity and the Rise of Islam* (Edinburgh: Edinburgh University Press, 2016); Urban, *Conquered Populations in Early Islam*.

33. There is therefore a sizable quantity of literature on the overlap in markets, routes, and representations between *sūdān* in the Arabophone and Persophone Indian Ocean and *Kunlun* in the Sinophone Indian Ocean. See, e.g., Philippe Beaujard, "Tang China and the Rise of the Silk Roads," in *The Worlds of the Indian Ocean: A Global*

Those with distant heritages in such regions, like the peripatetic Zuṭṭ, who are identified alongside the *ghurabāʾ*, or Strangers, as an itinerant ethnic group in the medieval Muslim world, continued to fall under the classification of "Blacks" in diaspora.[34] Guangtian Ha has argued that blackness's conceptual travels and Black people's movement across premodern Afro-Eurasian locales indicate a "subaltern transregionalism" that is especially ripe for racial analysis, born out of the fact that "both coastal East Africans and coastal Southeast Asians are referred to as being 'black' in medieval Arabic and Chinese accounts, and that both are employed in different legs of the trans-Indian Ocean journey," to which we might add many such people's further traversals of the Sahara and Mediterranean.[35]

The *bilād al-sūdān*, or "lands of the Blacks" to the world's general south, from which these transregional actors were said to originate in Arabic sciences, is also the only color-coded toponym that gained common currency in premodern Arabic besides, arguably, the *diyār al-ẓulumāt*, or "lands of darkness" to the earth's far north, so called for their lack of exposure to the sun.[36] There is, meanwhile, no commensurate "land of the whites," for to paraphrase the fourteenth-century thinker Ibn Khaldūn (d. 1406) on this disparity, people do not use the terms with which they identify to highlight difference.[37] In this sense, even the bitterly antagonistic Byzantine Christians of *Sīrat Dhāt al-Himma* do not approximate the semiotic range of their Black counterparts. Byzantine actors instead often participate in what Zayde Antrim has called an "erotics of sameness" with their Muslim peers, phasing easily into Arab families upon their conversion to Islam, which they have approached through their own civilized if mistaken monotheistic practices. The most sought after among them are just as

History, vol. 2 (Cambridge: Cambridge University Press, 2019). And more recently: Guangtian Ha, "From Baghdād to Baghpūr: Sailors and Slaves in Global Asia," in *Who Is the Asianist? The Politics of Representation in Asian Studies*, ed. Will Bridges, Nitasha Tamar Sharma, and Marvin D. Sterling (New York: Columbia University Press, 2022), 53–74.

34. Kristina Richardson, *Roma in the Medieval Islamic World: Literacy, Culture, and Migration* (London: I. B. Tauris, 2022), 26–27.

35. Ha, "Baghdād to Baghpūr," 57.

36. On the use of this term, see Ibn Faḍlān, *Ibn Fadlān and the Land of Darkness: Arab Travelers in the Far North*, trans. Paul Lunde and Caroline Stone (London: Penguin Classics, 2012), xvii.

37. This statement is discussed in Paul Hardy, "Medieval Muslim Philosophers on Race," in *Philosophers on Race: Critical Essays*, ed. Julie K. Ward and Tommy L. Scott (Oxford: Blackwell Publishers, 2002), 51; Ibn Khaldūn, *Muqaddimat Ibn Khaldūn*, ed. ʿAbd Allāh Muḥammad Darwīsh (Damascus: Dār Yaʿrib, 2004), 192.

likely as Junduba to be regarded as "ideal, moon-like types," having "some combination of dark eyes, arching brows, rosy or ruddy cheeks, and white teeth, often framed by black and/or curling hair and accentuated by a dark beauty mark or mole."[38] Indeed, as Remke Kruk has noted, the central problem with Byzantine women in the text is that they are too magnetic; they induce *fitna*, or civil strife, among Muslim characters because they embody an ideal to be pursued.[39] This, too, ramifies into conflict among the Arabs and their Black peers, as they vie against each other or take sides in their commanders' wars for Byzantine women's hearts.

Another way in which whiteness's emplotment as social and aesthetic baseline—as facilitator of movement, change, and transformation—emerges is in the arts of disguise and subterfuge in which trickster-heroes, or *ʿayyār*, regularly engage. In their case, whiteness at once expands opportunities for and undercuts the necessity of characters cultivating plausible alter-egos that bridge Muslim and Christian spaces. Where a blonde and multilingual al-Baṭṭāl, who regularly manipulates his appearance through changes to his hair and beard color, pretends by turns to be a Maghribi physician, an Anatolian monk, a jailor, a commander of Christian armies, and more, ʿAbd al-Wahhāb and his peers—often equally educated and silver-tongued—rarely attempt such elaborate cosmetic change.[40] They will still be Black, after all, and so they often find themselves instead playing at being slaves, mendicants, and street artists to slip past their enemies and pull off feats of cunning. At times, they pretend to have significant disabilities in order to make their presences sympathetic and unobtrusive. In a particularly illustrative moment in *Sīrat ʿAntar*, ʿAntar's Abyssinian half brother, Shaybūb, infiltrates another tribe's camp and earns one of the Arab women's sympathies—and a scrap of bread—by "acting like one of the begging poor of the Arabs [*fuqarāʾ al-ʿArab*] . . . he wrapped a turban around his head, dragged his right leg, and feigned blindness in his left eye and paralysis in his hands. He bent himself and limped so that he left a solemn impression [*ʿibra*] on anyone who saw him."[41] These antics in

38. Zayde Antrim, "*Qamarayn*: The Erotics of Sameness in the *1001 Nights*," *al-ʿUṣūr al-Wusṭā* 28 (2020): 9.

39. Remke Kruk, "The Bold and the Beautiful: Women and 'fitna' in the *Sīrat Dhāt al-Himma*: The Story of Nūrā," in *Women in the Medieval Islamic World: Power, Patronage, and Piety*, ed. Gavin R. G. Hambly (New York: St. Martin's Press, 1998), 99–116.

40. A full comparative study of trickster tales in the *sīras*, including a case study of al-Baṭṭāl, is available in Malcolm C. Lyons, *The Man of Wiles in Popular Arabic Literature: A Study of a Medieval Arab Hero* (Edinburgh: Edinburgh University Press, 2012).

41. *Sīrat ʿAntara b. Shaddād*, vol. 2 (Beirut: al-Maktaba al-Shaʿbiyya, n.d.), 331.

which the audience is, implicitly, in on what makes a ploy successful point to long histories of reification and interlocking modes of alterity.

Many scholars of race in the Middle East and North Africa have shown that "blackness," "whiteness," and "redness"—the triad of color signifiers used to encompass all human and natural variation from at least the Qurʾān and its early exegesis forward across a variety of Arabic-speaking societies—are not inherently somatic but are often lineage- or patriline- and class- or occupation-essentialist. They are distinctions that also often reflect past understandings of enslaveability or non-enslaveability and Muslimness or non-Muslimness. This matrix has been continually politically reanimated and evolved new meanings over time, even if only in "abstracted images that authenticated a past of honorable lineage and the wealth of slave ownership" for those to whom no ongoing, direct claims of property or patronage accrue.[42]

Blackness thus does not operate as a purely colorist or visually indicative qualifier in the sources. Very dark-skinned Arab individuals are typically not identified as being "Blacks," and when they are, this places them at the margins of Arabness. This is the case with the genealogically Arab yet black-skinned ʿAbd al-Wahhāb, whose status as the so-called "Black of the Tribe of Kilāb" structures his lived experience in re-racing ways. His heroic journey starts with a paternity suit to litigate whether his mother committed adultery with a Black man; his primary social affinities throughout the text are toward non-Arab Black people who have or have been migrated into central Islamic lands; and, in a testament to these classifications' relationality, it is not until he goes to East Africa that he begins to be referred to in the text as Arab, though then only by local East Africans themselves.

In other words, in the everyday—including in the fictive everyday lives of the Black heroes—these color terms can be somaticized, raising the prospect that despite one's claims to the alternative and despite the notional predeterminacy of one's ancestry at the level of entitlements and officialdom, one can still be widely perceived as Black at the level of snap judgment and popular opinion. But they can also not, or at least not in identical ways by all involved. This disjuncture deepens across time and

42. Afifa Ltifi, "Black Tunisians and the Pitfalls of Bourguiba's Homogenization Project," *POMEPS* 40 (2020): 71. Though Ltifi's study specifically examines a modern Tunisian politics of power and privilege, similar statements have been made of neighboring states as well, often alongside critiques of politicizing racialized divides in modern Arab states along lines that appear "Western" by invoking race and its economic effects. On these critiques, see Bruce S. Hall, "Reading Race in Africa and the Middle East," *Anthropologia* 7, no. 1 (2020): 33–44.

space, and as characters move, one sees the categories through which their identities are articulated by those around them shift. Their stories evince awareness of different epistemologies of difference.

Then there is the fact that color terms are also used in the *sīras* and related texts in ways that are specifically untethered from social-as-natural kind and that also merit our attention. Thus, in the intense clash of battle we are told:

> There were 1,800,000 [Byzantines], with the Muslims like a white blaze on a black bull. And the edges and flanks of the earth darkened, and silhouettes [*ashbāḥ*] swayed and blurred, and spirits were seized, and the winds of death raged. Squadron cleaved to squadron in battle, division upon division blended together, fate towered over them, and the day became like night.[43]

Of the medieval era, Cord Whitaker has recently written that, in Western European writings, the moralism of black and white is marked by their "contrariety," or their mutually necessary and constitutive natures, whereas modern race thinking "fixes" black and white as absolutes.[44] Similarly, Denise K. Buell has written of the fact that while color-coded race in modernity is a mutable category that pretends to permanence, in the premodern West its mutability is far more self-evident.[45] Premodern blackness and whiteness' contrariety and mutability are both on display in the passage above, in which the presumably white-skinned but numerous and providentially disadvantaged Byzantines are rendered "black" and shadowy while the rightly guided, small army of Muslims are "white" to create a specific sense of destabilization. Far from the earthly realms of the social or natural, we are confronted here with what Michael Mumisa refers to in his discussion of black-and-white Qurʾānic imagery concerning judgment and the afterlife—with which this passage presaging Muslim martyrdom echoes weightily—as an attempt at approaching the celestial and eschatological through human language that is doomed, inevitably, to fail. As Mumisa notes, early Muslim thinkers often recognized such language as figurative (*majāz*), but he further cautions that "[metaphor]

43. *Sīrat Dhāt al-Himma*, IX:55

44. Cord Whitaker, *Black Metaphors: How Modern Racism Emerged from Medieval Race Thinking* (Philadelphia: University of Pennsylvania Press, 2019).

45. Denise Kimber Buell, "Early Christian Universalism and Modern Forms of Racism," in *The Origins of Racism in the West*, ed. Miriam Eliav-Feldon, Benjamin Isaac, and Joseph Ziegler (Cambridge: Cambridge University Press, 2009), 113.

is something that can be understood here and now. These terms are used to refer to another world; a world that is beyond us."[46]

Arab-Islamic Epics

The phrase that will be translated as "popular epic" throughout this book is *sīra shaʿbiyya* (pl. *siyar shaʿbiyya*). The first word, *sīra* (life path, journey), goes back to early traditions of writing the biography of Muḥammad and his religio-political achievements; if one simply says "the *sīra*," in typical parlance that refers to *al-sīra al-nabawiyya*, or the traditional biography of the Prophet. Over time, though, this term also became a genre marker indicating the cycles of heroes typical of the epic tradition, who likewise earned their legendary legacies through piously minded conquest. The second term, *shaʿbiyya*, means "popular," and is a modern genre marker that relates to these works' mode of circulation: unlike prestige epics from throughout West and central Asia, popular epics are composed in semi-colloquial registers of language, anonymously and outside of patronage structures. With the possible exception of *al-sīra al-nabawiyya*, medieval Arabic does not have its own prestige epics; the corpus is instead of this popular stripe.[47] In this vein, *sīras* are typically "primary" epics, concocted from decades and centuries of orally performed tradition, rather than starting as a conscious textual enterprise.[48] Oral performances of some epics continue today and have developed their own artistry and compositional formulas distinct from their written versions.[49]

46. Michael Mumisa, "Towards an African Qurʾanic Hermeneutics," *Journal of Qurʾanic Studies* 4, no. 1 (2002): 73. On the verse to which Mumisa dedicates the most attention, Q 3:106, which declares that believers' and disbelievers' faces will be respectively whitened and blackened on the Day of Judgment, Christian Lange also has an insightful article. Christian Lange, "'On That Day When Faces Will Be White or Black' (Q3:106): Towards a Semiology of the Face in the Arabo-Islamic Tradition," *Journal of the American Oriental Society* 127 (2007): 429–45.

47. Todd Lawson has argued for an "epic" reading of the Qurʾān, with Muḥammad as a hero, but notes that his life becomes more consciously fleshed out in the *sīra* genre that is "umbilically wedded" to the Qurʾān. Todd Lawson, "The Qurʾan and Epic," *Journal of Qurʾanic Studies* 16, no. 1 (2014): 75.

48. On distinctions between primary and secondary epic, see C. S. Lewis, *A Preface to "Paradise Lost"* (London: Oxford University Press, 1969).

49. The oral-formulaic dynamics of performed versions of *Sīrat Banī Hilāl* in Bakātūsh, Egypt, are discussed at length in Dwight Reynolds, *Heroic Poets, Poetic Heroes: The Ethnography of Performance in an Arabic Oral Epic Tradition* (Ithaca, NY: Cornell University Press, 1995).

Being "popular" also announces that these texts are definitively not *adab*—a term with connotations of etiquette and refinement, used throughout history to delimit projects of text that embodied elite, learned enterprise, and typically translated simply as "literature," or else as "belles lettres." To contrast with their scholarly, veridical counterparts, Arabic epics are sometimes described through negation as "pseudo-histories," and related to works such as the embellished pseudo-*maghāzī* and *futūḥāt* (conquest chronicles).[50] One could also productively describe them in ways that evoke their ties with other medieval literary currents rather than their perceived rupture with Arabic high culture, speaking of them as chivalric literature or as romance, as the word *sīra* was often translated by early Orientalists. My choice of "popular epic" aligns with the present consensus of studies on the *siyar shaʿbiyya.*

"Popularity" moreover aligns with the status of the Black heroes themselves. By the ʿAbbasid era in which these narratives are first attested and in which several of them are also set, various forms of elite enslavement, concubinage, and patron-client relationships in society's uppermost tiers had evolved through which non-Arab actors increasingly earned elevated status and visibility in lands spanning the tales' core stomping grounds of Egypt, Syria, Arabia, and Iraq. The *sīras* bear significant imprints from ʿAbbasid historiography and written culture, and more tentatively from the Saljūq efflorescence in ʿAbbasid territories, under which Persian romances thrived and crystallized into a high-register genre that is nonetheless rich with parallels to their less decorated Arabic counterparts.[51] Yet despite their ties with ʿAbbasid memory, the contingent elite that evolved in this age rarely is the model for celebrated Black actors in popular epics. The assemblage of eunuchs, consorts, advisors, bureaucrats, and court functionaries through which some of the most prominent Black people in ʿAbbasid-era belles lettres emerge was most in contact and competition with administrators and learned socialites who were climbing the ladder themselves. In their construction of an aspirational history of Islam that

50. Peter Heath, "Styles in Premodern Arabic Popular Epics," in *In the Shadow of Arabic the Centrality of Language to Arabic Culture*, ed. Bilal Orfali (Leiden: Brill, 2011), 417–18; H. T. Norris, "Arabic Folk Epic and the Western *Chanson de Geste*," *Oral Tradition* 4, nos. 1–2 (1989): 125–50.

51. Daniela Meneghini, "Saljuqid Literature," in *Encyclopaedia Iranica*, ed. Ehsan Yarshater, updated May 25, 2010, https://www.iranicaonline.org/articles/saljuqs-v. On the "flurry of [romance or romantic epic] activity" in the Ghaznavid to Saljūq transitional era and its implications for how we might classify the genre, see Cameron Cross, "The Poetics of Romantic Love in *Vis and Rāmin*," PhD diss. University of Chicago, 2015, 71–78.

anticipates the *umma*'s future directions, popular epics tend instead to spotlight Black figures primed to take up its mantle because of their inborn *nasab* and nobility: generals and warrior-poets of tribal renown, princes, princesses, and even descendants of Muḥammad (*shurafāʾ*). Rather than threatening existing power structures or being ensconced in a layered administration, their characters embody enduring forms of both honor and accessibility.

The wave of Arabic epic production rolls over several centuries, with two significant crests.[52] The first can be hazily placed in the early medieval period, or Islam's formative centuries—the existence of a handful of epics is attested in an autobiographical and polemical text, *Ifḥām al-Yāhūd,* or *Silencing the Jews,* written by the Baghdad-based Samawʾal al-Maghribī (d. 1180), a rabbi's son who converted to Islam, in the mid- to late twelfth century. This earlier spate of the *sīras* includes the stories of pre-Islamic heroes such as ʿAntar, a local legend, and Alexander the Great, whose euhemerized life story had already crossed several other regional languages and cultures before being transmitted in Arabic. The listed text that deals with subject matter most proximal to Samawʾal's own lifetime is *Sīrat Dhāt al-Himma,* whose narrative closes with the ʿAbbasid caliph al-Wāthiq, who died in AD 847. In the words of Remke Kruk, events that the *sīras* explore offer little more than a *terminus post quem* for the texts themselves.[53] We do not know when, prior to Samawʾal's writing, the "great collections" (*al-dawāwīn al-kibār*) that he speaks of reading were first committed to the page or in precisely what form.[54]

More is knowable about what some characterize as a second efflorescence of Arabic epics, during the period of Mamluk rule in Egypt and Syria from the thirteenth to the sixteenth century. During this time, a

52. Danuta Madeyska, "The Language and Structure of the Sīra," *Quaderni Di Studi Arabi* 9 (1991): 193–218.

53. Remke Kruk, *Warrior Women of Islam: Female Empowerment in Arabic Popular Literature* (London: I. B. Tauris, 2014), 3.

54. In his autobiography, Samawʾal is lukewarm on the *sīras,* saying he encountered them as a child among what Moshe Perlmann refers to as "the Arabic fiction literature of his day—stories, anecdotes, popular romances of knighthood," but moved on in later life to more accurate histories. The examples listed in his treatise are the stories of *ʿAntar, Dhū-l-Himma wa-l-Baṭṭāl,* and *Iskandar dhū-l-Qarnayn*. Perlmann identifies the *dīwān* of *Dhū-l-Himma* as being a distinct text from that of *al-Baṭṭāl,* but this is likely in error. In the Ottoman period, though, al-Baṭṭāl does indeed receive his own separate treatment in the *Baṭṭālnāma.* See Moshe Perlmann, "Samauʾal al-Maghribī Ifḥām al-Yahūd: Silencing the Jews," *Proceedings of the American Academy for Jewish Research* 32 (1964): 15, 100.

series of works first appear with particularly timely resonances: the adventures of the Yemeni king Sayf b. Dhī Yazan prospecting for the Book of the Nile and warring against East African foes, the fantastic biography of Baybars, a prominent Mamluk sultan, and so on. Significantly, this is also the period in which extant manuscript versions of the prior epics emerge, and they emerge *en masse*. Unlike several of the texts that became various European countries' "national epics"—the *Cantar de Mio Cid, Chanson de Roland,* and *Beowulf*—through resuscitation in early modernity from single manuscripts, behind a given title of an Arabic *sīra* there lies an often very geographically diffuse plurality of physical versions, more or less tailored to local interests. Nearly all of these textual pathways originate in Mamluk territories, as does a robust record in marketplace manuals, their own marginalia, and other writings, of the epics being bought or rented out, volume by volume, in markets and recited in public spaces.[55] Often, when one looks at a handwritten *sīra* today, its volumes are no longer all together.

The Mamluk era also witnessed higher traffic in popular literature in general. Our earliest complete manuscript of *Alf Layla wa-Layla,* or the *1001 Nights,* hails from fourteenth-century Syria. Early copies of the only surviving Arabic shadow play scripts—another popular form of street entertainment—are from the late fourteenth through fifteenth centuries as well.[56] *Sīrat Dhāt al-Himma*'s tangible trajectory follows this same arc. Its earliest dated manuscript is from 1430.[57] The latest dated portion of a manuscript consulted for this book is from 1813, in a hand belonging to a man from Fes. As I discuss further in chapter 3, I attempted to cull from a mix of manuscripts and print versions that are on the same stemma, so as to closely compare, as well as from outliers that are rarer or more oriented to specific readerships. The print version of *Sīrat Dhāt al-Himma* that is most widely used in contemporary scholarship in general and in this book

55. Konrad Hirschler, *The Written Word in the Medieval Arabic Lands: A Social and Cultural History of Reading Practices* (Edinburgh: Edinburgh University Press, 2013), 165–80.

56. These plays also attest to yet another audience to and source of popular entertainments in the Mamluk period, in the form of performers and tricksters from the Banū Sāsān, Romani-like peoples examined by Kristina Richardson, who also collates a number of the plays' manuscripts in her reconstruction of the Banū Sāsān's language. Kristina Richardson, "Tracing a Gypsy Mixed Language through Medieval and Early Modern Arabic and Persian Literature," *Der Islam* 94:1 (2017): 139–43.

57. Magidow, "Epic of the Commander Dhat al-Himma," 4; Claudia Ott, "From the Coffeehouse into the Manuscript: The Storyteller and His Audience in the Manuscripts of an Arabian Epic," *Oriente Moderno* 83 (2003): 444.

as well was produced in Cairo in 1909 and subsequently reprinted in Beirut in 1980 with different formatting. The text's life in manuscript bleeds, temporally, into its life in print—the earliest printed version consulted for this book was written in the 1890s for a Tunisian Jewish audience. These aspects of how the texts were produced allow one to ask questions about ambient understandings of identity that simultaneously extended over vast spaces and times and can be populated with specific local details.

The diversity of the lead characters in epics brings into sharp focus the historical importance of narratives in which identities are navigated and negotiated among—and for—popular audiences. This is still the case today. Recently, stories from *Sīrat ʿAntar* have been brought to life anew in comic book form in both Arabic and English, and a primary reason adduced for interest in the works is the protagonist's mixed heritage and up-from-slavery heroic tale;[58] stories from *Sīrat Dhāt al-Himma* have been translated by Melanie Magidow in a recent, groundbreaking volume that audiences are promised will "contribute a frequently neglected face to the gallery of Arabic—and world—literature" in the personage of its defiant and unconventional heroine.[59]

Looking slightly further back, we see that interest in these tales had many ebbs and flows. *Sīrat Dhāt al-Himma* lived much of its life in the twentieth century as text rather than a performed narrative. Already in the nineteenth century Edward William Lane remarked on the scarcity of copies of *Sīrat Dhāt al-Himma* on the Cairene scene, attributing the tale's rarer performance—which often involved storytellers reading aloud from texts—to inaccessibility. He bemoaned the fact that out of the "fifty-five volumes" in which he was told the tale was rendered, he could only find the first three (a mere "302 pages" of the total).[60] Today, the aforementioned two main print versions of the *sīra* are somewhat easier to find and widely used by scholars. Printed abridgments are also available in

58. The publisher's blurb for the premier English-language ʿAntar comic, *Antar the Black Knight*, with words by Africanfuturist (a term of her own coinage, juxtaposing her focus on African continental cultural and storytelling paradigms with Afrofuturism's diasporic ones) novelist Nnedi Okorafor and art by Eric Battle, reads, "A despised camel driver born of an African slave mother and an Arab noble father, Antar proves that heroes are made by embracing who we are and dreaming about what we can become." Nnedi Okorafor "Antar the Black Knight," Nnedi.com, accessed 1 August 2023, https://nnedi.com/comics/antar-the-black-knight/.

59. *The Tale of the Princess Fatima, Warrior Woman: The Arabic Epic of Dhat al-Himma*, trans. Melanie Magidow (New York: Penguin Books, 2021), xviii.

60. Edward William Lane, An Account of the Manners and Customs of the Modern Egyptians (London: Alexander Gardner, 1895), 421–22.

multiple languages. In 1995, the Ministry of Culture in Egypt published an English translation that condenses the epic down to under 150 pages.[61] A chapbook version published in Arabic by ʿAbbās Khiḍr in Cairo in the 1960s was priced at a cheap 15 piastres, yet despite its ready availability the editor introduces the stories within as an example of the "buried treasure" of pre-*nahḍa* popular Arabic literature, lost to the public but recoverable by historians and litterateurs.[62] The epic was, in other words, portrayed explicitly as part of premodern "folk" heritage, waiting to be unearthed and reclaimed. Yet its performance tradition did live on throughout this period. The latest street performance of *Sīrat Dhāt al-Himma* to earn scholarly analysis was audited in 1997 in Marrakesh by Claudia Ott and Remke Kruk.[63] The stories have moreover been incorporated into Ramadan television series and children's cartoons.

In contrast to *Sīrat Dhāt al-Himma*'s relatively sharp decline in live performance, *Sīrat Banī Hilāl* enjoyed a longer trajectory as a semi-extemporized, oral composition, engendering a comparatively large and variable body of printed versions. In the first chapter on Black-Arab heroes' origin stories, I draw together a variety of iterations of *Sīrat Banī Hilāl*, allowing us to see in microcosm the way that Abū Zayd's birth narrative, and thus his racialization, transform in different compositional and cultural contexts. Among the several versions of *Sīrat Banī Hilāl* surveyed are a number of transcribed recitations from the Egyptian cities of Luxor and Bakātūsh, some of which have been made into storybooks and others of which have been incorporated into academic archives or monographs, and a printed edition from Beirut produced in the late twentieth century. Though I have highlighted recorded speech versions of *Sīrat Banī Hilāl* as well as versions conceived of and produced for print, much work remains to be done on its many manuscripts on which these later printings were based.[64]

By comparison, manuscript versions of *Sīrat ʿAntar* are well documented, and more importantly, they showcase a stunning amount of consistency

61. *Princess Dhat al-Himma: The Princess of High Resolve*, ed. and trans. Shawqi ʿAbd al-Hakim and Omaima Abou-Bakr (Giza, Egypt: Prism Publications, 1995).

62. *Dhāt al-Himma*, ed. ʿAbbās Khiḍr (Cairo: Maṭbaʿat al-Kīlānī), 1968.

63. Remke Kruk and Claudia Ott, "'In the Popular Manner': Sira-recitation in Marrakesh anno 1997," *Edebiyat* 10, no. 2 (1999): 183–97. This performance is also discussed in Magidow, "Epic of the Commander," 13.

64. An invaluable resource that contains recordings, transcriptions, and translations, including audience responses to the recitation, is Dwight Reynolds's *Sīrat Banī Hilāl* digital archive: *Sirat Bani Hilal Digital Archive*, Santa Barbara, CA, accessed August 1, 2023, https://siratbanihilal.ucsb.edu/.

for a work of popular prose.[65] Despite the fact that in places like Egypt ʿAntar's story became so synonymous with the trade of professional reciters that these men became known as *ʿAntarī*, their performances likewise typically involved reading aloud from a written work rather than extemporizing. The written substance of *Sīrat ʿAntar*—surmised by Harry Norris to have solidified in the "late medieval" period, under the textualizing influences of the Mamluk era—has a variety of identifiable literary forerunners that were brought into the text, sometimes with significant modification.[66] This includes many versions' frontmatter, featuring the stories of Ibrāhīm (Abraham) and Nimrūd (Nimrod) that echo those found in collected anecdotes about the prophets (*qiṣaṣ al-anbiyāʾ*), of the four brothers Iyād, Rabīʿa, Muḍar, and Anmār, who together are the storied progenitors of all of Arabia's tribes, and of various incursions into Africa, central Asia, and the Levant that draw on prior *maghāzī* literature. These stories were collected and copied with much faithfulness, such that, despite his complaints about inconsistency, a fifteenth-century Ottoman scholar was able to cobble together a critical edition to translate from three separate Arabic versions, an enterprise to which popular manuscripts rarely lend themselves, as modern translators have remarked.[67] In all of the manuscripts and printings of *Sīrat ʿAntar* that I consulted, the aspects of the hero's narrative that I analyze were virtually identical, and so I have ultimately only used one printed version in my discussions.

As medieval nonelite audiences' demand for a by-volume rental market attests, even though popular epics were typically economically fabricated with few inks and no illuminations, they nonetheless were of such great length that owning a whole epic was beyond the means of many. Narrators of the epic themselves would rent the volumes from which they would then recite, while by the nineteenth century, they were more likely to read from cheaply printed chapbook versions of the stories instead.

65. For a list of manuscripts and print editions of *Sīrat ʿAntar*, see Peter Heath, *The Thirsty Sword: Sīrat ʿAntar and the Arabic Popular Epic* (Salt Lake City: University of Utah Press, 1996), 232–39.

66. H. T. Norris, "The Futūḥ al-Bahnasā: And Its Relation to Pseudo-ʿMaġāzī' and 'Futūḥ' Literature, Arabic 'Siyar' and Western Chanson de Geste in the Middle Ages," *Quaderni di Studi Arabi* (1986): 80. Norris speculates that the versions of ʿAntar that have survived are from the late thirteenth century or later on the basis of style and intertexts: H. T. Norris, "From Asia to Africa: The 'Tuḥfat al-Albāb' by Abū Ḥāmid al-Gharnāṭī (473/1080–565/1169) as a Source of Chronology and Content of the 'Sīrat ʿAntar B. Shaddād," *Bulletin of the School of Oriental and African Studies* 57 (1994): 174.

67. Heath, *The Thirsty Sword*; *A Hundred and One Nights*, trans. Bruce Fudge (New York: New York University Press, 2016), xxix.

We know something about the identities of these tales' expert reciters, and one even finds occasional overlaps between the perceptions of members in this guild and the tales' Black heroes. In his ethnography of modern reciters of *Sīrat Banī Hilāl* in Bakātūsh in Egypt, Dwight Reynolds discusses the Ḥalab roots of many practitioners of the craft. Kristina Richardson has shown that the Ḥalab form is one subset of the aforementioned *ghurabā'*, "Strangers," who resided throughout Afro-Eurasia and are akin to the Roma, Yenish, and Travellers. Some Strangers were further grouped as Black in medieval Arabic writings. Reynolds notes one speculative etymology for Ḥalab relates to the community's dark skin, and elsewhere adds that oftentimes the Black epic hero's appearance and status lent him to disguising himself as an epic poet when passing through "enemy territory": the epicists of Bakātūsh might sing of Abū Zayd as presenting like one of their own, and being mistreated, overlooked, or underestimated for this fact.[68] *Sīrat Banī Hilāl* also has an extensive recitational tradition throughout Arabophone sub-Saharan Africa, though as I discuss further in chapter 1, sub-Saharan versions are said to de-emphasize the hero's blackness, either because it was not a salient marker of difference or because in these locales preserving histories of Arabization through the tales acquired particular importance.

The *Hilāliyya* is not the only epic whose sub-Saharan African elements and analogues have been traced; Hellen Blatherwick has demonstrated that the role of Solomon in the Mamluk-era *Sīrat Sayf b. Dhī Yazan* shares much with the fourteenth-century Ethiopian *Kebrä Nägäst* (*Glory of Kings*).[69] One of the text's central villains has moreover been identified with a Christian Ethiopian emperor from the mid- to late fourteenth century,[70] which puts the epic's action on the precipice of an era in which the Solomonic Ethiopian crown sent several unprecedented missions through Mamluk lands and into Europe.[71] Though Carl Petry writes that the "Mamluk Sultanate inherited a centuries-old world view from its Fatimid and Ayyubid forebears, compounded by dedication to preservation of the status quo in foreign affairs," they nonetheless also engaged diplomatically with parts of the "lands of the Blacks" in novel ways, from welcoming

68. Reynolds, *Heroic Poets*, 13–14.

69. Helen Blatherwick, "Solomon Legends in *Sīrat Sayf ibn Dhī Yazan*," *Mizan* 2, no. 1 (2017): 1–31.

70. Harry T. Norris, "Sayf b. Dī Yazan and the Book of the History of the Nile," *Quaderni di Studi Arabi* 7 (1989): 129.

71. Verena Krebs, *Medieval Ethiopian Kingship, Craft, and Diplomacy with Latin Europe* (London: Palgrave Macmillan, 2021).

Mali's kings to fielding pleas to stop illegal slave raids against their free Muslims subjects made by Bornu's rulers, the Sayfuwa, who take their name from the Sayf of *Sīrat Sayf b. Dhī Yazan*.[72]

These political transformations can in turn appear obliquely in the *sīras*. Andrea Crudu has noted that the conflict between the white- and Arab-identifying Muslim Sayfuwa and their "black and pagan opponents" earns further elaboration in later versions of the *sīra*.[73] Danuta Madeyska offers that the large quantity of Black enslaved and freed soldiers in *Sīrat Dhāt al-Himma* could be used to help date portions of the text in accordance with the fluctuating supplies of people from various of the Islamic world's peripheries into central Islamic lands, and hence their drawing focus in storytelling. In making an overall case for Fatimid influence on the text, Madeyska isolates the role potentially played by one leader, the Fatimid caliph al-Mustanṣir (d. 1094) and his Black mother and regent, Raṣad, in ramping up the purchase for military use of enslaved Black people through the trans-Saharan trade.[74] Yet *Sīrat Dhāt al-Himma*'s entanglements with goings-on related to the "lands of the Blacks" are otherwise largely unaccounted for in scholarship.

Others have offered rationales for the existence of Black heroes that coalesce around particular illustrious figures. As Peter Heath discusses, the nineteenth-century Orientalist Joseph von Hammer-Purgstall attributes ʿAntar's selection out of the panoply of well-known pre-Islamic warrior-poets to helm an epic to a clever move on the part of his *sīra*'s supposed compiler, the aforementioned ninth-century author al-Aṣmaʿī. Though al-Aṣmaʿī was responsible for one of the earliest anthologies of the historical ʿAntara b. Shaddād's (d. ca. 508) poetry, his attribution as the fashioner of his epic tradition is likely a metafictional device. Yet von Hammer-Purgstall made much of the fact that the grammarian and lexicographer was installed in the court of al-Maʾmūn (d. 833), a caliph who, like ʿAntar, was foreign on his mother's side and therefore perceived by some as a less legitimate heir to the caliphate than his half sibling.[75]

72. Carl F. Petry, *The Mamluk Sultanate: A History* (Cambridge: Cambridge University Press, 2022), 80; al-Qalqashandī, *Ṣubḥ al-Aʿshā* vol. 8 (Cairo: al-Maṭbaʿa al-Amīriyya, 1915), 117–18.

73. Andrea Crudu, "The Sudanese Elements in *Sīrat Sayf ibn Ḏī Yazan*," *Arabica* 61, nos. 3–4 (2014): 313.

74. Danuta Madeyska, "Reflections on the Origin of *Sīrat Ḏāt al-Himma*," *Rocznik Orientalistyczny* 43 (1984): 94–95.

75. Von Hammer-Purgstall reads the parallel more closely, mistaking the caliph al-Maʾmūn's maternal ancestry for African. In fact, his mother was of Persian heritage, born in present-day Afghanistan. Heath, *The Thirsty Sword*, 6.

Robert Brunschvig describes ʿAntar's story in more general terms as a *roman à thèse* designed to defend the birthrights of children born of slave concubinage, and adduces the *sīra*'s existence as "proof that the question [of such children] had some immediacy and demanded a liberal answer."[76] Nor do demands for reform through these Black heroes cease in Islam's early centuries. Particularly intriguing for our purposes is their sustained use to resist white supremacist medievalism before it was so named. Writing in Du Bois's journal, *Phylon*, in 1954, the British Indian polymath Cedric Dover compares ʿAntar (the "Black Knight") favorably both with King Arthur's European model of medieval chivalry and W. E. B. Du Bois's modern example as a "black warrior, who is also at heart a poet." He writes that ʿAntar rightly belongs in the annals of "the rising colored world."[77] Earlier still, the African American author and collector of African fables, Alphonso Orenzo Stafford, dubbed ʿAntar the "Achilles of the Arabian Iliad" and noted that this "mulatto" knight's tale had surely, in its most refined form, "preceded the romances of chivalry so common in the twelfth century in Italy and France."[78]

In light of ʿAntar's role as the Black protagonist of one of the first and best-known *sīras*, and indeed as this enduringly powerful archetype of chivalry, some have simply read other Black heroes in other epics as his avatars. At times, the sources themselves encourage this, as when in *Sīrat Dhāt al-Himma* a Black warrior from ʿAntar's tribe of ʿAbs brags that, had he been born centuries earlier in ʿAntar's time, legends would have extolled him instead (*law kunt fī zamān ʿAntar ibn Shaddād mā kān al-dhikr wa-l-fakhr ṭalaʿ illā lī*).[79] However, as the historical and ontological circumstances—as well as the different compositional milieus—that give rise to their Black heroes attest, these characters are laminated: they are both individuated and intertextual. A detailed study of ʿAntar's peers will bring to light yet more about their functions, past and present.

Structure and Chapters

This book consists of seven chapters divided into three parts—"Making Race," "Race through Time," and "Race through Space." Chapters 1

76. R. Brunschvig, "ʿAbd," in *Encyclopedia of Islam*, 2nd ed. ed. Peri Bearman et al. (Leiden: Brill, 2012).

77. Cedric Dover, "The Black Knight," *Phylon* 15, no. 1 (1954): 41.

78. A. O. Stafford, "Antar, the Arabian Negro, Poet, and Hero," *Journal of Negro History* 1, no. 2 (1916): 155.

79. *Sīrat Dhāt al-Himma*, XLI:55.

through 3 comprise part I, chapters 4 and 5 comprise part II, and chapters 6 and 7 comprise part III.

Chapter 1 explores the importance of origin stories in the fundamental making of heroes and in their racialization. Using *Sīrat ʿAntar* and *Sīrat Banī Hilāl,* I discuss the conventions of birth narratives in the epic tradition and the ways in which nonhereditarily Black heroes both support and subvert them. One of the primary features of heroic origins stories that narratives of differently racialized heroes amplify is the inspiration of *ʿajab,* a sense of "knowing wonder" at the intricate and deliberate structures of God's Creation. I demonstrate that, through both the subtle workings of *ʿajab* and the patency of their difference from their kin, these heroes make space for new ways of seeing. Chapter 2 turns to the yet more exceptional birth story of ʿAbd al-Wahhāb in *Sīrat Dhāt al-Himma,* which closely follows the hero from his conception to his paternity trial and adduces a range of both practical and esoteric possibilities for how his blackness comes to be. I argue that ʿAbd al-Wahhāb's construction does not fit neatly into transregional models of heroic hybridity that have been previously studied as sites of race-making in the Middle Ages, but rather invites us to rethink the overlap between gender and race, physiology and sexuality in medieval cultural productions. In chapter 3, I elaborate on this overlap further by departing from ʿAbd al-Wahhāb's birth story and its most immediate intertexts to explore the legal, medical, and etiological literatures with which it is also connected, conversancy in which showcases what I refer to as a popular science of difference that one can trace across various medieval Arabic-speaking Muslim societies.

Chapters 4 and 5 argue that the *sīras*' activations of social kind are chronopolitical—they evince an awareness of and a pious investment in people's perspectives on difference, community, and assimilation changing for the better over time. In *Sīrat Dhāt al-Himma,* this emerges through contrasts between the text's internal present and its past, prior to the full Islamization of Arabia. In chapter 4, I show that the upward mobility that ʿAbd al-Wahhāb epitomizes and enables is presented as impossible for Black people in the text's earliest episodes, which I suggest are best read as drawing on a *jāhilī* chronotope, or a didactic landscape hewn from receptions of the pre-Islamic Arabian past. In it, Black characters are typically enslaved and unable to be clientalized or wed into Arab tribal status, rendering them permanent community outsiders. This much becomes clear through the case of the "Three Slaves of Ṭayy," an episode whose significance is central to this chapter. Chapter 5, meanwhile, focuses on the transition out of this abject, temporally and socially regressed status quo through the heroic ascent of ʿAbd al-Wahhāb and his consolidation of a community of Black, Muslim comrades at his side, often through processes of purchase or capture, conversion, and manumission. A particularly involved narrative of this process, in which ʿAbd al-Wahhāb takes up with a Black soldier who had defected to the Byzantine side, is this chapter's backbone. As the Arab-pedigreed center of a burgeoning Black community—or at least its military component—within the text, I characterize ʿAbd al-Wahhāb's at once unique and emulable role as central to allegories of assimilation. His character's interactions instruct audiences in a range of social institutions that foster community attachments among Muslims through pseudo-agnatic kinship.

Chapters 6 and 7 show that the *sīras*' changeable approaches to difference have a spatial component as well in their capacity as a set of texts that have been regularly dubbed "frontier epics" and "pseudo-*maghāzī*" tales, or conquest works that recall and exhort Muslim expansion. The *sīras* play with the prospect of their heroes' identities and relationships changing as they move into geographic zones that as a whole are pregnant with the possibility of capture, conversion, and assimilation. I therefore apply the philosopher Michael Root's famed claim that "race does not travel" to analyze the ways in which African expeditions in Arabic epics depict identities in flux.[80]

While in *Sīrat Dhāt al-Himma*, Byzantine territories constitute the most immediate zone for interreligious conflict, I argue that the *sīra* presents East African portions of the *bilād al-sūdān* as an irreligious or areligious second frontier zone in which Christians and Muslims compete for the locals' souls. The East Africa of the *sīra* is also an interpenetrative, imaginative geography: though he largely remains within the *bilād al-ḥabash*, or roughly present-day Ethiopia and its environs, ʿAbd al-Wahhāb nonetheless meets peoples who, in medieval Arabic geographies, are located in regions spanning from the Horn's littoral to the Lake Chad basin and even farther west. In chapter 6, I explicate the strategic geocultural distancing of East Africa, and particularly Abyssinia, in the *sīra* by situating Abyssinians' interactions with Muslims in the narrative against the backdrop of traditionist historiography and the "mapping traditions" that arose in the ʿAbbasid era through a synthesis of traders' and travelers' reportage (*akhbār*) and the uptake of Greek writings. I show that by drawing on the theories of the climes and the material realities of Indian Ocean transport, the *sīra* selectively represents Black political entities as cosmopolitan to cultivate an aspirational history: audiences watch as a

80. Michael Root, "How We Divide the World." *Philosophy of Science* 67, no. 3 (2000): S628–39.

rich, implicitly untapped terrain in want of Muslim guidance transforms through heroes' sojourns abroad.

Chapter 7 considers what transpires when the heroes then return to the Byzantine frontier with their thousands of new Black recruits, and in ʿAbd al-Wahhāb's case with a new spouse, the East African princess Maymūna. Maymūna cycles through virtually every status imaginable for a woman in a *sīra* as hero, antihero, and villain. She moves from being a royal virgin to soldier and mother on the frontier, and from nascently Muslim to ascetically pious to converting to Christianity out of lust and love. I argue that Maymūna's mercurial arc and ultimate exit from the Muslim community must be read through her status as the only Black, female character of note in her portions of the text. Maymūna is aware of how she is perceived within the text's world: she asserts her true belief and chastity again and again to ʿAbd al-Wahhāb before their courtship blossoms; she notes that the Muslims' Byzantine foes especially fear Black soldiers; she recognizes the differences between the Byzantine-princess-turned-Muslim-warrior Nūrā's experiences of wifehood and motherhood and her own. She is also a particularly uncanny figure in how she subverts these perceptions. Even after converting to Christianity, Maymūna continues to bring the Muslims with whom she comes in contact oneiric and theophanic experiences. By interpreting Maymūna's character as an assemblage—a figure who, despite the seeming fixed points of her identity, constantly indicates these points' contingency and relationality—I offer a novel way of reading Black women's presences in Arabic popular literature.

Outlook and Scope

Though this book's subtitle gestures toward the idea that race has its makings in the medieval period, I also dissect some of the ways this point has been argued in the recent past, as well as the disciplinary terrains these arguments take up. Overall, this book intervenes in two contrasting narratives that have, until recently, structured the conversation on race in premodernity, and especially the precolonial "non-West." On the one hand, it is widely held that race is an invention of the modern Western state and its sciences, subjectivities, and colonial commitments, all of which serve to render "post-Enlightenment European bodies and social configurations as the sole signifiers of actualized universal reason."[81] Geraldine Heng has

81. Denise Ferreira da Silva, *Towards a Global Idea of Race* (Minneapolis: University of Minnesota Press, 2007), 101.

remarked on how this characterization of race's emergence ironically renders modernity "both *telos* and origin" in ways that are then, like race itself, totalized "through mechanisms of intellectual replication pervasive in the Western academy, and circulated globally."[82]

As this suturing of modernity, globalization, and Westernness implies, the dominant account of race's history is itself underwritten by cultural condescension. It assumes that only modern, Western (white) people rigorously positioned themselves as the ontological, intellectual, and moral centers of their universe, and implies that other historical, global subjects are exempt from engaging in what Denise Ferreira da Silva calls an "analytics of raciality" in any of their own efforts to do so.[83] This ironically undermines the humanity and complexity of those that "post-Enlightenment European" people have raced as "other" by alleging that structures like race—and, implicitly, those others' own sense of unconditioned subjectivity in the form of their relative independence from or agency in such structures—were historically unthinkable for them. This account has also prevented comparative thinking across languages and histories: as I discuss further in chapter 3, today a common thread in conversations in the Arabic-speaking world is the claim that race and racism did not arrive there until the colonial encounter, though there is a growing body of work that troubles this.

On the other hand, it is also widely held that virtually all premodern peoples have been unreflectively and virulently xenophobic, or, to use Aziz al-Azmeh's phrasing, that people's senses of peoplehood have been "sustained by exclusivity as if by a force of nature."[84] This reasoning would suggest that manifestations of Arab-Muslim antiblackness are merely one form of a transcultural rhetoric of "barbarism," typical also of Arabic writings on non-Arabs (*ʿajam*) in many forms. This argument, too, has a particular ideological trajectory: it maintains that what we now call racism is at worst an inevitable design flaw in the human mind and at best an inchoate holdover from our temporally and socially regressed forebears, making it out-of-place in, as opposed to unique to, modern life. In a progressive framework of history, the idea that racism's or related prejudices' most extreme iterations are located somewhere in the past or abroad forecasts a future in which sufficiently advanced societies might become "post-racial,"

82. Geraldine Heng, *The Invention of Race in the European Middle Ages* (Cambridge: Cambridge University Press, 2018), 20.

83. Silva, *Towards a Global Idea of Race.*

84. Aziz Al-Azmeh, "Barbarians in Arab Eyes," *Past & Present* 134 (1992): 3.

while those that are believed to be behind due to the heterogeneous march of civilizational time will languish in racial discord.

This argument has been tailored by Orientalist thinkers in several fashions, particularly in scholarship claiming that Europeans acquired their antiblackness by directly imbibing the prejudices of Arab slavers in al-Andalus and the Maghrib.[85] It also arises in paternalistic colonial and neocolonial projects that seek to remediate racism, alongside other "medieval" prejudices like those of sect and tribe, in the Arab-Muslim world and its diasporas. Though much scholarship analyzes the effects of "Arab superiority" in traditional histories, much likewise reifies the idea that Islam is inherently Arab and therefore subscribes to a racist vision of Muslim culture as permanently foreign to and unaffected by the contributions of its immense numbers of non-Arab members, including countless Black people throughout history.[86] As I discuss in chapter 7, at the heart of both this saviorism and this erasure of the Islamic world's diversity is the fact that when writing about racialization in the Arab-Muslim world, many have addressed only its most visible and virulent articulations such as bigotry toward enslaved Black people in Arabic literature, rather than considering how in societies where racialized categories are at play, everyone is subject to them.

Though neither of these argumentative extremes is adequate to the task of explaining racialization in medieval Arab-Muslim contexts, both describe an important caveat: racialized difference there and then was not constructed and used in the same ways as race here and now. This book offers ways to theorize racialization and the formation of social-as-natural kinds from vantage points that are not currently widely represented in English-language scholarship by reading popular literary sources from the premodern, Arab-Muslim world. In so doing, I build on a set of prior concepts. I understand race, per Stuart Hall, as "media-mediated": interpolation into identity categories that are racialized is a matter of what people represent, inscribe, and experience that interpolation to mean in communication with one another. And, as both Hall and Nicholas R. Jones would have us note, the commodification of media also plays a key role in discursively forming categories. That popular productions are derived not

85. See, for example: James H. Sweet, "The Iberian Roots of American Racist Thought," *William and Mary Quarterly* 54, no. 1 (1997): 143–66. I discuss several other examples in chapter 3.

86. Rudolph Ware, *The Walking Qur'an: Islamic Education, Embodied Knowledge, and History in West Africa* (Chapel Hill: University of North Carolina Press, 2014), 17–20.

through contemplative "aristocratic otium," but through lower classes' for-profit performances and acts of consumption in public spaces, imbues narrative choices with material resonances.[87] Jones, for example, comments that just as many Black people in early modern Spain were sold, so too were the characters and speech acts modeled on them publicly marketed. The trendiness of their stories was attended by accusations of vulgarity and anxieties over common taste that were not dissimilar to debates about storytellers among medieval Muslim elites.[88] At the same time, as Pierre Cachia assures us, popular Arabic artistry often looked "upward" for its inspiration, and as Konrad Hirschler demonstrates, elite opprobrium for the *sīra*s was born from direct interaction with them.[89]

Through tracking and analyzing both their repetitions and shifts, I demonstrate that the *sīra*s represented and crafted human difference in biobehavioral, socially intuitive, and intellectually supported terms that are generative to interpret alongside critical theories of race. I analyze how the discourses and techniques of racialization that iterate through and across the *sīra*s and their intertexts build out what Claudia Rankine and Beth Loffreda designate a racial imaginary, or the normative parameters in which racialized subjects were thinkable and writeable. These parameters are broad and allow for much contestation and contradiction while still working with various descriptive traditions. By focusing on the complexities of popular literature and its circulation, I reject the notion of nonelites as "dominated by discourse, not as active participants in its shaping"; they are, after all, its largest constituent of shapers.[90] Moreover, because of premodern Arabic literature's aforementioned dense interreferential quality and unapologetic indulgence in borrowing, sharing, and recycling, it is often difficult to discern clear directions of influence between the massive popular corpus of materials and elite presentations of analogous sources and ideas.

A word is also in order about what this book does not do. I do not propose a particular point of origin for race and racism, and I do not litigate the ultimate morality of these texts or seek to circumscribe an

87. Nicholas R. Jones, *Staging* Habla de Negros: *Radical Performances of the African Diaspora in Early Modern Spain* (University Park: Pennsylvania State University Press, 2019), 21.

88. Jones, *Staging* Habla de Negros, 23.

89. Pierre Cachia, "Arabic Literatures, 'Elite' and 'Folk,' Junctions and Disjunctions," *Quaderni di Studi Arabi* 3 (2008): 135–52; Hirschler, *The Written Word in the Medieval Arabic Lands*, 168–86.

90. David Nirenberg, *Communities of Violence: Persecution of Minorities in the Middle Ages* (Princeton, NJ: Princeton University Press, 1996), 6.

emotional and hermeneutic range for engaging with them. I supply context for my sources' problematics around tensions between earthly difference and transcendent unity—and concomitantly between hierarchy and universalism—that are common to human phenomena that aspire to far-ranging yet normative uptake. Rather than avoiding or eliding racialized difference in order to defuse these tensions, Arab-Islamic heroic literatures put its presumed facts and facets to dynamic use.

PART I
Making Race

1

Origin Stories of the Black-Arab Hero

ʿAjab . . . is a desirable feeling that stems from one's own inability to fully comprehend an event, object, or phenomenon because it is perceived as too strange, too great, or too complicated.

MATTHEW D. SABA

A distinction must be drawn between what might be termed the 'naïve' and the 'knowing' sense of wonder: that is, between the sense of amazement experienced upon encountering a phenomenon that, on first inspection, seems to defy the dictates of nature, and the subsequent amazement experienced when that phenomenon is revealed to be simply a manifestation of the orderly processes of nature, comprehended on a larger scale.

SUZANNE CONKLIN AKBARI

If she gives birth to a son and he is dark-skinned,
Think it not an evil act, O good one,
You see, her grandmother was black of color,
And her grandfather Black like slaves

SĪRAT BANĪ HILĀL

A storied set of heroes in the *siyar shaʿbiyya* are either Black or of what we might now call Afro-Arab heritage—ʿAntar, Abū Zayd al-Hilālī, Sayf ibn Dhī Yazan, and ʿAbd al-Wahhāb. I make a distinction between Black and Afro-Arab because the two do not perfectly overlap. ʿAntar has traceable African heritage through his Abyssinian mother, as does a Sayf who, despite having the same half-Abyssinian heritage as ʿAntar, is nonetheless depicted as white and Arab-leaning. Meanwhile, Abū Zayd al-Hilālī and ʿAbd al-Wahhāb are characterized by their seemingly spontaneous, nonhereditary blackness. Each is born Black to Arab parents who explicitly self-designate as white (*abyaḍ*) and receive their children's looks as a shock, spawning a litany of questions and theories around the children's mysteriously derived features. Did their mothers commit adultery with enslaved men? Did one of their fathers fantasize about a Black woman during conception? Is there a distant, forgotten Black ancestor whose traits were dormant until now? Is their parents' skin really as light and unfreckled as it seems, or does it carry some subtle, amplifiable dark cast? Both children quickly become associated with slavery and bastardy. Both are sifted through processes of legal recourse to either purge them from their families or resolve their belonging therein.

Each of the four heroes is thus made to experience literal and figurative trials of identity from birth. Even ʿAntar is subject to a set of contested paternity claims, though not because he is rejected for his visible difference from his parents but because his astonishing strength and size result in competing demands for ownership of him amid his father's tribe. ʿAntar and ʿAbd al-Wahhāb are said to resemble their Arab fathers, yet they are nonetheless also given elaborate stories depicting their "noticeable arrival," or what Sara Ahmed characterizes as the inevitable base condition for apprehending nonwhite bodies traversing white space.[1] Abū Zayd al-Hilālī being "Black like a slave" (though in some recitations he is said to nonetheless have "the same features as a white child"), meanwhile, results in his mother being divorced and him being disinherited.[2] Even Sayf, with whose story we will otherwise leave off here, has his loyalties questioned despite his Arab appearance, paternity, and royal pedigree. The sides between which he must choose have been in conflict for millennia: in one instance, Sayf avenges his forefather Sām, or Noah's son Shem, against his brother Ḥām, from whom his Abyssinian mother is descended, by acquiring Sām's ancient, stolen sword from his accursed brother's treasury.[3] Because of the gendered and classed associations in early Arabic literature between blackness and various forms of social dependency, ʿAntar, ʿAbd al-Wahhāb, and Abū Zayd are all meanwhile perceived from early infancy as socially inferior despite being born into elite tribal families, or, in the case

1. Sara Ahmed, "A Phenomenology of Whiteness," *Feminist Theory* 8, no. 2 (2007): 163.

2. Caroline Stone, "The Great Migration of the Bani Hilal," *AramcoWorld* (November 2016), 16. https://www.aramcoworld.com/Articles/November-2016/The-Great-Migration-of-the-Bani-Hilal.

3. Helen Blatherwick, *Prophets, Gods, and Kings in Sīrat Sayf ibn Dhī Yazan: An Intertextual Reading of an Egyptian Epic* (Leiden: Brill, 2016), 88–89.

of Abū Zayd, even being born to a *sharīfa,* a female descendant of the Prophet Muḥammad. Two main assumptions are common throughout the Black and Afro-Arab heroes' birth stories. First, that whiteness or lightness is unadulterated and ideal, whereas blackness is a product of mixing, contamination, or regression. Second, that female ideation, reproductive biology, and sexuality forms the domain in which these extraordinary changes occur. Each of these assumptions involves certain legal, medical, and social perceptions that we might deem realistic or verisimilar, tethering the texts' imaginative production of Black heroes to known arrangements of properties and bodies in the world.

At the same time, a common thread binding these heroes together is not only their racialization and reidentification vis-à-vis their tribesmen, but also the capacity for their unlikely beginnings, categorical indeterminacy, and grand purposes to produce *ʿajab*—a sense of contemplative wonder at the intricacies of God's creations that at once provides moral instruction and "metaphysical pleasure." Those things that are wondrous (*ʿajīb*) in Arabic literature are often paired with the strange or unexpected (*gharīb*), and it is worth noting that these two terms are used to describe many of the heroic adventures in Arabic epics. The bracketing phrase that the narrator offers after the extraordinary figure of ʿAbd al-Wahhāb is born in *Sīrat Dhāt al-Himma* is, "this Black boy will be met with wondrous events and strange affairs."[4]

Studies of the births of heroes in popular epics have emphasized the element of strangeness that inheres in tales not only of Black figures, but of the many socially liminal protagonists that are touchstones of the corpus. Nabīla Ibrāhīm declares that a hero is always "born strangely, as though life in its entirety is rejecting him."[5] Often, the hero's birth and imminent alienation is foreshadowed by dreams and visions had by his parents—a form of divine messaging subject in the medieval Islamic world to rigorous modes of human interpretation (*taʾwīl*) derived from "prophetic and scriptural tradition" in order to discern its truths.[6] In the cases of the Black heroes of Arabic epics, the abnormality signaled by such premonitions is either compounded or supplanted by the racialized differentiation from their kin that the heroes experience from their first

4. *Sīrat Dhāt al-Himma,* VII:15.

5. Nabīla Ibrāhīm, *Ashkāl al-Taʿbīr fī-l-Adab al-Shaʿbī* (Cairo: al-Dār Nahḍat Miṣr, 1966), 125.

6. Dwight F. Reynolds, "Symbolic Narratives of Self: Dreams in Medieval Arabic Autobiographies," in *On Fiction and* Adab *in Medieval Arabic Literature,* ed. Philip F. Kennedy (Wiesbaden: Harrassowitz, 2005), 263; Ibrāhīm, *Ashkāl al-Taʿbir,* 129.

moments of life. Aḥmad Shams al-Dīn al-Ḥajjājī notes that early in life a typical stage of the heroic experience is "estrangement and emigration," or *al-ghurba wa-l-ightirāb*; both share a root with the word *gharīb*, suggesting the strangeness of leaving one's family and homeland.[7] This flight into the unknown is usually precipitated by rejection from a father, which the Black heroes' difference readily facilitates and which is later remediated by their reuniting in an instance of mutual recognition and disclosure, *al-taʿāruf wa-l-iʿtirāf*.[8] The wondrous, meanwhile, has received less attention in explaining popular heroes' functions within their family units and home communities, and yet wonder is precisely what lies at the threshold of strangeness and recognition.

Studies of Arabic epics have instead emphasized their status as or incorporation of "wonder tales" by highlighting those stories that most explicitly hew to the genres to which *ʿajab* gives a name: adventures in faraway lands, confronting new peoples and creatures.[9] *ʿAjab* is most strongly linked in the premodern Arab-Islamic tradition with encyclopedic "wonders of creation" texts (*ʿajāʾib al-makhlūqāt*), sometimes likened to Latinate *mirabilia*. Works of *ʿajāʾib* in turn were close cousins to geographies and travel writing of the ilk discussed in chapter 6. Each body of texts is shot through with references to what are sometimes rendered as "monstrous" or "apocalyptic races" whose existence is entertained in both Christian and Muslim works. To be sure, Asa Mittman has pointed to the problem of such terminology in that it "[de-emphasizes] their (potential) humanity," making strange or rare humanlike forms seem more unlike ourselves than they may have appeared for medieval subjects.[10]

Yet wonder lies not merely at human (self-)knowledge's edges, but also at its very core. Alireza Doostdar explains that the wondrous was also commonly found in "everyday objects, phenomena, and events" that, upon closer inspection, reveal their profound complexity yet conceal their

7. Aḥmad Shams al-Dīn al-Ḥajjājī, *Mawlid al-Baṭal fī-l-Sīra al-Shaʿbiyya* (Cairo: Dār al-Hilāl, 1991), 94–130 passim.

8. Notably, here al-Ḥajjājī employs the same word for recognition that is used in the Qurʾān and commentaries to encourage different kinds of people to "know one another" (Q 49:13) across gradients of difference that exegetes often mapped onto Arabness and non-Arabness (*ʿajam*) or else onto color and the social kinds it connotes. Al-Ḥajjājī, *Mawlid al-Baṭal*, 131–88 passim.

9. Norris, "From Asia to Africa, 183.

10. See, e.g., Domenico Agostini, "Half-Human and Monstrous Races in Zoroastrian Tradition," *Journal of the American Oriental Society* 139, no. 4 (2019): 805–18. On the designation of monstrous "races" as such, see Asa Mittman, "Are the 'Monstrous Races' Races?" *postmedieval* 6 (2015): 36–51.

precise cause (*sabab*).[11] In other words, all of the writings that make use of *ʿajab* do so while presenting the reader with difference and foreignness, at times by defamiliarizing the familiar through eliciting new ways of perceiving.

A central component of *ʿajab* is therefore not only appreciating God's designs, but putting them to various human hermeneutics of sense and science. Far from wonderment at the construction of human difference militating against naturalizing and classifying racialized groups, the two go hand in hand. In keeping with Peter Wade's statement that concepts of race throughout history have been produced not solely through anthropocentric techniques of biologization, but also through naturalization, which positions humans "in dynamic relation to the environment," the racialization of heroes in the *sīra*s and its explication in their origin stories dynamically positions them within the ordered cosmos.[12]

This chapter offers an analysis of ʿAntar and Abū Zayd's narratives of birth, "preparatory youth," and early heroic achievement as producers of *ʿajab* within their tales.[13] Across versions, Abū Zayd's story scientizes and speculates on how a Black child could be born to white parents in a multitude of ways for which ʿAntar's origins do not provide occasion and thus its potential to provoke new insights is perhaps more readily apparent. However, reading ʿAntar's origins as simply incidental imposes a modern, secular paradigm of sexuality and reproduction on his narrative, which becomes far more extraordinary, contingent, and puzzling than at first it might appear when read against traditions of inspiring *ʿajab*. I argue that these figures' racialized difference is rendered as a key part of their wondrousness in its own way, and that through their blackness, the heroes promote new ways of seeing for other characters within their texts. The ways in which the heroes discipline the affects of their fellow characters raise questions about these heroes' receptions by audiences as well. What new ways of seeing do Black protagonists open up and promote for the everyday reader or listener? How might attending to texts and intertexts also help us attend to social life, and how not? Because these heroes experience becoming raced as Black in their infancy, their origin stories not only serve the typical objective of microcosmically

11. Alireza Doostdar, *The Iranian Metaphysicals: Explorations in Science, Islam, and the Uncanny* (Princeton, NJ: Princeton University Press, 2018), 80.

12. Peter Wade, "Race, Ethnicity, and Technologies of Belonging," *Science, Technology, & Human Values* 39, no. 4 (2014): 590.

13. I borrow this highly effective phrase from Peter Heath's account of ʿAntar's heroic childhood in his *sīra*. Heath, *The Thirsty Sword*, 72–74.

setting up the text's central conflicts, obstacles, and questions, but also of setting forth their limits of thinkability: what can a Black character be and do in the tale's world?

Michelle Karnes states that the possibility that marvels "might be real," and the "difficulty of discounting [them] conclusively" is what lends medieval works that deal in encountering the unexpected their particular force; Travis Zadeh similarly refers to this possibility as a "veridical ontological status," a positioning that relates, often uncannily, to reality.[14] Unlike with wonders and travel literature, though, in the *sīras* the marvels of the Black heroes' beginnings are always counterbalanced by another, far more quotidian yet chaotic possibility of unchecked sexual mixing and the usurpation of elite men. As such, their origin stories are double-edged: even as the blackness of their heroes and explanations for its occurrence elicit *ʿajab*, it also suggests the negative dimensions of rendering blackness archetypically nonnormative in a popular body of Arab-Islamic texts. The stories inform through wonders as well as through norms.

Paving the Way for ʿAjab: *Ibrāhīm and Nimrūd*

By the time of the first attested compilations of the early *sīras* in the mid-twelfth century, including a perhaps less fleshed-out version of *Sīrat ʿAntar*, Arabness had already come in classical Arabic writings to indicate a rhizome of collocated lineages that shared certain physical and dispositional features readable on the body and, to a lesser extent, in speech and gesture.[15] Nonetheless, Arabness was also fluid, and one could become Arabized (*mustaʿarab*) by adopting any number of these qualities,

14. Michelle Karnes, "The Possibilities of Medieval Fiction," *New Literary History* 51, no. 1 (2020): 216; Travis Zadeh, "The Wiles of Creation: Philosophy, Fiction, and the *ʿAjāʾib* Tradition," *Middle Eastern Literatures* 13, no. 1 (2010): 25

15. Peter Webb notes that ninth-century grammarians uncoupled Arabness from "monopolizing" the Arabic language in a logical turn that corresponded with the language's spread (and indeed many early lexicographers were of Persian descent), leading to a shift toward "closed-ended genealogical models that expressly operated to exclude Arabic speakers from the ambit of al-ʿarab." Webb, *Imagining the Arabs*, 309. These lineages were also attached to appearance and physiognomy, and indeed in his treatise on the favors of the Arabs (*Faḍl al-ʿArab*), Ibn Qutayba declares that skills in physiognomic scrutiny and somatomancy (*ʿilm al-firāsa*, *ʿilm al-qiyāfa*)—both of which are discussed in detail in chapters 2–3—are one of the Arabs' unique contributions to knowledge. Webb, 326. See Ibn Qutayba, *The Excellence of the Arabs*, trans. Sarah Bowen Savant and Peter Webb (New York: New York University Press, 2017).

assimilating to an Arab lineage, and intergenerationally transmitting this inheritance.[16]

One quality with which Arab characters in popular epics appear secure in identifying is "whiteness." Characters deploy terms designating their whiteness—most commonly, *abyaḍ*—in at once admiring and naturalizing fashion. In *Sīrat ʿAntar*, for example, ʿAbla, ʿAntar's beloved, is dubbed "white one" (*bayḍāʾ*) when ʿAntar panegyrizes her, while his mother Zabība's simultaneous blackness and attractiveness to his father Shaddād is represented as surprising.[17] However, "whiteness" in these tales is not best understood as a physically observable feature, though it also cannot be divorced from visual perception (others have noted that the early lexicographers glossed "*abyaḍ*" as something akin to the color of straw or wheat [*ḥinṭī*]—perhaps close to what early modern Anglophone Europeans would begin to call "tawny" when they observed the bodies of people from Arabia and its neighbors).[18] Instead, Arab identity in the

16. As Zóltan Szombathy notes, outright genealogical "forgery" was also a possibility, though likely one overrepresented in literary accounts. He enumerates the "payoffs" of such a risk—and particularly with the yet more sensitive forgery of prophetic lineage—as both business returns and royal fiscal rewards, including for relocating to a desirous ruler's kingdom, and relative legal impunity. Zóltan Szombathy, "Motives and Techniques of Genealogical Forgery in Pre-modern Muslim Societies," in *Genealogy and Knowledge in Muslim Societies: Understanding the Past*, ed. Sarah Bowen Savant and Helen de Felipe (Edinburgh: Edinburgh University Press, 2014), 24–27.

17. In many versions, "white" (*bayḍāʾ*) is the first word ʿAntar uses to describe his cousin in poetry during their iconic meet-cute, in which the women of the tribe, as was "the wont of Arab women at that time," are drinking camel milk together that their slaves let cool in the open air (*hubūb al-riyāḥ*) and then carry to them. It is during one of these portages that ʿAntar catches sight of ʿAbla having her hair brushed by her mother in her tent. She flees, her hair streaming behind her, and he recites "A white one who drags her hair [upon the ground] in its length, who vanishes in it as if it were the streaming night." This episode is typically preserved as such across editions, including in European abridgements. E.g., *Sīrat ʿAntara b. Shaddād*, vol. 1 (Cairo: Maṭbaʿat Būlāq, 1886), 148; *Extraits du roman d'Antar (Muntakhabāt min Sīrat ʿAntar ibn Shaddād al-ʿAbsī)* (Paris: Firmin Didot Frères, 1841), 9.

18. As Alexander Borg discusses, the terms we often translate as "white" and "black" from Arabic indicate not just a range of hues, but of intensity or brightness, including in modern Bedouin dialects. Alexander Borg, "Towards a History and Typology of Color Categorization in Colloquial Arabic," in *Anthropology of Color: Interdisciplinary Multilevel Modeling*, ed. Robert E. MacLaury et al. (Philadelphia: John Benjamins, 2007), 279–80. As if to gesture to this range, Ibn al-Manẓūr records that colloquially among some the "two white things" (*al-abyaḍān*) connoted water and wheat (*al-māʾ wa-l-ḥinṭa*): Ibn al-Manẓūr, *Lisān al-ʿArab*, 397. On the glossing of *abyaḍ* as wheat-colored, see Abdullah Bin Hamid Ali, *The 'Negro' in Arab-Muslim Consciousness* (Swansea, UK: Claritas Books, 2018), 239n36.

sīra is typically presented as a category that, by virtue of Arab dominance in the region in which the tales are principally set, assumes many of the qualities that are said to inhere in "whiteness" in postcolonial critique. Among these is what Sara Ahmed terms "worldliness," that is, its status as the default identity, predetermining whose presences are marked or unmarked.[19] A related aspect of whiteness in Arabic popular epics is that Arab characters can selectively and relationally identify themselves with it, and therefore use whiteness to rhetorically abnegate other differences among themselves in favor of particular affinities. This ability is typically not present for Black characters living among Arabs, who are grouped together whether or not they wish to be, and whose blackness overrides so much difference between them.

Group perceptions foreground ʿAntar's beginnings as if to present his salutary, heroic blackness as the antidote to a deeply historical series of fractures. Unlike many other Arabic epic heroes, ʿAntar's birth is not presaged by dreams or visions. Instead, it is foreshadowed by a series of linked, priming prefaces that are drawn from events of either genealogical or geopolitical significance, all of which lead ultimately to the rise to prominence of the Arabian tribe of ʿAbs, into which ʿAntar is born.[20] Early in the course of this series of stories, the audience encounters a birth whose circumstances defy the workings of the natural world: the prophet Ibrāhīm is born into a world tyrannized by the hulking, black-skinned king Nimrūd (directly descended from Ḥām's son, Kanaʿān, or Canaan), who fancies himself a god. After receiving revelation from God warning him that a prophet shall arise among those close to him to undermine his rule unless he changes his ways, Nimrūd slaughters his only son, Kūsh, and forbids anyone in his kingdom to have sexual intercourse with their wives except during their menses, hoping that this will prevent any pregnancies. Meanwhile, the menopausal wife of Nimrūd's favored advisor, Āzar, suddenly begins to menstruate again for the first time in years, and Āzar returns home one day to find that "her beauty and splendor and youth had returned to her, even better than it had been in the first place."[21] Following God's will, Āzar impregnates his wife—at which moment all the idols in the land prostrate themselves and the birds and beasts erupt into uproarious merrymaking, much to the consternation of Nimrūd's soothsayers and astrologers—and the prophet Ibrāhīm is born.[22]

19. Ahmed, "Phenomenology of Whiteness," 150.

20. Heath, *The Thirsty Sword*, 168–72. *Sīrat ʿAntara ibn Shaddād*, vol. 1 (Beirut: al-Maktaba al-Shaʿbiyya, n.d.), 1–100.

21. *Sīrat ʿAntara b. Shaddād*, 16–17.

22. *Sīrat ʿAntara b. Shaddād*, 18–19.

From an unusually young age, Ibrāhīm is able to speak in a way that bears no trace of childishness, and he uses this power to dispense both divine revelation and pieces of his own, preternatural wisdom. For the sake of Ibrāhīm's safety, his existence is kept secret from Āzar for a time, and in early infancy he is raised by the angel Jibrīl (Gabriel). Not only is Ibrāhīm born under supernatural conditions and thus rendered distinct from other human beings in his origins, but he is also physically separated from his kin at birth, mirroring the doubled alienation that Nabīla Ibrāhīm considers innate to the popular hero's birth narrative, wherein his uniqueness is preordained and then solidified through lived experience. This evolution begins after an often difficult parturition, leading Amanda Hannoosh Steinberg to refer to the maternity tales in the *sīras* and, by extension, in stories of the prophets as "heroic pregnancies" that provide their own form of foreshadowing.[23] As he grows into adulthood, Ibrāhīm valiantly defeats Nimrūd, takes control of Arabia, constructs the Kaʿba, goes on a diplomatic sojourn to Egypt that results in his acquiring Hājar, and bears his two sons, Isḥāq and Ismāʿīl (Isaac and Ishmael).

The aforementioned pattern of father-child separation in the *sīras* also reappears after Ibrāhīm has conceived Ismāʿīl with Hājar, a "Coptic slave-woman . . . of beauty and humility, stature and good proportions, and abounding intellect," who was gifted to Sāra (Sarah) by the king of Egypt. When Ibrāhīm takes her as a concubine and she conceives, Ibrāhīm implores Sāra to let Hājar into their home, at which point,

> [Sāra] said to our master Ibrāhīm, peace be upon him, 'I do not want Hājar to be with me in this household, so turn her away from me to wherever you will [*ḥawwalhā ʿanī ḥayth shaʾt*].' Then God, may He be praised and exalted, revealed to [Ibrāhīm] that He would send her to the Kaʿba [*al-bayt al-ʿatīq*] and brought forth [the flying horse] Burāq, who carried Hājar and our master, Ismāʿīl, peace be upon him, and placed them next to the House.[24]

Here, Ibrāhīm knows the whereabouts of his son, but he is nonetheless kept at a great physical remove because of domestic politics. ʿAntar's birth and early life emulates several elements of his prophetic forefathers' narratives: he is the product of an improbable match, he is separated from his father due to a kinship dispute, and in early childhood he exhibits a range of unique abilities.

23. Amanda Hannoosh Steinberg, "Wives, Witches, and Warriors: Women in Arabic Popular Epic," PhD diss. (University of Pennsylvania, 2018), 153.

24. *Sīrat ʿAntara b. Shaddād*, 47.

Parallels between the biographies of prophets and those of heroes are evident throughout Arabic epic traditions. In her work on *Sīrat Sayf b. Dhī Yazan*, Helen Blatherwick offers three categories under which references to the prophets in popular lore may be classified: cameos in diegetic, moral tales told by narrators or among the protagonists of the text, attribution as the former owners of heirlooms or relics acquired by the protagonists (a form of *waṣiyya*, or prophetic inheritance), and finally, subtler reference through "a variety of tale patterns, themes, and motifs which, however common, have their most universally recognised Semitic incarnation in the legends of the prophets."[25] This "prophetic intertext" cuts in both directions. Khalid Sindawi demonstrates the co-extensiveness between the images of popular heroes and those of prophetic or saintly figures in his study of *maqātil* (martyrological) literature and depictions of Ḥusayn b. ʿAlī (d. 680), identifying the work of hagiographers as "shap[ing] and embellishing their heroes and impart[ing] to them superior qualities."[26] He argues that the ideal saint or prophet is also a warrior for the faith. True to this, some of the early *sīras*, in the form of Arabic versions of the *Alexander Romance*, and numerous later ones such as *Sīrat Ḥamza al-Bahlawān*, render the lives of prophetic figures mentioned in the Qurʾān and members of the *ahl al-bayt*, or Muḥammad's family, into consummate heroic tales.[27]

ʿAntar's narrative accordingly resonates with and amplifies certain features of Ibrāhīm's within the text, including some that are not universal to its telling in anthologies of prophets' tales but are particular to the representational domain of the epic. The oppositional dynamic between Ibrāhīm and the Black, idolatrous despot, Nimrūd, positions ʿAntar's entrance as an intervention that complicates how we read the world's political and social organization, and even its natural one. We get a particularly striking glimpse of the contours of this organization when the child Ibrāhīm is with his mother one day, looking at his reflection:

> [Ibrāhīm] gazed at his face in the mirror [*fa-naẓar Ibrāhīm ilā wajhihi fī-l-miʾrāh*] and said to his mother, "O mother, who has a more beautiful

25. Blatherwick, *Prophets, Gods, and Kings*, 67.

26. Khalid Sindawi, "The Image of Ḥusayn ibn ʿAlī in 'Maqātil' Literature," *Quaderni di Studi Arabi* 20 (2002–2003): 80.

27. Though many of the full-length copies of Alexander tales in Arabic or in languages such as aljamiado using Arabic scripts are relatively late, dating to the sixteenth century or after, they appear to have far earlier forerunners that are no longer extant. On the development of the Arabic Alexander romance traditions, see Z. David Zuwiyya, "The Alexander Romance in the Arabic Tradition," in *A Companion to Alexander Literature in the Middle Ages*, ed. David Zuwiyya (Leiden: Brill, 2011), 73–112.

> [*aḥsan*] face—me or Nimrūd?" She replied, "O my son, you are more beautiful, because Nimrūd is black and swarthy [*aswad adbas*], frown-faced [*muʿabbis al-wajh*], squint-eyed [*aḥwal*], and flat-nosed [*afṭas*]." Ibrahim said, "If he were a god, he wouldn't be in this state [*mā kānat hādhihi al-ḥāla ḥālatuhu*] and look this way [*wa-lā hādhihi al-ṣifa ṣifatuhu*]."[28]

In a moment of physiognomic reasoning, as her son considers his face, Sāra declares her child more beautiful—*aḥsan* also connotes moral perfection—than Nimrūd because, implicitly, he is whiter, more smiling, and rounder featured. Her description of Nimrūd sends one of many fissures of disillusionment through Ibrāhīm's view of the cosmic order as Nimrūd presents it, with him its primary deity. This insight begins with a moment of looking (*naẓar*) at signs in his own face, which Travis Zadeh reminds us is not a mere superficial exercise, but an analytical process of "speculation" that was highly inflected by Greek rationalism in Islamicate contexts; mirrors, likewise, are a byword for the reflection of the inner realm in the outer, and the use of one here appears to be particular to the story's retelling in *Sīrat ʿAntar*.[29] In Sufi discourses on self-refinement, the moral dimensions of mirror-gazing achieve their richest metaphorical use, and in some cases play with black and white tableaux to do so. True to this, long after ʿAntar's tale is first attested, the fifteenth-century Persian poet Jamiʿ's (d. 1492) *Haft Awrang* (*Seven Thrones*) presents an essentially flipped vignette to Ibrāhīm's. A Black (*zengī*) man sees himself for the first time in a discarded mirror and is horrified at his appearance.[30] The author explains this as a representation of the pain of realizing one's own bad deeds and, concurrently, one's self-hatred—a negative manifestation of Suzanne Conklin Akbari's "'knowing' sense of wonder," in which probing the full truth of the unexpected reveals the alienation of the individual rather than the coalescence of the cosmos.

28. *Sīrat ʿAntara b. Shaddād*, vol. 1, 23.

29. Zadeh, "Wiles of Creation," 27–28.

30. Marianna Shreve Simpson, *Sultan Ibrahim Mirza's* Haft Awrang*: A Princely Manuscript from Sixteenth Century Iran* (New Haven, CT: Yale University Press, 1997), 188. On the role of the mirror in this and other related texts, see Gregory Minissale, *Images of Thought: Visuality in Islamic India 1550–1750* (Newcastle, UK: Cambridge Scholars, 2006), 174. As Cameron Cross has shown, elsewhere in the Persianate Sufi tradition black and white signal two necessary and dynamically interrelated "poles" on the spectrum of love, with black associated with concupiscence and white with purity: Cameron Cross, "The Many Colors of Love in Niẓāmī's *Haft Paykar*: Beyond the Spectrum," *Interfaces* 2 (2016): 52–96.

Ibrāhīm's interactions with Nimrūd culminate in Nimrūd's violent death and a complete overturning of the paradigms that he had instituted: his people revert to monotheism, all the idols to him are removed, and of course a Black man no longer holds the world in his thrall, having "grown in evil and corruption until he had seized many lands, one after the other, possessing their wealth and consolidating their treasuries . . . and impressing their armies and soldiers," including those of the west (*al-gharb*), the east (*al-sharq*), Yemen, and India.[31]

Though this tale is most overtly one of righteous triumph over idolatry and forced false worship, it is possible to read Sāra's vilification of the world conqueror Nimrūd and Ibrāhīm's heroic vanquishing of him against the grain as a demonstration of know-your-place aggression. This form of social policing is defined by Koritha Mitchell as "the flexible, dynamic array of forces that answer the achievements of marginalized groups such that their success brings aggression as often as praise."[32] By the time ʿAntar is born, the world into which he noticeably arrives is one where most of the Black people in his midst are enslaved. Those that he finds in East Africa when he ventures abroad—typically described, like Nimrūd himself, as the "children of Ḥām"—are predominantly still living a backward existence as idolaters, revering the *jinn* and the fires they produce or natural objects they inhabit in ways that lead the text to analogize them with the Magians of Persia, and even intermarrying their royal children with these otherworldly beings.[33] The brethren of Ibrāhīm, meanwhile, remain as rulers of Arabia and stewards of the Kaʿba he erected.

The undercurrent of racialized backlash against Nimrūd is compounded by Sāra's relationship to the "Coptic" Hājar. Copts (*aqbāṭ*), a term used in early Arabic writings for native Egyptians of any religion, were typically understood to also be progeny of Ḥām and are described as having dark skin (*suḥm*), textured hair (*jiʿād*), and inhabiting "black loam" (*ahl al-madara al-sawdāʾ*). This likely reflects the Egyptians' own descriptions of the fertile, black soil bordering the Nile, from which the Coptic name for Egypt derives.[34] Hājar's geocultural difference and enslavement, and

31. *Sīrat ʿAntara b. Shaddād*, vol. 1, 11.

32. Koritha Mitchell, "Identifying White Mediocrity and Know-Your-Place Aggression: A Form of Self-Care," *African American Review* 51, no. 4 (2018): 253.

33. *Sīrat ʿAntara ibn Shaddād*, vol. 5, 351.

34. Ibn Hishām, *Sīrat Ibn Hishām*, ed. Muṣṭafā al-Saqqā et al. (Cairo: Maktaba wa-Maṭbaʿa Muṣṭafā al-Bābī al-Ḥalabī wa-Awlādihi bi-Miṣr, 1955), 6; Hussein Omar, "'The Crinkly-Haired People of the Black Earth:' Examining Egyptian Identities in Ibn ʿAbd al-Ḥākim's *Futūḥ*," in *History and Identity in the Late Antique Near East*, ed. Philip Wood (Oxford: Oxford University Press, 2013), 162.

the raced and gendered associations they carry, at times become premises for interconfessional polemic between Muslims and Christians (it is, for example, the root of the "Saracen lie"),[35] as well as intraconfessional but interethnic contestation. Ibn Qutayba (d. 889) notes that "bigoted" Persian Muslims use tales of Hājar to deride their Arab peers' lineages. Some Arab-Muslim writings refute these claims as much with proofs of Hājar's chaste comeliness as of Ismāʿīl's prophecy. For his own part, Ibn Qutayba goes so far as to say that Hājar was "purified" for Ibrāhīm by God (*ṭahharahā Allāh*), and that she was highly prized and well regarded in Egyptian society, as otherwise she would not have been a fitting gift for Sāra.[36] Though we are assured in the *sīra* as well of Hājar's beauty and *transcendent* worthiness in contrast to Nimrūd's ugliness and unworthiness, it is on this very axis that Hājar succeeds beyond the bounds of her *social* station as a minoritized and enslaved woman. Where Nimrūd conquered the known earth, Hājar enchanted the heart of one prophet and gave birth to another. Though they are assigned different moral and sympathetic values in prophetic history, both Hājar and Nimrūd experience being put in their normative "proper place" subsequent to these successes, with Nimrūd summarily defeated and Hājar exiled, but also thereby restored to humble reliance on God's protection alone.

ʿAntar—born with a face described almost identically to Nimrūd's but with a social station and disposition more akin to Hājar's—presents at once a more complex and triumphant narrative in which he ultimately defies others' bigoted aggressions. His tale also conveys that the racialized hierarchies that Ibrāhīm's story puts to use are in fact devices through which God teaches humans. Thus, the epic announces ʿAntar's coming at its inception as follows:

> Our storyteller, al-Aṣmaʿī—may God Almighty have mercy on him—relates that the most fascinating, clearly-composed, veracious, and well-regarded and of these [aforementioned] illustrious events is the tale of the tribe of ʿAbs, sleek wolves all. The informants who transmit the words of the first Arabs [*kalām al-ʿurbān al-awwalīn*] from their brave predecessors in the *jāhiliyya* [*ʿan ḥadīth al-ʿurbān al-jāhiliyya al-shujaʿān*] tell of a time when all knelt to idols, people had strayed, and Satan held sway, until God tested them with humiliation and dispossession [*al-madhalla wa-l-ḥirmān*]. Before, one's only aim was to subjugate

35. Heng, *The Invention of Race in the European Middle Ages*, 111–12.

36. Ibn Qutaybah, *The Excellence of the Arabs*, trans. Sarah Bowen Savant and Peter Webb (New York: New York University Press, 2017), 20–21.

> his fellows and become the ultimate in authority and victory. No one feared or revered a higher power. So, when God wanted to smite their self-aggrandizement [*tajabburihim*] and arrogance [*takabburihim*], he easily vanquished them with the meanest, measliest of beings in His eyes [*aqall al-ashyāʾ ʿalayhi wa-aḥqarihim ladayhi*]—a slave, known as the Riverbed Snake, the sharp-minded, high-born [*ṭayyib al-mīlād*], and gifted [*ṣāḥib al-fuʾād*] ʿAntara b. Shaddād, who burst on the scene like a spark from a flint. God vanquished the tyrants of the *jāhiliyya* through him until order was restored in the land [*mahhad al-arḍ*] in advance of our master—the greatest of Creation—Muḥammad's arrival.[37]

Here, we see that the society into which ʿAntar is born has veered away from Ibrāhīm's pious correctives, becoming more like that of Nimrūd and his progeny, even as the men of ʿAbs are deemed worthier to receive a push in the right direction because of their bravery and lupine valor. As I discuss further in chapter 4, early understandings of the *jāhiliyya*, often translated as an "age of ignorance," construe it as more of a mutable phase of ignorance, into which peoples might stray or from which they can be redeemed. Similarly, the Qurʾān speaks of a "first *jāhiliyya*," implicitly distinct from the one into which the Qurʾān is delivered. Under this prior *jāhiliyya*, people allowed women to go on promenade (*tabarruj*) and display their ornaments heedlessly, promoting chaotic structures of gender and class much as Nimrūd promoted those of religion and kind.[38] Exegetes cite disagreement over periodizing this "first" state of ignorance, placing it at various intervals between prophets or contexts in which certain prophets emerged. Some gloss it as the time of Noah, some as the epoch between Noah and Idrīs, some as the times into which Abraham was born, some as the epoch between Jesus and Muḥammad, some between Adam and Jesus, and so on. Though the implication is that a state of ignorance is ultimately concluded by revelations from a prophet, the passage introducing ʿAntar modifies this expectation in significant ways: it is possible for others to pave that prophet's way and to do so through feats that straddle the boundary between working miracles and restoring our attention to a divinely ordered cosmos. In the aspirational history of Islam that the epics set forth, even racialized others existing outside the timeline of Islam are always already at its vanguard, and the text announces their didacticism openly.

37. *Sīrat ʿAntara b. Shaddād*, vol. 1, 5.
38. Q 33:33.

Thus, we are told that ʿAntar is meant to prepare the world (*mahhad al-arḍ*). He is uniquely suited to this because he flouts an existing social arrangement in which he, descended half from the people of Ḥām and half from those of Sām, is derided as unfree and of no account while his paternal kin wax in haughtiness and arrogance (*tajabbur wa-takabbur*). Their mismanagement perverts the hierarchy set in motion centuries before and foreshadowed in the text. Indeed, not long after ʿAntar is introduced the narrator adds, "dominion [*al-mulk*] is the province of the sons of Sām, self-aggrandizement and harshness [*al-tajabbur wa-l-qaswa*] that of the sons of Ḥām, and manliness and prophecy [*al-futuwwa wa-l-nubuwwa*] that of the sons of Yāfith," making the unnatural overlap between the temporary *jāhiliyya* of the Arabs and the indefinite inheritance of Nimrūd explicit.[39] Within this landscape of squandered Arabian sovereignty, the enslaved ʿAntar is paradoxically described as "high-born." Though this is superficially a reference to the tribe of ʿAbs' status, as the tale later discloses, it also reflects his pious mother's royal pedigree—an indication of alternate manifestations of dominion—that was effaced when she became enslaved. As ʿAntar's narrative unfolds, he restores himself to order as well, assuming a place in his tribe befitting his long-obscured bona fides.[40]

As Roy Mottahedeh notes, one of the central facets of wonder in Arabic literature is suspense, which necessarily prefigures discovery and also disciplines audiences in another self-refining art in the form of patience, or *ṣabr*.[41] Through a series of linked episodes that reveal ever more complication within the strict category formations that its racial imaginary presupposes, the leadup to ʿAntar's story as well as ʿAntar's legendary exploits themselves set the stage for multiple registers of appreciation for the grander designs they invoke. This is especially highlighted when, tens of generations after Ibrāhīm and tens of pages after our prospective protagonist was first introduced, the child ʿAntar is born in circumstances shrouded in mystification and re-enchantment with mundane processes of attraction and reproduction.

39. *Sīrat ʿAntara b. Shaddād*, vol. 1, 6.

40. After proving himself several times over, ʿAntar's paternity is formally claimed by his father through *ilḥāq*, a certification of legitimacy. On this institution and its pre-Islamic background, see M. S. Sujimon, "Istilḥāq and Its Role in Islamic Law," *Arab Law Quarterly* 18, no. 2 (2003): 117–43.

41. Roy Mottahedeh, "*ʿAjāʾib* in *The Thousand and One Nights*, in The Thousand and One Nights *in Arabic Literature and Society*, ed. Richard G. Hovannisian and Georges Sabagh (Cambridge: Cambridge University Press, 1997), 36.

Wondrous Attractions: The Birth of ʿAntar

At the level of biological legibility, or what Brigitte Fielder terms "familial genealogies of racial resemblance," ʿAntar's origins are the most uneventful of the three main Black heroes of Arabic epics.[42] However, the meet-cute between ʿAntar's mother, Zabība, and his father, Shaddād, quickly makes clear that in the narrative landscape, the attraction between the two and the sort of child that results are hardly inevitable. Instead, it is a moment layered with allusions that encourage one to reconsider the scene and search for hidden meanings, and to identify a "queer genealogy" of race that directs us toward manifestations of racialized kinship that defy or destabilize simplistic biosocial logics.[43] Initially, all we are told about Zabība is that she has been captured while the men of ʿAbs were raiding a neighboring tribe. She and her two children, ʿAntar's elder half brothers, Jarīr and Shaybūb, are tasked with herding the plundered livestock. Then, we are told:

> [Shaddād] turned, and the slave girl who had been driving the camels emerged into the prince Shaddād's view. She took hold of his heart and bewitched his innermost thoughts and intellect [*sarāʾirihi wa-lubbihi*]—he longed to have her. He was struck by the sight of the fullness of her limbs, the softness of her form, the beauty of her color [*ḥusn lawnihā*], the coquettishness of her eyes [*ghunj ʿuyūnihā*], the enchantment [*siḥr*] of her eyelids, the curve of her shape, the kindness in her face, the sheen [*lamīʿ*] of her cheeks, the sweetness of her speech [*ḥalāwat lafẓihā*], and the comeliness of her figure. She had eyes sharper than fate [*aḥadd min al-manāyā*], and the flash of her front teeth was more dazzling than mirrors [*al-marāyā*]. Her mouth was sweet and her posture straight. Some have said she looks like what has been spoken of [in other poetry].[44] Praise upon our master Muḥammad, guarantor of the gazelle,
>
> In darkness [*sumr*] lies meaning [*maʿnā*], if you grasped its eloquence
> [*law ʿalimt bayānahu*],
> Unlike what you've seen of whiteness or redness [*la-mā naẓarat*
> *ʿaynak bīḍ wa-lā ḥumr*]

42. Brigitte Fielder, *Relative Races: Genealogies of Interracial Kinship in Nineteenth-Century America* (Durham, NC: Duke University Press, 2020), 7.

43. Fielder, *Relative Races*, esp. 1–9.

44. This statement indicates that the narrator is borrowing at least part of the following poem from a previous work.

The shapeliness of [her] body and charm of [her] glance
Could teach the angel Hārūt to divine and entrance
For without a mole's blackness on a white face,
A lover would not know of imminent fate
Were musk not black, it wouldn't cost so dear
And were night not black, dawn could not break clear
Were it not for the blackness of [a beloved's] eye,
It could not besot her love at first sight[45]

The atypicality of Shaddād's attraction to this dark-skinned slave girl (who, we are told initially, has beautiful coloring) is made apparent in the text's immediate leap to its defense. Before finding that Zabība is Black, the audience is confronted with a poem extolling blackness that opens with an apologetic. Its style recalls the way that many lovesick poets working in the well-known *ʿudhrī* tradition of chaste yet passionately self-destructive ardor begin their poems by repelling criticisms from an unnamed censurer, or *lāʾim*, who finds the public expression of their love indecorous.

The appropriation of an offstage blamer into poetry about Black lovers occurs across verses collected in prose debates, or *munāẓarāt*, an epistolary genre that arose in the ʿAbbasid age and pitted opposites against each other in order to vindicate the underdog. Many feature micro-anthologies that meditate on the beauty of subjects commonly thought of as unenviable, be they disabled, blemished, Turkic, or Black.[46] The anthologized verses' attributions attest to the illustriousness of authors who took up the conventions of expressing antinomian stances on beauty that appear also in the verses about Zabība above. For example, a poem attributed to Abū Muḥammad al-ʿAbbāsī, also known by his caliphal title al-Hādī (d. 786), begins "I say to those who malign blackness foolishly—for with blackness comes resentment and accusers [*wa-li-l-sūd qawm ʿāʾibūn wa-ḥasad*]," and then goes on to praise blackness's similarity to musk, a lover's eye, and so on.[47] Another set of lines assigned to the ninth-century Iraqi poet Abū ʿAlī al-Baṣīr (fl. first half of the ninth century) close saying, "the outlandishness [*istiḥāla*] of her color earns no reproach from me, it is the hue of

45. *Sīrat ʿAntara b. Shaddād*, vol. 1, 72–73.

46. On one such anthology concerning "blighted" lovers, see Kristina Richardson, *Difference and Disability in the Medieval Islamic World* (Edinburgh: Edinburgh University Press, 2012), chap. 3.

47. Ibn al-Jawzī, *Tanwīr al-Ghabash*, 243.

youth's [black] hair."[48] The relationship between Shaddād's first sighting of Zabība and doomed, socially suspect forms of love is enhanced by the fact that the verse used to describe Zabība is most frequently ascribed to Qays ibn al-Mulawwaḥ (d. 688), also named Majnūn Layla (He who is mad over Layla), who was one of the main progenitors of the *ʿudhrī* tradition. Though some sources claim that Layla was "black like an Abyssinian," even more striking is that Majnūn himself—in another instance of outward appearances reflecting one's inner world and desires—is said to have wandered the desert in a lovelorn fugue for so long that he, too, became dark-skinned in the sun as he withered away.[49]

The apologetic overtones of Shaddād's encounter with Zabība are cued not only through literary and romantic convention, but also through reminders to the audience of esoteric ways to see and perceive. One must go beneath blackness itself and discern hidden meanings. Hints of this begin with the way that Zabība's effect on Shaddād is described as taking hold of his innermost thoughts, or *sarāʾir*, a play on the word for "secrets." She is also said to have captivated his *lubb*, a euphemism for the heart that also can refer to a nut, kernel, or marrow, and thus indicates something embedded and encased. Ibn al-Manẓūr's (d. ca. 1312) thirteenth-century dictionary defines *lubb* simply as anything "of which you consume the innermost part and discard the exterior."[50]

In the first line of the quoted poem, darkness is said to have "meaning" and "eloquence" that is discernible with sufficient difficulty that the addressee is presumed to not be able to appreciate it. The terms for meaning and eloquence both evoke different branches of the Arabic rhetorical arts (*ʿilm al-balāgha*), with the study of "meaning" (*maʿnā*) focusing on the "mental contents" intended by units of utterance and underpinned by the assumption that the latter does not perfectly communicate the former.[51] The study of "eloquence" (*bayān*), meanwhile, relates to the aesthetic tools of persuasion, and particularly to literary devices used to ornament and astound. In this fashion, the poetic overture claims that darkness marks or is marked in such a way that, when these markings are properly scrutinized, one brings forth their true consequence and significance.

48. Ibn al-Jawzī, 245.

49. Barbara Brend, *Perspectives on Persian Painting: Illustrations of Amīr Khusrau's* Khamsah (London: Routledge, 2003), 16.

50. Ibn al-Manẓūr, *Lisān al-ʿArab*, 3979.

51. I borrow this phrasing from Alexander Key, *Language between God and the Poets: Maʿnā in the Eleventh Century* (Oakland: University of California Press, 2018).

Promoting alternative ways of seeing blackness arises as a theme in other works of popular literature as well. Perhaps the most recognizable appearance of the first two hemistiches of Majnūn's poem occurs in the *Thousand and One Nights*, during an episode in which enslaved women of the court with varying colors and shapes (one light and one dark, one fat, one skinny, one blond, and one swarthy) satirize one another's appearances. After a white-skinned slave girl has taken aim at her darker-skinned counterpart, the Black woman retorts by saying the above words, then continues extolling her virtues along similar lines to the plaudits given to ʿAntar's mother,

> My form is beautiful, my curves are ample, and my color is desired by kings and lusted after by the wealthy and wastrel alike. I am lovely and clever and supple of body, high of price [*ghāliyat al-thaman*], and I am studied in witticisms, literature, and eloquence [*qad kamalt fī-l-malāḥa wa-l-adab wa-l-faṣāḥa maẓāhirī*]. My gestures and tongue are articulate, my temperament is lighthearted, and my amusements are a delight [*wa-laʿbī ẓarīf*]. As for you, you're pale like the *mulūkhiyya* stew served in Bāb al-Lūq, and all of it's just roots [*ʿurūq*]. Wretchedness upon you, o impurity of the scalps, o coppersmith's rust, o face of the owl and food of the *zaqqūm* tree.[52]

The Black woman then goes on to recite invective poetry of her own deriding whiteness as an indicator of undesirability and devaluation, citing the cheapness of lime compared with musk and the unfavorability of a white-eyed lover—with light eyes often associated with blindness and disease—versus a black-eyed one. The passage's final two images relate pallor directly to death with the owl's cry, which was a harbinger at ruins and burial grounds, and the fruits of the *zaqqūm* tree found only in hell and said in the Qurʾān to scald the insides as they are digested.[53] Across the riffs on Majnūn's poem, blackness meanwhile affirms ongoing vitality: an

52. "*Ḥikāyat al-Jawārī al-Mukhtalifa al-Alwān wa-mā waqaʿa baynahun min al-Muḥāwara*," in *Alf Layla wa-Layla, al-Juzʾ al-Thānī* (Calcutta II, 1839), 280–81. On this tale, see also: Robert Irwin, "The Dark Side of 'The Arabian Nights,' Critical Muslim, https://www.criticalmuslim.io/the-dark-side-of-the-arabian-nights/, accessed 18 September 2018.

53. Q 44:45. On the morbid symbolism of the owl lurking at graves, see T. Emil Homerin, "Echoes of a Thirsty Owl: Death and Afterlife in Pre-Islamic Arabic Poetry," *Journal of Near Eastern Studies* 44, no. 3 (1985): 165–84.

evening with a lover, the cyclic passage of night into day, or the twinkle of a healthy eye.

Yet in promoting its alternative way of seeing, the *Nights* draws a set of contrasts between blackness and whiteness that nonetheless shores up normative material realities. The web of images used in the *Nights* and in *Sīrat ʿAntar* suggests not only Zabība's and other Black women's comeliness, but also their fecundity and thus worthiness as concubines. The unnamed woman in the *Nights* refers to herself as expensive, a nod not only to the commodification of her entertaining skills in the rhetorical arts but also her physicality. Against the common contrivance of Black women as hypersexual and solicitous, the story of ʿAntar's mother therefore goes to great lengths to indicate that, despite having a body that appears without any effort on her part to flirt with "coquettish eyes" and seduce with "magical eyelids," she has a profound sense of personal honor. This is conferred through her noble pedigree and freeborn status—neither of which is typical to Black women in the world of the text:

> When the prince Shaddād b. Qurād saw such qualities in this slave girl [*ama*], she shone in his eyes, as [God] wills to disclose His secrets through hidden graces [*ka-mā shāʾ khafī al-alṭāf li-yaẓhar minhā maknūn sirrihi*]. At that point, Shaddād beckoned to her and departed, so she followed him to a far-off place, not knowing what he wanted. Then he asked to sleep with her, so she rejected him and was repulsed with the sordid matter, for, as shall emerge, *she was from a prominent family* [*bayt kabīr*]. [Shaddād] then said to her, 'Woe upon you! You will be my wife, and keep your children with me, and I will devote my efforts to honoring you.'[54]

Zabība agrees to Shaddād's promise, however the other men of the tribe who as yet have no "delivered law" (*sharīʿa*) to teach them right (*ḥalāl*) and wrong (*ḥarām*) also try to take advantage of her:

> She fled from their presence to the desert and repudiated their attempts, for *she was from an honorable family line* [*nasl qawm kirām*], not a blameworthy one [*ghayr liʾām*]. And we will recall the origins of her kin and the cause of her estrangement and separation [from them], but everything must be told in its [proper] place, with God's help and power . . .

54. *Sīrat ʿAntara b. Shaddād*, vol. 1, 73, emphasis mine.

Al-Aṣmaʿī then said: *When the slave woman had withdrawn from them and behaved like a free, honorable woman [al-ḥurra al-mukarrama], and did not assent to this hateful matter because she was—as we have remarked—from a great household [min bayt kabīr]*, then the prince Shaddād drove off [his companions] from her and said to them, 'I have placed her in my protection and I will be happy to take her as part of my share [of the raiding spoils].' [The other men] were pleased with this arrangement, so they retreated from her. Whoever had hoped [to proposition her] was disappointed. No one received [what he desired] from her save the designated prince Shaddād, for their judge ruled that she was his and said, 'O Shaddād, [her] newborn shall be deemed yours.'[55]

Unlike with the unexpectedly Black epic heroes whose mothers must refute aspersions of acts of lineage-depreciating adultery cast upon them after birth, for ʿAntar's mother such concerns are headed off at the pass. On the one hand, this is because of the relative commonality and acceptability of her sexual arrangement with Shaddād and, on the other, because the hidden truth of her elite identity underwrites her moral character. Zabība's regal propriety ironically does not permit her to trespass the conditions of her unfreedom. The discussion of Zabība's family background assumes the immutable essence of one's lineage in a similar fashion to the purportedly fixed natures of the children of Sām, Ḥām, and Yāfit, however, Zabība's royal and free heritage also trouble the connotations of racialized slavery endemic to the broader genealogical category into which she is fitted as an Abyssinian, even as she becomes enslaved. Moreover, because in the pre-Islamic period lineage had both its matrilineal and patrilineal components emphasized, her royal *nasab* holds immense explanatory power with respect to ʿAntar's own heroic destiny despite his being slave-born. The suspense and suspension of disbelief that her description overtly demands of readers—who are told that Zabība's heritage with be clarified in due time—is not resolved until well into ʿAntar's adulthood when he travels to Abyssinia himself along with his brother, Shaybūb, and his likewise half-Abyssinian wife, the warrior-princess Ghamra. There, they meet Zabība's noble sister, who reveals her true identity. Their encounter causes Shaybūb to experience a resurgence of knowledge (*maʿrifa*) about the lands of his childhood:

[The princess] said, "O Shaybūb, what is your mother's name?" [Shaybūb] replied, "Zabība," at which she said, "Whoever stole her changed

55. *Sīrat ʿAntara b. Shaddād*, vol. 1, 73, emphasis mine.

> her name—does your mother look like such-and-such? Does she not have jet-black eyes [*kaḥlā' al-ʿuyūn*]? And on her right cheek there was a birthmark, yes?" [Shaybūb] exclaimed, "By God, I know [*aʿrif*] the families in these abodes—I've not forgotten a thing! I know their every quarter still, down to the person [*a-lā mā khaff maʿrifat aḥad*]!"[56]

Zabība's story is one that many have shared. She is stolen from her home, enslaved, and renamed. However, in the epic, the capacity for her origins to be rediscovered after a long period of estrangement and narrative deferral, and for her lineage to continually assert itself despite appearances, cultivates polyvalent forms of marvel in the seemingly everyday. As with explanations of the unique priming and positioning of Hājar, Zabība's tale frequently emphasizes the non-arbitrariness and intricacy of the processes through which she is assimilated into the tribe of ʿAbs, the mutual recognition her past engenders between Arabia and Abyssinia, and the trajectory of communal preparation for Islam and Muslim expansion that she helps initiate.

ʿAntar's status as a slave-born child of a concubine in the pre-Islamic period is likewise a relatable one. Indeed, Robert Brunschvig proposes that ʿAntar's epic is best read as an instructive story meant, through a study in contrasts, to promote the acceptance in the Islamic era of children born through foreign concubinage.[57] As noted in the introduction, these children were legally recognized full Arabs, endowed with their fathers' *nasabs* through the institution of *umm walad*, or mother of the child, that guaranteed their legitimacy in the household and therefore promoted the growth of the Arab-Muslim community. Because of when he was born, ʿAntar does not have immediate access to Arabness as a *hajīn*, or mixed person, and instead must earn it through warriorship.[58] As with his mother, though, the text's first encounter with ʿAntar undermines a straightforward reading of these all too ordinary beginnings, encouraging further speculation:

> [T]hat night [Zabība] went into labor, as the Creator of Creation willed, and she did not stop screaming from the earliest portion of the

56. *Sīrat ʿAntara b. Shaddād*, vol. 5, 379.

57. R. Brunschvig, "ʿAbd."

58. Indeed, a stark difference between the poetry of ʿAntar's epic and of many poems more conclusively identified with ʿAntara as a historical figure is that the former depict him as self-consciously Black while in the latter the term *hajīn* or references to his mixed parentage are favored. For the full collection of ʿAntara's works, including selections from his epic, see ʿAntarah ibn Shaddād. *War Songs*, trans. James Montgomery (New York: New York University Press, 2018).

night until daybreak, then she gave birth to a son, and he was Black (*aswad*) and dark-faced (*adgham*)[59] like an elephant, flat-nosed and broad-shouldered, with wide eyes. The creation of the Glorious King was frown-faced, peppercorn-haired, large-mouthed, with mud-colored nostrils, broad-backed, solid of limb and bone, and had a large head and legs like chunks of cloud, with big ears and pupils that emitted sparks of fire, as the poet has said of him in these verses, praise upon the Lord of lords,

[This] Black man looks like the dark of night,
As though he were hewn from a stone
Far-spanning arms and towering height
We presage burdens [*aʿbāʾ*] and contagion [*awbāʾ*],
An unsettling sight, alike, to Black and white

(The narrator said) indeed he had the flanks and shoulders of Shaddād, and his limbs and shape resembled the build of his father Shaddād [as well], so the prince Shaddād rejoiced in him when he saw him and said, "praise upon He who created him and perfected him [*khalaqahu wa-sawwāhu*]," and he named him ʿAntar and entrusted his mother Zabība with him.[60]

In many ways, ʿAntar is identical to Nimrūd, his mother's beauty replaced in him with an exaggerated masculinity and a host of stereotypical Black African features; he, too, is said to be "black," "frown-faced," and "flat-nosed." At the same time, he bears an uncanny resemblance to his father that is instantly recognizable to Shaddād and those around him. The poetic excerpt that buttresses ʿAntar's description gestures toward ambiguity and hybridity, with its subject described as fearsome and strong, but also precarious. His powerful limbs are rendered as afflicting, beleaguering, or diseased. Though ʿAntar is described as dark like night's shadows (*ẓalām al-dujā*), he presents a disturbance (*muzʿij*) to other Black people (*li-l-aswad*) as well as white. ʿAntar is at once almost nonhuman—having an animalized, elephantine color, paradoxical and elemental muscles that are at once rock-solid and cloud-like, and eyes that emit sparks—and is caught between a variety of human identities. He demands a new way of seeing.

The full implications of his difference from those around him come to a very public head some years later after ʿAntar has been weaned and "news

59. This term, often used to describe horses, carries connotations of color and sound. It can mean both black about the muzzle and snuffling.

60. *Sīrat ʿAntara b. Shaddād*, vol. 1, 74.

about him [has] spread," at a banquet hosted by the local king, Zuhayr. The reason that ʿAntar is in attendance is because his growing fame has resulted in Shaddād's brothers coming forward and trying to claim the child for themselves as part of their raiding spoils, saying, "the Abyssinian slave girl . . . gave birth to a child whose form [*khilqa*] is like a lion, and we all say that he cannot have been part of [Shaddād's] share while he was hidden [*makhfī*] in his mother's belly." Their host responds with astonishment:

> When the king Zuhayr heard this, he became as amazed as one can [*taʿajjab ghāyat al-ʿajab*] over these affairs, and he said to Shaddād, "bring the slave you've all been fighting over to me, so these lords and I can see him for ourselves." At that, Shaddād left for a while and returned with the boy. When Shaddād had stood him before King Zuhayr, he and the others in attendance looked at him and saw that his face was like a threatened lion's and his eyes were like red blood, so the king and his guests were mystified [*iḥtār*], and all who were there said, "this is a lion of the forest!" King Zuhayr looked at his face [again] and marveled [*taʿajjab*] at his form [*khilqatihi*] and the size of his body—though ʿAntar was not yet four years old, he looked like youths of twenty. With that, King Zuhayr shouted at him and threw a cut of meat that he had in his direction. One of [Zuhayr's] dogs chased after it and snatched it up, and turned to run off, when the boy's eyes lolled and he raced up behind the dog, grabbing onto his neck in a fury, kneeling on him and taking the meat from his maw. Then, [the boy] reached into [the dog's] mouth, gripped him by the jawbones, and tore him in two—palate to shoulder blades [*fa-shaqq ḥanakahu ilā ḥadd kitfayhi*]. [The child] then went back, searching for his father Shaddād and eating the meat. . . . King Zuhayr was amazed as anyone can be [*taʿajjab al-malik Zuhayr ghāyat al-ʿajab*], and all the other lords were astonished [*bahat*]. King Zuhayr said, "By God, surely this feat is a mark [*dalīl*] of the valor of this boy [*ghulām*] named ʿAntar, and one day he will indeed be among the bravest heroes."[61]

Before first meeting ʿAntar, Zuhayr already expresses wonder at the stories told about him. As proofs of their truth unfold—as ʿAntar's complications multiply—Zuhayr's wonder only grows. Zuhayr dispatches the child to a local judge, who states that he is rightfully Shaddād's because he "resembles him in form," and as the dispute over ʿAntar's ownership (for he is

61. *Sīrat ʿAntara b. Shaddād*, vol. 1, 75.

raised not as Shaddād's son, but as his slave) fizzles, fear over his abilities and the threat they pose to the tribal power structure grow.

Like many a hero, ʿAntar's separation from his father means he must become an autodidact in martial arts, mostly practicing in thickets by wrestling animals and sparring with trees in a montage that many of his ilk will emulate. But, when ʿAntar kills a wolf who is threatening his flocks, his mother grows concerned. When he kills another slave who was terrorizing an old woman, Shaddād's siblings start to recognize the boy as a threat, and Shaddād himself declares, "I don't know what to do about what's happened with this Black slave. I'm afraid he might one day kill a great prince [*amīr kabīr*]." The plants and then beasts through which ʿAntar progresses begin to approach humankind in formidability, as if to evoke the great chain of being that became especially associated with the Islamic Neoplatonic tradition.[62] Moreover, as ʿAntar becomes ever more lethal, he also becomes ever more wild in ways that may allow for "reimagining social relations beyond normative kinship structures," but therefore also threaten these hierarchical and paternalist structures' existence.[63] When, in one of many moments of violent backlash, Shaddād and his siblings decide to do away with the twelve-year-old ʿAntar themselves, they catch sight of him killing, butchering, and eating a lion in the forest that, not unlike ʿAntar himself, is "frowning, flat-nosed, wily and courageous, with wide, whirlwind-like paws and large chest and head." This strongest of wild animals being brought low immediately tilts into another prospect: one brother exclaims that "maybe he'll kill one of us—maybe he's not full yet, and he'll eat us like he ate that lion!" This moment calls to mind tales of cannibals from the edges of the earth, and predominantly the *bilād al-sūdān*, that permeate taxonomic discourses on human kinds in wonders literatures, geographies, and epics, and that are often concerned at heart with ill-gotten gain and unmanaged predation by the powerful.[64]

Zuhayr, though, does not play out all of these destructive possibilities when he sees ʿAntar kill the dog in his salon. Instead, in the height of his astonishment at ʿAntar's created nature (*khilqa*), Zuhayr's response is unbound from immediate racialized, gendered, and classed anxieties about

62. Sarra Tlili, "All Animals Are Equal, or Are They? The Ikhwān al-Ṣafāʾ's Animal Epistle and Its Unhappy End," *Journal of Qurʾanic Studies* 16, no. 2 (2014): 45.

63. Allison Kanner-Botan, "Rewriting the Wild: Fiction, *adab*, and the Making of Majnun's Animal World," *postmedieval* 13, no. 3–4 (2022): 454.

64. *Sīrat ʿAntara b. Shaddād*, vol. 1, 92–95; Wendy Belcher, "Mary Saves the Man-Eater: Value in the Medieval Ethiopian Marian Tale of 'The Cannibal of Qəmər,'" *Digital Philology: A Journal of Medieval Cultures* 8, no. 1 (2019): 42.

his own elite standing vis-à-vis the child; he sees only ʿAntar's transformative potential, "comprehended on a larger scale."

The Birth(s) of Abū Zayd

As with the prefacing of ʿAntar's illustrious career with tales of the lives of the prophets, the birth of Abū Zayd al-Hilālī is often read as being freighted with divinely ordained significance. Susan Slyomovics accounts for the multilayered way in which Abū Zayd's miraculous origins are animated with prophetic allusions in performance through reference to the "miraculous beginnings" of the epic recitation in and of itself, which becomes linked to divine revelation through the reciter's "breakthrough into performance instigated by poems of praise," for God and Muḥammad.[65] This is in addition to the embedded genealogical relationship between the Prophet Muḥammad and the hero Abū Zayd, conferred through the heritage of Abū Zayd's mother Khaḍrāʾ, the daughter of a Meccan *sharīf* named Qirḍāb (sometimes Qirḍa). In some editions of the text, even the marriage of Khaḍrāʾ to the Hilālī chief, Rizq, is providential. Recitations recorded in both the Egyptian village of Bakātūsh and the city of Luxor narrate that Rizq is apprised of Khaḍrāʾ's eligibility by spiritual authorities, in one case a Sufi shaykh who foretells his future son's greatness, and in another the Hilālī elders.[66] In their ensuing marriage, Khaḍrāʾ fails to conceive a male child for a significant period of time (in some recitations, it is five to seven years, in others, as many as eleven) and, desperate, she begs God for a son. In some versions, the women of her tribe take it upon themselves to aid her in this endeavor, and they all go out to either a forest or a river together to watch birds gather, praying that their sons will mirror the qualities of the bird that each woman finds most appealing. In others, Khaḍrāʾ is walking in a forest or garden alone when she comes upon a number of birds that are either varicolored or all white. In all cases, a crow emerges and begins to terrorize the other creatures. Khaḍrāʾ asks that her child be as fierce as this dark, aggressive bird, and in an instance of what has been described elsewhere as "cosmic literalness of interpretation," her wish is answered, and she conceives a black-skinned son.[67]

65. Susan Slyomovics, "Praise of the Prophet and Praise of the Self: *Sīrat Banī Hilāl* and Epic Narrative in Performance," *Journal of Arabic Literature* 49 (2018): 68.

66. Reynolds, "Episode 1: The Birth of Abu Zayd (Part 1)"; al-Ḥajjājī, *Mawlid al-Baṭal*, 203.

67. I borrow this turn of phrase from Susan Slyomovics. See Slyomovics, "Praise of the Prophet, Praise of the Self," 66.

Abū Zayd's story, though, recurrently subverts the transparency of cosmic logic: as with ʿAntar's deceptively simple origins, the ostensible "literalness" of the cause of Abū Zayd's blackness conceals a tangle of intertexts adducing theories of heredity and creation that circulated in Late Antiquity and Islam. Abū Zayd's racialization also defies fixity, even at the most superficial, somatic level. This, too, is elaborated through the internally intertextual nature of *sīra* traditions, of which *Sīrat Banī Hilāl* is particularly emblematic because of its protracted life as a transregionally, orally performed work: in some recordings, Abū Zayd is said to be Black, in some piebald, in some dark-skinned, and in others a mixture of the foregoing depending on who is doing the perceiving. In other narratives still, particularly those from Sudan, Niger, Mali, and Chad, Abū Zayd's color does not figure in his narrative at all, and instead his racialized alterity takes another form entirely:

> The Shuwā Arabs disregard Abū Zayd's blackness, so it is not among the main points of the *sīra*. This is in harmony with the storytellers [themselves], because in this case Abū Zayd is of course Arab, but he is from the African Arabs [*al-ʿarab al-afāriqa*], and African Arabs from regions south of the Sahara have taken on blackness [*qad iktasabū al-sawād*], so it is difficult to differentiate their complexions from those of other Africans. The drama from the problem of the child's blackness has thus been transformed into a problem with the child's excessive strength, [which is so great] that his father fears him, and worries that his son might be from the *siʿlā* demon species, that is, a *ghūl* who eats human flesh.[68]

As Aboubakr Chraïbi has argued with respect to manuscripts of the *1001 Nights*, the addition of *ʿajab* and related ideas of wonder and strangeness is a literary embellishment that occurs within a primarily textual rather than oral environment, typical to works that have been written, rewritten, and edited in a spirit of literary "one-upsmanship." He adds that the result is, ultimately, to Islamize the tales, much as various prophetic traditions characterize the workings of prayer and intercession as ever more astounding.[69] In keeping with the far more colloquial and textually "unprocessed"

68. Al-Ḥajjājī, *Mawlid al-Baṭal*, 114.

69. Aboubakr Chraïbi, "Introduction," in *Arabic Manuscripts of the* Thousand and One Nights*: Presentation and Critical Editions of Four Noteworthy Texts Observations on Some Osmanli Translations*, ed. Aboubakr Chraïbi et al. (Paris: Espaces et Signes, 2016), 52–53.

manifestation of his *sīra* tradition, *ʿajab* plays a different and often more minimal formal role in Abū Zayd's birth narrative than in ʿAntar's. Rather than the gratification of acquiring a new lens on or knowledge of the cosmic order, *ʿajab* operates instead by signaling the sensation of finding order undone—the "naïve wonder" to which Akbari refers. The primary paradox of Abū Zayd's simultaneous blackness and chiefly paternity is eventually accepted on its face rather than resolved by uncovering an intricate hidden cause.

Many versions of *Sīrat Banī Hilāl* first forecast Abū Zayd's blackness with his mother's encounter with a crow. Audiences aware of the storyline sometimes avidly anticipate the bird's prescient appearance, knowing the hero quickly follows. In Dwight Reynolds's transcripts of his Bakātūsh recordings, listeners exclaim "This is Abū Zayd!" when the reciter arrives at the line "suddenly, from far off, a dark bird approached them" (*illā wa-ṭayr asmar min al-buʿd jā li-hum*). However, one version of the text, produced in Beirut, foreshadows Abū Zayd's unexpected appearance in a wholly different way.[70] After arranging her marriage and before his daughter departs with Rizq, the *sharīf* Qirḍāb offers words of parting:

> The valiant Qirḍāb has this to say,
> With tears flowing over his cheeks
> O prince Rizq, Khaḍrāʾ is yours today,
> Estranged, she will now take her leave [*gharība wa-rāḥat ilā bilād baʿīd*]
> I entrust her to you, o prince, to honor,
> And may she someday birth your boy
> If she bears you a son black in color [*idhā jāhā walad wa-kān asmar*],
> O good one, think it no ruinous ploy [*lā taẓunn fī fiʿl al-radā yā jayyid*]
> For her grandmother looked dark as well [*sittahā sawdā kān lawnuhā*]
> And her grandfather, Black like slaves [*wa-jadduhā kān aswad ka-l-ʿabīd*]
> Should you accuse Khaḍrāʾ of ill [*al-qubḥ maʿ al-radā*]
> And leave her deprived in dire straits
> She'll be friendless in the world

70. This version was produced in Beirut in the 1980s by the Maktaba Thaqāfiyya, or Cultural Library, a press that reproduced some of the popular *sīras* with glossy, kid-friendly cover designs in the late twentieth century. These productions were not necessarily original, but were instead reprints of prior printed versions, some of which were themselves edited from manuscripts. There is reason, therefore, to assume that this seemingly unique telling of the *sīra* has forerunners and is not an editorialization.

Save ever-flowing tears of mourning
They'll say, "That's the Sharīf's girl—
With good Prince Rizq, yet lusts wandering [*ṭāmiḥa*]"[71]

After the Sharīf's statement, Rizq responds with his own verses in affirmation that "your words, O king, have been registered," promising political fidelity and reiterating his interest in Khaḍrāʾ even if she "truly has meager grandparents" (*mankhūbat al-jaddayn bi-l-tawkīd*); this bond is later broken, of course, when Khaḍrāʾ does indeed give birth to a Black baby and Rizq repudiates her.[72] The reason given for his doing so is delivered in nearly identical language to Qirḍāb's warning. Rizq is in the midst of celebrating the birth of his one-week-old child—freshly named Barakāt, or blessings (Abū Zayd becomes his assumed name later in the tale) and assigned to a wet nurse—with a mass butchering of livestock and a feast hosted for local tribal leaders, likely a reference to the *ʿaqīqa* ceremony of making a sacrifice to commemorate a newborn. It is unclear in the story whether Rizq has seen his son before this point. As Kathryn Kueny has shown, often immediate postnatal care was a women-only affair similar to the birth itself, with children given over to a wetnurse for feedings until their mother's colostrum ceased coming in or until they could have a *taḥnīk* ceremony administered—a ritual of having a paste of masticated dates daubed on a newborn's palate representing its first food—typically by a male elder.[73] So, too, the naming ceremony and the sacrifice of livestock are hallmarks of a newborn son's "rebirth into the world as his father's child and a social being."[74] On the day of Barakāt's debut, one of the prominent luminaries in attendance, the prince Sirḥān, sees the child, bites his fingers in distress, exclaims "this child is black like a slave!" (*hādhā al-walad aswad mithl al-ʿabd*). He adds, in verse, "O prince Rizq, this isn't your progeny / *his father is surely a Black slave* [*hādhā abūhu ʿabd aswad*]. . . . O Rizq, you've squandered your chance for prophetic ancestry [*ḍayyaʿt naslak bi-l-nabī*] / happiness has been turned away, and disaster perdured [*wa-naḥsuk ṣamad*]."[75]

71. *Sīrat Banī Hilāl* (Beirut: al-Maktaba al-Thaqāfiyya, 1980), 37–38.

72. *Sīrat Banī Hilāl*, 38.

73. *Sīrat Banī Hilāl*, 38. See also Avner Gilʿadi, "Some Notes on Taḥnīk in Medieval Islam," *Journal of Near Eastern Studies* 47, no. 3 (1988): 175–79.

74. Kathryn Kueny, *Conceiving Identities: Maternity in Medieval Muslim Discourse and Practice* (Albany: State University of New York Press, 2013), 153.

75. *Sīrat Banī Hilāl*, 39, emphasis mine.

In an Upper Egyptian telling of the tale, recited by epicist ʿAwad Allāh, the fact of Abū Zayd's difference is a collective realization, rather than one impressed upon Rizq by a peer:

They drew near to the hero Abū Zayd and lifted the blankets,
They found the Hilālī dark [*asmar*], not like his father [*wa-lā jā li-bāh*],
They found the Hilālī blue-black [*azraq*], with the coloring of slaves [*bi-lawn al-ʿabīd*]
But his face was sweeter than grapes and raisins,
The prince Sirḥān said, "The working of God is wondrous [*ʿajīb*],
Through the compassion of the Creator, one is preserved from sinners.
His mother and father are white [*bīḍ*], and so who does he take after?"[76]

This passage indicates that everyone sees the problem Abū Zayd poses immediately, together. Yet the child's description also indicates the many ways, across various iterations, that Abū Zayd's fundamental difference in color can be articulated. In the poem, the terms *asmar* and *aswad* seem to be used interchangeably to mean black-skinned, as opposed to *asmar* connoting dark skin that nonetheless still places the child within the normative range of complexions among Arabs in the text. Instead, his being *asmar* is represented as strange and estranging, removing him from relationality with his father. That *asmar* should frequently be used interchangeably with *aswad* is perhaps surprising in view of the term's use historically and in modern dialects.

A variety of dictionaries compiled between the eighth and fourteenth centuries attest the evolution and flux of *asmar*'s specific connotations. Al-Khalīl ibn Aḥmad's (d. 791) *Kitāb al-ʿAyn*, the earliest known dictionary of the Arabic language, attests the use of *samrāʾ* as a generic flesh-tone similar to the color of wheat (*fatāh samrāʾ wa-ḥinṭa samrāʾ*), and says that the color is dark or "blackish" (*lawn ilā sawād*), but that it is not actually a true black; indeed the term *abyaḍ*, often translated as "white," is described nearly identically by other lexicographers.[77] And yet, associations between *samar* and the nighttime place the color's connotations in more direct overlap with *aswad*. A common *muzāwaja*, or aphoristic pair

76. Al-Ḥajjājī, *Mawlid al-Baṭal*, 210.

77. Al-Khalīl b. Aḥmad, *Kitāb al-ʿAyn al-Juzʾ al-Sābiʿ* (Baghdad: Dāʾira al-Shuʾūn al-Thaqāfiyya wa-l-Nashr, 1984), 255.

of terms that are often rhymed and are conceptually related, is *al-samar wa-l-qamar*, meaning the dark night sky and the moon. In his lexicon of Qurʾānic terms, *Mufradāt Alfāẓ al-Qurʾān*, al-Rāghib al-Iṣfāhānī (d. 1108) further associates the term with that which was once white but is no longer. He begins his entry on *samar* by claiming that the color is a composite of black and white (*aḥd al-alwān al-murakkaba min al-bayāḍ wa-l-sawād*), like the color of wheat or of thin milk whose color has turned (*al-laban al-raqīq al-mutaghayyir al-lawn*).[78]

Turning to the Qurʾānic text itself, the only verse in which a word derived from the root *s-m-r* is used alludes to a participant in nighttime conversations, or a *sāmir* (Q 23:67). Ibn al-Manẓūr's *Lisān al-ʿArab* further notes that *sumra* lies somewhere between white and black (*manzila bayn al-bayāḍ wa-l-sawād*), and is the color of humans, camels, and the like. It is a color that "shades into having a black cast" (*yaḍrib ilā sawād khafī*), like the color of the skin of the prophet Muḥammad (*wa-fī ṣifatihi ṣallā Allāhu ʿalayhi wa-sallam kān asmar al-lawn*).[79] The above definitions indicate that, at least for a time, *asmar* was understood as a term connoting the skin color thought to be typical of the Arabs themselves, and even archetypical, in that it was the color of the flesh of Muḥammad who was thought to epitomize masculine ideals of beauty. This is a link against which the *sīra* actively militates, and whose severance points to the increasing identification of Arabness with unambiguous whiteness in many later literatures.

Another term that co-occurs with *aswad* in the above poem is *azraq*, which is used in Qurʾānic Arabic to primarily indicate a light, rheumy or milky color, and which tends in classical Arabic to mean various shades of blue. In Egyptian and Sudanese Arabics, though, it comes to mean dark black. Used as a verb, *zarraq* may also be used to mean to bruise, which is to say, to purple or darken one's flesh.[80] The idea that a very deep black can appear to be blue or have a bluish cast is found in myriad cultures and literatures. Much like in Arabic, in Hebrew, the root *k-kh-l* indicates painting or lining the eyes (as with kohl), and also gives rise to the word *kakhôl*, blue.[81] *Kakhal* is often duly used in rabbinic literature in reference

78. Al-Rāghib al-Iṣfahānī, *Mufradāt Alfāẓ al-Qurʾān* (Beirut: al-Dār al-Shāmiyya, 1992), 425.

79. Ibn al-Manẓūr, *Lisān al-ʿArab*, 2090.

80. Martin Hinds and El-Said Badawi, *A Dictionary of Egyptian Arabic: Arabic-English* (Beirut: Librairie du Liban, 1986), 369.

81. William Gesenius and Edward Robinson, *A Hebrew and English Lexicon of the Old Testament* (Oxford: Clarendon Press, 1909), 471.

to eye cosmetics composed with antimony sulfides, which are an iridescent, bluish black.[82]

This is not only the case in Semitic languages: dark hair is described in Homeric epics as *kuaneos*, or "blue," although the epics are famous for their enigmatic (to us) use of color. Nor does everyone understand this term to simply mean "dark" when applied to either the mortal or immortal realm. R. Drew Griffith has suggested that a deep, lapis-colored blue might actually be the intended meaning of this term in the Homeric context, with the possibility that the conception of the gods and demi-deities being blue-haired is derived from earlier Mesopotamian and Egyptian depictions; Egyptians tended to render their gods in human form as lapis-haired and gold-skinned.[83] However, these qualities of Egyptian myth and art may themselves be stylized means of rendering beauty ideals such as dark hair and a bright complexion, which the gods would have expressed in their purest form.

Middle English geographical works and travelogues speak of Saracens who are "black and blue-black as lead," with Indian and Ethiopian peoples often being portrayed in analogous terms. Roland Betancourt argues of medieval Byzantine painting that holy Ethiopian figures were sometimes exalted by using the same blue-black pigment for their skin as the one artists selected to illustrate the firmament.[84] Descriptions of blue-black humans are likewise found in Old Irish and Welsh, with compound terms such as *blowmon* (blue person) designating black-skinned people.[85] Kathleen Ann Kelly reads such associations between what we might call more tropical peoples and blue skin as possibly derived from humoristic theories about how the climate affects one's physiology, with blue emerging as a mark of melancholia due to overexposure to heat and moisture. The ultimate work of these depictions was part of a "long literary tradition profoundly concerned with contrasting the known and the familiar with the strange, the exotic, the Other."[86]

The "bluish" description of Abū Zayd al-Hilālī is not the sole depiction that deviates somewhat from the more common descriptions of him as

82. BT Shabbat 95a, Shabbat 109a, Shabbat 151b, Yoma 9b, etc.

83. R. Drew Griffith, "Gods' Blue Hair in Homer and Eighteenth-Dynasty Egypt," *Classical Quarterly* 55 (2005), 329–34.

84. Roland Betancourt, *Byzantine Intersectionality: Sexuality, Gender, and Race in the Middle Ages* (Princeton, NJ: Princeton University Press, 2020), 195.

85. Betancourt, 332.

86. Kathleen Ann Kelly, "'Blue' Indians, Ethiopians, and Saracens in Middle English narrative texts," *Parergon* 11 (1993): 52.

asmar or *aswad* and, in so doing, points simultaneously to the *sīra*'s local entrenchments and to its parallels with transregional and transtemporal discourses of otherness. In her recordings of southern Tunisian recitations of *Sīrat Banī Hilāl*, Anita Baker finds that Abū Zayd's mother is represented praying over not a thoroughly pitch-black crow but a black bird with a white blaze on its chest, only to have Abū Zayd be born with a bright white torso and black limbs. He is referred to as *adraʿ* (mottled).[87] Abū Zayd is not history's only piebald epic hero. In the medieval German romance, *Parzival*, the figure Feirefiz is born of a "Moorish" mother and a white, Christian father, and emerges with flesh that has black and white patches, like a magpie. Geraldine Heng has argued that the pied nature of Feirefiz's skin may be read as physicalizing his father's "pied" ethics: while Feirefiz is a morally irreproachable hero, his father often has split loyalties in his military endeavors and is obsessed with acquiring personal lucre, such that his "interior is as piebald as the exterior of his miscegenated son."[88] There is perhaps a sense in which the striking interpenetration of black with white on Abū Zayd's body is emblematic of the conflictual conditions under which he comes into the world. His father Rizq has grown perilously impatient with Khaḍrāʾ's infertility. While Khaḍrāʾ is overjoyed to have a son "even if he is Black," his father rejects the child outright. Family structure and notions of honor are thus destabilized by this child whose social irresoluteness is inscribed upon his skin.

Among the *siyar*, another major hero born with an unusual birth mark is Sayf b. Dhī Yazan, whose cheek has a "greenish" mole that distinguishes him as a Yemeni king in his father's line. Here, the birthmark is not a nod to Sayf's hybridity of origin but rather a bulwark against it. Like Zabība, his mother Qamariyya is of royal Abyssinian heritage, and yet the birthmark constitutes a telltale sign that Sayf's paternal, Arab nobility remains an unassailable part of his identity.[89] True to his physical presentation, Sayf's fidelities lie with preserving his father's line against the Abyssinian aggressor and bringing the curse of Ḥām to its ultimate realization by subjugating East Africa. As the Black hero who will lead the Hilālī vanguard in warring against the Zenata Berbers, Abū Zayd inverts the aesthetic absolutes manifest in Sayf's narrative. His Black appearance—embellished with a telltale white mark near his heart as a sign of his true affinities—perhaps evokes his destined territorial conquests during the western migration (*taghrība*)

87. Cathryn Anita Baker, "The Hilālī Saga in the Tunisian South," PhD diss. (University of Indiana, 1978), 67–68, 652.

88. Heng, *Invention of Race*, 198.

89. Blatherwick, *Prophets, Gods, and Kings*, 31–32.

of his tribe into present-day Tunisia. Yet not unlike with the sub-Saharan versions of the *sīra* mentioned above, Dwight Reynolds explains that Abū Zayd's complexion may not be so foreign to the rural communities of southern Egypt that have preserved and delighted in the tale. They are, he notes, often classed as inferior to the "western-garbed, lighter-skinned, urban upper classes, the *affandiyah* or *effendis*," even as the rural *fallāḥīn* are often valorized for their strength and resilience.[90] And, as discussed in the introduction, the *Ḥalab* reciters of the text also layer in explicit instances of the hero imitating practitioners of their craft in appearance and skill.

In the Beirut version of the story, meanwhile, audiences are presented with a case in which darkness and the upper echelons of society are intimately connected. We get an inkling that Rizq's emphatic interest in his bride's lineal value as a *sharīfa* is either separable from or compatible with ancestral blackness. The combined patriliny and matriliny of Khaḍrāʾ's Black heritage implies the possibility of Black people who trace their descent to the Prophet Muḥammad through multiple routes, or perhaps of *sharīfs* who, in a colorist framework, became aligned with Black people in much the way that Abū Zayd will be throughout his life. The simile between Khaḍrāʾ's grandfather and slaves and the *apparent* blackness (*tarā sittahā sawdā kān lawnuhā*) of her grandmother, that Rizq is urged to literally "see," ambiguates the question of whether their blackness is being treated as the substance of their social kind or whether like Abū Zayd, contrary to appearances or perceptions, they are fully lineally Arab.

Nonetheless, the intimation that Muḥammad has a variegated family, the varied external traits of whom all map onto internal qualities of *sharaf*—honorability or nobility—is striking in that it defies a facile physiognomic calculus that would associate only a narrow set of idealized external qualities with the noblest of internal ones. Moreover, it goes a step further than many communities' attempts to align themselves with prophetic heritage through reimagining traditionist and pre-Islamic discourses. In addition to the myriad Black Muslim communities that trace their heritage, figuratively or literally, to the companion Bilāl, Xavier Luffin has noted that many African Muslim sovereigns in places historically thought to be of "the Blacks" unearthed genealogies that would link themselves to south Arabian tribes who shared the ancestor Qaḥṭān. These tribes were in turn said to be related to the prophet Ismāʿīl in Islamic prosopography, but as his cousins rather than in the prophet's direct line, which runs through

90. Dwight F. Reynolds, "Abu Zayd al-Hilālī: Womanizer, Warrior, Shaykh," *Journal of Arabic Literature* 49, nos. 1–2 (2018): 89.

the ancestor of the north Arabian tribes, Maʿadd, and thence to Muḥammad's tribe of Quraysh.[91] Claiming Qaḥṭānī heritage cautiously balanced one's proximity and distance to the original Muslim community and was made plausible through histories of migration between South Arabia and East Africa.

Peter Webb describes the symbolic importance of Qaḥṭān and his parallelism with Maʿadd as a result of consolidating legends and contending for legitimacy after south Arabian tribes entered Islam at a cultural disadvantage, temporally posterior and geographically displaced from their peers in the Ḥijāz. Thus, "a collective sense of exclusion from Maʿadd prompted an array of groups into a separate line of novel ethnogenesis as the Yamāniyya/Qaḥṭān faction of 'Yemenis.'"[92] Similar "mnemohistoric" logics are at work among many early, non-Arabian adopters of Islam. Sarah Bowen Savant has shown that Persian converts attributed their heritage in the Muslim community once again not to a direct kinship with Muḥammad, but to prior prophets such as Isaac or companions such as Salmān, to whom even some non-Muslim Persians traced their heritage, privileges, and protections in Muslim societies.[93]

Though the precise nature of its genealogical claims is perhaps purposefully unclear, the integration of ancestors who are raced as Black into Khaḍrāʾ's background in this telling of the *sīra* rationalizes Abū Zayd's advent by drawing not only on polyvalent meanings and manifestations of *sharaf*, but also on a theory of hereditary transmission that has its roots in antiquity. In *On the Generation of Animals,* Aristotle discusses the case of a woman who had intercourse with a Black person (an "Aethiop"), and did not bear a Black child, but nonetheless had a Black grandchild.[94] Such resemblances with one's distant kin can, according to Aristotle,

91. Xavier Luffin, "'Nos ancêtres les Arabes . . .' Généalogies d'Afrique musulmane," *Civilisations* 53 (2006): 182.

92. Peter Webb, "Ethnicity, Power, and Umayyad Society: The Rise and Fall of the People of Maʿadd," in *The Umayyad World,* ed. Andrew Marsham (London: Routledge, 2019), 81.

93. Sarah Bowen Savant, "Isaac as the Persians' Ishmael: Pride and the Pre-Islamic Past in Ninth and Tenth-century Islam," *Comparative Islamic Studies* 2, no. 1 (2006): 5–25; Sarah Bowen Savant, *The New Muslims of Post-conquest Iran: Tradition, Memory, and Conversion* (Cambridge: Cambridge University Press, 2013), 82–88.

94. Aristotle, *Aristotle on the Generation of Animals: A Philosophical Study,* trans. Johannes Morsink (Lanham, MD: University Press of America, 1982), bk I; cf. Devin Henry, "Aristotle on the Mechanism of Inheritance," *Journal of the History of Biology* 39 (2006): 434.

"recur at an interval of many generations."[95] Devin Henry has argued that Aristotle's preoccupation with genetic atavism stems mainly from this phenomenon acting as a counterpoint to the prevailing theory of "material pangenesis," wherein bodies transmit their form from one generation to the next through the use of composite reproductive tissue, constructed from bits of tissue "drawn from each part of the parent's body."[96] If this were the case, then people could only beget people who were physically analogous to themselves. Instead, Aristotle arrives at the conclusion that an organism's material that is passed on in reproduction must contain all the potentials of the entire lineage, certain among which are activated by "movements," which enable generational relapses.

In the medieval Arabic-speaking world, three of Aristotle's major works on biology, namely his *Historia Animalium*, *De Partibus Animalium*, and the *De Generatione Animalis* were all bundled together as one grand text—the *Kitāb al-Ḥayawān*—during the heyday of ʿAbbasid courtly translation. Because the text appears to have been translated directly from the Greek to the Arabic without a Syriac intermediary, Lou Filius speculates that the initial compilation and translation of the *Kitāb al-Ḥayawān* must have been quite early, before a courtly translation methodology became more standardized.[97] In addition to this compendium of Aristotle's works, there existed a large body of supplementary pseudo-Aristotelian zoological literature, much of which, according to Remke Kruk, expatiated the occult properties of parts of animals not addressed by Aristotle himself.[98]

The texts *De Partibus* and *De Generatione* are often regarded as the more theoretical portions of Aristotle's zoological corpus, and thus earned the attentions of a variety of Muslim philosophers.[99] However, as the story of Khaḍrāʾ attests, clearly certain ideas articulated in these more rarefied treatises had traction in the wider literary world as well, or else mapped onto ideas that were part of the common, preexisting milieu. As I discuss further in chapters 2 and 3, the belief that it was possible to physically incline (*nazʿ*) toward a more distant part of one's heritage, or be diverted (also *nazʿ*) from

95. Aristotle, *On the Generation of Animals*, I:18.

96. Henry, "Aristotle on the Mechanism of Inheritance," 433.

97. Lou Filius, "The *Book of Animals* by Aristotle," *Islamic Thought in the Middle Ages* 75 (2008): 267–273.

98. Remke Kruk, "Reception of Aristotle's *Historia Animalium* in the Arabic tradition," forthcoming in Historia Animalium *of Aristotle: The Arabic Version of Book I-X of the* Kitāb al-Ḥayawân, ed. L. S. Filius and J. N. Mattock (Leiden: Brill, 2017), 2.

99. Kruk, 5.

one's direct line, became utilized in both prophetic (*nabawī*) and "Greek" (*yunānī*) branches of medicine in the Islamic world to explain generational discontinuities in appearance that were often racialized. The belief in the spontaneous resurgence of old family traits was brought to bear in legal contexts to settle paternity in cases whose crux was almost always the etiology of blackness—with few exceptions, parents seem to not have heralded the birth of a much whiter child than themselves with equal alarm.[100] The *ḥadīth*, "there is no grounds for condemnation if a man does not identify with his child's color, for it is simply a root toward which [the child] has inclined [*huwa ʿirq nazaʿahu*]," longer and more intricate elaborations of which appear elsewhere, illustrates that the ideal outcome of such cases was to preserve family integrity and prevent the very fate that befalls Khaḍrāʾ in the *sīra*.[101] The aim was to put an end to the gendered moral panic that ferments among the *Hilālī* elders. True to this, in both this handful of *ḥadīth*s and in *Sīrat Banī Hilāl*, explanations for nonhereditarily Black children are unburdened of the fraught question of mastering understanding, and hence control, of the minute forces that act upon a body's reproductive organs that vexed Aristotle.

In his analysis of heroic births in the *siyar*, Aḥmad Shams al-Dīn al-Ḥajjājī picks up on the discrepancy between the textual version of the *sīra* and its orally performed counterparts, which, he claims, "interpret Abū Zayd's blackness of color with a cosmic reading, in which he emerges Black because his mother's prayer was answered."[102] One might view the introduction of Abū Zayd's ancestral blackness as working against this more cosmic logic, as well as against the logic of the work's social setting. Indeed, as if to put a fine point on the difference and distance between Khaḍrāʾ's ancestral status and associations with slavery, in some recitations her assets before marriage are explicitly stated to include "two hundred Abyssinian women from the highlands," and another hundred *mamlūk* slaves; if her forebears were ever in bondage, the dynamic has long been reversed.[103] However, the lack of strict geocultural delineation and hierarchization of Black and white people in the Beirut

100. One such exception occurs in al-Marzubānī, *Ashʿār al-nisāʾ*, ed. Sāmī Makkī al-ʿĀnī and Hilāl Nājī (Baghdad: Dār al-Risāla, 1976), 82.

101. Ibn Ḥajar and al-Bukhārī, "Bāb idhā ʿaraḍ bi-nafī al-walad," in *Fatḥ al-Bārī Sharḥ Ṣaḥīḥ al-Bukhārī* (al-Maktaba al-Islāmiyya, 1996), https://www.islamweb.net/ar/library/content/52/9693.

102. Ḥajjājī, *Mawlid al-Baṭal*, 115.

103. Ḥajjājī, *Mawlid al-Baṭal*, 205; cf. Elizabeth Wickett, *Seers, Saints, and Sinners: The Oral Tradition of Upper Egypt* (London: I.B. Tauris, 2012), 63.

recension ultimately coheres around the human acceptance of unknowability and indeterminacy in God's created order, of which only He has full knowledge.

After he divorces Khaḍrā', Rizq expels her from the tribe. Rather than point her howdah homeward, and fearing that her father will kill her, Khaḍrā' seeks the territories of the tribal ruler Zaḥlān. He takes her in and becomes Abū Zayd's foster parent, bringing him up alongside his sons and overseeing his classic, heroic "preparatory youth," which entails tutoring in Qur'ān, a diverse array of languages, sciences, and rhetorical and martial arts.[104] Sometime later, fighting breaks out between Rizq and Zaḥlān, who is wounded and whose horse is slain. Still not knowing they are kin, in reprisal Abū Zayd rides out against the Hilālīs, killing, wounding, and capturing them, but Rizq is on a hunt and away from the fray. When he returns, the prince Sirḥān apprises him, "O Rizq, Hilāl has been met with wondrous affairs [*ṣār bi-hilāl umūr ʿajā'ib*]," Abū Zayd has emerged against them.[105] At that same time, the *sharīf* Qirḍāb begins to sense he is dying, and he asks that word be sent to his daughter to visit him, only to be told she is no longer in Rizq's charge. He writes to the Hilālī leadership, "The valiant Qirḍāb says, truly, these times and this world have become wonders [*al-ayyām wa-l-dunya taswā al-ʿajā'ib*] . . . tell Rizq to send Khaḍrā' to us, in order to see her loved ones [*ahlahā wa-l-qarā'ib*]."[106] As Rizq's attempt to remove Khaḍrā' from his life begins to crumble around his ears, the world pitches into a carnivalesque landscape in which the inexplicable—yet, for those outside the narrative, fated—seems to overtake the everyday. All of this ultimately leads to father and son meeting in battle, and to Rizq disclosing their relationship. He explains as if to excuse himself, "My cousin Sirḥān came to me and said/ O Rizq, O face of the Hilālīs / give us the newborn so we can pronounce on him! / It was then we saw you were dark [*asmar*] and black-eyed / he said, 'this child looks like your slave / his face resembles starless nights,'" but that they have now returned to each other again nonetheless (*wa-l-tamm shamalī fīk baʿd shatātī*). At this, Abū Zayd responds:

> If someone told you to throw yourself into a pit, you'd throw yourself! What's more, you're contradicting the words of your Lord concerning

104. For a discussion of education as represented in this portion of the epic, see Arie Schippers, "An Episode in the Life of a Hero in the 'Sīrat Banī Hilāl': Abū Zayd as a Schoolboy," *Oriente Moderno* 22, no. 83 (2003): 347–59.

105. *Sīrat Banī Hilāl*, 49.

106. *Sīrat Banī Hilāl*, 51.

> the composition of His Creation [*takwīn khalqihi*] [by alleging] that if a son doesn't resemble his father, he's a bastard [*ibn zinā*].[107]

He then punctuates this statement with verse, saying that in heeding other men rather than observing the workings of God's Creation, Rizq has "destroyed [his] house by [his] own hand," and noting that "if you look at the whole of Creation, you find its forms are always different [*tarā ṣuwarahum dawm mukhtalifāt*]." A practitioner of reason (*aʿāqil*) would have been attentive to this, rather than to Sirḥān and his peers. Abū Zayd essentially extols human diversity through its play of extremes, with "him as white as the moon in the sky [*ka-annahu al-badr fī-l-samāʾ*], and him looking as if he were lumps of coal [*tarāhu yushbih faḥamāt*]," indicating, not unlike in Q 49:13 and Q 30:22, that differences are signs of God's creative genius.[108]

At this, Rizq apologizes to Khaḍrāʾ, stating that she is indeed of "great inherited merit [*ḥasab*] and lineage [*nasab*]," which remains the idiom of honor even as the optics of its embodiment are shifting within the narrative—as is true across the *sīra* traditions writ large. The family reunites, and when Zaḥlān passes away, Abū Zayd is installed as leader of his tribal faction (*ajlasū Abū Zayd ʿalā takht al-mulk*), effectively achieving parity of position with his father without replacing him; his father lives to witness and embrace demographic change in microcosm.[109] All of this comes to pass because the exceptional Abū Zayd—lineally fully Arab, schooled in theology and the arts of rhetorical persuasion in not one but seven languages, and well on his way to picaresque heroic stardom—vocally demands a new way of seeing within the world of the text. And, across his many manifestations

107. *Sīrat Banī Hilāl*, 53.

108. *Sīrat Banī Hilāl*, 54. These verses, which respectively declare that God in his wisdom created humankind in peoples and tribes and with varied tongues and colors, are often adduced in modern commentaries stating that there is no basis for racial discrimination in Islam: Chouki El Hamel emphatically declares that, "[N]either the Qurʾan nor the Hadith make any evaluative racial distinctions among humankind," saying that instead "religious" justification for color prejudice comes in through an apocryphal back door, in the form of the Ham's Curse, which was used to "extend Arab and Berber cultural prejudices about race that preexisted Islam." Bernard Lewis agrees, finding that "the Qurʾān expresses no racial or color prejudice." To be sure, exegetes were themselves divided on whether Q 30:22 implied the differentiation of humankind into broad, essentialized groups of "black, white, and red" peoples and those who spoke Arabic and non-Arabic (*ʿajam*) languages, or whether it implied myriad, intricately small differences of feature that all humans express despite all having "two eyes and two eyebrows and a nose and a forehead and a mouth and two cheeks." Ibn Kathīr, *Tafsīr al-Qurʾān al-ʿAẓīm*, vol. 11, ed. Muṣṭafā al-Sayyid Muḥammad et al. (Giza: Muʾassasa Qurṭuba, 2000), 21.

109. *Sīrat Banī Hilāl*, 55–56.

in different tellings and writings of his epic, the figure of Abū Zayd elicits new ways of seeing modes of racialization as they are "created, inhabited, transformed, and destroyed" in global perspective as well.[110]

Conclusion

Origin stories, writes film critic James Whitbrook, are so central to their making that they are now synonymous with superheroes: "It's the telling of that one crystallising moment for a character that raises them up from the unknown to the hero we know and love."[111] Much like today's superheroes, as evidenced by the listening session in Bakātūsh, the *sīra* heroes' origin stories are beloved and emotionally powerful in large part because of their familiarity and formalism. Audiences know them, instinctually and experientially, before the telling even begins. They certainly know the heroes themselves by reputation or, in the case of ʿAntar, as a historical person. Theirs is the gratification of, to paraphrase Tahera Qutbuddin, having their expectations appropriately set up and fulfilled by the shape of the genre.[112] Is it possible, therefore, that whenever someone rehearses the origins of ʿAntar or Abū Zayd, these tales still evoke new ways of seeing? Does the affect and didactic power of *ʿajab*—the gratification of new cosmic cognizance—work each time anew?

It is likely impossible to know for sure, at least for the medieval era with which we are most concerned, as most direct accounts of people witnessing the *sīra*s read or performed are from the eighteenth century and later. Indeed, as Dwight Reynolds has noted, we often hear about the popular *sīra*s earliest and in greatest detail from their critics.[113] A tantalizing, periodic history of attempts to crack down on their performance in Mamluk Cairo provides some leading insights. So, too, do notes on the broader preaching and storytelling landscape of the time, in which orators tried to elicit at once transformative and disruptive bouts of ecstasy and emotional release from audiences over and over again. Sometimes they did so through clever contrivance. Mustard was applied to the eyes to bring

110. Hochman, "Racialization," 1245.

111. James Whitbrook, "Why Are We So Fascinated by Origin Stories?" *Gizmodo*, November 16, 2014, https://gizmodo.com/why-are-we-so-fascinated-by-origin-stories-1663820928.

112. Tahera Qutbuddin, "*Khuṭba*: The Evolution of Early Arabic Oration," in *Classical Arabic Humanities in Their Own Terms: Festschrift for Wolfhart Heinrichs*, ed. Beatrice Gruendler (Leiden: Brill, 2008), 208.

113. Reynolds, *Heroic Poets*, 7. See also: Hirschler, *The Written Word in the Medieval Arabic Lands*, 168–86.

tears, a reformed dissenter was stationed in the crowd, or one presented before mixed-gender circles where women were perhaps more prone to screaming and rending their garments.[114]

Another speculative answer to whether the *sīras* were thought to retain their suasion and novelty meanwhile lies in the progressive approaches to reading practice and hierarchies of knowledge that circulated in various philosophical and ethical traditions. The belief that one encounters the world differently in different stages of socialization, education, and self-knowledge, whether acquired through age, gnosis, or privilege, flourished in various premodern Muslim discourses. At their most simplistic, philosophies divided humanity into the elect (*khāṣṣ*), typically indicating those who had an inborn capacity for developing rationality and right decision-making (*ʿaql*), and hence leadership, and the remainder of the wider populace (*ʿāmm*). This distinction often overlaps with indicators of pedigree like *nasab* and *ḥasab*, staples of the epic world; it also typically disfavored the producers and audiences of much-maligned, popular literature even as it was ingrained in the imaginaries of the texts themselves. Zahra Ayubi has beautifully dissected the gendered, classed, and raced ethical problematics of sifting the elect from the non-elect.[115] Louise Marlow has complicated this division in her analysis of thought systems inherited from Late Antique Persia and Greece that populated elite and nonelite strata further with various taxonomies of occupations and abilities.[116] For some, distinctions of rank and nature also affected the sorts of truths that a person could be expected to absorb and the mechanisms of delivery through which this was possible, with the philosopher al-Fārābī (d. 950) claiming in a well-known passage,

> Most men, either by nature or by habit, are unable to comprehend and cognize [first principles]; these are the men for whom one ought to represent the manner in which the principles of the beings, their ranks of order, the Active Intellect, and the supreme rulership, exist through things that are imitations of them.[117]

114. Jonathan P. Berkey, *Popular Preaching and Religious Authority in the Medieval Islamic Near East* (Seattle: University of Washington Press), 29–31.

115. Zahra Ayubi, *Gendered Morality: Classical Islamic Ethics of the Self, Family, and Society* (New York: Columbia University Press, 2019).

116. Louise Marlow, *Hierarchy and Egalitarianism in Islamic Thought* (Cambridge: Cambridge University Press, 1997).

117. Al-Farabi, "The Political Regime," trans. Muhsin Madhi, in *Medieval Political Philosophy*, ed. Ralph Lerner and Muhsin Madhi (Ithaca, NY: Cornell University Press, 1993), 40.

We see a similar, and similarly exclusive, division of who can imbibe which truths arise in both ʿAntar's and Abū Zayd's birth stories, only there it is not just abstract ultimate truths that are in question, but their worldly implications for how to engage racialized difference. Thus, only those capable of understanding deep meaning (*maʿnā*) and eloquent messages (*bayān*) can appreciate Zabība's beauty in full, despite its ample and almost salacious description in the foregoing text. Only one who actively exercises his rational faculties (rendered participially with *aʿāqil*) can connect human diversity not with human perfidy but with divine, creative order (*takwīn al-khalq*), especially where popular opinion works to the converse. When the sovereign Zuhayr immediately experiences positive, knowing wonder in the form of *ʿajab* in ʿAntar's story, this cements a mutual acknowledgment between kindred elites that is to endure for much of the epic. The strongest and most heroic man alive, meanwhile, is the "measliest of beings" to all the other Arabs, and must prove his worth again and again in trial after trial to gain wider recognition.

The genealogy of ideas behind scientizing Abū Zayd's difference through references to the concept of intergenerational atavism, originated by the "first teacher" of Muslim thinkers and put to marriage-preserving use by Muḥammad himself, may have impressed a more rarefied circle than the rest of the vignette. So, too, with what his blackness portends for the nature of prophetic lineage, or *sharaf*, and superior standing in the *umma*. Meanwhile, the succinct denunciation of racialized discrimination and disavowal of one's own child with the refrain that if your friends jump off a bridge, that doesn't mean you should, inflected also with a universalist piety about all creations being crafted by an intentional and omniscient God, would perhaps have greatest mileage with a wide range of people.

Like the histories these heroes will advance, the interpretive frameworks subtly embedded in their origin stories are aspirational: they envision potentials for one engaged in contemplation of the world, its peoples, and its narratives, to derive ever deeper insights, much as the characters do themselves. The tales envision new futures and possibilities apart from the everyday social ills with which their audiences contend. And if the texts urge, cajole, and encourage their own characters to see their Black peers, children, and champions in new ways, perhaps those in the audience can see each other and be seen by each other with fresh eyes as well.

✸ 2 ✸

Conceiving ʿAbd al-Wahhāb

Eventually, late-Umayyad and early Abbasid actors resolved this controversy [of caliphs with concubine mothers] by articulating a notion of purely patrilineal descent, which redefined concubines' children as full 'Arabs' and thus fully deserving of the caliphate.

ELIZABETH URBAN

In slave conditions, Islam insists on ascending miscegenation. If the father is Arab the child is Arab, regardless of whether the mother is a wife or concubine, and regardless of the nationality of the mother.

ALI MAZRUI

The text . . . refuses to say how Feirefiz's black-and-white dappling is patterned, so that some critics believe he is speckled; others imagine him with a white surface and black markings (like writing on parchment, an analogy the narrative supplies), or with a black surface and white markings; or . . . they believe him to be striped like a zebra.

GERALDINE HENG

The birth story of *Sīrat al-Amīra Dhāt al-Himma*'s signature Black hero, ʿAbd al-Wahhāb, offers the lengthiest and most theoretically dense account of nonhereditary Black birth to appear in the literature of the *sīras*, and arguably in medieval Arabic literature in general. When ʿAbd al-Wahhāb is born black-skinned, to the shock and dismay of all, his mother Fāṭima is almost immediately accused of committing adultery with a slave. At a glance, we might recognize this as a stock feature not only of the *sīras*, but of numerous Arabic genres, perhaps most infamously the *asmār* or nighttime tales of the *Thousand and One Nights*. But there is more: quickly, aspersions swirl around Fāṭima's milk sibling and squire, Marzūq, which if true would render Fāṭima guilty of incest as well as an extramarital affair. In a world in which the Arabness of one's *nasab* (lineage) gradually became patrilineally determined per Mazrui's and Urban's statements above, a woman like Fāṭima choosing a non-Arab Black man and tribal affiliate (*mawlā*) flouts ideals even if in wedlock. And even when relationships like that between ʿAntar's Arab father, Shaddād and his Abyssinian mother, Zabība, followed gender-normative fault lines and occurred at society's upper echelons, a child's racialized status was subject to contestation—to tensions between how they presented to society and what their paternity entitled them to claim. As a Black child with tribally elite Arab parentage, ʿAbd al-Wahhāb embodies these overlapping anxieties.

After a bout of local litigation concerning who his father might be, Fāṭima's Kilābī tribesmen go to Mecca with her and her son in tow. Once there, a fictionalized representation of the sixth Shīʿī imam Jaʿfar al-Ṣādiq (d. 765), whose authority is respected and trusted across confessional groups, pronounces a final verdict: ʿAbd al-Wahhāb is Black because he was conceived at the time of his mother's menses, of which his father, al-Ḥārith, was heedless in his lust. Fāṭima rejoices at her exoneration. ʿAbd al-Wahhāb is taken before the caliph and laureled with praise and gifts. Al-Ḥārith and his father, ʿAbd al-Wahhāb's uncle Ẓālim, remain so unable to accept the boy as theirs that they convert to Christianity and defect to Byzantium, only for ʿAbd al-Wahhāb—by then a righteous and accomplished Muslim warrior—to later kill them in battle.

ʿAbd al-Wahhāb is not the only character in a *sīra* to be born Black due to being conceived during his mother's menses; a villain in *Sīrat ʿAntar* shares a similar origin story.[1] Likewise, the Arabic corpus of prophets' tales is scattered with stories in which women's menses exert a blackening effect on other bodies, alongside similar effects produced through other imbalances in one's bodily fluids that take on sexualized and reproductive significance. ʿAbd al-Wahhāb is outstanding among these intertexts for his positive characterization as one of his epic's central protagonists, making the ascription of his blackness to such taboo origins striking. All of this leads us to ask how these tropes became entrenched in storytelling and what references to sexual deviance might reveal about the logic of producing and introducing difference in narrative.

1. Lyons, *Arabian Epic*, volume 3, 60.

At the level of their normative, collective reproduction, we have seen that etiologies of discrete human kinds tended to be explained by two, sometimes enmeshed theories in many sources that the *sīra* is at once versed in and actively remixing. There was the predominant climatological explanation discussed in the introduction, which regarded factors such as heat and humidity in a given location as giving rise to natural differences of social import through their effects on the humors (the *bilād al-sūdān*, e.g., being hot and dry, blacken their inhabitants and curl their hair). Then, there were the supernatural explanations given for large-scale human differentiation in prophetology, which in the Islamic tradition typically traces the beginnings of blackness to a curse on Nūḥ's son, Ḥām. Scriptural sources likewise provided for readings of humans as a product of both their lands and of their lineages, with the Qurʾān offering a split etiology for mankind as protoplast, in which Adam is made from specific kinds of earth, and as reproductive actor, in which man is made from the refinement of his own "water," or ejaculate, into flesh.

Theories about racialized difference used by the *sīra* meanwhile seem to extend into relatively unbiologized domains: though penetrative menstrual sex of the kind that leads to ʿAbd al-Wahhāb's skin color is prohibited on the basis of Q 2:222, which states that menstruation causes a woman pain and so men ought to abstain from "closeness" with their spouses for its duration, it does not forebode any bodily consequence to not doing so other than physical strain. Nonetheless, the *sīra* adduces a biological and physically discernible consequence for wayward sex by drawing on scientific and speculative notions about the body that were known by the mid-eleventh century across a vast geography—thinkers cited throughout this chapter span al-Andalus to Baghdad—at least half a century before the earliest *sīras*' existence as written texts is first attested in Samawʾal al-Maghribī's polemical treatise, *Ifḥām al-Yahūd*.[2] In other words, the *sīra* proposes that this nonhereditary change is possible by using concepts of heredity, considering the concoction of materials contributed by one's parents inside of a woman's womb.

This focus on maternity is perhaps unsurprising. As we have seen, the origin tales of Black heroes often reveal as much about the condition of the hero's mother as they do about the hero himself. In his alterity and paternal rejection, ʿAbd al-Wahhāb has often been read as mirroring his mother's experience of being given over to a nursemaid in childhood to be raised as her daughter because in a bet with her uncle, her father had staked his claim to chiefdom on who would be first to have a son. Shahzad Bashir

2. Perlmann, "Samauʾal al-Maghribī Ifḥām al-Yahūd," 15, 100.

duly writes, "Fatima's gender and ʿAbd al-Wahhab's blackness are marks of similar implications," and in her own translation of the epic, Melanie Magidow dubs the vignette in which the two first embark together on raids after the paternity trial's denouement "Like Mother, Like Son."[3] The story's parallel relationship between racialized and gendered precarity and tenacity is indicative of what Ania Loomba has called the comparative nature of racial thinking, which

> depended upon making particular kinds of comparisons between women, non-Europeans, blacks, religious minorities, the poor, sexual "deviants," and animals in order to deepen, broaden, and fine-tune the idea of a "natural" hierarchy between peoples and groups.[4]

Though Loomba situates this as part of a European genealogy of race, she also notes that we might use comparison to unthink a Eurocentric account of racialization's history and impact. As is apparent from the conflict between Junduba and Shamṭā in which her Black soldiers are ensnared at this book's beginning, already in centuries-old works there are comparisons to be made between Black masculinity and white, Arab womanhood—for we are assured that Fāṭima herself is "radiantly white." But there are also contrasts. Fāṭima is quickly rendered her Black son's staunchest advocate in the text, flexing her rhetorical prowess and threatening her tribesmen with violence, dishonor, and chaos if they deny him. Like Shamṭā the gray-haired, Fāṭima is conferred much of this power and responsibility over her child through an age differential that inheres in parenthood, but her control is also underpinned by the production of gendered "know-how": in the birthing room, Fāṭima's retinue offers to do away with the child, maximizing on their exclusive, feminine medical knowledge and survivalist skills with guarding information.[5] Fāṭima declines.

3. Shahzad Bashir, *A New Vision for Islamic Pasts and Futures* (Cambridge, MA: MIT Press, 2022), https://doi.org/10.26300/bdp.bashir.ipf.premodern-epic; *Tale of Princess Fatima*, 123.

4. Ania Loomba, "Race and the Possibilities of Comparative Critique," *New Literary History* 40, no. 3 (2009): 501.

5. I borrow this idea of midwives' privileged access and legal status from Avner Gilʿadi, *Muslim Midwives: The Craft of Birthing in the Premodern Middle East* (Cambridge: Cambridge University Press, 2015), esp. 128–29. I borrow the phrasing of gendered "know-how" from Nora Berend's use of the term to describe informal, traveling, and not inherently textual forms of knowledge. Nora Berend, "Interconnection and Separation: Perspectives on the Modern Problem of the 'Global Middle Ages,'" *Medieval Encounters* 29 (2023): 313.

However Fāṭima decides to deal with the facts of her child's existence, she does so as a respected woman exercising options available specifically to her. As Stephanie E. Jones-Rogers suggests, even when such options were adaptive countermeasures to circumvent patriarchal "legal doctrine that placed their persons and their goods under their husbands' control," the "extra steps" that women could and did take to secure rights evinced a significant keenness to participate in legal, economic, and political life rather than go against its rules.[6] As she arbitrates his paternity and bends the ear of imams and caliphs to do so, Fāṭima becomes more intimate with structures of authority than she was previously through stewardship of her Black child, and he does likewise.

In this chapter, I show that it is not an arbitrary choice to blacken a positive, heroic figure. Nor is the taboo choice to hinge this blackening on the workings of the pious and chaste but also maternal and menstruating female body merely convenient. I argue that what on the one hand appears a cautionary tale about the dangers of incorrect sex is, on the other, a crucial device for creating a Black-Arab hero whose unique, hybridized identity is putatively impossible on both physiological and legal axes yet is also key to defining the Muslim community within the story's world.

Hybridity, "mixedness," and identity transformation are signature elements in premodern heroic literatures and have previously been the subject of analyses of race in several European contexts, some of which I alluded to in chapter 1. Examinations of the black-to-white baptismal vignette in the Middle English *King of Tars*, the ill-mixed piebald protagonist of the German *Parzival* whose skin provokes so much ongoing speculation, and the monstrous composite species of the originally French travels of the intrepid John Mandeville all are key, echoing elements in the critical enterprise of defining race and identifying processes of racialization in medieval Europe.[7] Even one of the most analogous texts to

6. Despite Jones-Rogers's specific focus on white women's slave ownership in the US South rather than medieval paternity suits, her discussion of gendered incentives and obstacles to participating in legal and economic systems and securing proprietary rights is apropos. Stephanie E. Jones-Rogers, *They Were Her Property: White Women as Slave Owners in the American South* (New Haven, CT: Yale University Press, 2019), xvi.

7. On the *King of Tars* scene, see Geraldine Heng, *Empire of Magic: Medieval Romance and the Politics of Cultural Fantasy* (New York: Columbia University Press, 2003), 227–37; Cord J. Whitaker, "Black Metaphors in the *King of Tars*," *Journal of English and Germanic Philosophy* 112, no. 2 (2013): 169–93 and Whitaker, *Black Metaphors: How Modern Racism Emerged*, 20–48; Adam Hochman, "Is 'Race' Modern? Disambiguating the Question," *Du Bois Review: Social Science Research on Race* 1 (2020): 1–19. On *Parzival*, see Heng, *Invention of Race*, 181–256; on Mandeville, see

Sīrat Dhāt al-Himma—to which it is often compared and even tentatively connected—the Byzantine tale *Digenis Akritas*, recalls the triumphs of a literal "two-blood border lord," who is the child of a so-called Saracen *amīr* and a Byzantine noblewoman.[8] Within premodern critical race studies, such examples query the edges and flux of racialized categories by calling attention to the prospect of mixing and mixedness, as well as to the mechanisms that work to limit and prevent it.

ʿAbd al-Wahhāb's form of hybridity is radically different from the foregoing, as well as from that of ʿAntar or even Abū Zayd. First, it is disingenuous to simply call ʿAbd al-Wahhāb "mixed" without considering how this occurs at a fundamental (we might even say chemical) level. Rather than expressing the qualities of both of his parents through channels of male and female seminal activity that were conventionally understood at the time, he is concocted in the womb through other materials blending with these elements, particularly his mother's menstrual issue. As Liana Saif notes, various Muslim scholars of the Middle Ages offered "epigenic" models of the fetus's gradual formation and individuation in the womb that also treated even an emergent human as a microcosm, acted upon by external, astral, and cosmic forces as well as internal, biological ones.[9] Menstrual blood bridges this threshold further, being an internally generated substance considered both subject to the heavens and superordinate over one's natural surroundings and external world, as I discuss more in chapter 3.[10]

Second, it is misleading to interpret ʿAbd al-Wahhāb's Black-Arabness straightforwardly as "mixed" within the identity matrix typical to the

---

Suzanne Conklin Akbari, "Race, Environment, Culture," in *A Cultural History of Race in the Middle Ages*, ed. Thomas Hahn (London: Bloomsbury Academic, 2021), 47–66; Mittman, "Are the 'Monstrous Races' Races?," 36–51.

8. This is the direct translation of the hero, Basil's, cognomen that lends the story its title, as given by Denison B. Hull: *Digenis Akritas, the Two-blood Border Lord: The Grottaferrata Version*, trans. Denison B. Hull (Cincinnati: Ohio University Press, 1985).

9. Liana Saif, "The Universe and the Womb: Generation, Conception, and the Stars in Islamic Medieval Astrological and Medical Texts," *Journal of Arabic and Islamic Studies* 16 (2016): 187–88.

10. I mean this not just in the sense of symbolic links between menstruation and lunar cycles; heavenly encounters engender unique experiences regarding menstruation. For example, Muḥammad's daughter, Fāṭima, was said not to menstruate at all because the sperm-drop that produced her originated in Paradise. For an in-depth discussion of Fāṭima's conception narrative, see Michael Muhammad Knight, *Muhammad's Body: Baraka Networks and the Prophetic Assemblage* (Chapel Hill: University of North Carolina Press, 2020), 143–49.

ʿAbbasid era in which his tale is set, in which the very lineal categories that exist constrain the possibility of mixedness. The concept of mixture is fundamentally a political rather than biological one that hinges in large part on who "counts" in the constitution of ancestry and how much, with notions of hybridity in one's heritage frequently reinforcing contrasting ones of purity.[11] Literature from the pre- and early Islamic period attests to ambivalence about the workings of *nasab*, which had both matrilineal and patrilineal components. Gradually in most Islamic legal contexts, patrilineality became the determiner of ethnic identity, even if one was raced otherwise. Only at the extremes did bilateral descent still matter: for exceptional or elite women, like Muḥammad's daughter, Fāṭima, whose accolades were so striking that people actively argued for their intergenerational salience, or for marginalized women and children who, as a by-product of their matriline, had no one legally empowered to argue on their behalf.[12]

As, increasingly, elites were "mixed" according to prior hermeneutics, their goalposts of what Urban calls "full Arabness" moved through

11. On mixedness as political, see Josep Lluís Mateo Dieste, "Are There '*Mestizos*' in the Arab World? A Comparative Survey of Classification Categories and Kinship Systems," *Middle Eastern Studies* 48, no. 1 (2012): 125–38. For a concise theoretical discussion of how hybridity and purity interrelate, see Jennifer DeVere Brody, *Impossible Purities: Blackness, Femininity, and Victorian Culture* (Durham, NC: Duke University Press, 1998), 11–12.

12. For example, there is some evidence that the gender-reversed counterpart of the pre- and early Islamic *hajīn*, *muqrif* (taken from a word designating horses of lower pedigree due to their Arabian maternity and non-Arabian paternity), endured longer in the early Islamic period and merged with ideas of unfreedom. A tenth-century bill of sale entails the purchase of a woman born to a *muqrif*, whose father was enslaved and whose mother was free, and hence she was born into enslavement. Elizabeth Urban and Shaun Marmon discuss cases in the early period of *muwalladāt*, daughters said to have been born into slavery to enslaved mothers, who were denied their free fathers' *nasab* because they refused to acknowledge paternity. This in turn denied their mothers status as *ummahāt al-awlād*. On the relative prominence of bilateral descent claims vis-à-vis maternal nobility, reputation, and achievement, see Alyssa Gabbay, *Gender and Succession in Medieval and Early Modern Islam: Bilateral Descent and the Legacy of Fatima* (London: I.B. Tauris, 2020), esp. 23–24, 50–54. For the tenth-century bill of sale, see Naïm Vanthieghem, "Quelques contrats de vente d'esclaves de la collection Aziz Atiyya," *Journal of Juristic Papyrology* 44 (2014): 179. On *muwalladāt* who were not paternally recognized in the early period, see Elizabeth Urban, "Race, Gender and Slavery in Early Islamicate History," *History Compass* 20, no. 5 (2022): 7; Shaun Marmon, "Intersections of Gender, Sex, and Slavery: Female Sexual Slavery," in *The Cambridge World History of Slavery*, vol. 2, ed. Craig Perry, David Eltis, et al. (Cambridge: Cambridge University Press, 2021), 205–10.

contestation, restructuring, and ultimately naturalization. Within this matrix, ʿAbd al-Wahhāb gets caught in a "racial loophole" because the surrounding society views it as possible that he could only be one of two totalized identities—Black *or* Arab—not both. He is consistently mistaken for a slave and polemicized by his detractors as the "Black of the Banū Kilāb" and the bastard "son of Marzūq," Fāṭima's inferably Black milk sibling. He primarily keeps company with the Black contingents of his tribe's armies and is said to look like he is from East Africa, and he builds relationships with people who are Abyssinian, Zanji, and so on.[13] Indeed, ʿAbd al-Wahhāb's disputed origins place the authentic plurality of his world and the problems of navigating far greater differences than those between a Black-Arab child and his Arab peers center stage, with varied peoples raced as Black present in the Muslim community—in history and in potential—from the outset.[14]

13. Like *sūdān*, *zanj* is frequently used in early Arabic sources to indicate all Black Africans rather than a specific group, though in early sources it seems to have primarily indicated peoples from southeastern Africa, and many scholars have duly aligned the term with Bantu-speaking and proto-Swahili ethnicities (figures such as al-Jāḥiẓ refer to Zanj from Qanbalu and Lanjīya, for example, or Mkumbuu and Unguja in Zanzibar, while geographers also speak of an Indonesian raid on the "Zanj" lands of the Comoros and Sofala in Mozambique, etc.). In classical Persian and in turn in various Turkic languages, Black Africans are referred to as *zengi*, and this same word, combined with the Persian word for coast (*bār*), constructs the name of the modern nation of Zanzibar. These terms' superficial application—along with a host of at once more particular-sounding and similarly mutable ethnonyms, at times all coming to bear on the selfsame figures—in racecraft construct, in the words of Zavier Wingham, "ungeographic-yet-Black" presences in the Middle East. Al-Jāḥiẓ, *Kitāb al-Bayān wa-l-Tabyīn* vol. 3, ed. Muwaffiq Shihāb al-Dīn (Beirut: Dār al-Kutub al-ʿIlmiyya, 2009), 33; Marina Tolmacheva, "Toward a Definition of the Term *Zanj*," *Azania: Journal of the British Institute in Eastern Africa* 21, no. 1 (1986): 105–13; André Wink, *Al-Hind: The Making of the Indo-Islamic World*, vol. 3 (Leiden: Brill, 2004), 186; Zavier Wingham, "Arap Bacı'nın Ara Muhaveresi: Under the Shadow of the Ottoman Empire and Its Study," *YILLIK: Annual of Istanbul Studies* 3 (2021): 178.

14. Insofar as membership in society's upper tiers became subtended by blending into or laying claim to an Arab patriline, and insofar as being in enslaved or unfree classes was widely viewed as an intermediary and impermanent status, several scholars have remarked that what we might today recognize as Black ancestry and mixedness in nonblack Muslim cultures eludes the archive, particularly as an afterlife of slavery. Parisa Vaziri draws attention to a historiographical trend in which the stigma of racialized blackness and enslavement in the Indian Ocean leads to lamentations that the past "supposedly lacks a willing, live referent [. . .] claimed by neither survivors, nor, purportedly, their descendants." Dahlia Gubara notes a similar lamentation in studies of diaspora and enslavement in Arab and Ottoman contexts. My object here is not to salvage or "give voice" to genealogies that are occluded in the documentary

In view of the lengths to which the story goes in crafting and explicating ʿAbd al-Wahhāb's unique origins, certain questions therefore arise. Why produce difference in this way—why make the valorized, lineally illustrious bodies of a titular woman hero and her son the locus of anxiety about racial accident? Why not have the central Black hero of the text mirror more directly the experiences and heritages of his similarly raced peers? How does setting up characters of varying moral and social positions to respond to ʿAbd al-Wahhāb's unforeseen difference drive the narrative forward, and to what ends?

Dangerous Conception: Fāṭima's Pregnancy

Fāṭima's journey to motherhood begins with her vigorously resisting the idea of marriage and pregnancy. Rejecting a more conventional domestic role, Fāṭima favors the ascetic pursuits of a warrior. These exploits, as Remke Kruk notes, are often connected implicitly to virginal chastity.[15] Due to family politics, Fāṭima is reluctantly wed to her cousin al-Ḥārith through the machinations of her father, Maẓlūm (Oppressed), and her uncle, Ẓālim (Oppressor).[16] The two brothers have split authority over their tribe in the aftermath of their bet, and a marriage of their children will restore the chiefdom's unity. Even after being wed, it becomes clear that Fāṭima has no intention of committing to wifely duties, and al-Ḥārith claims that he fears approaching her to consummate their union because of her anger and strength. And so, al-Ḥārith conspires to have Fāṭima's milk sibling and lifelong companion, Marzūq, drug her with a tincture made by ʿUqba. Delivered in a winking, technical register, the elaborately pharmacological description of the villainous *qāḍī*'s concoction seems to prefigure the rigorous inquiry to which the ingredients of ʿAbd al-Wahhāb's identity will later be subjected:

> This was the drug that ʿUqba gave him: vaporous Cretan henbane, ground up with a blue-hued sulfur [*maṭḥūn bi-l-kibrīt al-azraq*]. Should

---

or anthropological record, but to point to how storytelling lays currents of exchange, dislocation, and reidentification bare in novel ways. Parisa Vaziri, "False Differends: Racial Slavery and the Genocidal Example," *Philosophy Today* (2022): n.p.; Dahlia E. M. Gubara, "Revisiting Race and Slavery through ʿAbd al-Rahman al-Jabarti's *ʿAjaʾib al-athar*," *Comparative Studies of South Asia, Africa and the Middle East* 38, no. 2 (2018): 233–34.

15. Kruk, *Warrior Women of Islam*, 45.

16. Names in the *sīras* are often symbolic of character and social role.

a camel taste even a grain of it, it would lose consciousness through the whole week. ʿUqba kept it concealed on his person because he was a lecher [*yakhfīhu maʿhu li-annahu fāsiq yuhwī al-niswān*], consumed with women, and if a lady came to call on him, hoping to hear him [speak of] piety and righteousness, he would instead drug her and take advantage of her.[17]

Though its formula is intricately described as if to suggest novelty or rarity, it is entirely possible that this specific tranquilizing recipe was readily recognizable to the initiated. In his thirteenth-century catalogue of con artists' tricks, the Syrian author al-Jawbarī (fl. ca. 1222) details the "most prodigious[ly]" used and "classiest" of sleeping pills on the market, made with a mix of henbane, opium, leek juice, and so on, and "fumigated with blue sulfur" that must first be crushed into a powder. By al-Jawbarī's time, this drug earned the nickname blue Cretan, "perhaps because of the association of blueness with darkness, and even with the Devil"—a connection made all the more evocative given that ʿAbd al-Wahhāb's own darkness comes on the heels of his mother's oblivion.[18] As with the coming question of ʿAbd al-Wahhāb's own concoction, we are invited here to contemplate how complex and even dangerous entities break down into familiar parts.

After returning from a hunt, Marzūq slips this drug into a parched Fāṭima's goblet. Upon drinking it, she falls unconscious and inert as a "plank of wood," at which point al-Ḥārith assaults her. His action is described in graphic terms and represented as a clear violation of Fāṭima's will, indicated even with tacit clues such as her clothing. Moreover, in one of the text's many oblique criticisms of corruption among the religio-legally trained classes (*ʿulamāʾ*), al-Ḥārith is aided and abetted by ʿUqba, a judge appointed by the caliph who is also a Byzantine spy and secret Christian. This foreshadows the mutually informing tension between the epic's sense

17. Though the original text writes what I have translated here as "Cretan henbane" as *aqarr baṭshī*, or very cold (?) and overpowering (?), this is almost certainly an error and should read *Aqrīṭishī*, or Cretan, which I did not account for in my 2017 article that included this passage. *Sīrat Dhāt al-Himma*, VII:9; Rachel Schine, "Conceiving the Premodern Black-Arab Hero: On the Gendered Production of Racial Difference in *Sīrat al-amīrah dhāt al-himmah*," *Journal of Arabic Literature* 48 (2017): 305.

18. Al-Jawbarī, *The Book of Charlatans (Kitāb al-Mukhtār fī Kashf al-Asrār)*, trans. Humphrey Davies (New York: New York University Press, 2020), 262n27.

of justice and its representation of the learned establishment's understandings of the same, both of which are brought to bear in uncovering the truth behind Fāṭima's assault:

> He undid her trousers, then found drawers beneath them made of well-worked, Taʾif leather [*taḥtihi sirwāl min al-ḥulal al-adīm al-Ṭaʾifī*], with tight-fitting legs [*maḥbūk al-sāq*], sculpted to her form [*li-annahā kānat ʿalā ṣīghatihā*]. Al-Ḥārith was bewildered and astonished [*taḥayyar al-Ḥārith wa-huwa yataʿajjab*] by [the measures she had taken] to safeguard herself and did not know what to do. He took a knife and gouged out a place in her undergarments as needed, and he penetrated her until her blood poured out [*wa-wāqaʿ ilā an nazal damuhā*]. After he finished satisfying his urges, he left her as she was and took off.[19]

The phrasing above suggests a causal relationship between the rape and Fāṭima's bloodshed. In particular, the word *penetrated* (*wāqaʿ*) can mean, depending on context, either "to attack" or simply "to have intercourse with." In this scenario, it appears to carry both meanings simultaneously. The term's warlike echoes are especially stark in light of Fāṭima's primary identity as a warrior, which often is pitted against her femininity as it was in the initial contracting of her marriage. We may therefore read this as a double entendre befitting the scene: al-Ḥārith is sexually attacking Fāṭima.[20] This too would seem to remove us into the text's moral environment rather than a strictly practical or juristic sphere of reasoning: though the question earned significant scrutiny, in Islamic law there is no concept of marital rape per se. Meanwhile, denying a partner sex was grounds to petition for divorce, though often with different time scales for husbands and wives. Sexual violence or coercion largely fell either within the remit of *zinā*, or adulterous and extramarital sex acts, or if it took place within a marriage and was sufficiently physically harmful or painful to a spouse, within the remit of harm (*ḍarar*). Harm also included other broad failures to fulfill a wife's financial, bodily, and social needs. In light of all of this, Fāṭima's ambiguous experience of being forced into consummation

19. Already in the pre-Islamic period, the Arabian city of Taʾif was well-known for its leatherworks. Gene W. Heck, "'Arabia without Spices': An Alternate Hypothesis," *Journal of the American Oriental Society* 123, no. 3 (2003): 569. *Sīrat Dhāt al-Himma*, VII:10.

20. Ibn al-Manẓūr, *Lisān al-ʿArab* (Beirut: Dār Ṣādir, 1955), 4896.

while insensate resists certain types of legal casuistry.[21] And yet the language imbues the scene with an unambiguous dynamic of proscription and intrusion.

The assault's description does not explicitly indicate that Fāṭima is menstruating, which surfaces only much later in a courtroom "grand reveal." Nor does the scene indicate that al-Ḥārith takes notice of the blood or cares. Rather, the audience is left believing that, because this is Fāṭima's first sexual encounter, the blood is a natural result of her hymen stretching or tearing, made particularly violent by al-Ḥārith's eagerness. Al-Ḥārith departs, unrepentant, and is subsequently compelled to flee from a remorseful Marzūq's wrath. He does not see Fāṭima again until after ʿAbd al-Wahhāb is born and rumors of his paternity eventually reach him.

As with the mundane birth circumstances of ʿAntar examined in the previous chapter, the description of ʿAbd al-Wahhāb's birth bears further analysis not because of its exceptional nature, but rather because of its normalcy. It is embellished with references to divine will and creative power, which serve to reinforce that bearing a child, regardless of kind, is a divinely ordained experience:

> She went into labor, as permitted by the Creator of Creation. Soon, a son appeared, as the singular Eternal One willed [*ka-mā yashāʾ al-fard al-ṣamad*]. All desire and will is preceded by [His] hidden, esoteric knowledge, with which [God] says "be," and so it is [*kun fa-yakūn*]. Thus He enabled the birth of this child, the unsheathed sword of God and shield of the grave [*sayf Allāh al-maslūl wa-turs qabr*] of the Prophet Muḥammad b. ʿAbdallāh, peace be upon him. Though at the time the pain frightened Dhāt al-Himma, she held fast, and the Master of Will [*ṣāḥib al-irāda*] helped her. She gave birth to a boy as dawn approached. His color was like the thick, roiling night [*lawnuhu mithl al-layl al-muʿtakir*], dark [*aswad aghbar*], taut of limbs, black of eyes, and with beautifully arched brows [*azajj al-ḥājibayn*].[22]

Particularly striking in the above passage—all of which is composed in stylized, rhyming prose—is the use of the title "eternal one," or *ṣamad*,

21. On the question of marital rape and the role of physical pain or injury in adjudicating coerced *zinā* wedlock and/or mistreatment of wives across various schools of law, see Wissam Halawi, "Zinā and Gender (In)Equality in Ismāʿīlī Druze Law," *Der Islam* 99, no. 2 (2022): 529–31; Hina Azam, *Sexual Violation in Islamic Law: Substance, Evidence, and Procedure* (New York: Cambridge University Press, 2015), 19.

22. *Sīrat Dhāt al-Himma*, VII:11.

for God. This epithet occurs once in the Qurʾān, in the *sūra* "The Sincerity" (*al-Ikhlāṣ*), which also features a monotheistic catechism refuting the existence of divine ancestors or descendants by affirming that God "neither begets nor is born."[23] This reference reminds the audience within the parameters of a broader birth narrative that although God has no descendants, which is to say, He does not reproduce, He nonetheless retains supreme *creative* power. Coupled with the reference to God as the "Creator of Creation," this effectively distinguishes the process of creation from that of reproduction and minimizes Fāṭima's direct responsibility for the appearance of her child in a moment when blame is about to be cast her way. With God as the ultimate architect of all beings, ʿAbd al-Wahhāb's looks are attributable ultimately to Him.

In a similar vein, when her attendants beg Fāṭima to confide her secret in them and confirm their suspicions that she has committed adultery, Fāṭima says simply, "Seek refuge in God . . . this child is a craft or handiwork [*ṣināʿa*] of the all-powerful king [*al-malik al-qādir*]," who alone, in her words, can raise the dead among the living and draw black beings from white ones. With this, Fāṭima molds the nearly universal trope of woman as a mere vessel for children of God's making into a justification for her child's condition. In keeping with this division between birthing and bringing into being, the birth scene also features a recurrent Qurʾānic formulation of God creating through speech. He merely says, "be," and it is (*kun fa-yakūn*);[24] several of these refrains about God's creative capacities will be repeated when Jaʿfar al-Ṣādiq adjudicates ʿAbd al-Wahhāb's paternity to substantiate that nonhereditary blackness is an act of an omniscient God with greater designs than humans can anticipate, as is everything in the world. In this fashion, ʿAbd al-Wahhāb's birth is represented as being both as common and as miraculous as any other act of creation. And so, even as the *sīra* creates difficulties for its Black hero and posits a negative worldly cause for his origins, it also places the hero within a cosmology that provides for his redemption.

ʿAbd al-Wahhāb emerges from the womb not only with his permanent complexion but also with other mature physiognomic markers, perhaps in keeping with the tradition in the *siyar* of heroes being born unnaturally large and exhibiting adult levels of strength and canniness from birth. In the above passage, the child's eyes and brows are described as black and beautifully arched; each of these qualities is indicative of quintessentially

23. Q 112:3.

24. Q 2:117, Q 3:47, Q 3:59, Q 6:73, Q 16:40, Q 19:35, Q 36:82, Q 40:68.

Arab handsomeness. A description identical to that of the newborn ʿAbd al-Wahhāb's brows appears in al-Bayhaqī's (d. 1066) *Dalāʾil al-nubuwwa* describing the brow line of the Prophet.[25] His eye color also registers as "normal." Kristina Richardson observes of Arab male beauty standards, read against the grain through her work on catalogs of blemishes (*ʿāhāt*), that:

> The normative body belongs to an Arab male who has dark (not blue or green) eyes, dark (not light) hair, a hooked (not flat) nose, a full (not thin) beard, and brown (not black) skin, and who stands at medium height.[26]

Deviations from this indicate features often perceived as ugly and, when far enough removed from the norm, as causing deformity or disability. ʿAbd al-Wahhāb's idealized facial features, meanwhile, offer an initial intimation of what is later confirmed by the first panel of judges before whom he is brought—although his black skin goes against the norm, ʿAbd al-Wahhāb otherwise shares his father's more conventional Arab looks. The *sīra* itself does not always acknowledge this, though, declaring that ʿAbd al-Wahhāb appears to be "from among the sons of Nubia" or calling attention in the voices of his detractors to his supposedly wide, "cow-like" nose (*furṭūsat al-ʿijl*).[27] The kind to which ʿAbd al-Wahhāb belongs is constructed not just through what his appearance socially signals and what affinities it invites, but through these counterfactual discourses that exaggerate, essentialize, and stereotype what blackness means as a principle for exclusion.

A Natural Childhood?

From the outset, ʿAbd al-Wahhāb's skin color puts him in harm's way, which in turn imperils his mother. This compels Fāṭima to hide him with one of her servants until, at the age of four, he is brought under her tutelage in Qurʾān study and martial skills, at which he brilliantly excels. The dangers begin on the day of his birth, when one of the women attending to Fāṭima notes his complexion and suggests cutting his umbilical cord and killing him immediately to "hide the affair, so that you're not dishonored

25. Abū Bakr Aḥmad b. Ḥusayn al-Bayhaqī, *Dalāʾil al-Nubuwwa*, vol. 1, ed. ʿAbd al-Muʿṭī Qalʿajī, ed. (Beirut: Dār al-Kutub, 1985), 214–15.
26. Richardson, *Difference and Disability*, 11.
27. *Sīrat Dhāt al-Himma*, VII:15.

from now until Day of Reckoning." Lest Fāṭima be accused of adultery, the attendant pragmatically advises that "the proper thing to do is to kill him, and not to perish because of him." The other women agree, though the whole group devolves into chaos, having thought Fāṭima incapable of promiscuity. It takes a poetic overture from Fāṭima to convince the women that she has a handle on the situation:

[al-Ḥārith] drugged me with a bind,
Addling my right-guided mind [*khawāṭir ʿaqlī maʿ rashīd madhāhibī*].
Tablet inscribed, it came to be,
God's judgment unmoving for me
He sent this child I now bear,
A starless night [*dujā*] of jet-black air [*ghayāhib*]
Surely this may wax into calamity—when it spreads
And swells over its boundaries with dread[28]

Fāṭima emphasizes not only that God has granted her this child according to His will but that she is a woman of superior intellect and morality. Though condensed in the above translation, she uses three terms across two lines of verse to describe her rational faculties—*khawāṭir*, desires or opinions; *ʿaql*, reason or logic; and *madhāhib*, modes of thought—along with the weighty modifier "right-guided" (*rashīd*). When deprived of these faculties, she was placed entirely at the mercy of God and her assailant. Here, though, Fāṭima upholds a narrative of submission to divine will rather than one of victimhood. She notes that her predicament will surely spiral, but also implies that this need not be the case.

Fāṭima moreover semiotically repositions her child's blackness using panegyric conventions of comparing a poem's celebrated subject with natural imagery. Fāṭima represents ʿAbd al-Wahhāb's blackness as a quality so innate to a constellation of other cosmic phenomena that it is etymologically inextricable from their identities. Both the words used for "starless night" and for "jet-black" are derived from roots that signify blackness itself, and that also have earthlier resonances with creatures designated by their dark color through double-entendres produced by homophony or homography, with the night (*dujā*) calling to mind a dark-feathered thrush (*dujjā*) and the word for jet-black darkness (*ghayāhib*) a deep black stallion (also *ghayāhib*). This attempt to naturalize her child's blackness through polyvalent references to the cosmos and its creatures draws descriptions

28. *Sīrat Dhāt al-Himma*, VII:12.

of her son's appearance into alignment with apologetic poetic traditions of vaunting the maligned and repudiating the censurer, which have previously been discussed. However, it simultaneously evokes traditions of (re)naming enslaved people with nonhuman terms, especially the names of various animals, colors, perfumes, foodstuffs, and precious stones—as with ʿAntar's mother being renamed Zabība (raisin or dried fig)—recalling idioms of connoisseurship, value, and commodification through which blackness becomes precious elsewhere as well.[29]

The double resonances of this line are made all the more distinct through its intertextuality with racialized tropes in Arabic poetry and prose. Fāṭima evokes a thrush over the most common avian analogue for black-skinned people in the poetic lexicon, namely, the crow (*ghurāb*). Elsewhere, she refers to her son's blackness as lustrous (*baṣṣāṣ*) and even likens it to the Kaʿba's sacred Black Stone, an aesthetically and religiously apologetic reference that binds the object's color to its sacred qualities. This same image is found in al-Jāḥiẓ's epistle in defense of blackness, *Fakhr al-Sūdān ʿalā-l-Bīḍān*, as well as in a lengthier exposition by Ibn al-Jawzī. The latter includes the stone in a list of black physical features, plants, and minerals that have health-giving effects (like ebony curing bladder stones, nigella seeds reducing phlegm, and so on), with touching the stone in sincerity ensuring a believer's standing in this life and the next.[30] In a moment when Fāṭima's relationship to ʿAbd al-Wahhāb introduces the seemingly imminent prospect of racialized and gendered violence, Fāṭima uses her verses as a form of reversal, styling herself as the divinely guided mother of a handsome, ennobled knight-to-be and making herself the picture of forbearance during hardship.

It does not take long before, as a youth, ʿAbd al-Wahhāb perceives that his color causes his mother social strife. Tearfully, he recites a few lines of poetry to his mother, beginning with the declaration "Although I am Black, my heart has white upon it, illumined with the light of day," and concluding that one's color does not matter, but rather one's deeds.[31] This line typifies sentiments expressed by the Umayyad inheritors of the

29. These naming practices endure into modernity, both in Ottoman and Persian sources as well as Arabic, though Nur Sobers-Khan notes that in Ottoman registers, concubines and eunuchs are most subject to receive "fanciful" names. On these trends, see Hekmat Dirbas, "Naming of Slave-Girls in Arabic: A Survey of Medieval and Modern Sources," *Zeitschrift für Arabische Linguistik* 69 (2019): 26–38; Nur Sobers-Khan, *Slaves without Shackles: Forced Labour and Manumission in the Galata Court Registers, 1560–1572* (Berlin: Klaus Schwarz Verlag, 2014), 233.

30. Al-Jāḥiẓ, *Rasāʾil al-Jāḥiẓ*, vol. 1, 219. Ibn al-Jawzī, *Tanwīr al-Ghabash*, 51–53.

31. *Sīrat Dhāt al-Himma*, VII:20.

traditions of the so-called "Crows of the Arabs" (*aghribat al-ʿarab*), or pre-Islamic *hajīn* poets of East African maternal descent who, through later anthological synthesis, became grouped as the premier Black authors of their age. Umayyad-era Black authors writing in a newer, more self-consciously defiant mode often exalted the "white souls" that lay beneath their dark appearances. The wording and cadence of ʿAbd al-Wahhāb's poem also overtly mimic a brief poem that is typically attributed to the historical personage of ʿAntara b. Shaddād (d. 608), whose piece is likewise composed in the *wāfir* meter:[32]

Although I am Black, my color is that of musk
And there's no curing the blackness of my skin
Yet impropriety keeps its distance from me,
Like the land is distanced from the air above[33]

Abd al-Wahhāb is now old enough to have developed a nuanced awareness of where his blackness places him in others' estimations, which is rendered parallel in spirit and expression to that of the archetypal epic persona of ʿAntar by routing his poetic expressions through ʿAntar(a)'s poetic oeuvre, and thus is clearly signposted for audiences. At this pivotal moment of maturation, articulated as dawning consciousness of his blackness, ʿAbd al-Wahhāb's father, al-Ḥārith learns of the child's existence despite his mother's attempts to conceal him. Al-Ḥārith convenes elders from the tribe and sets out to wrest a confession of adultery from Fāṭima. In advance of their arrival, al-Ḥārith's first encounter with ʿAbd al-Wahhāb is foreshadowed by a reorienting intervention in the text: the narrator of the *sīra* thrusts the reader back into the orally reported framework of the tale by offering a brief moralizing aside. He reminds the audience that though ʿAbd al-Wahhāb looks like a "Nubian" child, he has a good

32. Though I, like several editors of his *dīwān*, claimed in the piece "Conceiving the Pre-Modern Black-Arab Hero" that this poem was by ʿAntara b. Shaddād, the recent excellent work of James Montgomery to create a critical edition of the *dīwān* and personal correspondence with him have shown this poem to most likely itself have been lifted from *Sīrat ʿAntar* and placed into ʿAntara b. Shaddād's poetry collections retroactively; it was, in Montgomery's words, the practice of many editors to have "included [the *sīra* poems] willy nilly" based largely on taste. It becomes, then, an interesting piece of insight into intertextuality among the *sīra*s that this poem was a piece riffed off of in *Sīrat Dhāt al-Himma* as well! James Montgomery, personal correspondence, June 26, 2019. See also: James E. Montgomery, *Dīwān ʿAntarah ibn Shaddād: A Literary-Historical Study* (New York: New York University Press, 2018).

33. ʿAntara b. Shaddād, *Dīwān ʿAntara* (Beirut: Dār Ṣādir, 1958), 88.

heart, and such goodness renders a "black heart" (*qalb aswad*)—which is sometimes also used to mean cruel-hearted—white and immaculate (*abyaḍ naqī*). The offstage narrator then adds the crowning piece of foreshadowing: "This Black boy [*ghulām aswad*] will experience wondrous events and strange affairs, which we shall mention in due time, if God Almighty wills."[34] ʿAbd al-Wahhāb's heroic cycle thus begins with a reminder to listeners that a hero is presented from birth with challenges that test his virtue and prompt affective shifts in witnesses to his exploits.

That this testament to ʿAbd al-Wahhāb's future glory is displaced from the characters within the text and voiced instead by the narrator gives it a more generalized force. It interrupts the narrative with the views of a temporally and socially external figure, who speaks up to redeem the Black child. ʿAbd al-Wahhāb's struggles as a Black person are thus framed conspicuously as a retrospective on how people used to think. As will be discussed in part II, the *sīra*'s content details a layered set of pasts, bringing in narratives from the *jāhiliyya*, or pre-Islamic period, and the Islamization of Arabian tribes, as well as reaching a textual "present," consisting of Fāṭima's lifetime and that of her son. The narrator, meanwhile, stands outside of these temporal frames, contemporary with an imagined audience that is engaging with the epic as historical narrative. It is into this contemporary moment that the narrator inserts himself as a mediating character who instructs us to accept the Black hero. This comes alongside the numerous gestures of acceptance that his birth story entails, from recurrent references to God's creative power and stewardship to his mother's poetic ode, constructing a moral relationship with the past that is at once cyclic—anticipating that we, too, might need added coaxing in order to appreciate ʿAbd al-Wahhāb's significance—and progressive, believing we will.

Finding the Father: ʿAbd al-Wahhāb's Paternity Trial

Once al-Ḥārith and the other senior members of the tribe have confirmed the rumors of ʿAbd al-Wahhāb's unexpected appearance, legal proceedings ensue to determine the identity of his father. ʿAbd al-Wahhāb cycles through several appellate courts, represented by a provincial elder, a set of Meccan physiognomists (*qāʾif*, pl. *qāfa*), and finally Jaʿfar al-Ṣādiq himself. As Robert Hoyland has shown, physiognomic practices are attested from the pre- and early Islamic era in the form of *ʿilm al-qiyāfa*, or knowledge

34. *Sīrat Dhāt al-Himma*, VII:15.

of tracks and markings, a divinatory and esoteric practice among specialists in the Arabian Peninsula and the term by which ʿAbd al-Wahhāb's judges are designated.[35] Their techniques were later largely supplanted by the more "empirical" approach of what came to be called *ʿilm al-firāsa,* or the science of perspicacity, inflected by Greek physiognomic works such as the treatise of Polemon and, often, with Sufi conceptualizations of the body-soul connection. However, the two words *qiyāfa* and *firāsa* continued to coexist and be used relatively interchangeably through Ottoman times, at which point the sciences they designate became a fixture of royal courts and a set of principles for organizing a polity and meting out justice, making the ruler who used physiognomy well a "nexus between creator and creation."[36] In the process of their work, the physiognomists of the *sīra* likewise straddle divinatory technique and Islamic principles of justice. They touch on what at first appears a disconnected mélange of *ḥadīth*s, theories, and anecdotes that bear common associations with the adjudication of paternity in numerous stories about Muḥammad and his companions. They situate ʿAbd al-Wahhāb's extraordinary status in a familiar epistemology.

The primary physiognomist begins by citing Muḥammad's statement that "the son belongs to the [lawful] bed [*firāsh*]." This may be interpreted as meaning "that any child born to the mother (from any intercourse) should be considered the offspring of her husband or master," depending on whether she is free or enslaved.[37] The second half of this *ḥadīth,* which, though unmentioned in the *sīra* would have likely been known by much of its audience, is typically recorded as "and stoning is [decreed] for the fornicator [*wa-li-l-ʿāhir rajm*]."[38] Joseph Schacht has noted that this *ḥadīth,* were it taken seriously, would have decisively nullified the role of physiognomists in paternity disputes altogether.[39] Uri Rubin adds that claims of *firāsh* were indeed believed by some jurists to abrogate the role of physiognomists when used to formally contest a

35. Robert Hoyland, "Physiognomy in Islam," *Jerusalem Studies in Arabic and Islam* 30 (2005): 363.

36. Emin Lelic, "Physiognomy (ʿilm-i firāsat) and Ottoman Statecraft: Discerning Morality and Justice," *Arabica* 64 (2017): 626.

37. Uri Rubin, "'Al-Walad li-l-Firāsh' on the Islamic Campaign against 'Zinā,'" *Studia Islamica* 78 (1993): 5.

38. Ibn Ḥajar al-ʿAsqalānī and al-Bukhārī, "Bāb al-walad li-l-firāsh ḥurra kānat āw ama," in *Fatḥ al-Bārī Sharḥ Ṣaḥīḥ al-Bukhārī,* http://library.islamweb.net/newlibrary/display_book.php?idfrom=12367&idto=12370&bk_no=52&ID=3723.

39. Joseph Schacht, "Foreign Elements in Ancient Islamic Law," *Journal of Comparative Legislation and International Law* 32 (1950): 5.

diʿwa, or extramarital paternity claim. They moreover function to render a child's appearance immaterial to a case despite many attempts throughout the formative period to center appearance in paternity claims.[40] This notably still holds space for physiognomists to have certifying roles in cases where a rightful parent has denied paternity, as in ʿAbd al-Wahhāb's situation.

In opening with this *ḥadīth*, the Meccan physiognomists also recall Muḥammad's own use of physiognomists in a related scenario:

> ʿĀ'isha, may God be pleased with her, relates that the Prophet, peace and blessings be upon him, came to me pleased, with joy showing upon his face, and said, "Did you not see that Mujazziz looked previously at Zayd b. Ḥāritha and Usāma b. Zayd, and said that they have the same feet?" . . . In the narration that follows [this *ḥadīth*], [the physiognomist] went in and Usāma b. Zayd and Zayd had a blanket upon them covering their heads, and their feet were exposed. . . . During the *jāhiliyya*, the people of lineage [*nasab*] would attack Usāma's pedigree because he was deeply dark black, and his father Zayd was whiter than cotton, so when the physiognomist said what he said regarding the difference of their color, the Prophet, peace and blessings upon him, was gladdened by this for it made them stop mocking him, since they believed it.[41]

In addition to this depiction, there are a number of other *ḥadīth*s and anecdotes that discuss the deductive methods of physiognomists using media such as the stars and sand, and ichnomancy or podomancy, or divining using footprints and the soles of the feet, as is done above. The physiognomists who attend to ʿAbd al-Wahhāb combine the latter methods, instructing al-Ḥārith and ʿAbd al-Wahhāb to walk across a sand-strewn surface alongside several other men, and then identifying their family relationship from the footprints. This probative use of occult methods, framed by overt and implied references to Muḥammad and miracles of revelation, at once invokes exacting sciences of genealogy and the metaphysical affect derived from witnessing and interpreting wondrous natural anomalies with unseen causes.

40. Rubin, "Al-Walad li-l-Firāsh," 11–12.

41. Ibn Ḥajar and al-Bukhārī, "Bāb al-qā'if," in *Fatḥ al-Bārī Sharḥ Ṣaḥīḥ al-Bukhārī* (al-Maktaba al-Islāmiyya, 1996), http://library.islamweb.net/newlibrary/display_book.php?flag=1&bk_no=52&ID=12405#docu.

At the same time, even before proceeding with this test, the head physiognomist undercuts the need for dealing in the unseen by judging ʿAbd al-Wahhāb's paternity on the basis of superficial indicators, saying,

> Though thoughts occurred to [al-Ḥārith] [*dakhal ʿalayhi al-afkār*], for [the child] is Black, different in color, and blemished in form [*li-ajl sawādihi wa-taghyīr lawnihi wa-iḍṭirāb kawnihi*], by God the Great, this boy is surely al-Ḥārith's son, for [the child's] eyes are like his eyes, and likewise with his bone structure and [other] traits, and the palms of the hands, and the extremities, and the fingertips; I speak truthfully, not from ignorance [*innī aqūl ṣādiq ghayr jāhil*].[42]

In alluding to the ambient thoughts (*afkār*) that al-Ḥārith has failed to keep at bay—with *dakhal ʿalayhi* suggesting both sexual entry and a disruption to one's mental state—the physiognomist asserts that al-Ḥārith is the father of the child whether he believes so or not. Al-Ḥārith then attempts to invalidate the physiognomists' surmise, saying that these postulations are nothing but the tall tales of an old man (*wa-mā anta illā kharaft min kathrat al-sinīn*). This brief disagreement over the role of belief, imagination, and mental control in constituting the truth of another's social kind echoes intriguingly with a wholly different medical discourse found in several sources, both classical and medieval, about the role of a parent's visions and desires in shaping their child's looks before they even exist.

Cases of "image-imprinting," or impressing a birthmark or blemish on a child through acts of sexual fantasy or psycho-emotional fixation, are attested in many cultures.[43] One prominent instance in *adab* sources is found in Ibn Ḥazm's *Ṭawq al-Ḥamāma* (*The Dove's Neck-Ring*). Ibn Ḥazm, whose knowledge of Christian and Jewish scriptures was profound, relates the biblical account of Jacob stripping poplar branches and setting the

42. *Sīrat Dhāt al-Himma*, VII:34.

43. What is referred to here as "image-imprinting" is often designated "maternal impression," attesting to the oddity of this outcome being the responsibility of a male partner. Several literary works in the European tradition take maternal impression as a central element, and it features in Galenic medicine as well, though again with the mother empowered as the sole "impresser." See Graham Anderson, "Two Notes on Heliodorus," *Journal of Hellenic Studies* 99 (1979): 149; Cristina Mazzoni, *Maternal Impressions: Pregnancy and Childbirth in Literature and Theory* (Ithaca, NY: Cornell University Press, 2002), 16–17. On Middle Eastern folk beliefs about maternal impression during pregnancy, see Remke Kruk, "Pregnancy and Its Social Consequences in Mediaeval and Traditional Arab Society," *Quaderni Di Studi Arabi* 5–6 (1987–1988): 426–28.

wood before his flock's trough to engender piebald offspring.[44] After seeing the mottled bark whenever they feed, the sheep mimetically produce spotted lambs. To this, Ibn Ḥazm adds, "also, one physiognomist gives an account of a Black child brought forth from white parents." Then he recalls the tale of a white man and woman who give birth to a Black child because of a portrait of a Black man hung on the wall, upon which the woman fixed her eyes during sex.[45] Indeed, when Abū Zayd's mother Khaḍrāʾ spies her black crow and wishes for a child in its likeness, she may be putting this same type of process in motion, albeit more consciously.[46]

Like ʿAbd al-Wahhāb's physiognomists, the one in Ibn Ḥazm's tale looks at various bodily "signs" and sees beyond a doubt that the child belongs to his non-Black parents (*naẓar ilā aʿlāmihi fa-rāhu lahumā min ghayr shakk*). On further investigation of the couple's home, he finds the offending picture. For Ibn Ḥazm, this anecdote constitutes an example of how images stimulate lust, the cautionary aspect of which is clear. Implicitly, curating a woman's environment and limiting potential objects of her desires also limits reproductive risk. Her lack of mental control and a husband's lack of structural control are linked through their externalization in a child whose blackness links him with bastardy.

Unsatisfied with their findings, al-Ḥārith mocks the physiognomists' approach and threatens to kill his wife and son. Al-Ḥārith's father recites some palliative verses assuring him that ʿAbd al-Wahhāb is a bastard, likening his origins to those of dogs—an insinuation of Fāṭima's promiscuity—and his appearance to a crow. These verses are reminiscent of a poem recited earlier by al-Ḥārith when he accused Fāṭima of adultery, in which al-Ḥārith holds forth on his own self-perceived skin color:

> She bore a bastard son, not mine—the liar!
> Though she alleges the child's ours to share,
> My color is white, beautiful, and fair [*wa-lawnī abyaḍ ḥasan jamīl*]
> While that color of his is a suspect mire. [*wa-hādhā lawnuhu ḥalak marīb*]

44. Gen. 30:37–39.

45. ʿAlī b. Aḥmad b. Ḥazm, *Ṭawq al-Ḥamāma*, ed. Muḥammad Muḥammad ʿAbd al-Laṭīf et al. (Cairo: al-Maṭbaʿa al-Madanī, 1975), 11.

46. The rabbinic text of *Bemidbar Rabbah* reverses Ibn Ḥazm's and Khaḍrāʾ's dynamic, featuring a "black" king of the Arabs and his wife who bear a white son due to her seeing white images in their home during sex. For a discussion of this passage, see Wendy Doniger, "The Symbolism of Black and White Babies in the Myth of Parental Impression," *Social Research* 70, no. 1 (2003): 9.

This child resembles tar [*qaṭrān*], per Arab claims,
And my color is white—what unease. [*wa-lawnī abyaḍ hādhā ʿajīb*]
Can cucumbers sprout from date-trees? [*raʾitum nakhal taḥmil qaṭṭ qittā*]
Or moist dates from burning flames? [*wa-nīran li-hā ruṭab raṭīb*]
Leave off with this, I won't take heed
I won't stand here and bear this screed[47]

The young brown dates (*ruṭab*) simmering in flame evoke not only the paradoxical production of water from fire, but perhaps also Fāṭima's nonnormative passions for the dark-skinned man that al-Hārith imagines as his wife's lover. The bizarre and priapic image of the cucumbers hung from date palms further accentuates an underlying theme of sexual deviance. Insulting ʿAbd al-Wahhāb's complexion as resembling "tar" draws on a common refrain that is also embedded in Qurʾānic images of a darkened hell, whose dwellers are tar-covered.[48] And yet, the young dates also recall the Qurʾānic image of when Maryam (Mary), while in the throes of a painful labor similar to Fāṭima's, is given a date palm by God and instructed to sustain herself with its fruits (Q 19:25). Both Maryam and Fāṭima endure complicated pregnancies, each attended by accusations of untoward behavior. Both share in the remove between their husbands and their children. In *Sūrat Maryam*, the miraculous appearance of a palm in full fruit that is recalled in the poem above reflects Maryam's deservingness and comforts her in her isolation. Even when impugning her, al-Ḥārith selects images that ironically reinforce Fāṭima's chastity and maternal rights. When Fāṭima later seeks to validate ʿAbd al-Wahhāb's paternity, his extraordinary difference from her will once again be likened to ʿIsā (Jesus) being virgin-born. The most repeated image throughout the poem, though, is al-Ḥārith's assertion of his own whiteness.

Not all agree with al-Ḥārith's view of his own complexion. In the midst of the argument, one of Fāṭima's defenders says, "Have you seen a newborn whose mother is radiantly white, while his father though fair is mottled [*ashqar abqaʿ*], come forth with his color—a leathery black?"[49] The term *abqaʿ* again derives from animal husbandry and was used to indicate its own form of mixedness in which a horse's or other creature's "whiteness mixes with another color [*al-abqaʿ mā khālaṭ bayāḍuhu lawn ākhar*]." The

47. *Sīrat Dhāt al-Himma*, VII:16.
48. Q 14:50.
49. *Sīrat Dhāt al-Himma*, VII:16.

lexicographer Ibn al-Manẓūr elaborates further, explaining how this term fits into a broader civilizational taxonomy:

> It is said that [some] are called *buqʿān* because of their differences of color and their descent from two kinds [*li-ikhtilāf alwānihim wa-tanāsulihim min jinsayn*]. Qutaybī said: *al-buqʿān* are those who have whiteness and blackness in them, thus you would not call someone who is entirely white and not mixed with black *abqaʿ*, so how could the Byzantines [*al-rūm*] be deemed *buqʿān* when they are purely whites [*wa-hum bīḍ khullaṣ*]?[50]

Conjuring the idea of being *abqaʿ* into a text seeking to explain intergenerational, dramatic change in color resonates with medieval Latinate writings that derived terms for human "races" from preexistent "identifiably biological ideas about animal breeding and reproduction."[51] In using causal language to render al-Ḥārith's complexional tell as the catalyst for ʿAbd al-Wahhāb's black skin, the anonymous commenter implies that Al-Ḥārith's allegedly "mottled" skin tone may carry a hereditary potential that is expressed in exaggerated fashion in his child's complexion. This line of reasoning is demonstrative of Brigitte Fielder's aforementioned description of race's transpositions as queering how kinship and resemblance are typically thought to flow: rather than al-Ḥārith passing his identity lineally to his child, his child's difference elicits a backward projection into the father's ancestry. Though al-Ḥārith's forefathers are not described, the implication is that ʿAbd al-Wahhāb presents in full force traits that al-Ḥārith carries forward from them, and even presents, though in an attenuated way. This passage subtly references the theory of atavism that was discussed at some length above with respect to Abū Zayd al-Hilālī's distant Black ancestry—blackness (or whiteness) from generations past can, according to theories inherited in the Islamic context from Greco-Roman forerunners, resurface at random in one's descendants. This pithy rationalization does not recur elsewhere in the *sīra*, but its use indicates at least tangential familiarity within yet another popular work with a principal classical understanding of how blackness can emerge seemingly spontaneously from whiteness.

To return to the tale, at the suggestion of the physiognomists, Jaʿfar al-Ṣādiq is sought to offer his opinion. The imam is described early on in

50. Ibn al-Manẓūr, *Lisān al-ʿArab*, 326.

51. David Nirenberg, "Was There Race before Modernity? The Example of 'Jewish' Blood in Late Medieval Spain," in *The Origins of Racism in the West*, ed. Miriam Eliav-Feldon et al. (Cambridge: Cambridge University Press, 2009), 252.

a manner indicating that his is the ultimate authority and his judgment will be final. First, his kinship with Muḥammad is referenced. He is then described as a "trove of virtue [*futuwwa*]," who dispels anxieties and showers generosity upon the downtrodden. When the assembled crowd sees him, they remark on the greatness of his "ʿAlid brilliancy [*al-bahiya al-ʿalawiyya*] and Hashemite roots [*al-salāla al-Hāshimiyya*]," or his evident inherited qualities from both Muḥammad's son-in-law and Muḥammad's clan, once again underscoring the significance of physiognomy in discerning one's genealogy—and concomitantly, one's destiny.[52]

During his judgment, Jaʿfar al-Ṣādiq compels al-Ḥārith to confess that he had sex with Fāṭima while she was menstruating. In light of this, Jaʿfar blames the coloring of the fetus on the mixing of menstrual blood with the embryogenic *nuṭfa*, or seminal drop. In so doing, though, he must explain how it is that such a mixture would tint the fetus black and not red. Jaʿfar al-Ṣādiq's character finds recourse in a distinction that is highly debated in early exegesis and jurisprudence, namely, the difference between a woman who is a *ḥāʾiḍ* (menstruant) and one who is a *mustaḥāḍa* (metrorrhagic, or "spotting"):

> The imam Jaʿfar turned his face to them and said, "O, people, has not the judgment of God been revealed—that white may come from black and black from white? This poses no difficulty for God, nor does anything exhaust the power of God—not one thing! . . . He created ʿIsā son of Maryam without a father. Black from white is no difficult thing for Him, as nothing is beyond His power. With that in mind, I alert you that if a man has intercourse with his wife and she is menstruating, the child will emerge black [*al-rajul idhā jāmaʿ zawjatahu wa-hiya ḥāʾiḍ jāʾ al-walad aswad*]. For God, blessed and glorious, created the souls in their sublimity [*khalaq al-anfus ʿalā jalālatihā*], from a sperm-droplet just as He set the trees to germinate [*min al-nuṭfa ka-mā badaʾ al-ashjār ʿalā manābitihā*]. So, too, He enfolds and assembles a white, handsome, noble body [*hādhā al-jism al-abyāḍ al-wasīm al-karīm*] from this vulgar droplet in the darkness of the womb [*min hadhihi al-nuṭfa al-ḥaqīra fī ẓulumāt al-aḥshāʾ*], and He conducts it however He wills."[53]

Jaʿfar then questions al-Ḥārith, who admits that Fāṭima was menstruating at the time of their sexual encounter. To this, Jaʿfar responds using

52. *Sīrat Dhāt al-Himma*, VII:36.
53. *Sīrat Dhāt al-Himma*, VII:39.

an analogous case that was brought before his forefather, the Prophet Muḥammad:

> [Muḥammad] said of the man that if he had intercourse with his wife while the blood was black and stopped-up at the beginning portion of the menses, this [would cause] the boy to become red-brown [*aḥmar*] in color, while if he had intercourse with her at the end of the menses, when the blood is pure [*ṣafā al-dam*], the child comes to resemble his father. Such was my ancestor's judgment. And you, o Ḥārith, had sex with your wife while there clung to her whatever adheres to women from the menses—and during metrorrhagia [*istiḥāda*], a woman's blood is red, and the menses is black and the sperm droplet is white and a woman's blood is dark-colored [*aghbar*]. The red and white and black and dark-colored [materials] mixed together [*ijtamaʿ*] and the Creator created and arranged [him].[54]

Jaʿfar's explanation, though seemingly sufficient to his audience, is far from straightforward. Yet it is also not the only instance of blaming blackness on menstruation in a *sīra* tradition. In *Sīrat ʿAntar*, the child of the ruler ʿAbd Hubal, whose name implies worship of a pre-Islamic Arabian god but who presides over India and whose wife is a queen of Sind, is also born a "black slave" (*ʿabd aswad*) unexpectedly. Like ʿAbd al-Wahhāb, his paternity is clarified in part through his persistent strong resemblance to his father, though this is done much more expeditiously:

> When [ʿAbd Hubal] saw [the child] he said, "How on earth is this boy black like this when we're white [*mā bāl hādhā al-walad aswad hakadhā wa-naḥnu bīḍ*]?" The queen explained her story to him instantly [*ṭalʿatan*], saying that she had been menstruating [*ḥāʾiḍ*] at the time that he took advantage of her [*waqt iqtināṣihā*], and [the blackness] was from menstruation, though otherwise he resembled his father in his form [*i-lā annahu yushbih abīhi fī khilqatihi*]. Indeed, he was greater than his father in shape and features [*aʿẓam minhu fi-l-khilqa wa-bi-l-awṣāf*].[55]

Where in the antagonist ʿAbd Hubal's case, his wife's testimony seems to have sufficed, Jaʿfar calls upon all of his already evident authority in

54. *Sīrat Dhāt al-Himma*, VII:39.
55. *Sīrat ʿAntara b. Shaddād*, vol. 6, 187.

making his judgment, including his prophetic lineage, perhaps because here the Black child is to be not vilified, but redeemed. Indeed, Jaʿfar's presence in this vignette may stem from his particular stake and legitimacy in assessing the paternity of a noble child who is raced as black but is lineally Arab. The historical Jaʿfar al-Ṣādiq famously took an East African woman, Ḥamīda—whose *nisba* indicates that she is from the Barbaria region, bordering the Red Sea coast—as a concubine, and she became the mother of the imam Mūsā al-Kāẓim (d. 799), who is sometimes described as having a dark or black complexion. Relationships with women native to North and East Africa are common in the lives of later imams as well, and the reception and representation of these genealogies remains fraught, as Amina Inloes has shown.[56] In the following chapter, I further discuss the layering of precedents referenced in this case, including the standard set by an analogous suit brought to the Prophet Muḥammad, as well as Jaʿfar's standing as not only a religious but also a folk-medical authority. Here, though, I wish to address the varieties of menstrual issue that, according to Jaʿfar, all play a distinct role in fashioning ʿAbd al-Wahhāb's appearance.

A number of early *tafsīr* works grapple with the distinction between the status of a menstruant (*ḥāʾiḍ*) and someone who is spotting (*mustaḥāḍa*), particularly with respect to the Q 2:222, "And should they ask you about menstruation, say, 'it is harm [*adhā*], so withdraw from women during menstruation.'" Many of these debates focus on the question of timing. Some attest that *istiḥāḍa* represents random spotting, while others define it as the condition when the length of menstruation extends beyond a certain point, often ten or fifteen days.[57] Al-Qurṭubī (d. 1273), writing after these parameters were first defined, adds a distinction with respect to the type of blood being discharged, claiming that *dam al-ḥayḍ* is initially black

56. I am indebted to Kristina Richardson for this observation. On the ancestries of various imams and their racialization, see Amina Inloes, "Racial 'Othering' in Shiʿi Sacred History: Jawn ibn Huwayy 'the African Slave,' and the Ethnicities of the Twelve Imams," *Journal of Shiʿa Islamic Studies* 7 (2014): 411–40.

57. Though his *tafsīr* postdates most of the featured primary sources in this chapter, al-Qurṭubī cites the views of earlier jurists on this debate, with al-Shāfiʿī (d. 820), for example, asserting that a woman is metrorrhagic if she bleeds for less than one full day or exceeding fifteen days; Abū ʿAbd Allāh Muḥammad b. Aḥmad al-Anṣārī al-Qurṭubī, *al-Jāmʿi li-aḥkām al-Qurʾān*, vol. 3 (Cairo: Dār al-Kutub, 1967), 83; Marion Katz, "Scholarly versus Women's Authority in the Islamic Law of Menstrual Purity," in *Gender in Judaism and Islam: Common Lives, Uncommon Heritage*, ed. Firoozeh Kashani-Sabet and Beth S. Wenger (New York: New York University Press, 2015), 73–105.

and thick, but is later overtaken by red blood.[58] That is, al-Qurṭubī, like the fictional Jaʿfar al-Ṣādiq above, offers a color- and consistency-based timetable of menstrual blood types.

Fāṭima is not asked to confirm whether she was menstruating or which stage of her cycle she was in. Rather, the evidence is clearly inscribed on her son's flesh. Nor does Fāṭima's assault become a feature of legal consideration. Instead, the seeming violence of her being coerced, unknowingly, into sex is minimized by Jaʿfar's judgment: Fāṭima having been left bleeding by her husband no longer connotes possible battery or her hymen tearing, but simply an instance of lust prevailing over perspicacity—al-Ḥārith may not have even noticed her bleeding prior to his attack.

There is a critical disconnect, however, between the Fāṭima's emission of this "black" blood and the resemblance that it forges between the child and al-Ḥārith—as the physiognomists and Jaʿfar have both confirmed, though ʿAbd al-Wahhāb is Black, he does have some of his father's features. Jaʿfar al-Ṣādiq enigmatically mentions that the "purity" of the blood toward the end of the menses causes this paternal resemblance. If we are to encounter the 1909 Cairo edition on its own terms and try to make sense of this anecdote as presented, the above allusion to the purity of the blood in the later stages of the menses may refer to chromatic saturation, meaning that it is a very consistent, intense black; in the next chapter, I propose that the ambiguity about what is meant by blood's purity may be due to a departure in the 1909 Cairo edition from a clearer, prior telling of ʿAbd al-Wahhāb's story that appears in the *sīra*'s manuscript tradition. There, "purity" signifies the end of the menses entirely.

Reading solely through the logic of the present version, though, the purely black blood's causal link to paternal resemblance is not immediately intelligible. The double entendre through which the word for "purity" (*ṣafāʾ*) may alternatively mean "pleasure" or "contentment" is perhaps suggestive, and also draws us to another commonplace understanding of reproductive biology in Arab-Muslim writings. In a tradition recorded by the historical Jaʿfar al-Ṣādiq and his students about the color, viscosity, and potency of male and female *nuṭfas*, the first individual to ejaculate during sex was thought to bear primary responsibility for the child's appearance. The *ḥadīth* states that if "the water (= the ejaculate) of the man precedes the water of the woman," then the child will resemble the father's line, and vice versa. Elaborations on this statement also note that a woman's ejaculate is categorically weaker and less influential, being thinner and yellower

58. Al-Qurṭubī, 82.

than the man's whiter, thicker counterpart.[59] By extension, though, if menstruation is a harm or pain for a woman, and her blood meanwhile does not preclude enjoyment for her male partner and even heightens it, the mother's blood could lead the child to resemble his father by ensuring that his ejaculate is the first or only motive substance in the womb.

Jaʿfar's ascription of agency to the man's sperm as well as the woman's blood in fashioning the child's appearance draws on two seemingly contradictory reproductive models that were both prevalent in Islamic medicine, from Aristotle and Hippocrates; Kathryn Kueny notes that, despite Aristotle's revered status as the "first teacher" in dialectics, in medical literature the Hippocratic model tended to predominate.[60] For Aristotle, women had no part in the constitutive process and simply housed the fetal tissue that men made. For Hippocrates, both men and women produced ejaculates that combined to make up a fetus. In al-Ḥārith's case, he has contributed the initial force to which Aristotle refers when discussing the male's active and activatable ejaculate vis-à-vis the woman's inert womb. Meanwhile, in place of her own *nuṭfa,* Fāṭima unwittingly and unwillingly has provided an added coloring element in the form of her menstrual blood, in addition to the inert blood of her womb upon which al-Ḥārith's biological material acts. As it is expanded, dissected, and re-narrated throughout the *sīra,* this critical moment of mixing deepens the significance of ʿAbd al-Wahhāb's racialized difference by calling upon classical theories of human reproduction and intergenerational flux as well as Islamically inflected understandings of female biology and of man as microcosm, a complex manifestation of God's manifold creative powers. The sexual moralism of prosecuting ʿAbd al-Wahhāb's origins is tempered by an often piously phrased epistemological humility about what his unique body may be meant to do and become.

After Jaʿfar's pronouncement that distills all of the above, Fāṭima is overcome with joy at the resolution. ʿAbd al-Wahhāb earns Jaʿfar's special favors: he describes the boy as a guardian of the Prophet Muḥammad's grave (*turs qabr al-nabī*) and presages that ʿAbd al-Wahhāb will grow into a valiant *mujāhid,* or warrior for the religion. ʿAbd al-Wahhāb is the only heroic figure in the text to take the title of one who defends the specific site of the Prophet's tomb, and its resonances waver between valorizing him and diffusing apprehensions around the child's preternatural virility and strength. Historically, Muḥammad's burial place in Medina was serviced

59. Jaʿfar al-Ṣādiq, *Ṭibb al-Imām al-Ṣādiq,* ed. Muḥsin ʿAqīl (Beirut: Muʾassasat al-Aʿlāmī, 1998), 520.

60. Kueny, *Conceiving Identities,* 31.

and maintained by a contingent of enslaved eunuchs, ʿAbbasid-era records of which say they were a mix of "Slavs" (*ṣaqāliba*) and Black people or Abyssinians (*ḥabash*). By the late Ottoman era, "the majority, if not all, of the eunuchs of the Prophet were African in origin," with many of them bought in childhood and trained for years to assume the role.[61] In Jaʿfar's court, ʿAbd al-Wahhāb stands as a pre-sexual, beardless youth who does not yet participate in a libidinal world in which Black men are recurrently presented as hypermasculine, carnal, and threatening. As if to underscore his sexual innocence and present him as emphatically untarnished by the preceding affairs, the narrative obliquely links his role to that of these sacred, castrated figures, many of whom looked not unlike the young hero.

On the momentum of Jaʿfar's favorable prognostication about ʿAbd al-Wahhāb's career, the Kilābīs set out again. They ride to Baghdad and the seat of the caliphate, then under the ʿAbbasid ruler al-Hādī, before moving homeward. Al-Ḥārith and his father continue to resist the recurrent proofs of ʿAbd al-Wahhāb's paternity along the way, including a dream the caliph has in which Muḥammad himself verifies Jaʿfar's hypothesis. This culminates with al-Ḥārith and his father's public renunciation of Fāṭima and her child before the royal court, with the caliph censuring the two for their noncompliance with prophetic law (*ṭaghā fī-l-sharīʿa al-Muḥammadiyya*). Al-Ḥārith and his father subsequently decide to convert to Christianity and move to Byzantium, fully exiling themselves from the community of believers out of prejudicial spite; their antiblackness literally places them outside of the *umma*. In contrast, in the caliph's court ʿAbd al-Wahhāb is showered with lucre that is commensurate with his predicted station in elite Arab-Muslim society but also ironically representative of the racialized associations that he is fated to navigate therein: he is gifted an ass from Nubia with a bejeweled bridle and twenty slaves, all of whom are "Black sons of Ḥām" (*ʿishrīn ʿabīd sūdān min awlād Ḥām*). ʿAbd al-Wahhāb's reception of this present further presages the arc of his identity: "ʿAbd al-Wahhāb rode off on his steed with the Blacks, and his heart inclined toward them [*wa-qalbuhu qad māl ilayhim*]."[62]

Conclusion

Key to the process of naturalizing race is attaching it to rationalist notions of cause and effect that are generated organically in and across bodies,

61. Marmon, *Eunuchs and Sacred Boundaries*, 33, 100.
62. *Sīrat Dhāt al-Himma*, VII:44

rather than originating in social perception. How nonnormative, intergenerationally (if differently) embodied conditions become associated with racialized difference is therefore central to explaining how ʿAbd al-Wahhāb's extraordinary origin tale achieves verisimilitude within a narrative that purports—like much premodern Arabic storytelling—to offer reliable reportage. Though it is often thought that premodern racisms do not share in modernity's "scientific" (qua secular and Enlightened) dispositions, the stories of the *sīras*' Black heroes and the intellectual traditions in which they are situated perturb such a clean temporal and cultural break.[63] ʿAbd al-Wahhāb's story would seem to signal that a defining feature of modern constructions of race—namely, their formulation as scientific and rigorous in order to underwrite their application as a tool of rational social control—should be understood as continuous with rather than distinct from trends in premodernity. Nonetheless, ideas of what falls in the realm of speculative inquiry and what constitutes a mechanism of causality have changed over time. Thus we find that ʿAbd al-Wahhāb's tale offers a twist on hereditary mechanisms while maintaining that the bodily environment in which inheritance should occur is central to his making.

At its most superficial, ʿAbd al-Wahhāb's birth story is a cautionary tale warning believing Muslims against menstrual sex. However, it is also a multivalent commentary on the possibilities of redemption through humanely confronting otherness. Al-Ḥārith is so unwilling to accept his child even after the final, authoritative verdict is rendered that he and his father, Ẓālim, convert to Christianity and live out the remainder of their lives fighting ʿAbd al-Wahhāb and his mother on the side of the Byzantines, only to be killed by ʿAbd al-Wahhāb. ʿAbd al-Wahhāb, meanwhile, becomes a hero in his own right. His destiny is certified not only by Jaʿfar al-Ṣādiq, but also by numerous other sacred authorities throughout his journeys. Throughout the epic, it is villainous, non-Muslim figures like al-Ḥārith, Ẓālim, and ʿUqba who will repeat the sharpest racialized invectives against ʿAbd al-Wahhāb, referring to him as "son of Marzūq" (*ibn Marzūq*), a "bastard slave" (*ʿabd zanīm*)—which is also used against other Black characters—and the "Black of the Banū Kilāb" (*aswad Banī Kilāb*). Though, as we will see in the ensuing

63. I have thus used *scientific* as a descriptor throughout in order to provoke awareness of transregional and transtemporal continuities as well as certain fallacies about modernity's monopoly on the concept of science. For a thorough historicization of the application of terms like *science*, *scientific*, and *sciences* in describing premodern Islamicate knowledges (*ʿulūm*), see Justin K. Stearns, *Revealed Sciences: Natural Sciences in Islam in Seventeenth-Century Morocco* (Cambridge: Cambridge University Press, 2021).

chapters, even the story's most pious characters have their moments when racialized prejudice bubbles to the surface, particularly in considering life-cycle events like marriage and birth and in tenser moments of encounters with foreign cultures and strange lands.

The cautionary elements of ʿAbd al-Wahhāb's tale extend far beyond observations of ritual purity, reaching to the very heart of how societies should imagine themselves and grapple with the inclusion of historically othered groups. This question is made particularly pressing by the pregnant period in which the story is set, amid the Arab-Byzantine conflicts of the seventh to ninth centuries, the ramp-up of the trans-Saharan slave trade, and the overturning of Umayyad power in Islam's central lands in favor of the ʿAbbasid regime. This question is also made physically central to the sacred geography of Islam and to the foundational, Arabian milieu of the *sīra* through the trial's passage from the tribal lands of the Kilāb to the holy city of Mecca and subsequently to the seat of the caliphate in Baghdad, with ʿAbd al-Wahhāb ultimately assuming a heroic title that evokes Muḥammad's resting place in Medina.

In light of al-Ḥārith's impious characterization, we may read the results of his illicit sexual act, namely, a child that is both Black and uncannily similar in appearance to himself, as a mechanism for moral refraction. The father who conceived a child while his partner was menstruating, upon meeting that child, is met with a dark mirror. In rejecting his child by claiming that he is a product of sin—in this case, of adultery—al-Ḥārith ironically repudiates his own behavior, infusing the whole conception narrative with didactic force.

Added to the malefaction of menstrual sex is al-Ḥārith's unwillingness to claim his resultant child. Paternal rejection is common in the *sīra* tradition; rejection because she is a girl precipitates Fāṭima's own heroic ascent, and in the previous chapter we saw that ʿAntar and Abū Zayd al-Hilālī both experienced a similar rupture in their families. Mortified at having had a daughter instead of a son, Fāṭima Dhāt al-Himma's father nearly commits infanticide. He is narrowly coaxed out of doing so by an enslaved woman, who then takes Fāṭima into her care, only to be captured by a rival tribe during a raid. It is in this environment of estrangement, fatherlessness, and male duress that Fāṭima began to show her martial prowess.[64] Both instances of rejection buttress the *sīra*'s refrain that one's actions can overturn certain social deficiencies or indignities, though the natural basis of this is still provided

64. For a translation of episodes from Fāṭima's early life, see Magidow, "Epic of the Commander Dhat al-Himma," 1–62.

by a free and elite *nasab*, or lineage. For both the captive Fāṭima and the Black ʿAbd al-Wahhāb, their temporarily obscured lineages offer the strongest rebuttal to their perceived slave status and fulfill the commonplace notion in popular and prophetological sources that one's birth station, free or unfree, will always ultimately assert itself. Others' sustained experiences of enslavement, meanwhile, eddy around their narratives in much the way they do for heroes throughout the *sīra* traditions discussed in chapter 1, with Fāṭima and ʿAbd al-Wahhāb both provided helpmates in the form of enslaved characters, almost all of whom are raced as Black and whose narrative importance is contingent on their proximity to the text's central heroes. This simulates the social dependencies of the unfree on those with freeborn and secure lineages while also weaving an aspirational history in which these dependencies are salutary and effective at bringing people into community. Those who reject the widening scope of their families and social worlds, like al-Ḥārith, are meanwhile ejected from them entirely.

As was noted at this chapter's beginning, the formative challenges faced by both mother and son stem from their deviation from the *sīra*'s unstated ideal of a masculine, Arab warrior-poet, that is, from their gender and racialized kind. This is thrown into sharp relief by the results of the paternity trial. Fāṭima's exoneration comes at the price of having aspects of her bodily functions put on public display, after having already been violated and impregnated against her will. ʿAbd al-Wahhāb's blackness is moreover rendered not only as a source of social chaos, but also as ensuing from biological chaos. His blackness' characterization as the result of a trespass on human norms that obey nature's rhythms undermines his mother's attempts to naturalize blackness by associating it with benign, cosmic images.

Although the alternative taboo of Fāṭima having committed adultery with her milk sibling and Black servant is disproven, this is only achieved through the exposure of a mystifying act that thwarts conventions of heredity and still renders ʿAbd al-Wahhāb an *ibn ḥayḍa* (child of a menstruant) if not an *ibn zinā* (bastard). This carries its own often analogous stigmas: a *ḥadīth* narrated by Abū Hurayra and recorded in the *Jāmiʿ* of al-Suyūṭī states that, "A (morally) beautiful nature is divested only from the child of menstruation or adultery" (*al-khulq al-ḥasan lā yunazzaʿ illā min walad ḥayḍa aw walad zāniya*).[65] In some strains of Shīʿī discourse, the moral impoverishment of such children leads them to reproduce their

65. Al-Munāwī, *Fayḍ al-Qadīr Sharḥ al-Jāmiʿ al-Ṣaghīr*, 6 vols. Cairo: Al-Maktaba al-Tijāriya al-Kubrā, 1978, 4129. Abū Hurayra has earned significant scrutiny as a narrator in Muslim feminist scholarship, beginning with Fatima Mernissi in *The Veil and the Male Elite*. On Mernissi's critiques and various *ʿālims'* responses at the time, see

parents' taboo behavior and turn away from the imamate, as in the saying, "no one reviles you, O ʿAlī, except the child of fornication, the child of menstruation, or the hypocrite" (*lā yabghuḍuk yā ʿAlī illā ibn zinā aw ibn ḥayḍa aw munāfiq*).[66]

As we will see in the coming chapter, though, the text is not merely concerned with menstruation as such, but with the specific workings of menstrual blood as a black or blackening material. It is rendered a uniquely problematic chemical and biological substance rather than as one of several similarly ritually impurifying emissions. That ʿAbd al-Wahhāb's nonhereditary blackness is debated in a series of scientific idioms hinging on mixing within the womb, on atavism, and even touching on maternal impression, indicates that people sought to phrase what Bruce Hall has called "racial arguments"—rhetorical strategies that trade on ideas of organically grouped difference to make political and social claims—in medicalized terms, even in cases when typical notions of racial genealogy are being subverted.[67] It also indicates that these arguments were relevant for world-building within fictive, popular accounts, attesting both to their wide circulation and to their centrality such that they merited inclusion when creating a verisimilar narrative.

Scholars have noted that *Sīrat Dhāt al-Himma*, unlike the Alexander Romance or the story of Sayf b. Dhī Yazan, tends to read more like a chronicle and is aligned with the pseudo-*maghāzī* strain of Arabic epic; it is less concerned with the magic, occultism, and miraculous creatures such as dragons and rocs that populate other works of a similar ilk.[68] True

---

Raja Rhouni, *Secular and Islamic Feminist Critiques in the Work of Fatima Mernissi* (Leiden: Brill, 2010), 219–25.

66. For background on this *ḥadīth* and others like it, see Etan Kohlberg, "The Position of the 'Walad Zinā' in Imāmī Shīʿism," *Bulletin of the School of Oriental and African Studies, University of London* 48 (1985): 239.

67. Bruce Hall, *A History of Race in Muslim West Africa* (Cambridge: Cambridge University Press, 2011).

68. Somewhat by contrast to how I have phrased this, Remke Kruk characterizes *Sīrat Sayf* as uniquely magical vis-à-vis the remainder of the *siyar* and discusses anthropological interviews in which Moroccan audiences seem to agree. Remke Kruk, "Review: *Prophets, Gods and Kings in Sirat Sayf ibn Dhi Yazan: An Intertex Reading of an Egyptian Popular Epic* (Brill Studies in Middle Eastern Literatures) by Helen Blatherwick," *Bulletin of the School of Oriental and African Studies*, University of London 80, no. 2 (2017): 379. On magic in *Sīrat Sayf*, see Samantha Pellegrino, "The Gender of Magic: Constructions of nonbinary gender categories in Sīrat Sayf ibn Dhī Yazan," *postmedieval* 13, nos. 3–4 (2022): 351–70. On magic as a dividing line in *sīra* periodization, see Faustina Doufikar-Aerts, "*Sīrat al-Iskandar*: An Arabic Popular Romance of Alexander," *Oriente Moderno* 22, no. 2 (2003): 516.

to this, its figuring of racialized difference is viscerally preoccupied with the real. ʿAbd al-Wahhāb's story maps onto a broad set of speculations on social kind's true, natural, and ordained ontology that manifest across elite and popular genres, from medicine and geographies to prophetologies and legends. It cycles through these speculations and methods as the narrative progresses, considering each in turn until the final resolution is reached. The ultimate value that lies in this truth having been revealed is the authentication of ʿAbd al-Wahhāb as a particularly effective heroic hybrid, primed through his "full Arabness" to link others at the margins to whom his "heart inclines" with the story's center, and primed through his blackness to be able to activate the value of their presence.

3

The (Popular) Science of Difference

If a man has intercourse with his wife while she is menstruating, the child will be either black [*aswad*] or defective [*nāqiṣ*] or mentally ill [*ma ʿtūh*] because of the corruption of the menstrual blood.

SĪRAT DHĀT AL-HIMMA

I heard Asmāʾ say that she asked the Prophet—peace and blessings upon him—about menstrual blood staining clothing. He said, "Rub it off, then scrape [across the surface] with water and moisten it, then you may pray in it."

. . . Al-Shāfiʿī said, "In this lies evidence that menstrual blood is impure, just like every other [type of] blood [*wa-fī hādhā dalīl ʿalā ann dam al-ḥayḍ najas wa-kadhā kull dam ghayrihi*]."

AL-SHĀFIʿĪ

In every case we could claim that we had discovered within these religions the actualization of one potential among many: the potential to map the reproduction of culture onto the reproduction of the organism. . . . But we should not imagine that the actualizations we discover constitute the origins of racism or the essence of those religions. For when we do so, we ourselves yield to a historical logic of lineage that is itself akin to that family of concepts we call race.

DAVID NIRENBERG

In his ascent as the premier Black-Arab hero of the epic *Sīrat Dhāt al-Himma,* audiences find that ʿAbd al-Wahhāb's race is a product of blood, though not exactly in the way that is normally meant: rather than being born to parents whose self-declared white and Arab identities predetermine his own, his skin is darkened at conception by his mother's menstrual blood because his father unthinkingly engages in a forbidden sexual act. In the tale's imaginary, the mixing of his mother's menstrual discharge with his father's *nuṭfa* (ejaculate) produces a difference between the hero ʿAbd al-Wahhāb and the rest of his family that is racialized from early on: he is presumed by outsiders to be slave-born, to be of Black African heritage, and to be a bastard. He becomes known as the "Black of the Tribe of Kilāb" (*aswad banī kilāb*), distancing him from the Arabness of his tribe by using the racialized moniker *aswad*, typically applied to people from the *bilād al-sūdān*, with whom he shows particular affinity as the head of military contingents composed mostly of Black enslaved and manumitted people. In fact, though, ʿAbd al-Wahhāb's *nasab* (lineage) is fully Arab on both his mother's and his father's side. His skin color derives from blood, but not from bloodline.

In this chapter I revisit ʿAbd al-Wahhāb's birth narrative. I demonstrate that naturalizations of social kind in Arabic literature showcase the dynamic and malleable relationship between humans, their environment, and the universe, but also bind human physiology to organic processes to which social choice is then rendered subordinate. Intellectual connections between mannered genres of literature and natural philosophy, legal works, and medicine come together to form the popular science of difference that is in evidence in the *sīra*. I show how popular works that circulated beyond the purview (often to their dismay) of *ʿulamāʾ*, or the religio-legally learned, and *udabāʾ*, or courtly cognoscenti, participate in racialization in ways that we may read as responsive to rather than merely derivative of these classes' cultural productions.

Using emic physiological models, I analyze how the *sīra* locates lived experiences of difference within the altered physicality of its Black hero. Though it may seem that the hero's stunning transformation suggests blackness is its own chaotic force in the world, I read the ways in which the hero's body is reinterpolated into society in the narrative as an aspect of racialization—of reinforcing where blackness *should* fit within an earthly order even as the hero's identity otherwise troubles this.

This chapter opens with a discussion of how an overlapping collection of bodily elements and the broader forces that govern them shape individual and group identities in early medieval Arab-Muslim thought. It then returns to the contexts of ʿAbd al-Wahhāb's birth narrative and the slight yet significant differences in the biological expressions used to explicate his blackness across several variant manuscripts and print editions of the epic. To reiterate, *Sīrat al-Amīra Dhāt al-Himma* was a diffuse and frequently oral tradition between the twelfth and fifteenth centuries—or between when mention of the story of *Dhāt al-Himma* first appears in writing and the dating of its earliest known manuscripts—and subsequently engendered polyvalent written traditions across the Middle East and North Africa. In written form the *sīra*s were often still part of economies of secondary orality, with storytellers by trade reading parts of *sīra*s aloud in public and semi-public locations.[1] Variations in how the *sīra* crystallized in text showcase compositional creativity and flexibility with the makings of social and/as natural kind with which this chapter is concerned.

As is clear in ʿAbd al-Wahhāb's birth narrative, the physiological properties of a range of bodily materials—in the story we see blood of at least two kinds and ejaculate as well as the substance of the womb—can have an indelible effect on one's constitution. Superficially this sketch of physiology would seem to accord with aspects of both the genealogical and climate-based humoral understandings that were typical to medieval Muslim learning as discussed in the prior chapter. However, the workings of bodily fluids that are prominent across Islamic discussions of racialized difference, inspired largely by Hippocratic and Galenic medicine, also complicate both climate-based and lineage-essentialist models of human difference by providing for the prospect of movement, mixing, and even sudden racialized change across generations and kinship groups. Such changes also, analogically, are related to the seemingly spontaneous construction of other forms of difference, as in the epigraph above adducing both physical and mental disability in addition to blackness as possible consequences of wayward, menstrual sex. I therefore attend to how versions of the *sīra* aggregate or separate out human differences along lines of alterity, social dependency, and ability and disability (or hyper-ability).

A primary point of departure between the *sīra*'s techniques of biologization and others that are perhaps more familiar to a contemporary Anglophone readership is what Foucault identifies as a "thematic of blood." He argues that this thematic became coupled with "devices of sexuality" in the nineteenth century to produce a politics in which the state actively intervenes in one's property, health, family, and everyday life. These interventions hinge on a "mythical concern with protecting the purity of the blood and ensuring the triumph of the race."[2] Bloodlines in their most

1. Walter Ong, *Orality and Literacy: The Technologizing of the Word* (London: Routledge, 2012 [1982]), 11–16.

2. Michel Foucault, "Right of Death and Power over Life," in *The Foucault Reader*, ed. Paul Rabinow (New York: Vintage Books, 2010), 270–71.

literal sense and ideas of blood purity and blood nobility have long been regarded as formative to modern understandings of race. Under modern bodily epistemologies, ideas about blood and heredity have been key to race's mobilization as a covert construction, that is, as a set of classifications fashioned through social practices but interpreted as natural facts.[3]

In the burgeoning conversation around premodern concepts of race, tracing their origins has therefore often taken the form of trawling for another, related etiology: the instance when controlling for blood purity first acquired salience at the level of the state. As a result, many authors have moved the needle backward in time to a seemingly pivotal moment in late medieval Spain. In 1449, the first edicts of blood purity (*limpieza de sangre*) were put in place by a state seeking to cordon off and gradually rid itself of its not-"natively"-Christian populace. Those who had converted (*conversos* if formerly Jewish, *moriscos* if formerly Muslim) were to be permanently excluded from Christian society because of their religious pasts, which were rendered ever-present, racialized identities. Other authors locate the shift instead in Portugal, following a thread of Great Man history in which Henry the Navigator's fifteenth-century missions along the West African coast and his court chronicler, Gomes de Zurara's depictions of the same rendered them the "first race maker[s] and crafter[s] of racist ideas."[4] Monica Green, meanwhile, notes that this was an era of accelerated encounter between many and various actors, in which Christian Iberians developed direct relationships with Sahelian traders who had their own ideas of social kind as well.[5] Common to these narratives is the fifteenth century as a period of such pregnant coincidences and its unprecedented quality as the era in which continental Europe turned overtly toward a politically activated formulation of what was increasingly called "race."

These arguments about blood's mobilization have a significant and often overdetermining influence on fields of study focused on other regions when seeking to understand what racialization might mean for a range of local contexts. The prevalent view—in which racialization's origins are located in Europe, period aside—gives Western racial formations and projects outsized narrative power that is itself anachronistic to the

3. On the effects of serological studies and genetic nationalism in the modern history of the Middle East, see Elise Burton, *Genetic Crossroads: The Middle East and the Science of Human Heredity* (Stanford, CA: Stanford University Press, 2021).

4. Ibram X. Kendi, *How to Be an Antiracist* (London: Oneworld, 2019), 39.

5. Monica H. Green, "The Diversity of Human Kind," in *A Cultural History of the Human Body in the Middle Ages*, edited by Linda Kalof and W. F. Bynum, (London: Bloomsbury, 2010), 173–90 and 268–71.

so-called Middle Ages. These narratives' seductiveness cannot be divorced from a now-commonplace belief about the Middle East and North Africa, namely, that racialization, concepts of natural slavery, and more were brought to the region through European colonial encounters. This belief has been called into question in recent work by Africanists and Arabists such as Bruce Hall, Michael Gomez, Ismael Montana, Hannah Barker, and Chouki El Hamel.[6] And, as Justin Stearns suggests in his critique of Geraldine Heng's concept of a general medieval *homo europaeus*, historical excavations of the white, Western, Christian subject as race maker also risk reinscribing racial essences in a subtler fashion. Europeans are re-presented as having the degree of civilization requisite to forecast the true value of race-making and perfect it into a violent and lucrative epistemology, while other societies' constructions of racialized kinds are reduced to pale imitations, intelligible only through comparison or tributary connection to the real thing. In this framework, eliding the complexity and contestation in Islamic discourses on racialized blackness is an essentialist erasure, and so is presuming such discourses' categorical absence.[7]

But, of course, histories of racialization that quest after its origins and find them outside of Europe are not innocent either. Rather, they are part of a long history of Orientalist projection, Islamophobic fearmongering, and European abolitionist displacement. This legacy regularly culminates in calls for foreign interventions in conflicts that are framed as "Arab vs. African," as if the two were essential and mutually exclusive, or else in the positing of "white Arab vs. Black African" animus as the inspiration for European racial hierarchies. Typically, this inspiration arrives via the Islamic world's *maghrib*, or west, beginning in Iberia, West Africa, or, as Hisham Aïdi shows, Morocco, regarded as a composite of the two. In a review of El Hamel's *Black Morocco*, Aïdi cautions that his project at once conflates early modern Moroccans' methods of racial reckoning with a system of blood quantum that was wholly alien to them and treats Morocco as an almost inevitable, "quasi-mystical" space in which such a system would arise: "a

6. Hall, *A History of Race in Muslim West Africa, 1600–1900*; Michael A. Gomez, *African Dominion: A New History of Empire in Early and Medieval West Africa* (Princeton, NJ: Princeton University Press, 2018); Chouki el Hamel, *Black Morocco: A History of Slavery, Race, and Islam* (New York: Cambridge University Press, 2014; Hannah Barker, *That Most Precious Merchandise: The Mediterranean Trade in Black Sea Slaves, 1260–1500* (Philadelphia: University of Pennsylvania Press, 2019); Ismael Montana, *The Abolition of Slavery in Ottoman Tunisia* (Gainesville: University Press of Florida, 2013), esp. 13–24.

7. Stearns, "Race in the Islamicate Middle East."

tree with roots in the Sahel, and leaves that sway to the European breeze."[8] Such critiques compel us to ask how we might think with "race before race" while divesting from both teleology and claims to firstness or uniqueness, the pursuit of which Sarah Pearce trenchantly describes as a neocolonial enterprise and Margo Hendricks likens to a doctrine of discovery.[9]

Transregional studies of premodern race, many of which focus on literary sources, have further been critiqued for their emphasis on text and story rather than on material impact. Despite many a cliché about the pen's might over the sword's (a staple in medieval Arabic works as well), discourses do not themselves have coercive power. Feisal Mohamed is incisive when declaring that premodern critical race studies' accounts of Elizabethan English literature at times render a "skulking minor player on the world stage . . . chastened by Spanish and Ottoman power," into a highly *effective*, as opposed to active, white ethnonationalist polity of global import before its time.[10] Indeed, attached to the notion of European colonizers as disseminators of racialization is the idea that racial construction is an exclusive tool of the nation-state, an argument that manifests also in the tendency to trace the first evidence of racial formations to the "state-sanctioned" and state-documented discriminatory practices of Spain and Portugal. In a recent study, Jonathan Brown uses what we might call the coercion corollary somewhat differently. He explains that certain premodern legal rulings by Malikī jurists on *kafāʾa*, or spousal sufficiency, may appear antiblack but are not so—or at least not in a way for which the jurists are responsible. Rather, such rulings are made based on the established juristic practice of considering local customs (*aʿarāf*), albeit in places where Black people had become collectively devalued. Antiblackness, then, is an external reality that jurists were enjoined to concede and powerless to either change or enforce in the absence of state backing.[11]

8. Hisham Aïdi, "Moulay Ismail and the Mumbo Jumbo: *Black Morocco* Revisited," *Islamophobia Studies Journal* (2023): 10.

9. S. J. Pearce, "The Inquisitor and the Moseret: *The Invention of Race in the European Middle Ages* and the New English Colonialism in Jewish Historiography," *Medieval Encounters* 26 (2020): 145–90; Margo Hendricks, "Coloring the Past, Rewriting Our Future: Raceb4Race," "Race and Periodization Symposium," September 2019, https://pressbooks.claremont.edu/clas114valentine/chapter/coloring-the-past-rewriting-our-future-raceb4race/.

10. Feisal G. Mohamed, "On Race and Historicism: A Polemic in Three Turns," *ELH* 89, no. 2 (2022): 379.

11. Jonathan A. C. Brown, *Islam and Blackness* (London: Oneworld 2022), esp. 196–97.

To tease this apart, we may analyze how customs and the consciously shared traditions of knowledge in which they are embedded have constituted feedback loops through which racialization operates, and how they have normative potentials rather than coercive ones. This is not to imply that racialized violence did not occur in premodern Arab-Muslim contexts—the aforementioned work shows it did—but that connections between lived and epistemic violence are made, not given. In medieval Arab-Muslim domains, discursively bounded by intellectual traditions and reading cultures and peopled with scholastic bureaucracies, the sociopolitical influence of systems of knowledge is vast, but often in ways that are mundane and difficult to name. Strikingly similar ideals and terminologies for social kind reverberate across forms and audiences, manifesting in poetry and slaving manuals, philosophical excurses and nighttime tales. The communication structures and networks of trade and exchange developed within empires certainly had some hand in circulating these ideas, and as Marina Rustow has persuasively argued, we ought to think of royal courts and their interlocutors' use of these structures in terms of statecraft.[12] However, to privilege state actors as the sole or even the main architects of racialized norms overlooks what some have called a politics of the everyday, in which lower rungs of society strategically formulate their own "skills and competencies that can be acquired and transmitted" in order to pursue their interests.[13]

As Neda Maghbouleh demonstrates, popular culture is a fertile terrain for exploring the everyday politics of race. People wed ideas of their own and others' authenticity and identity within a group to what is widely, vividly amplified on the screen and page and in the public square. Likely in construct with the recurrent lower-status position of Black people within a hierarchy of roles and occupations both domestic and public, Black people become the archetypal slaves (*ʿabīd*) in Arabic popular literature, as well as loci of dangerous desire and gendered discord.[14] Recent work

12. Marina Rustow, *The Lost Archive: Traces of a Caliphate in a Cairo Synagogue* (Princeton, NJ: Princeton University Press, 2020), 63–66.

13. Sociologists have also troubled Foucault's top-down formulation of race-making and biopower in modern states. On how contemporary non-statist constructions of race exert an impact on governmental policies and structures, see Maghbouleh, *The Limits of Whiteness*; I borrow this definition of the everyday politics of nonelites within premodern states and empires from Michael Szonyi's fascinating study of military conscription in Ming China: Michael Szonyi, *The Art of Being Governed: Everyday Politics in Late Imperial China* (Princeton, NJ: Princeton University Press, 2017), 8.

14. On the racialization of enslaved characters in popular Arabic works, see Malcolm Lyons and Robert Irwin, *Tales of the Marvelous and News of the Strange* (London:

by Lamia Balafrej on thirteenth-century Arabic manuscript illustrations notes similar trends of typification in visual culture as well, with skin color used to "create social order *among* slaves."[15] She argues that enslaved people's blackness is often paired with visual indicators of objectification and containment, while enslaved people's whiteness is paired with indicators of dialogue, suggesting fluidity or common ground with white owners. This typology is what lends the Black heroes of the *siyar shaʿbiyya* their particular didactic force, as figures who must recurrently prove their piety and nobility despite appearances that would confine them to a reified underclass. Meanwhile, Byzantine, Turkic, and Armenian characters in *Sīrat Dhāt al-Himma,* who were also typically subject to enslavement in the Islamic world, are not made to undergo similar trials of identity.[16]

We may therefore ask, how do the Black heroes' bodies—down to their literal viscera—become the staging ground for social dramas? How is blackness constituted in the body in ways that are a priori challenging to social norms and perceived natural orders? And how does a popular science of racialized difference take shape through narratives about complicated and dramatic bodies?

Becoming Black: Blood, Bile, and Bodily Transmission

The bodily substances that are most relevant to ʿAbd al-Wahhāb's tale and its intertexts differ from the four standard humors that were intrinsic to ideas of how the external climate affected the body: black bile, yellow bile, blood, and phlegm. Rather, they include blood, black bile, semen, and to a lesser extent, milk. Each of the latter was understood to be formed from or conducted in the blood. Their transmission among humans could forge the affective channels of family and community. Nursing created kinship

---

Penguin Books, 2014), xxiv–xxv; Irwin, "The Dark Side of the Arabian Nights." As several scholars have recently noted, the largest yet most textually invisible form of enslavement in the premodern Islamic world was domestic. Domestic slavery was also heavily female, which is generally underrepresented in popular sources like the ones discussed in this book. Craig Perry, "Historicizing Slavery in the Medieval Islamic World," *IJMES* 49 (2017): 133–38.

15. Lamia Balafrej, "Domestic Slavery, Skin Color, and Image Dialectic in Thirteenth-Century Arabic Manuscripts" *Art History* 44, no. 4 (2021): 2 (emphasis in the original).

16. Malcolm Lyons, for example, notes that Armenian characters virtually disappear from the texts after being introduced as such, a process he refers to as assimilatory, with their "origins being forgotten," and which he notes is tantamount to them being "allowed no racial characteristics." Lyons, *Arabian Epic* vol. 1, 22.

connections in analogous fashion to womb kinship.[17] Black bile, which was thought to circulate like a precipitate in the bloodstream, is inextricable from discourses of disease as well as those of skin pigmentation, both with respect to ephemeral changes in tone and one's permanent complexion.[18] Though ʿAbd al-Wahhāb's particular narrative is concerned with kinship through the exchange of fluids in their literal sense, elsewhere more abstracted pathways of exchange also construct kinship in ways tied, metaphorically, to physiology. In her recent work on early modern Persianate identities, Mana Kia notes that kinship itself forms a "spectrum" in Muslim societies. Many affinities beyond biological ones—articulated most often as womb kinship—such as one's relationship to fellow scholars or soldiers or mendicants, are spoken of in familial terms, expressed through ties to a shared place of origin or settlement that are in turn given meaning through shared Noahic heritage.[19] These metaphors are not strictly patriarchal: Eyad Abuali finds that *shaykhs*, or elder figures who mentor Sufi disciples, are recurrently likened in biographical literature to wet nurses, and thus milk-parents, to their charges.[20]

17. In Islamic contexts, this principle is often expressed through the *ḥadīth*, "nursing prohibits the same relationships that descent prohibits" (*yaḥram min al-raḍāʿ mā yaḥram min al-nasab*). On milk kinship arrangements in popular storytelling tropes, see Rachel Schine, "Nourishing the Noble: Breastfeeding and Hero-Making in Medieval Arabic Popular Literature," *al-ʿUṣūr al-Wusṭā* 27 (2019): 165–200. Milk bonds also figured in late medieval Spanish understandings of kinship. See Carolyn A. Nadeau, "Blood Mother/Milk Mother: Breastfeeding, the Family, and the State in Antonio de Guevara's *Relox de Príncipes* (*Dial of Princes*)," *Hispanic Review* 69:2 (2001): 153–74.

18. Both of these dimensions of physiognomy—as a guide for discerning a person's permanent worth and for discerning their impermanent state of health—are brought together in institutions such as slave purchasing. Manuals by such temporally and geographically distant figures as Ibn Buṭlān in the tenth century and al-ʿAynṭabī in the fifteenth century attest to the continued use and development of these understandings in construct with practices of slaving in different Arab-Muslim regions; Ibn Buṭlān, "Risāla Jāmiʿa li-Funūn al-Nāfiʿa fī Shirā al-Raqīq wa-Taqlīb al-ʿAbīd, in Nawādir al-Makhṭūṭāt," vol. 2, ed. ʿAbd al-Salām Hārūn (Cairo: Muṣṭafā al-Ḥalabī, 1973); Muẓaffar al-Dīn Abū-l-Thanāʾ Maḥmūd b. Aḥmad al-ʿAynṭabī al-Amshāṭī al-Ḥanafī, *al-Qawl al-Sadīd fī Ikhtiyār al-Imāʾ wa-l-ʿAbīd* (Ms. orient A 1237, Universitäten Erfurt/Gotha). On the practicalities of how these knowledges informed the inspection of slaves, see Barker, *That Most Precious Merchandise*, 100; Hannah Barker, "Purchasing a Slave in Fourteenth-Century Cairo: Ibn al-Akfānī's *Book of Observation and Inspection in the Examination of Slaves, Mamlūk Studies Review* 19 (2016): 1–23.

19. Kia, *Persianate Selves*, 103.

20. Eyad Abuali, "'I tasted sweetness, and I tasted affliction': pleasure, pain, and body in medieval Sufi food practices," *The Senses and Society* 17, no. 1 (2022): 61–64.

Biological reasoning is thus a practice that can help people make sense not just of their own bodies, but of land, history, and society in ways that are elective and often advantaging. Naturalizing one's kind makes the reverse appear true: that our social practices and affinities—our advantages and entitlements—are biologically contingent and obscure or thwart agency. In focusing on race-qua-bloodline in premodernity, we flatten a complex physiological model in which multiple parts of the body are put to work in making and transmitting likeness in ways that do not necessarily flow linearly across generations. We overlook commonplace ways that people situated their bodies in other types of kinship network through a biological idiom that they are at once empowered to define and that, notionally, works its own suprahuman and independent effects.

But how do we arrive at the *sīra*'s portrayal of blood—menstrual or otherwise—as playing a role in the transmission of black skin? Blood is generally conceived of as necessary for reproduction in Islamic thought. Although blood is intrinsic to basic human processes, it is also used by God to wondrous and sometimes unexpected ends; this is manifest in the *sīra*'s claim that, using blood's various forms, God can bring black from white and vice versa as He wills. Many polymaths, including al-Jāḥiẓ, his near-contemporary Ibn Qutayba, and the historical Jaʿfar al-Ṣādiq, offered theories about the specifics of blood's reproductive functions. All share the common belief that the blood that a woman would otherwise lose through menstruation is diverted to the womb to encase and nourish the fetus. Other fluids, such as the male and/or female ejaculate (*nuṭfa*), mingle prior to the embryo's movement into the woman's blood-filled womb. Though this would seem to signal the *nuṭfa*'s distinctness from blood in substance and function, in classical Islamic medicine the production of semen was the result of one of many chemical processes that occur in the blood.[21]

As previously discussed, medieval Muslim physicians and theologians were divided on whether the *nuṭfa* was indeed a mixture of substances contributed by both male and female, or whether it was exclusively male; this debate roughly follows the divide between the Hippocratic and Aristotelian theories of reproduction.[22] Whereas for Hippocrates, both male and female could produce a seminal discharge, Aristotle averred not only that women could not emit semen, but that their menstrual blood was moreover a result of the same physiological process through which males

21. Kueny, *Conceiving Identities*, 31.

22. Etin Anwar, *Gender and Self in Islam* (London: Routledge, 2006), 75; Kathryn Kueny, *Conceiving Identities*, 28–31.

generate semen, namely drawing nourishment from one's organs to then produce and nourish another body. Aristotle held, by analogy, that semen acted on menstrual blood to create the embryo. This quickening effect works much "the way rennet curdles milk in the making of cheese."[23]

Thinkers sometimes negotiated among these viewpoints. Similar to Jaʿfar al-Ṣādiq's previously-cited claim that women's "water" is weaker than that of men, Ibn Sīnā (d. 1037) holds that women produce seminal fluid, but that it is less effectual than men's, and moreover that it is a result of further processing one's menstrual blood. This relegates women's *nuṭfa* to "the same function Aristotle assigned to the menses," and therefore to a passive role mirroring that of the blood in the womb.[24] Undergirding the belief that women could not produce semen—or that they could not produce semen of equal strength to men's—is the notion that women's bodily humors are imperfectly balanced, rendering them reproductively deficient and dependent.[25] In standard humoral reasoning, men were said to be internally warmer and drier than women, and their body heat was a productive resource in generating seminal fluid.

The Qurʾān does not deal in humoral pathology, but its statements on human reproduction were interpreted as falling within or certifying certain among the above models. Often, the philosophers mentioned above differed on when a fetus became a coherent entity, that is, when the materials requisite for its existence became properly mixed and situated within the woman's body. The following passage, from *Sūrat al-Muʾminīn* (Q 23:12–14), draws particular focus in these discussions:[26]

> We created man of an essence of clay, then We placed him as a drop of fluid in a safe place, then We created of the drop [*al-nuṭfa*] a clinging form [*ʿalaqa*], and We made that form into a lump of flesh [*muḍgha*], and We made that lump into bones, and We clothed those bones with flesh, and later We made him into other forms—glory be to God, the best of creators!

23. Lincoln Taiz and Lee Taiz, *Flora Unveiled: The Discovery and Denial of Sex in Plants* (Oxford: Oxford University Press, 2017), 325.

24. Sherry Sayed Gadelrab, "Discourses on Sex Differences in Medieval Scholarly Islamic Thought," *Journal of the History of Medicine and Allied Sciences* 66:1 (2011): 67.

25. Basim Musallam, *Sex and Society in Islam: Birth Control before the Nineteenth Century* (New York: Cambridge University Press, 1983), 43–44. On the four humors in the body as well as in the environment, see Joshua T. Olsson, "The World in Arab Eyes: A Reassessment of the Climes in Medieval Islamic Scholarship," *Bulletin of the School of Oriental and African Studies* 77:3 (2014): 488.

26. Kueny, *Conceiving Identities*, 28.

In this passage, blood first becomes relevant to the reproductive process after the *nuṭfa* is formed, though before the fetus itself becomes a mass of blood, flesh, and bone. It is evoked in the word *ʿalaqa*, typically interpreted as a blood clot or an embryo. Theoretically, blood should not interact with other sexual fluids until the stage at which the *ʿalaqa* lodges itself in the blood-filled uterus. Across many medieval Arabic medical-scientific texts, blood diverted for gestational uses is not evaluated as impure or repugnant in the way menstrual blood generally is, because it remains inside the body and therefore cannot in any way invalidate ablution or influence ritual performance. This moral neutrality meant that a mother's blood was also not thought to have any contaminating effect on the fetus, which, as in the Hippocratic model, comes into being as a comprehensive, formable, and "ensoulable" entity when the flesh, blood, and bone take shape.[27]

This ambivalence toward the womb's blood as both ritually innocuous and life-giving is notably not upheld, however, in the case of the Nuṣayrī wisdom text, *al-Haft al-Sharīf* (*The Noble Set of Seven*). The eighth-century work is attributed to Jaʿfar al-Ṣādiq, the same Shīʿī imam who appears within the text of *Sīrat al-Amīra Dhāt al-Himma* to pass final judgment on ʿAbd al-Wahhāb's origins. It is said to have been recorded by Jaʿfar's student, Mufaḍḍal ibn ʿUmar al-Juʿfī.[28] One of Jaʿfar's recorded sayings claims that God employs the bloody environment of the womb to torture unbelievers (*kāfirūn*) by "ensouling" their bodies earlier than their believing counterparts. His explanation of how this unfolds follows the arc of Q 23:12–14:

> Then, when [the embryo] becomes an attached thing [*ʿalaqa*], the angels take a spirit from among the spirits of the unbelievers, and they put it into that attached mass. Then, the spirit of the unbeliever is tortured in the [layers of the] womb, in the blood and the menstrual secretion and the darkness and the obscurity until it becomes a body, for [the purpose of] castigation. All the while, the spirit of the believer is luxuriating in the Garden. The enfeebled spirit of the unbeliever is meanwhile

27. Kueny, 128.

28. This work is also known by the title *al-Haft wa-l-Aẓilla*; see Jaʿfar al-Ṣādiq and Mufaḍḍal b. ʿUmar al-Juʿfī, *al-Haft al-Sharīf*, ed. Muṣṭafā Ghālib (Beirut: Dār al-Andalus, 1964). See also Farhad Daftary, *Ismaili Literature: A Bibliography of Sources and Studies* (London: I. B. Tauris, 2004), 163; Mushegh Asatryan, "Mofaẓẓal Al-Joʿfi," in *Encyclopedia Iranica* (New York: Encyclopedia Iranica Foundation, 2012), http://www.iranicaonline.org/articles/mofazzal-al-jofi.

> tortured until it becomes a small lump of flesh [*muḍhgha*]. At that point, one of the spirits of those who have lapsed into unbelief is taken, and that body is lodged in the womb, then it is turned upside down... and the spirit of the tortured unbeliever is inverted in the blood and menstrual secretion and other things that are within the belly, until the body has reached its term. Then, the angels gather around the spirit that is in the garden and give it the primordial covenant [*mīthāq*], then the woman begins labor to take custody of the spirit, and however much the spirit tarries in its descent is however long labor extends for the woman and her pain intensifies.[29]

Although the author imagines the womb's blood as forming a hellish space for the unbeliever, contrasting this with the believer's spiritual stay in the heavenly Garden and hesitant departure, he does not imply that the blood in any way taints the unbeliever or permeates his body. And yet, this passage is seemingly unique in its view that blood negatively affects the fetus when exposed to it for too long; in other writings, being surrounded by blood is an unremarkable, natural condition of the womb. Jaʿfar's sayings provide a rare, explicit instance of blood's moral instrumentality in scholarly dress—blood, when put to use, is a didactic tool for disciplining the unbeliever, much in the way that blood, when put to misuse, produces ʿAbd al-Wahhāb's black complexion with the effect of disciplining the sexuality of his peer characters and of his story's audience. In words attributed to Jaʿfar al-Ṣādiq, it is intimated that blood can physically and socially differentiate human experiences, even before those humans are born. However, *al-Haft al-Sharīf* does not adumbrate a visible physical difference between believers and unbelievers, and so the role of blood here does not aid in constructing phenotypes or helping humans visually sort one another on the earthly plane.

In other texts focused on human reproduction, such as the section of al-Jāḥiẓ's creation treatise, *al-ʿIbar wa-l-Iʿtibār*, that concerns the fashioning of the body, blood has a more explicit effect on skin color and appearance. However, this is a temporary feature of the gestational process. Unlike in *al-Haft al-Sharīf*, al-Jāḥiẓ's epistle renders blood as benign sustenance for the fetus. In a forerunner of the "you are what you eat" adage, he proposes that different types of nourishment have distinct complexion-altering effects:

29. Al-Ṣādiq and al-Juʿfī, *al-Haft al-Sharīf*, 83.

> From the blood of his mother, [the fetus] receives that which nourishes him, like water irrigating plants, and his food supply does not abate until his creation has been completed . . . and when he has been born, that which nourishes him shifts from the blood of his mother to her breasts, and his coloring becomes fair and pure and beautiful when his taste is sweetened.[30]

Implicitly, al-Jāḥiẓ observes that children emerge pink, or "blood-colored" from the womb, and are lightened—that is, given a more normative skin tone—through nursing. Whereas al-Jāḥiẓ attributes the subsequent change in a child's coloring to an improvement in one's type of nourishment, *ḥadīths* collected by his near-contemporary Ibn Qutayba instead state that breast milk creates a conduit between mother and child, or wet nurse and child, that results in the child's skin tone coming to resemble her own.[31] Ibn Sīnā cautions, likely in part on these grounds, that wet nurses should be chosen for their beauty as well as for their ethics and youthful fitness.[32] Indeed, in pre-Islamic poetry, breast milk was sometimes thought to have the opposite effect of that proposed by al-Jāḥiẓ, with one preserving one's fair complexion from birth so long as they nursed minimally and from a narrow pool of women.[33] Because customarily Muslims could not acquire non-Muslim wetnurses, superstitions about wetnurses of different religions and/or racialized kinds did not typically arise, though they are observed in other medieval cultures.[34] However, in

30. Al-Jāḥiẓ, *al-ʿIbar wa-al-Iʿtibār*, ed. Ṣābr Idrīs (Cairo: Al-ʿArabī, 1994), 78.

31. ʿAbd Allāh b. Muslim b. Qutayba, *ʿUyūn al-Akhbār*, vol. 2, ed. Abī Muḥammad ibn Qutayh al-Dīnwarī (Cairo: al-Muʾassasah al-Miṣriyyah al-ʿĀmma lil-Taʾlīf wa-l-Tarjamah wa-l-Nashr, 1964), 68.

32. Ibn Sīnā, *al-Qānūn fī-l-Ṭibb*, ed. Muḥammad al-Dīn al-Ḍannāwī (Beirut: Dār al-Kutub al-ʿIlmiyya, 2009), 114.

33. Ibn Qutayba al-Dīnawarī, *ʿUyūn al-akhbār*, ed. Aḥmad Zakī al-ʿAdawī (Cairo: Dār al-Kutub al-Miṣriyya, 1925), 2:68.

34. Scholars of the Latin West identify the new prohibitions of "cross-cultural wet-nursing" in the *Siete Partidas* in thirteenth-century Spain as a key moment in using the "milk-as-blood" model to racialize religion and constrain interreligious interaction in ways that then placed new forms of scrutiny on the social class of wetnurses instead. Emilie L. Bergmann, "Milking the Poor: Wet-Nursing and the Sexual Economy of Early Modern Spain," in *Marriage and Sexual Economy in Medieval and Early Modern Iberia*, ed. Eukene Lacarra Lanz (London: Routledge, 2002), 90–114. On the application of ideas about milk-as-bloodline by British colonizers in the Americas in ways that are classed, raced, and religiously inflected, see Carla Cevasco, "'Look'd Like Milk': Colonialism and Infant Feeding in the English Atlantic World," *Journal of Early American History* 10 (2020): 147–78.

interpretations of the story of Mūsā's (Moses's) childhood in the Qurʾān, it is sometimes said that had he nursed from a pagan or "transgressive" Egyptian woman (*mukhālifa*) or a wild beast (*waḥsha*) rather than his mother, he would not have been fit for transmitting prophecy.[35] The physical and moral effects of one's lineal kinship, produced in the womb, could be altered by milk consumed once outside of it.

Though the wisdom found in elite literature eschews blood's connection to impurity for the unborn, popular sources—some of which gave themselves elite imprimaturs through citation and quotation—offer quite a different story, in which blood is a tool for discipline and differentiation between individuals with positive and negative heritages or destinies. Milk, meanwhile, is widely viewed in both popular and mannered sources as meting out physical markings of such differences, which comes with cautionary instruction about whom one should draw into one's kin networks through nursing. With the exception of al-Jāḥiẓ's surmise, though, this marking does not rely on a syllogistic relationship between the color of a fluid and the color of one's skin, and in his case it only allusively does so.

Narratives in *qiṣaṣ al-anbiyāʾ*, or "stories of the prophets" anthologies, offer perhaps the most robust set of literary precedents for the direct, skin-tinting effects brought about by mixing corrupting or colorful bodily fluids. These compilations were often made by renowned exegetes, grammarians, and anthologists. Their labors complemented orthodox sources on the prophets' lives in the Qurʾān, *ḥadīths*, and *tafsīr* with backgrounding collections of *isrāʾīliyyāt*, or stories from Christians and Jews. They therefore toed the line between popular and canonical forms. In these works, other substances take the place of blood in exerting an influence on human appearance. Most prominent are black bile (*mirra sawdāʾ*) and ejaculate (*nuṭfa*). Across their distinct iterations of the same prophet's biography, their appearance shows that there was not a fixed consensus in storytelling practices around how bodies and their substances can affect one another, which has implications for explaining the origins of racialized groups as well as for how one's kind may be reproduced or altered intergenerationally. In al-Thaʿlabī's (d. 1035) and al-Kisāʾī's (d. 805) respective accounts of the story of Nūḥ and his sons, a different mixture of substances transforms Nūḥ's son Ḥām and his offspring into the first Black people ever to exist, bringing into effect the so-called

35. Abū ʿAbd al-Raḥmān Muḥammad b. al-Ḥusayn al-Sulamī, *Ḥaqāʾiq al-tafsīr*, ed. Sayyid ʿUmrān (Beirut: Dār al-Kutub al-ʿIlmiyya, 2001), 101; Rūzbihān al-Baqlī al-Shīrāzī, *ʿArāʾis al-bayān fī ḥaqāʾiq al-Qurʾān*, ed. Aḥmad Farīd al-Mizyadī (Beirut: Dār al-Kutub al-ʿIlmiyya, 2008), 80.

"Curse of Ham" and also participating in a formal, universal-historical tradition of offering "etiologies" for the world's peoples.[36]

For al-Thaʿlabī, the possibility of starkly differentiated human groups was latent in Ādam (Adam), who was made from clay of all colors, pulled from all parts of the earth; realizing these differences in his offspring merely required a catalyst.[37] This comes during the great flood, when Nūḥ prohibits his family members from sexual intercourse while they are in the ark. Ḥām defies this ban, and Nūḥ then curses him—God therefore alters his *nuṭfa* so that he bears Black offspring.[38]

Rather than imagining Ādam as racially prismatic, al-Kisāʾī pictures him as transcending the paradigm of standard human types entirely, though we might note that his imagined default for physical ambiguity is still related to lightness—Ādam is described as looking like pale silver (*al-fiḍḍa al-bayḍāʾ*), recalling the descriptions of the *houris* that dwell in heaven, and who are discussed further in the next chapter.[39] Ḥawwāʾ's (Eve's) skin, meanwhile, is said to be yet more delicate (*araqq*) and fairer (*aṣfā*) than Ādam's. The leadup to Ḥām's curse in al-Kisāʾī's account more closely mirrors the biblical narrative, wherein Ḥām "sees" his father's nakedness and is then censured.[40] Ḥām, according to al-Kisāʾī, laughs when Nūḥ's robe slips in his sleep and his genitals are exposed, causing Nūḥ to stir and utter, "What is this laughter? Do you laugh at your father's genitals? May God change your created form (*khalqak*) and blacken your face!" Immediately, Ḥām's visage turns black. Nūḥ then adds, "may slave women and slave men come from Ḥām's line, until the Day of Judgment." This command is fulfilled when, while Ḥām is having intercourse with his wife, God splits open his gallbladder and that of his spouse, so that the black bile produced in the gland mixes with their *nuṭfas*, resulting in a "black (slave) boy and (slave) girl [*ghulām wa-jāriya aswadayn*]" being born.[41]

36. See David Goldenberg's description of the "etiology of race" story type, in David M. Goldenberg, *The Curse of Ham: Race and Slavery in Early Judaism, Christianity, and Islam* (Princeton, NJ: Princeton University Press, 2003).

37. Aḥmad b. Muḥammad al-Thaʿlabī, *Qiṣaṣ al-Anbiyāʾ: al-Musammā bi-l-Arāʾis al-Majālis*, ed. ʿAbd Allāh b. Asʿad Yāfiʿī (Cairo: Maktabat al-Jumhūriyya al-ʿArabiyya, 1900), 22.

38. Al-Thaʿlabī and Ibn Asʿad Yāfiʿī, 49.

39. Muḥammad b. ʿAbdallah al-Kisāʾī, *Vitae Prophetarum, Auctore Muhammed Ben Abdallah Al-Kisai: Ex Codicibus Qui in Monaco, Bonna, Lugduni-Batavorum, Lipsia et Gothana Asservantur*, ed. Isaac Eisenberg (Leiden: Brill, 1922), 27–32.

40. Gen. 9:21–27.

41. Al-Kisāʾī, *Vitae Prophetarum*, 99–100. The use of the terms *ghulām* (young boy) and *jāriya* (young girl) for enslaved people into adulthood has been remarked

Black bile in the stories of Ḥām and black menstrual discharge in ʿAbd al-Wahhāb's birth narrative in the *sīra* behave in an analogous fashion. Their overproduction or redirection punishes parents, or rather, fathers, for illicit acts by imposing a physical change upon their children. Al-Kisāʾī's writing is not the only instance in which these two fluids are put to similar divine, didactic use: menstrual blood also plays a specific role in dyeing or otherwise affecting other fluid substances in tales of yet other prophets. As has been noted in comparative studies of Jewish and Muslim approaches to menstruation by Eve Krakowski and Haggai Mazuz, Islamic law differentiates between impurifying contact with menstrual blood or the orifice out of which it flows and innocuous contact with the menstruant in general, while Jewish law tends to treat the menstruant herself as able to ritually impurify other people and objects even through chaste touch. In practice, people from these respective religious communities sometimes bridged approaches: Mazuz shows that in Muḥammad's time, Medinans regularly followed or brought questions about Jewish menstrual and purification norms to the Prophet, from seclusion outside the home to handling ritual objects and undoing one's braids before immersion. Rejecting imitation of Jewish practices becomes a recurrent theme of *ḥadīth*s concerning menstruants.[42] Krakowski shows that in Maimonides's (d. 1204) Cairo, some Jewish women ceased to immerse in a mikvah at the end of their cycle, preferring to use bathhouses or drawn water that would be sufficient for Muslim *ghusl*—and for biblical rather than rabbinic laws of purification—and prompting juristic reform.[43]

---

on regularly, and it is likely that the polysemy here is intended. On "juvenilizing" language for the enslaved, see Marmon, "Intersections of gender, sex, and slavery," 202.

42. Haggai Mazuz, "Menstruation and Differentiation: How Muslims Differentiated Themselves from Jews regarding the Laws of Menstruation," *Der Islam* 87, nos. 1–2 (2012): 204–23. Interestingly, some medical literatures recall that pre-Islamic Arabs loathed sex during the menses as a cultural habit rather than due to regional religious influences. The tenth-century Cordovan author ʿArīb ibn Saʿīd claims that pre-Islamic Arabs would call conceiving from menstrual sex a negligent pregnancy (*ḥamalat ʿalā sahw*) or a wasted/squandered pregnancy (the edition reads *tudʿan* but should likely be *taḍyīʿan*, or perhaps *ḍayʿan*)—he writes of such pregnancies occurring but does not mention them ever resulting in Black children. Ibn Saʿīd does, however, mention the concept of atavism, writing, "some say that a woman had a white daughter with a Black man, then the girl wed a white man and gave birth to a Black child." *Kitāb Khalq al-Janīn wa-Tadbīr al-Ḥabālā wa-l-Mawlūdīn*, ed. Nūr al-Dīn ʿAbd al-Qādir (Noureddine Abdelkader) and Henri Jahier (Algiers: Libraire Ferraris, 1956), 10, 28.

43. Eve Krakowski, "Maimonides' Menstrual Reform in Egypt," *Jewish Quarterly Review* 110, no. 2 (2020): 253.

In various prophet stories taken into or elaborated on in Islamic sources, the line between a menstruant's blood and her body, and thus her ritual impurity and others' impurification through nonsexual contact, likewise becomes blurred: direct interaction between a bodily fluid and the material or environment it manipulates need not be made. In his universal history containing much prophetic lore, *al-Kāmil fī-l-Ta'rīkh* (*The Complete History*), Ibn al-Athīr (d. 1233) cites a story in which Ibrāhīm helps a community build a well, but contact with a menstruating woman causes the water to run dry:

> Ibrāhīm left Egypt [with Sāra] for the Levant, out of fear of the Pharaoh, and settled in Sabaʿa in the land of Palestine, and Lūṭ settled in the overturned city [*al-mu'tafik*], which was a day and a night's journey from Sabaʿa. God sent him there as a Prophet, and Ibrāhīm fashioned a well and a place of worship in Sabaʿa, and the well's water was clear and pure, but the people of Sabaʿa abused him, so Ibrāhīm departed from them. The water then ran dry, so they followed him, asking him to return to them, which he did not do, instead giving them seven goats. He said: when you bring them to the water, it will well up until it is clear and pure, so drink from it and do not allow a menstruating woman [*ḥā'iḍ*] to ladle from it. They left with the goats, and when they stopped at the watering hole, the stream reappeared to them. They were drinking from it, but then a menstruating woman [*ṭāmith*] ladled from it, so the water dissipated to the way it is to this day.[44]

Here, it is not contact with menstrual blood itself but rather with a woman who is menstruating that renders the well unusable. The cleanness of the well's liquid, described as clear (*maʿīn*) and pure (*ṭāhir*) is juxtaposed with the ritual impurity of the menstruant (*al-ṭāmith*), generated by the liquid issuing from her womb, with the latter overpowering and cutting off the former. Notably, the term used for the menstruant in question here is not the more generic term, *al-ḥā'iḍ*, but rather one that evokes the deflowering of a virgin or the onset of menarche. In other words, it is a term that may be applied to bleeding for the first time from various causes suggesting sexual maturity, placing the woman on the medical and moral threshold of womanhood in addition to being in a ritually liminal condition. In the above tale, a lack of control over this liminal body affects not only the woman herself, but the entirety of her community, implying

44. Ibn al-Athīr, *al-Kāmil fī-l-Ta'rīkh*, vol. 1 (Beirut: Dār al-Kitāb al-ʿArabī, 1997), 92.

a link between the management of sexually mature women and the maintenance of society as a whole.

In al-Ṭabarī's (d. 923) *Ta'rīkh al-Rusul wa-l-Mulūk* (*History of Prophets and Kings*), in which the above narrative also appears, menstruating women are directly linked with the alteration of a material that is still observable and sacrosanct to this day, namely the Black Stone in the Kaʿba. Here, the perils of not controlling menstruants' behavior again both reflect on society in the abstract and are made concrete by transforming an object that has passed through prophets' hands:

> Al-Ḥārith relayed to me that Ibn Saʿd said, via Ibn Hishām b. Muḥammad, via his father, via Abū Ṣāliḥ, that he heard from ʿAbbās that, "When Adam fell from the Garden, the Black Stone was sent down with him, and it was more intensely white than snow, and Ādam and Ḥawwāʾ cried over what they had lost, meaning the luxury of the Garden, for hundreds of years. And they neither ate nor drank for forty days, then they resumed eating and drinking, and on that day, they were on Mount Būdh, where Ādam had fallen, and he did not draw near Ḥawwāʾ for a hundred years."
>
> Abū Humām said that his father told him via Ziyād b. Khaythuma that he heard from Abī Yaḥya, the fodder seller, that "While we were sitting in the mosque, Mujāhid said to me, 'do you see it?' I said, 'O Abū'l-Ḥajjāj, [you mean] the stone?' He said, 'That's what it's called?' I said, 'Is it not a stone?' He said, 'By God, ʿAbdallāh b. ʿAbbās told me that it was a white gem with which Ādam left the Garden, and which he showered generously with his tears, for Ādam's tears did not cease from the moment he left the Garden until his return two thousand years later, when Iblīs could no longer compel him to anything.' So I said to him, 'O Abū'l-Ḥajjāj, then what blackened it?' He replied, 'Menstruating women would touch it during the *jāhiliyya*.'"[45]

Again, unlike with ʿAbd al-Wahhāb's tale, the effect of menstrual blood is not brought about through direct contact between the affected material and the substance itself. Rather, contact between the sacred stone—sent down from the heavenly Garden with Adam—and impure menstruating women exerts a blackening effect, implicitly due to mixing the sacred with the profane. However unlike in medieval Christian romantic narratives

45. Al-Ṭabarī, *Taʾrīkh al-Rusul wa-l-Mulūk* vol. 1 (Beirut: Dār al-Kutub al-ʿIlmiyya, 1988), 85.

such as the *King of Tars*, in which whitening of the skin readies one for the baptismal font,[46] or yet more proximal, mystical narratives like that of Dhū'l-Nūn al-Miṣrī's (d. 859) eyewitness account of a Black man who spontaneously yet temporarily whitens "whenever he recalls God" (*kullamā dhakar Allāh*), the question of whether reconsecrating the Black Stone to monotheism might cause its color to revert is absent in al-Ṭabarī's historical landscape.[47]

Other *akhbār* sources, or histories based on reportage, do not always include this tradition that freights the women of the *jāhiliyya* with all the blame for the Black Stone's loss of its original coloring. Instead, they claim that the generally sinful conduct of people during the *jāhiliyya* gradually corrupted the stone's nature, a tradition that al-Ṭabarī also features alongside this more extended explanation.[48] And as we saw in the prior chapter, other writers cite the blackness of the Black Stone as a mark of its beauty, not desecration. They place the stone alongside articles like musk and brass or discuss the soul-nourishing effect of touching it alongside the healing properties of other black substances, as if to say that blackness corrects unsound bodies, rather than being caused by them.

Al-Ṭabarī's relayed indictment of women's behavior during the *jāhiliyya* not only furnishes audiences with a pointedly gendered rebuke of paganism but also refers to normative legal precepts about the limitations placed on women's activities during menstruation. Menstruants are permitted to perform every activity during the *ḥajj* pilgrimage except for circumambulating the Kaʿba and, according to some, hastening between the hills of Safa and Marwa. Muḥammad gave ʿĀ'isha permission to do the remaining rites after she began menstruating during the pilgrimage and inquired as to what she should do. Circumambulation (*ṭawāf*) and hastening (*saʿy*) are generally regarded as the most strenuous portions of *ḥajj*, and so reducing women's ritual obligations in this way is in keeping with Q 2:222, in which it is advised that women's menstruation is physically harmful. In al-Ṭabarī's report, we glimpse a complimentary explanation that is exemplary of how popular discourses about menstruation could remain

46. Often, the *King of Tars* tale has been read as one in which the act of baptism whitens the convert, however, Cord J. Whitaker has shown in a recent study that the more compelling reading depicts the Saracen being turned "fair" prior to baptism, and that this mark of God's grace in fact impels his enthusiastic conversion. Whitaker, *Black Metaphors*, 23.

47. Abū Nuʿaym al-Iṣfaḥānī, *Ḥiliyat al-Awliyā' wa-Ṭabaqat al-Aṣfiyā'*, vol. 9 (Beirut: Dār al-Fikr, 1990), 278.

48. Al-Iṣfaḥānī, 278.

entrenched and were often insulated from criticism, if not actively taken up, by the learned. Alleging dire consequences in non-legal scenarios for interacting with menstruants in the deep past shores up the contemporary legal system and the status quo it aims to promote.

Finally, and most closely related to ʿAbd al-Wahhāb's story, is a seemingly minor tradition within the spectrum of tales about the prophet and ruler Sulaymān (Solomon). Sulaymān's status as a judge of course predates the Islamic tradition, but his discernment and rationality became sufficiently noteworthy in Muslim traditions to render him a locus for debates about whether prophets judge using their own reasoning (*ijtihād*) or through divine intercession (*naṣṣ*), and in what ways. Several elaborations on this debate occur across exegeses of the Qurʾānic verse that states, "We gave Sulaymān understanding" (Q 21:79), along with exemplary judgments that Sulaymān subsequently gave. In one widely attested case, one people's flock consumes the vegetation of another people's field, and Sulaymān judges on entitlement to the sheep. Then there is the famous tale of Sulaymān's proposal to divide a baby with two claimants to being his mother. One finds a third judgment linked up with this verse—in which Sulaymān rules that a child's face is literally blackened (*sawwad Allāh wajhahu*) as "punishment" (*ʿuqūba*) for a couple having had menstrual sex—but seemingly only in Sufi exegesis. This tradition appears in commentaries such as Ismāʿīl Ḥaqqī al-Burūsawī's (d. 1725) compendious *Rūḥ al-Bayān*, and across a handful texts relating to the fundamentals of jurisprudence such as Aḥmad b. ʿImād al-Aqfahsī's (d. 1409) *Kashf al-Asrār*, whose contents also assume the diffusion of "Ṣūfī themes and values into mainstream juristic discourse."[49]

As I discuss in chapter 7, many have remarked on the didactic use of blackness in Sufi writings to literally mirror dynamics of moral abjection and introspection or, at times, to suggest that earthly debasement and spiritual exaltedness go hand in hand. Here, though, blackness is straightforwardly instructive as a stain incurred through doing the forbidden. The language in which this is explained unmistakably recalls the terms in which Nūḥ repudiates Ḥām in the above stories, and in which God repudiates nonbelievers at Judgment (Q 3:106) by blackening their faces. For some interpreters, the face becomes a metonym for the body, and a euphemism for shame becomes a physical reality. However, unlike with

49. Marion H. Katz, "The Study of Islamic Ritual and the Meaning of *Wuḍūʾ*," *Der Islam* 82 no. 1 (2005): 124; al-Aqfahsī, *Kashf al-Asrār ʿammā Khafī ʿalā-l-Afkār*, ed. al-Sayyid Yūsuf Aḥmad (Beirut: Dār al-Kutub al-ʿIlmiyya, 2010), 131; al-Burūsawī, *Rūḥ al-Bayān fī Tafsīr al-Qurʾān*, vol. 6 (Beirut: Dār al-Kutub al-ʿIlmiyya, 2003), 382.

Ḥām's gall bladder and more like with *jāhilī* women tainting the Black Stone, blackness is fashioned not by the blood as carrier or colorant, but by social violation itself. That the *sīra*'s depiction of ʿAbd al-Wahhāb's near-identical birth story directs audiences toward Muḥammad's precedent as a judge in a similar case rather than Sulaymān's is perhaps remarkable given how prominently Sulaymān figures in other Arabic epic traditions, such as *Sīrat Sayf b. Dhī Yazan.*[50] And given how frequently the *sīras* otherwise draw on esotericism, it is noteworthy that ʿAbd al-Wahhāb's blackness is not related directly to punitive and moralizing unseen intervention in the text.[51] Instead, his color is tied much more expressly to embodied processes, and variants of his tale suggest that these same processes have the capacity to produce other forms of external markedness and behavioral abnormality. The narrations are concerned with the very substance of difference, while its ultimate meanings are left to unfold with the hero's life.

Speculative Inquiry and Variant Theories of Blackening in the Sīras

Far-ranging myths around menstruants and the perils of mingling with them were shared across a number of Near Eastern cultures, and a tacit permissibility around apocryphal notions that shore up religio-legal

50. Blatherwick, "Solomon Legends."

51. I use the phrase "esotericism" here and throughout to indicate that these strains in the *sīra* corpus, while piously embracing the resonances of the unseen and metaphysical in one's worldly life, are not necessarily Sufi. The Byzantine borderlands in which *ghazwa* was enacted and on which *Sīrat Dhāt al-Himma* dwells were, for example, noteworthy for a shared Christian and Islamic ascetic disposition that Thomas Sizgorich has called "militant devotion." As shown in chapter 7, characters' *taṣawwuf* does not earn emphasis in these stories, but their *zuhd* and *ʿubūdiyya* does, and as Megan H. Reid notes, the titles *zāhid(a)* and *ʿābid(a)*, or ascetic and devotee, continue to be used in bio-bibliographical literature to describe pietists through the Mamluk period—the two occur side-by-side in descriptions of Fāṭima Dhāt al-Himma herself. To be sure, by the time the *sīras* are composed, it may be that much of their account of militant devotion is routed through later Sufi practice. Occasionally the heroes of the *sīras* can be found being referred to as Sufi elders or ascetics and learning under them, though this is seemingly most pronounced in the *Sīrat Banī Hilāl* tradition. On this motif in *Sīrat Banī Hilāl*, see Reynolds, "Abū Zayd al-Hilālī," esp. 91–92; Megan H. Reid, *Law and Piety in Medieval Islam* (Cambridge: Cambridge University Press, 2013), 21–25; Thomas Sizgorich, *Violence and Belief in Late Antiquity: Militant Devotion in Christianity and Islam* (Philadelphia: University of Pennsylvania Press, 2009).

consensus may in part explain their persistence in Islamic contexts. As these myths move and merge, the ramifications of wayward interactions with menstruants appear to multiply and to tie in with discourses not just on material contamination or social contagion as above, but also on racialization, disability, and disease. Across versions of the *sīra*, each of these possibilities arises, and manuscript or print variants of small details in ʿAbd al-Wahhāb's birth story seem to tug, selectively, at the threads that connect the three. But what exactly binds disease, disability, and blackness together, and why are these connections drawn, or else rejected, in a given context?

The oldest dated manuscript of the *Sīrat Dhāt al-Himma* is from 1430–1431. Like many iterations of the text, it is not complete. It begins in medias res and does not contain ʿAbd al-Wahhāb's birth story. I therefore consulted later manuscripts that contained this vignette, which occurs relatively early in the epic. All were produced in the Levant and North Africa between the seventeenth and twentieth centuries. Using nearly thirty different manuscripts of the *sīra*, Claudia Ott established various stemmata for the text, including its linkages with copies of tales from the *1001 Nights* that co-occur in or are modeled in the *sīra*'s prose. My comparison of BnF MS Arabe 3840 and Cambridge MS Qq 247—with the former a composite manuscript of texts brought together around 1820, but with the oldest hands from around 1600, and the latter dated to the early 1800s—looks at two versions that Ott notes have a "probably direct" connection yet finds meaningful differences in how they depict ʿAbd al-Wahhāb's birth. I also look laterally at the same vignette in BnF MS Arabe 3855; though the particular *juzʾ* containing his birth story is undated, one of its prior volumes is dated to 1641.[52]

In working with related or near-contemporary manuscripts of the text that nonetheless have critical differences, I gesture to both scribal technique and to interpretative proliferation even in one stream of tradition. I also use Qq 247 to untangle an idiosyncrasy in the 1909 Cairo printing despite being unable to consult a copy that was more closely connected to it. By pulling in a fascinating outlier—a heavily edited Tunisian printing of

52. Ott also traces direct similarities between the 1909 print version from Cairo that is most widely used in scholarship and was the basis for the likewise widely used 1980 printing in Beirut to a 1727 manuscript now housed in Gotha, but does not identify other texts in the 1909 edition's chain of predecessors. The Gotha manuscript is missing the volume in which ʿAbd al-Wahhāb's birth story would occur. Nonetheless, there are quite clear and often nearly verbatim parallels between the 1909 edition and the manuscripts analyzed in this section. Claudia Ott, *Metamorphosen des Epos*, 101–37.

the text in Judeo-Arabic—I show how the tale of ʿAbd al-Wahhāb's birth also reaches across significant intercommunal boundaries. In all cases, certain consistencies abide in the account of ʿAbd al-Wahhāb's origins. In the final assessment, the incongruously black-skinned hero is ruled to be the legitimate child of parents who committed an illicit sexual act during his mother's menses, though the specific relationship between menstruation, menstrual blood, blackness, and other potential consequences varies.

Reading Jaʿfar al-Ṣādiq's final pronouncement on ʿAbd al-Wahhāb's paternity as it appears in several versions, it is possible to extract a list of socially and physiologically detrimental alleged consequences to menstrual sex, all of which are visited upon one's progeny rather than a member of the couple that commits the act. In BnF 3855, dated to within the same century as the earliest hands in the composite manuscript BnF 3840,[53] menstrual sex is said to result in children that are physically and socially incapacitated in one of a few ways. They may be born Black, "lacking"—which is to say not fully realized or intact—or mentally infirm. Typical or idealized bodies are meanwhile said to be white and handsome (*al-abyaḍ al-wasīm al-karīm*),

> "As for black from white, such a thing is not hard for God, mighty and exalted. Behold—all that exists, he is capable of [bringing into being]. With his creative skill, he fashions the white and black, and no one can make the white black nor the black white save God." He said, "For God, mighty and exalted, is able to say to a thing 'be' [*kun*] and it will be, commanding it between the 'b' and the 'e.'[54] He created ʿIsā son of Maryam without a father. Likewise, if a man has sex with his wife while she is menstruating, the child will be either Black [*aswad*] or deficient [*nāqiṣ*] or mentally ill [*maʿtūh*][55] because of the corruption of the menstrual blood [*li-ajl fasād dam al-ḥayḍ*], for God,

53. Ott identifies BnF 3840 as the progenitor text for a number of other copies made throughout the nineteenth century as well. Ott, *Metamorphosen des Epos*, 112.

54. The Arabic command "be," is "*kun*," and is comprised of two letters (*kāf* and *nūn*), hence this phrase is the equivalent of saying that God commands something to "be" and it comes into existence between uttering the "b" and the "e."

55. "Mentally ill" is an openly anachronistic rendering of this term, which means something more like "imbecilic." As Geert van Gelder has noted, psychological afflictions in the medieval Muslim context lay on a spectrum between madness and stupidity, and even these were not always delineated in the lexicon. Geert Jan van Gelder, "Foul Whisperings: Madness and Poetry in Arabic Literary History," in *Arabic Humanities, Islamic Thought*, ed. Joseph E. Lowry and Shawkat M. Toorawa (Leiden: Brill, 2017): 155–56.

blessed and praised, created souls in their gloriousness from drops of sperm, like trees are made to grow [from seeds], by the graces of the Giver, and He enfolds and conducts this white, handsome, venerable body [originating] from this vile sperm drop in the shadows of the bowels, and He designs it as He wills"[56]

Comparing this version with the printed edition from 1909 in Cairo, we find a large amount of verbatim overlap between the two; what stands out above is the range of ramifications that ʿAbd al-Wahhāb could have experienced instead of becoming Black, but did not. MS Arabe 3840 also raises the possibility that a range of body types and bodily infirmities may be produced through menstrual sex, but in more limited fashion. There, only blackness and deficiency, or being *nāqiṣ*—an ambiguous term that literally means "lacking" or "defective," and here seems to connote an embodied difference—are mentioned. Jaʿfar states:

"I inform you that should a man have intercourse with his wife while she is menstruating, the child will be born either Black or defective [*jā al-walad aswadan amā nāqiṣan*] because of the corruption [*fasād*] of the blood."[57]

Perhaps the prospect of being *maʿtūh* comes into other iterations in order to indicate both physical *and* mental defects might be possible, or else to delineate the meaning of *nāqiṣ* more clearly. Both of these versions divorce the color or quality of his mother's menstrual blood from directly impacting ʿAbd al-Wahhāb's skin color, and instead identify a symbolic commonality between the conceived child's manifold prospective forms and the "corruption" (*fasād*) of menstrual issue. Other editions of the *sīra*, though—including the print version used throughout this book—instead relate the colors of menstrual blood to a range of possible complexions through a syllogism.

In keeping with the view of most Islamic medical and legal scholars that the color of menstrual issue is not uniform throughout the course of one's menses, some versions of the *sīra* propose that children conceived at different points in a woman's cycle would be colored in different ways. As discussed previously, in the 1909 Cairo printing, the stages and colors of the menses are mapped onto time and regularity (that is, whether one

56. Bibliothèque Nationale de France, MS Arabe 3855, fol. 173v.
57. Bibliothèque Nationale de France, MS Arabe 3840, fol. 379v.

is experiencing metrorrhagia or not) and correlate with the color of a menstruant's child:

> "[Muḥammad] said of the man that if he had intercourse with his wife while the blood was black and stopped-up at the beginning portion of the menses, this [would cause] the boy to become red-brown [*aḥmar*] in color, while if he had intercourse with her at the end of the menses, when the blood is pure, the child comes to resemble his father. . . . You, O Ḥārith, had sex with your wife while there clung to her whatever adheres to women from the menses—and during metrorrhagia [*istiḥāda*], a woman's blood is red, and the menses is black and the sperm droplet is white and a woman's blood is dark-colored [*aghbar*]. The red and white and black and dark-colored [materials] mixed together and the Creator created and arranged [ʿAbd al-Wahhāb]."

A similar phrasing appears in a Tunisian Judeo-Arabic version of the *sīra*, printed in the 1890s. Rather than Jaʿfar explaining this reasoning, though, the narrator of the text articulates it as an instructive aside in which he states that concealed sins never remain so due to markings like ʿAbd al-Wahhāb's telltale physical difference. Unlike with the 1909 Cairo version, which expounds lengthily on the exact way in which reproductive materials combine to bring about a color change in the embryo, the Judeo-Arabic version simply pronounces that Black children resulting from menstrual sex is a prospect "of which there is no doubt," indicating that perhaps over time or among certain populations this myth became more stable, canonical, and commonplace:

> There is a truthful saying that if a man has sexual intercourse with a woman and at that time her menses is at its height, while [the blood] is pouring forth and [its level] is elevated, it is determined that the newborn will come out black [*yaḥtaqq al-mulūd yajī akḥal*], and if it is at the final stage of the menses, then the little one will come out dark-colored [*asmar*]. This is something in which there is no doubt [*hādhā shayʾ mā fī shakk*], and through this nothing can stay hidden in plain sight [*kullihi bāsh mā yuqaʿdshī qubir fī ẓahr*].[58]

This narration parallels the 1909 Cairo edition in assigning different shades of skin tone to the child depending on the stage of the menses

58. Eliezer Farḥī and Ḥai Sitruk, eds., *Sīrat al-Dalhama* (Tunis: Farhi and Sitruk, 1890), 382.

during which conception occurs. The sureness with which the relationship between menstrual sex and a child's transfiguration is asserted here may also depend, to some extent, on the context of the Judeo-Arabic version's audience. They may have been familiar with both Jewish and Muslim views on menstruants, and perhaps even the relationship between the two.

Haggai Mazuz observes that as long as notions inherited from the pre-Islamic period or from adjacent cultures did not conflict with the precepts of Islamic law, there was seemingly no serious opposition to them among the scholarly class. In his words, "on one hand the Muslim sages rejected the Rabbinic Jewish laws of menstruation, and on the other hand they still adopted the Jewish Aggada on the subject," with the rejected law being Jewish stipulations that wives must withdraw from husbands during menstruation not only with respect to sexual relations, but also to sharing food and a bed. Aggadot (rabbinic narratives) that anecdotally depict perilous yet implausible consequences to violating purity laws were nonetheless absorbed into popular Muslim discourses.[59] As discussed below, rabbinic literature portends dire physical consequences for sexual intercourse during menstruation.[60] For an audience for whom the wisdom dispensed in these lines of the *sīra* would echo with other sources of communal norms and theological truths, it may have been uncontroversial to declare that there was "no doubt" in the text's specious medical assertions.

Cambridge MS Qq 247 most closely approximates the text of the 1909 Cairo version in the thoroughness and particularities of how it explains ʿAbd al-Wahhāb's blackness. An overt differentiation between menstruation and metrorrhagia is made on the basis of timing and color,

> "Know, o prominent Arabs and people of rank and esteem, that this is like a case brought before my ancestor, the Messenger of God—peace and blessings upon him—he was presented with a child like this one, a Black child whose father and mother were both white. So, my ancestor judged that he was their child because of the accordance with [the time of] women's menstruation. He stated that if a man has intercourse with

59. Haggai Mazuz, "Midrashic Influence on Islamic Folklore: The Case of Menstruation," *Studia Islamica* 108 (2013): 201.

60. The literature produced by the Christian clergy in Late Antiquity shares these beliefs as well, as with the church father Jerome, who claims that fetuses conceived during menstruation will be deformed due to the corrupting effects of the menstrual blood—a sentiment that is reproduced nearly word for word in the *sīra*. On this, see Sharon Faye Koren, "The Menstruant as 'Other' in Medieval Judaism and Christianity," *Nashim: A Journal of Jewish Women's Studies and Gender Issues* 17 (2009): 33–59.

> his wife and the blood is black and flowing profusely at the beginning of the menstrual period, the child will come out a deep black [*ʿamīq al-sawād*], and if he has sex with her at the end of the menses (*ʿind intihā al-ḥayḍ*), at which time the blood is unmixed and the womb is clean [*wa-ṣafā al-dam wa-naḍāfat* (*sic*) *al-raḥim*], the child will emerge looking like his father [*shabīh abīhi*]. This was the judgment of my ancestor, and you, o Ḥārith, had sex with your wife while she was menstruating and there clung to her that which clings to women from her menses, and the blood of metrorrhagia is red and that of the menses is black and the sperm drop is white and the woman's blood is dark, so the black and red and white and dark color mixed and created this creation and design[ed it]."[61]

This version of the *sīra* could also be used to interrogate an ambiguity in the 1909 Cairo edition, namely the question of what is meant by *ṣafāʾ* (purity, but also delight or pleasure) in relation to the condition of one's blood. In the preceding chapter, the most obvious reading of the Cairo edition's description of the end of the menses is as the bleeding's final stage rather than the time after which it has elapsed. I therefore speculated that *ṣafāʾ* could, through a double entendre, indicate both the off-limits pleasure that comes from menstrual sex and the comparative purity or intensity of the blood's color. Black blood is likened in various sources to a mixture or suspension, like ink sediment. Thus, *ṣafāʾ* might characterize the thoroughness or consistency of this mixture.[62]

In the above passage, though, "end" more clearly indicates the time at which the menses has finished and the womb reverts back to its typical state: filled with blood, but not contaminated by the fact that menstrual issue is exiting the body and rendering it ritually impure. Rather, the womb is described as being "clean." During the menses, the line between inside and outside is being actively transgressed as the uterine lining sloughs off, making it impossible to discern "clean" portions of the womb from "unclean" ones; the child accordingly is said to become Black during the peak of a woman's flow. In this manuscript, as in Islamic discourses more broadly, the blood in a ritually pure womb exerts no ill effect, and, if anything, it makes space for the salutary consequences of normative conception with a healthy male *nutfa* by helping to ensure the child will resemble his father. Meanwhile, how ʿAbd al-Wahhāb becomes both black-skinned and similar to his father in the 1909 Cairo edition remains ambiguous.

61. Cambridge MS Qq 247, folios not numbered.

62. Haggai Mazuz, "Islamic and Jewish Law on the Colors of Menstrual Blood," *Zeitschrift der Deutschen Morgenländischen Gesellschaft* 164 (2014): 100.

Taken together, the variant renderings of ʿAbd al-Wahhāb's birth narrative supply the following consequences for menstrual sex: one's children may be red-brown or Black, depending on the stage of the menses; they may be physically impaired or flawed; or they may be mentally ill. Evoking such outcomes in popular literature is a scare tactic that militates against nonnormative and religio-culturally prohibited sexual practices. But possibilities as to why these specific consequences became the devices for policing ritual and sexual boundaries across a variety of popular texts and prophets' stories is to be found in works that circulated beyond and long before the *sīra*'s immediate context.

Connecting the Dots: From Isrāʾīliyyāt *to* Sīras, *from Leprosy to Blackness*

In his indispensable work on the representation of Black people in medieval Arabic literature, *Tamthīlāt al-Ākhar: Ṣūrat al-Sūd fī-l-Mutakhayyal al-ʿArabī al-Wasīṭ* ("Representations of The Other: The Depiction of Blacks in the Medieval Arab Imaginary"), Nādir Kāẓim regards the choice of ascribing ʿAbd al-Wahhāb's blackness to menstruation as a clever maneuver on the part of the *sīra* composers.[63] Through it, the narrators combine a few disparate myths and notions about menstruation and racial difference in such a way as to simultaneously explain ʿAbd al-Wahhāb's nonhereditary blackness, indict al-Ḥārith for his rape of Fāṭima, and suit the sensibility of an urbane literary audience that is used to seeing human difference but, perhaps, is unacquainted with its prevalent explanations through analogies to animal husbandry in early Islamic works. To this last point, Kāẓim notes that one of the only *ḥadīth*s that explicates how one can be born Black to white parents does so through the metaphor of camel-breeding, in which offspring differing in color from their parents is a common enough occurrence:

> A man from the Banū Fazāra approached the Prophet, peace and blessings upon him, and said, "My wife gave birth to a Black boy," so the Prophet, peace and blessings upon him, said, "Do you have camels?" [The man]

63. Nādir Kāẓim, *Tamthīlāt al-Ākhar: Ṣūrat al-Sūd fī-l-Mutakhayyal al-ʿArabī al-Wasīṭ* (Beirut: al-Muʾassasa al-ʿArabiyya li-l-Dirāsāt wa-l-Nashr, 2007), 343–44. Happily, this book has recently been translated into English by Amir al-Azraki. All translations here are my own and were done prior, though I am grateful to have been able to consult al-Azraki's renderings! Nader Kadhem, *Africanism: Blacks in the Medieval Arab Imaginary*, trans. Amir al-Azraki (Montreal: McGill-Queen's University Press, 2023).

replied, "Yes." [The Prophet] said, "And what are their colors?" He said, "Red." [Muḥammad] replied, "Are there ash-colored ones?" He said, "Sure, there are ash-colored ones among them." [Muḥammad] said, "So how did that come about?" [The man] said, "It's possible that it's an interruption of the breed [*laʿallahu nazaʿahu ʿirq*]." [Muḥammad] replied, "And this could be an interruption [of the child's origins]."[64]

In this dialogue, Muḥammad helps a man confounded by his newborn son's appearance to reason through an explanation based on his lived experience, rather than offering the simple aforementioned pronouncement of *al-walad li-l-firāsh*, or "the child is for the marriage bed," which is used elsewhere to resolve cases of contested legitimacy. This is perhaps because here the aim of Muḥammad's rhetoric is not to scuttle an accusation of adultery, but rather to dispel the family's perplexity over a seemingly irrational or impossible result.

As to why this *hadith* was not simply quoted to explain ʿAbd al-Wahhāb's case, but nonetheless is a probable intertext, Kāẓim offers:

> As we mentioned a bit earlier, it is known that the Messenger of God (peace and blessings upon him) interpreted the birth of a Black child to a white mother and father as a kind of "reversion of origin" [*nazʿ al-ʿirq*] as happens among camels, and when the shocked parents heard this explanation they understood it, for they were Bedouin Arabs and camel owners. The society of the *sīra*, though, seems to be a settled, urbanized society that does not live with camels or have experience with them, and for this reason the choice of the Messenger of God's interpretation would not be understood among them, nor would it be persuasive for them.[65]

He adds, moreover, that the ascription of a child's maladies to having been conceived during his or her mother's menses is a feature of Islamic—and particularly Shīʿī—legal discourse, per the maligned image of the *ibn ḥayḍa* that was previously discussed. However, many such cases describe the child as fated to be leprous (*majdhūm*), a condition that often turns the skin white rather than black. Perhaps through a clever decision (*ikhtiyār dhakī*), the *sīra* authors have married these two concepts—having sex with a menstruant can alter the condition of the child's skin, and a child can naturally

64. Ibn Ḥajar and al-Bukhārī, "Bāb idhā ʿaraḍ bi-nafī al-walad," in *Fatḥ al-Bārī Sharḥ Ṣaḥīḥ al-Bukhārī* (al-Maktaba al-Islāmiyya, 1996), https://www.islamweb.net/ar/library/content/52/9693.

65. Kāẓim, *Tamthīlāt al-Ākhar*, 346.

be born a wholly different, darker color than its parents—to contrive a resolution for ʿAbd al-Wahhāb's tale that can plausibly be linked to both the Prophet and to a prominent Shīʿī thinker in the form of Jaʿfar al-Ṣādiq.[66]

While Kāẓim has found a plurality of important elements that could all play a constitutive role in ʿAbd al-Wahhāb's story, in investing the *sīra*'s composers with sole creative control, we perhaps overlook other, more culturally ambient influences on the association between blackness, sickness, and menstruation. We need not think of blackness and leprosy as being unrelated or opposite conditions; rather, the two are intimately connected for Muslim thinkers and their forerunners in several ways.

The notion that menstrual blood can cause darkening, disease, and putrefaction is an ancient one. In his *Natural History*, Pliny the Elder details the effects of menstruation on a woman's surrounding environment: storms can be kept at bay, the color of linens is altered even by the ash of the blood, metals corrode, crops are contaminated, vermin flee, and contact with a menstruant can cause men fatal diseases and make other women miscarry.[67] As with Ibn al-Athīr's menstruant at the well, one need not even make physical contact with the blood itself to experience many of the menstruant's polluting effects, but may scent it in the air.

Ancient Iranian culture ascribes menstruation to a curse inherited from the activity of daevas, supernatural beings that unleash disorder into nature: according to the *Bundahišn*, a Zoroastrian collection of creation stories, the first menses occurs when his lover, Jeh, tries to rouse the demon ruler Ahriman from a coma-like state by offering to do all sorts of polluting deeds on his behalf, saying she will "vex the water, . . . vex the plants, . . . vex the fire of Ohrmazd, [and will] make the whole creation of Ohrmazd vexed."[68] Ahriman awakens, kisses Jeh on her forehead as a reward, and she starts to bleed from her vagina.[69] The Zoroastrian *Dēnkard* carries Jeh's sinister promises forward, saying that menstruating women still make

66. Kāẓim, 344.

67. Pliny the Elder, *Natural History*, trans. A. C. Andrews, D. E. Eichholz, W. H. S. Jones, and H. Rackham, Loeb Classical Library (Cambridge, MA: Harvard University Press, 2014), 56–61.

68. *The Bundahishn ("Creation") or Knowledge from the Zand*, trans. Edward William West (Oxford: Oxford University Press, 1897 [digitized 1997 by Joseph H. Peterson]), 5.

69. A mythos about cursed deities explains menstruation's origins in ancient Indian culture as well. The *Dharmashastras*, a collection of Sanskrit legal maxims, caution men not to take food from women during their menses because it has sinful pollutants latent in it, dating from women's primordial covenant to share the guilt of the god Indra after he had killed another deity; a menstruant sitting in a high-caste household

food lose its taste, poison water, and cause mental infirmities and loss of memory in their interlocutors. Shai Secunda asserts that this Zoroastrian association of menstruation with the demonic and demon-possession is also reflected in the Babylonian Talmud's extremely negative views on menstruants, which stand apart from the Hebrew Bible and Jerusalem Talmud's stances on purity law.[70] It is also likely via this connection that menstrual sex becomes associated explicitly with the potential for fatality or affliction of sexual partners and offspring, with the infliction of leprosy (*tsaraʿat*) upon one's offspring first attested in midrashic literature such as Leviticus *rabbah*, composed around 500–600 CE.

Many rabbinic understandings of leprosy's effects mirror those caused by menstrual blood in the sources above—water and food is contaminated and should not be shared with the unaffected, the leprous body emits an offensive stench, and people are cautioned to withdraw physically from the afflicted in either case and take extreme measures to quarantine him or her.[71] The man who has sex with his wife while she is menstruating is made to have a child whose daily life is a constant reminder of the taboo conditions in which his father took a moment's pleasure. The metaphor of leprosy being applied to toxifying femininity also appears elsewhere in rabbinic literature, deepening the link between a woman's excesses and the affliction of men and their households. In tractate *Sanhedrin*, evil wives are compared to leprosy that is alleviated by divorce.[72]

Connections between menstrual sex and leprosy persist in Islamic exegetical and prophetic literature: a number of *ḥadīth*s attest that should a man copulate with his wife and conceive a child, "[the child] will be afflicted with leprosy [*judhām*], and he'll certainly have no one to blame but himself [*fa-lā yalūmann illā nafsahu*]," in keeping with the view of man as

downgrades the house's caste status temporarily. Janet Chawla, "Mythic Origins of Menstrual Taboo in Rig Veda," *Economic and Political Weekly* 29 (1994): 2819.

70. Shai Secunda, "The Fractious Eye: On the Evil Eye of Menstruants in Zoroastrian Tradition," *Numen* 61 (2014): 88.

71. On the connection between illness and menstruation in the Babylonian Talmud and the medical implications of menstruation in ancient Persian culture writ large, see Shai Secunda, "The Construction, Composition, and Idealization of the Female Body in Rabbinic Literature and Parallel Iranian Texts: Three Excursuses," *Nashim: A Journal of Jewish Women's Studies and Gender Issues* 23 (2012): 60–86. On the punishment of leprosy for intercourse with a menstruant, see Mazuz, "Midrashic Influence on Islamic Folklore," 197–99. Cf. BT *Peṣahim* 111a; Leviticus *rabbah* 15:5; Midrash Tanḥūmā, Leviticus, Meṣōraʿ 39:22b, etc.

72. Sanhedrin 100a, quoted in: Joseph Zias, "Lust and Leprosy: Confusion or Correlation?" *Bulletin of the American Schools of Oriental Research* 275 (1989): 30.

the fundamental initiator accountable for sexual action.[73] Other traditions stipulate in particular against men having sex with women after their periods have ended but before they've performed the major ablution (*ghusl*) in order to avoid afflicting a child.[74] In much the way that menstruation "vexes the water" in antiquity, so too does it implicitly vex the "disdained water" (*māʾ mahīn*) of the *nuṭfa* during conception.

Though these ideas appear in collections of *ḥadīths*, they are largely absent from legal literature on menstruation; their appropriation into popular literature implies that they may have held particular sway in a genre that often is lukewarm in its views on the juristic class. After all, the principal villain in *Sīrat Dhāt al-Himma* is a Muslim judge, or *qāḍī*, who has secretly become a Christian spy but is nonetheless able to use his prodigious traditionist learning to convince even the caliphs of his piety. Traditions forecasting extremes of contamination through menstrual blood were in fact in tension with legal precepts such as that which appears in the epigraph from al-Shāfiʿī's (d. 820) *Kitāb al-Umm*, which casts contact with menstrual blood as no more or less sullying than contact with any other out-of-body blood.[75] Nonetheless, they support the overarching legal aim of minimizing sexual contact with menstruants. Their particular use in the *sīras* at once builds on and complicates Mazuz's assertion that preexistent, widespread myths about menstruation became felicitous tools for "Muslim sages," who resituated them within the *qiṣaṣ al-anbiyāʾ* genre. Indeed, the specific trajectories of these myths speak to competition between different social groups that circulated unorthodox knowledge in materials that some viewed as impinging on traditional interpretative authority. By the Mamluk era, these tensions periodically resulted in attempted legal crackdowns on the sale and recitation of the *sīras* entirely.[76]

And yet, in the case of apprehensions about menstrual sex, popular understandings ultimately shored up legalistic aims, and there was no apparent effort by the *ʿulamāʾ* to stymie them even if they were not incorporated into formal discourse. The catastrophic depiction of the consequences of menstrual sex that the *sīras* and prophetological literature contain may

73. Al-Munāwī, "*Bāb ḥarf al-mīm*," 9078. Kecia Ali has analyzed the normative role of the male partner as sexual initiator in Islamic law in depth in her hallmark study on sexual ethics, particularly with respect to menstrual sex. Kecia Ali, *Sexual Ethics and Islam: Feminist Reflections on Qurʾan, Hadith, and Jurisprudence* (London: Oneworld, 2015), 163–65.

74. Abū Ḥamīd al-Ghazālī, *Iḥyāʾ ʿUlūm al-Dīn*, vol. 2 (Jakarta: Maktaba wa-Maṭbaʿa Kiryāṭa Fūtrā, 1957), 56.

75. Al-Shafīʿī, "Bāb dam al-ḥayḍ," 70.

76. Hirschler, *The Written Word*, 169.

even have had more day-to-day force than legal deterrents. The punishment by law for men who were caught copulating with their wives during their menses—already a dim possibility—was typically a fairly minor, penitential fine amounting to between a half dinar and a dinar depending on whether her blood was "fresh" or "yellowed," with sex at the height of the menses more reprehensible than sex during its wane.[77]

The Arabic term typically used for leprosy in the comparatively potent admonitions one finds outside the juristic context is *judhām*, or elephantiasis, the most visible symptom of which is the exaggerated swelling of the limbs. One who is afflicted is either *majdhūm*, *ajdham*, or sometimes *mujadhdham*. There are a few ways in which the condition of being *majdhūm* could have come to be associated with blackness. Prevalent understandings of humoral pathology during the medieval period ascribed leprosy to the spread of black bile throughout the body;[78] it is the overproduction or loosing of the same substance upon the other internal organs that was instrumental to the creation of the original Black bodies in al-Kisāʾī's etiology of human kinds. That is, uncontrolled black bile could result in either leprosy or epidermal blackness, and so the two may have come to be popularly regarded as related conditions.

Leprosy could also simply appear black in specific instances, and blackness leprous. Despite Kāẓim's point that leprosy is commonly associated with hypopigmentation, medieval Arabic medical literature accommodated a wide range of leprosy-like diseases, some of which caused blackening or darkening. In Al-Jāḥiẓ's treatise *Kitāb al-Burṣān wa-l-ʿUrjān* ("Book of the Lesioned and the Limping"), *baraṣ*, which typically is defined as a form of leprosy resulting in white, scaly skin, instead is rendered an umbrella category for dermatological ailments resulting in changes to skin pigmentation. An example of this is *barash*, a form of discoloration that tends to raise black spots on the fingernails, as well as black patches on the skin of the armpits or the genitals (*wa-l-sawād yaʿtarī al-nās kathīra fī mawāḍiʿ min julūdihim yaʿtarī al-ḥaṣā wa-l-madhākīr wa-rubbamā iʿtarā julūd al-ābāṭ wa-jild al-ʿijān*), and can cause black tufts of hair to grow on the head.[79] Likewise, Ibn Sīnā cites a type of *judhām* in his *Qānūn fī-l-Ṭibb* that manifests in dark ulcerations, engorged lips, and blackening of the skin. He

77. Kāẓim, *Tamthilat al-Akhar*, 344; al-Thaʿlabī, *Tafsir al-Thaʿlabī*, ed. Majdī Bāslūm (Beirut: Dār al-Kutub al-ʿIlmiyya, 2004), 346.

78. Timothy S. Miller and John W. Nesbitt, *Walking Corpses: Leprosy in Byzantium and the Medieval West* (Ithaca, NY: Cornell University Press, 2014), 65–67.

79. Al-Jāḥiẓ, *Kitāb al-Burṣān wa-l-ʿUrjān wa-l-ʿUmyān wa-l-Ḥūlān* (Baghdad: Dār al-Rashīd li-l-Nashr, 1982), 70.

also classifies conditions such as hyperpigmentation and vitiligo—literally referred to as "black patching," or *bahaq aswad*—alongside leprosy.[80]

More plausible still is that insofar as it was sometimes considered a deformity or blight (*ʿāha*),[81] blackness was lumped together with a range of other bodily defects related to physical health. Slavery sometimes was, too, for both legitimate and illegitimate reasons, as I explain below. The experiences presaged for ʿAbd al-Wahhāb's character as a result of his color mirror those typical to social practices around the leprous, much as with metaphoric alignments between seclusion, leprosy, and menstruation in rabbinic writings. Lepers in the Arab-Muslim world were often pitied, shunned, and outcast, though at much less extreme levels than in Western Europe. Concomitantly, the figure of the leper looms less singularly large in medieval Arabic literature than its Latinate counterparts. Instead, a diverse range of disabilities and sicknesses are prominent, which perhaps imparts a degree of literary interchangeability and abstraction. The use of illness and disability as a metaphor for one's social or cosmological position is common in Arabic works. Indeed, al-Jāḥiẓ militates against associating blackness with illness, as well as with ideas of divine disfavor arising from stories of Ḥām, in his defense of a strictly climate-based model of human difference in *Fakhr al-Sūdān ʿalā-l-Bīḍān*: "[Color] is not the result of a distortion [*maskh*] or a punishment [*ʿuqūba*], or a disfigurement [*tashwīh*] or defect [*taqṣīr*]."[82] Because leprosy's most visible symptom was typically its effects on the skin, this may have engendered slippages between nonnormative skin colors that were racialized in ways that curtailed one's social life and skin-altering conditions perceived as congenital that did the same. And like the intergenerational suppression and resurgence of skin color in Aristotle's discourse on atavism, leprosy was sometimes thought to be carried, inertly and invisibly, by women and come to light only through sexual relations whose acceptability was predicated on factors such as her and her partner's raced, classed, religious, and reputational standing.[83]

80. Ahmed Al Sharif, "Judham, Baras, Wadah, Bahaq and Quwaba': A Study of Term and Concepts in 'Al Qanun Fit Tib' of Ibn-Sina," *JISHIM* 5, no. 10 (2006): 32; Ibn Sīnā, *al-Qānūn fī-l-Ṭibb*, vol. 3, ed. Muḥammad al-Dīn al-Ḍannāwī (Beirut: Dār al-Kutub al-ʿIlmiyya, 2009), 361.

81. Kristina Richardson, *Difference and Disability*, 6; 36; 112.

82. Al-Jāḥiẓ, *Rasāʾil*, 220.

83. Fears of leprosy latent in women obtained not only in Near Eastern representations of leprosy's spontaneous activation due to female impurity, but also in those affected by accusations of leprosy in the Latin West. David Nirenberg raises the case in fourteenth-century Aragon of a woman being accused of leprosy, which he relates

In Arabic, the ambivalences between leprosy and related physical and social conditions operates at the level of language as well as of metaphor, particularly in the legal corpus. Similar to the English usage of "leper," outside of the purview of medicine, the designation of being leprous, or *ajdham*, works both as a medically discreet and socially relational category. This is especially vivid in discussions of sexual transaction. Leprosy coincides with a number of conditions that all rendered an individual more socially dependent, less freely marriageable, and so on. A tradition narrated by Ibn ʿAbbās describing blemishes that devalue a woman indicates a range of leprosy-like or leprosy-adjacent symptoms:

> Four [types of women] are fit neither for sale nor marriage: the crazed woman [*al-majnūna*], the elephantiasis-afflicted woman [*al-majdhūma*], the leprous woman [*al-barṣāʾ*], and the woman with a pudendal hernia [*al-ʿaflāʾ*]. All of these women are [referred to as] mutilated [*wa-l-jamʿ min dhālik jadhmā*], as with [the terms] mentally deficient and foolish [*mithl ḥamqā wa-nawkā*].[84]

Jadhmā being used to collectively characterize the women suffering this range of afflictions—many of which relate also to fertility or sexual availability—recalls another meaning of *ajdham*, "amputated," that is, someone who is missing a normatively integral part of themselves. Such missing parts, if discovered after marriage or sale, could be used in suits to contest for annulment or reimbursement. It does not seem coincidental that, though leprosy itself is not mentioned at all in the explanations of ʿAbd al-Wahhāb's coloring, terms that echo those in this list relating to mental and physical lack are invoked.

A yet more overt link between the legal status of Black people and those afflicted with the above infirmities is formed in a ruling that is effectively a gender-reversed peer to Ibn ʿAbbās's statement, attributed to the famed Tunisian jurist Saḥnūn, which states, "If a man wishes to wed his daughter to a madman, one with elephantiasis, a leper, a Black man [*aswad*], or one inadequate to [her station] [*man laysa li-hā bi-kafʾ*] and the daughter refuses, the ruler should prevent him on grounds of

---

to other, less verifiable accusations of "infamy, such as adultery, usury, or concealing a treasure trove," all of which in turn have classed implications in their ability to ruin an individual's reputation and their precipitation of the legal seizure of property or restitutive measures. David Nirenberg, *Communities of Violence: Persecution of Minorities in the Middle Ages* (Princeton, NJ: Princeton University Press, 1996), 106.

84. Ibn al-Manẓūr, *Lisān al-ʿArab*, 579.

harm [*ḍarar*]."[85] Such rulings also are in keeping with the general practice in Islamic marriage law of insulating partners from harm by cultivating matches that are equal in certain socially important ways, such as freedom/unfreedom, health, piety, and prominence of *nasab*.[86] These considerations were grouped as part of discerning *kafāʾa*, or spousal sufficiency, which Saḥnūn references directly.

Similar rulings preventing harm to free women through marriage choice interchange "Black" and "slave," despite the latter's far clearer implications for marital unfitness, possibly indicating milieus in which *black* had already come to essentially indicate enslaved status or ancestry. Of a near-identical ruling to Saḥnūn's attributed to al-Shāfiʿī that uses the term *slave* (*ʿabd*) rather than *black man*, al-Māwardī explains, "A man may not wed his daughter to a slave, or one with an indenture contract (*mukātaba*), or one to be manumitted on his owner's death (*mudabbar*), or anyone with any portion of obligations of enslavement [*riqq*]," for all of these conditions are lesser (*naqṣ*) than the free status of his potential spouse.[87] Here, ideas of social insufficiency merge with those of physiology in a yet different arrangement, with blackness becoming synonymous with enslavement that is in turn synonymous with lack. There were, to be sure, scenarios in which the interrelation of slavery and leprosy took on much more tangible form; as a source of "connectivity" between regions and persons through the intimacies of "sexual as well as labour exploitation" throughout the medieval world, the traffic in enslaved people may have contributed to the dispersal of leprosy across Indian Ocean routes.[88]

Less tangibly, there are many ambient similarities between the treatment of *majdhūm* people and other marginal members of medieval Arab-Muslim society in the day-to-day, outside of marital situations. Though some narrations from the Prophet Muḥammad contravene received images of leprosy's transmissibility and advocate treating lepers with closeness and charity, several others advise bodily comportment around one

85. Al-Tasūlī, *al-Bahja fī Sharḥ al-Tahfa*, ed. Muḥammad ʿAbd al-Qadr Shāhīn (Beirut: Dār al-Kutub al-ʿIlmiyya, 1998), 411.

86. On the importance of *nasab* to the expectation of marriages that were mutually suitable to the partners' social stations (*kafāʾa*), see Marlow, "Ḥasab o Nasab." On the role of gendered injury or harm (*ḍarar*) in rulings on marriage and divorce, see Ali, *Sexual Ethics and Islam*, 27.

87. Al-Māwardī, *Kitāb al-Ḥawī al-Kabīr*, vol. 9 (Beirut: Dār al-Kutub al-ʿIlmiyya, 1994), 135.

88. Monica H. Green and Lori Jones, "The Evolution and Spread of Major Human Diseases in the Indian Ocean World," in *Disease Dispersion and Impact in the Indian Ocean World*, ed. Gwyn Campbell and Eva-Maria Knoll (London: Palgrave, 2020), 38.

who is *majdhūm* that suggests *judhām* was understood to be fairly contagious or to warrant avoidance on some other grounds. One finds sayings like "run from a *majdhūm* person as you would from a lion," or "speak with a *majdhūm* person with a spear's length or two between you."[89] Lepers were given protected status across most legal schools (*madhāhib*) that reflected the dependency and social inferiority their condition produced. The company that lepers keep within the legal structure is perhaps remarkable when contemplating the potential for slippage between lepers and other marginal figures,

> Leprosy is not discussed in the Arabic legal texts as a separate subject; rather, it is treated as a disability within such broad areas as marriage, divorce, inheritance, guardianship, and interdiction of one's legal capacity [*ḥajr*]. Because leprosy is considered a mortal illness, the leper is limited in his legal rights and obligations—*along with the minor, the bankrupt, the insane, and the slave.*[90]

Even as they are legally protected, leprosy and blackness-qua-slavery or slavery-qua-blackness (the conflation of which could occur at the level of legally effectual citations as well as popular prose, as indicated by the disparity between the pronouncements attributed to Saḥnūn and al-Shāfiʿī) are popularly regarded as recompense for immoral conduct, with slave populations in the Muslim world being so because they were historically non-Muslim. Both constitute imprecations invoked against bad actors.[91] According to Michael Dols, though the Qurʾān states that there is no crime in being blind, lame, or sick, this did not stop some from calling down

89. Ibn Ḥajar and al-Bukhārī, "Bāb Ālamna Shifāʾ li-l-ʿAyn," in *Fatḥ al-Bārī Sharḥ Ṣaḥīḥ al-Bukhārī* (al-Maktaba al-Islāmiyya, 1996), http://library.islamweb.net/newlibrary/display_book.php?flag=1&bk_no=52&ID=10434.

90. Emphasis my own. Michael Dols, "The Leper in Medieval Islamic Society," *Speculum* 58, no. 4 (1983): 897. See also Matthew L. Long, "Leprosy in Early Islam," in *Disability in Judaism, Christianity, and Islam*, ed. Darla Schumm and Michael Stoltzfus (New York: Palgrave Macmillan, 2011), 43–61.

91. In fourteenth-century Iberia, such an imprecation was treated with grave seriousness. David Nirenberg writes, "The word 'leper,' like 'sodomite,' 'whore,' 'traitor,' or 'Saracen' (to a non-Muslim), represented an insult actionable as slander when used against 'respectable' people. Accusations of leprosy, like those of infamy, seem to have been used by communities to expel people perceived as troublemakers." He adds that this features in both Christian and Muslim legal codes of the time. See Nirenberg, *Communities of Violence*, 105. See also Dols, "The Leper in Medieval Islamic Society," 902.

leprosy on their peers in a disciplinary manner that echoes Nūḥ's curse of blackness upon his son.[92]

The parallels between leprosy and blackness as supposed punishments for a violation of norms are especially visible in the case of their being purported consequences of menstrual sex and deterrents against violating ritual purity. With the sustained demand for a salient countermeasure against menstrual sex, the list of menstrual sex's ill effects may have moved from the specificity of a single form of illness or battery of illnesses into the combined and compounding set of plights attested in the *sīra*'s variant editions. Their ranging from physical to mental to structural ills reflects not only on a milieu that placed the enslaved person (who, in popular literary depictions, is most often Black) on similar footing with the otherwise socially dependent, but on a comparative idiom—common to so many social hierarchies—that associates the raced-as-other individual with the deficient, dependent, and liminal.

Conclusion

In the Arabic epic traditions' popular science of difference, associative reasoning is in full force. It therefore seems a smaller leap to blackness amid the web of comparative alterities that ties leprosy in with other forms of biological-cum-social marginality than the leap of a unilateral, calculated reversal on the part of the *sīra* author. As with its inclusion amid lists of blights in the medieval Arabic-speaking world, blackness seems to have likewise been tacked onto a broad array of socially alienating and physically stigmatizing conditions in the case of those versions of the *sīra* that list possible maladies afflicting progeny conceived during menstruation.

The syllogistic versions of ʿAbd al-Wahhāb's birth story in particular go to great lengths to tease out a physical connection between black menstrual blood and racialized blackness, which suggests an interest on the part of the text in upholding some measure of biological plausibility. Yet the precedents for this connection are themselves largely found in homiletic prophet stories rather than medical or anatomical works. In effect, these versions of the *sīra* offer a robust account of several fluids thought to construct and reproduce human phenotypes, from both partners' ejaculate to the woman's uterine blood in its several forms; apparent mixing or imperfect reproductions of a parent's image can result from but one of these externally invisible substances being altered through errant sex,

92. Q 48:17.

rather than solely from either sexual partner's identity and heritage. In other words, the *sīra* models concepts of both biological inheritance and change, each with implications for one's perceived kind.

The non-syllogistic versions of ʿAbd al-Wahhāb's birth story function less on a strict logic of commensurability between a mother's effluvium and a child's mark, than on a seemingly widespread version of the belief that interactions with a menstruant can entail communicable uncleanliness, debilitation, stigma, or contagion. These interactions occur on a spectrum varying from ritual violation—as with the blackening of the Black Stone—to communal or domestic violation—as with a dried-up well or afflicted progeny. The suspicion that such effects could be produced through chaste touch may be orthogonal to Islamic legal ethics, but it nonetheless circulates widely in interreligious storytelling. Rather than conceiving of ʿAbd al-Wahhāb's blackness resulting from menstrual sex as discontinuous with other accounts of the consequences of violating purity law in Islamic and pre-Islamic contexts, we may think of this vignette in *Sīrat Dhāt al-Himma* and its analogue in *Sīrat ʿAntar* as thematically and functionally dovetailing with its companions across a number of traditions.

The primary lesson in ʿAbd al-Wahhāb's conception story is thus a recurrently elaborated one. Much in the way that the leper and the menstruant receive similar treatment in Jewish law and society, in which the rules governing the segregation of menstruating women are stricter than in Islam, the unexpectedly Black child and the illicit fornicator receive similar treatment in Arab-Muslim society, such that al-Ḥārith's punishment for menstrual sex is having a son whom he and others are bound to reject.[93] That the crime of menstrual sex reflected more harshly on men in general is patent in the Qurʾān's characterization of a menstruant's physical pain, in the legal corpus, and in the corrective projection of blame in the *sīra* itself onto al-Ḥārith, not Fāṭima. This points to popular works' didacticism

93. The purported alternative punishment of one's progeny being *nāqiṣ* due to menstrual sex may operate in a similarly reflexive fashion, blighting the child with a reminder of the condition of his/her mother at the time of his/her conception, in that menstruation is often linked in traditional sources with Eve's punishment for transgressing God's will in the heavenly Garden, resulting in all women being "lacking in rationality and in religion" (*nāqiṣāt ʿaql wa-dīn*); in al-Thaʿlabī's anthology of prophetic tales, these two punishments are listed together among the fifteen reprisals for Eve's actions. In the *ḥadīth* tradition quoted in the text, a lack of rationality explains women's being only partial legal witnesses vis-à-vis men's full capacity to witness, while the lack of religion is ascribed to the lessened prayer and fasting obligations for women due to menses and pregnancy. See al-Thaʿlabī, *ʿArāʾis al-Majālis*, 25–26.

concerning aspects of family law and overarching social norms, though often not in ways that mainstream authorities pursued. Moreover, it shows that legal and social norms became entangled with popular belief not just via enacting the rules and customs outlined by the *ʿulamāʾ*, but via storytelling itself.

Bodies of antique and medieval normative knowledge about natural and/as social kinds were synthesized and promulgated in polyvalent traditions of text among the *ʿulamāʾ*, *udabāʾ*, and common folk. Above I touched primarily on prophetological, legal, and medical or humoral-pathological discourses that pertain to ʿAbd al-Wahhāb's conception story. Also pertinent are the geographic and cosmological traditions that formed the backbone of climate-based and esoteric reasoning about why earthly differences arise and what they might teach us. I deal with these further in ensuing chapters. Already, we see that authors adduced intricate causal relationships between colorful substances, the coloring effects of humors and environments, and differently colored and constituted peoples. In conjunction, authors speculated on the susceptibilities of women's biology and a community's standing when these things combined to ill effect, rendering gender central to the question of how racialized difference is made and how it ought to be managed. Some drew further conclusions from the social analogousness of various biologized others, thinking across race, gender, unfreedom, disability, and disease.

Although blood—typically the primary carrier of race in modern imaginings—played a significant role in producing many of these conditions, this could be harmonized with or take a backseat to other bodily matter and modes of relationality that could carry or avert heredity, which in any case did not travel in "bloodlines." Transmission of kind in medieval Arab-Muslim contexts often works similarly to what Brigitte Fielder has called the "queer genealogy" of race, central aspects of which are race's non-linearity across generations and its resistance to single-answer scientization, as well as anxieties these variabilities produce about social control.[94] Though the *sīra* does not cite its sources, it is clearly conversant with the physiological models discussed above and is invested in presenting audiences with their mundane workings even when discussing an extraordinary case. And though it thwarts fictions of perfect reproducibility and declares that appearances do not tell the full story, the *sīra* nonetheless reaffirms the existence of a visceral and innate bodily substrate that underlies socially meaningful differences. Unexpected manifestations of that

94. Fielder, *Relative Races*.

substrate matter profoundly, with the story conjuring legal imbroglios and expert testimonies to probe the strangeness of a new difference's origins.

At the same time, as his illicitly wrought yet divinely mediated blend of Arab lineage and blackness follows ʿAbd al-Wahhāb throughout the story, its grander significance to the text's aspirational history emerges. Blackness poses an epistemic and embodied challenge in the world at hand. For ʿAbd al-Wahhāb, this challenge structures his experiences in ways that presage his heroic legacy as, moving against the grain, he fosters veritable armies of assimilated Black Muslim clients and manumittees, travels to East Africa to woo remote civilizational "others," and models pious wartime virtues for his growing community in a form theretofore unseen.

PART II

Race through Time

✷ 4 ✷

The Past

So the ontological bottom line is that even if, in our hearts of darkness, we are all savages, nonwhite savagery is paradigmatic—natural and inescapable for them—while at least we (white, culturally evolved, normatively self-regulating) are capable of knowing and doing better, located at a different position in humanity's moral evolutionary timeline, though vulnerable to lapses.

CHARLES W. MILLS

Truly, O foremost of the Arabs, not a one among you has had anything like my story transpire. . . . I left with her in the night, and she was of indescribable beauty, so the Devil whispered to me of being with her in a valley near [the chief] Dārim's land. What was proper left my mind, and the gates [of reason] closed in my face as a fire flared within me, then I told her of this and what I wanted from her. She said, 'Truly I would never do such a thing, even at pain of death,' and when I heard this statement from her, I let go her mount's reins, then I unsheathed my sword and struck her with its flat.

SALLĀM'S SPEECH, *SĪRAT DHĀT AL-HIMMA*, 1:26

Time in Arabic popular epics is a slippery thing: journeys across vast spaces are improbably short, people live eerily long, and a mere month can consume hundreds of pages while whole years are skipped over in a flash. Characters can also appear to manipulate time, with heroic figures that predate Islam such as Sayf b. Dhī Yazan and ʿAntara b. Shaddād appearing as pious "proto-Muslims," or with Alexander the Great meeting in the earthly plane with a Methuselan al-Khiḍr.[1] It may seem difficult, if not impossible, to track developments within the worlds of these texts as narrative time progresses at this erratic pace. Common to many of the *sīras*, though, is that the times in which they are set are consciously turbulent; the world needs heroes, for change is on the horizon, be it the tribe of Hilāl's drought and famine-induced westward migration, the Frankish invasions repelled by a legendized Baybars, or the imminent arrival of the Prophet Muḥammad and his message. This last form of marking time looms large throughout Islamic historiography, with the sacred time enacted by the rise of Islam separated from profane time, or *jāhiliyya*, often translated as an "age of ignorance." In turn, a notional *jāhiliyya* acts in *Sīrat Dhāt al-Himma* as a pivot-point around which new prospects for community arrangement emerge. The text presents the change from ignorance to Islamization as a transition from which Black people in particular stand to benefit.

This is not simply due to the fact that, unlike *jāhiliyya*-era tribalism as construed in the text, Islam offers a "big tent" system of belief that transcends the earthly confines of social kind. Rather, the betterment of racialized others' prospects is attributable in large part to new modes of kinship and social affiliation that are introduced by Islamic law. Institutions arise such as *umm walad*, which entitled children born in concubinage relationships to take the ancestral name, or *nasab*, of their father and the inheritance entitlements it implies. There also arose a retooled and expanded system of *walāʾ*, whereby non-Arabs could affiliate with Arabian tribal lines through a dependent relationship with a family after being manumitted from slavery or—in the early period—by being contracted into clientage. In the world of the *sīra*, these relational institutions are instrumental in the assimilation of Black people into the early Muslim community, with its dominant Arab core.

Islam is not presented as an eternalized reality for the Arabs in the text, though. Rather, the *sīra* is all too aware of the existence of a time and set of lifeways that precede Islam in Arabia. The story traces a detailed arc from un-Islamization—or perhaps, partial and incomplete Islamization—among Arabia's heroic and prideful Bedouin tribesmen to submission not just to Islam but to the supra-tribal and unifying authority of a sovereign whom they previously viewed as not being of their own. Though *Sīrat Dhāt al-Himma* technically begins within the temporal pale of Islam,

1. On possible connections between this encounter and Dhū al-Qarnayn's proximity to al-Khiḍr in the Qurʾān, see Branon Wheeler, "Alexander," in *Medieval Islamic Civilization: An Encyclopedia*, vol. 1, ed. Josef W. Meri (New York: Routledge, 2006), 29.

during the mid-Umayyad period, its early phase is bookended by the transitional personality of the caliph ʿAbd al-Malik ibn Marwān (d. 705), who is often represented as reverting the decadent Umayyads to pious ideals of rule. In traditional historiography, ʿAbd al-Malik's metamorphosing role is discussed in terms of the storied revolutionary measures through which he consolidated power and re-righted the ship of his office, meant to stand as both a theological and political head. He is credited with having standardized the Arabic script and its administrative use, systematized weights and measures, minted coins (famously the first to contain professions of faith), and supervised construction of the Dome of the Rock in Jerusalem.

In the *sīra*, ʿAbd al-Malik sends his son, Maslama (d. 738), known in his lifetime for conducting warfare against the Byzantines in an apocalyptically tinged push toward Constantinople, as an emissary from Damascus to the tribes of the Najd region in central Arabia.[2] His task is to strengthen the caliph's hold in the region by helping him to deputize a "king of the Arabs." They coronate Ṣaḥṣāḥ, ʿAbd al-Wahhāb's distant ancestor. Prior to this feat of diplomacy, though, the Arabians of the Najd appear unruly and uninterested in altering their old ways, an anxiety found in much traditional historiography. In early portions of *Sīrat Dhāt al-Himma,* the tribes of the Najd cling to Bedouinism and refute caliphal authority over their affairs. When ʿAbd al-Malik attempts to elevate the chief of the Banū Kilāb, his rival tribesmen exclaim,

> Who is ʿAbd al-Mālik b. Marwān to the Bedouins who have taken the desert as our abode and the rope halters [of camels; alt: mountains][3] as our homelands? We obey not a soul, either from the Bedouins or from the settled folks.[4]

This pronouncement is quite similar to the characterization of the more conventional pre-Islamic chronology into which ʿAntar emerges in his *sīra*:

> Due to the ignorance of the Bedouin horsemen of the *jāhiliyya,* it was their belief that any time someone acquired something, it was licit

2. On Maslama's role in Islamic apocalyptic, see Antoine Borrut, *Between Memory and Power: The Syrian Space under the Late Umayyads and Early Abbasids (c. 72–193/692–809),* trans. Anna Bailey Galietti (Leiden: Brill, 2023), 238–50.

3. Different versions of the *sīra* write *jibāl* as opposed to *ḥibāl.* Cf. *Sīrat Dhāt al-Himma,* II:76 and *Sīrat al-Amīra Dhāt al-Himma,* vol. 1, ed. al-Maqānibī et al. (Beirut: al-Maktaba al-Shaʿbiyya, 1980), 201.

4. *Sīrat Dhāt al-Himma,* II:76.

(*ḥalāl*) for him, for they were very ignorant and wayward (*li-kathrat al-jahl wa-l-ḍalāl*).[5]

Yet we are also promised in the tale's first pages that the half-Abyssinian, slave-born ʿAntar is a premonitory figure, sent to test them and to lead the Bedouins out of their ways through his valiant yet humble example in the century before Islam's arrival. In *Sīrat Dhāt al-Himma*, the heady era of Bedouin independence prior to Maslama's ministry has particularly negative consequences for tribal outsiders, who have no upward mobility or way of integrating with Arabian society and who are almost categorically represented in the story as Black. An especially prominent instance, and the one that will comprise this chapter's case study, occurs when the chief of the tribe of Ṭayy comes to covet a particular emblem of prestige: the peerless steed of the Kilābī chief Junduba, the most beautiful and well-bred creature in the region. The chief sets three Black slaves to the task of stealing the horse, promising each to his exquisite, noble daughter Salmā in turn. Each suddenly dies on the threshold of marriage—much to his would-be bride's joy, whose elite lineage remains untainted by these low-class, tribeless men.

Approximately a century of history and several hundred pages of narrative separates ʿAbd al-Wahhāb from this bleak past. ʿAbd al-Wahhāb's heroic advent in the early ninth century coincides with a period of particularly large proportions of enslaved Black Africans serving in the ʿAbbasid army, followed by a late-century decline that Jere Bacharach attributes to the stymying effect of the Egyptian Tulunid dynasty on overland trade from the west.[6] The period of ʿAbd al-Wahhāb's ascent within the text also notably aligns with what Peter Webb identifies as the formative era for Arabness itself beyond the text, a dawning ethnic consciousness that braided many different Arabian genealogies together in an age of accelerated movement, conquest, and encounter.[7] Though the Bedouins throughout the *sīra* are always characterized as "Arab," we might note shifts within the story of

5. *Sīrat ʿAntara b. Shaddād*, vol. 1, 73.

6. This decline seems either temporary or incidental in the long view of history. The eleventh-century traveler Nāṣir Khusraw attests witnessing "30,000 Zanjī and Abyssinian slaves" in Arabia during his ventures. Jere L. Bacharach, "African Military Slaves in the Medieval Middle East: The Cases of Iraq (869–955) and Egypt (868–1171)," *International Journal of Middle East Studies* 13 (1981): 474; Craig Perry, "Slavery and the Slave Trade in Western Indian Ocean World," in *The Cambridge World History of Slavery*, vol. 2, ed. Craig Perry, David Eltis, et al. (Cambridge: Cambridge University Press, 2021), 131.

7. Webb, *Imagining the Arabs*.

what this can mean: through his Muslimness and his Blackness, ʿAbd al-Wahhāb's Arabness likewise becomes capacious and extendable, touching people and groups it previously would not have done.

Time itself is freighted with racial resonances. In the previous chapter, we encountered the notion that race has been ascribed a much-debated periodicity. The standard narrative of race's Enlightenment-era advent and particular formativeness of global capitalist modernity is increasingly troubled, not unironically, by the contemporary expansion of the scope of what "race" might mean once we acknowledge it to be socially constructed, fluid, contingent on local histories, and arising not in biology but in regimes of metaphysical knowledge *about* nature, the human, and the soul.[8] In what follows, I also consider how historical periods have been ascribed raciality. I argue that the action in the *sīra* prior to ʿAbd al-Malik's direct intervention in Bedouin life is patterned on a *jāhilī* chronotope. Writing of al-Andalus, or Islamic Iberia, as a Bakhtinian chronotope for modern Arabic novels, William Granara demonstrates that the mythicization of al-Andalus as a "a space that represents the expanding boundaries of the Islamic jihad, of spreading the faith and bringing order to a chaotic world," and a "time of political stability and cultural florescence," allows readers to tap into a wellspring of collective memory, desire, and critique through literary form.[9]

To be sure, the pre-Islamic Bedouin aesthetics of the *sīra*'s early sections are not consciously deployed in the way that a novel's author deploys a chronotope. Instead, these sections are likely a product of how popular epics were collectively composed, preserving the labors of prior storytellers layered over by later ones. Marius Canard has hypothesized that *Sīrat Dhāt al-Himma* incorporates two loosely related, large storytelling sequences, one that is Arabian and comprises the early portions of the epic focused on tribal intrigue in the Peninsula, and the other that is Anatolian and focuses on Fāṭima Dhāt al-Himma, ʿAbd al-Wahhāb, and al-Baṭṭāl's frontier wars.[10] This fits with the contrastive style of how Black

8. Some, such as William Chester Jordan, adduce this irony as part of their misgivings about race's hermeneutical utility for the deeper past because, "on the matter of race, the racists *have* won," and so any attempt to expand critically on its analytical potentials works to opposite effect. William Chester Jordan, "Why Race?" *Journal of Medieval and Early Modern Studies* 31, no. 1 (2001): 168.

9. William Granara, "Nostalgia, Arab Nationalism, and the Andalusian Chronotope in the Evolution of the Modern Arabic Novel," *Journal of Arabic Literature* 36, no. 1 (2005): 58–59.

10. Marius Canard, "Dhū'l Himma," *in Encyclopedia of Islam*, 2nd ed., ed. Peri Bearman, et al. (Leiden: Brill, 2012).

characters are represented in the text's *jāhilī* and Islamized stages. The details of reprocessing the first cycle and joining it with the second in the epic as it has survived to us today are perhaps unknowable. Here, I treat the *sīra* as a coherent narrative organism that wants to bridge its various parts. Read in this way and against the backdrop of ʿAbbasid historiography, *Sīrat Dhāt al-Himma* presents audiences with a powerful case that "others" are better off in the *umma* than outside of it, at least from the early Marwanids on.

Thus, the *jāhilī* chronotope of the *sīra* has a racialized dimension: within it, Black characters are frozen out of social life, unable to wed, manumit themselves, secure consistent patrons, gain their own glory in raiding or war, or otherwise socially advance. As with Junduba's appeal to Shamṭā's Black warriors at the beginning of this book, their fates are entirely bound to the vicissitudes of Arab interests and conflicts. The emergence from the text's *jāhiliyya* is also an emergence into a social world where new types of mobility and incentive are possible, and material improvements are then conferred through one's ontological orientation. Arab characters can shrug off their myopia by becoming Muslim or embedding themselves more deeply into Muslim modes of learning and authority. Doing so provides them with the tools to see others' relative disadvantage not as a flatly hypostatic position, but a dynamic matter of relative moral and spiritual evolution, to draw on Charles W. Mills's formulation. As the Bedouins expand their Islamic networks and this future takes shape, lingering in ignorance is increasingly embodied by non-Arab, mainly Black figures who have become synonymous with the non-Muslim or heterodox and unlearned peoples at their world's edges, even as Islam affords them greater leeway to change this status. This changeability also points to a disparity between being figured as one who is *jāhil*, or ignorant, and as a *kāfir*, or unbeliever, with the former implying someone who has not encountered Islam and its truths and the latter someone who has but has not accepted them. As the primary aggressors in the text who are believing Christians yet deeply and polemically aware of Islam, Byzantines are regularly presented as *kuffār* but more infrequently appear as being in some form of *jāhiliyya*. For Black non-Muslims, this is reversed.

Much as the Andalusi chronotope involves both nostalgia for a gilded age of Muslim-led coexistence and ambitions for a rosy future in which this may again become true, the *jāhilī* chronotope involves an admonitory cyclicality: *jāhiliyya* can recur or persist in new times and places. Peter Webb notes that in early Islamic traditions, the word *jāhiliyya* appears not to connote a particular period at all. Rather, it is a "fluid state of being" that reflects collective amorality or denial of religious authority, and into which any society can lapse.[11] In a related fashion, in his work on chronopolitics, or how dynamics of domination are latent in the ways that we relate different human collectives to time, Charles W. Mills declares that "whose space it is depends on whose time it is." He adds that "temporal cartographies for populations internal and external" to a given nation or stage of civilization are strategic and racializing. For Mills, in early modernity, "white temporality" became the vanguard—white, European Christians wrote themselves as farthest advanced in time because of their whiteness and vice versa.[12] Their self-narratives had myriad salvific and paternalist components. The ramifications of this "allochronic" or hetero-temporal view for Arabs and Muslims have been eloquently dissected by Edward Said, who notes that the Middle East is often represented as in a state of "arrested development"—typically a medieval one—and as needing colonial stewardship in order to progress.[13] In arguing that cultural productions from the Islamic Middle Ages themselves espouse a chronopolitics, my aim is neither to implicate them in Mills's white temporality, nor to fix them as artifacts of "backward" racial thinking. Rather, I show that the *sīra* uses concepts of time to engage with the possibility that one's own identity and perceptions of others can change, creating a developmental communal narrative.

Sallām and the Three Slaves of the Banū Ṭayy

Until ʿAbd al-Wahhāb's heroic ascent in the text, Black characters tend to appear only allusively and in fulfillment of certain staid archetypes; many of the early heroes of the *sīra* acquire a sidekick in the form of a servant who aids them on their journeys, most of whom the audience may infer are raced as Black. Such men are often suggested to be assets to their owners in name and deed, designated by monikers with which they were not born, as with the king Ṣaḥṣāḥ's loyal steward, Najjāḥ (Exceedingly Successful), or one of the young ʿAbd al-Wahhāb's first Black slaves, Nāfiʿ (Beneficial). Occasionally, these names take on an ironic cast, as with the figure of Sallām (Exceedingly Protective). Arriving early in the text, before its first fully fledged hero, Junduba, has even been born, Sallām assumes the role of prurient slave attempting to seduce a chaste and noble widow after his owner, Junduba's father al-Ḥārith, has perished. His widow, Arbāb

11. Peter Webb, "Al-Jāhiliyya: Uncertain Times of Uncertain Meanings," *Der Islam* 91, no. 1 (2014): 69–94.

12. Mills, "Chronopolitics," 301, 308–9.

13. Edward Said, *Orientalism* (New York: Random House, 1979), 307.

(alternatively: Rabāb), who at the time is pregnant with Junduba, initially trusts Sallām with her life and asks him to help her escape from her tribe's lands in the night because she fears that al-Ḥārith's chiefly succession will become a bloody affair. In a sense, Sallām is her only option: all of al-Ḥārith's other slaves are said to have "each taken one of the enslaved maidens and sought out the wasteland, fearing [the coming] strife and warfare." While on the road, though, Sallām attempts to do with Arbāb "what men do with women," only for her to resist him and for her labor pangs to begin. In a rage, Sallām accuses her of having begun her labor at that moment on purpose. After a long altercation, he strikes off her head and absconds. Sometime later, a newborn Junduba is found by another local chief, shrouded in the protection of desert animals and suckling at his slain mother's breast.[14]

Sallām's vignette is also laced with a few key indications that the world is evolving around him and his peers, and that the tribes still vacillate between old ways and new. When we first meet the Kilābīs whom he serves, we are already in the Umayyad period, but the locals still rely on preexistent forms of spiritual authority: when Arbāb has a disturbing dream during her pregnancy, al-Ḥārith seeks the interpretation of a *kāhin*, or priestly figure strongly associated with pre-Islamic polytheistic and oracular practice. The Kilābī elder bears forward ancestral knowledge in order to divine coming events, saying, "I discern among the sagacious nations [*al-umam al-aʿārifa*] that transmitted the texts of those nations that forbore them that [your wife] will have a great child, and what greatness!"[15] Characters speak of interminable fate, or *dahr*, having its own hand in people's affairs, a common refrain in pre-Islamic writings that ebbs as it is "dissolved into the concept of divine providence" in Islamic thought.[16] The Arabians can be seen swearing oaths in their dialogue by the touchstones of Meccan pilgrimage that predate Islam but are imbued with restored meaning on its arrival—the Kaʿba, the Well of Zamzam, and the Black Stone—as well as by a supreme God who creates all beings. When Sallām attempts to ravish her, Arbāb tells him to stop and seek shelter in God, "the All-Hearing and Most Knowing," and to be heedful of his rearing (*tarbīya*), which is said to have been ministered by Arbāb herself (in some versions, Sallām is said to be a *muwallad* slave, or one born to a non-Arab but raised among Arabs). Implicitly, his education involved instruction in

14. *Sīrat Dhāt al-Himma,* I:7–14

15. *Sīrat Dhāt al-Himma,* I:4–5.

16. Pavel Pavlovich, "The Concept of Dahr and Its Historical Perspective in the Ǧāhiliyya and Early Islam," *The Arabist: Budapest Studies in Arabic* 26–27 (2003): 58.

God's omniscience.[17] Yet there is everywhere a seeming absence of learned leadership that is reinforcing such guidance.

Other forms of knowledge are deferred within the narrative as well, though less to build the world than its characters. At first, Sallām's color is not discussed; he is referred to only as a *ghulām*, or servant boy, and repeatedly dubbed *zanīm*, ignoble and lowborn in a way that often connotes foreignness. However, he repeatedly couches his wayward lusts for Arbāb in blackening terms, speaking of them as an affliction in his heart's dark core (*suwayd al-qalb*), and describing his liver as diseased with love (*suwād*). Long after, when Junduba has reached adulthood and begun his own adventures, Sallām's identity is vividly revealed. While exchanging campfire stories one night amid a neighboring tribe, a "Black slave" (*ʿabd aswad*) emerges and blithely regales Junduba with the tale of Arbāb's death. Afterward, Junduba asks, "What was the name of your master, boy?" When Sallām replies "al-Ḥārith ibn ʿĀmr al-Kilābī," Junduba leaps up and kills him with one blow.[18]

The ways in which Sallām's blackness is alluded to throughout his tale recall the layered play on "the semantic fields and associations of blackness" that characterizes the narrative of the first king Shahzaman's cuckolding in the frame tale of the *1001 Nights*. Though the kind of slave with whom his wife slept goes unmentioned, their affair is surrounded by allusions to darkness.[19] Furthermore, the circumstances in which Sallām appears are unmistakably similar to the *Nights'* opening, in which an enslaved man takes advantage of a powerful owner's absence in order to tryst with his mistress. Sallām's character is flat, inveterate, and remorseless; where the enslaved Black men of the *Nights'* frame are flushed from the narrative before they might be redeemed, a self-interested Sallām is given a second act and proves himself unchanged. He enchants the camp with a story that he promises, grandiosely, is unlike any they have ever heard, casting blame on the Devil for his desires but not for his violence against an imperiled woman. With a foreboding hubris he adds that he took his money, likely stolen that night from his mistress, and used it to rise to the command of his own party of raiders. Junduba makes short work of Sallām and his pretensions to social ascent.

Although premodern Arabic storytelling often names the kinds and colors of characters who stand outside the social default—and, as Mohamad Ballan reminds us, imputations of color difference as a "marker of

17. BNF MS Arabe 3840, fol. 5v.

18. *Sīrat Dhāt al-Himma*, I:27.

19. Ferial J. Ghazoul, *Nocturnal Poetics*: The Arabian Nights *in Comparative Context* (Cairo: The American University of Cairo Press, 1996), 26.

identity" are never neutral, but rather indicate what J. Reid Miller calls an "evaluative field" through which subjects are constituted—blackness can nonetheless also be an implicit feature in narrative.[20] It can be conjecturally evoked in the audience's imagination through paronomasia, euphemism, and cliché. Elsewhere, as we will see below, Black presences are suggested through the staging of narrative encounters in which whiteness, usually invisible, suddenly leaps into view. Though in Sallām's case his initially unspoken blackness could be symptomatic of the conflation between enslavement and blackness—we are meant to see Sallām as Black from the first—it could also be a piece of information that is consciously withheld, even if presumed, for the purpose of setting up a moral and social proving ground. A picture of Sallām's true nature sharpens as he fails, recurrently, to surpass it.

In her discussion of the stakes and legacies behind the study of Indian Ocean slavery, Parisa Vaziri notes the ambivalent position of a subfield that is at once made legible through and resists an overdetermining relationship with studies of Atlantic world enslavement. She focuses on Indian Ocean historians' insistence on regional enslavement's nonracial quality and their concern that, because blackness "enfleshes" slavery in the modern, Western imagination, "racial blackness refuses to release slavery to a transparent and objective historiographical account of itself."[21] Another, companion "disavowal" that is common to the study of enslavement in Islamic contexts, both bordering the Indian Ocean and in points northward, has been the insistence that enslavement was not a form of abjection or not purely so. Often, this disavowal has been accomplished by using postcolonial theories of agency and resistance. And often it has further been accomplished through drawing contrasts with a particular turn, around forty years ago, within slavery studies toward the contemplation of what Orlando Patterson termed "social death." In conditions of enslavement, Patterson explained that one was berefted of personal, bodily and spiritual control as well as answerability, in the sense of both full standing and full culpability within the legal systems of recourse and inheritance designed to protect human autonomy and individual right. One's labor, abilities, and honor are not one's own, but work to the enhancement or

20. Mohamad Ballan, "Borderland Anxieties: Lisān al-Dīn ibn al-Khaṭīb (d. 1374) and the Politics of Genealogy in Late Medieval Granada," *Speculum* 98, no. 2 (2023): 493; J. Reid Miller, *Stain Removal: Ethics and Race* (Oxford: Oxford University Press, 2017), 114.

21. Parisa Vaziri, "No One's Memory: Blackness at the Limits of Comparative Slavery," *POMEPS* 44 (2020): 17.

degradation of owners. Social death is also discursive. It can take the form of representing the enslaved as external or "foreign" to the social body, or as internal but "fallen" from the social body.[22]

Frank B. Wilderson III writes Blackness as a "loss of loss," or the condition of not ever having had the "plenitude" and "transformative capacity" of humanity that Patterson claims one relinquishes through social death and might therefore regain.[23] Wilderson sees Patterson's phrasing as too ephemeral because, in teasing apart enslavement from Blackness, he muddles the prospect of transformable conditions for some with the fact that there must then always be someone occupying the "paradigmatic position" of inertness through which change becomes thinkable. Meanwhile, various scholars of slavery in Islamic contexts have understood Patterson's phrasing as too absolute. They seek out the ways that mostly elite enslaved persons flexed their transformative muscle in history, finding *qiyān*, or highly trained female entertainers, who bent the ears of the powerful at court, or *mamlūks*-turned-sultans who sent for their kin in their homelands despite their natal alienation being "both assumed and desired by their contemporaries."[24] Or more acerbically, one finds statements such as,

> Patterson argues that slave elites in Islamic civilization were still effectively powerless because their fate still hung on the whim of their masters. But the frequency with which Egyptian Mamluks and Ottoman Janissaries summarily executed their masters when it suited them strongly suggests otherwise.[25]

So what do we make of narratives from Islamic contexts in which Blackness-qua-enslavement is indeed presented as a vortical condition from which one tries but fails to escape, or in which one is trapped physically and mentally? Are we to interpret these representations as implying an erstwhile reality because they occur in the narrative past, or as indicating an enduring model of abjection that one could draw on in narrative within and without specific temporal frames? Though figures like Sallām

22. Orlando Patterson, *Slavery and Social Death: A Comparative Study* (Cambridge: Harvard University Press, 1982), 39–42.

23. Frank B. Wilderson III, *Afropessimism* (New York: W. W. Norton, 2020), 16, 102.

24. Hannah Barker, "Reconnecting with the Homeland: Black Sea Slaves in Mamluk Biographical Dictionaries," *Medieval Prosopography* 30 (2015): 90; Kristina Richardson, "Singing Slave Girls (Qiyan) of the ʿAbbasid Court in the Ninth and Tenth Centuries," in *Children in Slavery through the Ages*, edited by Gwyn Campbell, Suzanne Miers, and Joseph C. Miller. Athens, OH: Ohio University Press, 2009), 105–18.

25. Jonathan A. C. Brown, *Slavery & Islam* (London: Oneworld, 2019), 121.

acquire added significance within *Sīrat Dhāt al-Himma*'s *jāhilī* chronotope, we also see them in other timelines. We also see how Sallām's condition is generalized: when not encountering Black men as singular characters, one comes across them in early portions of the *sīra* instead in faceless collectives as bands of raiding men acting at an Arab overlord's behest, broadly designated as sons of Ḥām and disaggregated from either a lineal or contemporary social account of the text's Arabian landscape.

It is against this total exclusion that the three slaves of Ṭayy most visibly struggle. Shortly after Sallām's story closes, the *sīra*'s primary heroic lineage is once again pulled into relationality with a series of Black figures. The tale begins with Ghaṭrīf, the chief of Ṭayy and rival to Junduba, chief of the tribe of Kilāb and great-grandfather to the text's eponymous heroine, Fāṭima Dhāt al-Himma. Junduba is the owner of a much-coveted mare, pitch-black of eye and bright white of flank, whose tale the narrator forecasts as "a wondrous [*ʿajīb*] affair and a travail hounded by strangeness [*gharīb*]"—perhaps this tale, like those of ʿAntara and Abū Zayd in chapter 1, will elicit a new way of seeing.[26] Ghaṭrīf becomes so bent on acquiring the mare that he disastrously gambles the tribe's livelihood on her capture. The narrator claims that "many people died because of [the horse], after which [Ghaṭrīf] left off his pursuit of her, despite still deeply desiring her [*inqaṭaʿ ʿan ṭalabihā ṭamiʿ al-ṭāmiʿ*]."[27] A short while later, when Ghaṭrīf's beautiful daughter, Salmā, comes of age and noble suitors begin plying her father for her hand, Ghaṭrīf seizes the opportunity to instead auction Salmā off to whichever man is able to procure Junduba's steed. We are then introduced to the first contender, a slave named Jaffāl:

> There was amid the tribe of Ṭayy a man called Jaffāl, and he was nicknamed "Imposter" [*yulaqqib bi-l-muḥtāl*]. He was of repugnant form [*shanīʿ al-khilqa*], with no hope of getting into Salmā's bed [*lā yuṭammiʿ fī Salmā bi-l-wiṣāl*] nor of suiting her station. But when Ghaṭrīf made his offer, Jaffāl grew confident that his wish would be realized, so he rose hastily and said, "Salmā is meant for no one but me [*mā taṣluḥ Salmā illā lī*]!" Then he mounted his she-camel and took leave of his family and fellows, speeding across the deserts and plains.[28]

Catching sight of Jaffāl, Salmā immediately begins to pray for his failure, calling him "a profligate, deceitful devil who has stripped into a human

26. *Sīrat Dhāt al-Himma,* I:41.
27. *Sīrat Dhāt al-Himma,* I:42.
28. *Sīrat Dhāt al-Himma,* I:42.

visage [*insalakh fī ṣūrat insān*], with a repulsive mustache, a reeking stench, a deviated nose [*anf aʿwaj*], and offset jaws [*fakk aflaj*]." Even more damning, Salmā laments that her father is satisfied to wed her, "a dove," to Jaffāl, "a crow."[29] This claim reveals that in addition to being variously disfigured, Jaffāl is Black.

In her work on blighted bodies in medieval Islamic discourse, Kristina Richardson notes that *ʿāhāt*, or disfigurements, were often defined broadly to incorporate deviations from Arab norms of beauty, such as black skin, flat noses, or blue eyes, as well as disabilities such as lameness, congenital diseases, and the visible symptoms of recent illness (like boils or hair loss). Certain types of blight, especially one-eyedness, narrow eyes, or dark skin, are often associated with nightmarish figures like Satan or the antichrist-like demon, al-Dajjāl, while bodily excessiveness is—as we see in Salmā's own words—often attended by perceptions of appetitive excessiveness and libertinism. In the *sīra*, though the extreme grotesqueness of Jaffāl works in part to comedic effect, his description would also have recalled a particularly nightmarish spectacle to the audience: he is marked as a condemned man.

Jaffāl's vilified appearance sharply contrasts with Salmā's famed beauty, which given her description as "the pearl solitaire [*farīda*] of her age and jewel of her era" seems to fit the reversed ideal of light skin, delicate features, and black eyes that is also reminiscent of images of the next world. Jaffāl even notes this overlap when, before stealing into the Kilābīs' camp, he remarks inwardly that if he perishes in the attempt to win Salmā he will have risked himself for the likes of a houri (*ḥūr al-ʿayn*). Though in general heaven's contrast to hell consists in the fact that it is a riot of color—a verdant garden festooned with embroidered textiles—descriptions of its human figures more overtly contrast whiteness and lightness with the darkness of hell's souls. The maidens of heaven, or *ḥūr*, are described in scripture as well-hidden eggs (*bayḍ*)—the whiteness of which is etymologically embedded in the *b-y-ḍ* root—and pearls (*lūʾlūʾ*).[30] The *ḥūr* carry in their name the image of one whose eyes have great contrast between sclera and iris, with *ḥ-w-r* connoting the "intensifying of the whiteness of the eye and a blackening of the blackness of it, [by which is meant] that which encircles the pupil," with this contrastive bright-whiteness of a sclera that does not blur into one's iris being associated not merely with beauty but with youth, health, and even hydration.[31] Jaffāl's medical

29. *Sīrat Dhāt al-Himma*, I:43.
30. Q37:49, Q56:22–23.
31. Ibn al-Manẓūr, *Lisān al-ʿArab*, 1043.

complications modify and exaggerate this picture of dewy vitality, with Salmā at one point cautioning that if her betrothal comes to pass, youthful onlookers should be particularly afflicted, urging, "then wail in despair and cry, my young [friends] [*fa-nūḥū ḥasratan wa-abkū shababī*]."[32]

Yet despite his physical extraordinariness, Jaffāl proves a master of shape-shifting disguise. He infiltrates the tribe of Kilāb by morphing himself into a mendicant preacher:

> Jaffāl had long, white hair and a pleasant bearing [*malīḥ al-hayba*], so he donned black sackcloth and exposed his head. He had hair that was long as a horse's tail, and a face black like the darkness of night. He hunched his back, slackened his chin [*arkhā dhaqnahu*], and draped his hair over his shoulders, then he teased out his beard [*nafas laḥiyatahu*] and loosed it upon his chest. He entered the village, reciting poetry.[33]

Jaffāl then dazzles the men of Kilāb with a stirring memento mori (*waʿẓ*), recalling abandoned campsites, mortal heroes, and places of feasting gone feral:

> Where are the tribes and where the kin? [*ayn al-ʿashāʾir wa-l-qabāʾil*]
> Where the friend and sultan great? [*ayn aṣḥāb al-maḥāfil/ayn al-salāṭīn al-kibār*]
> They've perished, but their campsites stay [*halakū fa-mā tabaʿathum al-manāzil*]
> They've taken much, but so has fate
> Now their shrines but waste away
> They drank death's brew, and now sip not
> On wining and dining days—
> O you who give death not a thought, [*yā ghāfilūn ʿan al-fanāʾ*]
> Know that Death does not forget! [*lays al-fanāʾ ʿankum bi-ghāfil*]
> So wake up, 'fore Judgment Day
> Lest your Judgment be what's met!
> None is perfect, safe from flames [*lam yanj min nār al-jaḥīm*]
> Except the hero with Godly aims [*siwā fatā li-llāh ʿāmil*].[34]

Jaffāl's poem is filled with recollections of God's impending judgment, and in the wildness of his appearance his audience finds its own pious

32. *Sīrat Dhāt al-Himma*, I:43.
33. *Sīrat Dhāt al-Himma*, I:43.
34. *Sīrat Dhāt al-Himma*, I:43.

eloquence; they take him for a true preacher, and Junduba thanks him for encouraging them to meditate on their sins and abjure the world (*dunya*). Jaffāl has effectively transformed his fearsome looks from an intrinsic, alienating condition into a sign of his voluntary withdrawal from humanity as an act of piety.

The resonance of Jaffāl's portrayal as a black-skinned, ascetic primitive who dwells in the wilderness, emerging to dispense wisdom to urbane society, echoes both forward and backward in time and radiates upward and downward in its genres of intertext. It harkens to the marginal pre-Islamic figures of the *ṣaʿālīk*, or vagabond poets, one of the most famed of whom is the half-Abyssinian Taʿabbaṭa Sharran (d. c. 530). In later collections such as al-Suyuṭī's (d. 1505), Taʿabbaṭa Sharran is classified among the *aghribat al-ʿarab* as one of the pre-Islamic era's most accomplished Black poets, though his descent from an Abyssinian woman is contested.[35] Jaffāl's persona also plays explicitly on the self-designedly marginal *zuhhād*, or ascetics, charlatan parodies of whom populate the high-literary genre of *maqāmāt*, or tales of imposture in which false mendicants and itinerants dazzle and deceive through rhetorical acrobatics. Yet the reality of Jaffāl's classed situation could not be more dissonant with these literati-turned-slummers.

Jaffāl's characterization additionally evokes a wider array of contexts for rhetorical performance and contest, including in early anecdotes about Black people in their native lands. For example, the Zanj—a nebulous term that frequently balloons from denoting certain East Africans to designating all Black Africans in Arabic, Persian, and later Turkish sources—are said to have many gifted orators (*khuṭabāʾ*) "in their own tongues" (*bi-alsanihim*). In one of the earliest Arabic-language Indian Ocean travelogues, their preaching is portrayed as having ancestral and renunciant components. They would stand leaning on a staff from dawn to dusk, "describing to [listeners] the fate of their people who have died."[36] This is not wholly unlike the bedraggled, hunched Jaffāl, who opens his sermon to the Kilābīs with a harrowing *ubi sunt*. Similar links between Bedouin and Black orality are attested elsewhere, though satirically. In his treatise on rhetorical expression, *al-Bayān wa-l-Tabyīn*, al-Jāḥiẓ imagines a dialogue in which a set of boastful Persians, or *shuʿūbīs*,

35. Shawqī Ḍayf, *Tārīkh al-Adab al-ʿArabī: al-ʿAṣr al-Jāhilī* (Cairo: Dār al-Maʿārif, 1986), 377.

36. Ibn Faḍlān and Abū Zayd al-Sīrāfī, *Two Arabic Travel Books: Accounts of China and India and Mission to the Volga*, trans. James Montgomery and Tim Mackintosh-Smith (New York: New York University Press, 2014), 120–21.

conscious of their long legacy of urbane settlement and courtly eloquence, directly relate the speech and song of Bedouins who orate while wielding sticks to the Zanj in a unifying discourse of primitivism:

> "There is no link between a stick and speech, nor any attribution between it and the bow. They simply distract the intellect and divert one's thoughts, and muddle reason with that which mimics it; carrying them does not strengthen one's reasoning, and gesturing with them does nothing to bring forth meaningful speech. Those skilled in song say that one who has musical accompaniment with their singing falls short of one who does not. Carrying a stick resembles the manners of the coarse-voiced, and is a mark of the Arabs' roughness and the Bedouins' self-importance; it is like [their] persistence in leading their camel herds on the path, and indeed [its appearance] resembles it."
>
> They [also] said, "Oratory is something all nations have, and each people is in utmost need of it. This is even true of the Zanj, in their ignorance and excessive simplicity, with their dulled wits and crude sentiments and imbalanced temperaments—they wax long in speechifying! They exceed the remainder of the non-Arabs in doing so, even if their meaning is most coarse and rough and their utterances most idle and foolish."[37]

Perhaps Jaffāl is especially persuasive to a set of ignorant, *jāhilī* Bedouins who, though they have oratorical knowledge, have yet to pair its forms with truer meaning. Looking forward and crosswise, Jaffāl's meditative pastoralism—and perhaps that of his audience as well—also shares much with the "noble savages" who began to populate the proto-colonialist and colonialist imaginations of Europe from around the sixteenth century, arising out of a primitivist nostalgia for the European man's pre-Enlightenment, pre-industrial connection with nature. Authors channeled this nostalgia by conjuring up idealized, bucolic images of the Black and brown peoples with whom Europe was increasingly in contact in Africa and the New World, rendering them, in the words of Edna L. Steeves, "a symbol of perfectibility" that was predicated not on development and futurism, but on a return to simplicity.[38] One role of the noble savage is to perturb notions of the linear march of time and its corollary of progress by suggesting that time has wended its way through the world

37. Al-Jāḥiẓ, *Kitāb al-Bayān wa-l-Tabyīn,* 3:12–13.

38. Edna L. Steeves, "Negritude and the Noble Savage," *Journal of Modern African Studies* 11 (1973): 97.

heterogeneously, placing some peoples at more advanced stages than others in the same historical moment. This early phase of the *sīra* likewise marks a proliferation of possible timelines: the borders of the Islamic world are expanding, cross-cultural interactions are increasing, and tribal groups are shown fighting among themselves within a shifting political dynamic that has been, in many ways, corrosive to Bedouin mores. At its edges remain figures like the one Jaffāl has styled himself to be, a man still unused to civilization and its comforts, though of course this is in large part because he is as yet barred from them. Swarthy, aged, and desert-weathered, Jaffāl arrives on the scene and begins his appeal to the Kilābīs by playing off of the tribesmen's longing for bygone glory.

His words hit their mark and Jaffāl gains access to Junduba's abode and stables. Later that night, he sneaks out to fetch the horse, only to find he has been beaten by a doppelgänger. A Black slave named Fātik from a neighboring tribe, "dark brown of color, handsome of composition, and thin of waist as though he were a woman," has taken advantage of his dainty frame to dress in drag and steal into the Kilābī camp in the guise of a maid.[39] Just as Jaffāl is hoping to be rewarded with a betrothal, so too is Fātik smitten with a highborn woman from his tribe: identically to Jaffāl, he rides to the lands of Kilāb singing poetry the whole way panegyrizing his beloved. After Jaffāl pilfers the horse just before Fātik has the chance, the two meet in a clearing and exchange words about the respective merits of their putative future wives. This perfect duplication of Jaffāl's plight is, again, ostensibly a humorous flight into the absurd, but it also serves to make the problem of unworthy Black slaves coveting and conspiring over betrothals to elite Arab women appear ubiquitous—perhaps every tribe has their own Jaffāls or Fātiks. The two men come to blows, and Jaffāl is killed. Yet the audience is told in an aside using an aphorism attributed to figures from the caliph Abū Bakr (d. 634) to Muḥammad himself, that Jaffāl's defeat is an omen (*fāl*) that was brought on by his own utterances (*muwakkal bi-l-manṭiq*). After all, in his sermon he had toyed with sacred matters, his reasons for doing so notwithstanding. Jaffāl's trespass of higher truths both makes him less mournable and indicts those that enabled him. The mare is not held by Fātik after this for long, though. Junduba learns of what has happened and quickly retrieves her. The game is afoot again.

Following a failed attempt to avoid the "severe disgrace" (*ʿār shadīd*) of marrying Salmā off to a slave by simply betrothing her to Junduba

39. *Sīrat Dhāt al-Himma*, I:47.

directly and extorting the mare from him as a bride-price, another man soon emerges to take up the challenge. The man's name is Maymūn, but he is nicknamed "Raging One" (Hāʾij). Like Jaffāl, he is said to be articulate (*faṣīḥ al-lisān*). Encouragingly, he already has a reputation as a "horse-thief and deceitful devil," a skill set well suited to Ghaṭrīf's task. Less encouragingly, he is said to be extremely lustful (*mashghūf bi-ḥubb al-niswān*).[40] Upon seeing him, Salmā—who has dressed herself in a coarse black hair-shirt that accentuates not only her mournful demeanor but also her comparative whiteness and softness—says resignedly to her father, "If you wed me to the lowliest of slaves, I shall be a bondmaid [*ama*] to him."

Maymūn succeeds in procuring the mare, but is so badly wounded while doing so that, by the time he has returned, he senses he is dying. His wounds are self-inflicted. Suspicious that this second slave who has arrived out of the blue with blandishments is also after his horse, Junduba has Maymūn beaten and chained to the steed. Maymūn lulls the other enslaved men who are charged with watching him but are nonetheless endeared to him (for "kind harkens to kind") to sleep with grand stories, then cuts off his own foot to free himself rather than damage the prized mare and risk Salmā's hand. On his return journey, he then kills another knight after lying about seeking his protection, leaving him stranded in the desert, at which the narrator relates, "This is not the work of decent folks [*awlād al-ḥalāl*]," and "this slave, son of vile and blameworthy ones, deserves death in any case." Having returned bleeding profusely and now crippled as if to further echo Jaffāl, Maymūn is hurriedly wed to Salmā. His bride enters into the ceremony with "her face radiant with light" (*wa-wajhuhā yatalaʾlaʾ nūran*), not out of joy but as a mark of her pale beauty.[41] Lying with his head innocently cradled in her lap and the marriage unconsummated, Maymūn expires after reciting a few morbid lines of poetry:

We've met with great and terrible terror,
As, afflicted, we gave over our labor.
Our ardor's incurable, we're just now together, [*iltaqaynā wa-mā shafaynā ghalīlan*]
Yet soon we shall part, as though we were never [*wa-iftaraqnā ka-annanā mā iltaqaynā*][42]

40. *Sīrat Dhāt al-Himma*, I:65.
41. *Sīrat Dhāt al-Himma*, I:66.
42. *Sīrat Dhāt al-Himma*, I:66.

The ironically luckless Maymūn (whose name suggests good fortune) issues a shuddering gasp and dies. Immediately, Salmā rejoices at narrowly evading sex with her repulsive, short-lived spouse (*fariḥat bi-dhālik farḥan shadīdan*). As with Sallām, we are never told explicitly about Maymūn's color or appearance, but throughout his interactions with the people of Kilāb and Ṭayy, he is consistently referred to as a bastard born of adultery (*zinā*), whose lineage has been cursed for thousands of generations (*ibn alf malʿūn*); when he dies, we learn he has a brother named Zaytūn (Olive) and a fellow slave and close comrade named Zand al-Fīl (Elephant's Arm) whose names evoke darkness and gargantuan size. All of this, coupled with his obvious parallelism to his predecessor Jaffāl, suggests that Maymūn is the second lowborn Black slave to become a casualty of Ghaṭrīf's greed.

In the aftermath of Maymūn's death, Zaytūn and Zand al-Fīl decide to restore the mare to Junduba in the hopes of ingratiating themselves with the powerful and wealthy chief. When they have nearly reached Kilābī territory, Zaytūn is overcome with a bout of anxiety, thinking of his traveling companion, "If I arrive before them with a slave of this sort, they'll assume that we are the same." He advises Zand al-Fīl to ride behind him in the stead of a servant, but Zand al-Fīl retorts that they ought to reverse roles. The interchangeability of Black men, and the presumption that all of them must be enslaved or previously so, again distends to tragicomic proportions: in the course of arguing who should (re)play the slave, Zaytūn and Zand al-Fīl fall upon one another with daggers and kill each other, leaving the mare to run homeward.[43] Another reset.

A third and final enslaved Black man emerges to retake the mare. This time, Salmā's would-be betrothed is both Black and light-eyed due to blindness. As with connections between Jaffāl's blackness, facial abnormalities, and the demonic or hellish, the rare and symbolically potent combination of black skin and blue eyes has roots that project into the pre-Islamic past. In a line of poetry attributed to ʿAntara ibn Shaddād, a dune-dwelling demoness, or *ghūl*, is portrayed as having "blue eyes, a black face, and nails like scythes."[44] So, too, in *Sīrat ʿAntar*, the prehistorical but postdiluvian figure of Kūsh (one of Nūḥ's grandchildren) appears as "dark-colored, light-eyed, large of body, strength, and frame, and having nails like beasts' claws."[45] The use of blue eyes in perhaps incongruous or unexpected figures in *Sīrat Dhāt al-Himma* may also recall audiences to the work's primary spiritual antagonists. Some exegetes linked having blue

43. *Sīrat Dhāt al-Himma*, I:66.
44. Jūrjī Zaydān, *ʿIlm al-Firāsa al-Ḥadīth* (London: Hindāwī, 2011), 78.
45. *Sīrat ʿAntar*, vol. 1, 16.

eyes with earthly unbelief because the Rūm, or Byzantines, were notoriously light-eyed.[46]

Vilifications of the dark-skinned and light-eyed in early Arabic writings are also taken up in a fascinating way in modernity, in a moment when having light skin and light eyes had become a globally known ideal through colonial enterprises. The nineteenth-century Lebanese historical fiction author Jurjī Zaydān (d. 1914), who was invested in writing an account of Arabness that used "the tools of cultural and especially physical anthropology available during his day," additionally wrote a treatise titled *ʿIlm al-Firāsa al-Ḥadīth* (*Modern Physiognomy*).[47] He proposed to offer certain expansions and corrections to works by the German physiognomist Johann Caspar Lavater and American phrenologist Samuel Wells through classical Arabic sources. In an account of various combinations of qualities and their significance, Zaydān—who is quick to note that Arabs do not share Europeans' unequivocal love of blue eyes—writes "the ugliest [situation] of blue eyes for the Arabs is against skin that is dark or black," adding that "this indicates that the [important] qualities of the eye lie not in their color, but their clarity [*ṣafāʾihā*] and cloudiness [*kadūrihā*], in their movement and stillness, and their shininess and brilliance."[48]

The dual associations of dark skin and light eyes with a lack of clarity, illumination, or radiance is echoed as well in eschatological imagery: denizens of hell in the Qurʾān are at times depicted as rheumy-eyed, a physical inscription of their blindness to God's truth and the intense thirst associated with those parched by hell's punishing fires. They are elsewhere figured as black-faced, which some interpreters saw as euphemistic and others as physicalized. Still others associated these images with the physicality of God's deputies who doled out postmortem fate, so that "this image of the dark-skinned, green-eyed sinner echoes the descriptions of the two angels Munkar and Nakīr, who interrogate and punish the dead in their graves."[49] The damned are enrobed in multilayered darkness, garbed in clothing made from tar and draped in shadow that, unlike the shade of this world, is "neither cool nor goodly."[50]

46. Kristina Richardson, "Blue Eyes and Green Eyes in the Islamicate Middle Ages," *Annales islamologiques* 48, no. 1 (2014): 17.

47. Orit Bashkin, "On Noble and Inherited Virtues: Discussions of the Semitic Race in the Levant and Egypt, 1876–1918," *Humanities* 10, no. 3 (2021): 6.

48. Zaydān, *ʿIlm al-Firāsa al-Ḥadīth*, 78.

49. Richardson, "Blue and Green Eyes," 20.

50. Q56:44.

In *Sīrat Dhāt al-Himma*, this final slave's superficial relationship to both demons and the damned is rendered quite literally in his description as an "old man, bleary-eyed and blind, woolly-haired and gap-toothed, flat-nosed, blue of eyes and dun-colored like an *ʿifrīt* from among the reviled people."[51] The man's name is Jamrat al-Ḥaddād, or The Blacksmith's Embers, likely in reference to his complexion; in his adventures he is accompanied by his son, Sharāra, Spark. These names seem tailor-made to provoke laughter—even the self-serious Junduba openly derives horrified amusement when he hears them (*fa-tashawwash Junduba wa-nafar min hādhihi al-asmāʾ*).[52] Jamra is a practitioner of arts reminiscent of the eloquent charlatans Jaffāl and Maymūn, though with his own added flair for the occult. He pretends to be far blinder than he actually is, alleging that though he cannot visually navigate the earth he "sees" through astrological prognostication. He offers his soothsaying wisdom to Junduba. Junduba, perhaps now feeling quite desperate, accepts the blind seer's proposal and asks him to cast apotropaic spells to protect the mare. Once again, sacred invocations are toyed with in the process: Jamra declares that he will not cast a spell without payment, saying, "For the Prophet, peace and blessings upon him, said, 'There is no charm without a bribe [*lā raqwa illā bi-rashwa*],'" at which Junduba passes him a dinar. Permissiveness around a trade in spellcasting—and accepting kickbacks—in which Muḥammad is typically emphatically said to *not* have participated is dressed up in his supposed words. After proving he can compose effective incantations, Jamra asks that Junduba's slaves prepare the horse in her stables, during which time he doses the men with a sedative drug slipped into their drinking cups, kills them, and makes off with her.[53]

When Jamra emerges as the latest contender for her heart, Salmā openly despairs; her mother consoles her with the prospect that this man, too, may perish through God's intervention. Her mother proves to have been prescient: when Jamra returns, he is riddled with injuries incurred on his escape from the lands of several neighboring tribes. Adding to his losses, Jamra's son has been killed by a wild beast, dragged off and eaten when he went to relieve himself on their journey homeward through the desert. Reunited with his prize, Ghaṭrīf bridles the horse with jeweled garlands, swaths her in silk, and parades her into the village, then calls for doctors to nurse Jamra to health.

51. *Sīrat Dhāt al-Himma*, I:68.
52. *Sīrat Dhāt al-Himma*, I:72.
53. *Sīrat Dhāt al-Himma*, I:70–71.

Jamra's condition only worsens, so like Maymūn, he urges that the marriage be hastened. When the ceremony is completed and Salmā is ordered to "enter into the presence of [her] husband," she laments to Ghaṭrīf, "Yesterday you gave me over to a slave of little value, today to an elderly blind man [who looks like] the *ʿifrīts* of the wasteland!"[54] Jamra's likening—as with many other Black characters—to an *ʿifrīt*, a towering, dark demon, carries significances beyond the superficial similarities that also apply to the *ghūl* and the *jinn*.[55] Black figures are frequently referred to as *aghbar*, or dust-colored, throughout the *sīra*, and likewise one of the colors of a woman's blood in the story of ʿAbd al-Wahhāb's birth. The root *ʿ-f-r* is likewise related to dust and grime, compounding the fact that like many varieties of *jinn*, *ʿifrīts* are typically represented as ground dwellers who occupy an underworld distant from yet parallel to that of mortal humans.[56] Kathryn Kueny notes the preference in various Islamic narratives of human creation for the use of earth and clay as the materials from which one is hewn over the use of dust more commonly associated with the Hebrew Bible:

> In contrast to the Hebrew dust (*ʿafār*), the Qurʾānic God prefers clay (*ṭīn*) in his molding of humanity: "It is he who created you from clay (*ṭīn*) then decreed a term." However, the Qur'ān does not limit him to ṭīn alone. Other verses mention God's use of potter's clay (*ṣalṣāl*); mud (*ḥamaʾ*); sticky clay (*ṭīn lāzib*); and dust (*turāb*).[57]

Then, there is the intertextuality of the *ʿifrīt*'s haunting representation across various genres of Arabic storytelling. Revisiting the frame tale of the *1001 Nights*, a woman held prisoner by a hulking black *ʿifrīt* forces

54. *Sīrat Dhāt al-Himma*, I:77.

55. *ʿIfrīts* are in some contexts particularly associated with fire and lamps, perhaps evoked in Jamra's name, meaning ember, as well as with the chthonic realm through their etymological linking with dust. Christian Lange, "Revisiting Hell's Angels in the Quran," in *Locating Hell in Islamic Traditions*, ed. Christian Lange (Leiden: Brill, 2016), 82.

56. See J. Chelhod, "ʿIfrīt," in *Encyclopedia of Islam*, 2nd ed., ed. Peri Bearman et al. (Leiden: Brill, 2012); Robert Shaham, "Masters, Their Freed Slaves, and the Waqf in Egypt (Eighteenth–Twentieth Centuries)," *Journal of the Economic and Social History of the Orient* 43, no. 2 (2000): 162–88. On the chthonic nature of the *jinn*, see Simon O'Meara, "From Space to Place: The Quranic Infernalization of the Jinn," in *Locating Hell in Islamic Traditions*, ed. Christian Lange (Leiden: Brill, 2016), 56–72. On the difference between the idea of creation from dust and from clay or earth, see Kueny, *Conceiving Identities* 21.

57. Kueny, *Conceiving Identities*, 21.

herself upon the cuckolded brothers Shahriyar and Shahzaman in a scene that simultaneously amplifies and reverses the dynamics of the fatal liaisons between the kings' wives and their Black slaves.

In certain eras, the image of the *ʿifrīt* may also have recalled a more tangible, ritualized form of collective fright. At the time of the Mamluk sultanate in Egypt potentates setting out for pilgrimage often did so as part of grand processions, or *maḥmils*. During these festivities, entertainment was supplied in part by young men (discussed by Mamlūk historians as rabble, or "men on the fringes") who masqueraded as *ʿifrīts* and made mischief, to the point that the spectacle was temporarily banned in the mid-fifteenth century.[58] This is the same period conventionally most closely associated with heightened production of tales of the *Nights* as well as with the large-scale textualization of a number of *sīras* for which prior manuscripts do not survive.

Jamra's literal demonization plays with an affect of fear that works at once to render violence against him acceptable within his vignette and to haunt the characters with their complicity in the narrative's longue durée. When our figurative *ʿifrīt* finally expires, Salmā's marriage once again remains unconsummated. Salmā emerges from the boudoir praising God for her luck, and her father inquires about what has made her so elated. She says, "My husband died." Her father, seemingly at a loss, laughs and responds, "You are not very blessed when it comes to spouses." At this point, Salmā has the last word: "O my father, you have failed to grasp my meaning, truly God has wasted neither my rank nor my lineage [*fa-mā ḍayyaʿ Allāh ḥasabī wa-lā nasabī*]."[59]

In a few words at the tale's denouement, Salmā—who is never to appear in the *sīra* again—encapsulates the violence of genealogical protectionism in a world in which one is either enslaved or free and the layered, pseudo-agnatic nets of dependency, guardianship, and protection that will typify the Muslim *umma* in the text are not yet entrenched. The only way to gain social purchase in this prior realm is to marry into it, and three enslaved Black men have died in the attempt, to Salmā's joy. Their fatalistic narratives share far more in common with the most rote, stereotypical, and caricaturing elements of popular storytelling than with the elaborate moral construction of heroes. The characters with whom they interact are likewise less morally complex than their descendants—if they are to have

58. Boaz Shoshan, *Popular Culture in Medieval Cairo* (Cambridge: Cambridge University Press, 1993), 72; Annemarie Schimmel, "Some Glimpses of the Religious Life in Egypt During the Later Mamlūk Period," *Islamic Studies* 4, no. 4 (1965): 366–67.

59. *Sīrat Dhāt al-Himma*, I:78.

descendants, that is. Throughout, they remain committed to a cosmography in which one's ancestors and legacy are especially revered, and fate is the fearsome and interminable force that spirits them away. Consistently, we see various Arabian characters seek comfort in false preaching and magical method concerning ancestry and descent. We may note that in protecting her *ḥasab* and her *nasab*, Salmā has ended her journey in the text alone. Her father is without both a steed and an heir. Like the *jāhiliyya* itself, the Ṭayyī tribesmen have become a nonviable relic of a changed world order in their own lifetimes. Yet in the new world to come we will still rarely see "doves" wed to "crows." Instead, Black people are given a wider array of modes of filiation and belonging that nonetheless remain sexually constrained.

Conclusion

Antoine Borrut argues that though the ʿAbbasid historiographical "vulgate" generally took a dim view of the Umayyads, it also configured the reign of ʿAbd al-Malik and his policies as a premonitory moment in a narrative that culminates in the establishment of the ʿAbbasid state. Borrut further argues for the overlooked, ongoing importance of Syria to the ʿAbbasids, where much of *Sīrat Dhāt al-Himma*'s action takes place. He places the end of a period of relatively coherent policy and statecraft initiated by ʿAbd al-Malik with the demise of Hārūn al-Rashīd (d. 809), during whose reign ʿAbd al-Wahhāb does some of his most intricate proselytizing work in the *sīra*.[60] The ʿAbbasid conceptualization of history worked both to elide the violence of the dynasty's bloody revolution and to define its relationship, strategically, with the undeniable, physical traces of the built Umayyad past in their midst.[61] Borrut's explanation of how the ʿAbbasids remembered and wrote themselves into the passage of time impels us to consider how popular narratives that spotlight the same key political figures engage with time as well. As we have seen above, in the text of *Sīrat Dhāt al-Himma*, the pre-ʿAbd al-Malik period in the Arabian Peninsula is mapped as a time and space of *jāhiliyya*, ensconced in internecine tribal warfare, Bedouin raiding culture, and exclusive intimacies between insular kinship groups. These intimacies exert a disabling and, ultimately, lethal

60. Antoine Borrut, "Vanishing Syria: Periodization and Power in Early Islam," *Der Islam* 91, no. 1 (2014): 56–59.

61. On the multiple meanings of such sites of memory, see Antoine Borrut, "Remembering Karbalāʾ: The Construction of an Early Islamic Site of Memory," *Jerusalem Studies in Arabic and Islam* 42 (2015): 51.

force on those who dwell in the Arabian Peninsula but live outside the bounds of local kinship, articulated with marked consistency as *nasab*.

Throughout the tale of the three slaves of Ṭayy, the tribal Arabs' preoccupations with accruing the trappings of pedigree, be it through noble marriage or remarkable steeds, comes with the false promise and ultimate withholding of these same prospects from a large, expendable supply of Black slaves. Recurrently, the text's universe takes pains to snatch the Black characters from the world of the living at the moment that they are about to consummate their marriage with Salmā and thus secure their posterity, bringing unhealable wounds to bear or contriving tragicomic run-ins with doppelgänger slaves from other tribes who are also doomed in love. This serves to underscore the fact that the slaves are being punished in the *sīra* not so much for their thievery and dissimulation as for their ambitions to advance in the social ranks through marriage to Arab women, which gives rise to these desperate measures. The measures, meanwhile, serve to make their deaths less lamentable and their abjection more reasonable, and are even treated within the story as the most proximate cause of their suffering.

Yet each one's suffering is also not solely his own. Despite their inability to reproduce themselves through sexual intercourse, the Black men in the text do have a regenerative capacity in that the vanished body of one is replaced swiftly by another. In the words of Bakhtin, "in the grotesque body," an excessive, exaggerated physicalizing of political conflict and critique, "death brings nothing to an end, for it does not concern the ancestral body, which is renewed in every generation."[62] Likewise, we see that the fates of the Black figures who follow on one another's heels in this episode all are ineluctably connected despite their lack of any but the most superficial biological or social relation—each of their bodies prefigures and compounds the significance of the next, dramatizing the classed and racialized threat against a highborn Arab woman's honor. Though, as we already saw in the heroes' birth stories, Black boys' and men's bodies continue to be objects of reproductive anxiety throughout the narrative present and not just in the chronotopic *jāhilī* past, we shall see in the next few chapters that Black male figures are simultaneously imbued with another type of symbolism and purpose as engines of Islamic territorial expansion.

As with the fear and anxiety they elicit, so too the humor that the three slaves of Ṭayy provoke turns on their sexual and somatic excesses: the

62. Mikhail Bakhtin, *Rabelais and His World*, trans. Helene Iswolsky (Bloomington: Indiana University Press, 1984), 322.

absurd descriptions of the men's prevailing lusts even as their bodies bleed and their organs fail, Jaffāl's and Jamra's deformities and Maymūn's maiming, and Sharāra's demise while urinating in the woods are all elements that might prompt laughter at the text's Black subjects, even as their positioning in a bygone thought-world frames this racialized humor as outré. Notably, the derisive humor that characterizes the three slaves of Ṭayy's narrative largely disappears from the *sīra* by the time ʿAbd al-Wahhāb takes center stage; mocking the Black Muslim body comes to be presented as crassly derogatory, and insofar as he is the target of mockery by others for his skin color, ʿAbd al-Wahhāb is held up as a paragon of patience and resolve. Those who are most unkind to him in this regard are branded as villains. At the same time, though, the invective against the three slaves of Ṭayy makes use of a form of racial thinking that continues throughout the text, which Cord Whitaker has identified as enthymematic logic. Enthymematic logic stitches together people perceived to be of the same kind and makes them accountable to legacies—or, in rhetorical terms, unstated premises—that are not theirs to authorize. It thwarts the possibility of unalloyed deduction. In explaining how enthymeme works to fix racialized identities and perceptions, Whitaker writes:

> This [example of] inductive enthymeme speaks to its subjects' character; it asserts that those who have failed before are not to be trusted, even though the evidence from the past might not necessarily predict current or future failure. Such enthymematic logic easily shades over into racial judgments in which the character flaw of one person leads to the presumption of the same flaw in someone who shares a defining yet unrelated characteristic.[63]

Though the slaves of Ṭayy are a special case and earn special critique, the general practice of judging Black men with greater scrutiny endures. This scrutiny obtains at the level of pedantic physiognomic prognostication and inquiries into paternity, to say nothing of the standards of heroism through which Black men merit redemptive narration.

The slaves of Ṭayy are not the only ones being satirized in the above vignette. Throughout, Salmā stands as a symbol of snobbish recalcitrance: the aloof beauty who must be continuously reminded by her father that a wife's duty is to obey, that enslaved people are human, and that a man's worth lies in his good deeds rather than his lineage. Her father Ghaṭrīf,

63. Whitaker, *Black Metaphors*, 129.

meanwhile, emblematizes decadence and naivety: he is willing to squander his daughter's *ḥasab* and *nasab* over a horse. Ironically, the creature would itself have had its quality certified through sciences of pedigree verifying its elite *nasab*, which was often deployed to chart the breeding of prestige animals like horses, camels, and falcons. Read in this light, his pretensions to putting the pedigree of his potential sons-in-law aside and advising Salmā to do likewise ring hollow.

Ghaṭrīf pursues his aim single-mindedly, against the counsel of his advisors, his wife, and his child. In addition to the obvious cost to the tribe's Black slaves, the text's determined preclusion of exogamy renders Salmā paralyzed in place, as her posterity is forestalled again and again by her own desire to preserve her lineage and the astonishing plot devices that continuously enable this. The text thus imagines the tentatively Islamized pre-ʿAbd al-Malik environment as untenable, lacking moral clarity and a vision for the future. This untenability disproportionately imperils the survival of Black characters, who therefore stand to gain a particularly great amount from the coming of Islam. These gains are articulated as the ability for Black people to access and assimilate into the elite *ansāb* so studiously guarded by Salmā and her ilk, yet which continue to be framed as divinely assigned. Using *nasab* advantageously, heroes throughout the ensuing tale who have been graced with prodigious talents and stand as their community's paragons gradually bring rootless and nonelite characters under their wing through kin-like channels. These relationships are largely predicated on marginal figures' former enslavement and conversion rather than marriage. Nonetheless, they are offered a prospect that appears impossible in the *sīra*'s quasi-*jāhiliyya*. Through forms of Muslim piety that are mediated by contact with caliphs and luminaries, racialized and othered subjects become instantiated within the religio-legal apparatus that helps them contend more effectively for their inclusion.

5

The Present

God has angels that convey people of the same kind to one another.

HADĪTH

Sharing a common group history cannot be a criterion for being members of the same group, for we would have to be able to identify the group in order to identify its history.

KWAME ANTHONY APPIAH

The primary hero of a *sīra* must be of a prominent line [*karīm al-nasab*].

AḤMAD SHAMS AL-DĪN AL-ḤAJJĀJĪ

Sīrat Dhāt al-Himma's Black characters and their degrees of freedom mark time, teleologically, representing the prospects of those racialized and othered in the un-Islamized *jāhiliyya* differently and more negatively than in the text's Islamized narrative present. Much as across the epic tradition heroic lineages that extend into the pre-Islamic age are presented as preternaturally pious or "proto-Muslim," *Sīrat Dhāt al-Himma* presents its audiences with an exaggeration of the pre-Islamic masses' genealogical myopia, treating their non-tribesmen as perpetual, derided outsiders. The advent of ʿAbd al-Wahhāb as the central Black-Arab hero of the text and a leader of the Muslim armies, who is referred to deferentially as the "shield of the Prophet Muḥammad's grave" (*turs qabr al-nabī*), introduces a transition from one form of racialized time to another: Black people are no longer irrevocably banished from Arabness because they can instead seek community as Muslims, a by-product of which is that they will indeed culturally Arabize. But first, they must link themselves into Arab genealogies through various agnatic and quasi-agnatic channels. Where this process is articulated literally in the tale through a hero who is born Black to an elite, Arab lineage in the tribe of Kilāb, it is expressed more figuratively through the experiences of conversion and incorporation on the part of myriad other Black figures.

As mentioned previously, the state of being *jāhil*, or ignorant, is increasingly displaced onto figures beyond Arabia as the Peninsula comes under ever more direct caliphal control in the tale. Ignorance gives occasion for conversion and education in Islamic practices, ideals, and social structures. Conversion in the *sīras* is described by Helen Blatherwick, following Richard van Leeuwen, as extending beyond changes to personal religion, instead ushering in a wholesale shift from "chaos" to "order" and from "non-history" to "history."[1] Because this educational process is presented in *Sīrat Dhāt al-Himma* through individual snapshots and character pairings, one watches the social order evolve gradually and unevenly, with certain types of people eliciting different, more protracted, or more urgent techniques of incorporation. Often, new converts and freedmen's experiences of community are channeled through genealogical processes, creating proximity to more socially secure individuals who had been Islamized for far longer or to an illustrious prophetic past. During the early Islamic period, the project of "recovering" and codifying proximity to specific Arabian lineages was frequently enacted on behalf of precarious and new Muslims, who compensated for their lack of standing by imagining themselves as part of a more multiethnic, primeval prophetic network or else as descendants of non-Arab companions of the Prophet Muḥammad, if not by directly "grafting" themselves into Arabian family trees.[2] In the words of Sarah Bowen Savant, these reworkings were "profoundly assimilationist in character and reflected an earnest effort to imagine . . . a better place within an Islamic society still respectful of Arab norms."[3]

ʿAbd al-Wahhāb's centrality to the project of envisioning Black Muslim collective betterment through normative, genealogical Arab channels is premised on his unique hybridity: he is not only of high birth, but also is the same kind as many who are not. A particularly lengthy and involved example of activating this hybridity is ʿAbd al-Wahhāb's encounter

1. Blatherwick, *Prophets, Gods, and Kings*, 66; Richard van Leeuwen, "Conversion as a (Meta-)Historical Concept in the Epic Stories of the *Thousand and One Nights*," in *Fictionalizing the Past: Historical Characters in Arabic Popular Epic*, ed. Sabine Dorpmueller (Leiden: Uitgeverij Peeters en Departement Oosterse Studies, 2012), 135.

2. I borrow this use of the concept of "grafting" from Zoltán Szombathy. Zoltán Szombathy, "Genealogy in Medieval Muslim Societies," *Studia Islamica* 95 (2002): 5–35.

3. Savant, "Isaac as the Persians' Ishmael," 6.

with the Black warrior Abū'l-Hazāhiz, or "Father of Convulsions"—a titanic figure said to have the strength of tens of men, who first cycles through several communities before finding a true home in normative Islam (which is to say, with Muslim peers not labeled as *khārijī*, or separatist, in the world of the text). ʿAbd al-Wahhāb acts as his steward on the last legs of his spiritual journey. The meeting of the two allegorizes assimilation into both cosmic and worldly orders: with ʿAbd al-Wahhāb's guidance, Abū'l-Hazāhiz can be seen acquainting himself with concepts of an elaborately ranked universe filled not just with masses of human worshippers, but also celestial figures like angels and human intermediaries like Messengers. Moreover, he acquaints himself with the far worldlier hierarchical dimensions of how he is racialized among his fellow Muslims, his dependent status as ʿAbd al-Wahhāb's lower *mawlā*, or post-manumission client, and his duties as a soldier beholden to God's vicegerent, the ʿAbbasid caliph.

This chapter demonstrates that Abū'l-Hazāhiz's allegory of assimilation—a tale in which cosmic and earthly forces nest neatly to the end of educating and incorporating an "other"—is meant to educate an audience, too. "Allegory" is not a sui generis category in early Islamic thought. However, Peter Heath demonstrates that a variety of narrative forms, from Sufi anecdotes to epistolary prose and reportage (*akhbār*) "create their polysemous structures by contrasting everyday experiences against several major cultural codes." They perform an allegorical function in that they inculcate habits of recognizing and appreciating the duality of having tangible principles that are discernible in intricate figurative tableaux.[4] I also use "allegory" to suggest that would-be-assimilated Black characters' semiotic richness is paired with their subjective elision, or the "representative surplus and referential lack" through which racialized subjects are so often made knowable.[5] Their malleability can also render them transgressive and unbound from specific moments, events, or individuals.

As one such malleable figure, Abū'l-Hazāhiz has an ambiguous biography such that it is far more difficult to be concerned with him as a person

4. Peter Heath, "Allegory in Islamic Literatures," in *The Cambridge Companion to Allegory*, ed. Rita Copeland and Peter T. Struck (Cambridge: Cambridge University Press, 2011), 85.

5. I borrow this very useful phrasing from Aravamudan's theorization of resistivity in representations of colonized peoples, which as representations are at once diminutions of a "real" and, interpretatively, are larger than their own anticipated lives. Srinivas Aravamudan, *Tropicopolitans: Colonialism and Agency, 1688–1804* (Durham, NC: Duke University Press, 1999), 5.

in the tale than with what he might mean. He is presented as originless and pliable. He moves across a variety of religious persuasions before settling firmly on (Sunni) Islam and developing a relationship of service to and tutelage from ʿAbd al-Wahhāb that the text at times overtly portrays as childlike. Indeed, the status of being someone's *mawlā* connotes a form of guardianship that is regularly compared to filiation. Alongside tens of peers who make up the topmost ranks of the "noble Blacks," or *al-sūdān al-anjāb*, in the story, Abū'l-Hazāhiz's more elaborate narrative imparts specific affects and sensibilities around what to do with difference. That an especially urgent form of difference to be assimilated is represented, recurrently, by uprooted and hypermobile Black men throughout the text indicates not just how blackness is racialized and charged with signifying something far larger and more morally weighty than one's external qualities in narrative, but also how Muslimness can unlock its purpose.

One might be compelled to read Abū'l-Hazāhiz's arc as a following a straightforward tale-type: the reformation of the savage or wild man. This much was surmised in a 1996 article by Jean-Patrick Guillaume, who reads Abū'l-Hazāhiz as an "incarnation" of the giant, Black, primitive, and often-anthropophagic "ogre" archetype that he traces across popular Arabic storytelling, with Abū'l-Hazāhiz's story showing the triumph of the forces of faith over nature.[6] I instead explore how an utterly human Abū'l-Hazāhiz illustrates the utility of specific social structures in enticing and keeping one faithful—structures of family and racialized status that people have tended to think of as themselves emanating from nature.

I am far from the first to argue that the *sīras* in particular, and popular literature in general, have didactic functions concerning macrocosmic formations of society and identity. In his foundational study of epicists in the Egyptian town of al-Bakātūsh, Dwight Reynolds describes the marginalized poetic performers of *Sīrat Banī Hilāl* as using their craft as a source of identity in ways that run parallel to lineage, and as a tool for instructing locals in the poets' would-be social standing:

> Their attachment to specific customs and traditions seems to be involved in the poets' sense of separateness from the larger society, that

6. Jean-Patrick Guillaume, "Les Ismaéliens dans le *Roman de Baybarṣ*: Genèse d'un type littéraire," *Studia Islamica* 84 (1996): 162–63. See also: Jean-Patrick Guillaume, "Quelques avatars du géant au tronc d'arbre dans la tradition épique arabe et ailleurs," in *Medioevo romanzo e orientale: Temi e motivi epico-cavallereschi fra Oriente e Occidente*, ed. Gaetano Lalomia and Antonio Pioletti (Soveria Mannelli, Italy: Rubbettino, 2010), 163–78.

is, an aspect of differential identity, and seems to be specifically engaged with the Arabic concept of *aṣl*, or origin, through the establishment of a persona that is more Arab than that of neighboring social groups.[7]

A command over genealogical knowledge and its cultural production was a matter not just of knowing a given *sīra* or related work, but also the "paratexts" through which an audience might apprehend and appreciate the story, acting "like a fine skin over its body."[8] Pasha Khan notes that in the tradition of Persian and Urdu *qiṣṣas*, staple "extra-generic" Islamic features like opening praise of God and the Prophet work to orient audiences, but that scholars often take them for granted as workaday rather than as tailored yet familiar entry points into a text's world.[9] Melanie Magidow states that it is through these pious formulas that one may interpret *Sīrat Dhāt al-Himma*'s opening claims to ethos as well.[10] We might also add to this the extra-generic, paratextual feature of the genealogical chain by which one's past and legacy might be reckoned, which, Magidow notes, consists in the *sīra*'s opening list of prior reciters. Such chains are elsewhere recalled by a range of terms, such as an *isnād* or a *silsila*, depending on the ideas of intergenerational continuity to which they are most germane. In the *sīra* itself, intergenerational chains typically are instead phrased as *ansāb*, to which the audience's attention has already been turned through its frame.

Within *Sīrat Dhāt al-Himma*, the passage of time and rise of new, linked generations is a key facilitator for dispensing lessons about identity. By the time that ʿAbd al-Wahhāb and Abū'l-Hazāhiz meet, the tribes of the Arabian Peninsula are firmly within the fold of the ʿAbbasid caliphate under the rule of Hārūn al-Rashīd. This is largely due to a meeting and mutual esteeming of grand lineages: Maslama, son of ʿAbd al-Malik b. Marwān and famed fighter on the Anatolian frontier, develops an intimate friendship with Junduba's successor to the Kilābī chiefdom, Ṣaḥṣāḥ, and ultimately helps to align him with caliphal interests and secure the position of "King of the Arabs," presiding over a loose federation of tribes. In the aftermath of the tribes' reinvigorated Islamization, *ḥasab wa-nasab*, or the inherited rank and kinship ties so precious to Salmā in the prior chapter, have not lost their importance. As Touria Khannous puts it, it

7. Reynolds, *Heroic Poets*, 89–90.

8. Pasha M. Khan, *The Broken Spell: Indian Storytelling and the Romance Genre in Persian and Urdu* (Detroit: Wayne State University Press, 2019), 14.

9. Khan, 124.

10. Magidow, *Tale of Princess Fatima*, xi.

has virtually always been the case that denizens of Arabia "[viewed] blood and biological descent as fundamental to one's racial identity," though we might modify this slightly in light of chapter 3 to emphasize lines via womb-blood and semen, rather than blood in its more generalized sense and with its contemporary resonances with racial quantum.[11] Although these lines remained fundamental to concepts of social belonging, their connotations evolved in the early Islamic period, engendering a new set of genealogical priorities and possibilities.

Lines and Time

In the early Islamic background to *Sīrat Dhāt al-Himma*, the passage of time entails the collection, proliferation, and divergence of interpretations of Islam's foundational texts and traditions with respect to modeling community and hierarchy. Throughout this book, we have seen various expressions of the notion that the intricacy of a highly diverse world—and differentiation and plenitude as such—are manifestations of divine genius, and that so too is its order. For various early Muslim thinkers, the specifics of social stratification could nonetheless be subject to change. According to Louise Marlow, learned individuals often made the "Qurʾānic piety clause" their discursive foundation for "pious opposition" to aspects of social inequality among Muslims, that is, the sentiment expressed in Q 49:13 that one's righteousness (*taqwā*) is paramount over one's tribe or people. For confronting social inequalities grounded in lineage, various other scriptural precedents also existed. In Q 25:54, God is ascribed the role of sole architect of all human relations of womb kinship (*nasab*) and marital affinity (*ṣihr*), rendering these relationships parallel forms of filiation that are both contingent on divine rather than human authority.[12] The Qurʾān also assures believers that on the Day of Judgment, bonds of lineage (*ansāb baynahum*) will be rendered meaningless, perhaps signaling the obsolescence of pre-Islamic notions of ancestral intercession.[13] And in various traditions, Muḥammad reconfigures the definition of *nasab*'s companion, *ḥasab*, or inherited merit, to refer to one's level of religiosity or strength of personal character, in contrast to its *jāhilī* connotation as a legacy of ancestral feats and virtues. *Ṭaʿn fī-l-ansāb*, or the practice

11. Touria Khannous, "Race in Pre-Islamic Poetry: The Work of Antara Ibn Shaddad," *African and Black Diaspora: An International Journal* 6:1 (2013): 69.

12. A. J. Arberry, *The Koran Interpreted: A Translation* (New York: Touchstone, 1996), 61.

13. Q 23:101.

of artfully satirizing others on the basis of birth station, earns increasing opprobrium.[14]

However, rather than rendering *nasab* obsolete, the early Islamic period witnessed new ways to capitalize on social flux and create, link up, or revalue lineages. As the Prophet, his forebears, and his companions became the new elite, many actors with roots outside of the region saw an opportunity to weave themselves into esteemed genealogies by claiming an agnatic relationship with pre-Islamic prophets or non-Arab companions of Muḥammad, thus sidestepping the traditionally coveted Arab lines while still privileging the use of *nasab* as a tool for gaining social purchase. Muḥammad himself sets scripts for what this process might look like, as in a *ḥadīth* tradition known as the *waṣiyya bi-l-aqbāṭ* (exhortation concerning the Copts, or native Egyptians), which makes it incumbent for Muslims to take Coptic populations into their care through duties of protection (*dhimma*) because of their familial ties. These are stated as bonds of womb kinship (*raḥim*), issuing from Ibrāhīm's Egyptian slave woman, Hājar, mother of Ismāʿīl, who is the progenitor of Arabia's populace as discussed in chapter 1.[15] Other traditions attest not only to Hājar's relation to Copts but also more generally to people with specific shared features and shared space, and who have common "lineage and matrilineal relation (*nasab wa-ṣihr*)" with the Arabs.[16] Thus, they are distinct yet related. Xavier Luffin finds a diverse range of pathways through which peoples historically seen as Black in Arabic sources linked their *ansāb* to Arab and Arab-Muslim figures of note, from those in parts of Ethiopia who trace themselves to dispersed early converts from the Banū Makhzūm clan of Quraysh, to Muslims in Chad who trace their heritage to the pre-Islamic Yemeni sovereign Sayf b. Dhī Yazan.[17]

Arab-identifying groups were also sensitive to the political value of historicizing their Muslim identity, with the result that tracing common north Arabian tribal lineage to the ancient pagan ancestor Maʿadd b. ʿAdnān was supplanted by a connection with the yet more chronologically distant figure of Ismāʿīl. Some traditions synthesize the two, making Ismāʿīl

14. Muslim b. Ḥajjāj al-Qushayrī and Ṣafī al-Rahmān al-Mubārakpūrī, *Minnat al-Munʿim fī Sharḥ Ṣaḥīḥ Muslim*, vol. 2 (Riyadh: Dar al-Salām al-Nashr wa-l-Tawzīʿ, 1951), 53; "Ḥasab wa-Nasab."

15. Nathaniel Miller, "Warrior Elites on the Verge of Islam: Between Court and Tribe in Arabic Poetry," in *Cross-Cultural Studies in Near Eastern History and Literature*, vol. 2, ed. Saana Svärd and Robert Rollinger (Münster: Ugarit-Verlag, 2016), 145.

16. Ibn Hishām, *Sīrat Ibn Hishām*, 6.

17. Luffin, "'Nos ancêtres les Arabes,'" 177–209.

a forefather of Maʿadd, and hence of the northern Arabs (Qaḥṭānī, or southern, Arabian lineages are less frequently traced to Ishmael and instead said to go back to Joktan).[18] Thus goes the tradition that opens Ibn al-Kalbī's (d. 819) *Jamharat al-Nasab*, the earliest extant comprehensive genealogical register of the Arabs:

> The Messenger of God, peace be upon him, held back until the completion of [the recitation of] the *nasab* up to Maʿadd b. ʿAdnān. Then he said, 'The genealogists have lied [*kadhab al-nassābūn*]. God, praised be He, said, 'And many generations between them.'[19] Ibn ʿAbbās said, 'And had the Messenger of God desired to instruct [the reciter], surely he would have informed him that, as he has said, 'between Maʿadd b. ʿAdnān and Ismāʿīl are thirty fathers.'[20]

Through such interventions, people of many tribal Arabian heritages are able to fashion their sense of particularity and cohesion as a people around the figure of Maʿadd while also embedding their genealogical bona fides within the more universal fabric of Muslim sacred history.

The prohibition against satirizing one's peers on the basis of *ansāb* was often taken to mean not a moratorium on the scientific practice of tracing genealogy nor an undermining of genealogy's social value in this world, but instead a call to wield *nasab* to illuminating rather than derogating ends. Indeed, keeping track of lineage could prove an invaluable resource for those who were not lineally advantaged and could not readily bring new details of their past to light. In the early Islamic period, an option for those without tribal standing was to subordinate oneself to those that had it through ties of *walāʾ*, often translated as "clientage," and derived from the idea of being drawn close to another being in a relationship of dependency or "unfreedom." In her work on the famed *mawlā* (one in a relationship of *walāʾ*) of the Prophet, Abū Bakra, and his maligned half brother Ziyād ibn Abīhi (d. 673), Elizabeth Urban has shown that in their foundational "morality tale," being a humble *mawlā* rather than pretending to a tribal lineage one

18. Webb, "Ethnicity, Power, and Umayyad Society"; Martin Wittingham, *A History of Muslim Views of the Bible: The First Four Centuries* (Berlin: De Gruyter, 2021), 69.

19. This passage is found in verse 38 of *Sūrat al-Furqān*, in which it is said that God destroyed the pre-Islamic empires of ʿĀd and Thamūd, the People of the Well, and many intervening generations.

20. Al-Kalbī, *Jamharat al-Nasab*, 1:65. On Arabic prosopography, the rise of the *jamhara* genre, and the reification of genealogies, see Tarif Khalidi, "History and Hadith," in *Arabic Historical Thought in the Classical Period*, 17–83 (Cambridge: Cambridge University Press, 1994).

did not have was represented as the pious, honest route to belonging, thus tying in righteousness and worthiness with accepting one's station.[21]

According to tradition, relationships between upper and lower *mawlās* were analogous to *nasab* in terms of their non-fungible social value: "*walāʾ* is a form of kinship like the kinship of *nasab*, and can be neither sold, gifted, nor bequeathed."[22] One of the main ways of entering into a relationship of *walāʾ*—and the only one that endured beyond the early ʿAbbasid period—was manumission from slavery, which rendered one a permanent client to their prior owners.[23] In some parts of the world, these patron-client relationships rooted in former enslavement have endured across generations, becoming part of people's family names, patterns of settlement and migration, and labor structures. In enfolding the Black, formerly enslaved Abū'l-Hazāhiz into his family through *walāʾ*, ʿAbd al-Wahhāb presents an audience already primed to associate blackness with slavery or dispossession with a legible, allegorical case of the assimilation of one outstanding Black man into the Muslim community through a proven pathway.

Many of the most prominent examples of Black characters experiencing a rags-to-riches ascent in the *sīra* tradition are men similarly engaged in homosocial, paternalistic structures with male heroes. In steadily consolidating a Black community around himself through masculine bonds of service and compact, ʿAbd al-Wahhāb configures a subset of society bounded not only by racialized kind, but also by gender.[24] As with the birth stories of the *sīras*' incongruously, nonhereditarily Black heroes, relationships of *walāʾ* among Black brethren succeed not only in offering tales of advancements made and glories gained, but doing so in ways that tidily leave aside alternative imaginings of the same. In both tale-types—the hero's unlikely origin story and the evolution of a soldierly confraternity—Black men experiencing marriage and fatherhood is kept largely offstage, even as the critical importance of extending kinship ties to meritorious figures is centered.

21. Urban, *Conquered Populations*, 69.

22. Al-Bayhaqī, *Fahāris Aḥādīth wa-Āthār al-Sunan*, vol. 11, ed. Ibrāhīm Shams al-Dīn (Beirut: Dār al-Kutub al-ʿIlmiyya, 2003), 494.

23. On the endurance of manumissive cliental or dependent relations beyond the Umayyad era, see Daniel Pipes, "Mawlas: Freed Slaves and Converts in Early Islam," in *Slaves and Slavery in Muslim Africa*, vol. 1, ed. John Ralph Willis (London: Routledge, 2014), 222–23.

24. On the trope of homosocial mentor-mentee relationships in *Alf Layla wa-Layla*, see Fedwa Malti-Douglas, *Woman's Body, Woman's Word: Gender and Discourse in Arabo-Islamic Writing* (Princeton, NJ: Princeton University Press, 1991).

Before meeting Abū'l-Hazāhiz, several other of these homosocial arrangements arise. For example, ʿAbd al-Wahhāb encounters the analogous figure of Simlaq, thunder-voiced and formidable, serving Arab-led armies and arriving from Basra as if to recall the urban center's history as a hub for enslaved Zanj and Zuṭṭ workers in Iraq, each of whom staged rebellions in the ninth century.[25] On seeing ʿAbd a-Wahhāb, "kind yearns for kind" (*ḥann al-jins ilā-l-jins*). The moment is enhanced by Simlaq's appreciation of ʿAbd al-Wahhāb's superior beauty even among this "kind" and his elevation "by the people and the caliph"; Simlaq is further impressed by the Black men in ʿAbd a-Wahhāb's cohort, who flank him "clothed in Greek silk and Melkite brocade"—a far cry the treatment Simlaq has received thus far. Simlaq infers that these must be the goods that frontier plunder can procure, along with the "daughters of unbelievers" (*banāt al-kuffār*). He and his men quickly take an oath of allegiance to the Black hero, vowing to fight and die in his service exclusively.[26]

The *sīra* is not unique in conjuring Black individuals as the test cases for navigating competing discourses of genealogy and merit. Work that was far more explicitly concerned with the sciences of lineage did likewise. Thus opens Ibn Ḥazm's *Jamharat Ansāb al-ʿArab*, an eleventh-century comprehensive genealogical register:

> Indeed God, the praised and gloried, has said, "Truly we created you male and female and made you into peoples and tribes in order that you may know each other [*li-taʿārafū*]. Verily the most honorable of you before God is the most righteous of you." . . . We were told by Saʿīd b. Abī Saʿīd, who is al-Maqburī, via his father, via Abū Hurayra, that [they said], "O messenger of God! Who is among the most honorable of people?" He responded, "The most righteous of them!" They said, "This is not what we are asking you about." He said, "Yūsuf, the prophet of God, son of the prophet of God, son of the comrade [*khalīl*] of God." They replied, "This is not what we are asking you about." [The Prophet] said, "Then, are you asking me about the origins of the Arabs? The best

25. Simlaq appears to be coded in the story as Zanjī, particularly through his fascination with silks. However, his name is identical with that of a general in the Zuṭṭ rebellion, implying that oral lore around the two events and peoples—one East African and the other South Asian—may have merged over time. Richardson, *Roma in the Medieval Islamic World*, 26. On the role of silks in the Zanj rebellion's closure, see Philip Grant, "Entangled Symbols: Silk and the Material Semiosis of the Zanj Rebellion (869–83)," *al-ʿUṣūr al-Wusṭā* 30 (2022): 573–602.

26. *Sīrat Dhāt al-Himma*, VII:67–69.

of them in the *jāhiliyya* is the best of them in the [age of] Islam, if they comprehend [it]."

And truly God Almighty has pronounced that the most honorable [individual] is the most righteous, even if he is the bastard son of a Zanjī woman [*ibn zanjiyya li-ghayya*], and indeed the most disobedient unbeliever is diminished in rank [*maḥṭūṭ al-daraja*], even if he is the son of two prophets. Thus the mutual knowledge [*ta'āruf*] of people by means of their *nasab* is an objective that the Almighty had in creating us peoples and tribes, hence it must be the case that the science of *nasab* is a science of high regard [*jalīl rafī'*], for with it comes mutual knowledge [*ta'āruf*].[27]

Ibn Ḥazm justifies the practice of *'ilm al-nasab* as a means of generating mutual knowledge (*ta'āruf*) across peoples, per the Qur'ān's instruction, but is at pains to say that this knowledge is only instructive insofar as people have lived up to their lineages through righteousness. Yet as the putative "worst case scenario" of the bastard child of a Zanjī woman suggests, historical, cross-cultural dynamics of domination and exploitation mean that many people who were marginalized in the past will continue to bear a larger burden of proof, because at issue is not whether they have furthered their illustrious origins, but whether they have exceeded baser ones.

Sīrat Dhāt al-Himma is not itself a work of traditionist interpretation grounded in a specific set of methods and knowledges (*'ulūm*), though it draws on many such works. In many respects, the narrative seems to follow a genealogy for no end other than the excellence of that genealogy itself. It is remarkable, then, that the cyclical generations of heroes by which the *sīra*—the "life path"—is known gather to themselves bands of marginal figures of whom they make new kin in new ways that become available to them as the text progresses. We may then ask: Why do they do so? Who merits this incorporation? And through what means?

Abū'l-Hazāhiz and a Quest for Origins

When we first meet Abū'l-Hazāhiz, he is doubly marginalized and on a path to ruin. Not only is he Black, but he heads up a battalion of other Black people fighting the Byzantines on behalf of the self-proclaimed savior, Mahdī'l-Zamān (Messiah of the Age), who is referred to as a "*khārijī*" agitator because he is contesting Hārūn al-Rashīd for the title of caliph.

27. Ibn Ḥazm, *Jamharat Ansāb al-'Arab*, 1–2.

Though the political and theological leanings of his first patron are a blip in Abū'l-Hazāhiz's greater tale, they are highly symbolic. Among the many things for which people who fought under the Khārijī banner were known—rapine, heresy, regicide—was the principle that one's heritage carries no aspect of entitlement, but rather piety alone. When one trespasses the responsibilities that their piety had earned them, so goes one's authority. The defining events in Khārijī formation are their dissent from and eventual murder of the fourth caliph, ʿAlī (d. 661), after he agreed to bring his predecessor ʿUthmān's (d. 656) killers to justice when, in their view, ʿUthmān's death had been deserved and even ordained. However, as Hannah-Lena Hageman shows, Khārijī motivations are more often pronounced on from the outside; the term *Khārijī* quickly becomes a byword for fractiousness within normative Muslim historiography and a cautionary narrative device.[28] The Khārijī messiah of the *sīra* may thus not be aligned with the seventh-century political movement, but rather simply named as such because he contests the ʿAbbasids and professes Islam.

At times, the exaggerations of heresiographers about the Khārijīs map uncannily onto racialized conflations of blackness and status that we have seen before: Patricia Crone identifies a pervasive notion in both modern scholarly and medieval heresiographical sources beginning with al-Shahrastānī's (d. 1153) *Kitāb al-Milal wa-l-Niḥal*, or *Book of Factions and Creeds*, that the Khārijīs would allow a "slave" (*ʿabd*) to become caliph. Crone considers this unlikely because "a slave is not his own master," instead favoring the view that here *slave* is meant to indicate a "non-Arab," though more trenchantly in the text's play of opposites, it may also be read as a Black person.[29] The appeal of Kharijism's more quietist cousin, Ibāḍī Islam, to peoples of so-called Berber and Black heritage in North Africa and the Sahel throughout Islam's first centuries is likewise often attributed in part to its "egalitarianism" and favorable view of low-status individuals.[30] Moreover, the instances in which the *sīras*

28. Hannah-Lena Hagemann, *The Khārijites in Early Islamic Historical Tradition: Heroes and Villains* (Edinburgh: Edinburgh University Press, 2021), 5–6.

29. This is indeed how Crone seems to read it, though for different reasons: she translates *ʿabd* as "black slave" specifically rather than as a generic slave. Patricia Crone, "'Even an Ethiopian Slave': The Transformation of a Sunnī Tradition," *Bulletin of the School of Oriental and African Studies* 57, no. 1 (1994): 66. Al-Shahrastānī, *Kitāb al-Milal wa-l-Niḥal*, ed. William Cuerton (Leipzig: Harrassowitz Verlag, 1923), 87.

30. See, e.g.: Phillip C. Naylor, *North Africa: A History from Antiquity to the Present* (Austin: University of Texas Press, 2009), 69; Elizabeth Savage, "Berbers and Blacks: Ibadi Slave Traffic in Eighth-Century North Africa," *Journal of African History* 33 (1992): 351–68.

activate this sectarian language are pregnant ones, particularly in view of the fact that elsewhere in the corpus internecine conflicts within the *umma* are strategically erased: in the Mamluk-era *Sīrat Baybars*, for example, the Nizārī Ismāʿīlī "assassins" of northern Syria whom the historical Baybars (d. 1277) brought to heel are instead rendered as his helpmates, practicing the "Sunnism strongly marked with fraternal Sufism that constitutes the religious background of the romance," and stepping in on behalf of the "community of the Prophet" with valiance.[31]

Nonetheless, the nature of Abū'l-Hazāhiz's possible Kharijism and what it might signal about his background is of little immediate bearing to other characters within the text's world. Upon seeing Abū'l-Hazāhiz, the Byzantine soldiers are struck instead by the fact he and his ilk seem even more ferocious than the "Blacks of ʿAbd al-Wahhāb," immediately drawing these quite ideologically separated Black men into comparison with each other. Abū'l-Hazāhiz is described vividly as looking:

> Like a hunk of solid stone [*qiṭaʿa min ḥajar jalmad*], broad-shouldered and with formidable arms, a huge head and wide nostrils, thick lips [*ghalīẓ al-shafatayn*] and a deeply black brow line [*ʿamīq sawād al-ḥājibatayn*], as though it were hewn from rock. He was tall like a pillar.[32]

This leads the Byzantine king, from his perch on a "throne encrusted with pearls and jewels" to exclaim, "if this Black man were to enter my religion and lead the fight in my name, surely I would grant him Amorium, which each day would yield him a thousand dinars!"[33] The Byzantines thus embark on a gambit to capture Abū'l-Hazāhiz and groom him as their own warrior. Implicit in this aim is that the Byzantines believe they must fight fire with fire: the only way to defeat their Black adversary, ʿAbd al-Wahhāb, is to acquire a superior specimen of his kind for themselves. In order to do this, the Byzantine king is even willing to bestow on such a man his plushest principality—a bargain that echoes Ghaṭrīf's grand promise of betrothal to Salmā to the victor who brings him his steed.

The Byzantines plot to capture Abū'l-Hazāhiz the way one might trap a wild boar. They dig a trench in his warpath and cover the ground over with thatch and dirt. The plan works, and Abū'l-Hazāhiz's forces tumble into the pit and are forced to surrender. Once extracted from the trap,

31. Guillaume, "Les ismaéliens," 146.
32. *Sīrat Dhāt al-Himma*, X:24.
33. *Sīrat Dhāt al-Himma*, X:24.

Abū'l-Hazāhiz is brought before the Byzantine king and, at the king's command, is presented with the piles of lucre he might enjoy if he converts and complies:

> They brought forth riches and showed them to him, then they brought water and washed his body. The king commanded that he be brought fine clothing, so they dressed him in [finery] and presented a robe of honor in which they enrobed him, then they brought [more] riches and dumped them from their boxes, pouring them upon him until they reached his chest [*fa-sakabūhu ḥattā annahu waṣal ilā ṣadrihi*], and they placed a money-box [*khizāna*] from King Manuel's treasuries [*khazā'in*] in his hands. Then they presented ten slave girls[34] with ample breasts to him, like moons [*qaddamū ilayhi ʿashr jawār nahd akbār ka-annahun al-aqmār*], and the king said to him, "Name any province among the territories of Byzantium and I shall give it to you on the condition that you enter my religion and propound our words [*tadkhul fī dīninā wa-taqūl bi-kalimatinā*]. Then standards, banners, and flags shall be raised over your head, and you shall ride your mount with a hundred thousand [men], and the king shall repay them all."[35]

This display of wealth would have been particularly striking to Abū'l-Hazāhiz, who, true to the fashion of Black African characters represented across *maghāzī* and pseudo-*maghāzī* genres, is depicted as fighting in little clothing. This fact is embedded in a host of other descriptors that ostensibly make a spectacle of him as bestial, but perhaps also gesture to particular integumental and bodily aesthetics and preferences. Before battle, Abū'l-Hazāhiz had thus,

> Removed all his rags from his body [*khalaʿ min ʿalā jasadihi aṭmārahu*], until he was stripped down to his trousers [*ḥattā baqiy bi-l-sirwāl*] and set forth against Rūm as if he were the lead camel of the herd [*jamal min al-jimāl*], and he roared and stormed and sparks flew from his eyes

34. The ambiguous unfreedom of *jawār*, which can connote either enslaved or young women, is heightened here by the presentation of them as an example of Byzantine immodesty (it is later said that the Byzantines do not veil their women and here their chests are clearly at least somewhat visible); enslaved women in Muslim households also do not veil, so one must wonder whether the object is to show that Byzantines treat even their free young women as if enslaved or whether these enslaved women are standing in for all Byzantine women.

35. *Sīrat Dhāt al-Himma*, X:32.

[*ṭār min ʿaynayhi-l-sharar*], and there were breakage-points along his teeth [*ʿalā anyābihi kasr*].[36]

What may well be a quasi-ethnographic nod to practices of anterior dental chipping dispersed across sub-Saharan Africa, as well as habits of battle dress and battle cries, is here reduced through Abū'l-Hazāhiz's deracination: to which culture or people might we ascribe these attenuated references?[37] The text instead directs us to the animal and elemental—to nakedness, lowing camels, and fire. The productive contrast between "detailed descriptions of the Coptic and Byzantine attire of the Christian warriors on the one hand, and, on the other, the terrifying spectacle of wild men from the deserts of the Sūdān" has been described by Harry Norris as a means of enhancing the drama of battle narratives, depicting the varied shows of strength and barbarity across the Arabs' spectrum of enemies.[38] Posing a contrast between civilizational poverty and wealth provides yet

36. *Sīrat Dhāt al-Himma* X:22.

37. Joel D. Irish, "Knocking, Filing, and Chipping: Dental Modification in Sub-Saharan Africans," in *A Worldview of Bioculturally Modified Teeth*, ed. Scott E. Burnett and Joel D. Irish (Gainesville: University Press of Florida, 2017), 33–47.

38. This is a phenomenon that carries over into European representations of combined Arab-African fighting forces as well. Some fourteenth-century Spanish chronicles that represent the Almoravid siege of Valencia describe a contingent of Black women who fought on the Muslim side with their heads uncovered, such that their topknots were visible; see Elena Lourie, "Black Women Warriors in the Muslim Army Besieging Valencia and the Cid's Victory: A Problem of Interpretation," *Traditio* 55 (2000): 181–209. Several testimonials about pious Black men who lived at the time of the Prophet collected in Ibn al-Jawzī's *Tanwīr al-Ghabash* relate that the men often wear scant clothing compared to their Arab peers. They are typically said to wear "two garments," with one piece of fabric wrapped at the waist and another piece of fabric draped across the chest. Imran Hamza Alawiye, "Ibn al-Jawzī's Apologia on Behalf of the Black People and Their Status in Islam: A Critical Edition and Translation of *Kitāb Tanwīr al-Ghabash fī Faḍl al-Sūdān wa'l-Ḥabash*" (PhD diss., University of London SOAS, 1985), 180–89. Many early manuscript illuminations from the Islamic Middle East depicting Black Africans similarly display them in relatively little garb, with their chests bare. See Robert Hillenbrand, "The Image of the Black in Islamic Art: The Case of Islamic Painting," in *The Image of the Black in African and Asian Art*, ed. David Bindman, Suzanne Preston Blier, and Henry Louis Gates, Jr. (Cambridge, MA: Harvard University Press, 2017), 215–53. These images likely depict an actual sartorial disparity between Black Africans (especially those from territories in the Horn of Africa) and Arabs, however, the comparative nudity of Black men also becomes an evocative trope indicating difference and at times bestiality, as suggested in the depictions of Abū'l-Hazāhiz. For Norris's review of this trend in *maghāzī* literature, see Norris, "The Futūḥ al-Bahnasā," 78.

a different form of drama. The putative susceptibility of recent Muslim and recent Christian converts to reversion to their prior faiths, when plied with a salary and good treatment, is a common trope in crusade-era literary works.[39] Those who are represented as particularly wretched are also particularly buyable.

Within this matrix of religion and class, Abū'l-Hazāhiz's pared down attire starkly contrasts with the Byzantines, who outfit themselves for battle with textiles and precious metals that incorporate every color of the rainbow; they emerge in "frocks of yellow like the daytime sun, black like the color of the depth of night, and gold, the color of a *dīnār*, and blue the color of the twilight sky and lapis that dazzles the mind and the eye, and violet like [the flush of] a lover bereft of his kinsfolk and abodes."[40] As the Byzantine king's riches mount before his eyes, Abū'l-Hazāhiz is placed in the position of finally being able to procure the wealth that was only ever dangled before him while fighting on the Muslim side. Nevertheless, he has some quibbles with his reward being conditioned on conversion:

> He said to them, "I must recall my companion [*rafīqī*], Muḥammad, one time each month and say, "There is no god but God and Muḥammad is his Messenger." [The Byzantines] laughed at his words and said to him, "Woe to you, you may not keep saying such things, Muḥammad is not part of our religion." Then [Abū'l-Hazāhiz] said, "When you've all recalled Jesus I do not anger, yet when one mentions Muḥammad—peace and blessings upon him—you are incensed? Surely, I have entered your religion, but I still have a companion that I shall miss, [and shall recall] each month once or twice, and I will say, "There is no god but God and Muḥammad is his Messenger." At this, King Manuel laughed until he fell over backwards and said to them, "Summon him [*di'ūhu*] so that he comes around and observes your worship rites and attends your churches."[41]

King Manuel and his retinue do not rely on theological persuasion alone to convince Abū'l-Hazāhiz to convert. Rather, they continue to entice him with material and sexual incentives:

39. Hannah Barker finds several examples of this, as well as of suspicions about and strategies involving the use of conversion to avoid enslavement during various interreligious conflicts. Barker, *That Most Precious Merchandise*, 186–208.

40. *Sīrat Dhāt al-Himma*, X:24.

41. The phrase "summon him," or urge or call to him, indicates proselytizing to Abū'l-Hazāhhiz. *Sīrat Dhāt al-Himma*, X:33.

> They ordered Abū'l-Hazāhiz to sit, and he sat because he is ignorant of religions [*jāhil bi-l-adyān*]. They feared he might flee, so they presented him with the finest of food. He looked upon the spread, the likes of which he had never seen, and the variety of which he had never consumed, and ate much because he is a rustic and ignorant man [*rajul badawī wa-jāhil*] in every way.... Then [Abū'l-Hazāhiz] gazed upon the maidens in his midst—because the women of Byzantium do not veil their daughters before men, and these maidens were like full moons—and Abū'l-Hazāhiz lost all reason and was charmed by them. He said, "It is not so bad for me [*mā ʿalayya min baʾs*] if I am Christian by day and Muslim by night, then on the Day of Judgment I shall have followed whoever had the ultimate truth [*man kān maʿhu al-ḥaqq tabaʿatuhu*]."[42]

Layered into this scene is not only the aforementioned fact of Abū'l-Hazāhiz's crude provisioning and his attendant appetite when presented with wealth and nourishment, but also his prurient interest in light-skinned women. Happily, his own clichéd desires harmonize well with the trope of Byzantines' lax modesty norms; as Nadia El Cheikh has demonstrated, this stereotype persisted even in cases of Byzantine women trafficked into Muslim territories, with taking a Byzantine concubine regarded by some as a sure "road to perdition."[43] Another point of overlap between the unbelieving Byzantines and their captive is highlighted in Abū'l-Hazāhiz's deficient religious literacy, which renders his understanding of the *shahāda*, Muḥammad's prophethood, and the implications of conversion from one confession to another superficial at best.

This portrayal is double-edged, and also represents a critique of Abū'l-Hazāhiz's prior incorporation into a heterodox or heretical movement competing with the ʿAbbasid caliphate. However, to read it solely as a simultaneous dig at Byzantines and "bad Muslims" elides the structural sources of his ignorance of Muslim norms: as a Black man trafficked into the empire for use as a fighter, with no prior knowledge of Islam, Abū'l-Hazāhiz has no premise for being able to appreciate the theological sophistication of caliphal Islam vis-à-vis the other options at hand. Thus, we find him referred to as a rustic or rural figure (*badawī*) who is said to have no

42. Malcolm Lyons offers his own, more lyrical translation of this line in his synopsis of the *sīra*: "It won't be bad for me if I am a Christian by day and a Muslim by night, and then on the Day of Judgment I shall follow whoever is right." *Sīrat Dhāt al-Himma*, X:33; Lyons, *Arabian Epic*, vol. 3, 336.

43. Nadia Maria El Cheikh, *Women, Islam, and Abbasid Identity* (Cambridge, MA: Harvard University Press, 2015), 8.

comprehension of any religion (*jāhil bi-l-adyān*). Images of Black African pagans and *jāhilī* Bedouin mercenaries like the erstwhile Ṭayyī tribesmen or the present-day Kharijites conflate and reverberate in this phrase, with pre-Islamic "Bedouin" ignorance coming to reside in the body of a Black character in sacred time. Abū'l-Hazāhiz is portrayed as knowing nothing of religion prior to his contact with Arabs and Byzantines, and has still not learned much along his way. Moreover, in his time enslaved in the army of Mahdī'l-Zamān, Abū'l-Hazāhiz has not had a mediator symbolically and ideologically suited to the task of indexing Islam's true values for him—this is where ʿAbd al-Wahhāb comes in.

"Like Inclines toward Like": Abū'l-Hazāhiz and ʿAbd al-Wahhāb

ʿAbd al-Wahhāb and Abū'l-Hazāhiz are fated to meet from the outset, and are subject to comparison from the latter's earliest appearance in the *sīra*. Abū'l-Hazāhiz is represented as a fitting adversary to ʿAbd al-Wahhāb, and indeed, Abū'l-Hazāhiz's textual function both parallels and inverts that of his implied mate; much as ʿAbd al-Wahhāb will do for him with Islam, Abū'l-Hazāhiz acts as a medium for the conversion and militarization of his fellow Black men. He calls them to the Byzantine side with promises not of honor and community, though, but of worldly wealth. After converting, he tells his fellow captives:

> O people of Ḥām! O people of Ḥām [*yā āl Ḥām yā āl Ḥām*]! Whoever among you wants first-rate clothes and cash [*al-qumāsh al-muftakhar wa-l-amwāl*], hasten to me and enter into the Christian religion. If you don't, I'll beat it [into you] with a Yemeni sword![44]

Many of the Black soldiers heed his threat, while tellingly the Arab captives remain skeptical, saying, "There is no doubt after certainty [*i-lā kufr baʿd al-īmān*]"—a Qur'ānic refrain warning against turning one's back on belief after they have found the faith—and refusing to defect from Islam.[45] Perhaps they are indeed more pious, or perhaps without the loose sense of kinship conferred as fellow "people of Ḥām," they are less certain that Abū'l-Hazāhiz has their interests at heart.

44. *Sīrat Dhāt al-Himma*, X:33.
45. E.g., Q 16:106.

As a mouthpiece of the Byzantines, Abū'l-Hazāhiz's focus on money is hardly new. In narratives of travel and intercultural encounter from throughout the early medieval period, anxieties over the seductiveness of Byzantine riches are often given vent. Ibn Jubayr (d. 1217) meditates on the stirring sight of a Byzantine bride and her wedding retinue at Acre, wreathed in gold and luxurious dress.[46] Similarly, in an anecdote recorded by the jurist ʿAbd al-Jabbār (d. 1025), the munificence of the Byzantines proves fickle, especially when coupled with the wiles of their women; after wedding a woman for her beauty and wealth (*jamāl wa-māl kathīr*), a formerly Muslim convert is sent on a forty-day trip by the Byzantine ruler, then finds that his wife has acquired a lover in his absence—an occurrence said to be normal among the Byzantines but scandalous to him.[47] Nadia El Cheikh reads this anecdote as strongly "discourag[ing] the Muslims from marrying Byzantine women," but the pretext for doing so in the first place is worthy of note as well. Before our ex-Muslim begins to explain his marriage, we are told that the Byzantine ruler in whose service he was employed had encouraged the converts of his court to "look for a Christianized woman of wealth (*min dhuway al-yasār*) to wed in order to better their station."[48] Women and wealth are inextricably linked factors in making Byzantine Christianity attractive to outsiders, and in the *sīra* as well as ʿAbd al-Jabbār's account, this seems to be by design. For figures such as Abū'l-Hazāhiz who have only tenuously Islamized and not to their tangible benefit, this proves a dangerously potent combination in the story.

Having successfully wooed their Black captives, the Byzantines set out with newly swelled ranks against ʿAbd al-Wahhāb and his troops, who are said to be marching toward Malatya after successfully pillaging Constantinople. The encounter between ʿAbd al-Wahhāb and Abū'l-Hazāhiz is foreshadowed by a narrator's aside that points to some significant contrasts between Abū'l-Hazāhiz's fitness to be a leader of Black troops and that of ʿAbd al-Wahhāb:

46. Ibn Jubayr, *The Travels of Ibn Jubayr: A Medieval Journey from Cordoba to Jerusalem*, trans. Ronald Broadhurst (London: Bloomsbury, 2019), 340; Ibn Jubayr, *Riḥlat Ibn Jubayr*, ed. Ibrāhīm Shams al-Dīn (Beirut: Dār al-Kutub al-ʿIlmiyya, 2003), 237.

47. Al-Qāḍī ʿAbd al-Jabbār, *Tathbīt Dalāʾil al-Nubuwwa*, vol. 1 (Cairo: Dār al-Muṣṭafā, 2010), 171.

48. Nadia M. El-Cheikh, "Describing the Other to Get at the Self: Byzantine Women in Arabic Sources (8th–11th Centuries)," *Journal of the Economic and Social History of the Orient* 40:2 (1997): 242; al-Qāḍī ʿAbd al-Jabbār, *Tathbīt*, 171.

> When the prince [*amīr*] saw a Black [person], he became joyous [*yafriḥ bihi*] and if he were a slave, he would go to extremes to purchase him [*wa-in kān raqīq yubāligh fī shirāhu*], or if he were free [*ḥurr*], he became intent on making him one of his companions [*yaḥraṣ an yajʿaluhu min aṣḥābihi*].[49]

He feels these sentiments even in encounters with enemy battalions. When ʿAbd al-Wahhāb sees the armies of an East African ruler, who is discussed in the next chapter, advancing against the Muslims with "their bodies gleaming like the blackness of musk," it is said:

> When the prince ʿAbd al-Wahhāb saw this, his face lit up with joy at the Blacks who approached for combat with him, hoping that they might become part of his group of comrades [*min jumlat aʿawānihi*]. The prince Abū Muḥammad [al-Baṭṭāl] said to him, "You'll keep loving them even when Allah has sent you every Black man on earth [*mā zalt tuḥibbuhum ḥattā arsal Allāh ilayk kull al-sūdān alladhīn fī-l-dunya*], while I ask God Almighty to spare us their wickedness."[50]

Not only is ʿAbd al-Wahhāb a singular Black hero, but he is also an enthusiastic medium for the development of Black networks and communities, with the high rank and means to purchase slaves and attract devoted followers without bribes and threats. Abū'l-Hazāhiz, meanwhile, has used his Black cultural network to draw people away from Islam and to subordinate them to other powers, fulfilling their interests in only a temporary sense.

Yet in either case, the men are able to draw on a preternatural connection between themselves and others who look like them. Throughout the *sīra,* the natural affinity among people of who have been grouped as social kinds is phrased in terms of "like inclining toward like," echoing a sentiment similar to al-Jāḥiẓ's presentation of *wiʾām,* or social harmony, in this book's introduction. Euphonic societies are built not from the contented mixing of various kinds of beings, but rather from the non-conflictual coexistence of many different groups that do not infringe on each other. Al-Jāḥiẓ's definition of harmony as the maintenance of homogeneous communities harkens to an idea diffused throughout the Arabic tradition in a number of poetic, aphoristic, and traditional references. Perhaps its most known expression is to be found in a *ḥadīth* that appears across

49. *Sīrat Dhāt al-Himma,* X:39.
50. *Sīrat Dhāt al-Himma,* XXXVI:2.

collections of "weak" or fabricated attributions to the Prophet Muḥammad: "like inclines toward like (*al-jins ilā-l-jins yamīl*), and intimacy with those unlike oneself is a torment (*ʿadhāb*)." Often, this statement also appears, unattributed, in collections of *ḥadīth* in relation to the sounder tradition, "*al-arwāḥ junūd mujannada*," or roughly, "people band together," both in mutual agreement with those like them and common vilification of a perceived "other side." Elsewhere, one finds the aphorism, "birds land with their kind," the *ḥadīth*, "one is drawn to his semblance," the idea that angels help people find their kind in the afterlife, the negative sentiment that "the bleakest of prisons is intimacy with one's opposites," and so on.[51] Solomon is, for example, said to have threatened the hoopoe with being stripped of his feathers or banished from his kind, the two being functionally the same. The former relates to cause—being stripped of one's marks of belonging—and the latter to consequence.

In the *sīra*, like inclining toward like takes on an extreme color-coded significance when even the aforementioned band of East African men being drawn to the black basalt fortifications of a the Anatolian city of Āmid is explained by the phrase "nature inclines towards nature" (*al-ṭabʿ yamīl ilā-l-ṭabʿ*).[52] In romantic narratives, this notion tends to pertain to the happy pairing of individuals. Cameron Cross has related its occurrence in Perso-Arabic contexts to antique analogues such as Aristophanes's dialogue in the *Symposium* and Plotinus's idea of *suggenia*, and Zayde Antrim likewise identifies an "erotics of sameness" that endures in the tales of the *1001 Nights*.[53] As we see in the application of this concept in the chivalric prose of the *sīra*, the erotics of sameness works to explain collective affinities, not just those between lovers. It is a glue that coalesces racialized groups and explicates the efficacy and esprit de corps of military units organized by human type.

As discussed previously, a preponderance of Muslim traditions present an egalitarian ethic that is largely ambivalent toward one's ancestral roots

51. All of these *ḥadīth*s except the final one listed are arranged together in the following: Muḥammad b. Khalīl al-Qāwūqjī, *al-Lūʾlūʾ al-Marṣūʿ fī-mā Lā Aṣl li-hu aw bi-Aslihi Mawḍūʿ* (Beirut: Dār al-Bashāʾir al-Islāmiyya, 1994), 102. The final *ḥadīth* is often cited in exegeses of the punishment Sulaymān threatened for the *hud-hud* in Q 27:21, which is said to possibly refer to a number of tortures, from losing all of his feathers to losing his social circle. Al-Qurṭubī, *Mukhtaṣir Tafsīr al-Qurṭubī*, vol. 3, ed. ʿIrfān Ḥassūna (Beirut: Dār al-Kutub al-ʿIlmiyya, 2001), 335.

52. *Sīrat Dhāt al-Himma*, XXXVI:2–3.

53. Cameron Cross, *Love at a Crux: The New Persian Romance in a Global Middle Ages* (Toronto: University of Toronto Press, 2023); Antrim, "*Qamarayn*: The Erotics of Sameness in the *1001 Nights*," 1–44.

while acknowledging the reality of those roots' widespread meaning and use. This is visible in the re-premising of *ḥasab*, or inherited merit, on one's piety and the denouncing of prejudicial practices such as *ṭaʿn fī-l-ansāb*, or insults to pedigree. A concept of essential, spiritual equality need not also entail an aim of social integration across those nominally equal groups, though. In the words of Louise Marlow,

> Few Muslims (or at least, few of those whose opinions have been recorded) were prepared to extend the religious ideal [of equality] to the social sphere, and widely acknowledged, if informal, conceptions of social hierarchy were a part of common experience in pre-modern Islamic communities as elsewhere.[54]

In the case of the above aphorisms and *ḥadīths*, though several are widely rejected as weak, the notion that humans fall into predetermined, natural groupings is nonetheless being packaged in a legitimating, learned form. The fact that some felt the need to give such thoughts a prophetic voice betrays not only their perceived importance, but perhaps also their fragility in a new system of belief with a competing view of sociability. True to this ambivalence, none of these sayings explicitly promotes a hierarchization of the "kinds" under discussion. Yet the assertion that well-defined kinds exist among humans—be they biologized, classed, or some mixture of the two[55]—obscures one's ability to see connections *across* groupings. Instead, forging too much familiarity across seemingly opposed groups is represented as unnatural at best, torturous and punitive at worst.[56]

For their own part, despite their destined connection on the grounds of their racialized sameness, Abū'l-Hazāhiz's and ʿAbd al-Wahhāb's meeting carries all the drama of a clash of imminent foes. In the thick of battle with the Byzantines:

54. Marlow, *Hierarchy and Egalitarianism in Islamic Thought*, 6.

55. Another prominent way in which humans were arrayed into "kinds" was by occupation, and therefore by allotment of talent. On this, see Marlow, *Hierarchy and Egalitarianism*, 143–74.

56. As noted by J. Reid Miller and in contrast with thinkers such as Kwame Anthony Appiah, who hold that it is possible to conceive of people in terms of different but not hierarchized essences, beliefs in the existence of such clear-cut groupings are necessarily supported—indeed, preceded—by a belief in the worth of an evaluative system for constituting groups, and thus in groups' relative and relational value. Miller, *Stain Removal*; Kwame Anthony Appiah, "The Conservation of 'Race'" *Black American Literature Forum* 23, no. 1 (1989): 44.

Suddenly someone called out, "Look out, O prince!" [ʿAbd al-Wahhāb] wheeled around faster than a lightning flash [*asraʿ min al-barq*]. Before him stood a man like an elephant, who gave a roar and a bray [*li-hu hadīr wa-ṣahīl*]. The prince screamed in the face of the advancing knight—a terrible shout that would split stones and uproot trees. With this scream [*ṣarkha*], the steed that was beneath the knight—who was Abū'l-Hazāhiz—reeled backward [*tuqahqir*], so [the knight] dismounted faster than a dazzling lightning bolt [*fa-tarajjal min ʿalayhi asraʿ min al-barq al-khāṭif*].[57]

The congruence of the two knights' movements sets them up as strikingly similar opponents. Each maneuvers faster than lightning, and each shouts loud enough to be heard above the fray. Before they fall to blows, though, ʿAbd al-Wahhāb prefaces their combat by reasserting their differences. Their dialogue is poetic, and as is the convention of self-aggrandizing flytings (*naqāʾiḍ*)—common to pre-battle exchanges as well as courtiers' competitions—the two volley a few rounds of verse. ʿAbd al-Wahhāb begins:

O, vilest of the Blacks [*ardhal al-sūdān*], beware Black one [*dunak aswad*]!
Enemies, by sword and blade, shall meet their fates.
I'm the shield of the grave of Muḥammad the Hashemite,
Prophet of divine guidance, exalted over man and [earthly] domains [*nabī al-hudā fāq al-warā wa-l-ʿawālim*].
You shall find that your combat worries me not,
The likes of me does not fear battling with lions
You are nothing but the meekest of sheltered wives [*aḍʿaf ḥurma*],
Whose husband returns to her by night, bearing spoils
So be on your guard, I give blows that break armor
Wearing out the likes of countless chiefs [*ghalāṣim*]
Has it not reached you that I am their champion,
On days when horses stumble over the field of skulls?
I've killed my own two kinsmen in God's service,
I slayed Ḥārith with my sword, then Ẓālim
And compassion did not move me when I fought them,
For they had left the enduring, ultimate religion
Beware battle with me, you shall meet your fate swiftly

57. *Sīrat Dhāt al-Himma*, X:43.

From a black hand, pouring generously [*kaff aswad sājim*]
I've not sought out any bribe [*rashwa*] for piety,
Nor can any censurer usurp my place with God[58]

This poem distills many of the major themes of this section of the *sīra* with great economy of language. Concepts of lineage and status loom large, especially insofar as they tie one in simultaneously with a religious and lineal elite. ʿAbd al-Wahhāb begins by calling Abū'l-Hazāhiz the vilest of the Blacks, implying there is an offstage multitude of other vile Black men, with Abū'l-Hazāhiz superlative among them. In light of ʿAbd al-Wahhāb's own blackness, which he references proudly, we may read this as a gesture toward ʿAbd al-Wahhāb's unlikely success in surpassing his peers' base station. Abū'l-Hazāhiz, by contrast, has failed to do so. Even the first reference that ʿAbd al-Wahhāb makes to the Prophet Muḥammad is bound up with genealogy; he calls Muḥammad "the Hashemite," invoking his clan's name and thus Muḥammad's and his family's standing within the renowned tribe of Quraysh. When ʿAbd al-Wahhāb boasts of men whom he has killed in the past, he highlights their chiefly status as if to say that such men are worthier, more impressive opponents than Abū'l-Hazāhiz. They are described as *ghalāṣim*, also meaning throats or larynges, and the polysemy of this term connects the figure of a tribal chief with the speech and vitality of his whole social unit.

There are also moments in the poem, though, in which social ranks and relations appear flimsy in comparison with religious obligations, faithfulness to which is one of the main things that differentiates ʿAbd al-Wahhāb from the turncoat Abū'l-Hazāhiz. ʿAbd al-Wahhāb revisits his murder of his highborn father and grandfather, al-Ḥārith and Ẓālim, which was in reprisal for (among other things) their conversion to Christianity. The consequence of social standing among men may also be mooted by transcendental concepts, as in the Qurʾānic formulation of the irrelevance of *ansāb* on the Day of Judgment. Thus, in the poem, the Prophet Muḥammad is designated not merely as a member of the earthly, Hashemite elite, but also as the axial figure within the cosmic order: he is said to rise above (*fāq*) the reaches of the worlds (*ʿawālim*) and their mortal inhabitants (*warā*). All of this resonates deeply not only with the scriptural priority on personal righteousness over generational merit, but also with a collection of related aphorisms about how piety (*taqwā*, *dīn*, etc.) can act as a stand-in for birth rank (*ḥasab*, *nasab*) that were, according to

58. *Sīrat Dhāt al-Himma*, X:47–48.

Louise Marlow, formulated in Islam's earliest periods and subsequently "watered down" into ennobling courtly platitudes rather than activated as real-world social models.[59] Perhaps the popular hero ʿAbd al-Wahhāb—for whom the sword is usually mightier than the pen—is able in his fictive realm to enact an otherwise taboo form of social usurpation, leveraging his greater piety to overturn generational order.

Overall, the poem resolves into a three-part, cosmic hierarchy: God, the Prophet, and the remainder of humankind. God, referred to with the epithet al-Qāʾim, the maintaining and enduring, is immovably positioned in the highest rank, while the Prophet "exceeds" mankind and thus occupies an interstitial, and perhaps intercessory, role between earth and heaven. Humankind, meanwhile, is superficially arrayed according to one's natal social standing, but one may exceed or fall short of this through one's actions. The fact of Abū'l-Hazāhiz's low rank and compounding self-debasing actions is articulated not only through the reference to his relatively "vile" expression of blackness but also through the emasculating remark that likens him to a cloistered woman waiting on her husband to bring home spoils, which again recalls him contracting himself into servitude with the wealthy but morally bankrupt Byzantines.

Incensed at ʿAbd al-Wahhāb's words, Abū'l-Hazāhiz retorts with a poem of his own, referring to ʿAbd al-Wahhāb as "son of Marzūq," his mother's milk-brother and alleged lover. Abū'l-Hazāhiz then adds that ʿAbd al-Wahhāb is the one who is a *ḥurma,* a cloistered woman, awaiting the treasures her husband may bring, and concludes that "the likes of you cannot hope to defend [himself] against calamity, nor recourse when the tyrant (*ẓālim*) approaches," playing off of the name of ʿAbd al-Wahhāb's slain grandfather (Ẓālim) and implying that he shall be his avenger.[60] In his rebuke, one registers a feature of the poem above that Abū'l-Hazāhiz found most offensive, namely its emasculating jibe. This is so affronting to Abū'l-Hazāhiz that it renders him nearly inarticulate, and he is only able to throw the exact words of his opponent back in his face. In the poem's play on gender we are also reminded of the fact that Abū'l-Hazāhiz's conversion to Christianity was clinched by the promise of being able to do what he sees ʿAbd al-Wahhāb's putative father, the black-skinned Marzūq, as having done: gain sexual access to elite, light-skinned women.

ʿAbd al-Wahhāb has a final, brief poetic word, during which he refers to Abū'l-Hazāhiz several more times as a slave (*ʿabd*) and concludes by

59. Marlow, *Hierarchy and Egalitarianism,* 93.
60. *Sīrat Dhāt al-Himma,* X:47–48.

saying, "By God, O slave of the blameworthy and their progeny, you shall learn that I am from honorable stock (*min sulāl al-akārim*)," effectively refuting Abū'l-Hazāhiz's claim about his bastardy and emphasizing his foe's debased rank as a mere slave to the ignoble Christians. When the two engage in combat, they go at it for several days with neither being able to best the other. Abū'l-Hazāhiz is quickly impressed by ʿAbd al-Wahhāb's comportment on the battlefield; he switches to referring to him as *Ibn Dhāt al-Himma*, or "son of Dhāt al-Himma," and states that "your virtues in combat have amazed me" (*ʿajabatnī shamāʾiluk ʿind al-nizāl*). Referring to the hero's matriline is a seemingly odd choice, as it still positions him as having potentially dubious paternity. Yet it at once acknowledges Fāṭima's unparalleled heroism as well as al-Ḥārith's conversion to Christianity and thus loss of community standing, and it may recall the fact that several prominent Black figures in the Arabic tradition have been likewise known by their matriline inasmuch as it was considered the source of their blackness, and thus their mutual identification. Though figures like the pre-Islamic poets Khufāf ibn Nabda and Sulayk ibn al-Sulaka were so known because they were *hajīns*, or "mixed," in a context when bilateral descent had widespread import, after Islam bilateral descent was still selectively highlighted when an outstanding woman's role stood to be significant for her descendants, as Alyssa Gabbay has shown.[61] Use of a matronymic may also obliquely reference Abū'l-Hazāhiz's origins outside of a community in which patrilineality predominates; many of the same societies at the western reaches of the early Islamic world that became most aligned with Ibāḍī and Khārijī movements were likewise associated with matrilocality and matriliny.

Despite a huge differential in size, with ʿAbd al-Wahhāb said to barely have the bulk of one of Abū'l-Hazāhiz's thighs, ʿAbd al-Wahhāb subdues his opponent and brings him back to the Kilābī troops' encampments. The men prepare a meal and offer Abū'l-Hazāhiz the best cuts of meat. Unlike in the court of the Byzantines, this is given without further conditions, though al-Baṭṭāl quips that if ʿAbd al-Wahhāb were to fill his ward's mind with Islam, perhaps he would "get full and not eat all the meat in Malatya." Abū'l-Hazāhiz also therefore has the fetters around his arms removed in a symbolic act of limited liberation and trust. Retiring for bed, ʿAbd al-Wahhāb commences his *ʿishāʾ* prayers with his captive in the room. Ecstatic in his piety, ʿAbd al-Wahhāb weeps and swoons during prayer. Just as on the battlefield, Abū'l-Hazāhiz is struck by ʿAbd al-Wahhāb's virtue, but

61. Gabbay, *Gender and Succession*.

nonetheless he resolves to kill him and abscond. After the devil whispers a scheme into Abū'l-Hazāhiz's ear, he leaps up and takes ʿAbd al-Wahhāb's sword from the beam on which it hangs, then:

> [Abū'l-Hazāhiz] raised up his hand, wielding the sword so high that the blackness of his armpits was exposed. He made to strike the prince, but suddenly there was a sound like clashing thunder and storming wind and [something] took the sword from him and said, "O enemy of God, did you not hear what God said in His great Book? Those who carry out the compact of God and do not violate the covenant, and who are worthy of us and exult us are indeed slaves in our service [*ʿabdanā fī khidmatinā*]. We do not guard with our watchful eye nor guide under our protection he who opposes [us]."
>
> When Abū'l-Hazāhiz lifted his gaze to look upon the speaker, sure enough there was a figure standing at ʿAbd al-Wahhāb's head, and his face was embraced by the clouds of the sky though his legs [reached] to the lowest bounds of the earth. Two wings spread out over him and he had a lance in hand, aglow with light. Abū'l-Hazāhiz was stupefied [*ṣār ḥāʾir*] by what he saw and grew regretful [*nadam*], saying, "Truly this one is of great station with God (*wallāhi inn li-hādhā manzila ʿaẓīma ʿind Allāh*)."[62]

Confronted with this spectacular sight, Abū'l-Hazāhiz immediately repents and gathers everyone in the camp to witness his conversion. He recites the *shahāda,* to ʿAbd al-Wahhāb's glee. In accepting Islam, Abū'l-Hazāhiz becomes a differently orientated version of his former self; rather than being a slave to an earthly master, he becomes servant of God. This is made explicit in the above narrative, in which worship is represented in the narrative as a form of service (*khidma*) performed by a slave (*ʿabd*).

In acting as the medium for Abū'l-Hazāhiz's conversion, though, ʿAbd al-Wahhāb continues to reinforce earthly channels of devotion even as they are being subordinated to cosmic ones. Having proved his high pedigree and the gentility that accompanies it by leaving Abū'l-Hazāhiz unchained, nourishing him with superior food, and trusting him enough to prostrate himself in his presence, ʿAbd al-Wahhāb is well placed to become Abū'l-Hazāhiz's patron, mentor, and ultimately, father figure. All of these forms of paternalist interaction are entwined in the relationship of *walāʾ* that ʿAbd al-Wahhāb has recently established with Abū'l-Hazāhiz in all

62. *Sīrat Dhāt al-Himma,* X:53.

but name by capturing him in war, liberating him with a literal unshackling, and admitting him into his entourage as a recent convert. In this relationship, ʿAbd al-Wahhāb occupies the position of the upper *mawlā*, a patron on whom Abū'l-Hazāhiz, the lower *mawlā*, is dependent. But there remains one further mode of earthly authority for the newly Islamized Abū'l-Hazāhiz to discover and submit to: the ʿAbbasid caliph, Hārūn al-Rashīd.

Caliph of the Whites and Blacks

Shortly after converting, Abū'l-Hazāhiz approaches his army of Black soldiers and converts them all back to Islam as well, merging his troops with those in ʿAbd al-Wahhāb's charge. Just then, ʿAbd al-Wahhāb receives word from the caliph that Baghdad is under imminent siege from a horde of fire worshippers marching from Khorasan and that he is commanded to return to Iraq and fight. As the men prepare to leave, Abū'l-Hazāhiz begins asking about the source of the caliph's sovereignty, to which ʿAbd al-Wahhāb replies, "All of us are servants and slaves [*khadam wa-ghilmān*] to him."[63] Confused, Abū'l-Hazāhiz responds, "O prince, we truly know no caliph except for you, and we do not want anyone to command us and forbid us except for you. Why do you not take the caliphate with the sword, and we shall send down humiliation and harm upon all who oppose you?"[64]

This statement again recalls Abū'l-Hazāhiz's heterodox early introduction to Islam by speaking to the aspirational yet also Kharijism-tinged logic that anyone of sufficient merit could be caliph regardless of genealogy, appearance, or personal history. Abū'l-Hazāhiz's allusion to this fringe position gives occasion for ʿAbd al-Wahhāb to explain that the caliphate is inherited through the line of the Prophet Muḥammad, and so one cannot take it by force even if one wills (*laysat al-khilāfa bi-l-yad al-qawiyya li-annahā warathahā min Muḥammad al-muṣṭafā*). Once again, the importance of one's ancestry in assaying rank and political capital within the Muslim community is being impressed upon Abū'l-Hazāhiz, though in the context not of Arabness or non-Arabness, but of prophetic lineage or lack thereof. Despite what Abū'l-Hazāhiz has seen of ʿAbd al-Wahhāb's nobility, fitness, and piety, due to his identity, none of these characteristics can ultimately gain him entry to the highest echelons of power. While ʿAbd

63. *Sīrat Dhāt al-Himma*, X:61.
64. *Sīrat Dhāt al-Himma*, X:61.

al-Wahhāb is seemingly content with this truth, it continues to disturb Abū'l-Hazāhiz throughout his encounter with al-Rashīd in Baghdad:

> [ʿAbd al-Wahhāb] arrived at the main square and there the Caliph of the Age met him, flanked by the jurists and the scholars and servants. When ʿAbd al-Wahhāb's gaze fell on al-Rashīd he knelt, and all those who were with him dismounted, except for Abū'l-Hazāhiz. Indeed, he did not dismount for al-Rashīd. Instead, he exclaimed, "Hey, you with the big turban and the wide ears, why do you not dismount for ʿAbd al-Wahhāb like he did for you and do right by him as he has done by you? For if you are the caliph of the whites, then he is caliph of the Blacks [*fa-in kunt anta khalīfat al-bīḍān fa-huwa khalīfat al-sūdān*]!" Then the general ʿAmr b. ʿUbayd Allāh shouted at him, "Shut up! Shut your mouth and recant [*sakat ḥissuk wa-baṭal naṣṣuk*]! You talk to the Caliph of the Age in this way? Get down and kiss the earth!" When [Abū'l-Hazāhiz] heard his words, his eyes rolled backward in his head, his hand felt for the hilt of his sword, and he said, "Woe to you, ʿAmr, would you dare compel me . . . ? Then there is nothing for me to do but hoist you up by this sword! I shall not obey any caliph, or any sultan, or any reigning king except for the prince ʿAbd al-Wahhāb, who dealt generously with my spirit [*jād ʿalayya bi-rūḥī*] when he captured me in battle."
>
> ʿAmr said to himself, "By the goodness and truth of the Merciful, we had no relief when we had only one Black man, and then came even more of them [*kunnā bi-aswad wāḥid wa-lā bi-nakhluṣ kayf wa-qad ṣār hādhā wa-tilk al-sūdān*]. Each of them has a devil inside of him, and there is nothing for me to do but try to annihilate him with a well-poured glass of ruin, because he is mad [*majnūn*], and there is not a single person who exists for him [*wa-mā fī ʿaynihi min aḥad*]." Then ʿAbd al-Wahhāb called to him, "O Abū'l-Hazāhiz, O my son [*yā waladī*], the general has spoken rightly," so Abū'l-Hazāhiz dismounted, having been shamed by ʿAbd al-Wahhāb.[65]

Underlying Abū'l-Hazāhiz's misguided expectations of how the meeting with Hārūn al-Rashīd would transpire is the fact that the soldier's world is so rigidly segmented into Black and white that he feels any Black person who occupies a position of leadership must do so on parallel footing with a white equivalent. He has spent the majority of his time in homogenously Black militias, and now is at the command of one led by the Black-Arab

65. *Sīrat Dhāt al-Himma*, X:62.

ʿAbd al-Wahhāb. Moreover, ʿAbd al-Wahhāb's claim to authority is manifest to Abū'l-Hazāhiz both in the financial idiom on which he has been weaned throughout his time among the Kharijites and the Byzantines and in the new religio-political framework to which he has recently been introduced: Abū'l-Hazāhiz has witnessed ʿAbd al-Wahhāb's vast wealth and munificence as well as the respect that he is visibly conferred by all but the caliph. Both these material and spiritual dimensions of ʿAbd al-Wahhāb's governance are encoded into Abū'l-Hazāhiz's claim that he "dealt generously with my soul."

ʿAbd al-Wahhāb also presents an embodiment of power to which Abū'l-Hazāhiz is happy to submit, as he is apparently the same kind as himself. Conversely, he must be compelled to pay his respects to al-Rashīd, whom Abū'l-Hazāhiz envisions as presiding over a population of solely whites, rather than the entire Muslim world. The logic of like inclining toward like rears its head again, though this time it presents an urgent plight—how can individuals accustomed to being arrayed according to their kinds understand the legitimacy of a sovereign's claim over a large, plural society defined not by racialized commonality but shared religion? In the case of Abū'l-Hazāhiz, creating a new kinship tie that incorporates him first into an Arab clan and then, by extension, into the Muslim polity facilitates this new understanding. This familial tie is articulated in quite literal terms when, remonstrating his behavior, ʿAbd al-Wahhāb refers to Abū'l-Hazāhiz as his son. In a word, ʿAbd al-Wahhāb concretizes his paternal relationship with Abū'l-Hazāhiz that, though not adoptive *stricto sensu*, constitutes a form of filiation through Abū'l-Hazāhiz's status as ʿAbd al-Wahhāb's lower *mawlā*.[66]

His fatherly chiding succeeds, and when ʿAbd al-Wahhāb directs Abū'l-Hazāhiz to kneel before al-Rashīd, he does so without further objection. This turnabout underscores the fact that Abū'l-Hazāhiz's acknowledgment of the political figurehead of the Muslim world and integration into the Muslim community is contingent on an intermediary relationship with

66. Legal adoption, in the sense of conferring one's family name to someone outside one's natal line, is prohibited in the Qurʾān (Q 33:5, Q 33:37), but other types of fosterage are permitted, most typically that established not through *walāʾ* but through milk-kinship, which integrates an infant into a family through a biological process. For more on fosterage in Islamic law, see J. Schacht, J. Burton, and J. Chelhod, "Raḍāʿ or Riḍāʿ," in *Encyclopaedia of Islam*, 2nd ed., ed. Peri Bearman et al. (Leiden: Brill Online, 2012), http://dx.doi.org/10.1163/1573-3912_ei2glos_SIM_gi_03811. On adoption, see E. Chaumont, "Tabannin," in *Encyclopaedia of Islam*, 2nd ed., https://referenceworks.brillonline.com/search?s.f.s2_parent=s.f.book.encyclopaedia-of-islam-2-Glossary-and-Index-of-Terms&search-go=&s.q=Tabannin.

ʿAbd al-Wahhāb. ʿAbd al-Wahhāb seemingly articulates this relationship in terms of a biological bond, and goes beyond the technical bounds of clientage in doing so. Certain types of familial invocation are a form of address that the Qurʾān encourages among the community of Muslim believers. In the course of explaining that adoptive sons must not be referred to in the same terms as one's literal children but must instead continue to be called by "the names of their fathers," the fifth verse of *Sūrat al-Aḥzāb* also advises referring to people whose parentage is obscure as "brothers in faith," *ikhwānukum fī-l-dīn* and as one's "clients," or *mawālī*, rendering fraternal and cliental relationships analogous in the eyes of the community.[67] At the same time, this would seem to make clear that referring to another's child as one's own is still discouraged.

Perhaps though Abū'l-Hazāhiz cannot be a literal son to ʿAbd al-Wahhāb, as a recent convert he is as yet more like a child than a sibling. As I have shown elsewhere with respect to how *Sīrat Dhāt al-Himma* uses narrative to instruct on the laws concerning milk kinship and nursing women's maintenance (*nafaqa*), the *sīras* at times vernacularize or informalize legal concepts so that their sense is conveyed—as when a henpecked husband offers his wife a fortune (*al-māl al-kathīr*) to nurse a foundling rather than framing this as a normative transaction whose amount was meant not to be excessive or burdensome, but in keeping with local custom (*ʿurf*).[68] Though ʿAbd al-Wahhāb may seem literally to claim paternity of Abū'l-Hazāhiz here, more likely his cry of "O my son" functions to avoid highlighting Abū'l-Hazāhiz's lack of a known father as well as to circumvent the term *mawlayya* (my *mawlā*), used almost exclusively in the text for royals and high-ranking figures whom one serves rather than the reverse. It also perhaps evokes the semantic range of companion terms for servants such as *ghilmān* (boys), which subordinate through a notional age gradient.

Referring to Abū'l-Hazāhiz as his son may be modeling another, affective dimension of *walāʾ* as well. A common refrain in *fiqh*, or positive law, concerning the status of *walāʾ* is that it is a form of kinship (*luḥma*) tantamount to hereditary kinship (*ka-luḥmat al-nasab*).[69] The very use of *luḥma* as the mot juste for expressing this kinship has a corporeal resonance; the homonymic term *laḥma* with which it shares a root means a lump of meat or flesh. As seen in ʿAbd al-Wahhāb's fatherly claim on

67. Q 33:5.

68. Schine, "Nourishing the Noble," 191.

69. Ibn Ḥajar and al-Bukhārī, "Bāb ithm man tabarraʾ min mawālīh," in *Fatḥ al-Bārī Sharḥ Ṣaḥīḥ al-Bukhārī*, vol. 12, ed. ʿAbd al-Qādir Shaybat al-Ḥamd (Riyadh: Maktabah al-Malik Fahd al-Waṭanī Athnāʾ al-Nashr, 2001), 45.

Abū'l-Hazāhiz, this biologization of companionship between upper and lower *mawālī* renders society's power structures more intuitive through a commonplace language of authority: children are subordinate to parents, and all are subordinate to the state. Patricia Crone portrays this set of relationships in terms of private and public legal dependencies, saying:

> All non-Arab newcomers to Arab society, be they freeborn or freed, converted or unconverted, were thus affiliated to individual members of this society [through *walā'*], not directly to Arab tribes, let alone directly to the Arab state; and . . . the relationship in which they were placed was an unequal one: in public law freedmen and converts enjoyed the same rights and duties as other Muslims, but in private law they were dependents.[70]

Elsewhere, Crone refers to the institution of *walā'* as a form of "humiliation," through which "newcomers to the faith [were] attached to the person 'at whose hands' they had converted." However, as we see with Abū'l-Hazāhiz, a bond of *walā'* with a person whom he respects on grounds of friendship and identity actually mitigates the greater humiliation of serving a more remote, white caliph whose religious authority has not been proven before Abū'l-Hazāhiz's very eyes by an angelic apparition, unlike ʿAbd al-Wahhāb's. It is not until Abū'l-Hazāhiz has been prompted to recognize ʿAbd al-Wahhāb as a father figure that he is able to comprehend al-Rashīd's sovereignty and comport himself accordingly. Assimilation within the state is cast as posterior to and dependent on membership within a smaller, more intimate social unit, much as it was by law. In other words, Abū'l-Hazāhiz's conversion narrative—itself an allegory—is concluded with an allegorical depiction of the convert imbibing Arab-Muslim cultural norms under the guidance of his upper *mawlā*. That Abū'l-Hazāzhiz's *walā'* is implicitly post-manumission indicates the enduring power that ʿAbd al-Wahhāb has in the text as a Black hero to work within this institution: the ʿAbbasid era signaled the end of forms of *walā'* contracted between free men, but not between the free and freed. Blackness's recurrent link with slavery and enslaved pasts works in the text to open a pathway for allegorizing assimilation that has been foreclosed on for other characters and groups due to the march of narrative time.

70. Patricia Crone, *Roman, Provincial and Islamic law* (Cambridge: Cambridge University Press, 1987), 36.

The meeting with al-Rashīd sketches the boundaries and possibilities that structure Abū'l-Hazāhiz's new world. One of the clearest implications of ʿAbd al-Wahhāb not in fact being the "caliph of the Blacks" is that his authority is limited. Because the Black people under his command and incorporated into his clan through *walāʾ* cannot supersede the rank of their manumitter, they are in a yet lower social position that manifests in the tale mostly in a chain of military command. ʿAbd al-Wahhāb's Black comrades are aggregated together and insulated from the broader Muslim community, even as they gain appreciable status through attachment to ʿAbd al-Wahhāb's Kilābī Arab line. It is perhaps for this reason that, despite the protective familial relationship implied in early definitions of *walāʾ*, scholars who examine the carryover of such systems of clientage into contemporary societies find that they appear disturbingly analogous to relations of ownership, and moreover that they tend to disproportionately affect diasporic sub-Saharan peoples who are made to "retain, because it is imposed upon them, the indelible traces of a servile past."[71]

Black characters in the *sīra*, too, often begin their lives in the text enslaved. Though their servile past, situated within the sacred time of the Islamic period, has very different contours and implications from the perpetual and fatal servility of the *jāhiliyya* embodied by the slaves of Ṭayy, Islamic society only provides for a restricted form of upward social mobility. In order to join the Muslim community, figures such as Abū'l-Hazāhiz must pass from one form of dependency to another, rather than from dependency into total freedom. Black characters in the text are subsumed into Arab social structures and acculturated to Arab norms through the hybrid Black-Arab figure of the hero, ʿAbd al-Wahhāb, who enacts an allegory of assimilation for audiences to the *sīra* that intertextually resonates with a variety of legal and theological discourses. Though this rarely was the case in real-world relationships of *walāʾ*, racialized enclavism underpins ʿAbd al-Wahhāb's role as the sole architect of these relationships. His naturalized avidity for buying and manumitting or soliciting the companionship of Black characters renders him the access point for particular racialized "others" to broader social membership in the Muslim *umma*.

In the transition from the pre-Islamic era to the narrative present, and from the age before Black heroes to the assurgency of ʿAbd al-Wahhāb and his forces, the racial imaginary of the text has shifted through the formulation of a Muslim identity that admits Black people into the community

71. Inès Mrad Dali, "De l'esclavage à la servitude: Le cas des Noirs de Tunisie," *Cahiers d'Études Africaines* 45 (2005): 936.

much more readily than erstwhile, *jāhilī* institutions, on the condition of their profession of faith and fidelity to the political order. Though their acceptance is far from complete, it nonetheless is premised upon a basic egalitarian notion of what makes a Muslim a Muslim. The representation of Black Muslim experiences in this milieu may easily have bested the imagined *jāhiliyya*'s restive Black parvenus for a range of audiences to the *sīra*, who would witness not only the lot of Black figures in the text improving under Islam through new pathways to communal betterment, but also the Muslim realm benefiting as a whole from the growth of an elite fighting force of recently converted, loyal Black men.

Conclusion

The ways in which ʿAbd al-Wahhāb pulls exceptional Black characters, allegorically and selectively, out of states of ignorance bear some striking parallels with a much more contemporary form of transitional narrative, that of "racial uplift." Racial uplift ideology was popularized by some nineteenth- and twentieth-century African American thinkers and promoted the belief that the outsized talents of a few exemplary members of a historically oppressed group can illuminate a path to liberation for all. Since its formulation, the theory of racial uplift has drawn criticism for its elitism, its derision of poorer Black people, and its subordination to a white, masculine optics of success. In the words of Kevin Gaines, racial uplift ideology "cannot be isolated from dominant modes of knowledge and power relations structured by race and racism."[72] We might therefore attend to the subtler hierarchical structures at work in the *sīra*'s account.

Institutions like *walāʾ* point to the fact that earning membership status in a given society is often predicated on acceding to its existing power structures; indeed, a society's newest members are often arrogated into its most dependent, and therefore most vulnerable, ranks, be they newborns, new arrivals, or the newly freed. In other words, "uplift" inherently entails a submission to the status quo, which in the world of the *sīra*—in its vision of Arabness, of caliphal Islam, and of means of community building—is heavily structured by genealogy. At first glance, it is perhaps surprising that this truth perdures in the transition from the *jāhiliyya* into Islam, given the Qurʾān and *hadith* corpus's emphases on faith and not class status as the primary metric for heavenly and worldly favor.

72. Kevin Gaines, *Uplifting the Race: Black Leadership, Politics, and Culture in the Twentieth Century* (Chapel Hill: UNC Press, 1996), xiv.

However, this egalitarian conception of the emergent Muslim community was shortly tempered by a form of cultural determinism that predated Islam but worked well within the parameters of ascribing the human condition to an omniscient God: inequalities clearly exist, and so these must be divinely inscribed ways of organizing human society, structuring interactions, and engendering human co-dependencies and cooperation across firms.[73] Marlow traces the movement of egalitarian sentiments from fragmentary, radical expressions found in idioms from the early period to the courtly works of the ʿAbbasid era that conscripted such adages into the cause of elite self-discipline and decorum rather than grassroots action, and we might say that *Sīrat Dhāt al-Himma* traces a similar trajectory. It moves from the convulsive attempts at overturning tribal hierarchies as Islam was dawning among the south Arabian Banū Ṭayy to the stable, institutionalized paths to assimilating marginal groups into their appropriate places within the *umma* as exemplified by ʿAbd al-Wahhāb and Abū'l-Hazāhiz's relationship.

Of particular interest is the way in which figures such as Abū'l-Hazāhiz can—and cannot—merge into Arab-Muslim society in the *sīra* tradition and its relatives. In the seemingly *jāhilī* tale of the three slaves of Ṭayy, the obstacles against Black men wedding the women of Arabia's tribes are explicit and fatal, echoing aspects of other popular stories such as those in the *1001 Nights* that draw on the fear of perfidy with an intimate underclass to unknowable and unacceptable effects for the reproduction of rank and power. Such a class-trespassing arrangement was implicitly forbidden when the woman was of noble, Arab birth, and this was often encapuslated in concern over spousal sufficiency (*kafāʾa*), in which a woman's partner should match her in piety, lineage, wealth, freedom, and health or ability so as to insulate her from legal and reputational harm (*ḍarar*).

The reverse dynamic of Arab men taking non-Arab women as partners, meanwhile, was permitted if not encouraged, particularly through concubinage and the legal invention of *ummahāt al-awlād*. This gendered disparity in sexual access and selectivity produces what Ali Mazrui has referred to as a structure of "ascending miscegenation," whereby the sexual relations of conquered or enslaved peoples with the predominantly Arab core of early Islamic society led to increasing Arabization on paper through lineal proliferation as Islam spread while simultaneously guarding against demographic change in the opposite direction.[74] In rendering him

73. Marlow, *Hierarchy and Egalitarianism*.

74. Mazrui, *The Politics of Gender and the Culture of Sexuality*, 88–93.

an exemplary yet coherent figure within the narrative, Abū'l-Hazāhiz's ambitions to wed ennobled and affluent white women are not quashed, but they are duly displaced into his journey in Byzantium. The ties he establishes when (re-)entering Islam are meanwhile focused on homosocial male community, arrayed by lineal and spiritual rank and structured through cliental and military command.

Abū'l-Hazāhiz's story therefore also points to where Black masculinity—which in him becomes a superpower, whereas for the slaves of Ṭayy it was associated with disability—is best thought to serve the Islamic world community. Black masculinity is ideally suited to the epic's system of pious warriorship, and this maps directly onto traditional historiographies and military structures in the medieval Arab-Muslim world. In the *sīra*, as the significance and uses of blackness change over time, and as Black people increasingly become a freeable, freed, or free part of Muslim communities rather than permanently enslaved tribal rejects, that infamous feature of racial uplift ideology, the performed respectability of the uplifted, comes to the fore. Where in the *jāhiliyya* Black men could not gain respectability because the only legal pathway was marrying into a tribe that did not want them, in the narrative present, community roles are renegotiated for Black men, who are strategically deployed to secure Arab Muslims while still being kept an arm's length from technically "mixing" with them. The didactic implications of this are clear. Though the *sīra* and its intertexts frequently conflate blackness with slavery, this same period is aspirationally inflected in the epic through the emergence of Black characters who exit slavery and pull the levers of mobility afforded them by Islamic legal structures. That is, racial time in the epic is progressive, and Islam is characterized by its capacity to ultimately bolster its underclass through religious and social assimilation.

To this end, Black ethno-cultural particularity is given only the most superficial attention. In the conversion story of Abū'l-Hazāhiz, rather than offering audiences a historicitous representation of the gradual conversion of various peoples designated as "Black" to Islam via conquest, trade, or the effects of diaspora across the central Islamic lands into which many migrated or were trafficked, we find a moralized narrative of a Black man converting to (Sunni) Islam that turns on the artifice of him leaving behind not his own religious, cultural, and geographic roots—which given blackness's capaciousness in medieval Arabic writings is most likely suggestive of Sahelian or sub-Saharan African descent, but also connects with South and Southeast Asian or Austronesian heritages—but Byzantium. We hear little of what becomes a muddled and speculative pagan, Ibāḍī, or Khārijī background to Abū'l-Hazāhiz's arrival as a soldier in a separatist Muslim army. His might and desirability as a warrior act as reason enough for his presence. Conveniently, he is finally ushered into the fold by an aptly designed peer who is simultaneously lineally Arab and raced as Black.

For all his didactic expressions of rebellion, confusion, and refutation of the constraints of caliphal Islam and cosmic and earthly servitude, Abū'l-Hazāhiz ultimately hews to the boundaries that contour his social ascent, marking out a dutiful passage through forms of dependency and tutelage, enslavement and kinship, as well as the perils of departure from this pathway. Through a web of literary conceits, he is idealized as a member of a conglomerate of carefully delineated but universally Muslim, Arabizing groups whose prior cultural ties are represented not through loss, but simply as absence waiting to be filled and ignorance awaiting remedy.

PART III
Race through Space

✵ 6 ✵

Venturing Abroad

The king Hadlamūs was fearsome like a buffalo, long-limbed and foam-mouthed, with a lion's face. He had big ears, powerful arms, huge palms, and tall stature like a pillar. He sat upon an ebony litter, and beneath him lay lion skins. . . . Men from the tribe of ʿUqfūr guarded him . . . . There were locked apparatuses over their mouths, and they were like lions on the hunt, they roared and raged, and their voices were like the braying of donkeys.

SĪRAT DHĀT AL-HIMMA, XXXV:54

In the absence of moral quandary [about slavery], why would scribes, chroniclers, and travelers fabricate a political landscape resplendent with enactments of African lordship alongside serial representations of African barbarism?

HERMAN L. BENNET

"We saw the whole earth darkened by the quantity of Blacks with them, like herds of buffalo, at least a million of them clad in coats of mail." King Michael's face hardened, and he said, "Woe upon you! I've not seen the likes of this save in a dream."

SĪRAT DHĀT AL-HIMMA, XXXVIII:53

Many of the popular *sīras* contain some form of sustained African expedition: *Sīrat Banī Hilāl* chronicles the conquest of present-day Tunisia, *Sīrat ʿAntar* takes us into Egypt and the Horn of Africa, and *Sīrat Sayf b. Dhī Yazan* draws its battle lines between Yemen and Abyssinia. *Sīrat Dhāt al-Himma* transports audiences to East Africa as well, chasing the text's central villain, the *qāḍī*-turned-Christian named ʿUqba (whom we have encountered previously, proffering the sedatives that helped al-Ḥārith rape the heroine Fāṭima Dhāt al-Himma). Once there, the Kilābī Arabs battle ʿUqba for various Africans' alliances in their countervailing attempts to convert the native populace and swell their armies' numbers. In the process, they encounter a variety of African peoples, from the above-mentioned Abyssinian king Hadlamūs, who converts almost immediately over to the Muslim side, to the cannibals of the tribes of ʿUqfūr and people of Damdam, many of whom wear locked grates over their mouths to keep themselves from eating the flesh of their fellows, and speak only in unintelligible, animal-like sounds.

Among studies of Arabic literature, analyses of medieval depictions of Africa and Africans have taken aim at the texts' penchants for exoticism, exaggeration, and ultimately racism. John Hunwick claims authors created a "region of the mind," pieced together in projects of knowledge reminiscent of Said's "imaginative geographies," in which multitudinous human phenomena such as language, religion, sexual and economic habits, are made knowable in ways that purport to stand outside of relationality, occupying a "fixed, more or less total geographic position" that one then has the prerogative to explore, investigate, and corroborate.[1] Of course, though, the lineaments of the "lands of the Blacks"—for the continent of "Africa" is not at hand as such in the sources—were always mutable. As has been discussed, the "lands of the Blacks," or *bilād al-sūdān*, is a spatial delineation that sutures together a human element (the "Blacks") with external, climatological and astrological causes: the exposure of relatively southern terrains of the earth to variable amounts of heat and humidity, as well as their being traversed by certain celestial bodies, creates and sustains particular forms of embodied difference. As Guangtian Ha writes, diaspora both disrupts and reinforces the spatialization of Black people on the medieval Islamic map. "B/black sailors and B/black slaves employed on seafaring journeys beyond Arabia and Persia" phase into and out of the horizons of historic writings "as ghosts and phantasmagorical beings," becoming objects of knowledge through travel, whether their own or that which they facilitate for others.[2]

1. John O. Hunwick, "A Region of the Mind: Medieval Arab Views of African Geography and Ethnography and Their Legacy," *Sudanic Africa* 16 (2005): 103–36; Said, *Orientalism*, 50.

2. Ha, "Baghdād to Baghpūr," 62–63. Ha toggles between capitalization and non-capitalization to gesture both to the emergence of Black, Afro-diasporic consciousness through these historical processes in the Indian Ocean, Atlantic, and Pacific, and to the fact that the history at hand is prior to this emergence. "Black" in its medieval

Arabic geographic sources that arose in the tenth century rigorously represented the world by sorting and synthesizing the translated writings of "ancients," from Aristotle and Ptolemy to Pliny and Hippocrates, the transmission of which was said to have been modeled and transferred to the Persians under the kingship of Alexander the Great, or Dhū'l-Qarnayn, and was viewed by ʿAbbasid rulers as part of their intellectual inheritance.[3] Authors then combined and complemented these works with the more contemporary reportage of the mobile merchant classes that plied their trades within the *mamālik al-islām*, or realms ruled by Muslims, and far beyond, with the earliest Arabic travel literature focused mainly on India and China.[4] By drawing on this tradition of knowledge, the *sīra* evinces another dimension of interest in "scientific" accuracy and verisimilitude, providing a notional cartography in which the plot unfolds. As Zayde Antrim writes, Islamic geographic works are densely interreferential and intertextual. Imitation is part of their art and its ethos, and it is key to reproducing a sense of belonging within overlapping geo-cultural formations:

> They used similar vocabulary to talk about land; they invoked similar historical and religious sources; and they represented territory at similar scales and in similar forms. In particular, they tended to envision plots of land as homes, cities, or regions, each of which associated some notion of attachment or belonging with land.[5]

Expressions of disaffinity and lack of attachment likewise have a common language. Examining ʿAntara b. Shaddād's African adventures, Harry Norris declares that the narrative's pronounced interest in titillating cultural curiosities (*ʿajāʾib*) is a defining feature of the *sīra*'s genre and motivation. Where in chapter 1 we explored the *ʿajab*, or affect of wonderment, that was possible to find at the limits of one's inner world,

---

Arabic, Persian, and Chinese usage admits a wider range of people, including South/east Asian and Oceanian cultures.

3. Dimitri Gutas, *Greek Thought, Arab Culture: The Graeco-Arabic Translation Movement in Baghdad and Early ʿAbbāsid Society (2nd–4th/8th–10th Centuries)* (London: Routledge, 1998), 88.

4. On the origins of the "travel literature" genre (including its fantastic offshoots such as Sindbad's adventures) in relation to overseas shipping, see Maria Kowalska, "From Facts to Literary Fiction, Medieval Arabic Travel Literature," *Quaderni di Studi Arabi* 5–6 (1987–88): 397–403.

5. Zayde Antrim, *Routes and Realms: The Power of Place in the Early Islamic World* (Oxford: Oxford University Press, 2012), 2.

ʿajāʾib, or wonders proper, are often thought to exist at the edge of one's physical realm. Where this edge is positioned is therefore key to interpreting what work it does. When explaining how *ʿajāʾib* are conjured specifically into the text's African landscape, Norris finds several persuasive parallels between a portion of *Sīrat ʿAntar* concerned with the East African king Ḥumām and sections of the travelogue of Abū Ḥāmid al-Gharnaṭī (d. 1170), the *Tuḥfat al-Albāb*, that are concerned with the Dagestan region of the Caucasus.[6] When one type of exotic locale is readily interpolated with another, and when so much of the *sīras*' action occurs at a *thaghr*—an inherently movable frontier—what does the specific movement into the lands of the Blacks do?

Using the East African cycle of *Sīrat Dhāt al-Himma*, this chapter argues that the text conjures a landscape that plays strategically with the possibilities of proximity and distance in order to heighten the drama and ultimate scale of its triumphs. This dynamic is hardly unique to the *sīras*, and indeed is exemplary of why the genre has sometimes been referred to as "pseudo-*maghāzī*," or as a play on chronicles of the early Muslim conquests. Fred Donner identifies a "heroic" disposition within these chronicles that lingers on the military and kerygmatic dimensions of expansion into exaggeratedly hostile territories (mostly Persian and Byzantine) in order to make the stakes of failure higher, the victories more glorious, and divine justice more readily apparent on the page.[7] Nor, of course, were Muslim cultural productions the only ones to set the expansionist scene in this way. As Geraldine Heng has shown, fabulating improbable and far-flung adherents or prospective adherents to the faith—as in renderings of the Black Saint Maurice in thirteenth-century Germany—was central to triumphalist narratives of Christianity as global and universal.[8] In the *sīra*, these various features come together: a large and polymorphous population of Black people in their native lands are pulled, with varying degrees of resistance, into relationality with Islam in ways that aggregate them, accommodate them to new purposes and authorities, and mobilize them to new frontiers. Below, I sketch a series of these charged encounters abroad, where they occur on the notional map, and why that might be.

6. Norris, "From Asia to Africa," 182.

7. Fred Donner, "Visions of the Early Islamic Expansion: Between the Heroic and the Horrific," in *Byzantium in Early Islamic Syria*, ed. Nadia Maria El Cheikh and Shaun O'Sullivan (Beirut: Dar El Kotob), 14–15.

8. Geraldine Heng, "An African Saint in Medieval Europe: The Black St. Maurice and the Enigma of Racial Sanctity," in *Saints and Race: Marked Flesh, Holy Flesh*, ed. Vincent William Lloyd and Molly Harbour Bassett (London: Routledge, 2014), 18–44.

Sīrat Dhāt al-Himma's East African cycle takes place entirely in lands designated *ḥabasha*, sometimes translated as Abyssinia but often indicating a wider radius incorporating northeastern African territories in the east of present-day Sudan and extending to Ethiopia, Eritrea, Djibouti, and into the northern Horn in modern Somalia. However, the *sīra* adduces different models of African sovereignty and evokes different parts of the interior as it goes: where Hadlamūs is fleetingly associated with the Abyssinian title "Negus" (*al-najāshī*), recalling the long pre- and early Islamic legacy of interactions with rulers who have borne that name, he is nonetheless presented in the text as pagan himself, and as having a guard who are troped as Central or Southeast African in many respects. The neighboring ruler, Damdamān, is on the one hand presented as a more littoral figure, networked with Yemen, enriched with goods from China, and aware of Islam. Yet he bears a name and set of alliances that invoke the Damādim, an onomatopoeic exonym for peoples around the highly embellished southern reaches of the Upper Nile, the Lake Chad basin, and beyond, from whom everyone to their north was said to raid for slaves.[9] In the *sīra*, this patchworking of different members of the *bilād al-sūdān* is at once what Srinivas Aravamudan calls "tropological"—representing others in ways that become parodic and malleable through a loss of detail—and is suggestive of frontiers *within* the *bilād al-sūdān* as well. Its parties and peoples migrate, resituate, and participate in strategic intraregional engagements.[10]

The future potentials of the epic's project of recruitment in East Africa are lent particular significance when considering the alarmed reactions of the Byzantines to the Muslims' growing numbers of Black troops, as exhibited in the epigraph above. In assigning Black soldiers a unique capacity to intimidate and effectively war against the Byzantines, we could say that the *sīra* restores what Kwame Anthony Appiah terms "horizontality," in contrast with the *sīra*'s often hierarchical scheme of human difference: Black people possess a particular signifying value that Arabs do not, especially in the view of the Arab Muslims' most immediate adversary. They

9. A byword for their unintelligible speech or, in some accounts, for their cannibalistic customs, variants of the much-recycled monikers *damdam*, *lamlam*, *niamniam*, and so on would eventually be picked up by European colonial ethnographers in the eighteenth century to describe the Azande people in parts of present-day South Sudan, Congo, and the Central African Republic. Paola Ivanov, "Cannibals, Warriors, Conquerors, and Colonizers: Western Perceptions and Azande Historiography," *History in Africa* 29 (2002): 92.

10. Aravamudan, *Tropicopolitans*.

help bring visions of a vast world filled with Muslims and their allies to life.[11] We could also say, though, that the Byzantines' response shows the ineluctable link between demographic logics and racialized symbolism. Jennifer Morgan has shown that quantitative reasoning about Africans was essential not only to their commodification in European sources, but to the logic justifying their continuous evacuation from the continent.[12] Again, this trope is not exclusive to early modern Europe even if it is activated in very different ways in different contexts—the proto-Muslim hero ʿAntar is apprised in his own *sīra* of the human plenitude of the *bilād al-sūdān* by his brother who was born there, and who tells him, "The lands of the Blacks have knights in greater number and of stronger mettle than anywhere [*akthar kull al-fursān ʿadadan wa-aqwāhā jaladan*]."[13]

To flesh out the *sīra*'s flexible picture of the world and situate various parts of the *bilād al-sūdān* within it, I compare the *sīra*'s contents with geographical works such as the writings of al-Masʿūdī (d. 956) and al-Idrīsī (d. 1165). Throughout the *sīra*, the territories of East Africa are represented as being situated in the scheme of the climes, the names of various tribes and leaders reflect the nomenclature used in geographical works, and even the grotesque images of cannibalism bear some relationship to attestations in writings such as Ibn Saʿīd al-Maghribī's (d. 1286) *Kitāb al-Jughrāfiyā* or al-Bakrī's (d. 1094) *Kitāb al-Masālik wa-l-Mamālik*. Such similarities indicate how the *sīra* works within and makes use of projects of knowledge that themselves quickly evolved from "[delivering] necessary information which was needed to establish and develop stable trade relations" to the stuff of erudition and fascination for collectors, anthologizers, and would-be adventurers.[14]

Despite emerging as a distinct formation through an imaginative geographic discourse, the *bilād al-sūdān* and their peoples are not inert in the story. They both act and are acted upon. Black characters across their lands organize themselves politically, have networks of trade and exchange, and express their own sense of lineal, physical, and cultural particularity vis-à-vis their Arab interlocutors, especially in ways that reposition the Black-Arab ʿAbd al-Wahhāb. At times, though, the ways in which the *sīra* evokes the diversity within the *bilād al-sūdān* takes on an air of connoisseurship present elsewhere in the text as well, as when

11. Appiah, "The Uncompleted Argument," 36.

12. Jennifer L. Morgan, *Reckoning with Slavery: Gender, Kinship, and Capitalism in the Early Black Atlantic* (Durham, NC: Duke University Press, 2021).

13. *Sīrat ʿAntar*, vol. 5, 273.

14. Kowalska, "From Facts to Literary Fiction," 397.

the Umayyad caliph ʿAbd al-Malik ibn Marwān is said to provision a caravan with, "slave girls, among whom were Turks and Byzantines and Abyssinians, all wearing beautiful garb, like gardens amid the wilderness," along with palanquins of all colors, all manners of banner unfurled, and so on—arrays in and of themselves connote access to what the world has to offer.[15]

Carefully curating an array, as with the factions of the Muslim armies in the *sīra,* is a mark of leadership and skill. Writing of early Portuguese expeditions down the West African coast in the fifteenth century, Herman Bennett describes how a recognition of the cosmopolitan sovereignty they found there fed back into the anticipation of "profit" and search for "specific commodities," partly because travelers likewise differentiated between African rule by (pagan) might and European rule by (Christian) law, which would regulate those commodities' movements and discipline their consumption.[16] By piecing together individual portraits of differently significant Black sovereigns like Hadlamūs who preside over great masses of souls ripe for conversion and bodies readied for war, the *sīra*s reveal their own intricate purposes for imagining the lands of the Blacks as ones of far-ranging, yet-unrealized promise for Muslims in general and the story's hybrid hero in particular.

The diversity of the *bilād al-sūdān* cuts in multiple directions. In his discussion of how different African ethnicities such as "Guinean," Wolof, and Manding, were conjured into early modern "Black speech" (*habla de negros*) plays in Spain, Nicholas R. Jones claims that though these populations were meaningful for Spaniards because of the slave trade, in the texts African subjects also use each other's ethnic distinctions as a "mode of signifying," or way of contesting representation *among* cultural insiders.[17] Similarly, in characterizing the representation of Black people in the *sīra*s solely in terms of negative and acquisitive modes of knowledge production and representation, we overlook the fact that by migrating their stories into new geographies, texts such as the *sīra*s present multiple, conflicting epistemologies of difference and foreignness within a single work: those held by the primary characters as they travel, and by the individuals and societies that receive them along the way. Encounters with human difference imply the possibility of incorporation. The extremes of that difference push characters to new forms of reckoning and negotiation.

15. *Sīrat Dhāt al-Himma,* II:34.
16. Bennett, *African Kings,* 112–13.
17. Jones, *Staging* Habla de Negros, 108.

Figuring Black Africans: Transcendental Darkness

To the medieval Arab-Muslim listener, the mention of kingship in the lands of *ḥabasha* would have likely called to mind a ruler and a people renowned for their faithfulness: the Negus of Abyssinia who reigned during Muḥammad's lifetime famously accepted the first band of *muhājirūn*—early believing Muslims who departed Mecca as persecuted refugees even before the more prominent *hijra* of 622. The Negus's dominion over a neighboring monotheistic power and storied good disposition toward Islam became embedded in the prophetic *sīra* tradition. His dynastic line also holds pride of place in some of the poems composed by the often half-Abyssinian successors to the "crows of the Arabs" (*aghribat al-ʿarab*), indicating that East African Muslims raced as Black in the Umayyad period consciously used him as a touchstone. Authors such as Xavier Luffin, ʿAbduh Badawī, and Bernard Lewis have identified an evolution in Islam's formative centuries following the legacy of the collective of pre-Islamic poets with Abyssinian mothers and Arab fathers who in their own times would have been considered *hajīns*, or mixed, but were later grouped and named the "crows" as *nasab* paternalized and their legacies transformed into those of great Black men of literary accomplishment. Over time, more and more poetry meditating on blackness becomes attributed to these figures, including many of the poems in ʿAntara's *sīra*. More Black poets also emerge who compose in an increasingly defiant, boastful mode that some have linked with the foundations of *shuʿūbiyya*, a supposed movement for ethnicized and classed recognition by Persian elites in the early ʿAbbasid period.

Though the real motivations and institutionalization of *shuʿūbiyya* itself are widely contested—with some scholars pointing to the fact that no one seems to have ever self-designated as a *shuʿūbī* but rather that it was a form of saber-rattling among the Arabized elite, and others noting its ironic quality as a movement of Persian pride pioneered using the prestige medium of their Arab peers—there is indeed poetry from this period that glorifies aspects of a Persian pre-Islamic past, and so too with odes to Abyssinian greatness.[18] Anthological projects such as al-Jāḥiẓ's *Fakhr al-Sūdān ʿalā-l-Bīḍān*, whose title plays on the idea of

18. Sarah Bowen Savant, "Naming Shuʿūbīs," in *Essays in Islamic Philology, History, and Philosophy: A Festschrift in Celebration and Honor of Professor Ahmad Mahdavi Damghani's 90th Birthday*, edited by K. A. Thackston et al. (Berlin: De Gruyter, 2016), 166–84; Karla Malette, *Lives of the Great Languages: Arabic and Latin in the Medieval Mediterranean* (Chicago: University of Chicago Press, 2021), 26–28.

rhetorical self-aggrandizement, attest lines in which Black composers recall prior righteous kings of Axum, such as Abraha ibn al-Ṣabbāḥ, who ruled at least 150 years before Muḥammad was born. They proudly juxtapose the acceptance of Islam and Muslims on the part of the Negus of the *muḥadram* period (that time which intersects with Muḥammad's own life), against sovereigns of the Byzantines, Sasanians, Ghassanids, and Copts.[19]

Abyssinia was also folded into a larger imaginative ground for rendering inevitable Muḥammad's and the Qur'ān's universal recognition. Living proofs of Muḥammad's prophecy—mainly rabbis and monks—who were said to have anticipated or spontaneously recognized Muḥammad's prophethood and thus to have been of a few select "true" Jews and Christians remaining on earth, "whose faith was unaffected by the tainted scripture and manmade doctrines," hail from places like Abyssinia and are converted through the efforts of Muḥammad's cousin Jaʿfar ibn Abī Ṭālib (d. 629), the *muhājirūn*'s emissary.[20] The trajectory of Jaʿfar's mission in turn binds Abyssinian and Syrian Christians together in these experiences; returning to Medina, Jaʿfar brings along named figures such as Baḥīra the monk, a Syrian who recognized Muḥammad's *fiṭra*, or fitness to receive God's word, even before the Qur'ān's revelation. Another such link is formed through the Axumite presence in Ḥimyar. This presence is associated not only with the year of Muḥammad's birth, widely known for being the year in which the Abyssinians attempted a siege on Mecca and God aided the Quraysh in safeguarding the Kaʿba, but also much more sympathetically with the persecution of the faithful that catalyzed Axum's renewed interest in the Peninsula. Several Syriac *martyria* present a tableau found also, according to most interpreters, in Qur'ān 85:4–6, a trial by fire of Christians in Najrān that occurred after the Negus's withdrawal from Jewish-ruled Himyar following a first punitive strike.[21] These verses act as an apocalyptic warning to those

19. The poetry of ʿUkaym and Hayqutan mentions Abyssinian royal ancestry and names the Negus as providing ancestry of note in their collected verses. For more on the *aghribat al-ʿArab*, see Abdūh Badawī, *al-Sūd wa-l-Ḥaḍāra al-ʿArabiyya* (Cairo: al-Hay'a al-Miṣriyyah al-ʿĀmmah li-l-Kitāb, 1976); Xavier Luffin "Peaux noires, âmes blanches: Les poètes Arabes d'origine Africaine face à leur négritude," *Quaderni di Studi Arabi* 5–6 (2010–11): 199–215; Bernard Lewis, "The Crows of the Arabs," *Critical Inquiry* 12, no. 1 (1985): 88–97.

20. Barbara Roggema, *The Legend of Sergius Baḥīrā: Early Christian Apologetics and Apocalyptic in Response to Islam* (Leiden: Brill, 2009), 42.

21. Vassilios Christides, "The Himyarite-Ethiopian war and the Ethiopian occupation of South Arabia in the acts of Gregentius (ca. 530 A.D.)," *Annales d'Ethiopie* 9 (1972): 126–27.

who would oppress believers, linked with images of the Pharaoh in Egypt and the tyrannical people of Thamūd.

As we will see in greater detail below, by the tenth century when the Muslim geographic tradition arises, various authors write of Christian Abyssinia and Nubia as exceptions to the norms of the *bilād al-sūdān*. Authors such as Ibn Ḥawqal (d. 988) and al-Iṣṭakhrī (d. 957) state that unlike their neighbors who "have failed in hitting this mark, and have no fortune in anything of the like," they possess governance and social organization, architecture and urbanity, hew to the rites and theologies [*madhāhib*] of Byzantium, and are among "the Blacks who are close to these [other] known kingdoms, and who *return* [*yarjiʿūn*] to religion, rationality, and wisdom."[22] The language of return implies movable points on a line, or a *telos*, with religion-as-rationality as the end from which these other structural elements emanate. Other parts of the *bilād al-sūdān* are perhaps on this line, but further regressed. Michael Gomez glosses this passage by saying that "al-Istakhrī assumes black civilizational distinction results from proximity to recognized models."[23] Already we see that proximity is more than a geographical conceit, and so too is distance.

At first, the meta-geographic role played by religion might seem at cross-purposes with another aspect of reasoned tradition, namely, the scheme of "climes," a discussion of which also appears in the *sīra*. These broad latitudinal bands of the earth were thought to be similarly affected by exposure to sun and water and their attendant humoral influences, which produce constitutional differences in humans and animals alike. As early as the third century AD, the Syriac philosopher Bardaisan of Edessa (known in Arabic as Ibn Dīṣān) addresses the tension between religion's transregional sprawl and the climes' deterministic relationship with human intellect and cultural development. He speaks of the Indian subcontinent as a paradoxical portion of the earth in which some incline toward vegetarianism and others to feasting on humans, not unlike the tribe of ʿUqfūr. He likewise recalls the maintenance of customs among diasporic peoples, as with Jews circumcising their sons eight days after birth regardless of birth house, alignment of the stars, climate in their birth region, and so on. Bardaisan is credited with a claim that is highly compatible with what we have seen of the Muslim geographers: "The laws of men are stronger than Fate, and they lead their lives according to their

22. Emphasis mine. Ibn Ḥawqal, *Kitāb al-Masālik wa-l-Mamālik* (Leiden: Brill, 1872), 9–10. Also, al-Iṣṭakhrī, *al-Masālik wa-l-Mamālik*, ed. Muḥammad Jābir ʿAbd al-ʿĀl al-Ḥīnī (Cairo: Dār al-Qalam, 1961), 16.

23. Gomez, *African Dominion*, 50.

own customs."[24] And so, within one clime, one witnesses a diverse range of customs based in some measure on people's religious learning or lack thereof. Rather than setting hard boundaries around whether one can receive religion in these places—which would seem to flout endeavors at realizing truth in the world—it sets softer ones around directionality of spread and, often, perfectibility of acquisition.

Perhaps because of its theological importance and civilizational proximity, the *sīra* first removes Abyssinia from normative knowledge and embeds it into further corners of the *bilād al-sūdān* by recalling a darkness that is not climatologically induced, or even of this earth, but instead belongs to the unseen. Before being apprised that Hadlamūs is himself, incongruously, an Abyssinian Negus who is neither Christian nor versed in Christianity, audiences to the *sīra* are introduced to this possibility through a series of allusions to his benighted realm that are voiced by a Christian character versed in Muslim traditions. The text's earliest incursion into Abyssinia is filtered through the villainous turncoat ʿUqba. At the time, ʿUqba is pretending to be a faithful advisor to the caliph al-Maʾmūn, who has had a falling out with ʿAbd al-Wahhāb and his family and written to Hadlamūs in the hopes of attracting him into service in Baghdad, following the familiar logic of pitting Black champions against one another. After traveling for a month and a half, ʿUqba arrives at the Abyssinian ruler's court. There, he is immediately struck by the spectacle of a retinue of troops from the tribe of ʿUqfūr (lit. "Calamities," though elsewhere they are called al-Maqfūr, the "Tracked") stationed around the sovereign. The ʿUqfūrī men produce animal sounds and wear locked muzzles on their faces, leading ʿUqba to fearfully declare, "These are the *zabāniya* described by God and Muḥammad b. ʿAbdallāh, prophet of the Muslims . . . on the day of judgment they drag people to Hell."[25]

In designating the people of ʿUqfūr as the beings who guard the passage to hell, ʿUqba's character instantly taps into a matrix of associations that align these Black men with a lack of free will and rationality, with the hellish and demonic, and with forbidding superhuman strength.[26] His descrip-

24. Bardaiṣan of Edessa, *The Book of the Laws of Countries*, trans. H. J. W. Drivers and G. E. van Baaren-Pape (Piscataway, NJ: Georgias Press, 2007), 53. On Bardaisan's "refutation of astral determinism," see also Ute Possekel, "Bardaisan's Influence on Late Antique Christianity," *Hugoye: Journal of Syriac Studies* 21, no. 1 (2018): 81–125.

25. *Sīrat Dhāt al-Himma*, XXXV:54. Cf. Q 66:6, 74:30.

26. Elsewhere, the ʿUqfūrīs index a dramatic difference between themselves and other Black peoples that is also evident in the way they interact with Hadlamūs in his court: Hadlamūs appoints another ethnic group, the people of Kardam, over them in battle and they hold back the ʿUqfūrīs who are bound in chains and muzzled until

tion invokes a robust iconographic register with which the audience might have been familiar; in visual depictions throughout the medieval period, the *zabāniya* appear as hulking, dusk-colored demon-like creatures with exaggerated facial features. Although extant illustrations of the *zabāniya* mostly arrive to us from Timurid territories in the fourteenth and fifteenth centuries, they are preconfigured by various traditions that speak of the *zabāniya* as having giant, terror-inducing bodies, or as being "black-faced and snarling" (*musawwada wujūhuhum kāliḥa anyābuhum*).[27] While color is not discussed in the earliest portrayals of these creatures, already in the *tafsīr* of Muqātil b. Sulaymān (d. 767) to verse 30 of *Sūrat al-Muddaththir*, in which God reveals that he has assigned nineteen angels to guard Hell, an elaborate portrait of the *zabāniya* has emerged:

> Their eyes are like dazzling lightning, their canines like spurs—meaning [shaped] like the horns of a cow—and their hair reaches down to their feet. Flames of hellfire emerge from their mouths, and traveling from shoulder to shoulder requires a seventy-year journey. The extent of one of their palms spans [the territory of] Rabīʿa and Muḍar, and all their mercy and kindness is replaced by rage. One of them can drive seventy thousand [souls to hell], and [God] casts them out of hell as He wishes, and may send one of them down into hell for a journey of forty years. The hellfire does not harm them because their light [from which they are fashioned] is more intense than the hellfire's heat. Were this not so they could not endure entering the fire for one instant.[28]

The interpretation of the *zabāniya* as Black could relate to the Qurʾānic verse that immediately precedes their mention, in which it is said that the fires of hell are "scorchers of the skins" (*lawwāḥatun li-l-bashar*), by which logic their "more intense" light might do so as well, or might prepare

---

fighting commences. This portrayal has echoes in the geographic tradition, where the Zanj are said to have a band of soldiers called the "Pierced Ones," whose noses are ringed and fitted with chains for this same purpose. *Sīrat Dhāt al-Himma*, XXXV:57; al-Sīrāfī, *Two Arabic Tales*, 120–21.

27. On Timurid depictions of demons in the *Siyāh Qalam* ("Black Pen") style, see Sheila S. Blair and Jonathan M. Bloom, *The Art and Architecture of Islam 1250–1850* (New Haven, CT: Yale University Press, 1994), 61–63. For a description of the *khazanat jahanam*, or "keepers of hell," as black and sharp-toothed, see Ibn Rajab al-Dimashqī, *al-Takhwīf min al-Nār wa-l-Taʿrīf Majāl al-Bawār*, ed. Bashīr Muḥammad ʿUyūn (Beirut: Maktabat Dār al-Bayān, 1988), 218.

28. Muqātil b. Sulaymān, *Tafsīr Muqātil ibn Sulaymān*, vol. 3, ed. Aḥmad Farīd (Beirut: Dār al-Kutub al-ʿIlmiyya, 2003), 417.

them for hell's conditions accordingly. This verse led various exegetes to conclude that the fires of hell blacken the bodies of its occupants due to the relationship between burning and charring. Or images of the *zabāniya* could simply be related to the artistic habit of indexing the demonic using darker, more somber or chthonic colors and playing with contrastive extremes.[29] Perhaps because of this array of features, as well as their linkage with the ranks of "severe" or "punishing" angels (*malāʾika ghilāẓ shidād*) in Q 66:6, the *zabāniya* sit in many interpretations between being akin to angels and demons. The constitutional overlap between angels fashioned of light yet stationed in hell—like the fallen Iblīs, according to some interpretations—and demons, or *jinn*, fashioned from smokeless fire, aestheticizes a process that Simon O'Meara calls "infernalization."[30] In the early Islamic period, portrayals of *jinn* increasingly show them as chthonic and hellish and subsume a massive range of once more individuated beings that had previously existed as "aerial" para-human creatures. At times, the liminal process of becoming a creature of hell was even vividly portrayed. As Amira El-Zein notes, outside of popular literature the *jinn* are rarely depicted as winged, that being a privilege of the angels;[31] Francesca Leoni finds that, in one rare image, Iblīs's rebellion among the angels is represented not just in stock characteristics like his blackness and horns, but with his having wings that appear singed at their edges.[32] With a single, concise reference by ʿUqba, the *sīra* similarly removes Hadlamūs's court to a realm that even God's emissaries experience as a type of exile.

The Abyssinia encountered by ʿUqba is then presented as plunged into ignorant paganism. Hadlamūs asks after the source of al-Maʾmūn's power, and ʿUqba explains his lineal ties to Muḥammad, to which Hadlamūs replies "If that is the case, then we are naught but astray [*ʿalā-l-ḍalāl*], for we neither know nor worship any gods [*lā naʿrif wa-lā naʿbud min al-arbāb*]," and so he asks ʿUqba to teach him of the caliph's religion.[33] Instead, the duplicitous ʿUqba makes an appeal to Hadlamūs using a set of Christian pietisms, and the king appears never to have heard of the faith or its tenets:

29. On depictions of demons as black or dark-skinned in Islamic art, see Hillenbrand, "The Image of the Black in Islamic Art," 216–53.

30. O'Meara, "From Space to Place," 56–72.

31. Amira El Zein, *Islam, Arabs, and the Intelligent World of the Jinn* (Syracuse, NY: Syracuse University Press, 2009), 50.

32. Francesca Leoni, "On the Monstrous in the Islamic Visual Tradition," in *The Ashgate Companion to Monsters and the Monstrous*, ed. Asa Simon Mittman with Peter J. Dendle (London: Routledge, 2013), 156.

33. *Sīrat Dhāt al-Himma*, XXXV:55.

> ʿUqba said to him . . . "O king of the age, I shall guide you to the religion of great kings, possessors of countries and cities. It guards its practitioner from dangers and saves him from the punishment of hellfire, but I cannot reveal anything [about it] until I receive your pledge and promise that if you are pleased with this religion, you will hide it and not reveal it to anyone. I am an old man, and my life has waned and my energy been drained from reading overmuch from old books and righteous [Islamic] discourses, until my soul became desirous of the one who spoke from the cradle while an infant [*dīn man takallam fi-l-mahd ṣabān*], and he who resurrected the dead from their graves and cured the blind and leprous [*al-abraṣ*], and fashioned birds from clay and brought us the Gospel from God the Eternal and clarified the forbidden and licit [*al-taḥrīm wa-l-taḥlīl*] for us within it,"[34] and ʿUqba began to describe Christianity. . . . King Hadlamūs assented, saying, "Teach me what to say in order to become a Christian [*ʿallimnī kayf aqūl ḥattā aṣīr naṣraniyya*]."[35]

Hadlamūs's curiosity about God and desire for religious knowledge ultimately paves the way for him to accept not Christianity, but Islam, thanks to a decisive tussle with the *sīra*'s principal heroine, Fāṭima Dhāt al-Himma, when her troops later clash with ʿUqba and Hadlamūs on their way to the Byzantine frontier. As if to preface this, the milestones in the life of Jesus offered above are all Qurʾānic; miracles such as breathing life into clay birds that are key to Jesus's story in the Qurʾān do not appear in Christian scripture, though they do emerge in written and illustrated apocrypha throughout Late Antiquity and the Middle Ages. His speaking from the cradle likewise occurs in infancy gospels and the Qurʾān, but not in canonical Christian scriptures.[36]

Hadlamūs's first explicit exposure to the Qurʾān meanwhile occurs in a battle between the Muslim armies and his troops, who are temporarily under ʿUqba's sway. In the fray, Fāṭima grabs hold of the king's head and squeezes so hard he nearly dies. Astonished by her strength, a captured Hadlamūs—who has become endeared to his captors on seeing that ʿAbd al-Wahhāb and Abū'l-Hazāhiz are Black because "kind is accustomed to kind" (*al-jins yaʾlaf al-jins*)—later exclaims, "When she grabbed hold of

34. Q5:110.
35. *Sīrat Dhāt al-Himma*, XXXV:55.
36. Mary Dzon, "Jesus and the Birds in Medieval Abrahamic Traditions," *Traditio* 66 (2011): 189–230.

my head, I felt as though the sky had fallen to the earth." Fāṭima then explains the divine source of her strength, saying:

> When I placed my hands on your head, I recited this sacred verse [*hādhihī al-āya al-sharīfa*], the word of the Almighty: "They have not appraised God with true appraisal, while the earth entirely will be in His grip on the Day of Resurrection, and the heavens will be folded in His right hand. Exalted is He and high above what they associate with Him."[37] And lately, you have committed *shirk* [i.e., assigning partners to God], O cursed one who is deceived and confused in his ignorance [*wa-man huwa bi-jahlihi maftūn wa-maghrūr*]![38]

As with many of the *sīra*'s conversion narratives, Hadlamūs's tale gives occasion both for plot advancement and for a pious exhortation to the *sīra*'s audience in the form of an allegory of assimilation. With divine and earthly forces moving in unison, Hadlamūs perceives the heavens violently descending upon him when he is startled into a realization of the Muslims' physical might. Then, moved by both Fāṭima's recitation and by her later sincerity in prayer as she tearfully performs 100 *rakʿa*s each night with ʿAbd al-Wahhāb, Hadlamūs asks, "Who is this God of yours?" Fāṭima duly replies:

> Our God is the One who sees when we sit and stand, and who has raised up the canopies of clouds [*sarādiq al-ghuyūm*], who knows the number of the stars [*ʿadad al-nujūm*] and who establishes fates [*wa-abram al-qaḍāʾ al-maḥtūm*]. He is God, and there is no God except for Him, the eternally living.[39]

Unlike ʿUqba's appeal, which is grounded in notions of sovereignty and conquest, Fāṭima couches the might of God in transcendental and cosmic terms, speaking of mastery over the very skies that had suddenly felt so close to Hadlamūs in her grip before. Together, these passages function almost as a *memento mori*, or *waʿẓ*, drawing the firmament close in one's mind and then recalling fate's imminence. Immediately, Hadlamūs comes to the conclusion that ʿUqba has hoodwinked him, and he curses him as a "one-eyed, ignorant, lying old man." He then states, "I was not brought up in a religious tradition [*kunt anā lā atadayyan bi-l-dīn*] and did not know

37. Q39:67.
38. *Sīrat Dhāt al-Himma*, XXXVI:7–8.
39. *Sīrat Dhāt al-Himma*, XXXVI:7–8; cf. Q2:255, Q3:2, etc.

the words of the Christians, nor of the Muslims," adding that he now sees that the Muslims honor the true faith.[40] An indication of there being an attenuated religious substrate in Abyssinian culture is given, briefly, when Hadlamūs goes to proselytize to his land's ten governors (*al-muqaddimīn wa-arbāb dawlatihi*) who have traveled with him to Iraq. After hearing his description of Islam, four convert, while the remaining six say, "We shall not know anything but the religion of the Messiah (i.e., Christianity) for all the years of our lives," having been converted by ʿUqba.[41] Al-Baṭṭāl later explains this in temporally hazy terms, saying,

> Among this people are those who became Muslim when the Negus became Muslim and those who are Christian. When ʿUqba went to them as a messenger he found the people had no reason [*ʿuqūl*], so he played with them until they became Christian, but now this group and those that follow them have become Muslim at the hand of the general ʿAbd al-Wahhāb.[42]

Is al-Baṭṭāl here referring to a lapse between Abyssinian religious practice at the time of the Negus who was contemporary with Muḥammad, said by some to have converted to Islam, and the present? Or is he referring to Hadlamūs's conversion in similar terms to this illustrious past? Were Hadlamūs's advisors aware of Christianity before ʿUqba's arrival, or were they truly areligious and lacking in reason? If the implication is that the Abyssinians have devolved into this state like the Arabs in the long span of time between Abraham and Muḥammad, then ʿAbd al-Wahhāb and his peers are not pioneers per se in teaching them religious laws (*sharīʿa*) and thought (*madhhab*), but rather restorers of a bygone order.[43]

This initial East African ambivalence toward religion serves to heighten the stakes of the Muslims' engagement with these spaces and peoples vis-à-vis the malignant ʿUqba, as they each vie to convert the peoples of the region over to their side in a fight for souls that may be retrojected deep into the past. The creation of Abyssinia's artificial distance, foreignness, and hostility is particularly striking in view of Islamic historiography, which writes of the first encounter between Muhammad's emissaries and the Negus as a moment in which Christians were shown to be especially amenable to conversion to Islam. Instead,

40. *Sīrat Dhāt al-Himma*, XXXVI:7–8.
41. *Sīrat Dhāt al-Himma*, XXXVI:16–17.
42. *Sīrat Dhāt al-Himma*, XXXVI: 30.
43. *Sīrat Dhāt al-Himma*, XXXV: 48.

like the unrepentantly warmongering lands of Byzantium against whom Muslims in the text are mainly engaged, Abyssinia is made to constitute another portion of the adamantly non-Muslim world, in which conflict is considered both legitimate and anticipated. However, unlike Byzantium, it is also a blank canvas where one can use different tactics and yield different results from lands in which Christian tradition is more entrenched. Rather than vying against an equally pious enemy in a different tradition, the Muslims who have entered East Africa bring with them the very concepts of piety and tradition themselves, along with the tutelage structures these entail. Hadlamūs's religious awakening leads him to submit himself willingly into the Muslim social order as Fāṭima's servant and soldier, where once he was an absolute sovereign, and to bring his ample armies along with him.

Hadlamūs's experience is not the only indication of the region's supposed lack—or, more fittingly, *loss*—of religion. Hadlamūs's territorial rival, the king Damdamān, himself presides over a formidable domain and is described as being "a man of great esteem, little religion, and great processions" (*rajul ʿaẓīm al-shaʾn qalīl al-dīn kathīr al-mawākib*). ʿAbd al-Wahhāb is kidnapped by a party of his men who are traveling back from Anatolia, having accompanied Hadlamūs's delegation to the caliph al-Maʾmūn. The characterization of Damdamān as having little religion is perhaps looser than Hadlamūs's clear denial of ever having been brought up with any; indeed, as we will see in the next chapter, Damdamān has furnished his daughter Maymūna with a form of religious education through a Muslim teacher from Yemen, and this learning prepares her to become a religious aspirant and avid soldierly wife to ʿAbd al-Wahhāb.

Nonetheless, Damdamān's idea of his own sovereignty is phrased in capacious terms on which concepts of religious authority do not easily infringe: when ʿAbd al-Wahhāb initially falls into his hands and Damdamān is apprised by his servants of what transpired to cause this, they tell him that the hero, who holds many fortresses and lands, had a disagreement with the "caliph that the whites have [*al-khalīfa alladhī li-l-bīḍān*]" and that the two had drawn battle lines, to which Damdamān replies, "Imprison him until he ransoms himself with money or dies." He has no intention of remitting ʿAbd al-Wahhāb to a caliph who is represented as a functioning figurehead only for "whites," under whom ʿAbd al-Wahhāb is in turn included, with the implication—similar to Abū'l-Hazāhiz's inference in chapter 5—that there is either a caliph for Black people or else an opening for one to exist. When ʿUqba attempts to make an arrangement with Damdamān similar to the one he had originally brokered with Hadlamūs, he is met with the response, "O shaykh, do not presume that we are like Hadlamūs, for he is not fit even to be a slave to us."[44] ʿUqba offers him not Christianity, but money and service, submitting himself wholly into Damdamān's debt. Not coincidentally, Damdamān's might is also analogized in the story with that of Nimrūd b. Kanʿān, the world-conquering ruler in Ḥām's line who, through the Prophet Ibrāhīm, met his downfall for playing at being God, as we saw in chapter 1. And not unlike with Ibrāhīm's triumph, Damdamān's tyranny renders his pious daughter's eventual patricide forgivable and even salutary.

Emblematic of his unbridled earthly rule, which is here tethered to a disinterest in serving higher powers, Damdamān reigns over and makes bedfellows of peoples who are impious in multivalent ways. When we are first introduced to Damdamān, we are told that he presides over a population not of Ḥabashī or Zanjī groups, though both are ethnonyms that he and his daughter will use, but rather of *Qarāmida*. Or at least in part—Damdamān, who has warred against Hadlamūs many times, has thirty villages in his midst from whom he has taken "100,000 Blacks" apiece, "for they are uncountable in the world."[45] The representations of Damdamān's avarice when negotiating with ʿUqba cannot but be parodic given the wealth and manpower already at his disposal.

Qarāmida is likely a corruption of *Qarāmiṭa*, or *Qarmatians*, a term used for a band of rebels who arose in the ninth century in Bahrain under the banner of a specific form of Ismāʿīlī Islam and whose militancy against the religio-political mainstream climaxed in a successful sack of the Kaʿba and seizure of its Black Stone, to the humiliation of its ʿAbbasid stewards. There is a slimmer chance that term may be a corruption two steps removed of *Qarmāṭiyyūn*, Garamantes, which is also attested in the Arabic corpus principally in bills of sale for slaves and in portrayals of the Zanj revolt.[46] This would place Damdamān's kingdom closer to the Fezzan and further from the lands of *ḥabasha*, where it is said to be located.[47] The more straightforward transposition of the letter *ṭāʾ* with *dāl*,

44. *Sīrat Dhāt al-Himma*, XXXVI:41–43.

45. *Sīrat Dhāt al-Himma*, XXXVI:41.

46. Al-Ṭabarī, *Tārīkh al-Rusul wa-l-Mulūk*, vol. 5 (Beirut: Dār al-Kutub al-ʿIlmiyya, 1986), 446; al-Muqaddisī, *Bibliotheca Geographorum Arabicorum* [*Aḥsan al-Taqāsīm fī Maʿrifat al-Aqālīm*], ed. M. J. De Goeje (Leiden: Brill: 1877), 242; Vantheighem, "Quelques contrats de vente d'esclaves," 168–72.

47. *Qarāmida* leads us in further directions as well that still eddy at once around the lands neighboring Abyssinia and the reaches of human difference. In several passages, Hadlamūs is said to be attended by the Banū Kardam, or Karādima, with the term *kardam* in classical Arabic indicating men of short height (sometimes rendered as "dwarves"). Yet Karadim is also a family name in northern Sudan, among the Shaiqiya

described as a *taṣḥīf*, or misspelling, is attested in a few places, including the thirteenth-century dictionary *Lisān al-ʿArab*, where the verbal form *qarmaṭa* (meaning to space lines closely on the page) is said to have become *qarmada* in vernacular.[48]

Qarmatian groups also have a long history of engagement with East Africa. The *Kilwa Chronicle*, which records the history of proto-Swahili cultures along the coast, recalls an influx of Qarmatians from the Persian Gulf into the Horn of Africa in the late eleventh or early twelfth century following their expulsion by the Buyids, at which time they are said to have had a hand in founding Somali cities such as Mogadishu and Barawa. Randall Pouwels makes the case for a prior, related period of migration, stating that "groups of schismatic Kharijites and Shiʿites," arrived as early as the tenth century.[49] The timing of these settlements, of course, does not align with ʿAbd al-Wahhāb's expedition, set in the early ninth century under the caliphate of the ʿAbbasid ruler al-Maʾmūn. Nor does it quite fit seamlessly with the *sīra* tradition's supposed origins in the eleventh century.[50] However, East African involvement with Qarmatian politics originates with the movement itself, bringing us at least to the late ninth

near the "heartland" of medieval Makuria, and Kardam ibn Abū'l-Dīs is the name of the ancestor to whom the Sudanese Jaʿlīya also trace their Arab lineage. Local communities often assigned an Arabic broken plural on which to pattern their family names. Jay Spaulding, "The Old Shaiqi Language in Historical Perspective," *History in Africa* 17 (1990): 286–90. *Kurdūm*, the common plural for those of short stature, is meanwhile attested in a few places in *Sīrat Sayf b. Dhī Yazan* in a long, stock list of names for various Black peoples, filled in with playful pairings such as "Fighters of Mules" (*malākim al-bighāl*) and "Troops of Dogs" (*dawwās al-kilāb*), and exaggerated with a final remark by the narrator that "we have fallen short of [all the] names of the Blacks for they wear out every tongue." E.g., *Sīrat Sayf b. Dhī Yazan*, vol. 2 (Cairo: Maktabat al-Jumhūriyya al-ʿArabiyya, 1970) 373. At times, the *Karādim* blur with the *Qarāmida* in ambiguous ways in the tale—likely a result of oral transmission rather than written—as when after joining al-Maʾmūn's ranks Hadlamūs is said to have dispatched a faction of his troops back to Damdamān to aid him, as that was their home country, thus merging the *Qarāmida* and members of the Banū Kardam (*Sīrat Dhāt al-Himma*, XXXVI:43). Whether an audience with variable degrees of geographic learning may have imagined the people of Kardam as being differently sized, differently religious, or simply as Black and foreign is unclear.

48. Ibn al-Manẓūr, *Lisān al-ʿArab* (Beirut: Dār Ṣādir, 1955–56), 3606.

49. Randall L. Pouwels, "The Medieval Foundations of East African Islam," *International Journal of African Historical Studies* 11, no. 2 (1978): 209.

50. On the relationship of the *sīras* and chronology and to genres of universal history and conquest history, see Thomas Herzog, "Orality and the Tradition of Arabic Epic," in *Medieval Oral Literature*, ed. Karl Reichl (Berlin: De Gruyter, 2012), 627–49.

century: troops of so-called Zanj are said to round out Qarmatian armies.[51] Records of large-scale overseas trade between Qarmatian Bahrain and Oman and the East African coast reach back into the tenth century.[52]

As if to again tilt our gaze toward these paths of exchange, Damdamān's daughter, Maymūna, is described as having a towering stone fortress with doors of "Chinese iron" (*al-ḥadīd al-ṣīnī*), a term now commonly used for black hematite but that likely indicated an alloy of copper and zinc, noted for its use in imported Chinese mirrors and precious enough to be the material in various caliphs' signet rings.[53] Hadlamūs is likewise said to ride into battle with a shield of the same material, which only he can lift.[54] That the possibility of Damdamān, situated on the routes that convey peoples and goods from around the Indian Ocean, himself being a Muslim ruler, is never raised may be a matter of oblivion or perception: several medieval authors continued to refer to areas settled by the Qarmatians in Africa as pagan, naively or polemically.[55]

Damdamān's paltry religiosity may also relate to another population over which he stands to exert control, the cannibal peoples of Damdam, whom he has set up through a royal betrothal to assume a similar role in his court to the ʿUqfūrīs in Hadlamūs's. Damdam is one of a set of monikers often associated with semi-fabled regions of the *bilād al-sūdān*, and is the stem on which the king Damdamān's own name is constructed.[56]

As Michael Gomez puts it, the name "Damdam" appears in many geographic sources as "at first a mere permutation" of other regional groups, and a strong seam of folklore runs through these sources, with the Damdam peoples said to eat the flesh of men. Damdamān's name links him aurally with these figures, among possible others—onomatopoeic epithets

51. Zoltán Szombathy, "Eating People Is Wrong: Some Eyewitness Reports of Cannibalism in Arabic Sources," in *Violence in Islamic Thought from the Qur'ān to the Mongols*, ed. Robert Gleave and István T. Kristó-Nagy (Edinburgh: Edinburgh University Press, 2015), 200–224.

52. Bruce Stanley, "Mogadishu," in *Cities of the Middle East and North Africa: A Historical Encyclopedia*, ed. Michael Dumper and Bruce Stanley (Santa Barbara, CA: ABC-CLIO, 2007), 252.

53. *Sīrat Dhāt al-Himma*, XXXVII:22; Florian Sobieroj, *Variance in Arabic Manuscripts: Arabic Didactic Poems from the Eleventh to the Seventeenth Centuries—Analysis of Textual Variance and Its Control in the Manuscripts* (Berlin: De Gruyter, 2016), 11; Anya H. King, *Scents from the Garden of Paradise: Musk in the Medieval Islamic World* (Leiden: Brill, 2017), 57.

54. *Sīrat Dhāt al-Himma*, XXXVI: 6

55. Philippe Beaujard, *The Worlds of the Indian Ocean*," 349n64.

56. *Sīrat Dhāt al-Himma*, XXXVI:41.

like *damdam* and *lamlam*[57] are sometimes used interchangeably, but sometimes refer to distinct peoples.[58] As with the term Berber (*barbar*) derived from the Greek *barbaroi* and applied to non-Arabophone peoples in North Africa and the Sahel, and the term *ʿajam* for the eastern non-Arabophone sphere, *damdam* and its relatives imply and sonically imitate unintelligible speech. *Damdama* is often rendered as "snarled" or "growled." This verbiage is used for other East African peoples' speech as well, and particularly the Zanj. Ibn al-Nadīm's (d. ca. 995) *Fihrist*, which opens with a discussion of the world's tongues and writing systems, records that the Zanj have no writing and speak instead in long oratorical sessions, with elocution that "resembles grumbling [*al-damdama*] and growling [*al-hamhama*]," yet from which they derive a sound view (*al-raʾy*) to put into action.[59] This portrait of Zanj rhetoric has many analogues; Ibn al-Nadīm himself cites al-Jāḥiẓ, but this representation also reverberates across the geographic corpus, arising in the work of Abū Zayd al-Sīrāfī and others.[60]

Gomez detects subtle differentiations between the peoples denoted by this series of terms, particularly between the cannibalistic practices alleged to occur among the *Damādim* and the seafood-based diets of the *Lamālim*, situated in some writings to medieval Ghana's south, toward the Atlantic. Many scholars have tried to excavate the specific ethnicities to whom these nebulous terms refer. Gomez locates the *Damādim* mainly in Central Africa, in parts of Chad and Niger. Correlating Arabic geographic materials with Dinka oral histories, Stephanie Beswick makes a compelling case that at least some references to the *Damādim* refer to populations in the southern Gezira region of modern Sudan.[61] Daniel Ayana argues that sev-

57. Some have proposed that one iteration of these usages, *Nam-nam* (or *Niam-niam* or *Nyam-nyam*) has its origins in the Dinka language of southern Sudan, in which *nyam-nyam* means "great eater." This also is substantiated by the fact that the term is often used for cannibal peoples, specifically. Others differentiate among these many designations, relating "lam" in Arabic to nothingness, "dam" to blood or to masses, and so on. On this, see Gomez, *African Dominion*, 386n15; S. H. F. Capenny, "The Khedivic possessions in the basin of the Upper Ubangi," in *Scottish Geographical Magazine* 15 (1899): 309–16.

58. Authors also relate the existence of Dahdam people, and elsewhere Namnam and Tamtam are attested. Gomez, *African Dominion*, 45; R. Mauny, "Lamlam," in *Encyclopedia of Islam*, 2nd ed., ed. Peri Bearman, Thierry Bianquis, C. Edmund Bosworth, E. J. van Donzel, and Wolfhart P. Heinrichs, accessed 20 March 2019, http://dx.doi.org.proxy.uchicago.edu/10.1163/1573-3912_islam_SIM_4636.

59. Ibn al-Nadīm, *al-Fihrist*, ed. Ayman Fuʾad Sayyid (London: Furqān, 2014), 43.

60. Al-Sīrāfī, *Accounts*, 120–21.

61. Stephanie Beswick, *Sudan's Blood Memory: The Legacy of War, Ethnicity, and Slavery in South Sudan* (Rochester: University of Rochester Press, 2004), 24.

eral variant names, including Yamyam, all refer to the people who become designated predominantly as Damdam in later sources, and references to them that date even to ancient Egyptian works. Ayana pieces these references together to contend that one can reconstruct Oromo migratory history through Arabic sources. In his reading, where many early sources appear to place them in the Nile valley, after the fourteenth century the Damdam people are increasingly identified with the northeast coastal regions of modern-day Kenya and Somalia.[62] Ayana's analysis is not without its flaws; he interprets the generic term *khuṭba,* or sermon, used by the geographer Abū Zayd al-Sīrāfī to describe the skill with which Zanj men orate in a similar fashion to Ibn al-Nadīm as being a specific malapropism of the Oromo *buttaa* ceremony, which features its own rhetorical feats. He reads the Zanj al-Damādim as a single nation, having missed an "and," or *waw,* separating the two in a list given by al-Masʿūdī. However, his fundamental premise that these groups seem to move over time in the sources rings true, perhaps more due to the travel of a discourse than of the people represented.

Indeed, many sources surrounding the *sīra* traditions complicate these attempts to "reveal the layer of history related to racial ideas" in teasing out the anthropological implications of records of the Damdam peoples. Instead, they are ensconced in the rhetoric of world wonders and pushed, relationally, to the map's edge.[63] For example, in his twelfth-century work, *Nuzhat al-Mushtāq fī Ikhtirāq al-Āfāq,* al-Idrīsī (d. 1165) has only this to say of them:

> The remainder of the land of Gao [*Kawkaw*] and Damdam lies in the south of this portion [of the second clime], and there is the rest of the [range of] the Lūniyā mountains. Their earth is white and soft, and it is said that there are short-bodied snakes there, all of which have two horns on their heads. It is also said that there are two-headed snakes [in this region].[64]

Scholars have debated whether the mountains referred to here map onto the Aïr range or the Tibesti range, in northern Niger or Chad, respectively; colonial expeditions across much of the Sahel in what became French and

62. Daniel Ayana, "The Northern *Zanj, Demadim, Yamyam, Yam/Yamjam, Habasha/Ahabish, Zanj-Ahabish,* and *Zanj ed-Damadam*–The Horn of Africa between the Ninth and Fifteenth Centuries," *History in Africa* 46 (2019): 89.

63. Ayana, 63.

64. Al-Idrīsī, *Nuzhat al-Mushtāq,* 116.

Anglo-Egyptian Sudan attest local legends in Arabic and Fulbe of cannibal peoples residing to the south with sobriquets similar to Damdam.[65] Well before this, narratives of the people of Damdam as eaters of men were elaborated across the works of various medieval geographers, culminating in the conclusion that they eat virtually anyone who falls into their hands, including their own peers. John Hunwick notes that such myths are especially virulent with regards to people living west of the Niger River, finding in this evidence that Arabic geographers' informants did not venture further than trading with the peoples to the river's immediate east. Penetrating further into "pagan" country, meanwhile, is rendered as "dangerous . . . for both body and soul."[66] The interchanging, or perhaps migration, of the peoples of Damdam from mountain lakes and riverbends to coasts and more figurative "edges," as well as the blurring in early sources of their distinctions from the Lamlam, does not reduce easily to a single point. It sprawls, resulting in a fertile array of racialized intertextualities with which popular traditions and lore compound to give an impression of meta-geographic and ethical distance. For example, geographers' descriptions of the Lamlam as shoreline-dwelling fish eaters resonate with both the itinerancy of the Damdam and with the more primordial dispersion of these groups' earliest putative ancestors in prophetological works. Al-Kisāʾī writes:

> When [Ḥām's] first two children were grown, they left seeking their father [who had fled from them], searching until they reached a village on the shore of the sea [*shāṭiʾ al-baḥr*]. There they settled, and God stirred lust in the slave-boy so that he copulated with his sister, who conceived by him. They established themselves in that village, with no food but the fish that they fished for and ate, then [the sister] birthed a Black slave-girl and slave-boy from her brother. . . . The latter two children departed in search of their siblings, searching until they arrived at a village on the coast [*al-sāḥil*], where they settled and reunited with their siblings. They tarried there and each brother defiled [*waṭiʾ*] his sister, so each birthed a Black boy and girl, until they grew in number and dispersed throughout the shore. From them are the Nubians and Zanj and Berbers and Sind and Hind, and all Blacks, so they are all from the children of Ḥām.[67]

65. Andrew James McGregor, *Darfur (Sudan) in the Age of Stone Architecture c. AD 1000–1750: Problems in Historical Reconstruction* (Oxford: Archaeopress, 2001), 137; Ivanov, "Cannibals, Warriors, Conquerors, and Colonizers," 95–100.

66. Hunwick, "A Region of the Mind," 114.

67. Al-Kisāʾī, *Vitae Prophetarum*, 101.

As discussed above regarding the works of Bardaisan, vegetarianism (or pescatarianism) and cannibalism could be of a primitivist piece in civilizational geographies. In this passage, the former winks at the latter through the metaphor of incest, which is linked across cultures with acts of consuming one's kin. Arthur P. Wolf cites an "unholy trinity" of taboos, "composed of incest, witchcraft, and cannibalism," which obtains in many of the same regions in which Arabic sources adduce participation in these forbidden acts.[68]

The Damdam/Lamlam people are thus coded as standing even far outside the norms of surrounding peoples within the *bilād al-sūdān* as an irredeemable or antisocial category that Gomez has argued is critical to "the machinery of enslavement."[69] That in the *sīra* the cannibals of the destructive, demonic Banū ʿUqfūr and Damdam have ended up residing in East Africa and serving a constellation of competing kings should likely be understood less as a flight of fancy or geographical conflation and more as strategically distilling the perceived fluidity of Black peoples' movement, competition, and slaving among themselves, for, as al-Idrīsī reminds us,

> The people of Salā and Takrūr and Ghāna are jealous of the land of Lamlam and revile its people. They remove them to their country then sell them among the traders who enter the region, so the traders bring them to the other regions [of the world].[70]

Much as with tales of cannibalism, these anecdotes about slave raiding simultaneously suggest barrenness and surplus: is the living so harsh and are the people so deprived of protection that they are continuously readily taken from their land by nations that envy and fear them or are consumed by their peers? Are they yet so multitudinous that they can readily be so? For cannibalism is rarely rendered as a matter of occasion or social class in these writings. Habitual cannibalism operates in stark contrast to cases of cannibalism in sub-Saharan African folktales, which feature anthropophagy as a rhetorical device to critique upper-class corruption, represented as leading to the literal "consumption" of the poor and vulnerable.[71] Cannibalism as a feature of identity (*Sīrat Dhāt al-Himma*'s narrator is at pains to remind us that the people of Damdam are "the ones

68. Arthur P. Wolf, *Incest Avoidance and the Incest Taboos: Two Aspects of Human Nature* (Stanford, CA: Stanford University Press, 2014), 87.

69. Gomez, *African Dominion*, 45.

70. Al-Idrīsī, *Nuzhat al-Mushtāq*, 26.

71. Belcher, "Mary Saves the Man-Eater," 42.

who eat the flesh of humans," saying, *wa-hum alladhīna yaʾkulūn luḥūm al-ādamīyūn*) also works within the *sīra* tradition in contrast with other representations of eating human flesh: there are a few instances of Byzantine rulers dismembering and consuming Muslim foes, but all of them are one-off instances with particularly sadistic royals rather than routine and widespread among entire peoples.[72] Instead, in Arabic as well as Persian writings, anthropophagy is depicted as a convention common to large groups in the *bilād al-sūdān*.[73]

According to some accounts, such indecencies could persist even after enslavement by Muslims—or rather, enslavement by the wrong kinds of Muslims—in ways that tie back in with questions of the constitution of the king Damdamān's subjects. Al-Thaʿālabī provides an anecdote in his poetic anthology *Yatīmat al-Dahr* (*The Unique One of the Age*) about the Qarmatians' Zanjī soldiers, who were routed in the Buyid occupation of Oman, delighting in the consumption of human palms.[74] The fact that this anecdote is situated in a triumphal conquest narrative against a maligned sect indicates that representations of the persistence of cannibalism under Muslim jurisdiction could be a means of differentiating righteous, civilizing Muslim rule from the decadence and illegitimacy of other powers. In another report ascribed to Buzurg b. Shahriyār, which Zoltán Szombathy reads in parallel with the al-Thaʿālabī narration, the cannibal peoples of the Mozambique coast give up eating humans due to the enlightening influence of "a king who had been 'civilized' by a stint in Baghdad as a slave."[75] Szombathy argues that the "ultimate" significance of cannibal stories is that, through them, "norms and boundaries of civilization are stressed and reaffirmed," and it is worth noting that this conclusion nests nicely in Gomez's point about the naturalization of slavery for peoples thought to lie

72. *Sīrat Dhāt al-Himma*, XXXVII: 18; e.g., Lyons, *Arabian Epic*, vol. 3, 466.

73. In Persian travel narratives and *dāstāns*—essentially a more prestigious, courtly iteration of the *sīra* genre—Africans are typically denominated widely as "Zanj," and these people are often represented as cannibals. Minoo Southgate, "The Negative Images of Blacks in Some Medieval Iranian Writings," *Iranian Studies* 17, no. 1 (1984): 3–36.

74. Szombathy, "Eating People Is Wrong," 222. Al-Thaʿālabī, *Yatīmat al-Dahr fī Shuʿarāʾ Ahl al-ʿAṣr* vol. 2 (Damascus: s.n., 1885), 92.

75. Szombathy, "Eating People Is Wrong," 211. Though this anecdote and the source in which it is housed, the *ʿAjāʾib al-Hind*, is often fancifully attributed to Buzurg ibn Shahriyār, Jean-Charles Ducène argues compellingly that the text is attributable, at least largely, to Abū ʿImrān Mūsā al-Sīrāfī. Jean-Charles Ducène, "Une nouvelle source arabe sur l'océan Indien au Xe siècle: Le *Ṣaḥīḥ min aḫbār al-biḥār wa-ʿAǧāʾibihā* d'Abū ʿImrān Mūsā ibn Rabāḥ al-Awsī al-Sīrāfī," *Afriques* 6 (2015): n.p.

outside these limits.[76] Both groups, the Qarmatians and *Damādim*, come together in Damdamān's realms in an allusive yet foreboding symbiosis, into which ʿAbd al-Wahhāb and Damdamān's daughter, Maymūna, will later intervene by joining his Muslim precepts with her local knowledge and far-ranging ambitions.

What few religiously identified actors are encountered in Damdamān's domain occupy a status that maintains the distinction between the thoroughly Christian landscape of the Anatolian frontier and the East African realm in which those who are religiously identifiable are a visible minority. Having been wounded before being captured by Damdamān, the hero ʿAbd al-Wahhāb is ministered to by a Jewish physician.[77] This is a rare instance of a Jew cropping up in the text of *Sīrat Dhāt al-Himma,* and on the surface, it seems less a commentary on the region's demographics and more a trope to suggest that ʿAbd al-Wahhāb was in competent hands. In much the way that we have seen associations of different denizens of the *bilād al-sūdān* with certain occupations and skills, Jewish involvement in the medical profession becomes a staple of medieval Arabic storytelling, such that the Cairo Geniza researcher Shelomo Dov Goitein writes that he was able to anticipate a preponderance of Jewish physicians, but only few surgeons, in the Geniza's documents because of "the many Jewish doctors known to us from Arabic literary sources."[78] In his demographic study, Efraim Lev adds that the eleventh century was a turning point for Jewish medical practitioners, who rise in number and prominence throughout the Fatimid and Ayyubid periods.[79] By the time of the Mamluk-era efflorescence of writing popular stories, this growth seems to leave an imprint. A tale found in the fourteenth century "Galland manuscript" of the *1001 Nights* is devoted to a Jewish physician whose tale moves between Mosul, Damascus, and Cairo; more appear scattered in the *sīra* corpus.[80]

We can then query the function of moving an external stock figure into the *bilād al-sūdān*: how might ʿAbd al-Wahhāb's physician further situate

76. Szombathy, "Eating People Is Wrong," 224.

77. *Sīrat Dhāt al-Himma,* XXXVI:40.

78. S. D. Goitein, "The Medical Profession in Light of the Cairo Geniza Documents," *Hebrew Union College Annual* 34 (1963): 191.

79. Efraim Lev, *Jewish Medical Practitioners in the Medieval Muslim World: A Collective Biography* (Edinburgh: Edinburgh University Press, 2021), 280.

80. Lyons cites a story in the popular tale of ʿAlī al-Zaybaq in which the eponymous hero disguises himself as a Jewish doctor; there is also the elaborated account of the Jewish doctor in variations on the "Hunchback's Tale" within the *1001 Nights.* Lyons, *Arabian Epic* vol. 3, 5; *The Arabian Nights Encyclopedia* vol. 1, ed. Ulrich Marzolph and Richard van Leeuwen (London: Bloomsbury, 2004), 242.

Damdamān's realm? A small Jewish presence never left the Ḥaḍramawt region of Yemen even after Axumite interventions in Ḥimyar and the rise of Islam, and so Damdamān's doctor could be another Yemeni import like his daughter's teacher.[81] Nor, according to Arabic geographic writings, was East Africa itself bereft of storied pockets of Jewish learning that may have been yet more local to the ruler. The semi-nomadic Beja, whose social makeup is heavily disputed in the geographic tradition, are presented by al-Bakrī as a highly syncretic people residing between the Nile and Red Sea and known for their monumental architecture (*li-hum qilāʿ kathīra*). Described ethnically as a subset of the *ḥabash*, they worship stone idols in the forms of young men yet abide by the laws of the Torah (*aḥkāmuhum aḥkām al-tawrāh*).[82] This account is refuted in other sources. Al-Masʿūdī, for example, claims that the Beja are mostly nonbelievers (*kuffār*) but have a population of Muslims among them, while numerous other geographers claim they are at least partially composed of Christians.[83] The Beja were particularly important for their relationship to the port of ʿAydhāb, a site of Jewish and Muslim mercantile activity as well as being on a pilgrimage route to Mecca and a launching point for ports southward and eastward.[84] Craig Perry writes that the Beja were the delimiters of Islamic expansion into East Africa in the medieval period. Some believe this to be because

81. As Simcha Gross and Mark Letteney have recently shown, though there were assuredly Jewish communities on Yemen's coast prior to the rise of Islam, and of course there was the Jewish kingdom of Ḥimyar, certain "discoveries" about that community, and most notably the so-called synagogue of Qanī', are overstated. Simcha Gross and Mark Letteney, "Reconsidering the Earliest Synagogue in Yemen," *Studies in Late Antiquity* 6, no. 4 (2022): 627–50. On Himyarite Judaism, see Christian Robin, "The Judaism of the Ancient Kingdom of Ḥimyar in Arabia: A Discreet Conversion," in *Diversity and Rabbinization: Jewish Texts and Societies between 400 and 1000 CE*, ed. Gavin McDowell et al. (Cambridge: Cambridge University Press, 2021), 165–270.

82. Al-Bakrī, *al-Masālik wa-l-Mamālik*, 324–25.

83. Adding further ambiguity is the fact that there is a distinction between Beja territory and the Beja people proper. For example, Al-Idrīsī identifies a regional nomadic group who some claim are Romans who have been Christian since the time of the Copts' conversion, and who are itinerant between the "land of the Beja and the Ethiopians," though he argues they are in fact followers of the Jacobite sect. Al-Idrīsī, *Kitāb Nuzhat al-Mushtāq fī Ikhtirāq al-Āfāq* (Cairo: Maktabat al-Thaqāfa al-Dīniyya, 2002), 40. See also al-Mas'ūdī, *Murūj al-Dhahab wa-Maʿādin al-Jawhar*, vol. 2 (Beirut: Maktaba al-ʿAṣriyya, 2005), 15.

84. François-Xavier Fauvelle, *The Golden Rhinoceros: Histories of the African Middle Ages*, trans. Troy Tice (Princeton, NJ: Princeton University Press, 2018), 208–9. The Cairo Geniza source on Jewish merchant activity in ʿAydhāb and the case of the concubine discussed therein by Fauvelle is translated in Goitein, *Letters of Medieval Jewish Traders*, 335–38.

Muslims maintained their borderland as a "slave reservoir," but Perry explains that they lacked the capacity to "bring these regions to heel."[85]

Karen Pinto writes of the Beja that their militant nomadism seems to have fascinated geographers, who fancied them a throwback to the archetypal Bedouins of pre-Islamic and un-urbanized Arabian space, making them "not just an extreme manifestation of the *other*," but also "a paradoxical manifestation of the *self*."[86] That even in Damdamān's irreligious kingdom one finds uncanny points of contact, from People of the Book to the occasional Muslim, perhaps works in a reverse fashion. ʿAbd al-Wahhāb—paradoxically othered in a land that has been figured through his nonhereditary blackness not as familially ancestral but as providentially destined—is ministered to by a figure made familiar through a degree of shared belief and practice, or at least through a well-worn cliché. Nonetheless, the picture of the *bilād al-sūdān* in the *sīra* thus far is one in which belief is the exception to the rule.

Figuring East Africans: Elemental Darkness

What Hadlamūs lacks in religiously inflected models of kingship prior to his conversion he makes up for with a cult of personality based on curating his subjects' material experiences of themselves and the world. In ornamenting his court, Hadlamūs fills his environment with items that Arabic sources stereotypically associated with the *bilād al-sūdān*. In the first scene at his hall, we find him kneeling on an ebony litter covered with lion skins. Often, Arabic sources focus on East African lands as sites for the export of rare animal products and pelts, which goes hand in hand with the image typical to travel literature, *maghāzī* texts, illumination traditions, and so on, of Black Africans as clad minimally in skins or printed textiles wrapped around the waist and across the chest, in contrast with the brocaded fabrics and multilayered garb that marked prestige and modesty throughout the Middle East.[87] Of course, the lion is a potent symbol in Arab culture, with the moniker *asad* reserved for formidable warriors. And yet the use of its pelt as the rarefied covering of Hadlamūs's throne encodes it as an article of savanna exotica, said to be especially coveted by regional kings

85. Perry, "Slavery and the Slave Trade in Western Indian Ocean World," 146–47.

86. Emphasis in the original. Karen Pinto, "Capturing Imagination: The Buja and Medieval Islamic Mappa Mundi," in *Views from the Edge: Essays in Honor of Richard W. Bulliet*, ed. Neguin Yavari, Lawrence G. Potter, and Jean-Marc Ran Oppenheim (New York: Columbia University Press, 2004), 167.

87. Balafrej, "Domestic Slavery, Skin Color, and Image Dialectic," 1022.

as well as trading partners in the Indian Ocean. Many East African peoples are cited in geographies as cladding themselves in varieties of more or less local animal products. The Nubians, for example, are said to sole their shoes with giraffe leather, while the Zanj wear the skins of large cats like panthers (*numūr*).[88] Al-Bakrī offers a particularly rich synthesis of these themes in his discussion of the Zanj in his *Book of Routes and Realms*:

> From their lands comes nacre, from the shells of turtles. And in their domains one finds the giraffe, which is among the creatures that they have domesticated and that they admire, and which is given as a gift to kings. They have red panther skins [*julūd al-numūr al-ḥumr*] that they use as their clothes, and their territories possess—of all God's provinces—the greatest quantity of elephants, to the point that they are left wild, and they do not tame or use them. . . . They supply all corners of the earth with elephants' tusks, sending the majority of them to Oman, and thence elsewhere. The Chinese use the greatest preponderance of ivory, making columns for their kings' audience halls. . . . They also use it for incense in their shrines [*buyūt aṣnāmihim*] and for their temples' censers.[89]

Though China, via the above-mentioned trade, is depicted as a land embellished with imported ivory, the *bilād al-sūdān*, including Hadlamūs' throne, are often conceived of literally and figuratively as a land festooned with ebony, a commodity typically brought from various Indian Ocean islands across the sea. Like ivory, ebony was an expensive good, known not only for its beauty but also for medicinal applications. Figuratively it was often used as a stand-in for skin color. Arabic poetry compares Black (female) lovers favorably with branches of ebony (*ghuṣūn min al-abnūs*), alongside other high-value items like aloeswood and musk. This appears in Ibn al-Rūmī's (d. 896) infamous poem about a Black courtesan, in which she is rendered a skirted and girdled ebony branch, "quivering with voluptuous fruits."[90] Romanticizing blackness, one poet declares, "An ebony

88. The local production of cloth receives little mention in accounts of these locales, with the thirteenth-century writer Ibn Saʿīd al-Maghribī specifically stating that textiles of cotton and wool are the purview of those Black peoples who have "mingled with whites" (*man khāliṭ al-bīḍ*) when speaking of the people of Takrūr "and others" (*wa-ghayrihim*) mostly wearing skins. Ibn Saʿīd al-Maghribī, Kitāb al-Jughrāfīyā (Beirut: al-Maktab al-Tijāriyya li-l-Ṭabāʿa wa-l-Nashar wa-l-Tawzīʿ, 1980), 91.

89. Al-Bakrī, *Kitāb al-Masālik wa-l-Mamālik* (Tunis: Dār al-ʿArabiyya li-l-Kitāb, 1992), 321.

90. Ibn al-Rūmī, *Dīwān Ibn al-Rūmī*, vol. 2, ed. Aḥmad Ḥasan Basaj (Beirut: Dār al-Kutub al-ʿIlmiyya, 2009), 468. A translation of this poem is available in Geert

branch appears, enveloping me with fruits of musk [*ghuṣn min al-ābnūs abdā min misk dārayna lī thimāran*] / When shaded by luxuriant night, thus perfumed, I long not for day!"[91] In keeping with this literary convention, when ʿUqba first attempts to broker an alliance with Hadlamūs, he does so with reference to the meeting not merely of Black and white men, but of the material and aesthetic beauty of combining precious black and white materials, likening himself to ivory and Hadlamūs to ebony. Such comparisons are applied to other racialized figures in the *sīra* as well, and Hadlamūs is not the only character to sit on a throne well-matched to his features: the Byzantine princess, Nūrā, is first found on a seat of gold and pearls, a reference not only to Byzantium's oft-noted riches, but to the pale beauty that Byzantine women supposedly possess. This also draws a link between Nūrā's appearance and the well-known trope of heavenly women as pearl-like—fair, bright, and well-hidden—connoting not only a rare beauty, but visions of Paradise obtained.

Ebony is not the only black material that Hadlamūs and his people prize. When ʿUqba instigates Hadlamūs to take his armies to Iraq and attempt to unseat the caliph al-Maʾmūn, Hadlamūs and his troops encounter a new dark material that they come to admire in the famed Roman-era basalt walls of Diyarbakir, or Āmid:

> Hadlamūs's Blacks [*sūdān*] were entranced by the blackness of the stone of Āmid's structures, and nature inclined toward nature [*al-ṭabʿ yamīl ilā-l-ṭabʿ*], so Hadlamūs said to them, "When we return to our country, we will take this stone with us and fashion our buildings from it, for it is the same color as us [*wa-hiya ʿalā alwāninā*]." News of this reached [the Caliph] al-Maʾmūn, and he laughed with amazement [*ḍaḥak ʿajaban*] and shook with amusement [*ihtazz ṭaraban*] and mused, "These are men of war."[92]

---

van Gelder, *Classical Arabic Literature: A Library of Arabic Literature Anthology* (New York: New York University Press, 2013), 53–57.

91. This poem is sometimes attributed to the ʿAbbasid-era poet ʿAlī b. al-Jahm, but often is cited anonymously, which is how it appears in a text on marriage written by a famed, Tunisian-born member of the Tijānī Sufi order now popular throughout West Africa, in which the author has amassed several examples of blackness being likened in its beauty to ebony. Muḥammad ibn Aḥmad al-Tijānī, *Tuḥfat al-ʿArūs wa-Mutaʿa al-Nufūs*, ed. Jalil al-Atiyah (London: Riad El-Rayyes, 1992), 233.

92. *Sīrat Dhāt al-Himma*, XXXVI:2–3.

As discussed previously, the notion that one's heritage (typically articulated as *nasab*) and "kind" exert an ineluctable pull on an individual's actions appears throughout the *sīra* in repeated variations on the aphorism, "like inclines toward like." It arises in ʿAbd al-Wahhāb's joy upon seeing other Black men regardless of their adversariness, and in his mother Fāṭima Dhāt al-Himma sensing deeply that she is a freeborn woman despite growing up in bondage as a war captive.[93] It also is axiomatic in the writings of various *udabāʾ* in the early medieval period, and is endemic to geographic consciousness as well. For his part, the jurist Abū Saʿīd Ḥasan al-Sīrāfī (d. 979), who also authored two no-longer extant geographical works, is cited in *Lisān al-ʿArab* as commenting on the stock phrase, "Were it not for harmony, man would surely perish" (*law-lā al-wiʾām la-halaka al-insān*), in which "harmony" indicates keeping to one's own kind, by saying that being of a shared kind is social rather than essential and speciated, *pace* al-Jāḥiẓ. He writes that the phrase means, "Were it not that [an individual] found a model to emulate, and to comport himself like, he would surely die." For this reason, when people live together the young one emulates the old and the ignoramus emulates the learned.[94] Knowing and surrounding oneself intentionally with commensurate peers in terms of origins or trajectory is the optimal approach.

In contrast, rarely is the concept of affinity of kind applied so explicitly to the lived relationships between humans and material objects as it is when Hadlamūs's men react to the basalt stones. The moral or social import of these types of relationality with one's environment is at first more opaque. The passage above is perhaps a remark not on the nature of the black objects at hand, but on the disposition of the Black soldiers of Hadlamūs who fixate on them. Recurrently, the Black cannibal tribes are described as being bereft of *ʿaql*, or rationality, which renders them particularly fearsome in the Arab troops' views within the text. ʿAbd al-Wahhāb's

93. Melanie Magidow has translated what might be termed Fāṭima's "coming of age" story in a standalone piece. In it, young Fāṭima is rejected by her parents and taken in by a nursemaid, only to be captured during a tribal raid. As Madigow notes, Fāṭima consistently demonstrates her sense of superiority with statements such as, *mā anā jāriya wa-lā khādima*, or "I am no slave-girl," and many are unsurprised when they ultimately discover her elite birth. See Magidow, "Epic of the Commander Dhat al-Himma," 19–20.

94. Ibn al-Manẓūr, *Lisān al-ʿArab*, 4749.

right-hand man, the light-skinned al-Baṭṭāl, expresses this anxiety upon first seeing the East African armies:

> He found the troops [of Hadlamūs] encamped there, like the pitch-dark night, so al-Baṭṭāl remarked, "I have seen armies, and none have struck fear into me but these, for a man ought only to engage an adversary of right mind, yet these people are like donkeys who fling themselves into death."[95]

The dynamics of encounter between Hadlamūs' men and the black stone structures of Āmid are turned on their head when al-Baṭṭāl witnesses the arrival of the Abyssinians' battalions. Each meeting evokes a form of fascination, one positive and the other negative—one in which men come upon stone and see in it something uncannily similar to themselves, and the other in which a man comes upon people and yet struggles to find any human link between himself and them.

In his analysis of the "prop-work" in the *1001 Nights,* Daniel Beaumont notes that objects often perform functions similar to the Lacanian concept of "extimacy," through which "the subject finds his very identity somehow bound up in some uncanny object outside himself."[96] Similarly, the black objects appointing the Black Africans' world reflect the identities of their users in ways that transcend their blackness while also being richly associated with it. Not only are the black stones of Āmid that earn so much interest from the ʿUqfūrī troops dark like the skin of their admirers, but they are also impervious and inert like the soldiers who, in al-Baṭṭāl's estimation, serve as Hadlamūs's unthinking or "unreasoned" bulwark against destruction. Nature inclining toward nature in this scenario signals something more expansive than color inclining toward color, suggesting also dehumanized beings inclining toward the realm of objects and away from other living things. This is at variance with, say, the treatment of Byzantines in the text, who exhibit no special taste for white objects despite their

95. *Sīrat Dhāt al-Himma,* XXXV:59. Malcolm Lyons was also struck by al-Baṭṭāl's expression here, and analyzes it as an expression of black people's perceived subhumanity vis-à-vis Muslims' "superhuman contempt for danger," though their faithfulness makes them ambivalent toward death because of their sense of honor and anticipation of the afterlife. Lyons, *Arabian Epic,* vol. 1, 54.

96. Daniel Beaumont, "*Min Jumlat al-Jamādāt.* The Inanimate in Fictional and *Adab* Narrative," in *On Fiction and* Adab *in Medieval Arabic Literature,* ed. Philip F. Kennedy (Wiesbaden: Harrassowitz Verlag, 2005), 55–68.

light skin, and for whom such accessories appear tacitly signifying rather than openly sought after, as in the case of Nūrā's pearl encrusted throne.

The idea that people are naturally habituated to being surrounded by items that reflect their color is not found, for the most part, in the remainder of the *sīra* narrative. Yet it may be traceable to the scheme of climes mentioned above, which was part of a taxonomic endeavor that took seriously the divine genius behind the arrangement of natural phenomena. Many stressed the importance of climate in dividing the world and making sense of its peoples' behaviors. Classically, one's natal (or ancestral) environment was thought to act directly on one's bodily humors, with the hotness, coldness, wetness, or dryness of one's surroundings correspondingly tipping one's internal balance of blood, phlegm, and black and yellow bile. This effected a deep-rooted state of acclimation, physically and attitudinally, to a given realm. Climes at the earth's far northern and southern extremes were thought to be particularly harsh on the body and mind, scorching southerners black and maddening them, and leaving northerners unpigmented and in a state of lassitude. The extent of over- or underexposure to sunlight and moisture, in other words, was thought to set key social parameters as well, and was often used to explain the extraordinary practices and natures of humans at the world's edges. Some thinkers extended this logic to allege that in the most extreme conditions, the entire environment would alter in response. When describing various lands of the Black peoples throughout the Indian Ocean, the geographer al-Idrīsī conjures up a mirror image of the islands of Indonesia across from those of the Zanj, like Madagascar and the Comoros,[97] in which all the flora and fauna is darkened by the heat:

> Facing the littoral lands of the Zanj is a chain of islands called Rānj, of which there are several and whose land is vast. Its people are extremely dark [*sumr jiddan*] and whatever grows there, such as sorghum and sugar cane and camphor trees, is black in color.[98]

Writing two centuries earlier, Abū Zayd al-Sīrāfī makes this same claim about black crops for all the lands of the Zanj, using near-identical wording.[99] The underlying idea that climates can create aesthetic regimes is also found in the writings of al-Jāḥiẓ. In his discussion of blackness in Arab

97. Dionysius A. Agius, *Classic Ships of Islam: From Mesopotamia to the Indian Ocean* (Leiden: Brill, 2007), 104.

98. Al-Idrīsī, *Kitāb Nuzhat al-Mushtāq fī Ikhtirāq al-Āfāq*, 61.

99. Al-Sīrāfī, *Accounts*, 121–22.

lands in *Fakhr al-Sūdān ʿalā-l-Biḍān*, al-Jāḥiẓ describes the central Arabian region of Ḥarra as a place where

> everyone who has settled [there] in addition to the tribespeople of Sulaym [*min ghayr Banī Sulaym*] are Black. Their shepherds and water carriers, as well as menial laborers and servants, are from Hispania [*min al-Ishbāniyyīn*] and their women are from Byzantium [*min al-Rūm*], yet they give birth for no more than three generations before their move to Ḥarra turns [their offspring] the color of the people of Sulaym. And it is said of Ḥarra that its deer and cattle and its insects and flies, its foxes and sheep and mules, its horses and birds, all of these are black.[100]

Taken together, these passages illustrate how one's climate exerts a totalizing effect not only on one's personal appearance, but on one's sensorium—in the *sīra*, this is extrapolated as producing effects on one's aesthetic preferences as well because of naturalized affinity. With the world so thoroughly blackened, one seeks to surround oneself with ever more blackness. By linking this desire with the rapaciousness of Hadlamūs's "men of war," the moral valence at hand emerges as well. Analogies of being enveloped in blackness with disbelief echo across various literatures that are apposite to the *sīra*, and Hadlamūs even cannily inverts one such metaphor when reviling the foreign, Christian ʿUqba as blind in one eye and ignorant after he has accepted Islam. These terms evoke images of the Dajjāl, or false messiah, and recall the ideological and physical darkness in which he lives. A particularly palpable example of the darkness of unknowingness appears in the Qurʾān, in *Sūrat al-Nūr*:

> Like shadows in a deep sea covered by waves upon waves, with clouds above—layer upon layer of darkness—if he holds out his hand, he is scarcely able to see it. The one to whom God gives no light has no light at all.[101]

However much they are conditioned by their environment, the differences in desires, identity constructions, and personal tastes on the part of East African subjects in the *sīra* cannot be dissociated from their lack of commitment to a monotheistic religion; physical darkness and metaphorical, mental "darkness" is consciously enmeshed in the tale and in

100. Al-Jāḥiẓ, *Rasāʾil*, 219.
101. Q 24:40.

topoi diffused throughout its literary network. At times, the physical and metaphorical create productive dissonance in the mind's eye, as when the honorable Muslim armies are likened in clashes with the numerically superior but depraved Byzantines to a "white blaze on a black bull." But in the story's East African setting, darkness takes on a more thoroughgoing quality that Black characters themselves are made to naturalize. *Sīrat Dhāt al-Himma* recurrently places its East African characters not merely outside the cultural realm of the Arab(ized) characters within the narrative, but selectively outside of the realms of normative Arab-Islamic knowledges and canonical intertexts. Instead, they are situated at the edges of the conceptual, ethical, and behavioral map.

At the map's edge, the principles that the geographers outlined become at once predictive and flexible. In his at times highly speculative geography, al-Idrīsī speaks of the southernmost portion of the third clime in the far west as comprised of many islands. Some are likely the Canaries, which marked a prime meridian for many medieval Muslim geographers, and others seemingly further west in the "murky" Atlantic Ocean, and thus at the map's boundary in terms of the *terra cognita* of his time.[102] Each is rife with humanoid creatures and megafauna that prey upon mankind. These range from sea-monsters who war with the ogre-like people of the island of Sāwa to dragons battled by Alexander the Great (Dhū'l-Qarnayn) himself.[103] Once again, this region conduces to vegetarianism as well, with the dark-skinned and broad-featured pygmies (*qiṣār*) of the island of Ḥasrān eating only from the plants that flourish in their midst.[104] In the estimation of medieval thinkers, the latitudinal climes containing Sahelian and sub-Saharan West Africa, these Atlantic isles, and South Asia share in being extremely hot, though with variable degrees of wetness or dryness. It therefore follows that they produce people on a similar spectrum of qualities, allowing al-Idrīsī's mapping of unexplored lands to seem verisimilar and coherent with the other attributes of the earth's peripheries.

At the map's edge also lies epistemological opportunity. In her work on what it might mean to speak of medieval fiction, Michelle Karnes writes that medieval fabulation did not necessarily rely on "ironic assent or a willing suspension of disbelief," but rather on audiences inhabiting the uncertainty of dividing the real from unreal, reveling instead in possibility.[105]

102. E. S. Kennedy and M. H. Reiger, "Prime Meridians in Medieval Islamic Philosophy," *Vistas in Astronomy* 28 (1985): 29–32.

103. Al-Idrīsī, *Nuzhat al-Mushtāq*, 217.

104. Al-Idrīsī, 218.

105. Karnes, "Possibilities of Medieval Fiction," 210.

To argue this, she draws on traditions of *mirabilia*, or marvels, in Latin, and their companionate genre of *ʿajāʾib wa-gharāʾib*, the astounding and strange, in Arabic. The probative value of wonders consists not in their own truth or untruth, but in the greater truth that creation is surprising, massive, and impossible for any human to know comprehensively. But how is the *sīra* manipulating this epistemological edge in its tale of East African adventure and discovery? Where would the lands of *ḥabasha* have been cartographically situated for many of the *sīra*'s interlocutors, and how does the text play overtly with this arrangement in order to create possibility?

It is first worth noting that the placement of divisions between the climes was a regular point of divergence among the geographers, and second that the climes were but one system of geographic division, albeit a dominant one in early medieval Arabic sources. Its primary alternative was the Persian *keshvar* system, which divided the earth in nested circles of increasing size ringed by seas, forests, and other geological barriers. The existence of seven *keshvars* is recalled in the Zoroastrian Avesta and carries into Islamic geographies, with authors pronouncing on their comparative merits with the Greek-derived climes and choosing between them.[106] Often the climes were arrayed by a given geographer in relative fashion depending on where one placed the world's navel; major contenders often tracked with where an author was from or had received education, or else with the moral-intellectual centers of their universes, such as Mecca, Baghdad, and Isfahan. Moreover, a space's qualities were typically dictated not only by its latitudinal position on the earth's surface, but also by its astrological ambit, offering two means through which to interpret relative closeness and distance. Because of the path of the sun, for example, some geographers explained China's advancement vis-à-vis points to their west but in the same latitude.[107] Where East Africa—physically neighboring the Arabian Peninsula—is schematically located by geographers indicates whether these authors regarded its territories as sharing in the same spectrum of qualities present in places far closer to their own homes or to their putative historical and spiritual heartland. So, we might ask whether East Africa's obvious proximity to the Arabian Peninsula poses a hermeneutic problem for the *sīra* and related writings.

106. A. Shapur Shahbazi, "Haft Kešvar," in *Encyclopaedia Iranica*, last updated March 1, 2012, http://www.iranicaonline.org/articles/haft-kesvar.

107. A. Miquel, "Iḳlīm," in *Encyclopedia of Islam II*, ed. Peri Bearman, Thierry Bianquis, C. Edmund Bosworth, E. J. van Donzel, and Wolfhart P. Heinrichs, accessed 20 March 2019, http://dx.doi.org/10.1163/1573-3912_islam_SIM_3519.

In the ʿAbbasid era, lands roughly intersecting with southern Iraq and northern Arabia were often said to lie in the most temperate—which is to say, the most bio-behaviorally favorable—zone, much as is found in Greek self-positionings. True to this, al-Idrīsī places the lands of west and central Asia mostly in the fourth of his seven climes, though some portions of the Arabian Peninsula lie as far south as the upper edge of the second clime. Of the harshest, southernmost climes, he says,

> The people of this first clime, as well as those of the second and some of those in the third, have black coloring and crinkly hair because of the severity of the heat and burning effect of the sun, as opposed to the people of the sixth and seventh clime.[108]

For al-Idrīsī, the land of the *ḥabasha* is set in the fifth portion of the first clime.[109] Many similarly described the first clime as proceeding roughly latitudinally from the west coast of sub-Saharan Africa to the south-easterly portions of China, passing through the Horn of Africa on the way. Those authors who depart from the seven-clime convention, envisioning instead sixteen or even twenty climes, or who have a non-radial scheme, jostle the land of the *ḥabasha* around accordingly, even as they maintain that the "lands of the Blacks" lie at or very near the earth's extremes. Accordingly, in al-Masʿūdī's abridged universal history, the *Kitāb al-Tanbīh wa-l-Ishrāf*, the Hijaz and Abyssinia both comprise the second of seven circular climes, while in Ibn Saʿīd al-Maghribī's layout, which accommodates polar regions (beyond the southern equator and beyond the habitable north) in addition to seven central climes, the areas in the province of the "Blacks" (*sūdān*) lie in their entirety in the first clime.

For Ibn Saʿīd, the first clime is then composed of ten subdivisions, with the territory of, among others, the man-eaters of Lamlam and the people of Takrūr's environs in its first habitable portion, while some Berbers, the Nubians, and the Abyssinians lie in the fourth portion of the first clime, and the mountains of Ḥaḍramawt in Yemen emerge into view in its fifth portion; like many, Ibn Saʿīd groups dwellers of Indian Ocean islands, such as Sri Lanka, among the earth's "Blacks" within his scheme. In a more novel move, he also explicitly outlines a latitudinal color-gradient, with the first clime being "black" (*sūd*) the third clime "brown" (*sumr*), and the second clime's population varying in color in accordance with their

108. Al-Idrīsī, *Nuzhat al-Mushtāq*, 18.
109. Al-Idrīsī, 42.

proximity to the first or the third.[110] Writing later than our other geographers, and also later than the origins of the *sīra,* Ibn Saʿīd is compelled to mention that several of the lands in the *bilād al-sūdān* described in geographies such as al-Bakrī's as idolatrous have since turned to Islam or else embraced trade and travel among Muslims.

In *Sīrat Dhāt al-Himma,* for reasons that are not explained, the lands inhabited by Damdamān and his people are said to be situated in the fifth clime. It is possible that this is a direct borrowing from writings that situate such lands in medial divisions (the fourth or fifth) of the first clime, however, if taken literally as the fifth clime, the ostensible effect is to align East Africa more closely with the world's temperate zones, placing it in their north, more on par with Byzantium. Despite this, the conditions of the weather and terrain are described as being inhospitable to the text's Arab warriors. This becomes pronounced during moments of heroic physical exertion, as in a vignette in which ʿAbd al-Wahhāb is battling a foe named Ghāsiq, the king of the people of Damdam who had been betrothed to the princess Maymūna. Upon being told her father has died, Ghāsiq views both her and her lands as rightfully his and confronts her new beloved, ʿAbd al-Wahhāb, to assert this.[111] As the narrator relates:

> O sirs, that land was extremely hot because it is in the fifth clime [*kaththīrat al-ḥarr li-annuhā al-iqlīm al-khāmis*], which is like the pitch-black night [*wa-hiya mithl al-layl al-dāmis*]. . . . The prince ʿAbd al-Wahhāb approached al-Ghāsiq, and his nervousness was increasing and his sweat running, and each of their tongues was hanging down to their chests from the intensity of their thirst, so [ʿAbd al-Wahhāb] said, "Hey, accursed one! It is obvious that neither of us would shy away from fighting his adversary [*mā yuqaṣṣir ʿan qitāl ṣāhibihi*], but let's postpone this matter until the day cools [*daʿ hādhā al-amr ilā an yabrud al-nahār*]." Ghāsiq replied, "Never, O cowardly one, used to sleeping in walled rooms and playing around with women [*al-muʿawwad bi-l-nawm bayn al-judrān wa-mulāʿibat al-niswān*]! And were you not gifted with such agility and lightness, I would have already removed your soul from your body!"[112]

110. Antrim, *Routes and Realms,* 92; Ibn Saʿīd al-Maghribī , *Kitāb al-Jughrāfiyā* (Beirut: al-Maktab al-Tijāriyya li-l-Ṭabāʿa wa-l-Nashar wa-l-Tawzīʿ, 1980), 81.

111. His name is also rendered within the text as Ghasaq. For the sake of consistency, I have written his name as Ghāsiq throughout.

112. *Sīrat Dhāt al-Himma,* XXXVII:30.

For Ghāsiq, hardiness and a capacity to withstand the conditions of his clime is a badge of honor in battle, as well as something to lord over his Arab foe, who is used to the luxuries afforded not by his clime so much as by the infrastructure erected in it to protect one from the elements. This perhaps recalls us to the statement by al-Istakhrī and Ibn Ḥawqal that, unlike Abyssinia and Nubia, neither the "Blacks [*al-sūdān*] in the Maghrib, nor the Beja, nor the Zanj, and what nations lie in their span" possess built institutions (*al-ʿimāra*) or the political organization to support them (*al-siyāsa al-mustaqīma*). In phrasing the differences between himself and ʿAbd al-Wahhāb as ones of lifestyle, rather than of natural constitution emanating solely from the environment, Ghāsiq also points to the difference between his more spartan existence—even as a king and therefore, presumably, a man of means—and ʿAbd al-Wahhāb's comparatively urbane customs.

Perceived levels of built and settled civilization were another premise for deduction that was instrumental to how Arab-Muslim geographers arrayed the peoples of the globe, in addition to that of relative climatic factors and revealed religions. Despite the ongoing resonance of the Bedouin past, itself always in evidence in the hardscrabble adventures of the *mujāhidūn* of the *sīra* tradition, by the mid-ʿAbbasid period in which the *sīra* is situated, the very definition of civilization had become encoded as a cosmopolitan urbanism populated by great works of architecture and the diverse luxuries afforded a settled entrepôt. For Joshua T. Olsson, this is the reason that as time went on, geographers like the Tunisian Ibn Khaldūn and the Sicilian al-Idrīsī who were in close contact with more northerly European interlocutors from illustrious cities and kingdoms "found it harder to maintain blanket assertions of the north as a wholly savage and barbarous environment, as the theories of humoral pathology and the climes stipulated."[113] Throughout the *sīra*, we meanwhile see a blending of ideas of East African dominion with images of sheer, unmanaged wealth. On the one hand, rulers seek and import luxury goods. On the other, they enjoy local natural abundance in the form of both animals and people who have not accustomed themselves to "walled rooms," being acclimated instead to the oppressive heat. Yet none of this is phrased in explicitly extractive terms. Ghada Talhami writes, similarly, that despite their region becoming eponymous for a kind of slave, "one is struck by the absence of any mention of slaves as a major export of the Zanj coast" in medieval Arabic and Persian geographies, where authors mainly "describe a variety of trade items, mostly gold and

113. J. T. Olsson, "The World in Arab Eyes," 507.

ivory."[114] The implication of enslaveability is latent in a layered discourse of human surplus, environmental extremes, and infrastructural lack.

In her work on the commodification of Africans in the early modern Atlantic, Jennifer Morgan likens the production of race to an alchemical process, both for the metaphor of value-generation (turning people into gold) and the role of faith in the process—alchemy is, in a strict sense, not "real," but a matter of believing in its power. For Morgan, much of this alchemy is achieved through narrative, including geographic representation:

> By the start of the seventeenth century, Africa was a conundrum for European writers. Its abundant population, flora, and fauna served as a provocation for theorists who were trying to understand changing notions of state, power, national wealth, and population growth. . . . A people incapable of assessing the value of what nature had provided was unworthy of claiming it. Thus, Africa became opened to European rational economies. And where settlement was impossible, Africans themselves became the extractable value.[115]

For medieval Muslim authors, meanwhile, assessing the value of the natural world was often framed as part of appreciating divine plans for an ordered cosmos. Audiences to the *sīra* are being invited to trust in the yields of an imaginative process that at once produces Black difference and promises a future where that difference has a reasoned purpose and can be accommodated to Arab-Muslim communities and needs.

The divergent reactions of Ghāsiq and ʿAbd al-Wahhāb to the local climate indicate the ways in which ʿAbd al-Wahhāb does or does not carry his kind and its significances from his home context into his East African one: despite being Black, he is not preternaturally accustomed to the very clime and its conditions that supposedly give Black people their color. This is a far cry from the anecdotes offered in geographies that attempt to theorize the effects of one's ancestral or primordial environment, in which physical markers are conferred by and confer an ineluctable predisposition toward certain landscapes and societies. ʿAbd al-Wahhāb is received by Ghāsiq not as an insider, but as an outsider and a threat to be disposed of, made easier by the fact that Ghāsiq is on familiar terrain. There is perhaps an aspirational note to this scene, in that a Black person dislocated from his putative homeland and immersed in another culture can be rendered

114. Ghada Hashem Talhami, "The Zanj Rebellion Reconsidered," *International Journal of African Historical Studies* 10 (1977): 446.

115. Morgan, *Reckoning with Slavery*, 121.

other in the eyes of his brethren, appearing to them an exponent of his new society. True to this, Damdamān similarly recognizes ʿAbd al-Wahhāb as an ersatz general to the "caliph that the whites have," whose position should readily afford him ransom and whose belonging and importance in his community is uncontroversial despite his blackness.

Yet this picture of acclimation is imperfect. The experiences that ʿAbd al-Wahhāb's appearance predetermines for him in Arabia and the Anatolian borderlands do not translate to the lands of *ḥabasha,* where he is recurrently coded as "Arab" in ways with which his fellow Arab Muslims visibly resist elsewhere. This is done explicitly at times, through verbal labeling, as when a soldier in East Africa calls the hero an "Arab" during a confrontation.[116] At others, it is done implicitly, as when Ghāsiq assumes a high-status individual such as ʿAbd al-Wahhāb would have access to extravagant shelter and female companionship back home. This status is rarely presumed to exist for Black men by those operating within the Arab-Islamic settings of the text, so conflated was blackness with being a slave or subordinated client. ʿAbd al-Wahhāb instead continuously has had to prove his privileged standing and heritage among his immediate peers. Ironically, it is only upon entering the "lands of the Blacks" that ʿAbd al-Wahhāb becomes patently distanced from what his blackness means, and for whom it is meaningful.

Conclusion

Representations of the *bilād al-sūdān* and its inhabitants occur across the *sīra* corpus. In *Sīrat Dhāt al-Himma,* these portrayals share striking commonalities with a rich tradition of geographical writing that evolved in the Arab-Muslim world near-contemporaneously with *sīras*' more fanciful narratives of exploration, adventure, and war, though with some important embellishments. Abyssinians—known in Islam's earliest traditional sources for being fervent adherents to Christianity—are presented as unacquainted with religion in all but the most superficial ways. Peoples often situated in distinct regions are densely collocated, with tribesmen from the ostensibly West-Central African Damdam serving people in East African Abyssinia and its neighbors in an evocation of historical trajectories of migration and enslavement, and of artificial distance. Courtly life is by turns robust and primitive, with palatial buildings a seeming rarity and yet with kings enthroned on precious ebony in halls flanked with multitudes

116. *Sīrat Dhāt al-Himma,* XXXVII:3.

of guards. East Africa is hot, dry, and inhospitable, but it is also situated incongruously in a different "clime" than the one in which it is placed in much of the geographic literature, putting the audience off the axis of a number of norms and conventions simultaneously, from those of mannered, scholarly tradition to their expectations of the very configuration of the world itself. All of this establishes a fantastically inflated divide between East Africa and Arabia that is both geographical and cultural, poising the former territories as ripe for wonder and exploration. That various of the kingdoms are so heavily interpolated or ethnonyms so ambiguous as to thwart cartography lends these geographies a plastic quality, molding them to composers' and audiences' meaning-making endeavors.

At a glance, such depictions seem to reinforce a simplistic impression of these terrains' otherness through a set of essentializing and even carelessly contradictory tropes. However, I have argued that *Sīrat Dhāt al-Himma*'s East African landscape is strategically calibrated to allow for certain narrative maneuvers, representing these lands as particularly ripe for Islamization and as terrains for the self-actualization of the text's provisionally Black hero, for in the *bilād al-sūdān,* he becomes something else. The use of East African spaces to probe the *umma*'s future is facilitated by its presentation as an impious or ignorant canvas for numerous proselytizing endeavors, both Christian and Muslim. The Abyssinians thus become a proxy for the Arab Muslims' much more immediate conflict with the Byzantines, and are positioned critically between the text's two main belligerents. Damdamān's more littoral sphere, demographically massive and notionally connected at once with the Sahel and with the Indian Ocean, shows what the Muslims stand to gain by pressing yet further, as well as the obstacles that stand in their way. These obstacles are multi-directional: in the next chapter, I use the tale of ʿAbd al-Wahhāb's courtship of the East African princess Maymūna to examine some of the ways in which race "travels" and fails to do so as ʿAbd al-Wahhāb ventures abroad and as Maymūna then leaves her homeland at one edge of the characters' world and approaches the Byzantine *thaghr*. On all sides, characters grapple with transmitting their identities and identity-expectations when confronted with new milieus, across which the meanings of Arabness and blackness markedly change.

The role of the East African landscape in developing the heroic self materializes in ambiguities cast on the extent to which one's behavior is predetermined by one's environment, as well as the extent to which one's racialized status—typically naturalized as a product of one's ancestral climate—allows an individual to move comfortably in spaces that, though new to them, link them with their distant pasts. Ultimately, one's social upbringing cannot be so easily disrupted by a change of setting. Indeed, it is vital to the text's expansionist vision that the reverse be true. Far from a land of fixed "others," the *bilād al-sūdān* thus becomes not just a site of fantasy, but one of directed, aspirational promise that emphasizes societies' points of flexion through encounters with figures such as the convert king Hadlamūs and the interregionally well-connected ruler Damdamān, whose peoples rival "the stars and [particles of] earth" in number.[117] In turn, one's environment is shown to be not nearly as formative as one's *nasab*, a lineal bond that reasserts itself continuously in the lives of *sīra* characters even across vast distances of time, space, and culture. Despite being a useful heuristic for understanding peoples in broad aggregates, one's natal or ancestral climate has relatively little effect on individual action. In East Africa, rulers convert because they are noble, have cross-cultural access, and seek education. They submit themselves to powers greater than themselves, or refuse to do so, as part of their experiences of power and prestige, as well as humility and growth.

Damdamān does not express any interest in Islam despite appointing a Muslim tutor in his court and seeming to preside over a fringe community of Muslim subjects, preferring instead the might of wealth and his own authority alone. Hadlamūs's own trajectory toward becoming a Muslim meanwhile suggests that his capacity for belief is so atrophied that in order to approach the ultimate truth, he must first come to understand an intermediary half-truth, not unlike the gradual administering of food to a starving person. Like Abū'l-Hazāhiz in the previous chapter, Hadlamūs passes first through Christianity to arrive at Islam, allegorizing a triumphalist narrative in which submission to Islam is also the inevitable, eventual state of Christendom—even, or perhaps especially, for its most liminal adherents and environs. As we saw with Hadlamūs and will see in the following chapter's discussion of Maymūna, the progression seeded by this construction of the East African setting entails the spread of Islam and investment in Arab-Muslim relationships and interests on the part of charismatic, elite Black figures. These figures in turn command and commit thousands of Black soldiers, under varying degrees of (un)freedom, to the Muslim armies.

In contrast to the methods of geographic literature, in the *sīra* the truism that one's culture can supersede one's climate is thus sketched in biographical detail, emerging especially in vignettes showing ʿAbd al-Wahhāb's fraught reception by his Black African peers or those peers' interactions

117. *Sīrat Dhāt al-Himma*, XXXVI:41.

with Islam more generally. Yet we also see that other cultures share similar concerns around practices of scrutinizing and categorizing, including and excluding, of which Ghāsiq makes climate and temperament a part. Actors within the *bilād al-sūdān* strategically modulate their proximity to and distance from the Arab-Muslim characters, too.

7
Returning Home

Concepts do not prescribe relations, nor do they exist prior to them; rather, relations of force, connection, resonance, and patterning give rise to concepts.

JASBIR PUAR[1]

This woman's mark is not like that of heroes.

SĪRAT DHĀT AL-HIMMA[2]

Home, as Zayde Antrim has shown, was a meaningful concept for premodern Muslims. It could be flexible, and one could call multiple places home and make new ones over time, but the category was most central when one was longing to return. The archetype of the homesick warrior seeking the familiar and undergoing alienation (*ghurba*) in strange lands looms large in literary anthologies. Home became a special "preoccupation" for hypermobile actors in "era[s] of territorial expansion and decentralization."[3] As the primary agents within the growing realm of the *sīra*—emblematized in the first pages' citation of the geographically and genealogically inflected Qurʾānic verse, "Praised be God . . . who gave you no blameworthy thing in religion. It is the creed (*milla*) of your forefather, Ibrāhīm. And He designated you Muslims."[4]—how do Arab Muslims extend not only their physical reach but also their social lives into new domains? How do hybrid figures like the Black-Arab ʿAbd al-Wahhāb, who sit uneasily in

1. Jasbir K. Puar, "'I Would Rather Be a Cyborg Than a Goddess': Becoming-Intersectional in Assemblage Theory," *philoSOPHIA* 2 (2012): 57.

2. *Sīrat Dhāt al-Himma*, XXXVII:33.

3. Antrim, *Routes and Realms*, 13.

4. Q 22:78.

the identity matrix of their homeland, fare in these crossings? And what consequences, if any, do the experiences of identity deconstruction and reconstruction undergone in transit portend for a character's return? Can one move between worlds ultimately unchanged?

In his essay, "How We Divide the World," the philosopher Michael Root makes a claim that has become axiomatic of how race is discussed in the "constructionist" model, that is, the set of discourses that argue race is a social construct rather than a natural, essential kind: "Race does not travel."[5] Concepts of race vary in accordance with one's context, and as such, one does not carry one's racial identity across spatial, temporal, and social boundaries. As Root puts it, "Some men who are black in New Orleans now would have been octoroons there some years ago or would be white in Brazil today."[6] Ron Mallon complicates this point by referencing the impact of subjective experience and discursive norms on one's perception of race; he argues for the importance of the act of *labeling*, or of having the group to which one is seen as belonging named and renamed as one moves through space and time.[7] Unless met with a new label, one may carry one's prior sense of racial identity along through new locales. Frantz Fanon further illustrates how one might violently project and enforce their regimes of labeling in new spaces, such that white people moving through a colonized domain impose their whiteness and its definition upon the local populace, rather than having their mode of racial self-identification shaped by the colonized culture.[8] This form of privileged movement becomes unconscious for Sara Ahmed, with whiteness being that which "lags behind," and that which one "[does] not have to face."[9]

Denise Ferreira da Silva phrases whiteness becoming unconscious as the very stuff of modern subjectivity—the "transparent I," as opposed to racialized and "affectable" others.[10] Though such binaries may make the boundary between self and other sound absolute, it is characterized by continuous, ambivalent encounters and modifications. Dynamic interrelations are particularly evident in the fluid conditions of ongoing expansionism. Homi Bhabha writes, for example, that in trying to conform the colony to the image of the metropole while still maintaining the metropole's primacy,

5. Root, "How We Divide the World," S631.

6. Root, S631–S632.

7. Ron Mallon, "Passing, Traveling, and Reality," *Noûs* 38 (2004): 659.

8. Frantz Fanon, *Black Skin, White Masks*, trans. Richard Philcox (New York: Grove Press, 2008).

9. Ahmed, "A Phenomenology of Whiteness," 156.

10. Silva, *Towards a Global Idea of Race*.

colonizers set up a dynamic of mimicry that is instable and ever-evolving, a "part-object that radically revalues the normative knowledges of the priority off race, writing, history," and even lays them bare to be mocked and critiqued, if never fully overturned.[11] But we might once again ask: are these types of encounter and the subjectivities they produce bounded by modern Euro-colonial times, spaces, and arrangements of governance, or can we generatively think with them in instances that are prior and elsewhere?

When ʿAbd al-Wahhāb enters East Africa, he does so as an outsider and member of an antagonistic nation that views itself as having numerous civilizational advantages over and higher objectives for denizens of the "lands of the Blacks," or *bilād al-sūdān*. And yet, ʿAbd al-Wahhāb is coded within his home milieu as a Black man with putative roots in the region. Rather than this coding simply *not* translating within East Africa per Root's dictum, and rather than simply subsuming those he encounters under his own ways of knowing, ʿAbd al-Wahhāb's identity instead becomes caught between multiple modes of signification. This is evident in the ways ʿAbd al-Wahhāb is labeled by those around him: ʿUqba, now also in the *bilād al-sūdān*, continues to refer to him as the "Black of the Banū Kilāb," while a local ruler, Damdamān, refers to him ambiguously as maternal kin. Most prominently, when the princess Maymūna, Damdamān's daughter, takes a romantic interest in ʿAbd al-Wahhāb, her various other suitors compete for her attention while referring to him, jeeringly, as a Kilābī Arab.

The suitors' polemical campaign fails; Maymūna instead turns on her own kin, kills her father, rejects her more suitable prospects, and makes a new home in ʿAbd al-Wahhāb's native land as his Muslim bride. She represents at once the greatest change to ʿAbd al-Wahhāb's circumstances after his journey to the *bilād al-sūdān* and is a potent touchstone for the aspirational history of Islam in her own right. In her own imperfect and incomplete attempts at belonging, she reflects and exaggerates the *umma*'s failings as well as its promises. After submitting to Muslim rule and bearing ʿAbd al-Wahhāb a son, a series of traumatic events establish Maymūna's descent into arch-villainy. She converts to Christianity, wars against the Muslims, and kills her own child. Perhaps the greatest change to ʿAbd al-Wahhāb's life after his time away takes the form of his bride navigating the return journey with him, apart from him, and then against him. This chapter shows how Maymūna occupies various critical positions that illustrate the possibilities and limits of belonging for Black Muslim women

11. Homi Bhabha, "Of Mimicry and Man: The Ambivalence of Colonial Disclosure," *October* 28 (1984): 131.

in the expanding world of the story, as well as the stakes of extending and rescinding that membership.

Though Maymūna's role in the *sīra* has earned some attention, it is primarily for her status as one of a cluster of illustrious warrior women—a staple of *Sīrat Dhāt al-Himma*, which takes a heroine as its eponym, and of the *sīras* more broadly. As I argue below, in emphasizing Maymūna's gender while glossing over her blackness, we miss much not only of her character's particular, individual resonance, but also of the impact it has on the development of the text's other figures including Fāṭima and ʿAbd al-Wahhāb. Maymūna may be seen as a complex assemblage of co-determinant attributes that do not form a constant and stable subject, but rather configure and reconfigure in relation to her social situation, and therefore "cannot be seamlessly disaggregated into identity formations" like woman, Muslim, Christian, Black, and so on.[12] Her femininity and foreignness get read in construct as aggressive and Zulaykha-like in their ostensibly pagan East African context by the piously chaste ʿAbd al-Wahhāb, but as key attributes of the idealized beloved upon her entrance into the realms of Islam. Her comparative beauty "among the Blacks" is reduced to a flat and masculinized fearsomeness in the lands of the Byzantines. At times, Maymūna consciously exploits her changeable resonances, at others, she resists them.

As a once-heroic Black woman in a world not made for her, it might appear that Maymūna is a perfect candidate for an intersectional reading, that is, a reading that attends to the historic, systemic causes that complicate seeing and relating the experiences of figures in which more than one form of difference overlap. This framework has been applied previously in medieval studies to illuminating effect.[13] Kimberlé Crenshaw, who first articulated the concept of intersectionality, cites one of its aims as "challeng[ing] groups that are after all, in one sense, 'home' to us, in the name of the parts of us that are not made at home," a challenge that Maymūna recurrently poses for her fellow Muslims within the text as she works to establish herself.[14] Scholars of queer studies and religious studies supplement and contextualize Crenshaw's concept in ways that enable us to see yet more layers in Maymūna's tale. Jasbir Puar notes that conceiving of individuals intersectionally is analogous to plotting them as identity positions on a grid. She adds that seeing them as assemblages,

12. Puar, "'I Would Rather Be a Cyborg'" 56.

13. Betancourt, *Byzantine Intersectionality*, esp. 14–15.

14. Kimberlé Crenshaw, "Mapping the Margins: Intersectionality, Identity Politics, and Violence against Women of Color," *Stanford Law Review* 43, no. 6 (1991): 1299.

or as relationally and affectively contingent in ways that defy pinpointing any enduring position, supplies useful "friction."[15]

Through their emphasis on mutability and "relations of force, connection, resonance," that transcend the individual and even the human, assemblages become pertinent for a variety of religious contexts. In discussing the physicality of renunciant Muslims who seek an experiential and sensory relationship with the divine, Shahzad Bashir shows that, far from the isolation that renunciation sometimes implies, the renunciant Sufi body becomes a shifting medium for environmental and cosmic conditions.[16] Elsewhere, Bashir ties this mode of signification in with the liminalized border warriors of *Sīrat Dhāt al-Himma* as well. He writes that the heroes' afflicted and embattled bodies, situated in an epical early ʿAbbasid age, stand in for chroniclers' meticulous curation of names and dates throughout that tumultuous era by collectively embodying history.[17] As I trace the arc of Maymūna's character from ʿAbd al-Wahhāb's fateful arrival at her father's court through her demise, I argue that this arc and her transformations within it contain overlapping theological and social-historical potentials. Well before becoming a villain, as a Muslim Maymūna sits at the frontiers of thinkability among her coreligionists, wavering between orthodoxy and heterodoxy, nobility and vulgarity, and home and abroad.

Damdamān's Court

At the inception of his travels in East Africa, ʿAbd al-Wahhāb does not follow ʿUqba directly into Hadlamūs's realm. Nursing recent battle wounds, he becomes increasingly emaciated and infirm. It is in this condition that he falls into the hands of his captor, the king Damdamān, ruler of a neighboring region that is still said to be in the lands of *ḥabasha*, a span that tends to include parts of East Africa east of modern-day Sudan, such as Ethiopia, and extends into Somalia. There, ʿAbd al-Wahhāb remains sick for a full year until a Jewish physician appears and

> attends to him, applying medication to him. The rotten, dead flesh was consumed and fresh flesh developed [in its place]. [The doctor] continued medicating him for a whole month until he was healed and

15. Puar, "'I Would Rather Be a Cyborg,'" 50.

16. Shahzad Bashir, *Sufi Bodies: Religion and Society in Medieval Islam* (New York: Columbia University Press, 2011).

17. Bashir, *Visions*, n.p.

> returned to an even better [condition] than before [*ʿād ilā aḥsan mi-mā kān ʿalayhi*].[18]

When Damdamān sees that ʿAbd al-Wahhāb is sufficiently healed to be dealt with as a proper prisoner, he lowers him into a deep pit, saying, "O cousin [*yā ibn khāla*], you won't be leaving here for any less than one thousand *qinṭārs* of gold," at which ʿAbd al-Wahhāb realizes "these people are mad."[19]

Damdamān calling ʿAbd al-Wahhāb his cousin is in seeming conflict with the treatment of his captive, and hardly in keeping with the ineluctable outpouring of tenderness toward people of the same *nasab* that is otherwise a marked pattern throughout the *sīra*, with "blood stirring for blood." Perhaps this is because Damdamān is simply expressing a matter of fact; in his physical form, he recognizes ʿAbd al-Wahhāb as an indirect but nonetheless discernible relation to himself. This is embodied in his use of the term for a maternally descended cousin, rather than the paternal term of address used for close kin. As if in subtle acknowledgment of the sorts of power structures—foreign concubinage, in particular—that might have produced such a man as ʿAbd al-Wahhāb, Damdamān invokes the simultaneous familial proximity and lineal disprivilege of his newest hostage. Indeed, in classical Arabic usage, the collective noun *khawl,* derived from the same root as *khāla,* or maternal aunt, indicates one's subordinates, both enslaved and dependent. *Khāl* continues to carry this resonance in various Arabic dialects today, particularly in the Gulf, where it has increasingly become merged with racialized blackness that is inscribed especially on populations ringing the Indian Ocean.[20]

Damdamān's ambivalent expression of intimacy with ʿAbd al-Wahhāb is unique vis-à-vis his East African peers, though, who mostly reject the Black hero outright and refer to him as an Arab. This negative reception intensifies after word begins to travel that while at Damdamān's court, ʿAbd al-Wahhāb manages to woo one of its other members: the beloved princess, Maymūna. Our first encounter with Maymūna occurs when she sees ʿAbd al-Wahhāb while in her father's capture. Immediately, she "longs

18. *Sīrat Dhāt al-Himma,* XXXVI:40.

19. *Sīrat Dhāt al-Himma,* XXXVI:40.

20. On the tensions around this term's use, see Idil Akinci, "The Multiple Roots of Emiratiness: The Cosmopolitan History of Emirati Society," *openDemocracy* February 15, 2018, https://www.opendemocracy.net/en/beyond-trafficking-and-slavery/the-multiple-roots-of-emiratiness/.

for him like Zulaykha longed for Yūsuf."[21] Zulaykha is, on the one hand, the name given in ensuing traditions for the cunning temptress who unsuccessfully attempts to seduce the Prophet Yūsuf (Joseph) in the Qur'ān and then cover this up with lies. On the other, in Sufi interpretations Zulaykha becomes the embodiment of pure love of God, represented by single-minded and self-destructive attachment to one of His messengers on earth.[22] Whether Maymūna is being presented as a morally dangerous deceiver or as a newly enraptured seeker of divine union, this moment signals a frisson.

Maymūna is also presented more overtly as being worthy of ʿAbd al-Wahhāb. As with her heroic beloved, Maymūna's qualities are said to defy those of her kind. Moreover, her upbringing inclines her toward Islam,

> She had a famed intellect [*ʿaql maʿrūf*] and vaunted beauty [*jamāl mawṣūf*], and those who saw her would recall that there had been none like her among the Blacks, nor her better, for she was resplendently dark, with large, black eyes, pert breasts, a thick rear, and kohl-rimmed lids [*makḥūlat al-muqal*], and this was in contrast to [other] Blacks [*wa-hādhā bi-khilāf al-sūdān*].... A man from Yemen, the land of Zabīd and ʿAden, came to them, one of intellection and virtue and moral discipline. From him, she had learned calligraphy and the histories of the Arabs and Persians, and had studied the Arabic language [*al-khaṭṭ bi-l-qalam wa-aḥādīth al-ʿarab wa-l-ʿajam wa-taʿallamat bi-lisān al-ʿarab*]. She was of honorable roots and lineage [*wa-kānat karīmat al-aṣl wa-l-nasab*].[23]

As is often done with the Black heroes of the *sīra* tradition, Maymūna's exposition as a hero-to-be is entwined in exceptionalisms and "despites," exempting her from the stereotypes that attend her blackness, and thus throwing these into sharp contrasting relief. Though her unique appearance, education, and pedigree poise Maymūna to be a fitting partner for ʿAbd al-Wahhāb, with both of them having distinguished themselves from the rest of their kind, ʿAbd al-Wahhāb's inborn Arabness is nonetheless distinct from Maymūna's Arabizing education.

21. *Sīrat Dhāt al-Himma*, XXXVI:46.

22. Gayane Karen Merguerian and Afsaneh Najmabadi, "Zulaykha and Yusuf: Whose 'Best Story'?," *International Journal for Middle East Studies* 29, no. 4 (1997): 47–50.

23. *Sīrat Dhāt al-Himma*, XXXVI:46.

Maymūna's description in this passage plays with another tantalizing possibility: Maymūna has not only become familiar with Arabs' literature and culture, but also is well acquainted with at least some aspects of Islam. We might recall that earlier discussions of her father's domain as populated by *Qarāmida* and networked with Yemen would seem to push Damdamān's domains toward the coast and thus toward the profoundly interconnected—and largely Muslim—Indian Ocean trade.[24]

Moreover, Maymūna thinks of herself as following a system of Islamic doctrines and doing so more intensively than those around her. Speaking of her ambitions as a ruler, she states,

> I have no want of wealth, for all the riches of peoples of the east and west are in my grasp [*amwāl ahl al-sharq wa-l-gharb kulluhā fī qabḍatī*]. I have resolved to travel with 100,000 of my people, conquering lands and establishing the laws of God Almighty [*ḥudūd Allāh ta'ālā*] therein. Everyone will know the truth of my words, though my people [*qawmī*] have no rationality with which to conduct themselves and worship the One who created them and gave them succor. I shall undertake to incline them toward this—my teacher commanded me to do so and acquainted me with the paths of the religion [*ṭarā'iq al-dīn*] and guided me toward service of the Lord of the worlds.[25]

Across these passages, Maymūna's characterization wavers between the global and the local. One form this takes is in the tension between universal Muslimness and wide variations of interpretation and practice, such that Maymūna's Yemeni teacher's practices are evaluated as better than those of her community, which is perhaps Muslim, but if so, is characterized in fractious or atrophied fashion. Another discrepancy arises between universal and particular webs of human lineage. We might recall that when applied locally, *nasab* was a system principally tailored to tribal Arabness. When scaled globally, Black people (as the children of Ḥām) were often placed beneath others. However, this placement is troubled by Maymūna's royal status, also phrased in terms of her roots and descent. Her geographic situation at a crossroads of transregional wealth (with east and west equally in her purview) does likewise. Meanwhile, the

24. On what it might mean to refer to trade routes as "Muslim," and the role of Muslimness in trading, see Patricia Risso, "Muslim Identity in Maritime Trade: General Observations and Some Evidence from the 18th-Century Persian Gulf / Indian Ocean Region," *International Journal of Middle East Studies* 21 (1989): 381–92.

25. *Sīrat Dhāt al-Himma*, XXXVI:47.

incongruity between different systems of reckoning lineage across these spaces becomes a device through which the princess's other would-be prospects express their affront at her falling in love with someone of a different ethnicity and culture. Maymūna's suitors, the warriors ʿAnqūsh and Ghāsiq, voice their condemnation forcefully and engage in direct combat with ʿAbd al-Wahhāb, with Maymūna as the putative prize.

When the prominent Yemeni fighter ʿAnqūsh arrives home from a military expedition, he resolves to betroth himself to Maymūna, who, upon hearing this, tells her father she wants no man and rides off.[26] ʿUqba, knowing of Maymūna's love for ʿAbd al-Wahhāb, dispatches a slave to convey to ʿAnqūsh that she has "become besotted with an Arab man of clean coloring and beautiful form [*naqī al-lawn malīḥ al-kawn*]."[27] Upon hearing this depiction, calibrated to offend, ʿAnqūsh joins several thousand men with Damdamān's armies and marches out against ʿAbd al-Wahhāb and Maymūna. When Maymūna and ʿAnqūsh meet on the battlefield, ʿAnqūsh recites satirical verse at her, picking a bone with ʿAbd al-Wahhāb's lack of legible prestige:

> How could you be pleased with a Kilābī as your man, [*fa-kayf raḍītī bi-l-kilābī ṣāḥiban*]
> When he has no noble lineage and no favor?[28] [*wa-laysa li-hu aṣl nabīl wa-lā faḍl*]

As has been discussed previously, ʿAbd al-Wahhāb is indeed from a well-known line of tribal leaders and heroes, and his favor is amply demonstrated in his moniker, the "shield of the Prophet's grave" (*turs qabr al-nabī*). However, this mainly provides clout in an Arab-Muslim social context, and as such ʿAnqūsh suggests that he will not bring Maymūna any *local* glory or esteem in marriage. This reference to disparate and non-transferable forms of social capital indicates that the *sīra* composers had an awareness that Arab superiority is a culturally relative phenomenon, rather than a universally upheld truth. In a moment of irony, the once-familiar Damdamān also derides ʿAbd al-Wahhāb's lineage when the two meet

26. This rejection of men is a common refrain in narratives of young, Bedouin heroines in training, whom Julia Bray describes as "forever chaste and unattainable." Julia Bray, "Men, Women, and Slaves in Abbasid Society," in *Gender in the Early Medieval World: East and West, 300–900*, ed. Leslie Brubaker and Julia M. H. Smith (Cambridge: Cambridge University Press, 2004), 138.

27. *Sīrat Dhāt al-Himma*, XXXVII:3.

28. *Sīrat Dhāt al-Himma*, XXXVII:4.

again in battle in a way reminiscent of the insults leveled at him among his Arab peers because of his blackness's associations with bastardy,

> When [Damdamān] saw the most excellent prince [ʿAbd al-Wahhāb] [*al-amīr al-mifḍāl*] amid the chaos, he called to him, "O son of whores [*ibn al-ʿawāhir*], O you of vile rearing [*tarbiyat al-andāl*]! You're the one who has caused this strife and brought this ordeal upon us [*anta alladhī kunt sabab hādhihi al-fitna wa-jalabt li-nā hādhihi al-miḥna*]!"[29]

Later on as the melee escalates, Damdamān modulates his invective against ʿAbd al-Wahhāb by once again harkening to their common ground:

> O black-skinned one [*aswad al-jild*], go in peace—
> Seek your men's camps and take leave
> Had I wanted it so, you'd be dead.
> Retreat safely, and be of clear head!
> Maymūna is caught in the fray,
> Wielding weapons for your battle-day
> But should you have a foe in our ranks
> He'll be struck from the armies' flanks.
> Lovesick or not, go back home, [*fa-ʿid naḥw dārik aw fī wajd*]
> Seek the comforts found near your abode,
> And my child, Maymūna? Let be, [*wa-lā tabhgī li-bintī Maymūna*]
> Or you'll meet a swift fate, dealt from me [*fa-talqā ḥimāmak bi-l-munṣul*]
> Tell no one these words, for I swear
> Such a breach is beyond all repair.[30]

The overall tone of the above verses is one of conciliatory exhortation, with "O black-skinned one" appearing to be an appeal to camaraderie rather than insult. Thus, Damdamān once again makes use of a crude language of affinity when he desires something from ʿAbd al-Wahhāb, suggesting the tenuous superficiality of their connection through physical likeness.

Meanwhile, Maymūna's second jilted devotee, Ghāsiq, refutes the very premise that he and ʿAbd al-Wahhāb share any likeness, instead choosing to highlight his own similarities with Maymūna as though they are exclusive. When he first meets the Muslims on the battlefield, vying to retain

29. *Sīrat Dhāt al-Himma*, XXXVII:6.
30. *Sīrat Dhāt al-Himma*, XXXVII:7.

Maymūna as his betrothed, Ghāsiq and ʿAbd al-Wahhāb's deputy, a man named Ṭāriq al-Ḥijāzī, trade verses, with Ghāsiq saying:

> I've repelled those of noblest stock [*al-ʿunṣur al-akram*],
> Not doing so beneath night's cloak [*bi-l-aswad al-adham*],
> I've not tasted drink's loosing bonds, [*lā dhaqt ṭaʿm al-sakrā thāniyan*]
> Nor supped on fine, fancy viands. [*wa-lā ʿasht fī lidhdhat al-maṭʿam*]
> Before I rout you from her domain,
> Leave your body bloodless and slain,
> I surely shall see your princely guide
> Brought to heel and bereft of his pride.
> And you'll cry, recalling the loss
> Of life and land's glory, turned dross.
> And I'll take Maymūna forthwith
> To repose 'gainst her breast and her wrist
> For my color is one that she shares, [*fa-lawnī ʿalā lawnihā mushabbah*]
> Alike in our darkness, a pair.[31] [*kilā-nā yushabbih bi-l-asḥam*]

Ghāsiq notes color as one of the most prominent features that he and Maymūna share, and in doing so he implicitly denies that ʿAbd al-Wahhāb can share this with her as well. There is some ambiguity, however, over whether Ghāsiq was yet fully aware of ʿAbd al-Wahhāb's appearance at this moment; both due to the ways in which the elite Arab generals clothe themselves and due to Ghāsiq's assumptions about Arabs' appearance, he seems unable to conceive of ʿAbd al-Wahhāb as dark-skinned. This becomes clear when the Abyssinian king Hadlamūs faces Ghāsiq in battle, clad in the full-coverage garb gifted to him by ʿAbd al-Wahhāb after his conversion:

> When Ghāsiq looked at Hadlamūs coming before him in that uniform, he assumed he was the prince ʿAbd al-Wahhāb, because nothing of him was visible save the skin around his eyes and the corners of the lids, so Ghāsiq said, "This ʿAbd al-Wahhāb can really only be a great king, for were he not, he would not be equipped in this way in these far-flung, distant lands [*hādhihi al-arāḍī al-wāsiʿa wa-l-bilād al-baʿīda*]"[32]

31. *Sīrat Dhāt al-Himma*, XXXVII:26.
32. *Sīrat Dhāt al-Himma*, XXXVII:27.

Ghāsiq then muses that perhaps Maymūna has become taken by this man because he is visibly wealthy, for, in his own words, "Blacks love wealth" (*al-sūdān yurīdūn al-māl*).[33] He is simultaneously impressed with and threatened by the Arabs' elaborate provisioning. The recurrent theme that Black Africans lust after finery—seen in chapter 5 in Abū'l-Hazāhiz's reaction to the temptations of Byzantine lucre—is here restated in the voice of a Black man. This lends the trope a veneer of authenticity and propounds the belief that the East Africans lack resources and urbanity, which is also reinforced by Ghāsiq's aforementioned mockery of ʿAbd al-Wahhāb for being accustomed to permanent dwellings. In assuming that Maymūna could only be interested in ʿAbd al-Wahhāb's money, Ghāsiq also rejects the potential for there to be any substantive attraction between the two, and thus upholds his own logic that their different kinds are not naturally inclined to mix.

As a further indication that Ghāsiq may not have anticipated ʿAbd al-Wahhāb's physical likeness to himself, when the two finally do meet in combat after Hadlamūs's feint, Ghāsiq's boastful poetry shifts focus from color to genealogy. He declares, "We are the people of Ḥām, who have no equal, and to us may be traced respectful and honorable [relations]."[34] Both Ghāsiq and ʿAnqūsh seek recourse against ʿAbd al-Wahhāb's budding relationship with Maymūna in lineal claims, with ʿAnqūsh noting ʿAbd al-Wahhāb's lack of local significance, and Ghāsiq distancing himself from ʿAbd al-Wahhāb as a son of Ḥām, rather than of Sām. Ghāsiq also distances himself from ʿAbd al-Wahhāb by vaunting his own (relative) blackness and, as seen in the previous chapter, his being acclimatized to the heat and sunlight of his home.

Yet appeals to ʿAbd al-Wahhāb's likeness to his East African peers are also grounded in color and kinship, with Damdamān referring to him as the "black-skinned one" and as a maternal relation. When these attempts fail, Damdamān thinks to put ʿAbd al-Wahhāb into retreat and tell Maymūna, falsely, that he killed him, only for Maymūna to then turn the sword on her own father. Though racialized aspects of identity travel in the text insofar as perceived lineage and appearance continue to signify, the webs of relation and community that they connote do not. Taken together, these negotiations have the effect of decentering ʿAbd al-Wahhāb's standing in his world and training the text's focus on how he relates instead to Maymūna's position in hers. This dynamic is reversed when Maymūna

33. *Sīrat Dhāt al-Himma*, XXXVII:27.
34. *Sīrat Dhāt al-Himma*, XXXVII:29.

transforms from being a princess in her own right to the heroic ʿAbd al-Wahhāb's foreign companion, after first battling a series of stereotypes and assumptions that underpin ʿAbd al-Wahhāb's and his family's response to her ambitions.

Maymūna, ʿAbd al-Wahhāb's East African Princess

As we have seen, *Sīrat Dhāt al-Himma* regularly emphasizes human "kinds" succeeding best when kept together—be it in the structuring of nominally homogeneous military units or in ʿAbd al-Wahhāb's unique attachment to the Black community. Romantic pairings, by contrast, hold space for culturally plural arrangements as an essential part of their own community-building functions: much like conversion, manumission, and *walāʾ* are tools of assimilating non-Arab men into Arab genealogies, marriage, concubinage, and reproduction have these effects for non-Arab women. Remke Kruk has identified the "foreign princess" as a staple of the *sīra* tradition, and "winning" her affections—which typically comes alongside winning her over to the love of men rather than the company of women, and thus ushering her into norms of sexual maturity—as its own strain of triumphalism in the corpus. Kruk reads Maymūna's early relationship with ʿAbd al-Wahhāb as conforming to this established pattern, saying,

> A foreign princess appears, and after a certain number of vicissitudes she marries one of the Muslim heroes, joins the Muslim cause, and becomes the mother of a son.[35]

To be sure, the status of Maymūna as a generically "foreign heroine" is in league thematically with ʿAbd al-Wahhāb's paramours Mayrūna and Nūrā, both of whom are from Byzantium. And yet, Kruk acknowledges that Maymūna is exceptional in some ways vis-à-vis her peer foreign heroines in that she—unlike most figures in the *sīras*—undergoes "a total, and lasting, change of character," by going to the "dark side," and ultimately becoming an enemy of ʿAbd al-Wahhāb and his mother, fighting in support of the Franks and Byzantines.[36] I argue that another significant point of divergence is that, as a Black woman, Maymūna has several unique barriers to entry into hero-wifehood. And though heavily foreshadowed, her

35. Remke Kruk, "The Princess Maymūnah: Maiden, Mother, Monster," *Oriente Moderno* 22 (2003): 429.

36. Kruk, 428.

subsequent departure from hero-wifehood is protracted and ambivalent as she tries to keep a foot in several conflicting realms.

Also noteworthy is that, in her exposition, Maymūna's foreignness to the hybrid hero is treated as a matter of perception: she is Black and noble like ʿAbd al-Wahhāb and thus a fitting match according to the logic of "kind," though she is East African in answer to ʿAbd al-Wahhāb's cultural Arabness, and her comrades visibly resist seeing these connections. From the outset, the two have a fraught courtship, due in no small part to a priori surmise. ʿAbd al-Wahhāb assumes that all of Maymūna's advances are attempts to lead him into committing *zinā*, or fornication, with an impious woman, rather than being born out of a sincere desire to champion Islam and have a legitimate relationship with him.

When Maymūna first attempts to initiate a courtship with ʿAbd al-Wahhāb, she does so with pure, if lovelorn, intentions—she expresses that she is attracted to his honorable bearing and she vows to protect him from the evil ʿUqba and even her own father's aggressions. However, ʿAbd al-Wahhāb's initial reaction to her is one of pearl-clutching indignation: "God forbid that I should seek out any relief [/vagina] save in Him" (*maʿādh Allāh an aṭlub al-faraj*[*/al-farj*] *illā minhu*).[37] In the paronomasia that plays out through the homonymous relationship between relief and the company of a woman, ʿAbd al-Wahhāb draws a line dividing the frivolous interest in worldly pleasure from the true pleasure that can be found in piety. He then writes her a poetic epistle—on the back of her own love note to him—declaring that he will not be led into sin and calling Maymūna's and his love unsound, carnal, and inappropriate (*kayf yarā ḥubbī ṣawāban wa-annahu sa-tubālī ʿuyūnī fī-l-thadā*[38] *wa-l-ʿiẓām . . . fa-mā lik fī ḥubbī ṣalāḥ fa-annanī raʾīt al-taqā raʾā li-dayhi salām*).[39] Stunned by his rebuke, Maymūna replies in a letter,

O servant [of God] [*ayyuhā-l-ʿabd*], unsparing in his religion [*ṣaḥḥ dīnahu*],
By my life, you are in league with the best men
And by the truth of your God, virtue-giving,
Who guided you rightly [*ʿarafak al-rashād*], son of great lineage [*ibn al-anāsib*],

37. *Sīrat Dhāt al-Himma*, XXXVI:48.

38. The original text reads *tharā*, as in, his eyes will be afflicted by her "wealth" and her limbs, but should likely read *thadā*, as in her "breasts" and her limbs, particularly given her response's reference to women with large breasts (*kawāʿib*).

39. *Sīrat Dhāt al-Himma*, XXXVI:48.

I shall wrangle my passions, I want no corruption,
Nor do I chase bacchanal [*al-faḥsh*], like other, buxom women [*mithl al-kawāʿib*]
But I know my heart, toward you, is keenly leaning [*qad māl maylatan*]
With honest affection that is in no way misleading [*ilayk muḥibb ṣādiq ghayr kādhib*]
I'll send you old ʿUqba's head, his time soon to be up,
And pour a hearty draught of death into his waiting cup![40]

It is clear from this testimony that Maymūna did not desire him in an adulterous or unchaste way (*mā raghibat fīhi min ṭarīq al-zinā*), but ʿAbd al-Wahhāb nonetheless continues to repel her advances out of fear of God. After losing patience with his evasions, Maymūna goes to confront him in person. ʿAbd al-Wahhāb lowers his eyes and refuses to look at her out of a sense of modesty. Hurt by this gesture that impugns her behavior, Maymūna proclaims, "People of honor comport [themselves] honorably, so raise your head and look at she who is tangled in love, and whom great strain [*jahd*] has struck, and over whom anxiety has a hold. Spare me the excuses and pretexts [*al-ʿilal wa-l-iḥtijāj*] and speak to me in a suitable way."[41] ʿAbd al-Wahhāb then admits that his mind has changed, and that his gaze is not lowered because he fears her indiscretion, but because he fears his own passions, especially as an older man, when he cannot afford to do anything that might anger God in advance of death.

Yet we might question why ʿAbd al-Wahhāb had assumed that Maymūna's desires were perfidious in the first place—is it perhaps because, believing her a pagan, he could not expect her values to align with his (and yet she swears by God's truth repeatedly in her communiqués)? Is it because she pursued him, while in most of his other romantic experiences ʿAbd al-Wahhāb had been the initiator? Or is it because he is primed to view her in a certain way as a Black woman?

An indication of the latter is given when, a short while later, Fāṭima Dhāt al-Himma and Maymūna encounter one another formally for the first time. Upon arriving at Maymūna's fortress, Fāṭima and her companions are greeted by five thousand "Blacks and Abyssinians," clad in multicolored fabrics that make them appear "like flowers in a garden," with

40. *Sīrat Dhāt al-Himma*, XXXVI:48
41. *Sīrat Dhāt al-Himma*, XXXVI:50.

Maymūna at the fore. Upon seeing her, ʿAbd al-Wahhāb's heart soars, and he turns to his mother, saying,

> O mother, this is the woman I described to you, and she went out [to the battlefield] with these Black men, like the jinn of Sulaymān, and to her [troops] were added the remaining Blacks from the companions of King Damdamān, and she raised this great army [*al-ʿaskar al-ʿaẓīm*] like the jet-black night [*al-layl al-bahīm*].[42]

Seeing how dark Maymūna herself is (*naẓarat ilā Maymūna wa-sawādihā*), Fāṭima cuts in, saying, "This is Maymūna?" ʿAbd al-Wahhāb replies, "Yes, O commander, this one with the night-like face who battles on horseback." Fāṭima then says, "Know, O my son, that this woman's mark is not like that of heroes [*mā sīmatuhā sīmat al-abṭāl*]."[43] She then tells her son to write Maymūna a letter apologizing to her and entreating her goodwill toward the Muslims, but says nothing of her son's own clearly expressed affections for the princess.

This moment gives occasion for exploring the relationship between Blackness, femininity, social class, and the ascetically pious heroic disposition that predominates in the *sīras*. At first glance, there is a glaring inconsistency in Fāṭima's reaction to Maymūna's Blackness and its preclusion of her heroic status. Fāṭima's son is, after all, a black-skinned hero who has distinguished himself in combat. Moreover, some of history and myth's greatest figures that would have been known to Fāṭima—from ʿAntara ibn Shaddād to the ʿAbbasid caliph al-Manṣūr (d. 775), through whose reign she lived, to a number of Shīʿī imams, including one of Jaʿfar al-Ṣādiq's children[44]—had mothers who were of East African descent. Yet the precise terms in which Fāṭima reacts to Maymūna's blackness carry multiple meanings for how appearance and reality might interrelate. *Sīma*, a literal "mark," fundamentally suggests the physically observable. Fāṭima easily maps the exterior onto the interior when moving between a surface-level mark and the abstract quality of a hero in ways reminiscent of physiognomic practice, which in Arab-Islamic sciences is a mode knowledge one can acquire about people's dispositions through *firāsa*, "perspicacity," or fixing the gaze on minute details of their outer forms. The term *sīma* also works affectively, though, signifying an abstract, extrinsic concept that has become a manifest sign in the physical world

42. *Sīrat Dhāt al-Himma*, XXXVII:33.
43. *Sīrat Dhāt al-Himma*, XXXVII:33.
44. Inloes, "Racial 'Othering' in Shīʿi Sacred History."

because of a person's inner refinement, as with a mark of prostration on the forehead recalling other believers to piety and steadfastness in prayer.[45] In esoteric writings, one can have a *sīma* of such things as truth and kindness. What marks might Fāṭima believe Maymūna possesses? How might they affect others?

Fāṭima is thinking of Maymūna not merely as a hero, but as a woman who is to be a marriage prospect for her pious, high-ranking son. This is perhaps why Maymūna's signification becomes fraught; pathways to personal piety and social preeminence do not always easily mesh for women like her. In her work on early Sufi women, Laury Silvers notes the prominence of Black women who are either enslaved or presumed to be so in moral tales, where they symbolize ideal renunciants because of their lack of worldly station, writing, "In some of these stories, black skin seems to articulate the ideal of spiritual poverty by connecting the lowest social status, an enslaved black woman, with the highest spiritual status."[46] One of the axes along which these women express their humility is chastity, a choice that enables one to transcend the body but that cannot be made unilaterally when the body is bought and sold. Indeed, cultivating sensual arts and sexual relationships as an enslaved woman constituted a primary way of climbing the social ladder and gaining access to the elite. Some of the most illustrious and powerful Black women to be widely documented in the ʿAbbasid era in which the tale is set are courtly concubines and entertainers (*qiyān*) owned and gifted around by royal men and their functionaries, as with the much-mentioned Danānīr (d. ca. 810), owned by several Barmakid advisors. Their daughters, such as ʿUlayya bt. al-Mahdī (d. 825), born to the caliph and his enslaved Black consort Maknūna, in turn were occasionally among the few free women recorded as becoming highly educated in the literary and musical arts, in addition to being noble in all other respects. However much they shared their mothers' skills, they did not share their identities.[47] The professional function of the *qiyān* was giving others various forms of pleasure, from artistic reverie (*ṭarab*) to release.

45. Andrew Rippin, "The trace of prostration and other distinguishing bodily marks in the Quran," *Bulletin of the School of Oriental and African Studies* 78, no. 1 (2015): 41–51.

46. Laury Silvers, "Early Pious, Mystic Sufi Women," in *The Cambridge Companion to Sufism*, ed. L. Ridgeon (Cambridge: Cambridge University Press, 2014), 43.

47. Fuad Matthew Caswell, *The Slave Girls of Baghdad: The Qiyān in the Early Abbasid Era* (London: I. B. Tauris, 2011), 5, 14.

Alongside the celebrated expertise of the *qiyān*, chroniclers duly record tropes of their bodily excess, decadence, and hypersexuality.[48] Courtiers often elegize Black women for their beauty through the idiom of monetary value and luxury, likening them to expensive goods like aloeswood and musk. The link between these impressions and East African women such as Maymūna was, of course, neither universal nor determinative. Some works advising on the purchase of enslaved women alternatively intimate that though East African women were ideal for household work, they were less coveted than their counterparts, such as Persians and Berbers, for concubinage and the familial and sexual responsibilities that it entails. The infamous exordium of the Iraqi physician Ibn Buṭlān's (d. 1063) eleventh-century epistle, "Risāla Jāmiʿa li-Funūn al-Nāfiʿa fī Shirā al-Raqīq wa-Taqlīb al-ʿAbīd" ("The Collected Arts of Use in Buying and Inspecting Slaves") declares that one ought to purchase Berber women for pleasure, Byzantine women for caregiving, Persian women for childbearing, Zanj women as wet nurses, and Meccan women as singers; Abyssinian women are left out here entirely, only to come up later, suggesting they are not epitomes of any of the foregoing skills.[49]

The fourth part of his epistle is devoted to an account of the uses of slaves and slave women by nation. *Ḥabashiyyāt*, or Abyssinians, of whom Maymūna is ostensibly one, are described as fragile—tending to be quite thin and sickly—but lovely in comparison with many of their Black peers, and said to offer "goodness and comfort, and docility under obligation." The trope of their sexualized graciousness but relative weakness or infirmity carries several centuries in related bodies of literature, with the Mamluk-era slave manual *al-Qawl al-Sadīd fī Ikhtiyār al-Imāʾ wa-l-ʿAbīd* by the Egyptian physician Maḥmūd al-Amshāṭī al-ʿAyntābī (d. 1496) in turn declaring that *ḥabashiyyāt* are devoted to their men (*rijālahun*), who take pleasure in their "warm wombs" (*bi-sukhūna arḥāmihun*), but that they nonetheless bear frail and petty children.[50]

A final telling remark with respect to Fāṭima's attitude is Ibn Buṭlān's statement that "whenever [Zanj slaves'] blackness is increased, their

48. And, as Pernilla Myrne shows, at times the *qiyān* directly addressed, embraced, or inverted these stereotypes. Pernilla Myrne, *Female Sexuality in the Early Islamic World: Gender and Sex in Arabic Literature* (London: I. B. Tauris, 2020), esp. 137–38.

49. Ibn Buṭlān, "Risālat Jāmiʿat al-Funūn al-Nāfiʿa fī Shirā al-Raqīq wa-Taqlīb al-ʿAbīd," 352.

50. Muẓaffar al-Dīn Abū-l-Thanāʾ Maḥmūd ibn Aḥmad al-ʿAyntābī al-Amshāṭī al-Ḥanafī, *Al-Qawl al-Sadīd fī Ikhtiyār al-Imāʾ wa-al-ʿAbīd* (Erfurt, Germany: Ms. orient A 1237, Universitäten Erfurt/Gotha), fol. 11v–12r.

countenances are uglier, their teeth sharper, and their usefulness diminished."[51] Elsewhere, when discussing the schemes used by slave-sellers (*nakhkhāsūn*) to entice buyers, Ibn Buṭlān notes some tips and tricks for altering aspects of skin color that are less-than-desirable; dark skin can be made to appear golden (*dhahabiyya*) if drenched a few times a day with caraway water, and black skin made to shine through the application of violet oil; white skin was subject to schemes that would remove redness and make it appear to glow.[52] Implicitly, brightening the skin in these ways made it appear healthier and more appealing. In responding strongly to Maymūna's blackness (*sawāduhā*), Fāṭima is perhaps enregistering Maymūna, incongruously, into a set of classed practices and standards of beauty that mean little for the princess in her homeland. Unlike ʿAbd al-Wahhāb, Fāṭima seems unable to recognize and navigate the cultural and social facts of her new surroundings.

Greater situational awareness is demonstrated by al-Baṭṭāl, albeit with specific ends in mind. Fāṭima tasks him with using his linguistic prowess to convey ʿAbd al-Wahhāb's parting missive to Maymūna. Maymūna had recently killed another Muslim messenger sent her way, and so the stakes of al-Baṭṭāl's tact are particularly high in an already heated moment:

> [Al-Baṭṭāl] called to her, saying, "O princess, God Almighty said that there is no task upon the Messenger save to give notice.[53] . . . I have come to you risking my soul, though I am indeed confident in the favor of your elegance and goodness of your lineage [*a-lā annanī wāthiq bi-jamīl ẓarfik wa-ṭīb ʿunṣurik*]. This is a letter addressed to you from the prince ʿAbd al-Wahhāb, and should you reply with kindness, then I shall give thanks and favors to my Lord, for He is known for kindness. And if not, then I shall return to him and relay the story to him, and I know he shall surely die of sorrow and bite his fingertips with worry."[54]

In appealing to her better nature, the clever al-Baṭṭāl takes care to flatter Maymūna's noble mien, addressing her as a princess and remarking on her elegance (*ẓarf*) and pedigree (*ʿunṣur*). Yet his overture also underscores a central difference between Maymūna's life as a heretofore unattached woman and her prospective future as ʿAbd al-Wahhāb's wife in the

51. Ibn Buṭlān, "Risāla Jāmiʿa li-Funūn," 374.

52. Ibn Buṭlān, 379.

53. This borrows from a recurrent phrase in the Qurʾān. See Q 5:99, Q 24:54, Q 29:18.

54. *Sīrat Dhāt al-Himma*, XXXVII:33.

lands of Islam: her wifely eligibility relies on assimilatory structures that hinge on what Sarah Bowen Savant calls the "essential human practice" of selectively remembering and forgetting one's prior genealogical affinities in order to embed in a new social order, employing "an ideology of election" that preserves and elevates the Arab and Arabized core of the Muslim *umma* in the text.[55] Although in less traumatic ways than with ʿAntar's mother, Zabība, Maymūna's kingly inheritance does not follow her substantively into her new life. Though she continues to be known by the rarefied title *malika*, queen, among her comrades, she principally becomes subsumed into the collective of *al-umarāʾ*, or the generals of the Muslims; she presides over movable armies rather than a territorialized realm. In a pattern reminiscent of discussions of *kafāʾa*, or spousal sufficiency, in which a partner's status is supposed to insulate their betrothed from reputational, financial, and legal harm (*ḍarar*), Maymūna's lineage only burnishes her suitedness to ʿAbd al-Wahhāb and enriches his position.

True to this, when Maymūna does ultimately wed, conform herself to ʿAbd al-Wahhāb and Fāṭima's form of Islam, and ride into battle against the Byzantines in their cause, she brings the entirety of her large, "jet-black" army with her into the fold. Within a new land and matrix of norms and expectations, Maymūna's blackness and that of her troops quickly becomes instrumental to her martial achievements because of its extraordinariness in many senses of the term. In one of her early battles against the Byzantines, Maymūna tells her army,

> "When you dismount on campaign, uncover your heads [*kashafū ruʾūsakum*] and go forth; I swear by He who compels the senses, I will snuff out the breath of anyone I see with a covered head [*mā raʾīt minkum mughaṭṭī al-raʾs akhmadt min al-anfās*]! I want nothing from this except that when [the Byzantines] see your countenances, they'll think they're the faces of demons [*ruʾūs al-ʿafārīt*], and death will overtake them. I shall be the first to expose my head [*awwal man yakshif raʾsahu anā*], and I'll dive into the battle's dust and murk, for there's no transgression [*faḍīḥa*] and no shame [*ʿār*] in me doing that if it is done in obeisance to the Great and All-Forgiving [God]." Not a moment later (O sirs!) the Byzantines marched forward, approaching like a deluge released from a milk-camel's teat, at which point Maymūna uncovered her head, her black hair gleaming like the dusk, and the other Blacks did the same.[56]

55. Sarah Bowen Savant, *The New Muslims of Post-Conquest Iran*, 22, 50.
56. *Sīrat Dhāt al-Himma*, XXXVIII:19.

Maymūna's move proves to have been prescient, for, as the narrator of the text explains to us,

> Among [the enemy general Qarāqūnā's] companions, there were peoples who had never before seen Blacks, nor had anyone whose color was black even once entered their thoughts, so when they looked that day upon the Black [soldiers], terror and trembling overcame them, and the Blacks attacked their ranks with sword-blows.[57]

Maymūna's blackness is not only a source of strategic advantage in battle, but moreover its use in intimidating the Muslims' foes constitutes a righteous act that defies religio-legal and sartorial convention. Elsewhere in the epic, covering one's hair becomes a way of signifying not only piety but nobility; as a young girl, Fāṭima continues to veil after being enslaved as a war captive to indicate her sense of freedom. Enslaved women were typically prohibited from covering their hair and had different prescriptions of *ʿarwa*, or physical thresholds of modesty, than the free.[58] By emphasizing the unique capacity that her blackness confers to perform acts that are simultaneously supportive of her new community and premised on bending both her class and her gender, Maymūna's character shores up the impression of Black people, and particularly Black women, as paradoxically dangerous and domesticable: when used to serve the Muslims in their own realm, Black femininity exerts a positive and contained power, where abroad it had connoted chaos and existential threat.

When a racialized individual travels and is re-raced, she becomes interpolated into new social structures and acquires different significances, and Maymūna is seemingly aware of this. She is also aware of the discomfort and destabilization that such a shift can cause, as are her new Muslim brethren; when Maymūna is captured in a battle, ʿAbd al-Wahhāb becomes instantly concerned that her freshly converted troops, brought in under the care of their once-and-future owner, will "recall their homeland" and defect. His fears are realized when a faction of the new Black troops tries to ransom him to the Byzantines—when Maymūna reunites with her army, she beats them into submission and retakes command.[59]

57. *Sīrat Dhāt al-Himma*, XXXVIII:19.

58. On the significance of maintaining a distinction between free and unfree Muslim women even in prayer, see Ash Geissinger, "'Umm al-Dardāʾ Sat in *Tashahhud* Like a Man': Towards the Historical Contextualization of a Portrayal of Female Religious Authority," *The Muslim World* 103 (2013): 313–14.

59. *Sīrat Dhāt al-Himma*, XXXVIII:18.

A brief flash-forward is likewise instructive: when much later Maymūna's remaining men convert *en masse* to Christianity, this time following Maymūna's directives, they are subsequently moved to revert to Islam not by the promise of serving ʿAbd al-Wahhāb or other Muslim warriors, but by the beauty of the Qurʾān itself. They find that they are innately able to preserve its chapters, while nothing of the Gospels (*al-Injīl*) has stuck. Though little of their day-to-day experience has changed—they are still a band of militants serving this or that commander and community—the soldiers profess shock at the totalizing effects of following Maymūna out of the religion on their mindfulness of the hereafter: "What is this forgetfulness that has enclosed us, as if we had never heard the Qurʾān or learned the *sharīʿa*?" In a didactic flood of recollection, the men then list off central obligations in the religion, such as the five daily prayers and congregating in the mosque and performing ablutions with water or sand—as opposed to Christians who boast of not having touched water for decades—and abstaining from illicit sex, lest they be punished with "100 lashes," unlike the Christians who are obsessed with women.[60] Where previously Maymūna had kept these tentatively Islamized men tethered to other Muslims through bonds of service, they are now able to recognize that Islam supersedes these bonds and depart Maymūna's service upon her Christianization.

In putting them to distinct uses, entailing discrete codes of behavior and standards of treatment, Maymūna has participated in enclaving the Black, newly Muslim soldiers in her charge even as they acquire the traditional knowledge that is so often adduced as the foundation for social mobility. She reifies her people's difference in laxer codes of modesty—a feature typical to underclasses in both medieval Christian and Muslim societies—and their subjection to exploitation and abuse. Like ʿAbd al-Wahhāb socializing his Black guards as *mawālī*, Maymūna ushers her troops into their new identities not only as Muslims but also as racialized and subordinated others operating within another culture's worldly structures. In this she is both an earthly commander and spiritual guide, and we are cued throughout that she began to ready herself for a version of this role in youth. For a time before her descent into villainy, Maymūna expertly serves the overarching moral interests of *Sīrat Dhāt al-Himma*, expanding Islam's reach and advancing its aims in terms of her Arab(ized) counterparts' aspirations at their geopolitical frontiers. When she begins to chafe at the zero-sum stakes of loyalty to her new community, though, it is ruinous.

60. *Sīrat Dhāt al-Himma*, L:36–37.

Questioning Power, Changing Loyalties, Courting the Cosmos

Like Abū'l-Hazāhiz in chapter 5, Maymūna quickly comes to take a dim view of the of the ʿAbbasid caliph in her time fighting Muslims' wars. By the time that Maymūna has ensconced herself in the Muslim armies, the days of al-Rashīd have long passed; his young son, al-Muʿtaṣim (r. 833–842), has succeeded an elder sibling on the throne. Perhaps the most illustrious of the caliph al-Muʿtaṣim's achievements is his development of an institution that would mark caliphates and sultanates across central Islamic lands from that point forward: the Turkic standing army, garrisoned under his rule at the new capital city of Samarra, just north of Baghdad.

To maintain Baghdad throughout this time, al-Muʿtaṣim relied heavily on Isḥāq b. Ibrāhīm, of the elite Persian Tahirid line. He kept as one of his military leaders and mentees the Turk Ītākh, about whom he can be seen complaining viciously to Isḥāq behind his back in the annals of al-Ṭabarī, with Isḥāq commiserating that in patronizing the Turks al-Muʿtaṣim has selected men for their "branches" but not their "roots."[61] The hierarchical dynamic between the two men, one a vizier and the other a *ḥājib*, or guard, is represented clearly in an anecdote from the Buyid advisor Hilāl al-Ṣabī''s (d. 1056) *Rusūm Dār al-Khilāfa (Illustrations of the Caliphal Court)*, in which al-Muʿtaṣim attempts to host an audience of jurists (*quḍāt*) while drinking a possibly boozy looking julep mixed with water from a luxe crystal vessel. After Isḥāq commands Ītākh to remove the goblet from al-Muʿtaṣim, allow their guests entry, and return it to him after they depart, the caliph retorts, "Do not contradict me! I wanted that julep, which was diluted with water." Isḥāq replies that the jurists may not have seen it as such: "Though one might say 'it was julep,' another might say, 'it was wine [*khamr*],'" at which the caliph concedes that he made the correct judgment. Isḥāq can verbally advise, disagree, and cajole, while Ītākh silently follows the orders of both men.[62]

Jere Bacharach observes that after a century of frequent references to "Zanjī" military slaves garrisoned in various parts of Iraq, from the 820s during the rule of al-Muʿtaṣim's predecessor until the Zanj revolt of the 870s and 880s, Black military units are de-emphasized in ʿAbbasid chronicles. He writes that "this may reflect their absence or, more likely, their

61. Matthew Gordon, The Breaking of a Thousand Swords: A History of the Turkish Military of Samarra (A.H. 200–275/815–889 C.E.) (Albany: State University of New York Press, 2001), 148–49.

62. Hilāl b. al-Muḥsin al-Ṣābi', *Rusūm dār al-khilāfa*, ed. Mikhā'īl ʿAwwād (Beirut: Dār al-Rā'id al-ʿArab, 1986), 73.

relative unimportance in the eyes of the chroniclers," whose attention instead is diverted to Turkic soldiery.[63] The *sīra* would seem to reflect this as well. Al-Muʿtaṣim is shown allying himself with the "King of the Turks," a man named Āt, and is the first ruler in the text to have done so. When the crypto-Christian *qāḍī* ʿUqba is serving duplicitously at al-Muʿtaṣim's court, he praises an independent Black warrior that the caliph had elevated in Malatya in a fit of anger against ʿAbd al-Wahhāb because, unlike the latter, this soldier doesn't incur the liability of "relying on the fighting [abilities] of vile Blacks [*wa-yattakil ʿalā qitāl al-sūdān al-andhāl*]."[64] Various scholars have rightly questioned the overextension of the argument that al-Muʿtaṣim's reign inducted a rigidly fixed system in which Turks would thenceforth comprise the upwardly mobile cavalry of Muslim armies and Black people the underprivileged infantry. This dichotomy is often signified by the association in translations and research of the term *mamlūk*, often used for cavalrymen, with whiteness, and *ʿabd*, for infantrymen, with blackness. Eve Troutt Powell shows that by the late Ottoman era this "Manichaean" usage had indeed solidified, as evidenced in the historical writings of Egyptian administrator ʿAlī Mubārak (d. 1893).[65] Hannah Barker notes, however, that for the Mamluks who acted as Ottomans' dynastic predecessors in Egypt, the word *mamlūk* may have still applied infrequently to East African soldiers, despite the men who gave the sultanate its name being themselves Turkic and Circassian.[66] We might nonetheless infer that in al-Muʿtaṣim's era a shift of power structures took place that threatened the possibility of the military's ethnic ranks closing in ways that achieved popular resonance.

The fictionalized al-Muʿtaṣim of the *sīra* frequently treats the heroic ʿAbd al-Wahhāb and his peers as expendable, to Maymūna's fury. When al-Muʿtaṣim captures ʿAbd al-Wahhāb in order to take the city of Āmid for himself, Maymūna cuts through Āt and his troops to reunite with him, driving a sword through the Turkic king's chest. She refuses to release ʿAbd al-Wahhāb and his comrades, though, until they promise her revenge against the caliph, intoning that she does not protect cowards and cautioning that if ʿAbd al-Wahhāb resubmits himself into al-Muʿtaṣim's service, "he will have lost his manhood [*ʿadam murūʾatahu*]."[67] Maymūna's

63. Bacharach, "African Military Slaves," 473.

64. *Sīrat Dhāt al-Himma*, XLI: 56.

65. Eve Troutt Powell, *Tell This in My Memory: Stories of Enslavement from Egypt, Sudan, and the Ottoman Empire* (Stanford, CA: Stanford University Press, 2012), 14.

66. Barker, *That Most Precious Merchandise*, 57 and 229n145.

67. *Sīrat Dhāt al-Himma*, XLI:23.

suspicions are realized when, not long after, al-Muʿtaṣim recaptures ʿAbd al-Wahhāb along with Fāṭima, al-Baṭṭāl, Maymūna herself, and several of their best Black generals. He imprisons them all underground for seven years, during which time they grow thin and unkempt; in their first battle after being released, Fāṭima notes that she can still see traces of starvation in Maymūna's disposition. While in prison, just when ʿAbd al-Wahhāb has finally sworn to serve no caliph nor imam and begun to hatch plans for either repairing to the Hijaz or, if that remains unsafe, carving out some portion of Byzantine territory in "Amorium or Makūriya" and ceasing his raiding, the band is sprung free by an anxious crowd of Muslims.[68] Baghdad is under new threat from a Byzantine usurper named Baḥrūn who has captured al-Muʿtaṣim and pitched the city into chaos. ʿAbd al-Wahhāb is quick to assert that "For the sake of the religion, we should not try to keep ourselves from them. God Almighty will not forgive us if we forsake them."[69] After himself being freed, in an act of abject humility, al-Muʿtaṣim goes to Fāṭima on foot and apologizes to her personally. Once again, Maymūna finds herself fighting in the caliph's interests as a proxy for that of all pious Muslims.

Her time in al-Muʿtaṣim's subterranean cells was not Maymūna's first experience of imprisonment. Eighteen years prior, while pregnant with ʿAbd al-Wahhāb's child, she had been captured alongside the princess Nūrā, herself pregnant with al-Baṭṭāl's. They were held by a Byzantine ruleã who abused them vigorously; after failing to coerce Maymūna into sex, he throws her newborn child into the Mediterranean and orders Nūrā's newborn child killed (he earns the name Madhbaḥūn, which evokes butchery, because his execution was ordained but not fulfilled). Upon being retrieved by the people who would raise him, Maymūna's lost child becomes known as Baḥrūn, a name evoking the sea, and rises to be the mighty warrior who now threatens the Muslim heartland. His sidekick and vizier is Madhbaḥūn, who is the spitting image of his father, al-Baṭṭāl. If her disenchantment with al-Muʿtasim's leadership is Maymūna's first ideological break with her peers, her reunion with Baḥrūn is the first emotional fissure.

Before Baḥrūn's identity is revealed, his vizier Madhbaḥūn's comes to light when, having been captured by the Muslims, Nūrā sees him and immediately faints. When she wakes, she asserts that he must be her child; to confirm it, his birthmarks are inspected and his adoptive

68. *Sīrat Dhāt al-Himma*, XLII:7. Makūriya may be identified with Malūriya, mentioned in other chronicles.

69. *Sīrat Dhāt al-Himma*, XLII:8.

mother summoned to explain. Madhbaḥūn immediately accepts Islam. Later, Maymūna sighs to Nūrā, "I've despaired of having children and immersed myself in *jihād* and obedience to the Lord of all worshippers."[70] Premonitorily, Nūrā comforts her by saying that God may yet grant her fortune in children.

Baḥrūn and his mother reconnect a short time later in the heat of battle, with the Byzantine commander making good on his threats to strike to the heart of the caliphate. Together, Fāṭima and Maymūna give chase as Baḥrūn leaves the battlefield, pursuing him into unknown territory and then dismounting and devolving into hand-to-hand combat. Fāṭima subdues Baḥrūn and is just about to strike off his head with her sword when Maymūna spots an amulet (*taʿwīdh*) on his person. Maymūna then relates the story of having given her newborn baby an amulet from her childhood while in the Byzantines' clutches in the hopes it would ward off the jinn. She adds that it was a locket-like talisman with a text (*kitāb*) inside—likely rolled into a scroll—that she wore on her forearm throughout her young life, with her name inscribed in it "in the language of the Zanj [*bi-kalām zanjī*]" on one side and an "image of a Black woman (*sawdāʾ*)" on the other.[71]

This detailed description of the amulet embeds a variety of geocultural references. Maymūna specifies the language used, but not the script, though the Zanj were said to lack their own writing system according to multiple Arab chroniclers. Implicitly, Maymūna's name is different in the language in which the locket is inscribed. Zanjī language also would seem to recall us to the East African coast, with many early medieval references to a "Zanj language" (*lughat al-zanj*) conveying into Arabic pieces of Swahili, Malagasy, and various Bantu dialects.[72] Is the image of a Black woman

70. *Sīrat Dhāt al-Himma*, XLIII:35.

71. *Sīrat Dhāt al-Himma*, XLIII:51–53.

72. In *Fakhr al-Sūdān*, al-Jāḥiẓ seems to cite Bantu-derived words for biting ants and dogs when discussing Zanzibari tribes, whom he states refer to themselves as "Ant" and "Dog," followed by glosses (*takfū wa-tanbū*). Marina Tolmacheva has noted that he among others uses Arabizations of the Swahili terms for some of the Zanzibar archipelago's islands, albeit he takes them to be tribal monikers. Edgar Gregersen, following Carl Mienhof, suggests that the earliest known recorded Bantu word is attested in medieval Arabic writings. The word *mganga*, for a healer or diviner, also appears in al-Idrīsī's geographic writings on the present-day Kenyan coast. Several authors mention "Zanji" terms for fruits and animals that are actually from Swahili. Tolmacheva, "Toward a Definition of the Term *Zanj*," 107; al-Jāḥiẓ, *Kitāb al-Bayān wa-l-Tabyīn*, vol. 3, 33; al-Jāḥiẓ, *Rasāʾil al-Jāḥiẓ*, 210–11; Edgar C. Polomé, "Swahili in Tanzania," in *Language in Tanzania*, ed. Edgar C. Polomé and C.P. Hill (London: Routledge, 1980), 81–82; Bernard Lewis: *Islam: From the Prophet Muhammad to the Capture of Constantinople*, vol. 2 (New York: Walker and Co., 1974), 117–18;

a god? A demon? An ancestor? A ruler? Scroll-and-case style amulets are used throughout both Muslim and Christian parts of East Africa, and their symbolic lexicon likewise crosses confessional lines; layering faces and eyes into Ethiopian medicinal amulets is especially common, but the earliest extant Ethiopian healing scroll hails from the early sixteenth century and their illustrations are part of a broader set of pictorial norms.[73] In their figural depictions of demons art historians have found the influence of Coptic talismans, and in their geometric patterning influence from Arab and Islamic sources. Methods for creating effective amulets continued to be circulated through the translation of occult texts in whole or part, as Geʾez versions of the Arabic *Shams al-Maʿārif* (*Sun of Knowledge*) attest.[74] Provenance notwithstanding, Maymūna either understood the talisman from her childhood as an apotropaic item to ward off jinn specifically or else she seamlessly integrated a ritual object from her prior system of belief into her Muslim practices, even while captured by Christians.

Baḥrūn quickly accepts that Maymūna could be his mother due to indicators of belonging with which he is intimately familiar. He states, "One sign that I am her child is that I have recognized my color differs from the Byzantines, for I am very dark [*asmar ghamīq al-samra*]." And, as a formidable leader, Baḥrūn asks after his father's *ḥasab* and *nasab*, or meritorious lineage, for further confirmation. On being apprised of ʿAbd al-Wahhāb's pedigree, he says, "by the Messiah, this is an honorable stock without any doubts, shame, degradations, or ignominy," and that he "knew" even before being told that this must have been so.[75] Yet there is one way in which Baḥrūn will continue to diverge from his parents: at first it is impossible for him to leave the religion he has known since childhood, but perhaps with time he will come to Islam of his own choosing. Maymūna clings to this vague possibility in much of what ensues.

In his discussion of the Persian and Urdu storytelling traditions most apposite the Arabic *sīras*, namely *qiṣṣas* and *dāstāns* such as the *Hamzanāma*, Pasha Khan notes that storytellers were practiced in and spoke openly

Edgar Gregersen, *Language in Africa: An Introductory Survey* (New York: Gordon and Breach, 1977), 91; Carl Meinhof, "Afrikanische Worte in orientalischer Literatur," *Zeitschrift für Eingeborenen-Sprachen* 10 (1919–20): 147–52. I am indebted to Kristina Richardson for these final few citations.

73. Kristen Windmuller-Luna, "Ethiopian Healing Scrolls," in *Heilbrunn Timeline of Art History* (New York: The Metropolitan Museum of Art, 2015), http://www.metmuseum.org/toah/hd/heal/hd_heal.htm.

74. Jacques Mercier, *Ethiopian Magic Scrolls* (New York: G. Braziller, 1979), 10.

75. *Sīrat Dhāt al-Himma*, XLI:52–53.

of the art of deferment.[76] In a sessions-based recitational milieu, extending a small plot point over many hours and hundreds of proverbial or real pages was an asset. Many threads throughout the *sīra* similarly reach, unresolved, into the future. It is rare, however, for one's actual religious standing to remain ambiguous; villains might dissimulate and budding heroes might convert, but to and from what is typically clearly defined. Maymūna, whose exact point of entry into Islam is itself ambiguous, meanwhile makes an extremely gradual exit. For a while, she attempts to balance supporting her newfound son in all his grand ambitions with maintaining her personal piety. ʿAbd al-Wahhāb and Fāṭima repeatedly tell her that this is impossible. The tension begins with star-crossed love. Baḥrūn becomes sick with affection for a Byzantine princess, Marjāna, who has converted to Islam. ʿAbd al-Wahhāb sees an opportunity. He asks that al-Muʿtasim offer Baḥrūn his desired bride if he accepts Islam. When Baḥrūn refuses, al-Muʿtasim betroths himself to Marjāna instead. At first, Baḥrūn resolves to kill his mother, spring a captive ʿUqba free, and return to Byzantine lands, but he then decides instead to "lament over his passions to her. He said, 'If I do not join with [Marjāna], I will surely die,' and after all, this is his mother and she has no son but him." Maymūna duly comes to his aid—the text reminds us that she has no wish to lose her son over a Byzantine concubine (*jāriya rūmiyya*) going to the caliph over him, when the "commander of the faithful has how many others like her [*wa-kam li-amīr al-muʾminīn mithlihā*]?" Maymūna kidnaps Marjāna and "corrupts" four thousand of her Black soldiers, and they abscond.[77]

Maymūna's increasing isolation and tenacious attachment to her son as she cuts this path brings her to a spiritual crossroads. While persuading her soldiers to join her, she does not overtly sway them from Islam, nor does she offer them the prospect of Christian conversion. Rather, she ambiguously announces that "we will follow our religion (*wa-naḥnu ʿalā dīninā*) and, wherever we are, will eat our bread from what we take with our swords."[78] This may imply reverting to the practices they had in their homeland and among their people or finding their own more proprioceptive approach to Islam in a non-Muslim realm, which comes with the hermeneutical and practical challenges of being unmoored from learned authorities. A similar phrase (*wa-kān ʿalā dīn qawmihi*) is used in both senses in exegetical debates about whether Muḥammad had religious intuition prior to receiving instruction in divine precepts, as with traditions

76. Khan, *The Broken Spell*, 116.
77. *Sīrat Dhāt al-Himma*, XLIV:4–8.
78. *Sīrat Dhāt al-Himma*, XLIV:6.

demonstrating that even before the Qurʾān's revelation, Muḥammad withdrew from idols, became circumcised, performed ablutions, and so on.[79]

ʿUqba takes it upon himself to begin to recommend Christianity to Maymūna's men as they approach Byzantium. He does so by recalling the soldiers' precarious and undervalued position in the Muslim community, saying the Byzantine king will reward them with robes and positions of honor as well as elite wives. Moreover, he will give them "rest from battle and confrontation, for they left their own country at ten thousand in number and only these four thousand remain. Were they to stay in the lands of Islam another year, there would be not a one left."[80] ʿUqba says this not unironically, having repeated before to both Byzantine and Muslim audiences that Black people are incentivized only by money and gifts because of "how they are." Maymūna and her men are meanwhile pulled in split directions not by an embarrassment of choice, but by a consistent pattern of seeking actualization within their religious communities while being kept in continued suspense.

Suspense is likewise laced through Maymūna's next meeting with ʿAbd al-Wahhāb, who has written her off as "irrational" and "blameworthy," and her son as "accursed." He rages that she has "disbelieved after having believed," which is among the gravest sins, to which Maymūna replies,

> No, by the truth of the Most Compassionate and Merciful, but necessities have compelled [*tulajjiʾ al-ḍarūrāt*] me toward risking perilous ventures [*ilā rukūb al-maḥdhūrāt*]. And you know that you have children besides him and you worry over each one, while as for me, I have no child other than him and have neither the capacity to separate from him [*wa-lā baqayt aqdar ʿalā firāqihi*] nor to command myself to distance from him [*wa-lā tuṭāwiʿnī nafsī ʿalā buʿdihi*]. I am following the religion of Islam and not his.[81]

ʿAbd al-Wahhāb then retorts that one cannot remain a true Muslim while serving the calamitous ends of a Christian unbeliever (*wa-tabghī naḥs kāfir min dīn al-naṣrāniyya*), to which Maymūna concedes, "You are correct, that is not permitted in the religion of the Eternal One, but Baḥrūn's unbelief will not last." Maymūna's language here toggles between expressions

79. For an example of this phrase's contested meaning that collects several scholars' opinions on the question, see al-Maqrīzī, *Imtāʿ al-Asmāʿ*, vol. 2 (Beirut: Dār al-Kutub al-ʿIlmiyya, 1999), 357.

80. *Sīrat Dhāt al-Himma*, XLIV:17

81. *Sīrat Dhāt al-Himma*, XLIV17.

of her own cognizance and control and a lack thereof. She is adamant that she continues to follow Islam and will not succumb to her son's influence through sheer proximity, yet she also acknowledges that she feels she has no power to deny herself that same proximity. Their closeness is at once potent and limited in its ultimate effects. Maymūna is proverbially at the reins of her experience, which she describes euphemistically through a reference to mounting camels (*rukūb*), at which she is quite expert—only rather than riding beasts she sits astride danger itself (*al-maḥdhūrāt*). At the same time, Maymūna acknowledges feeling pulled to do so by needs that seem to exceed her power. She is at once aware that her actions skirt the edge of permissibility and hopeful that her risk will be rewarded by her son's belief. Her statements will prove premonitory: Maymūna is indeed part of a greater plan in which her free will becomes implicated, and her son will indeed become Muslim in the process.

If in light of this ʿAbd al-Wahhāb's declarations of Maymūna's apostasy appear premature, they are quickly substantiated when Maymūna meets the aforementioned Byzantine king. Unlike Fāṭima and ʿAbd al-Wahhāb, he is immediately enamored of her inside and out, praising her eloquence, wisdom, "color like that of the glowering darkness," massive stature, and even her large ears. Maymūna is endeared to him, particularly his pale, "moon-like" face, long hair, and flirtatious (*ghazal*) eyes. The "devil enters her form," and when the king at first denies her a betrothal because she is not Christian, she instantly converts.[82] News of her full transformation reaches a gravely wounded ʿAbd al-Wahhāb, though not from Maymūna herself, but from forces well beyond her control. While sleeping, her former husband has a vision,

> In my dream, I saw the Messenger of God (peace and blessings upon him), being on the brink of death, and he was saying to me "O champion of the religion, rejoice in news of the Garden [*ibshir bi-l-janna*]." I replied, "O Messenger of God, pardon me, for I cannot get up for you though the truth of your presence—God's peace and blessings upon you—demands it!" He asked, "What is wrong?" So I told him of the wound and that it was inflicted by my son, Baḥrūn. He said, "May God curse his mother, who has been repelled from the gate of the Most Merciful and turned toward unbelief after belief and left you forever. Be on your guard with her [*khudh ḥidhrak minhā*] and turn your heart from her." So I cried, then he said, "Look." Suddenly, there appeared a dome

82. *Sīrat Dhāt al-Himma*, XLIV:25.

> of green emerald, upon which ran chains of jewels. He said, "Look at what is inside it." So I looked, and within it was a girl [*jāriya*] that, were the people of the lower world to see her, they would prize over the sun and moon. She was saying to me, "O son of the worshipful renunciant [*yā ibn al-zāhida al-ʿābida*], who cries over Maymūna though she has left Islam, I shall be her substitute [*anā akūn lik ʿiwaḍuhā*]."[83]

The dream continues, with Muḥammad striking the wounded part of ʿAbd al-Wahhāb's body and the site healing. ʿAbd al-Wahhāb then asks whether the promised hour—for Muḥammad has shown him a glimpse of the hereafter—will soon approach. Muḥammad replies affirmatively, listing signs including that the Byzantines will reach Alexandria, while the Muslims will take Amorium.

Dreams are a potent tool for legitimation. They allow the dreamer to form relationships that are otherwise beyond reach and claim experience that is otherwise contested. In her work on Muslim oneiromantic practice, Mimi Hanaoka demonstrates that visions of the Prophet in places that he never traversed, appearing before types of people with whom he never spoke in life, serve to write new social and spatial ventures into Islam's prehistory. Dreams create the possibility for "non-biological prophetic pedigree" by supplementing the authority latent in lines of kinship with that of unique, transcendent events.[84] Likewise, in his discussion of epistemologies of Muḥammad's body after his death, Michael Muhammad Knight shows that in dreamworlds, ethereal interactions with the Prophet postmortem are unbound from anxieties about his ongoing "intercorporeal" extensibility in the waking world.[85] At the same time, such appearances trouble the boundaries of the dreamer's self and of the independent actions and thoughts of those referenced in the dream. Dwight Reynolds states that in the widely accepted typology of dreams formulated in Islam's early period, "true dreams" are those dispatched by God, reaching a dreamer's inner world from the outside. These dreams come as *bushrā*, a form of "glad tiding," as above when Muḥammad tells ʿAbd al-Wahhāb to take heart in the imminence of the heavenly Garden (*ibshir bi-l-janna*). Their path was nonarbitrary: the receiver of such dreams must, somehow, matter.[86]

83. *Sīrat Dhāt al-Himma*, XLIV:26.

84. Mimi Hanaoka, *Authority and Identity in Medieval Islamic Historiography: Persian Histories from the Peripheries* (Cambridge: Cambridge University Press, 2016), 98.

85. Knight, *Muhammad's Body*.

86. Reynolds, "Symbolic Narratives of Self, 265.

ʿAbd al-Wahhāb's significance is further underwritten by a set of references throughout his prophetic encounter: he is referred to as *nāṣir al-dīn*, "champion of the religion," a title taken almost exclusively by leaders and military commanders. He is also lineally significant, with his heavenly mate referring to him as the son of a devout renunciant (*zāhida ʿābida*), a characterization frequently associated with those ascetic and mystical actors who pursue the types of gnosis (*maʿrifa*) that dreams and visions can enable.[87] Though Fāṭima is generally not characterized by her material renunciation or her gnosis, this description of her nonetheless resonates with myriad images of the ideal frontier warrior, or eponymous *mujāhid(a)*, as a person of exacting moderation, primed through self-mastery to "[conquer] the world's proud and decadent temporal powers."[88]

But what of the individual about whom the dream is most concerned? Although Maymūna has converted to Christianity of her own volition, ʿAbd al-Wahhāb's vision shows the Prophet himself cursing her and declaring that she has no path of return. Could she repent and revert to Islam if she wanted to? If her leaving Islam paved the way for ʿAbd al-Wahhāb to see the unseen, commune with Muḥammad, and have insight into the future, is she not still exerting a powerful presence in others' pious lives? After her former husband's dream, Maymūna continues to act as an uncanny instrument of fate for the text's Muslim heroes, evoking the superficiality of this world and the solidity of the next. She hones others' devotion through opposition and strengthens a community of which she has become bereft, the grander implications of which are not lost on her (she once accuses Baḥrūn of having made it impossible for her to reach the Garden herself).[89] When Baḥrūn converts to Islam himself and the two meet on the battlefield as enemies, Maymūna calls his newfound piety duplicitous, saying that he only had a change of heart when she had already sacrificed everything for him. When Maymūna then kills Baḥrūn with her own sword, this too has been foretold by a true dream, nearly identical to his father's. In Baḥrūn's, though, Muḥammad is not himself present and Baḥrūn knows his future heavenly bride—she is the even comelier mother of another Byzantine princess with whom he's since fallen in love on earth. Later, in the heat and dust of battle, Baḥrūn is seized by thirst. The heavenly woman reappears to him, glass of water in hand, and tells him his time is near, giving him the foresight to recite the *shahada* before his mother deals the fatal blow.[90]

87. On the specific uses of these titles, see chapter 3, note 51.
88. Sizgorich, *Violence and Belief*, 162.
89. *Sīrat Dhāt al-Himma*, XLIV:24.
90. *Sīrat Dhāt al-Himma*, XLIV:50–52.

Maymūna's ongoing, portentous intimacy with the unseen becomes especially clear when she and ʿAbd al-Wahhāb first clash in battle after her conversion. Their opposition is phrased in terms of the esoteric and exoteric meanings each holds for the other. As so often before, when Maymūna enters the fray, she introduces herself; however, the way in which she does so is new:

> For those who know me, you've been sufficed. For those who do not, I am Maymūna the Ḥabashiyya, daughter of King Damdamān, wedded to [the Byzantine King] Armanūs, Christianized into the religion of the church bell [*al-nāqūs*], and the Messiah has freed me from ʿAbd al-Wahhāb, he of the distressing face [*al-wajh al-kāliḥ*] and radiating blackness [*al-sawād al-lāʾiḥ*].[91]

That the Black princess Maymūna, here proudly proclaiming her East African royal lineage, also derides ʿAbd al-Wahhāb for his glowering expression and exterior darkness is at first incongruous, and even more so for its apparent eschatological overtones. The conspicuously pious ʿAbd al-Wahhāb, whose adherence to his beliefs left Maymūna struggling to accommodate even their own Christian son, is described as having a blackness that radiates or "scorches" like hellfire is said to in the Qurʾān. His face might on the one hand scowl, but on the other has the resonance of afflicting those whom he influences, and once again has resonances with the afterlife's fires that distort damned people's faces into grimaces (*wa-hum fīhā kāliḥūn*).[92] Phrased in active participles whose synonymy compounds, Maymūna seems to differentiate ʿAbd al-Wahhāb's darkness from her own in its nature and effects, using it to symbolize the otherworldly torment he inflicts, which no mortal human—save her—can sense. Following his vision, ʿAbd al-Wahhāb does indeed possess unique comprehension of Maymūna's fate, sealed by Muḥammad himself; perhaps she sees him as that fate incarnate. Upon hearing himself described in this way, ʿAbd al-Wahhāb is struck by horror (*al-zamaʿ*) and cannot stay in the saddle due to the force of his righteous indignation (*ghayra*).[93]

91. *Sīrat Dhāt al-Himma*, XLIV:28–29.

92. Q 23:104.

93. On the meanings of *ghayra*, which is often translated as "jealousy" but signifies a masculinized jealous guarding of one's honor and that of one's household—and especially its women—see Marion Katz, "Beyond Halal and Haram: Ghayra (Jealousy) as a Masculine Virtue in the Work of Ibn Qayyim al-Jawziya," *Cultural History* 8, no. 2 (2019): 202–25.

When one of ʿAbd al-Wahhāb's sons moves to defend his father against what he sees as an insult to his physical form, he depicts Maymūna in the reverse fashion. Where ʿAbd al-Wahhāb is characterized by numinous darkness, Maymūna is represented as being insubstantially, meaninglessly white. He says, "Look at your transparent whiteness [*bayāḍik al-shafāf*], such that you'd shame my father's blackness!" Maymūna then takes up this very phrase and turns it around in verse, intoning, "I have had good fortune in Armanūs, like a full moon ascendant, clouds yield to him / I meet his transparent whiteness and bejeweled body [*jism mujawhar*] with my intense blackness [*sawād fāḥim*]."[94]

The word *shafāf*, used here twice to modify "white," signals something that is clear in metaphor or actuality, or else diaphanous and see-through because it is so thin. Diamond, glass, and rock crystal are sometimes described as "transparently white" (*abyaḍ shafāf*). Is ʿAbd al-Wahhāb's son implying that Maymūna's whiteness-by-association with her spouse is invisible—a useless cover? Perhaps in inverting the insult and pairing it with a reference to his body being jewel encrusted, Maymūna implies that her new husband is so resplendently white that he is unaffected by her own blackness. That this is externalized in the form of bodily ornamentation may be a reminder of his worldly wealth. It may also be a reminder of the symbolism of surfaces themselves, as discussions of transparency and reflectivity bring to mind the knowledge of optics in the Arabic tradition, which elaborates the interactions between whiteness, light, shadow, and blackness. Consolidating and expounding the prior works of a variety of Muslim polymaths and "ancients" (*al-qudamāʾ*) in his commentary on his teacher, al-Ījī's (d. 1355) theological text, *al-Mawāqif fī ʿIlm al-Kalām*, the fourteenth-century Persian thinker al-Sharīf al-Jurjānī (d. 1414) discusses al-Ījī's section on theories of color, beginning with the Greeks' hypothesis that color is not intrinsic to objects, but an image given by the eye. He adds,

> If air that is illumined passes through a body (*jism*) that is entirely transparent, one perceives whiteness, and if [the air] is dark, then [one perceives] blackness, and if it is mixed, then a mixture of different colors depending on the degree of mixture. . . . Reflection only pertains to existent [colors] [*al-mawjūd*], and none exist except blackness, which does not reflect, or light that one perceives [*yukhayyal*] as whiteness.[95]

94. *Sīrat Dhāt al-Himma*, XLIV:29.

95. Al-Sharīf al-Jurjānī, *Sharḥ al-Mawāqif*, vol. 5, ed. Maḥmūd ʿUmar al-Damiyāṭī (Beirut: Dār al-Kutub al-ʿIlmiyya, 2012), 241.

Maymūna's whiteness here can only be an external reflection of her spouse's superficial form; her blackness can only yield to him as clouds do the moon in a play of light and perception, but not disappear. Nor does she seem to wish her own "intense blackness" away; it is ʿAbd al-Wahhāb's fulminating, esoteric darkness that disturbs her. Her new beloved's whiteness is phrased in sensorial terms, drawing on metaphors for the workings of the eye and the glow or clarity of materials, but does not approach her at once sacralizing and damning description of ʿAbd al-Wahhāb's blackness.

What are we to make of Maymūna's disenchantment with Islam, at first so slow and then immediate when presented with the prospect of marriage to a moon-like man who ensconces her in this "thin" or "crystalline," but also "delicate" whiteness? This might seem to fit the recurring pattern of Black men taking after Byzantine women, with the former following the rote trope of priapism and the latter of inducing gendered *fitna*, only now reversed by gender. Indeed, elsewhere Maymūna hews to tropes almost incongruously. She quickly follows up her newfound love with an apparently racialized backlash against her Black ex patterned directly on an uncomfortable theologization of his color in Muslim eschatological terms that cause ʿAbd al-Wahhāb to nearly fall off his mount and compel his son to rage, but that also is strongly associated with her new Christian interpretative touchstones. We have elsewhere seen Maymūna maximize while Muslim on Byzantine fears of Black people and demonization of blackness.

Thomas Nail exemplifies assemblages through the image of a constellation: nothing eternal and essential holds a constellation together, stars—or rather the light that reaches us from them—shift in our perspective through movement, birth, death, and those stars in a constellation have no intrinsic relation to one another in any case. It is the incident of recognizing relations that constitutes a constellation over and over, and that allows it to "change as the elements change in a kind of reciprocal feedback loop."[96] If we think about Maymūna's interactions with her world through the concept of assemblage, even within a consciously formulaic genre we need not see her as constrained to simply follow or subvert archetypes. Instead, each of her character's transformations is a relational event that transiently ties Maymūna to other forces and people, and that flows from gendered and raced trauma, misreading, or erasures and false equivalences. At times, she is openly critical of the supposed inflexibility of the social order through which this occurs. She resists being pigeon-holed into

96. Thomas Nail, "What Is an Assemblage?" *SubStance* 46, no. 1 (2017): 26.

particular expressions of heroism and anti-heroism, religiosity or irreligiosity, and at times even into Muslimness or Christianness. As a villain, Maymūna becomes the site of others' self-actualizing events, facilitating transcendent experiences by giving rise to dreams and visions through her actions despite, or perhaps because of, how she crosses these lines. When Maymūna is finally killed at Fāṭima's hand, after a cycle that spans over one thousand pages in modern editions, their fight is presaged by competing dreams, with each envisioning victory. For once, Maymūna's premonition is false, but this failure preserves what Kruk calls "narratological symmetry," balancing her explosive entrance into the story with her exit.[97] Throughout, she has remained unlike the other Christian foes while also becoming one of them, much as she had been among the Muslims.

Conclusion

This final chapter uses the closure of *Sīrat Dhāt al-Himma*'s cycle of travel in the *bilād al-sūdān* and the East African princess Maymūna's emergence from this episode into the text's wider world to illustrate three things: first, that in these narratives racialization of course cannot be divorced from gender, class, freedom/unfreedom, but also from movement. The way in which signifiers of identity travel or fail to do so in stories that span large geographic sweeps demonstrates an awareness of multiple, conflicting perspectives on how to construct a social body. In the *sīra*, we have encountered scenarios in which racialized language concerning Black Africans is used to conjure fear, imply the difficulty and triumph of the Muslims' proselytizing endeavors, create romantic tension, deepen irony, and valorize an underdog heroine's success or demonize her failures. Second, between the admittedly anachronistic poles of explicitly racist and anti-racist discourse, there lies a vast spectrum of ambiguous—even calculatedly ambivalent—racializing language that is no less othering for the fact that it is slipperier. Third, through Maymūna these more ambivalent articulations forge another faint and porous intracommunal boundary, namely, between perceived orthodoxy and heterodoxy among one's coreligionists.

The perception of Black African ways of embodying Islam as inherently nonnormative or heterodox—phrased as notional dichotomies between "authentic" local customs and "foreign" Arabized imports, although these are often carried to and fro by itinerant African Muslims themselves—has been an organizing principle in Orientalist studies and colonial endeavors.

97. Kruk, "The Princess Maymūnah," 439.

Rudolph Ware shows that it has also animated discourse among Muslims themselves.[98] Some trace perceptions of Black African heterodoxy to chronological causes, resulting from where Islam spread and when, others to geographical ones, resulting from who had close contact with whom. Following Chouki El Hamel and Bruce Hall, Ousmane Kane underscores the materially consequential ways that Muslims in West Africa have also participated in this discourse. They made and remade the category of "unbelief" among themselves, producing enslaveable populations and protected ones as well as the authority to delineate the two.[99]

Increasingly, intellectual historians provide correctives to how we think about people and ideas moving through time and space by de-emphasizing amorphous, uneven flows of influence in favor of multitudinous negotiations and exchanges. Though evocative, such descriptions still risk falling into a similar trap to what Shahab Ahmed has sketched with the erstwhile vogue of discussing many, if not infinite, "islams" rather than "Islam."[100] Attempts to resist essentializing both ignore insider discourses of universalism and sensationalize the existence of dissimilarities and differences that we take for granted in most other global human phenomena. Nonetheless, for the East African context of the *sīra*, M. N. Pearson's formulation of "coastal Islam" is germane in that it locates a "reciprocal" pattern of travel in the Indian Ocean, to and from institutions of traditional learning in southern Yemen.[101] With Maymūna we see a different alchemy of these same discursive and material elements. Her use of tutors, talismans, and habits of dress are emblematic of a heterogeneous zone of contact in the region Pearson refers to as "Ethiopia and the Horn," or *al-ḥabasha* in her story. These elements make it difficult to account fully for the timing and nature of Maymūna's own introduction to and acceptance of Islam, which is further overwritten by other characters' presumptions of her ignorance or impiety.

Within the *sīra* more broadly, racialized presumptions about how origins, status, and potential interact are explained using bodies of knowledge that are made available to the characters, be they genealogical and medical

98. Ware, *The Walking Qur'an*, esp. 22–25.

99. Ousmane Oumar Kane, *Beyond Timbuktu: An Intellectual History of Muslim West Africa* (Cambridge, MA: Harvard University Press, 2016), 61–64.

100. Shahab Ahmed, *What is Islam? The Importance of Being Islamic* (Princeton: Princeton University Press, 2016), 148–149.

101. M. N. Pearson, "The Indian Ocean and the Red Sea," in *History of Islam in Africa*, ed. Nehemia Levtzion and Randall L. Pouwels (Athens: Ohio University Press, 2012), 52–53.

or geographic and cosmological. Thus we find, for example, that the heat of the "fifth clime" is more than a civilized person—one used to living in walled buildings—can be expected to bear; common terms for tribes residing at the edges of the known world, such as Damdam and Lamlam, are appropriated into popular narrative with a view toward ethnographic verisimilitude. Even the language in which Fāṭima denies Maymūna's heroism (*mā sīmatuhā sīmat al-abṭāl*) has a physiognomic undertone, with the term *sīma* often used to describe aspects of the face, though it also has more numinous resonances. In Maymūna's bare-headed battle against the Byzantines, the signification of helpful servility through uncovering for the text's only Black woman hero, in contrast to the resolute veiling of its Arab ones, would seem to support Fāṭima's doubts, and her later apostasy even more so. If Abū'l-Hazāhiz's allegory of assimilation is complete, with cosmic and divine entities collaborating with earthly circumstance to bring him into the fold, Maymūna offers a portrait of what it looks like for these forces to be misaligned.

Because Maymūna passes from being a hero to a villain, we can see how her blackness is differently activated across this moral range. Scholarship on blackness in Arabic literature has often highlighted forms of racialization most familiar to a contemporary Euro-American readership, pointing to uncanny and painful echoes with modern representations, such as the description of Africans as having swollen lips, kinky hair, and defective intellects in Ibn Khaldūn's *Kitāb al-ʿIbar*, or enslaved Black men being represented as hypersexual and threatening to female purity in the *1001 Nights*. By comparison, cases in which admiration for Black people is expressed qua the same features that earn derision elsewhere—as when al-Jāḥiẓ extols Zanjī musicality in his *Fakhr al-Sūdān ʿalā-l-Bīḍān*, recalling the adage, "If a Zanj man fell from the sky, he'd hit the ground on the beat"—have at times been read as clarion, anti-racist reclamations, and therefore as resistive rather than as part of a parallel racializing discourse.[102] As we have seen throughout this book, not only does racialized invective construct race, but the equanimous appropriation of categories and tropes or vindicatory defense of others also does so. The condemnations of Maymūna's derisive remarks about ʿAbd al-Wahhāb's blackness and critical ironies of ʿUqba weaponizing his Black peers' poor treatment reify Black people as subject to specific conventions of literary and social engagement. Particularly salient to understanding how reification and destabilization are twinned

102. On this adage and the broader stereotype it connotes, see Bernard Lewis, *Race and Slavery in the Middle East: An Historical Inquiry* (Oxford: Oxford University Press, 1990), 93–94.

are the various mystical and esoteric traditions that are evoked subtly in Maymūna's tale, from her Zulaykha-like characterization as a newcomer in the community to her sustained role even outside of it as a bringer of dreams. These descriptions at once weave Maymūna into Muslim ways of making meaning and place her far outside the norm.

An ambivalent theophanic thread thus runs throughout Maymūna's narrative. Is she Zulaykha-like because she is a temptress, or because she is love manifest in its purest, most transcendent form? Are her qualities not like those of heroes on the physically observable and taxonomizable surface, or because her outward appearance guides Fāṭima to the heretofore unseen and uncategorized? Does she truly accept Islam and then apostatize, or was Maymūna in fact almost always Muslim in ways that went unnoticed in her early encounters with the *umma*'s Arab champions and long after she had parted from them? Does Maymūna bring others prophetic dreams and have her premonitions realized because the extent of her evil provokes divine intervention, or because she is herself a cipher for esoteric experience? That we cannot easily plot Maymūna's position in the aspirational history that I have outlined throughout the foregoing chapters is perhaps by design. She instead works, critically, at its limits.

Conclusion

Universal claims are always particular. They are made in specific contexts and represent specific interests in the name of all. What is interesting about universal claims is how they are developed, whom they serve, and with what implications.

DENISE KIMBER BUELL

I wrote this book in the hopes of rethinking the relationship of literature with history, of race with religion, of science with modernity, of blackness with Africanness, and of members of the Muslim world community with themselves and each other. I am aware that I have done so on the shifting terrain of both the sources and our present moment. I hope Remke Kruk will not mind my quoting a personal correspondence when I say that one of the complications of working with premodern popular literatures that, in their very materiality, are "epically" scaled is internal contradiction: "the minute you think you've reached a valid conclusion about a certain aspect, you almost immediately bump into a counterexample."[1] This is a problem noted by other scholars of the *sīra*s as well, particularly around the topic of racialization. Malcolm Lyons cites the seemingly paradoxical locutions of the Black hero ʿAbd al-Wahhāb, who "is made to say at the age of seven, 'God created me black because of his foreknowledge,' [then] can remark baldly, 'the blacks have no intelligence.'"[2] Blackness in these works oscillates between the symbolic and the real, the voiced and unvoiced, both because of the range of expressive norms and "availabilities"

1. Remke Kruk, personal correspondence, December 21, 2021.
2. Lyons, *Arabian Epic*, 1:25.

in which it is situated, and the many unique hands that have reworked the stories over time.

I have tried to lay out these tensions in the foregoing pages while also demonstrating that one can read these texts as indicating an ultimate coherence of function. They are both entertaining and didactic, exoticizing and assimilatory, literarily calibrated by craftsmen who were often lineal experts in their own right to heighten the stakes of an expanding world order but also to render that expansion as possible, and to grapple seriously with the pluralizing consequences of its ultimate success. I have argued that racialized protagonists, and particularly the Black ones that are central to the epics of ʿAntar, the tribe of Hilāl, and most especially of the princess/general Dhāt al-Himma, are a fulcrum around which the diversity of the Muslim world, and even the subterranean and superlunar beings that envelop it, is produced and fitted into its proper place. The way that this occurs looks different from text to text, even within a single *sīra*'s stream of tradition, yet to paraphrase from Denise Buell's work on early Christian sources, these texts all make particular universal claims about Muslim cohesion, Black-Arab relationality, and what brings people together and enables them to overcome, or else strategically deploy, their differences. Nonetheless, there may be a much different role for Black figures in other *sīra*s due to removes of time and space: those works that originated in the Mamluk era, which I have largely overlooked, make race differently with different geopolitical stakes in mind. Robert Irwin, for example, suggests that the overarching combat between descendants of Ḥām and Sām in the Egyptian *Sīrat Sayf* reflects the Mamluks' "interventionist" policies vis-à-vis the Nubian capital of Dongola to their south. At the same time, the fact that Black people are seen fighting alongside the Arab Muslims of the tale might reflect an interest in catering to fifteenth-century Cairo's diverse passers-by.[3]

Those *sīra* traditions extant in various parts of North Africa also continue to proliferate racial meanings in novel ways. A 2020 documentary series by Al Jazeera on the *sīra*s titled *Abṭālunā, Our Heroes,* shows one Egyptian guest expert discussing the raison d'être for Black heroes who team up with Arab ones in *Sīrat Dhāt al-Himma* as a rational outgrowth of the fact that the central conflicts of the *sīra*s are:

> Arab-Persian, Arab-Turk, Arab-Byzantine—struggles with [those whose skin is] the color white, and across time [*ṭūl al-waqt*], white-colored

3. Robert Irwin, "Review: The Adventures of Sayf ben Dhi Yazan: An Arab Folk Epic by Lena Jayyusi," *British Journal of Middle Eastern Studies* 24, no. 2 (1997): 322.

> folks have always repudiated the color black. Black people are [cast as] either primitives [*badu*] or uncivilized [*aghlaf*] or slaves [*ʿabīd*]. So these three heroes [Dhāt al-Himma, al-Baṭṭāl, and ʿAbd al-Wahhāb] arise, and among them there's ʿAbd al-Wahhāb in order to refute this view [*li-kay yarudd ʿalā hādhā al-raʾy*] and to say that 'these people who are black in color [*aṣḥāb hādhī al-lawn al-aswad*] are Arab, and so if Black people have any triumph [*ay intiṣār*], it's a triumph for the Arabs, and for the Arab race [*ʿirq al-ʿarab*].'[4]

At the same time, this picture of solidarity that bears forward echoes of postcolonialism and Pan-Africanism promotes a vision that, to many, is as yet unrealized. Across the Arabic-speaking world, scholars and activists are working to make sense of the ways that their experiences have been shaped not only by European colonialism, but by the region's own legacies of conquest, enslavement, migration, diaspora, and indigeneity and by the precolonial epistemologies of difference that worked to fix and hierarchize these flows of people. In doing so, they are working against what Ehud Toledano has called an "attitude hurdle": a prevailing view—all the more entrenched by Islamophobic and anti-Arab Western polemics that allege the extreme converse—that because Islam does not allow for the weaponization of differences of birth, wealth, origin, and so on among coreligionists, these things cannot have happened, or at least not on large enough social scales to be meaningful.[5]

Such characterizations of premodern Muslim-ruled and majority-Muslim societies go hand in hand with arguments discussed throughout this book against using the lenses supplied by theories of racialization to premodernity. These include the notion that racialization cannot occur in the absence of a strong, centralized state; that the lack of a specific, umbrella term for techniques of difference-making implies the absence of such techniques; that because race is constructed as a fixed biosocial category, fluidity of identities precludes racial resonances. Instead, throughout I have argued for the possibility of diffuse traditions of knowledge production and interpersonal literary-cum-moral cultivation within and across premodern empires doing racializing work. The various discourses

4. "al-Siyar al-Shaʿbiyya al-ʿArabiyya 9: al-Amīra Dhāt al-Himma," YouTube, uploaded by Al Jazeera Documentary (*al-Jazīra al-Wathāʾiqiyya*), accessed 10 July 2023, https://www.youtube.com/watch?v=03ybcjOqudY&list=PLmrET10kAE969YJBUlKVReAuY3LkSlApf&index=14, 7:35.

5. Ehud Toledano, *As If Silent and Absent: Bonds of Enslavement in the Islamic Middle East* (New Haven, CT: Yale University Press, 2007), 15–17.

explored here instructed audiences in the uneven experiences of how people with essentialized and embodied differences move through society. We have seen these differential experiences in even the most basic acts of labeling various characters as Black, and often not as white unless confronted with the prospect of blackness, as when ʿAbd al-Wahhāb's father al-Ḥārith digs in his heels about his complexion and ancestry. We have also seen blackness's disparate treatment emerge in more complex ways, as with Maymūna's constant difficulties with outwardly expressing and persuading people of her Muslimness, a unique problem within her broader narrative. Latent in the unevenness of various characters' mobility is whom the texts position as the default: who moves through the world at hand relatively unquestioned and with relative conversancy and ease? Whose claims on status and rightness carry the greatest weight? These are questions of how figures take on relative ontological value that gives their actions meaning distinct from that of others repeating the same actions. The conjoint racialization and moralization of bodies that occurs within the *sīra* is key, in other words, to why ʿAbd al-Wahhāb's heroism signifies differently than Fāṭima's or Maslama's, and why Maymūna's eventual villainy signifies differently from ʿUqba's.

There is of course a set of moral questions outside of the worlds of these texts as well. What is the point of reading the Islamic past with "race," beyond historicist concerns about the truth-telling capacity of doing so or the lack thereof? What claims and investments do such readings allow or disallow? Answering this question in her own fashion, Sarah Pearce offers the possibility of enriching one's "critical compassion," writing that

> this is not the trap of empathy, assuming that others experience the world in the same way or that these experiences can be rendered emotionally comparable; rather, it is an internalized, personal drive to use critical tools to come to a better personal understanding of the experience of another, whether in historical terms or not.[6]

Though Pearce does not quite say as much, there is already a companionate relationship between historicizing race and racialization and historicizing affect, as well as how people tap into both across time, hence the concern that our empathy can deceive and entrap. I would venture that analyzing the contours of others' expressions of empathy can, meanwhile, illuminate and transform our understandings. One of the recurrent

6. Pearce, "The Inquisitor and the *Moseret*," 148.

emotional dimensions of the *sīras* that one is unable to unsee once it becomes evident, for example, is that insults centered on their blackness cause characters pain: ʿAbd al-Wahhāb nearly falls off his horse in the middle of battle when Maymūna derides his hellish, blazing color, and his son rushes to his reputational defense. As a child, ʿAbd al-Wahhāb feels the onus of wanting to console his mother about his own color. He cries as he proclaims his worth to her—and the world—in verse. When, after converting to Christianity, a fellow Byzantine warrior curses Maymūna as "black of face and heart," and with a lineage from "dogs" (*nasl al-kalb*), Maymūna lets out a piercing, terrible (*hāʾila*) scream and moves on him like a deadly lioness (*labwa qātila*).[7] It is amply evident, in other words, that these texts did fundamentally racializing work, but I have also argued that they did this work critically and emotively. If characters within these worlds are so affected, what of the audiences who have born witness to the arresting, shocking, hurtful, or rage-inducing dimensions of an antiblackness that heroes are no freer of despite the eminence and valor that stamped their names, proudly, onto histories real and imagined?

Then there are the ongoing questions—likewise both historical and affective—of what to call this antiblackness, so recessed in the past, and how to redraw the lines of its legacies. Increasingly, when people in Muslim-majority, Arabic-speaking countries excavate the histories of their experiences of discrimination, they deploy the language of race and racism to cognize and mobilize those pasts, giving new language to old adversities. Recent work by Luca Nevola documents the *akhdām* (literally "servants," an underclassed population of East African origin) in Yemen decrying *ʿunṣuriyya*—racism—disseminated in part through stories about them that reach into the pre-Islamic past and trope them as deceitful and servile.[8] Laura Menin writes of Moroccan academics and journalists generating discourse on the continuities between *racisme ancien* and *racisme moderne*, figuring Morocco's history of enslavement of sub-/Saharan Africans as racialized history.[9] Afifa Ltifi draws attention to how Tunisians use the language of antiblackness to reach out via francophone, pan-African, and global Black solidaristic channels in ways that at once invoke a shared subjection to "hegemonic epistemes of racial world making" and reconstruct more localized relationships to "the haunting traces

7. *Sīrat Dhāt al-Himma*, L:6

8. Luca Nevola, "'Black People, White Hearts': Origin, Race, and Colour in Contemporary Yemen," *Anthropologia* 7, no. 1 (2020): 93–115.

9. Laura Menin, "'Dans la Peau d'un Noir': Senegalese Students and Young Professionals in Rabat, Morocco," *Anthropologia* 7, no. 1 (2020): 172.

of a trans-Saharan Arab slavery."[10] Dismissing non-Western articulations of race and racism in scholarly quests for "authenticity" selectively walls local intellectual engagements off from global interaction in both the past and present. Bruce Hall writes of those in places like Sudan and Mauritania taking up the language of race in order to stage a global dialogue that "there is nothing illegitimate about such a move, especially when the dominant culture (and its international academic spokespeople) refuse to acknowledge the continuing effects of racialized slavery on contemporary life."[11]

This is but a snapshot of the latest set of scholarly assessments of emic accounts of race, racialization, and racism in Muslim *milieux* that seek to connect the modern and premodern. And yet, despite decades of work that several of the scholars discussed throughout this volume have built on, cited, and synthesized, much recent scholarship produced under the banner of studies of medieval race has meanwhile rendered cultures beyond those of Latin Western Europe or its immediate neighbors as inchoate in their approaches to human difference.

A recent volume of essays at the intersection of histories of race and medieval studies is illustrative: most of the activities of Muslims across the essays, written about by several different authors, are simultaneously ignorant of and subordinated to racial projects. Reliance on "Greek and Arabic intellectual traditions" thus "obscure[s] the tenor and distinctive claims of medieval thinkers" about race, as if classical Arabic intellectual traditions are neither themselves medieval nor sufficiently distinctive from their ancient Hellenic counterparts to suggest their own strategies of uptake and interpretation.[12] Unbeknownst to them, the Mamluk importation of Circassians, characterized as "a white slave traffic," monopolized by the Genoese, "of boys who had initially been Christian," leads the Italian city state to agentively opt out of racial solidarity with people of the Caucasus—an affective tie that is presumed but not proven to exist—in favor of economic gain. Their race-betraying greed laterally helps the Mamluks build a "glittering culture" and achieve victories against crusaders.[13]

10. Afifa Ltifi, "Disarticulating Blackness or the Semantics of (Anti)blackness in Tunisia," *POMEPS* 44 (2021): 55–60.

11. Hall, "Reading Race," 39.

12. Maaike van der Lugt, "Race and Science: Black Skin in Medieval Medicine and Natural Philosophy," in *A Cultural History of Race in the Middle Ages*, ed. Thomas Hahn (London: Bloomsbury Academic, 2021), 81.

13. Geraldine Heng, "Race and Politics," in *A Cultural History of Race in the Middle Ages*, ed. Thomas Hahn (London: Bloomsbury Academic, 2021), 108–9.

Ibn Baṭṭūṭa (d. 1369) records being referred to with the racializing epithet "Saracen" when entering the royal complex at Constantinople, and despite the consummate traveler having committed it to text thirty years after the fact, we are encouraged to read this experience not as carefully curated, but as immediate and victimizing—Ibn Baṭṭūṭa is fearfully "[reduced] to a vulnerable body."[14] Only one of the essays centers on Muslim-authored sources directly, and then it does so comparatively, bridging Christianity and Islam in the Maghrib and Iberia.[15]

In the present volume, I have aimed to showcase subjects as deeply complex, as participants in local, imaginatively worlded, and tangibly transregional discourse, and as polyvocal in their conceptions of what I have called a collection of beliefs and analyses devoted to explicating social-as-natural kind, which is to say, premises and patterns of racialization. Simultaneously, I have attended to the disciplinary stakes and political histories of making claims—especially periodizing ones, which almost inherently imply chains of causation and descent—about others making what we have come to call race.

Further Research

I want to use the remainder of this space not to tie up loose ends, but to indicate where I believe I have left them in place and to suggest directions that others might pursue. Many of the works and corpora of *adab*, exegesis, geography, law, and medicine that I lightly touched on because of their intertextual value to this study could be the subjects of entire projects in themselves. Intersections with ideas of dis/ability, disease, labor, bondage, dependency, and more that have received only brief treatment in the foregoing could likewise be so. In dealing in the main with racialized blackness, I have also, needless to say, neglected the question of the racialization of collectivities such as the *ʿajam* (sometimes Persians, others "Easterners," others non-Arabs as a whole),[16] *ṣaqāliba* (often "Slavs," but really a large and essentialized northeastern geocultural formation),[17] and

14. Christine Chism, "Definitions and Representations of Race," in *A Cultural History of Race in the Middle Ages*, ed. Thomas Hahn (London: Bloomsbury Academic, 2021), 28.

15. Nirenberg, "Race and Religion."

16. "Easterners" is the rendering of choice, for example, in Webb and Savant's edition and translation of Ibn Qutayba's *The Excellence of the Arabs*.

17. See, e.g., Marek Jankowiak's explanation of *ṣaqāliba* as a catchall for Slavs and their "neighbors," and Henry and Renée Kahane's argument for the term's use to

the central antagonists of *Sīrat Dhāt al-Himma* themselves, the *rūm* (translated throughout this book as "Byzantines," though this exonymous term has itself been widely critiqued; even the Arabic adduces that the people at hand were, among themselves and in an ethnicized sense, Romans).[18]

In dealing in the main with stories told about the *umma* that engaged in race-craft and logics of "kind" from within Arabic-speaking parts of the Middle East and North Africa, many territories and togues have gone largely unaccounted for that were producing analogous works in the period with which I am concerned. This is perhaps most overtly clear with respect to Persianate literatures. Persian romances have significant cross-pollination with the *sīra* traditions, as I have occasionally mentioned, and studies of them are likewise increasingly concerned with the salience of theories and concepts of race for premodernity.[19] Much space thus exists for continued engagement with popular culture and its various producers in Islamic spheres as a locus for exploring histories of racialization.

Though I have endeavored to incorporate some sources from critical whiteness studies, I look forward to further analysis of premodern Arabness and whiteness from new approaches, which in turn stands to defamiliarize many of the paradigms of whiteness that have become absorbed into premodern critical race studies writ large. Human-animal and human-nonhuman connections gestured toward through this volume's references to animal imagery, practices of husbandry, and demonology could also be greatly expanded. If race can be located anywhere decisively, it is, after all, in human histories and projects.

Ultimately, I wrote this book with the aim of further grounding the subfield of the study of racialization in premodern Muslim societies and

---

indicate not merely ethnicity, but enslaveability or unfreedom. Marek Jankowiak, "What Does the Slave Trade in Saqaliba Tell Us about Early Islamic Slavery?" *International Journal of Middle East Studies* 49, no. 1 (2017): 169; Henry Kahane and Renée Kahane, "Notes on the Linguistic History of *Sclavus*," in *Studi in onore di Ettore Lo Gatto e Giovanni Maver* (Florence: Sansoni, 1962), 360.

18. Anthony Kaldellis argues this generatively in his book's first few pages: Anthony Kaldellis, *Romanland: Ethnicity and Empire in Byzantium* (Cambridge, MA: Harvard University Press, 2019), x–xiii.

19. In his introduction to his recent translation of the *Kushnāma*, an early twelfth-century Persian romance detailing the adventures of its tusked, superhuman hero, Kaveh Hemmat considers dynamics of racialization in the tale and its peers, and I look forward to in-progress and forthcoming work by Amanda Leong, Alexandra Hoffmann, and Sam Lasman on related questions. Iranshah, *The Kushnameh: The Persian Epic of Kush the Tusked*, trans. Kaveh Hemmat (Oakland: University of California Press, 2022), 26.

developing theories and methods for pursuing the questions it might continue to raise. A central term of use in the foregoing chapters has been aspiration. I have argued that the *sīras*—the popular epics with which I have been most concerned—are shot through with aspirational histories of Islam as Arab-centered yet capacious and worldly. Frequently, their didactic depictions of the past are staged as allegories in which highly visibilized, racialized others are assimilated into Arabness and Muslimness through confluences of cosmic order and human resolve. Aspiration and action are related. One does not weave aspirational histories without some galvanizing impulse to enact the futures they portend, nor provoke new ways of seeing without sensing a greater design in their purpose. I hope readers therefore will indulge me closing with my own aspirations here.

Acknowledgments

This book has its origins in my doctoral research, and so I begin with my deepest thanks to those who supported its earliest stages and prepared me to begin its undertaking. Tahera Qutbuddin is a model of erudition and a sea of knowledge. Dwight Reynolds and Geraldine Heng each lent generous insight and guidance, often from afar. Michael Sells commented incisively on some of this project's first chapter drafts. Franklin Lewis, of blessed memory, brought his abundant kindness and critical care to both the doctoral project and to my entire graduate school journey. I join the chorus of students who dearly miss him.

As is true for so much current scholarly production, this project also evolved over several different positions and in times of general flux. I researched and wrote at four separate host institutions and collaborated through multiple venues both physical and virtual. I am grateful to my colleagues, mentors, and friends at the University of Chicago, particularly Samantha Pellegrino, Zachary Ralston, Annie Greene, Jessica Mutter, Amy Levine, Sarale Ben Asher, Allison Kanner-Botan, Xelef Botan, Alexandra Hoffman, Chelsie May, Pelle Valentin Olsen, Carl Shook, Francesca Chubb-Confer, Alexander Higgin-Houser, Cameron Cross, Nathaniel Miller, Mohamad Ballan, Kay Heikkinen, and Ghenwa Hayek for offering many forms of companionship, conversation, and contemplation. While abroad chasing down some manuscripts, I was also warmly hosted by Arafat Razzaque and Elise Burton. Kaveh Hemmat took our seed of an idea for a year-long, remote Geography and Identity workshop and brought it to fruition, and it proved an invaluable forum for considering new approaches.

I was fortunate to spend two years with a brilliant array of people at the University of Colorado, Boulder, and I thank those who offered their feedback and colleagueship while I was there, including Levi Thompson, Emily Drumsta, Katherine Alexander, Isabelle Koster, Xiaojing Miao, Brian Catlos, and Fred Astren, who gave insightful comments on one chapter from afar. I was then fortunate to spend a year at New York University, Abu Dhabi, as a Humanities Research Fellow, where I benefited from fascinating discussions with Saqer Almarri, Maurice Pomerantz, Paulo Horta, Justin Stearns, Erin Pettigrew, and Nathaniel Miller once again. Special thanks also must go to Tom Abi Samra; though I was sad to miss him at NYUAD by a year, he commented on several chapters of the manuscript.

I am grateful to have found a home at the University of Maryland, College Park. I credit many people with making that possible, and in so doing facilitating this book's final stages. Antoine Borrut, Max Grossman, Ahmet Karamustafa, and Pete Glanville all are owed a debt of thanks. I would also like to express my gratitude to the students who participated in two upper-level seminars that I led in my first year on campus—"Islam and the Body" and "Islam in Africa and the African Diaspora." Their commitment, curiosity, and enthusiasm helped push my thinking on several of the topics to which this book relates.

I presented aspects of this research at several institutions through speaker series, thanks to many kind invitations. I would particularly like to highlight the responses and questions I received after various of these talks from Hannah Barker, Craig Perry, Michael Cook, Lara Harb, Xinyi Wei, Elias Muhanna, Alexander Key, and Matthew Keegan, which stuck in my mind and encouraged me to make a variety of tweaks or introduced me to new avenues and frameworks. I would also like to express my deep appreciation for early comments on a whole draft of the book by Remke Kruk, without whose pathbreaking work I could never have conceived of this project. Many thanks are also owed to the editors at the University of Chicago Press, and especially to Randy Petilos, for seeing this work to its final form.

In addition to many of the people mentioned above, whose involvement has been far deeper than what I have glossed it as here, and the several people I have forgotten and to whom I apologize sincerely, I have also been blessed by a veritable team of friends who have offered their time, intellectual stimulation, good humor, and inspiration throughout this process. Scholar-friends who commented directly on the book and related materials (or helped me escape their thrall in useful ways) include Kristina Richardson, Sarah Pearce, Esther Liberman Cuenca, Jonny Lawrence, Sheera Talpaz, Oishani Sengupta, Marina Rustow, and Alicia Andrzejewski. Friends who have been here all along include Dan Sullivan, Duncan Price, and Jyl Ristau. Family and found family who help me live a more meaningful life—to which a book does not always contribute—include Emily Cook, Kelly Dickinson, Mattie Feder, Aaron Hagler, Andrea Schine, Miriam Lee, Jonathan Lee, and Elliot Lee.

Because it is convention, I place them last while also recognizing the inadequacy of doing so, but here I thank the two most essential beings in all my successes. Bishop Schine is her own form of epic adventure, a tireless canine companion and, in the words of Ibn al-Marzubān (d. 921), better than almost all creatures who wear clothes. The singular exception being Nathan Schine, in whom every day I find all else that is good, vibrant, surprising, and compelling. My thanks begin and end with you, always.

APPENDIX

Character Charts for Sīrat ʿAntar, Sīrat Banī Hilāl, *and* Sīrat Dhāt al-Himma

Table 1. *Sīrat ʿAntar*

Name of Character	*Relationship to Hero*	*Additional Information*
ʿAntar(a) b. Shaddād	Self	Alternatively known as ʿAntar and as the Father of Knights (Abū'l-Fawāris), he also takes the *nisba* al-ʿAbsī after being recognized as legitimate by his father
Shaddād	Father	One of ten brothers with claims to chiefdom of the tribe of ʿAbs
Zabība	Mother	A former Abyssinian princess, enslaved in the tribe of ʿAbs
Shaybūb	Half brother and sidekick	Born in East Africa and enslaved in youth
Jarīr	Half brother	Shaybūb's elder full-sibling, and mostly an offstage presence after ʿAntara's early youth
ʿAbla	Love interest, cousin, and eventual spouse	Her father, Mālik, resists betrothing her to ʿAntara for much of the tale, and ʿAntara marries several other women, but she remains his ultimate beloved

(*continued*)

Table 1 (*continued*)

Ghamra	Spouse	Hails from Yemen, also has an Abyssinian mother, and has her tribal lands conquered by a series of East African rulers

Table 2. *Sīrat Banī Hilāl*

Name of Character	*Relationship to Hero*	*Additional Information*
Abū Zayd al-Hilālī	Self	Birth name is Barakāt, and he is born unexpectedly Black either because of his mother's prayer after seeing a crow, her latent Black ancestry, or some combination thereof
Khaḍrāʾ	Mother	Literally "The Green," she is of *sharīfan* descent and struggles to conceive a son, resorting to desperate measures in order to bring Abū Zayd into the world
Qirḍāb	Grandfather	Khaḍrāʾ's father and, thus, also a *sharīf*
Rizq	Father	A chiefly figure in the tribe of Hilāl, he rejects his son and wife but later changes course
Sirḥān	Fellow chief and father's close friend	The first to announce suspicions about Abū Zayd's lineage, Sirḥān is in many ways Rizq's moral and social compass during the hero's coming of age; he is father to Ḍiyāb, who is likewise a hero in the epic and fights alongside Abū Zayd

Table 3. *Sīrat Dhāt al-Himma*

Name of Character	*Relationship to Hero*	*Additional Information*
Fāṭima Dhāt al-Himma	Self	Member of the Tribe of Kilāb but enslaved in youth in the Tribe of Ṭayy
Junduba b. al-Ḥārith	Great-grandfather	Progenitor of Fāṭima's heroic lineage, chief of the tribe of Kilāb, and steward of an army of enslaved Black soldiers whom he wins by defeating the older female warrior, Shamṭā
ʿAbd al-Wahhāb	Son	Born Black unexpectedly after his father assaults his mother during her menses, is a primary hero alongside his mother
Al-Baṭṭāl	Sidekick	Alternatively known as Abū Muḥammad; from the rival tribe, Sulaym, but an undying friend to Fāṭima and ʿAbd al-Wahhāb and trickster-hero extraordinaire; his name, "Exceedingly Lazy One," is acquired in youth
Maẓlūm	Father	Rejects and later reconnects with Fāṭima due to a fated pact with his brother, Ẓālim
Ẓālim	Uncle	Converts to Christianity after the birth of ʿAbd al-Wahhāb
al-Ḥārith	Cousin and spouse	Also converts to Christianity after the birth of ʿAbd al-Wahhāb
ʿUqba	*Qāḍī* (judge) and *shaykh* (learned elder) invested with both local and caliphal authority over her	Secretly a Christian convert and spy for the Byzantines, he is the text's principle villain

(*continued*)

Table 3 (*continued*)

Abū'l-Hazāhiz	One-time adversary turned *mawlā* (client) to her son and a "Black general" (*min al-umarā' al-sūdān*) affiliated with the Tribe of Kilāb	Abū'l-Hazāhiz is a giant warrior, prized by Muslim separatists, Byzantines, and the Kilābīs alike; ʿAbd al-Wahhāb is instrumental in his conversion to Islam
Hadlamūs	One-time adversary turned "Black general" affiliated with the Tribe of Kilāb	Was a king in Abyssinia with connections to the caliphate of al-Ma'mūn and the Byzantines prior to conversion to Islam
Maymūna	Daughter-in-law	East African and daughter of King Damdamān, she bears the title of queen (*malika*) and *nisba* al-Ḥabashiyya; Maymūna becomes a Christian and villain after serving the Muslims for many years
Baḥrūn	Grandson	Son of Maymūna and ʿAbd al-Wahhāb who is lost in childhood, raised by Byzantines, converts to Islam, and is killed by his mother

Bibliography

Abdel Haleem, M. A. S., trans. *The Qur'ān*. Oxford: Oxford University Press, 2004.

Abuali, Eyad. "'I Tasted Sweetness, and I Tasted Affliction': Pleasure, Pain, and Body In Medieval Sufi Food Practices." *The Senses and Society* 17, no. 1 (2022): 52–67.

Abū-l-Layl, Khālid. *Riwayāt al-Sīra al-Hilāliyya fī Qana*. Cairo: al-Hay'a al-Miṣriyya al-ʿĀmma li-l-Kitāb, 2012.

Agius, Dionysius A. *Classic Ships of Islam: From Mesopotamia to the Indian Ocean*. Leiden: Brill, 2007.

Agostini, Domenico. "Half-Human and Monstrous Races in Zoroastrian Tradition." *Journal of the American Oriental Society* 139, no. 4 (2019): 805–18.

Ahmed, Sara. "A Phenomenology of Whiteness." *Feminist Theory* 8, no. 2 (2007): 149–68.

Ahmed, Shahab. *What is Islam? The Importance of Being Islamic*. Princeton, NJ: Princeton University Press, 2016.

Aïdi, Hisham. "Moulay Ismail and the Mumbo Jumbo: *Black Morocco* Revisited." *Islamophobia Studies Journal* (2023): 100–122.

Akbari, Suzanne Conklin. "The Diversity of Mankind in *The Book of John Mandeville*." In *Eastward Bound: Travel and Travellers 1050–1550*, edited by Rosamund Allen, 156–76. Manchester, UK: Manchester University Press, 2004.

———. "Race, Environment, Culture." In *A Cultural History of Race in the Middle Ages*, edited by Thomas Hahn, 44–76. London: Bloomsbury Academic, 2021.

Akinci, Idil. "The Multiple Roots of Emiratiness: The Cosmopolitan History of Emirati Society." *openDemocracy*, February 15, 2018. https://www.opendemocracy.net/en/beyond-trafficking-and-slavery/the-multiple-roots-of-emiratiness/.

Al Sharif, Ahmed. "Judham, Baras, Wadah, Bahaq and Quwabaʾ: A Study of Term and Concepts in 'Al Qanun Fit Tib' of Ibn-Sina." *JISHIM* 5, no. 10 (2006): 30–39.

Alawiye, Imran Hamza. "Ibn Al-Jawzī's Apologia on Behalf of the Black People and Their Status in Islam: A Critical Edition and Translation of Kitāb Tanwīr Al-Ghabash Fī Faḍl 'l-Sūdān Wa'l-Ḥabash." PhD diss., University of London, SOAS, 1985.

"The Alexander Romance in the Arabic Tradition." In *A Companion to Alexander Literature in the Middle Ages*. Edited by David Zuwiyya, 73–112. Leiden: Brill, 2011.

Ali, Abdullah Bin Hamid. *The 'Negro' in Arab-Muslim Consciousness*. Swansea, UK: Claritas Books, 2018.

Ali, Kecia. *Marriage and Slavery in Early Islam*. Cambridge, MA: Harvard University Press, 2010.

———. *Sexual Ethics and Islam: Feminist Reflections on Qur'an, Hadith, and Jurisprudence*. London: Oneworld, 2006.

Anderson, Graham. "Two Notes on Heliodorus." *Journal of Hellenic Studies* 99 (1979): 149.

ʿAntara ibn Shaddād. *Dīwān ʿAntara*. Beirut: Dār Ṣādir, 1958.

———. *War Songs*. Trans. James Montgomery. New York: New York University Press, 2018.

Antrim, Zayde. "*Qamarayn*: The Erotics of Sameness in the *1001 Nights*." *Al-ʿUṣūr al-Wusṭā* 28 (2020): 1–44.

———. *Routes and Realms: The Power of Place in the Early Islamic World*. Oxford: Oxford University Press, 2012.

Anwar, Etin. *Gender and Self in Islam*. London: Routledge, 2006.

Appiah, K. Anthony. "The Conservation of 'Race.'" *Black American Literature Forum* 23, no. 1 (1989): 37–60.

———. "The Uncompleted Argument." In *"Race," Writing, and Difference*, edited by Henry Louis Gates Jr., 21–37. Chicago: University of Chicago Press, 1985.

Al-Aqfahsī. *Kashf al-Asrār ʿammā Khafī ʿalā-l-Afkār*. Edited by al-Sayyid Yūsuf Aḥmad. Beirut: Dār al-Kutub al-ʿIlmiyya, 2010.

The Arabian Nights Encyclopedia, 2 vols. Edited by Ulrich Marzolph and Richard van Leeuwen. London: Bloomsbury, 2004.

Aravamudan, Srinivas. *Tropicopolitans: Colonialism and Agency, 1688–1804*. Durham, NC: Duke University Press, 1999.

Arberry, A. J. *The Koran Interpreted: A Translation*. New York: Touchstone, 1996.

Aristotle. *Aristotle on the Generation of Animals: A Philosophical Study*. Translated by Johannes Morinsk. Lanham, MD: University Press of America, 1982.

Asatryan, Mushegh. "Mofazzal Al-Joʿfi." In *Encyclopedia Iranica*. New York: Encyclopedia Iranica Foundation, 2012. http://www.iranicaonline.org/articles/mofazzal-al-jofi.

Ayana, Daniel. "The Northern *Zanj, Demadim, Yamyam, Yam/Yamjam, Habasha/Ahabish, Zanj-Ahabish*, and *Zanj ed-Damadam*–The Horn of Africa between the Ninth and Fifteenth Centuries." *History in Africa* 46 (2019): 57–104.

Ayubi, Zahra. *Gendered Morality: Classical Islamic Ethics of the Self, Family, and Society*. New York: Columbia University Press, 2019.

Azam, Hina. *Sexual Violation in Islamic Law: Substance, Evidence, and Procedure*. New York: Cambridge University Press, 2015.

Azmeh, Aziz al-. "Barbarians in Arab Eyes." *Past & Present* 134, no. 1 (1992): 3–18.

Bacharach, Jere L. "African Military Slaves in the Medieval Middle East: The Cases of Iraq (869–955) and Egypt (868–1171)." *IJMES* 13 (1981): 471–95.

Badawī, ʿAbdūh. *Al-Sūd wa-l-Ḥaḍāra al-ʿArabiyya*. Cairo: al-Hayʾa al-Miṣriyya al-ʿĀmma li-l-Kitāb, 1976.

Bakhtin, Mikhail. *Rabelais and His World*. Translated by Helene Iswolsky. Bloomington: Indiana University Press, 1984.

Al-Bakrī. *Kitāb al-Masālik wa-l-Mamālik*. Tunis: Dār al-ʿArabiyya li-l-Kitāb, 1992.

Balafrej, Lamia. "Domestic Slavery, Skin Color, and Image Dialectic in Thirteenth-Century Arabic Manuscripts." *Art History* 44, no. 4 (2021): 1012–36.

Ballan, Mohamad. "Borderland Anxieties: Lisān al-Dīn ibn al-Khaṭīb (d. 1374) and the Politics of Genealogy in Late Medieval Granada." *Speculum* 98, no. 2 (2023): 447–95.

Bardaiṣan of Edessa. *The Book of the Laws of Countries*. Translated by H. J. W. Drivers and G. E. van Baaren-Pape. Piscataway, NJ: Georgias Press, 2007.

Barker, Hannah. "Purchasing a Slave in Fourteenth-Century Cairo: Ibn al-Akfānī's *Book of Observation and Inspection in the Examination of Slaves*." *Mamlūk Studies Review* 19 (2016): 1–23.

———. "Reconnecting with the Homeland: Black Sea Slaves in Mamluk Biographical Dictionaries." *Medieval Prosopography* 30 (2015): 87–104.

———. *That Most Precious Merchandise: The Mediterranean Trade in Black Sea Slaves, 1260–1500*. Philadelphia: University of Pennsylvania Press, 2019.

Bartlett, Robert. "Medieval and Modern Concepts of Race and Ethnicity." *Journal of Medieval and Early Modern Studies* 31, no. 1 (2001): 39–56.

Bashir, Haroon. "Black Excellence and the Curse of Ham: Debating Race and Slavery in the Islamic Tradition." *ReOrient* 5, no. 1 (2019): 92–116.

Bashir, Shahzad. *A New Vision for Islamic Pasts and Futures*. Cambridge, MA: MIT Press. 2022. https://doi.org/10.26300/bdp.bashir.ipf.premodern-epic.

———. *Sufi Bodies: Religion and Society in Medieval Islam*. New York: Columbia University Press, 2011.

Bashkin, Orit. "On Noble and Inherited Virtues: Discussions of the Semitic Race in the Levant and Egypt, 1876–1918." *Humanities* 10, no. 3 (2021): 1–20.

Bayhaqī, Abū Bakr Aḥmad b. Ḥusayn al-. *Dalāʾil Al-Nubūwa*. Vol. 1. Edited by ʿAbd al-Muʿṭī Qalʿajī. Beirut: Dār al-Kutub, 1985.

———. *Fahāris Aḥādīth wa-Āthār al-Sunan*. Vol. 11. Edited by Ibrāhīm Shams al-Dīn. Beirut: Dār al-Kutub al-ʿIlmiyya, 2003.

Beaujard, Philippe. *The Worlds of the Indian Ocean: A Global History*. Vol. 2. Cambridge: Cambridge University Press, 2019.

Beaumont, Daniel. "Min Jumlat Al-Jamādāt. The Inanimate in Fictional and Adab Narrative." In *On Fiction and Adab in Medieval Arabic Literature*, edited by Philip F. Kennedy. Wiesbaden: Harrassowitz, 2005.

Belcher, Wendy. "Mary Saves the Man-Eater: Value in the Medieval Ethiopian Marian Tale of 'The Cannibal of Qəmər.'" *Digital Philology: A Journal of Medieval Cultures* 8, no. 1 (2019): 29–49.

Bennett, Herrman. *African Kings and Black Slaves: Sovereignty and Dispossession in the Early Modern Atlantic*. Philadelphia: University of Pennsylvania Press, 2019.

Berend, Nora. "Interconnection and Separation: Perspectives on the Modern Problem of the 'Global Middle Ages.'" *Medieval Encounters* 29 (2023): 285–314.

Bergmann, Emilie L. "Milking the Poor: Wet-Nursing and the Sexual Economy of Early Modern Spain." In *Marriage and Sexual Economy in Medieval and Early Modern Iberia*, edited by Eukene Lacarra Lanz, 90–114. London: Routledge, 2002.

Berkey, Jonathan P. *Popular Preaching and Religious Authority in the Medieval Islamic Near East*. Seattle: University of Washington Press.

Beswick, Stephanie. *Sudan's Blood Memory: The Legacy of War, Ethnicity, and Slavery in South Sudan*. Rochester, NY: University of Rochester Press, 2004.

Betancourt, Roland. *Byzantine Intersectionality: Sexuality, Gender, and Race in the Middle Ages*. Princeton, NJ: Princeton University Press, 2020.

Bhabha, Homi. "Of Mimicry and Man: The Ambivalence of Colonial Disclosure." *October* 28 (1984): 125–33.

Blair, Sheila S., and Jonathan M. Bloom. *The Art and Architecture of Islam 1250–1850*. New Haven, CT: Yale University Press, 1994.

Blatherwick, Helen. *Prophets, Gods, and Kings in Sīrat Sayf ibn Dhī Yazan: An Intertextual Reading of an Egyptian Epic*. Leiden: Brill, 2016.

———. "Solomon Legends in *Sīrat Sayf ibn Dhī Yazan*." *Mizan* 2, no. 1 (2017): 1–31.

Borg, Alexander. "Towards a History and Typology of Color Categorization in Colloquial Arabic." In *Anthropology of Color: Interdisciplinary Multilevel Modeling*, edited by Robert E. MacLaury et al., 263–93. Philadelphia: John Benjamins, 2007.

Borrut, Antoine. *Between Memory and Power: The Syrian Space under the Late Umayyads and Early Abbasids (c. 72–193/692–809)*. Trans. Anna Bailey Galietti. Leiden: Brill, 2023.

———. "Remembering Karbalāʾ: The Construction of an Early Islamic Site of Memory." *Jerusalem Studies in Arabic and Islam* 42 (2015): 249–82.

———. "Vanishing Syria: Periodization and Power in Early Islam," *Der Islam* 91, no. 1 (2014): 37–68.

Bray, Julia. "Men, Women, and Slaves in Abbasid Society." In *Gender in the Early Medieval World: East and West, 300–900*, edited by Leslie Brubaker and Julia M. H. Smith, 121–46. Cambridge: Cambridge University Press, 2004.

Brend, Barbara. *Perspectives on Persian Painting: Illustrations of Amīr Khusrau's* Khamsah. London: Routledge, 2003.

Brody, Jennifer DeVere. *Impossible Purities: Blackness, Femininity, and Victorian Culture*. Durham, NC: Duke University Press, 1998.

Brown, Jonathan A. C. *Islam and Blackness*. London: Oneworld 2022.

———. *Slavery & Islam*. London: Oneworld, 2019.

Brunschvig, R. "ʿAbd." In *Encyclopedia of Islam*, 2nd ed., edited by P. Bearman, Thierry Bianquis, C. Edmund Bosworth, and Wolfhard P. Heinrichs. Leiden: Brill, 2012.

Buell, Denise Kimber. "Early Christian Universalism and Modern Forms of Racism." In *The Origins of Racism in the West*, edited by Miriam Eliav-Feldon, Benjamin Isaac, and Joseph Ziegler, 109–31. Cambridge: Cambridge University Press, 2009.

———. *Why This New Race? Ethnic Reasoning in Early Christianity*. New York: Columbia University Press, 2005.

The Bundahishn ("Creation") or Knowledge from the Zand. Translated by Edward William West. Oxford: Oxford University Press, 1897 (digitized 1997 by Joseph H. Peterson).

Burton, Elise. *Genetic Crossroads: The Middle East and the Science of Human Heredity*. Stanford, CA: Stanford University Press, 2021.

Al-Burūsawī. *Rūḥ al-Bayān fī Tafsīr al-Qurʾān*. 10 vols. Beirut: Dār al-Kutub al-ʿIlmiyya, 2003/

Cachia, Pierre. "Arabic Literatures, 'Elite' and 'Folk,' Junctions and Disjunctions." *Quaderni Di Studi Arabi* 3 (2008): 135–52.

Canard, Marius. "Dhū'l-Himma." In *Encyclopedia of Islam*, 2nd ed., edited by Peri Bearman et al. Leiden: Brill, 2016. http://dx.doi.org/10.1163/1573-3912_islam_COM_0164.

Capenny, S. H. F. "The Khedivic Possessions in the Basin of the Upper Ubangi." *Scottish Geographical Magazine* 15 (1899): 309–16.

Caswell, F. Matthew. *The Slave Girls of Baghdad: The Qiyān of the Early Abbasid Era*. New York: I. B. Tauris, 2011.

Cevasco, Carla. "'Look'd Like Milk.: Colonialism and Infant Feeding in the English Atlantic World." *Journal of Early American History* 10 (2020): 147–78.

Chaumont, E. "Tabannin." In *Encyclopedia of Islam*, edited by Peri Bearman et al. Leiden: Brill, 2012. http://dx.doi.org.proxy.uchicago.edu/10.1163/1573-3912_islam_SIM_8913.

Chawla, Janet. "Mythic Origins of Menstrual Taboo in Rig Veda." *Economic and Political Weekly* 29 (1994): 2817–27.

Chelhod, J. "ʿIfrīt." In *Encyclopedia of Islam*, 2nd ed., edited by Peri Bearman et al. Leiden: Brill, 2012.

———. "Raḍāʿ or Riḍāʿ." In *Encyclopedia of Islam*, edited by Peri Bearman et al. Leiden: Brill, 2012. http://dx.doi.org/10.1163/1573-3912_ei2glos_SIM_gi_03811.

Chism, Christine. "Definitions and Representations of Race." In *A Cultural History of Race in the Middle Ages*, edited by Thomas Hahn, 27–46. London: Bloomsbury Academic, 2021.

Chraïbi, Aboubakr. "Introduction." In *Arabic Manuscripts of the* Thousand and One Nights*: Presentation and Critical Editions of Four Noteworthy Texts Observations on Some Osmanli Translations*, edited by Aboubakr Chraïbi et al. Paris: Espaces et Signes, 2016.

Christides, Vassilios. "The Himyarite-Ethiopian War and the Ethiopian Occupation of South Arabia in the Acts of Gregentius (ca. 530 A.D.)." *Annales d'Ethiopie* 9 (1972): 115–46.

Crenshaw, Kimberlé. "Mapping the Margins: Intersectionality, Identity Politics, and Violence against Women of Color." *Stanford Law Review* 43, no. 6 (1991): 1241–99.

Crone, Patricia. "'Even an Ethiopian Slave:' The Transformation of a Sunnī Tradition." *Bulletin of the School of Oriental and African Studies*, University of London, 57, no. 1 (1994): 59–67.

———. *Roman, Provincial, and Islamic Law*. Cambridge: Cambridge University Press, 1987.

Cross, Cameron. *Love at a Crux: The New Persian Romance in a Global Middle Ages*. Toronto: University of Toronto Press, 2023.

———. "The Many Colors of Love in Niẓāmī's *Haft Paykar*: Beyond the Spectrum," *Interfaces* 2 (2016): 52–96.

———. "The Poetics of Romantic Love in *Vis and Rāmin*." PhD diss., University of Chicago, 2015.

Crudu, Andrea. "The Sudanese Elements in *Sīrat Sayf ibn Ḏī Yazan*." *Arabica* 61, nos. 3–4 (2014): 309–38.

Daftary, Farhad. *Ismaili Literature: A Bibliography of Sources and Studies*. London: I. B. Tauris, 2004.

Ḍayf, Shawqī. *Tārīkh al-Adab al-ʿArabī: al-ʿAṣr al-Jāhilī*. Cairo: Dār al-Maʿārif, 1986.

Dedes, Georgios S. "The Battalname, an Ottoman Turkish Frontier Epic Wondertale: Introduction, Turkish Transcription, Translation and Commentary." PhD diss., Harvard University, 1995.

de Miramon, Charles. "Noble Dogs, Noble Blood: The Invention of the Concept of Race in the Late Middle Ages." In *The Origins of Racism in the West*, edited by Miriam Eliav-Feldon et al., 200–216. Cambridge: Cambridge University Press, 2009.

Dhāt al-Himma. Edited by ʿAbbās Khiḍr. Cairo: Maṭbaʿat al-Kīlānī, 1968.

Dieste, Josep Lluís Mateo. "Are There '*Mestizos*' in the Arab World? A Comparative Survey of Classification Categories and Kinship Systems." *Middle Eastern Studies* 48, no. 1 (2012): 125–38.

Digenis Akritas, the Two-blood Border Lord: The Grottaferrata Version. Translated by Denison B. Hull. Cincinnati: Ohio University Press, 1985.

Dirbas, Hekmat. "Naming of Slave-Girls in Arabic: A Survey of Medieval and Modern Sources." *Zeitschrift für Arabische Linguistik* 69 (2019): 26–38.

Dols, Michael W. "The Leper in Medieval Islamic Society." *Speculum* 58, no. 4 (1983): 891–916.

Doniger, Wendy. "The Symbolism of Black and White Babies in the Myth of Parental Impression," *Social Research* 70, no. 1 (2003): 1–44.

Donner, Fred. "Visions of the Early Islamic Expansion: Between the Heroic and the Horrific." In *Byzantium in Early Islamic Syria*, edited by Nadia Maria El Cheikh and Shaun O'Sullivan. 9–30. Beirut: Dar El Kotob, 2007.

Doostdar, Alireza. *The Iranian Metaphysicals: Explorations in Science, Islam, and the Uncanny*. Princeton, NJ: Princeton University Press, 2018.

Doufikar-Aerts, Faustina. "*Sīrat al-Iskandar*: An Arabic Popular Romance of Alexander." *Oriente Moderno* 22, no. 2 (2003): 505–20.

Dover, Cedric. "The Black Knight." *Phylon* 15, no. 1 (1954): 41–57.

Ducène, Jean-Charles. "Une nouvelle source arabe sur l'océan Indien au Xᵉ siècle: Le *Ṣaḥīḥ min aḫbār al-biḥār wa-ʿaǧāʾibihā* d'Abū ʿImrān Mūsā ibn Rabāḥ al-Awsī al-Sīrāfī." *Afriques* 6 (2015): n.p.

Dzon, Mary. "Jesus and the Birds in Medieval Abrahamic Traditions." *Traditio* 66 (2011): 189–230.

Editors. "Ḥasab wa-Nasab." In *Encyclopedia of Islam*, edited by P. Bearman et al. Leiden: Brill, 2012.

El Cheikh, Nadia Maria. "Describing the Other to Get at the Self: Byzantine Women in Arabic Sources (8th–11th Centuries)." *Journal of the Economic and Social History of the Orient* 40, no. 2 (1997): 239–50.

———. *Women, Islam, and Abbasid Identity*. Cambridge, MA: Harvard University Press, 2015.

El Hamel, Chouki. *Black Morocco: A History of Slavery, Race, and Islam*. New York: Cambridge University Press, 2014.

Eliav-Feldon, Miriam, Benjamin Isaac, and Joseph Zeigler, eds. *The Origins of Racism in the West*. Cambridge: Cambridge University Press, 2009.

El Zein, Amira. *Islam, Arabs, and the Intelligent World of the Jinn*. Syracuse, NY: Syracuse University Press, 2009.

Extraits du roman d'Antar (Muntakhabāt min Sīrat ʿAntar ibn Shaddād al-ʿAbsī). Paris: Firmin Didot Frères, 1841.

Hall, Bruce. *A History of Race in Muslim West Africa, 1600–1900*. Cambridge: Cambridge University Press, 2011.

———. "Reading Race in Africa and the Middle East." *Anthropologia* 7, no. 1 (2020): 33–44.

Hall, Stuart. "Race, Culture, and Communications: Looking Backward and Forward at Cultural Studies." *Rethinking Marxism* 5, no. 1 (1992): 10–18.

Hanaoka, Mimi. *Authority and Identity in Medieval Islamic Historiography: Persian Histories from the Peripheries*. Cambridge: Cambridge University Press, 2016.

Hardy, Paul. "Medieval Muslim Philosophers on Race." In *Philosophers on Race: Critical Essays*, edited by Julie K. Ward and Tommy L. Lott. Oxford: Blackwell Publishers, 2002.

Hayes, Edmund. "The Death of Kings: Group Identity and the Tragedy of *Nezhād* in Ferdowsi's *Shahnameh*." *Iranian Studies* 48, no. 3 (2015): 369–93.

Heath, Peter. "Allegory in Islamic Literatures." In *The Cambridge Companion to Allegory*, edited by Rita Copeland and Peter T. Struck, 83–100. Cambridge: Cambridge University Press, 2011.

———. "Styles in Premodern Arabic Popular Epics." In *In the Shadow of Arabic the Centrality of Language to Arabic Culture*, edited by Bilal Orfali, 413–41. Leiden: Brill, 2011.

———. *The Thirsty Sword: Sīrat ʿAntar and the Arabic Popular Epic*. Salt Lake City: University of Utah Press, 1996.

Heck, Gene W. "'Arabia without Spices': An Alternate Hypothesis." *Journal of the American Oriental Society* 123, no. 3 (2003): 547–76.

Hendricks, Margo. "Coloring the Past, Rewriting Our Future: Raceb4Race." "Race and Periodization Symposium." September 2019. https://pressbooks.claremont.edu/clas114valentine/chapter/coloring-the-past-rewriting-our-future-raceb4race/.

Heng, Geraldine. "An African Saint in Medieval Europe: The Black St. Maurice and the Enigma of Racial Sanctity." In *Saints and Race: Marked Flesh, Holy Flesh*, edited by Vincent William Lloyd and Molly Harbour Bassett, 18–44. London: Routledge, 2014.

———. *Empire of Magic: Medieval Romance and the Politics of Cultural Fantasy*. New York: Columbia University Press, 2003.

———. *The Invention of Race in the European Middle Ages*. Cambridge: Cambridge University Press, 2018.

———. "Race and Politics." In *A Cultural History of Race in the Middle Ages*, edited by Thomas Hahn, 97–112. London: Bloomsbury Academic, 2021.

Henry, David. "Aristotle on the Mechanism of Inheritance." *Journal of the History of Biology* 39, no. 3 (2006): 425–55.

Herzog, Thomas. "Orality and the Tradition of Arabic Epic." In *Medieval Oral Literature*, edited by Karl Reichl, 627–49. Berlin: De Gruyter, 2012.

"Ḥikāyat al-Jawārī al-Mukhtalifa al-Alwān wa-Mā Waqaʿa Baynahun min al-Muḥawira." In *Alf Layla wa-Layla*. Vol. 2. 2nd ed. Calcutta, 1839.

Hillenbrand, Robert. "The Image of the Black in Islamic Art: The Case of Islamic Painting." In *The Image of the Black in African and Asian Art*, edited by David Bindman, Suzanne Preston Blier, and Henry Louis Gates, Jr., 215–53. Cambridge, MA: Harvard University Press, 2017.

Hinds, Martin, and El-Said Badawi. *A Dictionary of Egyptian Arabic: Arabic-English*. Beirut: Librairie du Liban, 1986.

Hirschler, Konrad. *The Written Word in the Medieval Arabic Lands: A Social and Cultural History of Reading Practices*. Edinburgh: Edinburgh University Press, 2012.

Hochman, Adam. "Is 'Race' Modern? Disambiguating the Question." *Du Bois Review: Social Science Research on Race* (2020): 647–65.

———. "Racialization: A Defense of the Concept." *Ethnic and Racial Studies* 49, no. 8 (2018): 1245–62. https://doi.org/10.1080/01419870.2018.1527937.

Homerin, T. Emil. "Echoes of a Thirsty Owl: Death and Afterlife in Pre-Islamic Arabic Poetry." *Journal of Near Eastern Studies* 44, no. 3 (1985): 165–84.

Hoyland, Robert. "Physiognomy in Islam." *Jerusalem Studies in Arabic and Islam* 30 (2005): 361–402.

A Hundred and One Nights. Translated by Bruce Fudge. New York: New York University Press, 2016.

Hunwick, John O. "A Region of the Mind: Medieval Arab Views of African Geography and Ethnography and Their Legacy." *Sudanic Africa* 16 (2005): 103–36.

Ibn Aḥmad al-ʿAynṭabī al-Amshāṭī, Muẓaffar al-Dīn Abū-l-Thanāʾ Maḥmūd. *Al-Qawl al-Sadīd fī Ikhtiyār al-Imāʾ wa-l-ʿAbīd*. Ms. Orient A 1237. Erfurt, Germany: Universitäten Erfurt/Gotha, n.d.

Ibn Aḥmad, al-Khalīl. *Kitāb al-ʿAyn*. Baghdad: Dāʾira al-Shuʾūn al-Thaqāfiyya wa-l-Nashr, 1984.

Ibn al-Athīr. *Al-Kāmil fī-l-Taʾrīkh*. Vol. 1. Beirut: Dār al-Kitāb al-ʿArabī, 1997.

Ibn al-Jawzī. *Tanwīr al-Ghabash fī Faḍl al-Sūdān wa-l-Ḥabash*. Edited by Marzūq ʿAlī Ibrāhīm. Riyadh: Dār al-Sharīf, 1998.

Ibn al-Kalbī, Hishām. *Jamharat al-Nasab*. Vol. 1. Kuwait: Wizārat al-Iʿlām, 1983.

Ibn al-Nadīm. *Al-Fihrist*. Edited by Ayman Fuʾad Sayyid. London: Furqan, 2014.

Ibn al-Rūmī. *Dīwān Ibn al-Rūmī*. Vol. 2. Edited by Aḥmad Ḥasan Basaj. Beirut: Dār al-Kutub al-ʿIlmiyya.

Ibn Buṭlān. "Risāla Jāmiʿa li-Funūn al-Nāfiʿa fī Shirā al-Raqīq wa-Taqlīb al-ʿAbīd." In *Nawādir al-Makhṭūṭāt*, edited by ʿAbd al-Salām Hārūn, 2:351–410. Cairo: Muṣṭafā al-Halabī, 1973. http://shamela.ws/browse.php/book-21514/page-281#page-337.

Ibn Faḍlān. *Ibn Fadlān and the Land of Darkness: Arab Travelers in the Far North*. Translated by Paul Lunde and Caroline Stone. London: Penguin Classics, 2012.

Ibn Faḍlān and Abū Zayd al-Sīrāfī. *Two Arabic Travel Books: Accounts of China and India and Mission to the Volga*. Translated by James Montgomery and Tim Mackintosh-Smith. New York: New York University Press, 2014.

Ibn Ḥajar. *Fatḥ al-Bārī Sharḥ Ṣaḥīḥ al-Bukhārī*. Vol. 2. Medina: Maktabat al-Ghurbāʾ al-Athariyya, 1996.

Ibn Ḥajar and al-Bukhārī, "Bāb idhā ʿaraḍ bi-nafī al-walad." In *Fatḥ al-Bārī Sharḥ Ṣaḥīḥ al-Bukhārī*. Al-Maktaba al-Islāmiyya, 1996. https://www.islamweb.net/ar/library/content/52/9693.

Ibn Ḥajjāj al-Qushayrī, Muslim, and Ṣafī al-Rahmān al-Mubārakpūrī, *Minnat al-Munʿim fī Sharḥ Ṣaḥīḥ Muslim*. Vol. 2. Riyadh: Dar al-Salām al-Nashr wa-l-Tawzīʿ, 1951.

Ibn Ḥawqal. *Kitāb al-Masālik wa-l-Mamālik*. Leiden: Brill, 1872.

Ibn Ḥazm, ʿAlī b. Aḥmad. *Jamharat Ansāb al-ʿArab*. Cairo: Dār al-Maʿārif, 1948.

———. *Ṭawq Al-Ḥamāma*. Edited by Muḥammad Muḥammad ʿAbd al-Laṭīf. Cairo: al-Matbaʿa al-Madanī, 1975.

Ibn Hishām. *Sīrat Ibn Hishām*. Edited by Muṣṭafā al-Saqqā. Cairo: Maktaba wa-Maṭbaʿa Muṣṭafā al-Bābī al-Ḥalabī wa-Awlādihi bi-Miṣr, 1955.

Ibn Jubayr. *Riḥlat Ibn Jubayr*. Edited by Ibrāhīm Shams al-Dīn. Beirut: Dār al-Kutub al-ʿIlmiyya, 2003.

———. *The Travels of Ibn Jubayr: A Medieval Journey from Cordoba to Jerusalem*. Translated by Ronald Broadhurst. London: Bloomsbury, 2019.

Ibn Kathīr. *Tafsīr al-Qurʾān al-ʿAẓīm*. 13 vols. Edited by Muṣṭafā al-Sayyid Muḥammad et al. Giza: Muʾassasa Qurṭuba, 2000.

Ibn Khaldūn. *Muqaddimat Ibn Khaldūn*. Edited by ʿAbd Allāh Muḥammad Darwīsh. Damascus: Dār Yaʿrib, 2004.

Ibn Manẓūr, Muḥammad b. Mukarram. *Lisān al-ʿArab*. Beirut: Dār Ṣādir, 1955.

Ibn Qutayba, ʿAbd Allāh b. Muslim. *ʿUyūn al-Akhbār*. Vol. 2. Cairo: al-Muʾassasa al-Miṣriyya al-ʿĀmma li-l-Taʾlīf wa-l-Tarjama wa-l-Nashr, 1964.

Ibn Qutaybah. *The Excellence of the Arabs*. Translated by Sarah Bowen Savant and Peter Webb. New York: New York University Press, 2017.

Ibn Rajab al-Dimashqī. *Al-Takhwīf min al-Nār wa-l-Taʿrīf Majāl al-Bawār*. Edited by Bashīr Muḥammad ʿUyūn. Beirut: Maktabat Dār al-Bayān, 1988.

Ibn Saʿīd, ʿArīb. *Kitāb Khalq al-Janīn wa-Tadbīr al-Ḥabālā wa-l-Mawlūdīn*. Edited by Nūr al-Dīn ʿAbd al-Qādir (Noureddine Abdelkader) and Henri Jahier. Algiers: Libraire Ferraris, 1956.

Ibn Saʿīd al-Maghribī. *Kitāb Al-Jughrāfiyā*. Beirut: al-Maktab al-Tijāriyya li-l-Ṭabāʿa wa-l-Nashar wa-l-Tawzīʿ, 1980.

Ibn Sīnā, *al-Qānūn fī-l-Ṭibb*. Edited by. Muḥammad al-Dīn al-Ḍannāwī. Beirut: Dār al-Kutub al-ʿIlmiyya, 2009.

Ibn Sulaymān, Muqātil. *Tafsīr Muqātil ibn Sulaymān*. 5 vols. Edited by Aḥmad Farīd. Beirut: Dār al-Kutub al-ʿIlmiyya, 2003.

Ibrāhīm, Nabīla. *Ashkāl al-Taʿbīr fī-l-Adab al-Shaʿbī*. Cairo: Dār Nahạt Miṣr, 1966.

Al-Idrīsī. *Kitāb Nuzhat al-Mushtāq fī Ikhtirāq al-Āfāq*. Cairo: Maktabat al-Thaqāfa al-Dīniyya, 2002.

Inloes, Amina. "Racial 'Othering' in Shiʿi Sacred History: Jawn Ibn Huwayy 'the African Slave,' and the Ethnicities of the Twelve Imams." *Journal of Shiʿa Islamic Studies* 7 (2014): 411–40.

Iranshah. *The Kushnameh: The Persian Epic of Kush the Tusked*. Translated by Kaveh Hemmat. Oakland: University of California Press, 2022.

Irish, Joel D. "Knocking, Filing, and Chipping: Dental Modification in Sub-Saharan Africans." In *A Worldview of Bioculturally Modified Teeth*, edited by Scott E. Burnett and Joel D. Irish, 33–47. Gainesville: University Press of Florida, 2017.

Irwin, Robert. "The Dark Side of the 'Arabian Nights.'" *Critical Muslim* 13 (2015). https://www.criticalmuslim.io/the-dark-side-of-the-arabian-nights/.

———. "Review: The Adventures of Sayf ben Dhi Yazan: An Arab Folk Epic by Lena Jayyusi." *British Journal of Middle Eastern Studies* 24, no. 2 (1997): 321–23.

Al-Iṣfahānī, Abū Nuʿaym. *Ḥiliyat al-Awliyāʾ wa-Ṭabaqat al-Aṣfiyāʾ*. Vol. 9. Beirut: Dār al-Fikr, 1990.

Ivanov, Paola. "Cannibals, Warriors, Conquerors, and Colonizers: Western Perceptions and Azande Historiography," *History in Africa* 29 (2002): 89–217.

Jaʿfar al-Ṣādiq. *Ṭibb al-Imām al-Ṣādiq*. Edited by Muḥsin ʿAqīl. Beirut: Muʾassasat al-Aʿlāmī, 1998.

Ja'far al-Ṣādiq and Ju'fī, Mufaḍḍal b. 'Umar al-. *Al-Haft al-Sharīf*. Edited by Muṣṭafā Ghālib. Beirut: Dār al-Andalus, 1964.

Al-Jāḥiẓ, Abū 'Uthmān 'Amr b. Baḥr. *Al-'Ibar wa-l-'Itibār*. Cairo: al-'Arabī, 1994.

———. "The Boasts of the Blacks Over the Whites" (*Fakhr al-Sūdān 'alā-l-Bīḍān*). Trans. Tarif Khalidi. *Islamic Quarterly* 25 (1981): 3–51.

———. *Kitāb al-Bayān wa-l-Tabyīn*. Vol. 3. Edited by Muwaffiq Shihāb al-Dīn. Beirut: Dār al-Kutub al-'Ilmiyya, 2009.

———. *Kitāb al-Burṣān wa-l-'Urjān wa-l-'Umyān wa-l-Ḥūlān*. Baghdad: Dār al-Rashīd li-l-Nashr, 1982.

———. *Rasā'il al-Jāḥiẓ*. Cairo: Maktabat al-Khanjī, 1964.

Jankowiak, Marek. "What Does the Slave Trade in Saqaliba Tell Us about Early Islamic Slavery?" *International Journal of Middle East Studies* 49, no. 1 (2017): 169–72.

Al-Jawbarī, Jamāl al-Dīn 'Abd al-Raḥīm. *The Book of Charlatans*. Trans. Humphrey Davies. New York: New York University Press, 2020.

Jones, Nicholas R. *Staging* Habla de Negros: *Radical Performances of the African Diaspora in Early Modern Spain*. University Park, PA: Pennsylvania State University Press, 2019.

Jones-Rogers, Stephanie E. *They Were Her Property: White Women as Slave Owners in the American South*. New Haven, CT: Yale University Press, 2019.

Jordan, William Chester. "Why Race?" *Journal of Medieval and Early Modern Studies* 31, no. 1 (2001): 165–73.

Kadhem, Nader. *Africanism: Blacks in the Medieval Arab Imaginary*. Trans. Amir al-Azraki. Montreal: McGill-Queen's University Press, 2023.

Kahane, Henry, and Renée Kahane. "Notes on the Linguistic History of *Sclavus*." In *Studi in onore di Ettore Lo Gatto e Giovanni Maver*. 345–60. Florence, 1962.

Kaldellis, Anthony. *Romanland: Ethnicity and Empire in Byzantium*. Cambridge, MA: Harvard University Press, 2019.

Kane, Ousmane Oumar. *Beyond Timbuktu: An Intellectual History of Muslim West Africa*. Cambridge, MA: Harvard University Press, 2016.

Kanner-Botan, Allison. "Rewriting the Wild: Fiction, *adab*, and the Making of Majnun's Animal World." *postmedieval* 13, nos. 3–4 (2022): 1–18.

Karnes, Michelle. "The Possibilities of Medieval Fiction." *New Literary History* 51, no. 1 (2020): 209–28.

Katz, Marion. "Beyond Halal and Haram: Ghayra (Jealousy) as a Masculine Virtue in the Work of Ibn Qayyim al-Jawziya." *Cultural History* 8, no. 2 (2019): 202–25.

———. "Scholarly versus Women's Authority in the Islamic Law of Menstrual Purity." In *Gender in Judaism and Islam: Common Lives, Uncommon Heritage*, edited by Firoozeh Kashani-Sabet and Beth S. Wenger, 73–105. New York: New York University Press, 2015.

———. "The Study of Islamic Ritual and the Meaning of *Wuḍū'*." *Der Islam* 82, no. 1 (2005): 106–45.

Kāẓim, Nādir. *Tamthīlāt al-Akhar: Ṣūrat al-Sūd fī-l-Mutakhayyal al-'Arabī al-Wasīṭ*. Beirut: al-Mu'assasa al-'Arabiyya li-l-Dirāsāt wa-l-Nashr, 2004.

Kelly, Kathleen Ann. "'Blue' Indians, Ethiopians, and Saracens in Middle English Narrative Texts." *Parergon* 11 (1993): 35–52.

Kendi, Ibram X. *How to Be an Antiracist*. London: Oneworld, 2019.

Kennedy, E. S. and M. H. Reiger. "Prime Meridians in Medieval Islamic Philosophy." *Vistas in Astronomy* 28 (1985): 29–32.

Key, Alexander. *Language between God and the Poets: Maʿnā in the Eleventh Century*. Oakland: University of California Press, 2018.

Khalidi, Tarif. "History and Hadith." In *Arabic Historical Thought in the Classical Period*, 17–83. Cambridge: Cambridge University Press, 1994.

Khan, Pasha M. *The Broken Spell: Indian Storytelling and the Romance Genre in Persian and Urdu*. Detroit: Wayne State University Press, 2019.

Khannous, Touria. "Race in Pre-Islamic Poetry: The Work of Antara Ibn Shaddad." *African and Black Diaspora: An International Journal* 6, no. 1 (2013): 66–80.

Kia, Mana. *Persianate Selves: Memories of Place and Origin Before Nationalism*. Stanford, CA: Stanford University Press, 2020.

King, Anya H. *Scents from the Garden of Paradise: Musk in the Medieval Islamic World*. Leiden: Brill, 2017.

Kisāʾī, Muḥammad b. ʿAbdallāh al-. *Vitae Prophetarum, Auctore Muhammed Ben Abdallah Al-Kisai: Ex Codicibus Qui in Monaco, Bonna, Lugduni-Batavorum, Lipsia et Gothana Asservantur*. Edited by Isaac Eisenberg. Leiden: Brill, 1922.

Knight, Michael Muhammad. *Muhammad's Body: Baraka Networks and the Prophetic Assemblage*. Chapel Hill: University of North Carolina Press, 2020.

Kohlberg, Etan. "The Position of the 'Walad Zinā' in Imāmī Shīʿism." *Bulletin of the School of Oriental and African Studies* 48 (1985): 237–66.

Koren, Sharon Faye. "The Menstruant as 'Other' in Medieval Judaism and Christianity." *Nashim: A Journal of Jewish Women's Studies and Gender Issues* 17 (2009): 33–59.

Kowalska, Maria. "From Facts to Literary Fiction, Medieval Arabic Travel Literature," *Quaderni di Studi Arabi* 5–6 (1987–88): 397–403.

Krakowski, Eve. "Maimonides' Menstrual Reform in Egypt." *Jewish Quarterly Review* 110, no. 2 (2020): 245–89.

Krebs, Verena. *Medieval Ethiopian Kingship, Craft, and Diplomacy with Latin Europe*. London: Palgrave Macmillan, 2021.

Kruk, Remke. "The Bold and the Beautiful: Women and 'Fitna' in the 'Sirat D–h––āt al-Himma': the Story of Nura," in *Women in the Medieval Islamic World: Power, Patronage, Piety*, edited by Gavin Hambly, 99–116. New York: St. Marin's Press, 1999.

———. "Pregnancy and Its Social Consequences in Mediaeval and Traditional Arab Society." *Quaderni Di Studi Arabi* 5– 6 (1988–1987): 418–30.

———. "The Princess Maymūnah: Maiden, Mother, Monster." *Oriente Moderno* 22 (2003): 425–42.

———. "Reception of Aristotle's Historia Animalium in the Arabic Tradition." In *Historia Animalium of Aristotle: The Arabic Version of Book I–X of the Kitāb Al-Ḥayawân*, edited by L. S. Filius and J. N. Mattock, 15–22. Leiden: Brill, 2019.

———. "Review: *Prophets, Gods and Kings in Sirat Sayf ibn Dhi Yazan: An Intertex Reading of an Egyptian Popular Epic* (Brill Studies in Middle Eastern Literatures) by Helen Blatherwick." *Bulletin of the School of Oriental and African Studies* 80, no. 2 (2017): 379–81.

———. *The Warrior Women of Islam: Female Empowerment in Arabic Popular Literature*. New York: I.B. Tauris, 2014.

Kruk, Remke, and Claudia Ott. "'In the Popular Manner': Sira-recitation in Marrakesh anno 1997." *Edebiyat* 10, no. 2 (1999): 183–97.

Kueny, Kathryn. *Conceiving Identities: Maternity in Medieval Muslim Discourse and Practice*. Albany: State University of New York Press, 2013.

Landau-Tasseron, Ella. "The Participation of Ṭayyiʾ in the *Ridda*." *Jerusalem Studies in Arabic and Islam* 5 (1984): 53–71.

Lane, Edward William. *Manners and Customs of the Modern Egyptians*. New York: Cosimo, 2005.

Lange, Christian. "'On That Day When Faces Will Be White or Black' (Q3:106): Towards a Semiology of the Face in the Arabo-Islamic Tradition." *Journal of the American Oriental Society* 127 (2007): 429–45.

———. "Revisiting Hell's Angels in the Quran." In *Locating Hell in Islamic Traditions*, edited by Christian Lange, 74–100. Leiden: Brill, 2016.

Lawson, Todd. "The Qur'an and Epic," *Journal of Qur'anic Studies* 16, no. 1 (2014): 58–92.

Lelic, Emin. "Physiognomy (ʿilm-i firāsat) and Ottoman Statecraft: Discerning Morality and Justice." *Arabica* 64 (2017): 609–46.

Leoni, Francesca. "On the Monstrous in the Islamic Visual Tradition." In *The Ashgate Companion to Monsters and the Monstrous*, edited by Asa Simon Mittman with Peter J. Dendle, 151–72. London: Routledge, 2013.

Lev, Efraim. *Jewish Medical Practitioners in the Medieval Muslim World: A Collective Biography*. Edinburgh: Edinburgh University Press, 2021.

Lewis, Bernard. "The Crows of the Arabs." *Critical Inquiry* 12 (1985): 88–97.

———. *Islam: From the Prophet Muhammad to the Capture of Constantinople*. Vol. 2. New York: Walker and Co., 1974.

———. *Race and Slavery in the Middle East: An Historical Inquiry*. New York: Oxford University Press, 1990.

Lewis, C. S. *A Preface to "Paradise Lost"*. London: Oxford University Press, 1969.

Long, Matthew L. "Leprosy in Early Islam." In *Disability in Judaism, Christianity, and Islam*, edited by Darla Schumm and Michael Stoltzfus, 43–61. New York: Palgrave Macmillan, 2011.

Loomba, Ania. "Race and the Possibilities of Comparative Critique." *New Literary History* 40, no. 3 (2009): 501–22.

Lourie, Elena. "Black Women Warriors in the Muslim Army Besieging Valencia and the Cid's Victory: A Problem of Interpretation." *Traditio* 55 (2000): 181–209.

Ltifi, Afifa. "Black Tunisians and the Pitfalls of Bourguiba's Homogenization Project." *POMEPS* 40 (2020): 69–72.

———. "Disarticulating Blackness or the Semantics of (Anti)blackness in Tunisia." *POMEPS* 44 (2021): 55–60.

Luffin, Xavier. "'Nos ancêtres les Arabes . . .' Généalogies d'Afrique musulmane." *Civilisations* 53 (2006): 177–209.

———. Peaux noires, âmes blanches: Les poètes Arabes d'origine Africaine face à leur négritude." *Quaderni di Studi Arabi* 5–6 (2010–11): 199–215.

Lyons, Malcolm. *The Arabian Epic: Heroic and Oral Storytelling*. 3 vols. New York: Cambridge University Press, 1995.

———. *The Man of Wiles in Popular Arabic Literature: A Study of a Medieval Arab Hero*. Edinburgh: Edinburgh University Press, 2012.

Lyons, Malcolm, and Robert Irwin. *Tales of the Marvelous and News of the Strange.* London: Penguin Books, 2014.

Madeyska, Danuta. "The Language and Structure of the Sīra." *Quaderni Di Studi Arabi* 9 (1991): 193–218.

———. "Reflections on the Origin of *Sīrat Ḏāt al-Himma,*" *Rocznik Orientalistyczny* 43 (1984): 91–96.

Maghbouleh, Neda. *The Limits of Whiteness: Iranian Americans and the Everyday Politics of Race.* Stanford, CA: Stanford University Press, 2017.

Magidow, Melanie. "Epic of the Commander Dhat Al-Himma." *Medieval Feminist Forum, Subsidia Series* 9, Medieval Texts in Translation 6 (2018): 1–62.

Malette, Karla. *Lives of the Great Languages: Arabic and Latin in the Medieval Mediterranean* Chicago: University of Chicago Press, 2021.

Mallon, Ron. *The Construction of Human Kinds.* Oxford: Oxford University Press, 2016.

———. "Passing, Traveling, and Reality." *Noûs* 38 (2004): 644–73.

Malti-Douglas, Fedwa. *Woman's Body, Woman's Word: Gender and Discourse in Arabo-Islamic Writing.* Princeton, NJ: Princeton University Press, 1991.

Maqānibī, ʿAlī b. Mūsā al-, and Ṣāliḥ al-Jaʿfarī. *Sīrat al-Amīra Dhāt al-Himma.* 7 vols. Cairo: Maktabat al-Maṭabaʿa al-Ḥusayniyya, 1909.

Al-Maqrīzī. *Imtāʿ al-Asmāʿ.* 14 vols. Beirut: Dār al-Kutub al-ʿIlmiyya, 1999.

Marlow, Louise. "Hasab o Nasab." In *Encyclopedia Iranica.* Updated March 20, 2012. http://www.iranicaonline.org/articles/hasab-o-nasab.

———. *Hierarchy and Egalitarianism in Islamic Thought.* Cambridge: Cambridge University Press, 1997.

Marmon, Shaun. *Eunuchs and Sacred Boundaries in Islamic Society.* Oxford: Oxford University Press, 1995.

———. "Intersections of Gender, Sex, and Slavery: Female Sexual Slavery." In *The Cambridge World History of Slavery.* Vol. 2, edited by Craig Perry, David Eltis, et al., 185–213. Cambridge: Cambridge University Press, 2021.

Al-Marzubānī. *Ashʿār al-nisāʾ.* Edited by Sāmī Makkī al-ʿĀnī and Hilāl Nājī. Baghdad: Dār al-Risāla, 1976).

Al-Masʿūdī. *Murūj al-Dhahab wa-Maʿādin al-Jawhar.* Vol. 2. Beirut: al-Maktaba al-ʿAsriyya, 2005.

Al-Māwardī. *Fayḍ Al-Qadīr.* Al-Maktaba al-Islāmiyya. Accessed March 20, 2019. http://www.islamweb.net/newlibrary/display_book.php?flag=1&bk_no=304&ID=18191.

———. *Kitāb al-Ḥawī al-Kabīr.* Vol. 9. Beirut: Dār al-Kutub al-ʿIlmiyya, 1994.

Mauny, R. "Lamlam." In *Encyclopaedia of Islam,* edited by Peri Bearman et al. Leiden: Brill, 2012. https://referenceworks.brillonline.com/entries/encyclopaedia-of-islam-2/lamlam-SIM_4636?s.num=60&s.start=60.

Mazrui, Ali A. *The Politics of Gender and the Culture of Sexuality: Western, Islamic, and African Perspectives,* edited by Etin Anwar. Lanham, MD: University Press of America, 2014.

Mazuz, Haggai. "Islamic and Jewish Law on the Colors of Menstrual Blood." *Zeitschrift der Deutschen Morgenländischen Gesellschaft* 164 (2014): 97–106.

———. "Menstruation and Differentiation: How Muslims Differentiated Themselves from Jews regarding the Laws of Menstruation." *Der Islam* 87, nos. 1–2 (2012): 204–23.

———. "Midrashic Influence on Islamic Folklore: The Case of Menstruation." *Studia Islamica* 108 (2013): 189–201.

Mazzoni, Cristina. *Maternal Impressions: Pregnancy and Childbirth in Literature and Theory*. Ithaca, NY: Cornell University Press, 2002.

McGregor, Andrew James. *Darfur (Sudan) in the Age of Stone Architecture c. AD 1000–1750: Problems in Historical Reconstruction*. Oxford: Archaeopress, 2001.

Meinhof, Carl. "Afrikanische Worte in orientalischer Literatur." *Zeitschrift für Eingeborenen-Sprachen* 10 (1919–20): 147–52.

Meneghini, Daniela. "Saljuqid Literature." In *Encyclopaedia Iranica*, edited by Ehsan Yarshater. Updated May 25, 2010. https://www.iranicaonline.org/articles/saljuqs-v.

Menin, Laura. "'Dans la Peau d'un Noir': Senegalese Students and Young Professionals in Rabat, Morocco." *Anthropologia* 7, no. 1 (2020): 165–88

Mercier, Jacques. *Ethiopian Magic Scrolls*. New York: G. Braziller, 1979.

Merguerian, Gayane Karen, and Afsaneh Najmabadi. "Zulaykha and Yusuf: Whose 'Best Story'?" *International Journal for Middle East Studies* 29, no. 4 (1997): 485–508.

Miller, J. Reid. *Stain Removal: Ethics and Race*. Oxford: Oxford University Press, 2017.

Miller, Nathaniel. "Warrior Elites on the Verge of Islam: Between Court and Tribe in Arabic Poetry." In *Cross-Cultural Studies in Near Eastern History and Literature*, edited by Saana Svärd and Robert Rollinger, 2:140–73. Münster: Ugarit-Verlag, 2016.

Miller, Timothy S., and John W. Nesbitt. *Walking Corpses: Leprosy in Byzantium and the Medieval West*. Ithaca, NY: Cornell University Press, 2014.

Mills, Charles W. "The Chronopolitics of Racial Time." *Time & Society* 29, no. 2 (2020): 297–317.

Minissale, Gregory. *Images of Thought: Visuality in Islamic India 1550–1750*. Newcastle, UK: Cambridge Scholars, 2006.

Miquel, A. "Iḳlīm." In *Encyclopaedia of Islam*, 2nd ed., edited by Peri Bearman et al. Leiden: Brill, 2012. https://referenceworks.brillonline.com/entries/encyclopaedia-of-islam-2/iklim-SIM_3519?s.num=0&s.f.s2_parent=s.f.book.

Mitchell, Koritha. "Identifying White Mediocrity and Know-Your-Place Aggression: A Form of Self-Care." *African American Review* 51, no. 4 (2018): 253–62.

Mittman, Asa. "Are the 'Monstrous Races' Races?" *postmedieval* 6 (2015): 36–51.

Mohamed, Feisal G. "On Race and Historicism: A Polemic in Three Turns." *ELH* 89, no. 2 (2022): 377–405.

Montana, Ismael. *The Abolition of Slavery in Ottoman Tunisia*. Gainesville: University Press of Florida, 2013.

Montgomery, James E. *Dīwān ʿAntarah ibn Shaddād: A Literary-Historical Study*. New York: New York University Press, 2018.

Morgan, Jennifer L. *Reckoning with Slavery: Gender, Kinship, and Capitalism in the Early Black Atlantic*. Durham, NC: Duke University Press, 2021.

Mottahedeh, Roy. "ʿ*Ajāʾib* in *The Thousand and One Nights*. In The Thousand and One Nights *in Arabic Literature and Society*, edited by. Richard G. Hovannisian and Georges Sabagh, 29–39. Cambridge: Cambridge University Press, 1997.

Mrad Dali, Inès. "De l'esclavage à la servitude: Le cas des Noirs de Tunisie." *Cahiers d'Études Africaines* 45, no. 179/180 (2005): 935–55.

"MS Arabe 3840." Bibliothèque nationale de France, n.d.
"MS Arabe 3855." Bibliothèque nationale de France, n.d.
Mumisa, Michael. "Towards an African Qur'anic Hermeneutics." *Journal of Qur'anic Studies* 4, no. 1 (2002): 61–76.
Al-Munāwī. *Fayḍ al-Qadīr Sharḥ al-Jāmiʿ al-Ṣaghīr*. 6 vols. Cairo: al-Maktaba al-Tijāriya al-Kubrā, 1978.
Al-Muqaddisī. *Bibliotheca Geographorum Arabicorum* [*Aḥsan al-Taqāsīm fī Maʿrifat al-Aqālīm*]. Edited by M. J. De Goeje. Leiden: Brill: 1877.
Musallam, Basim. *Sex and Society in Islam: Birth Control before the Nineteenth Century*. New York: Cambridge University Press, 1983.
Myrne, Pernilla. *Female Sexuality in the Early Islamic World: Gender and Sex in Arabic Literature*. London: I. B. Tauris, 2020.
Nadeau, Carolyn A. "Blood Mother/Milk Mother: Breastfeeding, the Family, and the State in Antonio de Guevara's *Relox de Príncipes* (*Dial of Princes*)." *Hispanic Review* 69, no. 2 (2001): 153–74.
Nail, Thomas. "What Is an Assemblage?" *SubStance* 46, no. 1 (2017): 21–37.
Naylor, Phillip C. *North Africa: A History from Antiquity to the Present*. Austin: University of Texas Press, 2009.
Nevola, Luca. "'Black People, White Hearts': Origin, Race, and Colour in Contemporary Yemen." *Anthropologia* 7, no. 1 (2020): 93–115.
Nietzsche, Friedrich. "On Truth and Lying in a Non-Moral Sense." In *The Birth of Tragedy and Other Writings* edited by Raymond Guess and Ronald Speirs, 139–53. Cambridge: Cambridge University Press, 1999.
Nirenberg, David. *Communities of Violence: Persecution of Minorities in the Middle Ages*. Princeton, NJ: Princeton University Press, 1996.
———. "Race and Religion." In *A Cultural History of Race in the Middle Ages*, edited by Thomas Hahn, 67–80. London: Bloomsbury Academic, 2021.
———. "Was There Race before Modernity? The Example of 'Jewish' Blood in Late Medieval Spain." In *The Origins of Racism in the West*, ed. Miriam Eliav-Feldon et al., 232–64. Cambridge: Cambridge University Press, 2009.
Norris, H. T. "Arabic Folk Epic and the Western *Chanson de Geste*." *Oral Tradition* 4, nos. 1–2 (1989): 125–50.
———. "From Asia to Africa: The 'Tuḥfat Al-Albāb' by Abū Ḥāmid Al-Gharnāṭī (473/1080–565/1169) as a Source of Chronology and Content of the 'Sīrat ʿAntar B. Shaddād." *Bulletin of the School of Oriental and African Studies* 57 (1994): 174–83.
———. "The Futūḥ Al-Bahnasā: And Its Relation to Pseudo-ʿMaǧāzī' and 'Futūḥ' Literature, Arabic 'Siyar' and Western Chanson de Geste in the Middle Ages." *Quaderni Di Studi Arabi* 4 (1986): 71–86.
———. "Sayf b. Ḏī Yazan and the Book of the History of the Nile," *Quaderni di Studi Arabi* 7 (1989): 125–51.
Okorafor, Nnedi. *Antar the Black Knight*. Nnedi.com. Accessed August 1, 2023, https://nnedi.com/comics/antar-the-black-knight/.
Olsson, J. T. "The World in Arab Eyes: A Reassessment of the Climes in Medieval Islamic Scholarship." *Bulletin of the School of Oriental and African Studies* 77, no. 3 (2014): 487–508.
Omar, Hussein A. H. "'The Crinkly-Haired People of the Black Earth:' Examining Egyptian Identities in Ibn ʿAbd al-Ḥākim's *Futūḥ*." In *History and Identity in the*

Late Antique Near East, edited by Philip Wood, 149–67. Oxford: Oxford University Press, 2013.

O'Meara, Simon. "From Space to Place: The Quranic Infernalization of the Jinn." In *Locating Hell in Islamic Traditions*, edited by Christian Lange, 56–73. Leiden: Brill, 2016.

Ong, Walter. *Orality and Literacy: The Technologizing of the Word*. London: Routledge, 2012 (1982).

Ott, Claudia. "From the Coffeehouse into the Manuscript: The Storyteller and His Audience in the Manuscripts of an Arabic Epic." *Oriente Moderno* 22 (2003): 443–51.

———. *Metamorphosen des Epos: Sirat al-Mugahidin (Sirat al-Amira Dat al-Himma) Zwischen Mündlichkeit Und Schriftlichkeit*. Leiden: Universiteit Leiden, 2003.

Patterson, Orlando. *Slavery and Social Death: A Comparative Study*. Cambridge, MA: Harvard University Press, 1982.

Pavlovich, Pavel. "The Concept of Dahr and Its Historical Perspective in the Ğāhiliyya and Early Islam." *The Arabist: Budapest Studies in Arabic* 26–27 (2003): 51–60.

Pearce, S. J. "The Inquisitor and the Moseret: *The Invention of Race in the European Middle Ages* and the New English Colonialism in Jewish Historiography." *Medieval Encounters* 26 (2020): 145–90.

Pearson, M.N. "The Indian Ocean and the Red Sea," in *History of Islam in Africa*, edited by Nehemia Levtzion and Randall L. Pouwels, 38–59. Athens: Ohio University Press, 2012.

Pellegrino, Samantha. "The Gender of Magic: Constructions of Nonbinary Gender Categories in Sīrat Sayf ibn Dhī Yazan." *postmedieval* 13, nos. 3–4 (2022): 351–70.

Perlmann, Moshe. "Samauʾal Al-Maghribī Ifḥām Al-Yahūd: Silencing the Jews." *Proceedings of the American Academy for Jewish Research* 32 (1964): 57–104, 135–36.

Perry, Craig. "Historicizing Slavery in the Medieval Islamic World." *IJMES* 49 (2017): 133–38.

———. "Slavery and the Slave Trade in Western Indian Ocean World." In *The Cambridge World History of Slavery*. Vol. 2. Edited by Craig Perry, David Eltis, et al., 123–52. Cambridge: Cambridge University Press, 2021.

Petry, Carl F. *The Mamluk Sultanate: A History*. Cambridge: Cambridge University Press, 2022.

Pinto, Karen. "Capturing Imagination: The Buja and Medieval Islamic Mappa Mundi." In *Views from the Edge: Essays in Honor of Richard W. Bulliet*, edited by Neguin Yavari, Lawrence G. Potter, and Jean-Marc Ran Oppenheim, 154–83. New York: Columbia University Press, 2004.

Pipes, Daniel. "Mawlas: Freed Slaves and Converts in Early Islam." In *Slaves and Slavery in Muslim Africa*, vol. 1, edited by John Ralph Willis, 199–247. London: Routledge, 2014.

Pliny the Elder. *Natural History*. Translated by A. C. Andrews, D. E. Eichholz, W. H. S. Jones, and H. Rackham. Loeb Classical Library. Cambridge, MA: Harvard University Press, 2014.

Polomé, Edgar C. "Swahili in Tanzania." In *Language in Tanzania*, edited by Edgar C. Polomé and C. P. Hill. 79–102. London: Routledge, 1980.

Possekel, Ute. "Bardaisan's Influence on Late Antique Christianity." *Hugoye: Journal of Syriac Studies* 21, no. 1 (2018): 81–125.

Pouwels, Randall L. "The Medieval Foundations of East African Islam," *International Journal of African Historical Studies* 11, no. 2 (1978): 393–409.

Powell, Eve Troutt. *Tell This in My Memory: Stories of Enslavement from Egypt, Sudan, and the Ottoman Empire*. Stanford, CA: Stanford University Press, 2012.

Princess Dhat al-Himma: The Princess of High Resolve. Edited and translated by Shawqi ʿAbd al-Hakim and Omaima Abou-Bakr. Guizeh, Egypt: Prism Publications, 1995.

Puar, Jasbir K. "'I Would Rather Be a Cyborg Than a Goddess': Becoming-Intersectional in Assemblage Theory." *philoSOPHIA* 2, no. 1 (2012): 49–66.

Al-Qāḍī ʿAbd al-Jabbār. *Tathbīt Dalāʾil al-Nubuwwa*. Vol. 1. Cairo: Dār al-Muṣṭafā, 2010.

Al-Qalqashandī. *Ṣubḥ al-Aʿshā*. 14 vols. Cairo: al-Maṭbaʿa al-Amīriyya, 1915.

Al-Qāwūqjī, Muḥammad b. Khalīl. *Al-Lūʾlūʾ al-Marṣūʿ fī-mā Lā Aṣl li-hu aw bi-Aslihi Mawḍūʿ*. Beirut: Dār al-Bashāʾir al-Islāmiyya, 1994.

"Qq 247." Cambridge, n.d.

Qurṭubī, Abī ʿAbd Allāh Muḥammad b. Aḥmad al-. *Al-Jamiʿ li-Aḥkām al-Qurʾān*. Vol. 3. Cairo: Dār al-Kutub, 1967.

———. *Mukhtaṣir Tafsīr al-Qurṭubī*. Vol. 3. Edited by ʿIrfān Ḥassūna. Beirut: Dār al-Kutub al-ʿIlmiyya, 2001.

Qutbuddin, Tahera. "*Khuṭba*: The Evolution of Early Arabic Oration." In *Classical Arabic Humanities in Their Own Terms: Festschrift for Wolfhart Heinrichs*, edited by Beatrice Gruendler, 176–273. Leiden: Brill, 2008.

Rāghib al-Iṣfahānī. *Mufradāt Alfāẓ al-Qurʾān*. Beirut: al-Dār al-Shāmiyya, 1992.

Rankine, Claudia, and Beth Loffreda. "'On Whiteness and the Racial Imaginary: Where Writers Go Wrong in Imagining the Lives of Others.'" In *The Racial Imaginary: Writers on Race in the Life of the Mind*, edited by Claudia Rankine, Beth Loffreda, and Max King Cap, 13–22. Albany, NY: Fence Books, 2015.

Reid, Megan H. *Law and Piety in Medieval Islam*. Cambridge: Cambridge University Press, 2013.

Reynolds, Dwight. "Abū Zayd Al-Hilālī: Trickster, Womanizer, Warrior, Shaykh." *Journal of Arabic Literature* 49, nos. 1–2 (2018): 78–103.

———. "Episode 1: The Birth of Abu Zayd (Part 1)." In *Sirat Bani Hilal Digital Archive*. Santa Barbara, CA. Accessed September 18, 2018. http://www.siratbanihilal.ucsb.edu/node/425.

———. *Heroic Poets, Poetic Heroes: The Ethnography of Performance in an Arabic Oral Epic Tradition*. Ithaca, NY: Cornell University Press, 1995.

———. "Symbolic Narratives of Self: Dreams in Medieval Arabic Autobiographies." In *On Fiction and* Adab *in Medieval Arabic Literature*, edited by Philip F. Kennedy, 261–86. Wiesbaden: Harrassowitz, 2005.

Rhouni, Raja. *Secular and Islamic Feminist Critiques in the Work of Fatima Mernissi*. Leiden: Brill, 2010.

Richardson, Kristina. "Blue and Green Eyes in the Islamic Middle Ages." *Annales Islamologiques* 48, no. 1 (2014): 13–30.

———. *Difference and Disability in the Medieval Islamic World: Blighted Bodies*. Edinburgh: Edinburgh University Press, 2012.

———. *Roma in the Medieval Islamic World: Literacy, Culture, and Migration*. London: I. B. Tauris, 2022.

———. "Singing Slave Girls (Qiyan) of the ʿAbbasid Court in the Ninth and Tenth Centuries." In *Children in Slavery through the Ages*, edited by Gwyn Campbell, Suzanne Miers, and Joseph C. Miller, 105–18. Athens, OH: Ohio University Press, 2009.

———. "Tracing a Gypsy Mixed Language through Medieval and Early Modern Arabic and Persian Literature." *Der Islam* 94, no. 1 (2017): 115–57.

Rippin, Andrew. "The Trace of Prostration and other Distinguishing Bodily Marks in the Quran." *Bulletin of the School of Oriental and African Studies* 78, no. 1 (2015): 41–51.

Risso, Patricia. "Muslim Identity in Maritime Trade: General Observations and Some Evidence from the 18th-Century Persian Gulf/Indian Ocean Region." *International Journal of Middle East Studies* 21 (1989): 381–92.

Robin, Christian. "The Judaism of the Ancient Kingdom of Ḥimyar in Arabia: A Discreet Conversion." In *Diversity and Rabbinization: Jewish Texts and Societies between 400 and 1000 CE*, edited by Gavin McDowell et al., 165–270. Cambridge: Cambridge University Press, 2021.

Roggema, Barbara. *The Legend of Sergius Baḥīrā: Early Christian Apologetics and Apocalyptic in Response to Islam*. Leiden: Brill, 2009.

Root, Michael. "How We Divide the World." *Philosophy of Science* 67, no. 3 (2000): S628–S639.

Rubin, Uri. "'Al-Walad Li-Firāsh' on the Islamic Campaign against 'Zinā.'" *Studia Islamica* 78 (1993): 5–26.

Rustow, Marina. *The Lost Archive: Traces of a Caliphate in a Cairo Synagogue*. Princeton, NJ: Princeton University Press, 2020.

Saba, Matthew D. "ʿAbbasid Lusterware and the Aesthetics of ʿ*Ajab*." *Muqarnas* 29 (2012): 187–212.

Al-Ṣābiʾ, Hilāl b. al-Muḥsin. *Rusūm dār al-khilāfa*. Edited by Mikhāʾīl ʿAwwād. Beirut: Dār al-Rāʾid al-ʿArab, 1986.

Said, Edward. *Orientalism*. New York: Random House, 1979.

Saif, Liana. "The Universe and the Womb: Generation, Conception, and the Stars in Islamic Medieval Astrological and Medical Texts," *Journal of Arabic and Islamic Studies* 16 (2016): 181–98.

Savage, Elizabeth. "Berbers and Blacks: Ibadi Slave Traffic in Eighth-Century North Africa." *Journal of African History* 33 (1992): 351–68.

Savant, Sarah Bowen. "Isaac as the Persians' Ishmael: Pride and the Pre-Islamic Past in Ninth and Tenth-Century Islam." *Comparative Islamic Studies* 2, no. 1 (2006): 5–25.

———. "Naming Shuʿūbīs." In *Essays in Islamic Philology, History, and Philosophy: A Festschrift in Celebration and Honor of Professor Ahmad Mahdavi Damghani's 90th Birthday*, edited by K. A. Thackston et al., 166–84. Berlin: De Gruyter, 2016

———. *The New Muslims of Post-Conquest Iran: Tradition, Memory, and Conversion*. Cambridge: Cambridge University Press, 2013.

Schacht, Joseph. "Foreign Elements in Ancient Islamic Law." *Journal of Comparative Legislation and International Law* 32 (1950): 9–17.

Schimmel, Annemarie. "Some Glimpses of the Religious Life in Egypt during the Later Mamlūk Period." *Islamic Studies* 4, no. 4 (1965): 353–92.

Schine, Rachel. "Conceiving the Pre-Modern Black-Arab Hero: On the Gendered Production of Racial Difference in *Sīrat al-Amīrah Dhāt Al-Himmah*." *Journal of Arabic Literature* 48, no. 3 (2017): 298–326.

———. "Nourishing the Noble: Breastfeeding and Hero-Making in Medieval Arabic Popular Literature." *Al-ʿUṣūr al-Wusṭā* 27 (2019): 165–200.

Schippers, Arie. "An Episode in the Life of a Hero in the 'Sīrat Banī Hilāl': Abū Zayd as a Schoolboy." *Oriente Moderno* 22, no. 83 (2003): 347–59.

Secunda, Shai. "The Construction, Composition, and Idealization of the Female Body in Rabbinic Literature and Parallel Iranian Texts: Three Excursuses." *Nashim: A Journal of Jewish Women's Studies and Gender Issues* 23 (2012): 60–86.

———. "The Fractious Eye: On the Evil Eye of Menstruants in Zoroastrian Tradition." *Numen* 61, no. 1 (2014): 83–108.

Al-Shāfiʿī. "Bāb Dam al-Ḥayd." In *Kitāb al-Umm*. 8 vols. Beirut: Dār al-Fikr, 1990.

Shaham, Robert. "Masters, Their Freed Slaves, and the Waqf in Egypt (Eighteenth–Twentieth Centuries)." *Journal of the Economic and Social History of the Orient* 43, no. 2 (2000): 162–88.

Shahbazi, A. Shapur. "Haft Kešvar." In *Encyclopaedia Iranica*. Last updated March 1, 2012. http://www.iranicaonline.org/articles/haft-kesvar.

Al-Shahrastānī. *Kitāb al-Milal wa-l-Niḥal*. Edited by William Cuerton. Leipzig: Harrassowitz Verlag, 1923.

Al-Sharīf al-Jurjānī. *Sharḥ al-Mawāqif*. 8 vols. Edited by Maḥmūd ʿUmar al-Damiyāṭī. Beirut: Dār al-Kutub al-ʿIlmiyya, 2012.

Al-Shīrāzī, Rūzbihān al-Baqlī. *ʿArāʾis al-bayān fī ḥaqāʾiq al-Qurʾān*. Edited by Aḥmad Farīd al-Mizyadī. Beirut: Dār al-Kutub al-ʿIlmiyya, 2008.

Shoshan, Boaz. *Popular Culture in Medieval Cairo*. Cambridge: Cambridge University Press, 1993.

Silva, Denise Ferreira da. *Towards a Global Idea of Race*. Minneapolis: University of Minnesota Press, 2007.

Silvers, Laury. "Early Pious, Mystic Sufi Women." In *The Cambridge Companion to Sufism*, edited by L. Ridgeon, 24–52. Cambridge: Cambridge University Press, 2014.

Simpson, Marianna Shreve. *Sultan Ibrahim Mirza's* Haft Awrang*: A Princely Manuscript from Sixteenth Century Iran*. New Haven, CT: Yale University Press, 1997.

Sindawi, Khalid. "The Image of Ḥusayn Ibn ʿAlī in 'Maqātil' Literature." *Quaderni Di Studi Arabi* 20 (2003 2002): 79–104.

Al-Sīrāfī. *Accounts of China and India*. Trans. Tim Mackintosh-Smith. New York: NYU Press, 2014.

Sīrat ʿAntara ibn Shaddād. Beirut: al-Maktaba al-Shaʿbiyya, n.d.

Sīrat Banī Hilāl. Beirut: al-Maktaba al-Thaqāfiyya, 1980.

Sīrat Sayf ibn Dhī Yazan. Cairo: Maktabat al-Jumhūriyya al-ʿArabiyya, 1970.

"al-Siyar al-Shaʿbiyya al-ʿArabiyya 9: al-Amīra Dhāt al-Himma." YouTube. Uploaded by AlJazeera Documentary (*al-Jazīra al-Wathāʾiqiyya*). Accessed 10 July 2023. https://www.youtube.com/watch?v=03ybcjOqudY&list=PLmrET10kAE969YJBUlKVReAuY3LkSlApf&index=14.

Sizgorich, Thomas. *Violence and Belief in Late Antiquity: Militant Devotion in Christianity and Islam*. Philadelphia: University of Pennsylvania Press, 2009.

Slyomovics, Susan. "Praise of the Prophet and Praise of the Self: *Sīrat Banī Hilāl* and Epic Narrative in Performance." *Journal of Arabic Literature* 49 (2018): 50–77.

Sobers-Khan, Nur. *Slaves without Shackles: Forced Labour and Manumission in the Galata Court Registers, 1560–1572*. Berlin: Klaus Schwarz Verlag, 2014.

Sobieroj, Florian. *Variance in Arabic Manuscripts: Arabic Didactic Poems from the Eleventh to the Seventeenth Centuries—Analysis of Textual Variance and Its Control in the Manuscripts*. Berlin: De Gruyter, 2016.

Southgate, Minoo. "The Negative Images of Blacks in Some Medieval Iranian Writings." *Iranian Studies* 17, no. 1 (1984): 3–36.

Spaulding, Jay. "The Old Shaiqi Language in Historical Perspective." *History in Africa* 17 (1990): 283–92.

Stafford, A.O. "Antar, the Arabian Negro, Poet, and Hero." *Journal of Negro History* 1, no. 2 (1916): 151–62.

Stanley, Bruce. "Mogadishu." In *Cities of the Middle East and North Africa: A Historical Encyclopedia*, edited by. Michael Dumper and Bruce Stanley, 251. Santa Barbara, CA: ABC-CLIO, 2007.

Stearns, Justin K. "Race in the Islamicate Middle East: Reflections after Heng." *Cambridge Journal of Postcolonial Literary Inquiry* (2022): 114–21.

———. *Revealed Sciences: Natural Sciences in Islam in Seventeenth-Century Morocco*. Cambridge: Cambridge University Press, 2021.

Steeves, Edna L. "Negritude and the Noble Savage." *Journal of Modern African Studies* 11, no. 1 (1973): 91–104.

Steinberg, Amanda Hannoosh. "Wives, Witches, and Warriors: Women in Arabic Popular Epics." PhD diss., University of Pennsylvania, 2018.

Stone, Caroline. "The Great Migration of the Bani Hilal." *AramcoWorld* (November 2016), 16. https://www.aramcoworld.com/Articles/November-2016/The-Great-Migration-of-the-Bani-Hilal.

Sujimon, M. S. "Istilḥāq and Its Role in Islamic Law." *Arab Law Quarterly* 18, no. 2 (2003): 117–43.

Al-Sulamī, Abū ʿAbd al-Raḥmān Muḥammad b. al-Ḥusayn. *Ḥaqāʾiq al-tafsīr*. Edited by Sayyid ʿUmrān. Beirut: Dār al-Kutub al-ʿIlmiyya, 2001.

Sweet, James H. "The Iberian Roots of American Racist Thought." *William and Mary Quarterly* 54, no. 1 (1997): 143–66.

Szombathy, Zoltán. "Eating People Is Wrong: Some Eyewitness Reports of Cannibalism in Arabic Sources." In *Violence in Islamic Thought from the Qurʾān to the Mongols*, edited by Robert Gleave and István Kristó-Nagy. Edinburgh: Edinburgh University Press, 2015.

———. "Genealogy in Medieval Muslim Societies." *Studia Islamica* 95 (2002): 5–35.

———. "Motives and Techniques of Genealogical Forgery in Pre-modern Muslim Societies." In *Genealogy and Knowledge in Muslim Societies: Understanding the Past*, edited by Sarah Bowen Savant and Helen de Felipe, 24–36. Edinburgh: Edinburgh University Press, 2014.

Szonyi, Michael. *The Art of Being Governed: Everyday Politics in Late Imperial China*. Princeton, NJ: Princeton University Press, 2017.

Al-Tabari. *Tārīkh al-Rusul wa-l-Mulūk*. Vol. 1. Edited by Muḥammad Abū-l-Faḍl Ibrāhīm. Cairo: Dār al-Maʿārif, 1967.

Taiz, Lincoln, and Lee Taiz. *Flora Unveiled: The Discovery and Denial of Sex in Plants*. Oxford: Oxford University Press, 2017.

The Tale of the Princess Fatima, Warrior Woman: The Arabic Epic of Dhat al-Himma. Translated by Melanie Magidow. New York: Penguin Books, 2021.

Talhami, Ghada Hashem. "The Zanj Rebellion Reconsidered." *International Journal of African Historical Studies* 10 (1977): 443–61.

Al-Tasūlī. *Al-Bahja fī Sharḥ al-Tahfa*. Edited by Muḥammad ʿAbd al-Qadr Shāhīn. Beirut: Dār al-Kutub al-ʿIlmiyya, 1998.

Thaʿālabī, Abū Manṣūr al-. *Yatīmat al-Dahr fī Shuʿarāʾ Ahl al-ʿAṣr*. Vol. 2. Damascus: s.n., 1885.

Thaʿlabī, Aḥmad b. Muḥammad al-. *Tafsir al-Thaʿlabī*. Edited by Majdī Bāslūm. Beirut: Dār al-Kutub al-ʿIlmiyya, 2004.

Thaʿlabī, Aḥmad b. Muḥammad al-, and ʿAbd Allāh b. Asʿad Yāfiʿī. *Qiṣaṣ al-Anbiyāʾ: al-Musamma bi-l-Araʾis al-Majālis*. Cairo: Maktabat al-Jumhūriyya al-ʿArabiyya, 1900.

Al-Tijānī, Muḥammad ibn Aḥmad. *Tuḥfat al-ʿArūs wa-Mutaʿa al-Nufūs*. Edited by Jalil al-Atiyah. London: Riad El-Rayyes, 1992.

Tlili, Sarra. "All Animals Are Equal, or Are They? The Ikhwān al-Ṣafāʾ's Animal Epistle and Its Unhappy End." *Journal of Qurʾanic Studies* 16, no. 2 (2014): 42–88.

Toledano, Ehud. *As If Silent and Absent: Bonds of Enslavement in the Islamic Middle East*. New Haven, CT: Yale University Press, 2007.

Tolmacheva, Marina. "Toward a Definition of the Term *Zanj*." *Azania* 21, no. 1: 105–13.

Urban, Elizabeth. *Conquered Populations in Early Islam: Non-Arabs, Slaves, and the Sons of Slave Mothers* (Edinburgh: Edinburgh University Press, 2019).

———. "Race, Gender and Slavery in Early Islamicate History," *History Compass* 20, no. 5 (2022). https://doi.org/10.1111/hic3.12727.

van der Lugt, Maaike. "Race and Science: Black Skin in Medieval Medicine and Natural Philosophy." In *A Cultural History of Race in the Middle Ages*, edited by Thomas Hahn, 81–96. London: Bloomsbury Academic, 2021.

van Gelder, Geert Jan. *Classical Arabic Literature: A Library of Arabic Literature Anthology*. New York: New York University Press, 2013.

———. "Foul Whisperings: Madness and Poetry in Arabic Literary History." In *Arabic Humanities, Islamic Thought*, edited by Joseph E. Lowry and Shawkat M. Toorawa. 150–75. Leiden: Brill, 2017.

Van Leeuwen, Richard. "Conversion as a (Meta-)Historical Concept in the Epic Stories of the *Thousand and One Nights*." In *Fictionalizing the Past: Historical Characters in Arabic Popular Epic*, edited by Sabine Dorpmüller, 125–37. Leiden: Uitgeverij Peeters en Departement Oosterse Studies, 2012.

Vantheighem, Naïm. "Quelques contrats de vente d'esclaves de la collection Aziz Atiyya." *Journal of Juristic Papyrology* 44 (2014): 163–187.

Vaziri, Parisa. "False Differends: Racial Slavery and the Genocidal Example." *Philosophy Today* (2022): n.p.

———. "No One's Memory: Blackness at the Limits of Comparative Slavery," *POMEPS* 44 (2020).

Wade, Peter. "Race, Ethnicity, and Technologies of Belonging," *Science, Technology, & Human Values* 39, no. 4 (2014): 587–96.

Ware, Rudolph T. III. *The Walking Qur'an: Islamic Education, Embodied Knowledge, and History in West Africa*. Chapel Hill: University of North Carolina Press, 2014.

Webb, Peter. "Al-Jāhiliyya: Uncertain Times of Uncertain Meanings." *Der Islam* 91, no. 1 (2014): 69–94.

———. "Ethnicity, Power, and Umayyad Society: The Rise and Fall of the People of Maʿadd." In *The Umayyad World*, edited by Andrew Marsham. London: Routledge, forthcoming.

———. *Imagining the Arabs: Arab Identity and the Rise of Islam*. Edinburgh: Edinburgh University Press, 2016.

Wheeler, Branon. "Alexander." In *Medieval Islamic Civilization: An Encyclopedia*. Vol. 1. Edited by Josef W. Meri. 29–30. New York: Routledge, 2006.

Whitaker, Cord J. *Black Metaphors: How Modern Racism Emerged from Medieval Race Thinking*. Philadelphia: University of Pennsylvania Press, 2019.

———. "Black Metaphors in the *King of Tars*." *Journal of English and Germanic Philosophy* 112, no. 2 (2013): 169–93.

Whitbrook, James. "Why Are We So Fascinated by Origin Stories?" *Gizmodo*, November 16, 2014. https://gizmodo.com/why-are-we-so-fascinated-by-origin-stories-1663820928.

Wickett, Elizabeth. *Seers, Saints, and Sinners: The Oral Tradition of Upper Egypt*. London: I.B. Tauris, 2012.

Wilderson, Frank B. III. *Afropessimism*. New York: W. W. Norton, 2020.

Windmuller-Luna, Kristen. "Ethiopian Healing Scrolls." In *Heilbrunn Timeline of Art History*. New York: The Metropolitan Museum of Art, 2015. http://www.metmuseum.org/toah/hd/heal/hd_heal.htm.

Wingham, Zavier. "Arap Bacı'nın Ara Muhaveresi: Under the Shadow of the Ottoman Empire and Its Study." *YILLIK: Annual of Istanbul Studies* 3 (2021): 177–83.

Wink, André. *Al-Hind: The Making of the Indo-Islamic World*. Vol. 3. Leiden: Brill, 2004.

Wittingham, Martin. *A History of Muslim Views of the Bible: The First Four Centuries*. Berlin: De Gruyter, 2021.

Wolf, Arthur P. *Incest Avoidance and the Incest Taboos: Two Aspects of Human Nature*. Stanford, CA: Stanford University Press, 2014.

Zadeh, Travis. "The Wiles of Creation: Philosophy, Fiction, and the *ʿAjā'ib* Tradition." *Middle Eastern Literatures* 13, no. 1 (2010): 21–48.

Zaydān, Jūrjī. *ʿIlm al-Firāsa al-Ḥadīth*. London: Hindāwī, 2011.

Zias, Joseph. "Lust and Leprosy: Confusion or Correlation?" *Bulletin of the American Schools of Oriental Research* 275 (1989): 27–31.

Index

ʿAbbasid empire, 13, 21, 74, 166, 197, 220, 231, 236, 265, 295; and Abū'l-Hazāhiz, 205; and army, 164; and caliphs, 191, 193, 295; and al-Hādī, 110; and Islam, 112, 200; and al-Maʾmūn, 247; and al-Manṣūr, 288; and *munāẓarāt*, 55; and *qiyān*, 289; and race, 87; and Hārūn al-Rashīd, 193, 216; and *sīras*, 267, 277; and state, 184; and trade, 31; and al-Wāthiq, 22

ʿabīd (slaves), 3, 123, 315. *See also* enslaved people; enslavement; slavery

Abū Bakr, 146, 177, 196

Abū'l-Hazāhiz, 202, 211, 225, 245, 284; and ʿAbd al-Wahhāb, 193, 197–98, 207–8, 210, 212–21, 223, 242; and assimilation, 191, 310; and Black masculinity, 224; and blackness, 199; and Black troops, 206–7; and Byzantines, 201–2, 204–7; and conversion, 215; depictions of, 203n37; and deracination, 203; and faith, 192; as father of convulsions, 191; and Hadlamūs, 271; and Kharijism, 201, 224; and Maymūna, 295; and "ogre," 192; and Harūn al-Rashīd, 199–200, 217; and religious literacy, 205; and social structures, 192; story of, 192, 200; and *wālaʾ*, 197, 219

Abū Zayd al-Hilālī, 6, 67–68, 70, 77–78, 86, 112, 172; and Bakātūsh, 27; and birth narrative, 25, 43, 64, 80; and blackness, 39–40, 65–66, 71–72, 75, 104; and Khaḍrāʾ, 64, 71, 102; and *sharīfa*, 41; and *sīras*, 73; and Zaḥlān, 76

Abū Zayd al-Sīrāfī, 249–50, 261

Africa, 231; and Abū'l-Hazāhiz, 202–3, 205; and Arabia's tribes, 26; and Arabic epics, 31; and Arabs, 65, 121; and Black Africans, 61, 88n15, 118, 121, 164, 176, 203n37, 230, 256, 260; and eunuchs, 110; and fables, 29; and *al-Hilāliyya*, 27; and *jāhilī*, 206; and landscape, 232; and literature, 230; and migration, 73; and Muslim sovereigns, 72; and slavery, 24n58, 164, 235; sub-Saharan, 27, 203, 224, 252, 263, 265

Africanness, 313

aghbar (dark-colored), 92, 106, 142, 182

ahl al-bayt, 48

ʿajāʾib, 42, 231–32; and *gharāʾib*, 264

amulets, 298–99

Anatolia, 5, 17, 165, 193, 209, 245, 254, 269; and ʿAbd al-Wahhāb, 5–6, 89, 99–100, 137, 142, 151, 192, 201, 303–4, 317; and Abū'l-Hazāhiz, 191, 193, 197–98, 206–7, 210–21, 223, 242, 245; and Arabness, 165; and assimilation, 31; and birth narrative, 30, 92–94, 111–12, 118–19, 133, 138–39, 145, 147, 156, 182; as Black hero, 81–82, 124, 164, 189, 208, 271–73, 296, 313, 315–16; and blackness, 39–41, 84, 88, 95–97, 104, 108, 114–15, 138, 143, 145, 158, 222, 234, 256, 259, 285, 310, 316; and complexion, 94, 107, 129; and conception

Anatolia (*continued*)
story, 156–58; and Damdamān, 278, 282, 284; and Fāṭima, 165, 300; and Ghāsiq, 266–69, 283–84; and *ḥadīths*, 146; and hybridity, 86, 190; as *ibn ḥayḍa* (child of a menstruant), 113; and identity, 90, 110, 275; and Hadlamūs, 239, 243, 245; and kinship, 125; and Maymūna, 32, 254, 270, 276–79, 281–88, 291–94, 297, 299, 301–2, 305–7; and menstrual discharge, 133, 135; origins of, 128; and paternity, 93, 98–99, 101–2, 106, 110, 140; and peers, 17; and race, 117; and racialized difference, 109; and Hārūn al-Rashīd, 184; and religious laws, 244; and Ṣaḥṣāḥ, 163; and *sīras*, 133, 138, 184, 186, 296; and skin color, 18, 83, 94, 103, 141, 144, 153, 186; and slavery, 167

Arabian Epic, The (Lyons), 8

Arabian genealogy, 164

Arabian heredity, 13, 190, 195–96

Arabian maternity, 87

Arabian Peninsula, 99, 184–85, 193, 262, 264–65

Arabian society, 163–65, 168, 172, 256

Arabian sovereignty, 53

Arabian tribes, 1, 5–6, 46, 72–73, 98, 162, 195

Armanūs, 305–6

asmar (dark), 66, 68–69, 71, 76, 81, 142, 299

Axum, 237

Axumite, 237, 255

Banū Ṭayy, 5, 167–68, 223

Baṭṭāl, al- (Baṭṭāl Ghāzī), 5–6, 17, 22n54, 165, 208, 214, 244, 260, 291, 297, 315

Beirut, 24–25, 66, 72, 76, 139n52

bilād al-sūdān ("lands of the Blacks"), 230, 253, 266, 269–72, 275, 308; and ʿAbd al-Wahhāb, 254; and Arabic sciences, 16; and *aswad*, 118; and Black heroes, 7; and cannibalism, 63; and Damdam, 248, 252; and diversity, 234–35; and Hadlamūs, 257; and landscape, 83; members of, 233; norms of, 238; regions of, 248; and *sīras*, 31, 233–34, 239, 256

birthmarks, 60, 71, 101

birth narratives, 1, 25, 40, 75, 93, 118–19, 133, 145, 185, 197; and ʿAbd al-Wahhāb, 30, 81, 93–94, 98, 111–12, 118–19, 133, 138–40, 145, 156, 182; and Abū Zayd al-Hilālī, 25, 43, 64, 66–67, 80; Afro-Arab, 41; and ʿAntara b. Shaddād, 46–47, 59, 80, 92; and heroes, 41, 47; and Junduba, 4; and Khaḍrāʾ, 67; and Rizq, 67. See also *sīra*

birthrights, 29

Blackness, 4, 7, 27, 82, 126, 141, 208, 214, 241, 296; and Abū'l-Hazāhiz, 213, 215; and ʿAbd al-Wahhāb, 30, 85, 97, 113–15, 118, 138–39, 143, 145, 156, 158, 165, 197, 212, 269, 276, 284, 305–6, 310, 316–17; and Abū Zayd al-Hilālī, 65–66; and Africanness, 313; and al-Jāḥiẓ, 96, 151, 261; ancestral, 72, 75; and antiblackness, 33–34; apparent, 72; and Arabic literature, 15, 40, 43, 46; and Arabness, 270; and bastardy, 102; beginnings of, 83; and Black Africans, 260; and Black movement, 16; demonization of, 307; and enslaved people, 124; and enslavement, 154–55, 170–71, 224, 290; etiology, 75; and exclusion, 94; and Hadlamūs, 258, 262; and heroes, 43–44; and Jaffāl, 179; and leprosy, 150, 155; and masculinity, 84; and Maymūna, 279, 288, 291–93, 306–7, 310; and menstruation, 106, 119, 140, 147, 156; and Middle East, 18; nonhereditary, 40, 93, 114, 145, 256; and North Africa, 18; and poetry, 55, 57, 236, 257; premodern, 9, 19; racialized, 89, 121, 192, 200, 278, 319; and Sallām, 169; seeing, 57; and social dependency, 40; and Sufi writings, 137; and whiteness, 18, 41, 46, 58, 104, 173; and Zabība, 45, 56

Black soldiers, 3, 32, 84, 206, 216, 233, 259, 271, 295, 300

blood, 11, 119, 120, 124, 129–31, 144, 182, 219, 249n57, 261; and blackness, 138; menstrual, 86, 105–9, 114, 118, 126–28,

133–35, 140–43, 147–49, 156; and purity, 108, 120, 131; quantum, 14, 121; and race, 117, 157; and sex, 91–92, 142, 150; and *sīras*, 126, 278; and *Sīrat Dhāt al-Himma*, 11n21; womb, 128–29, 194
bloodline, 118, 126, 130n34
boundaries, 11, 52, 88, 95, 165, 221, 225, 239, 253, 274, 303; intercommunal, 140; intracommunal, 308; and maps, 263; sexual, 145; social, 274
Byzantine Christians (*al-Rūm*), 5, 16, 104, 207, 257, 262
Byzantines, 32, 86, 124, 206, 232, 284; and agency, 16; and Arab conflicts, 112, 314; and borderlands, 138n51; and Christianity, 207; and frontiers, 242; and rulers, 201–4, 207, 253, 258, 297–98, 300–302, 304–5; and soldiers, 201, 317; and spies, 91; and territories, 31, 297; and *thaghr*, 270; and veiling, 202n34; and warfare, 5; and women, 17, 202n34, 205, 207, 258, 290, 307

Cairo, 24–25, 78, 108, 133, 139, 141–44, 254
caliphs, 82, 91, 110, 191, 198, 216–18, 220–21, 269, 289, 295–97, 300
Caucasus, 5, 232, 318
Christianity, 205–6, 232, 235–39, 254, 255n83, 276, 294, 299–302, 318–19; and ʿAbd al-Wahhāb, 214, 305; and Abyssinia, 238–39, 269; and ascetic disposition, 138n51; Byzantine, 5, 16, 207; and Christian apocrypha, 4; and Christian armies, 17; and Christian Europeans, 8, 167; and Christian Iberians, 120; and Christian writings, 42; and clergy, 143n60; and converts, 32, 82, 110–11, 204, 212–14, 275, 294; and Ethiopians, 27; and Hadlamūs, 242, 244, 271; and legal codes, 155n93; and *majdhūm*, 154; and Maymūna, 304, 307–8, 317; and Muslims, 31, 51, 166, 244, 255; and Muslim spaces, 17; and pietisms, 241; and proselytization, 270; and race-making, 121; and romantic narratives, 135; and scripture, 101, 242; and *Sīrat Dhāt al-Himma*, 5, 149; and tradition, 245; and ʿUqba, 5, 91, 229, 244, 246, 262, 296, 301; and warriors, 203
commodification, 34, 58, 96, 234, 268
conception narratives, 86n10, 112
conquest narratives, 253
Copts, 50, 195, 237, 255n83; *ahl al-madara al-sawdāʾ* (people of the black loam), 50

Damdamān, 233, 253, 255, 270, 280–82, 284, 288, 305; and ʿAbd al-Wahhāb, 254, 256, 269, 277–78; and *ḥabasha*, 246; and Hadlamūs, 245, 247n47, 271; and Islam, 271; and Maymūna, 248, 254, 275; and Muslims, 256; and religiosity, 248; and *Sīrat Dhāt al-Himma*, 266; and sovereignty, 245; and tyranny, 246; and ʿUqba, 246
ḍarar (harm), 91, 153, 223, 292
darkness, 56, 72, 95, 173–74, 262–63, 283, 302, 306–7; and ʿAbd al-Wahhāb, 90, 305; lands of, 16; and menstruation, 128; and *sumr*, 54
dark skin, 18, 27, 40, 173, 291; and ʿAbd al-Wahhāb, 283; and Abū Zayd al-Hilālī, 65; and dark-faced (*adgham*), 61; and demons, 241n29; and enslaved girls, 55; and Fāṭima, 103; and Mūsā al-Kāẓim, 107; and Majnūn, 56; and Maymūna, 288; and *qiṣār*, 263; and *suḥm*, 50; and vilification, 180; and Zanj, 261
Dhāt al-Himma, Fāṭima, 93, 113, 138n51, 165, 172, 259n93, 290, 304; and ʿAbd al-Wahhāb, 5, 81–82, 84–85, 95–96, 98, 103, 113, 243, 259, 276, 291–92, 297, 300, 302; and adultery, 95, 97; and al-Ḥārith, 89–92, 102–5, 110, 145, 157, 214, 230; and chastity, 103; and conception narrative, 86n10; and Hadlamūs, 245; as heroine, 112, 242–43; and Islam, 311; and Jaʿfar, 108–10; and marital prowess, 112; and Marzūq, 82, 88; and Maslama, 316; and Maymūna, 287–89, 291, 293, 297–98, 308–10, 316; and Maẓlūm, 5; and menstruation,

Dhāt al-Himma, Fāṭima (*continued*) 92, 108; as mother, 93–94, 103; and Muḥammad, 87; and *nuṭfa*, 109; and pregnancy, 89, 103; and promiscuity, 102; and race, 84; and rape, 91, 108; and sex, 92, 108; as warrior, 89
didactic narratives, 7, 78, 112, 124, 129, 133, 137, 192, 224, 314, 321
dīn (religion; pl. *adyān*), 12, 205–6, 212
dreams, 41, 46, 110, 168, 302–4, 308, 311

East Africa, 247–48, 252, 254–57, 264, 266, 268, 272, 288, 299, 310, 317; and ʿAbd al-Wahhāb, 158, 275–78, 284, 286, 305; and Abyssinia, 31, 39, 88, 269; and Arabness, 18; and armies, 260; and Beja, 15, 255, 255n83, 256, 267; and Black East Africans, 308–9; and Blackness, 16; and environments, 5, 270; and Ḥām, 71; and Ḥamīda, 107; and imams, 107; and maternal descent, 97; and Maymūna, 32, 305, 208; and migration, 73; and Muslims, 236, 245, 308; and Qarmatians, 247–48; and religion, 244; and rulers, 208; and Sayf b. Dhī Yazan, 23; and *sīras*, 31, 209, 234, 262, 267, 309; and *Sīrat Dhāt al-Himma*, 229, 232–33, 263; and slavery, 50; and soldiers, 269, 296; and women, 290; and Zanj, 88, 175, 198n25, 249, 253n73
enslaved people, 2, 10n18, 30, 40, 45n17, 132n41, 168, 178, 186, 215–16, 224, 233; and ʿAbd al-Wahhāb, 110; and Abū'l-Hazāhiz, 197; Abyssinia, 6, 12, 164; and afterlife of slavery, 88n16; and ʿAntara b. Shaddād, 53; in Arabic literature, 24, 34, 89n18, 113; Black, 28, 30, 34, 50, 66, 68, 88n16, 118, 164, 167, 177, 179, 183, 185, 187, 230, 310; and Blackness, 4, 72, 75, 124, 155, 197, 220, 224; and bodily defects, 151; as elites, 171; and eunuchs, 110; as export, 267; and genealogical protectionism, 183; and Indian Ocean, 170; inspection of, 125n18, 290; and Iraq, 198; and Islamic world, 171; and *jawār*, 202n34; and Junduba, 181; and *khāl*, 278; and leprosy, 154; and Mahdī'l-Zamān, 206; *mamlūk*, 75; and manumission, 162, 197; and Maymūn, 178; military, 5; and mothers, 87; and natural slavery, 121, 253; purchase of, 208, 246; and race, 59, 318; renaming of, 96; and sexual relations, 223; and *sīras*, 221; and *Sīrat ʿAntar*, 17; and social death, 171; and social order, 124; and status, 153, 155; and Ṭayy, 172, 185–86, 221, 223–24; and the *1001 Nights*, 169; traffic of, 154; and troops, 3; uncastrated, 3; and whiteness, 124; and women, 51, 53, 57, 59–60, 87, 99, 112, 124n14, 168, 289–90, 293; and Zanj, 198, 290, 295
enslavement, 269, 317; and Atlantic world, 170; birth into, 87; and blackness, 89n16, 154, 170–71; conditions of, 170; and conversion, 204n38; elite, 21; experience of, 113; former, 187, 197; and Hājar, 50; and Islamic world, 124, 253; and kinship, 225; legacy of, 315; machinery of, 252; obligation, 153
ethnicity, 3n4, 9–10, 14n29, 15, 23n56, 88, 88n15, 281, 235, 249, 296, 320n17; and ethnic consciousness, 164; and ethnic groups, 16, 239n26; and identity, 87

Fakhr al-Sūdān ʿalā-l-Bīḍān (*The Boasts of the Blacks over the Whites*), 10, 96, 152, 236, 262, 310
fathers, 42, 65, 67–68, 76–77, 100, 105, 149; and ʿAbd al-Wahhāb, 40, 82–83, 94–98, 106, 108, 144, 212–13, 218–20, 277–78, 306, 316; and Abū'l-Hazāhiz, 215; and Abū Humām, 135; and ʿAntara b. Shaddād, 6, 24n58, 40, 63, 82; Arab, 236; and al-Baṭṭāl, 297; and Blackness, 143, 197, 306; and Christianity, 71; and father-child separation, 47, 63; and Ghaṭrīf, 187; and *hajīn*, 14; and Ḥām, 3–4, 132, 251; and al-Ḥārith, 82, 101–4, 110–12, 167, 316; and *ilḥāq*, 53n40; and illicit acts, 133; and *ḥasab*, 299; and Jesus, 140; and Junduba, 1, 167; and kinship disputes, 47; and lineage, 71, 109, 142; and Madhbaḥūn,

297; and Mary, 140; and Maymūna, 266, 275, 277, 280–81, 284, 304; and Maẓlūm, 89; and *muqrif*, 87; and *nasab*, 60, 87, 118, 162, 299; and *nuṭfa*, 118, 144; and Salmā, 172–73, 178, 183–84; and Shaddād, 45, 54, 61–62; and ʿUqba, 286; and Zabība, 45, 54
fitna, 17, 307
fursān (knights), 3, 29, 178, 211, 234

gender, 79, 82, 84–85, 87, 123, 136, 153, 197, 213, 276, 293, 307–8; and anxiety, 63; and associations, 40, 51; and Black soldiers, 3; and categories, 114n70; and class, 52, 88; and disparity, 223; and moral panic, 75; and race, 30, 113, 157; structures of, 52; and violence, 96
genealogy, 189–90, 196, 198, 292, 309; and Arabs, 18; and genealogical claims, 73; and genealogical forgery, 45n16; and genealogical knowledge, 193; and genealogical models, 44n15; and genealogical priorities, 194; and genealogical protectionism, 183; and genealogical relationships, 64; and genealogical sciences, 14n30; and genealogical standing, 7, 46, 59; and genealogical thinking, 12, 119
Ghāsiq, 266–69, 272, 281–84
God, 2, 52, 92–93, 135–36, 193, 251; and Abū'l-Hazāhiz, 204, 214; and ʿAbd Hubal, 106; and ʿAbd al-Wahhāb, 101, 208, 215, 287, 297; and Blackness, 140, 143, 298, 313; and blood, 126; and curse of Ḥām, 132; and dreams, 303; and Fāṭima, 95, 103, 243; and Hadlamūs, 242; and Ibrāhīm, 47, 51, 246; and Jaʿfar, 128; and *Jamharat Ansāb al-ʿArab*, 198–99; and Maymūna, 280, 286, 291–92; and menstruation, 105; messenger of, 143, 146, 196, 302; and Muḥammad, 100; and love, 279; and nonbelievers, 137; and Nūrā, 298; and *nuṭfa*, 132; and omniscience, 80, 223; Oneness of, 6; and piety, 13; and poetry, 64, 68, 77n108; and al-Qāʾim, 213; and Qurʾān, 93, 182, 273; and Quraysh, 237; revelation from, 46; and Sabaʿa, 134; and Sallām, 168; and Salmā, 183; and *ṣamad*, 93; and Shaddād b. Quarād, 58; and *Sūrat al-Muʾminīn*, 127; and *Sūrat al-Nūr*, 262; and womb kinship, 194; and *zabāniya*, 239–40

Hādī, al-, 55, 208
Hadlamūs, 239n26, 244, 259–60, 262, 271; and ʿAbd al-Wahhāb, 239, 243; and Banū Kardam, 246n47; and *bilād al-sūdān*, 256–57; and conversion, 230; and Damdamān, 246, 247n47, 248; and Ghāsiq, 283; and Maymūna, 248; as Negus, 233; and *sīras*, 235; and ʿUqba, 241–43, 245–46, 258
Ḥām (Ham), 206; and Black bile, 133; children of, 5, 50, 53, 59, 110, 172, 251, 280, 284, 314; and curse, 3, 4n6, 71, 83, 131–32; and menstruation, 133; and Noah, 13, 40, 83, 131–32, 137; and poetry, 2; and Sām (Shem), 40, 53; and wife, 132
Ḥārith, al-, 82, 89–92, 95, 97–98, 100–105, 108–13, 135, 145, 156–57, 167–69, 212, 214, 229, 316
heroes, 1, 11, 20, 62, 78, 80, 162, 174, 232, 235, 300, 304, 308, 311; and ʿAbd al-Wahhāb, 5–6, 30, 41, 81, 98, 109–13, 115, 158, 164, 167, 208, 213, 221, 245, 254, 266, 281, 285–86, 296, 313–16; and Abū Zayd al-Hilālī, 64, 66, 68, 71, 76; Afro-Arab, 41; and ʿAntara b. Shaddād, 6, 24n58, 26, 59, 63, 234; Arab, 8, 15, 36, 85, 117, 189, 269; and *ʿayyār*, 17; and birth narratives, 47, 185; and al-Baṭṭāl, 5; Black, 7, 15, 18, 21, 25, 27–30, 39, 41–44, 54, 59, 81, 83, 85, 89, 93, 98, 111, 117, 124, 140, 186, 189–90, 197–98, 220–21, 270, 278, 314; and blackness, 27, 44, 46, 118, 317; and Fāṭima Dhāt al-Himma, 5, 112–13, 172, 230, 242, 288; forms of, 5; and *Ḥalab*, 72; and al-Ḥārith, 214; and identity, 31, 40, 118; and Junduba, 167; and lineage, 189; and *maqātil* (martyrological) literature, 48; and Maymūna, 285–89, 310; and moral construction, 183;

heroes (*continued*)
and *nasab*, 187; and paternity suits, 18; pre-Islamic, 22; and race, 30, 43; and Sayf b. Dhī Yazan, 6, 71, 161; and *sīras*, 32, 47, 111, 138n51, 172, 279; and *Sīrat Banī Hilāl*, 66; and *Sīrat Dhāt al-Himma*, 24, 41, 199, 276–77; and *siyar shaʿbiyya*, 39, 71, 75, 93; in *Tale of the Princess, Possessor of Ambition*, 3; in *The Take of the Pious Warriors*, 5; and women, 89
Ḥumām, 135, 232
hypersexuality, 58, 290

Ibn ʿAdnān, Maʿadd, 195–96
Ibn al-Ḥārith, Junduba, 1–2, 17, 167, 175, 181; and Blackness, 4; and Black soldiers, 3; and *fuḥūl*, 3; and Ghaṭrīf, 172; and Ḥām, 3–5; and Kilābī, 164; and Maymūn, 178–79; and Maẓlūm, 5; and Sallām, 168–69; and Salmā, 177; and Shamṭā, 84; as warrior, 4
Ibn Kanaʿān, Nimrūd (Nimrod), 26, 53, 246; and ʿAntara b. Shaddād, 48, 51–52, 61; and Hājar, 51; and Ibrāhīm, 47, 49–50, 52; and Kūsh, 46
Ibn Marwān, ʿAbd al-Malik, 163, 165, 184, 187, 193, 235
Ibn Qurād, Shaddād, 58–59
Ibn Shaddād, ʿAntara (ʿAntar), 28–29, 45n17, 52, 54–58, 61–63, 82, 112, 161–64, 179, 231, 288; and ʿAbd al-Wahhāb, 40, 86, 97; and ʿAbla, 45; and ʿAbs, 46; and Abū Zayd al-Hilālī, 78; and Afro-Arab heritage, 39; and Arabness, 60; and birth, 43, 50–54, 92; and Black people, 50, 314; and court of al-Maʾmūn, 28; and Egypt, 26; and enslavement, 53; as hero, 6, 22, 234; and paternity, 40; and Shaybūb, 17; and Zuhayr, 62
Ibrāhīm, 26, 44, 46–53, 134, 273
Islam, 266, 275–76, 309, 315, 319, 321; and ʿAbd al-Wahhāb, 206, 214–15, 286, 292, 300; and Abū'l-Hazāhiz, 208, 216, 271; and Arabian tribes, 73; and Arabness, 34, 162; caliphal, 205, 222, 225; coming of, 187, 223, 255; and conversion, 16, 22, 244; and cultural determinism, 223; and Damdamān, 233, 255, 271–72; and expansion, 60; and Fāṭima, 292; and heredity, 65; and heroic figures, 161; history of, 21, 52; Ismāʿīlī, 246; and *jāhiliyya*, 199; and *kuffār*, 166; and Maymūna, 279–80, 294, 299, 301–4, 307, 311; and Meccan pilgrimage, 168; and menstruating women, 156; and *muḥadram*, 237; and *nasab*, 12; normative, 191; and racial discrimination, 77n108; and relationality, 232; and sacred geography, 112; and sacred time, 162; and *sīras*, 200, 222, 236, 242; and *Sīrat al-Amīra Dhāt al-Himma*, 5; Sunni, 192, 224; and ʿUqba, 262; and ʿUthmān, 13; and Yemen, 255n81
Ismāʿīl (Ishmael), 47, 51, 72, 195–96

jāhiliyya, 51, 163, 166, 189, 199, 222, 224; and Islamization, 98; and menstruating women, 135–36; and *nasab*, 100; and Qurʾān, 52; and servility, 221; and *sīras*, 187; temporary, 53; and tribalism, 162; and tribal warfare, 184
Jāḥiẓ, al-, 126, 130, 208, 236, 249, 259, 261–62, 298n72, 310; and blackness, 96, 151; and creation treatise, 129; and *Fakhr al-Sūdān ʿalā-l-Biḍān* (*The Boasts of the Blacks over the Whites*), 10; and *Kitāb al-Burṣān wa-l-ʿUrjān* ("Book of the Lesioned and the Limping"), 151; and *sīras*, 11; and skin color, 131; and Zanj, 88n15, 175
Jewish apocrypha, 4
Jewish scripture, 101
Jews, 8, 24, 120, 133, 133n42, 143, 156, 237–38, 254–55, 277
jinn, 50, 182, 182n56, 241, 288, 298–99

Kebrä Nägäst (*Glory of Kings*), 27
Kilāb, 1, 281; and ʿAbd al-Mālik b. Marwān, 163; and ʿAbd al-Wahhāb, 6, 18, 88, 110, 118, 214, 221, 281; and Banū Kilāb, 163, 275; and blackness, 111, 118, 169, 190; and chiefdom, 193; and Jaffāl, 173–75, 177; and Junduba,

164, 172; and Levant, 5; and Mecca, 82, 112; and Ṣaḥṣāḥ, 193; and Sallām, 168–69; and Sulaym, 5, 262; and Ṭayy, 179; and tribe members, 168, 172, 175, 179, 230; and troops' encampments, 214; and ʿUqba, 230, 275; and Zaytūn, 179

King Manuel, 202, 204

King of Tars, 85, 136, 136n46

kinship, 47, 63, 73, 104–55, 119, 125–26, 162, 184–85, 193, 206, 218, 225, 284, 303; lineal, 131; milk, 125n17, 218n65, 219; pseudo-agnatic, 31; racialized, 54; and *walāʾ*, 197; womb (*raḥim*), 14, 14n28, 194–95

Kitāb al-ʿAyn, 68

Kitāb al-Burṣān wa-l-ʿUrjān, 151

Kitāb al-Ḥayawān, 74

Kitāb al-ʿIbar, 310

Kitāb al-Jughrāfiyā, 234

Kitāb al-Milal wa-l-Niḥal, 200

Kitāb al-Tanbīh wa-l-Ishrāf, 265

Kitāb al-Umm, 149

Kurds, 8

language, 9, 19, 76, 212, 230–31, 310; of affinity, 282; Arabic, 3, 6, 44n15, 48n27, 68, 152, 175, 279; and authority, 220; Dinka, 249n57; juvenilizing, 133n41; non-Arabic, 77n108; of race, 8, 308, 317–18; regional, 22; registers of, 20; of return, 238; Semitic, 70; Turkic, 88n15; Zanj, 298

law, 60, 98, 108, 118, 147, 150, 152, 157–58, 219–20, 319; and adoption, 218n65; and Blackness, 153, 155; Christian, 235; delivered, 58; and harm, 223, 292; Islamic, 87, 91, 133, 141, 143, 149n75, 153–56, 162, 218n65; Jewish, 133, 156; and legal casuistry, 92; and legal doctrines, 85, 136, 221; and legal impunity, 45n16; and legal literature, 30, 149, 154; and legal perception, 41; and legal recourse, 40; and legal reification, 14n29; and legal standing, 7, 84n5, 153, 219; and legal systems, 137, 170, 224; and legal rulings, 122; and paternity, 75; professionals, 90–91; prophetic, 110; purity, 148, 156; and religion, 138–39, 187, 293; and rights, 154; and scholars, 141

leprosy, 145, 149–55; and *baraṣ*, 151; and blackness, 147; and expulsions, 155n93; and *judhām*, 149; and menstruants, 148n73; and *tsaraʿat*, 148

Levant, 5, 26, 134, 139

Lyons, Malcolm, 8–9, 124n16, 205n42, 254n80, 260n95, 313

majāz, 19

Maʾmūn, al-, 28, 239, 245, 258

Manṣūr, al-, 288

marriage, 7, 14n29, 64, 66, 75, 112, 146, 152–54, 164, 182–83, 185, 187, 207, 258n91, 281, 285; and Black men, 197; and consummation, 178; and fatherhood, 197; and femininity, 91; and Maymūna, 289, 307; and *nasab*, 153n88; and pregnancy, 89; preservation of, 80; and sex, 91

Maymūna, 32, 275–78, 285, 289–90, 298–300, 307–11; and Abū'l-Hazāhiz, 295; and ʿAbd al-Wahhāb, 278–79, 281–82, 284, 286–88, 293–94, 296, 301–6, 317; and betrothal, 266; and Damdamān, 245, 248, 254, 275; and Fāṭima, 291–92, 297; and Ghāsiq, 283–84; and Islam, 271, 280; and race, 270

Maẓlūm, 5, 89

menses, 46, 82, 106, 108, 127, 133n42, 140–45, 147–48, 148n71, 150, 157n95

menstrual sex, 141, 144, 147–50, 155–57; and ʿAbd al-Wahhāb, 83, 145; and Muslim ideology, 111, 119, 140; and paternity, 112; and pregnancy, 133n42, 142–43; and punishment (*ʿuqūba*), 137

menstruants, 107, 133, 139, 143, 156; children of, 113–14; and impurity, 134–37, 147; and myths, 138

menstruation, 46, 85, 151, 157n95; and ʿAbd al-Wahhāb, 86, 106; and blackness, 145; and blood, 108–9, 114, 118, 126–28, 134–35, 140–41, 147–49; and discharge, 118, 128–29,

menstruation (*continued*)
133; and Fāṭima, 86n10, 92, 105, 108; and al-Ḥārith, 112; and impurity, 149; and Jaʿfar, 105–7; and Jewish laws, 143; and pain, 83, 109; and purity, 133–36; and racial difference, 145
Middle East and North Africa, 249, 320; and Black heritage, 200; and blackness, 18; and natural slavery, 121; and *sīras*, 314; and *Sīrat Dhāt al-Himma*, 139; and written traditions, 119
military slaves, 5, 295
modernity, 19, 125, 180, 335; and Anglophone Europeans, 4; and Arabic-speaking states, 18n42; and capitalism, 165; and genre, 20; and race, 19, 111, 120, 123n13, 157; and science, 111n65, 313; and sexuality, 43; and *sīras*, 23; and slavery, 170; and subjectivity, 274; and translation, 26; and the West, 32
mothers, 32, 67–68, 98–99, 107, 137, 168, 289; and ʿAbd al-Wahhāb, 82–83, 90, 111, 118, 156, 213, 285, 288, 317; and Abū Zayd al-Hilālī, 64, 66, 71, 75, 102; Abyssinian, 6, 39–40, 82, 236; and adultery, 18, 40; and ʿAntara b. Shaddād, 28, 45n17, 53–54, 57–61, 96, 292; and Baḥrūn, 298–300, 302, 304; Black, 28; and blackness, 113; and blood, 109, 128, 130; concubine, 14; enslaved, 24n58, 87; and Fāṭima, 5, 81, 84, 89, 94, 96–97, 103, 259, 285; and Hagar, 195; and Ibrāhīm, 48; and Jamra, 181; and Khaḍrāʾ, 64, 102; and kinship, 131; and lineage, 146; and Maymūna, 299; and menstruation, 86, 118, 140–41, 147, 157n95; and Nūrā, 32; and Shaddād, 62; and *sharīf*, 64; and Shaybūb, 59–60; and *sīras*, 113; and *ummahāt al-awlād*, 87; and *waḥsha*, 131; and Zabība, 45, 54, 59, 71, 292
Muḍar, 26, 240
Muslims, 120, 166–67, 203n37, 205, 210, 222, 225, 237, 243, 317–20; and ʿAbd al-Wahhāb, 191, 208, 275, 285; and Abyssinians, 12, 31; African, 72, 308; and antiblackness, 33; and apocrypha, 4; Arab, 4, 6, 33–34, 51, 60, 108, 110, 118, 123, 151, 154, 156, 158, 195, 223–24, 233, 236, 269–73, 281, 295–96, 314; and Arabic speakers, 15, 30; and armies, 3, 189, 235, 242, 163; Black, 72, 158, 186, 190; and blackness, 9, 147, 165; and Byzantines, 32, 245, 307; and Christians, 51, 244; and community, 32, 73, 85, 88, 125, 162, 197, 216, 218–19, 221, 223–24, 268, 301; and converts, 204, 207, 230; and culture, 88n16, 232; and Damdamān, 248, 253–56; and East Africa, 245; and elites, 35, 110; and expansion, 60; and geographers, 238, 163, 267; and *ghusl*, 133; and households, 202n34; and identity, 195, 221; and Jews, 143; and Kharijism, 191, 200; and kinship, 31; and martyrdom, 19; and Maymūna, 32, 276–77, 288, 293, 302; and medieval era, 4n6, 7, 16, 86, 119, 140n55; and menstrual sex, 111; and menstruation, 133, 143; and merchants; 255; and Muslimness, 18, 192, 280, 308, 316, 321; and Nūrā, 32; and philosophers, 74, 80; and physicians, 126; and piety, 187, 297; and polymaths, 306; premodern, 79; proto-, 161, 189, 234; and sages, 143, 150; and *sīras*, 11; and slave populations, 155; and social inequality, 194; and trade, 231, 266; and traditions, 137, 209, 220, 239, 299; and *umma* (world community), 7, 183, 218, 221, 292, 311, 313; and warriors, 82, 294; and West Africa, 309; and wetnurses, 130
Mustanṣir, al-, 28
Muʿtasim, al-, 295–97, 300

narrative time, 162, 220
nasab (lineage), 3–4, 9–11, 44, 74, 119, 162, 183, 185, 197, 199, 223, 236, 259, 286, 291; and ʿAbd al-Wahhāb, 113, 118, 212, 278, 281, 305; and Abū Bakra, 146; and adultery, 59, 179; Arab, 14, 45, 51, 158, 190, 195–96, 247n47; and Arabic literature, 11; and Arabness, 82, 280; and Baḥrūn, 299; bonds of, 194; and

curses, 179; elite, 113, 164; global, 13; and Hājar, 51; and *ḥasab*, 12, 77, 79, 184, 187, 212, 299; heroic, 172, 189; honorable, 18, 279; and identity, 192, 284; importance of, 153, 271; inborn, 22; interpretation of, 13–14; and Islam, 12; and kinship, 193–94; and Maymūna, 292, 305, 317; meritorious, 299; prophetic, 45n16, 80, 107, 216; royal, 59, 305; and Salmā, 186–87; sciences of, 14n30, 198; and scripture, 83; and *sīras*, 11; and Ṭayy, 186; as tool, 195–96; tribal, 195; and Usāma, 100; webs of, 280; workings of, 87; and Zabība, 59–60
nezhād, 10
non-Arabian parentage, 13, 87
Nūḥ (Noah), 2–4, 13, 52, 131–32, 137

Pan-Africanism, 315, 317
popular culture, 123, 320
popular epics, 20–23, 25–26, 32, 34–35, 41, 44–46, 57, 66n70, 78–79, 104, 145, 165, 229, 254, 310, 321; and ʿAbd al-Wahhāb, 213; and Abū'l-Hazāhiz, 192; and didacticism, 157; and enslaved characters, 123n14, 155; and fatalism, 183; and genres, 115, 150; and *ḥadīths*, 131, 149; and *isrāʾīliyyāt*, 131; and *jinn*, 241; and perfidy, 223; premodern, 313; and race, 251; and racial uplift ideology, 222; and reproductive anxiety, 185; and *tafsīr*, 131; and time, 161, 184
popular heroes, 42, 47–48, 213
popular opinion, 18, 80, 136, 143
popular science, 30, 118, 124, 155
premodernity, 8–9, 16, 33–34, 96n31, 123–24, 126, 273, 315, 320; and Arab-Islamic tradition, 42; and Arabic literature, 35, 111, 169, 313; and critical race studies, 86; and folk heritage, 25; and heroic literatures, 85; and Islamic communities, 210; and Islamicate knowledges, 111n65; and legal rulings, 122; and Muslim discourses, 79; and race, 32, 120, 122; and West, 19
Prophet Muḥammad, 54, 92, 133, 136, 181, 204, 209, 239, 300–301; and ʿAbd al-Wahhāb, 99–100, 138, 212, 216, 244, 303–4; and Abū Zayd al-Hilālī, 64; and Abyssinians, 236–37; and *ahl al-bayt* (family), 48, 72, 105; arrival of, 162; biography of, 20; and Black people, 72; companions of, 99, 190, 195; and Fāṭima, 86n10, 87; and *fiṭra*, 237; grave of, 189; and *ḥadīths*, 146, 195; and Jaffāl, 177; and Jaʿfar, 107, 109–10; and Jesus, 52; and kinship, 73, 105; and leprosy, 154; and lineage, 80, 241; and Medina, 112; and *ḥasab*, 194; and Maymūna, 305; and Mecca, 237; and *muḥadram*, 237; and *muhājirūn*, 236–37; and Negus, 244; and physiognomists, 99–100; and poetry, 211; and Quraysh, 73; and sexual intercourse, 142; and *shahada*, 205; and *sharīfa*, 41; and *shurafāʾ*, 22, 72; and skin color, 69; and son-in-law (ʿAlī), 105; and wife (ʿĀʾisha), 106

qāḍī (Muslim judge), 5, 90, 149, 229, 296
Qurʾān, 18, 20n47, 48, 52, 57, 76, 77n108, 83, 93, 155, 219, 237, 262, 279, 294; and al-Khiḍr, 162n1; and Day of Judgment, 194; and *ḥadīths*, 222; and hell, 180, 305; and humoral pathology, 127; and Jesus, 242; and Moses, 131; and prophets' lives, 131; and tutelage, 94

race, 10–12, 18, 31, 43, 113, 119, 275, 313–14, 319; and ʿAbd al-Wahhāb, 117, 270; Arab, 315; and Arab-Muslim world, 34; and Arabness, 321; and Arabic-speaking world, 33; and backlash, 50; and blackness, 15, 89n16, 121, 189, 200, 278, 319; and blood, 157; concepts of, 43, 120, 274; constructions of, 111, 120, 310, 315; and critical race studies, 86, 122, 320; critical theories of, 35; defining, 85; etiology of, 132n36; European genealogy of, 84; ideas of, 14n28; and Islam, 316; and Islamic world, 75; and kinship, 14n28; language of, 8, 317–18; markers, 121; mixed, 8; and modernity, 19; and *nasab*, 14; naturalizing of, 110;

race (*continued*)
and Nimrūd, 50; and periodicity, 165; politics of, 123; and power relations, 222; and prejudices, 77n108; and premodernity, 32; production of, 268; queer genealogy of, 54, 158; and race-making, 9, 30, 32, 121, 123n13; and race-qua-bloodline, 126; and racialization, 7–12, 15, 18n42, 25, 30, 34–35, 41, 43, 65, 78, 85, 107n58, 118, 120–23, 139, 152, 162, 185, 187, 191–92, 210, 274, 293–94, 307–10, 313–20; and racialized alterity, 65; and racialized anxiety, 63; and racialized associations, 110; and racialized categories, 12, 34, 86, 88, 121, 131, 197, 209; and racialized commonality, 218; and racialized difference, 7, 34–36, 43, 80, 83, 109, 111, 115, 119, 124, 130, 145, 157; and racialized differentiation, 41; and racialized discrimination, 80; and racialized divides, 18n42; and racialized enclavism, 221; and racialized heroes, 30; and racialized hierarchies, 51; and racialized identity, 120, 186, 284; and racialized intertextualities, 251; and racialized invectives, 111; and racialized kinship, 54; and racialized others, 52; and racialized precarity, 84; and racialized prejudice, 112; and racialized slavery, 59, 318; and racialized status, 82, 270; and racialized symbolism, 234; and racialized violence, 96, 123; and Shamṭā, 3n4; and *sirā*, 166, 258; and thinking, 19; "travel," 270; and tropes, 96; use of, 9
racism, 33–35, 222, 230, 317–18
Rashīd, Harūn al-, 199, 216
religion, 77n108, 90, 138, 187, 190, 192, 201–2, 204–5, 210, 230–31, 239, 254, 256, 262, 267, 272; and ʿAbd al-Wahhāb, 109, 297, 304; and assimilation, 224; and authority, 107, 166, 220, 245; and Byzantines, 218; and Christianity, 120, 206, 269, 305; and class, 204; and community, 133, 301; and conflict, 31; and coreligionists, 277, 308, 315; and differences, 130; and Egyptians, 50; and interreligious storytelling, 156; and Maymūna, 280, 293–94, 300; and *mujāhid*, 109; and Nimrūd, 52; and obligations, 212; and politics, 20, 246; and race, 130, 313; and rationality, 157n95, 238; and religiosity, 194, 248, 308; and religious fidelity, 12; and religious knowledge, 242; and religious minorities, 84; and religious traditions, 243–44; and sexual practices, 145; and standing, 7; and Sufism, 201; and *ʿulamāʾ*, 118
Rusūm Dār al-Khilāfa (*Illustrations of the Caliphal Court*), 295

al-Ṣādiq, Jaʿfar, 82, 93, 98, 104–8, 111, 126, 128–29, 140–42, 147, 237, 288
Ṣaḥṣāḥ, 163, 167, 193
Salmā, 164, 172–74, 177–79, 181–87, 193, 201
Salmān (the Persian), 73
servants, 5, 94, 216–17, 219, 245, 262, 317
sexual deviance, 82, 84, 103
sexual intercourse, 44, 46, 59, 101, 105, 118, 132, 142–43, 152–54, 289–90; and access, 213, 223; and fluids, 128; and habits, 230; and reproductive significance, 82
sexuality, 30, 41, 43, 110, 129, 149, 156; and Blackness, 184–85; devices of, 119; and incentives, 204–5; and maturity, 134–35, 285
sexual moralism, 109
sexual practices, 145
sexual violence, 91–92, 112, 140
Shahzaman, 169, 183
Shamṭā, 1, 3–5, 7, 84, 166
sharīf (pl. *shurafāʾ*), 22, 41, 64, 66–67, 72, 76, 328
Shūmdaris, 5–6
sīra, 3n3, 20, 138n51, 142, 147, 199, 212, 238–39, 254, 261, 271, 300; and ʿAbd al-Malik, 163, 165; and ʿAbd al-Wahhāb, 82, 94, 109, 133, 139, 145, 167, 184, 206, 234, 259, 273, 278, 316; and Abū'l-Hazāhiz, 206, 223; and Abū Zayd al-Hilālī, 73; and African sovereignty, 233; and Al-Muʿtaṣim,

296; and ʿAntara ibn Shaddād, 236; and Arab identity, 46, 69, 164, 222; and authors, 156; and Bedouins, 164; and *bilād al-sūdān*, 256, 266, 269; and biological inheritance, 156; and Black difference, 268; and blackness, 104, 163, 224, 262; and Black people, 93, 182, 197–98, 221–22, 232, 279; and blood, 158; and communal norms, 143; and creativity, 119; and difference, 118–19, 268; and divinatory technique, 99; and East Africa, 234, 262, 264, 267; and erotics of sameness, 209; and etiology, 83; and frontier zones, 31; and *ḥadīths*, 99, 146; and Hadlamūs, 241, 258, 262; and Hājar, 51; and Ḥām, 172; handwritten, 23; and intergenerational chains, 193; and Islam, 112, 200, 209; and Islamic world, 177; and Jaffāl, 173, 177; and *jāhilī*, 166; and Khaḍrāʾ, 75; and Khārijī messiah, 200; and Maslama, 163; and Maymūna, 276, 281, 309; and menstruation, 106, 141, 157; and Muslim armies, 235; narrator of, 97; and nonhereditary change, 83; and oral versions, 75, 119; and racialized difference, 83, 258, 308; and scientific accuracy, 231; and periodization, 114; print, 24; and *ṣafāʾ*, 144; and Salmā, 183; and Sayfuwa, 28; and slavery, 185–86; and textual versions, 75, 119; and theology, 143; and time, 167; tradition, 65–66, 77, 112–13, 223, 236, 247, 250, 253, 267, 285, 314, 320; versions of, 72; and wayward sex, 83; and *wiʾām*, 208; and women, 32, 207. *See also* popular epics
sīra al-nabawiyya, al-, 20
sīra sha ʿbiyya (pl. *siyar sha ʿbiyya*), 20. *See also* popular epics
Sīrat al-Amīra Dhāt al-Himma (*Tale of the Princess, Possessor of Ambition*), 1, 3, 23–24, 86, 97n34, 114, 138n51, 139, 165–66, 199, 254, 276–77, 314; and ʿAbbasid era, 184, 223; and ʿAbd al-Wahhāb, 30, 41, 81, 117–18, 128, 193, 285; and antagonists, 320; and Bedouinism, 163–64; and *bilād al-sūdān*, 269, 308; and blood, 11n21; and blue eyes, 173, 179–80; and Byzantine territories, 31; and cannibalism, 252; and characters, 124, 149, 189; and Christianity, 5, 16; and Damdamān, 266; and East Africa, 229, 232–33, 263, 270; and *fitna*, 17n39; and Islam, 5, 162–63, 194; and *jāhiliyya*, 162, 172, 184, 190; and Maymūna, 294; and narrative, 219; performances of, 25; and race, 9; and Samawʾal al-Maghribī, 22; and *Sīrat ʿAntar*, 156; and slavery, 181; and soldiers, 28; and warriors, 29
Sīrat al-Mujāhidīn (*The Tale of the Pious Warriors*), 5–6
Sīrat ʿAntar, 6, 17, 24–26, 30, 44, 49, 58, 82, 97n34, 106, 156, 179, 229, 232
Sīrat Banī Hilāl, 20n49, 25, 27, 30, 65–66, 71, 75, 138n51, 192, 229
slavery, 40, 133n41, 151, 154; afterlife of, 88n16; Arab, 318; and Blackness, 4, 75, 155, 170, 197, 220, 224; and daughters, 87; domestic, 124n14; and enslaved mothers, 87; and Ḥām, 4; and Indian Ocean, 170; Islamic, 171; and manumission, 162, 197; natural, 121; and naturalization, 253; racialized, 59, 318; and *Sīrat Dhāt al-Himma*, 24
social-as-natural kind, 10, 12, 19, 34, 319
social control, 111, 158
social death, 170–71
social harmony (*wiʾām*), 10–11, 208, 259
social inequality, 194
social institutions, 31
social kinds, 9, 30, 42n8, 72, 101, 115, 118, 120, 123, 157, 162, 208
social life, 43, 152, 166, 273
social order, 124, 190, 245, 292–93, 307
social organization, 48, 238
social standing, 11, 192, 212–13, 289
social station, 51, 153n88, 221
South Arabia, 73
Sudan, 65, 69, 233, 246n47, 249, 251, 277, 318

sūdān, al- ("Blacks"), 15, 88n15, 192, 203, 211, 258, 265, 267
sūdān al-anjāb, al-, 6
Sulaym, 5, 262

tafsīr, 107, 131, 240
talismans, 298–99, 309
Tanwīr al-Ghabash fī Faḍl al-Sūdān wa-l-Ḥabash (Illuminating the Darkness: On the Virtues of the Blacks and Abyssinians), 12
Taʾrīkh al-Rusul wa-l-Mulūk (History of Prophets and Kings), 135
1001 Nights, 23, 65, 139, 169, 182, 209, 254, 260
traditions, 13, 34–35, 72, 97, 111, 123, 132, 139, 149, 157, 192–96; and *ʿajab*, 43; and *akhbār*, 136; Arab-Islamic, 42, 48, 83, 137, 166, 208–9, 214, 239, 306, 318; Christian, 245; epic, 20, 28, 30, 48, 138, 155–56, 189, 199; esoteric, 99, 311; ethical, 79; European, 101n45; and genealogical literature, 14n30; and *ḥadīths*, 157, 195; Islamic Neoplatonic, 63; mapping, 31; literary, 70; and *mirabilia*, 264; oral, 20, 119; performance, 25; poetic, 96; recitational, 27; religious, 243; scriptural, 41; *sīra*, 65–66, 77, 106, 108, 112–13, 197, 223, 231, 236, 247, 250–53, 267, 279, 285, 314, 320; and *siyar*, 93; Sufi, 49n30; textual, 14, 20, 119; and *ʿudhrī* (star-crossed romance), 55–56
triumphalist narratives, 253, 271
Turks, 8, 235, 295–96

udabāʾ, 118, 157, 259
ʿulamāʾ, 91, 118, 150, 157
ʿUqba, 239–40, 262, 275, 277, 281, 286–87, 296, 300–301, 310, 316; and ʿAbd al-Wahhāb, 90, 239; and Damdamān, 245–46; and Fāṭima Dhāt al-Himma, 242–43; and Hadlamūs, 241–42, 244, 258; and al-Ḥārith, 91, 111, 229–30; and Shūmdaris, 5–6; and *sīras*, 241

West Africa, 120–21, 235, 258n91, 263, 309
white, 69, 76–77, 93, 97, 103–4, 124, 274, 291, 315–16; and *abyaḍ*, 40, 68; and *abyaḍ naqī*, 98; and Abū'l-Hazāhiz, 220; and Abū Zayd al-Hilālī, 73, 71; and Arabs, 28, 39, 84, 118; and *bayḍāʾ*, 45; and Black children, 43, 102; and blackness, 55, 69, 96, 258, 306; and Black people, 45n18, 61, 217, 222; and children, 102; and ethnonationalism, 122; and Fāṭima, 84; and God, 126, 140–42; and Hadlamūs, 258; identity, 118; and leprosy (*majdhūm*), 147; and moralism, 19; and Muslims, 19, 28; and paternity, 133n42, 142–46; race, 6, 105–6, 121; and *sīras*, 11; and slaves, 57, 318; temporality, 167; and the West, 33; women, 85n6, 224
whiteness, 17, 57; and Arab characters, 45–46; and Arabness, 69; and blackness, 58, 104, 170, 296; and Christians, 167; and Christian spaces, 17; and enslaved people, 124; and al-Ḥārith, 103; imposition of, 274; and lightness, 41, 173; and Maymūna, 306–7; and Muslim spaces, 17; paradigms of, 320; premodern, 19; and race, 18; reading, 7; and Salmā, 178
white supremacy, 29
women, 1–3, 64, 89, 108, 169, 177, 223, 304; and ʿAbd al-Wahhāb, 90, 266, 286; Abyssinian, 75, 290, 175; Arab, 5, 45n17, 177, 185, 223; and Aristotle, 73, 109, 126; Black, 40, 58, 102, 133n42, 203n37, 275–76, 285, 287, 289–90, 293, 298, 310; and breast milk, 130; and breasts, 286; Byzantine, 17, 202n34, 205, 207, 258, 262, 290, 307; and childbirth, 129; and East Africa, 107; Egyptian, 131, 195; elite, 87; enslaved, 47, 51, 57–59, 63, 85, 112, 132, 195, 202n34, 289–90, 293; and Fāṭima, 82, 93–95; freeborn, 259; and *ghayra*, 305n93; and *ḥurma*, 213; and Islam, 275, 293n58; and *jāhiliyya*, 136; and *jāhilī*, 138; Jewish, 133; and Khaḍrāʾ,

64; and leprosy, 152, 152n85; light-skinned, 207, 213; marginalized, 87; and marriage, 153; and Maymūna, 32, 276; and men, 168; and menstruation, 83, 105–9, 126, 134–36, 142, 144, 148–49, 148n71, 156, 157n95; and miscarriages, 147; and *muqrif*, 87; non-Arab, 285; and North Africa, 107; Persian, 290; and postnatal care, 67; and racial thinking, 84; and rationality, 157n95; and rights, 85; and seminal fluid, 127; and sex, 142, 149, 152; sexually mature, 134–35, 285; and *sīras*, 79; and *tabarruj* (promenade), 52; and the *1001 Nights*, 182; and wealth, 207; white, 224; Zanj, 199, 290

world, 79–80, 168, 180, 197, 239, 310; and Arabness, 82; Arabic-speaking, 33–34, 74, 151, 156, 224, 269, 315; Atlantic, 170; and Black Africans, 260, 262; building, 114, 169, 317; colored, 29; diverse, 194; inner, 56, 231, 303; Islamic, 75, 124, 177, 214, 234, 269; libidinal, 110; literary, 24, 74; and *mahhad al-arḍ*, 53; and *majāz*, 20; mapping of, 13; and Maymūna, 307–8; medieval Islamic, 41; Muslim, 7, 16, 34, 151, 155, 218, 224, 245, 269, 313–14; natural, 46, 268; New, 176; order, 184; and plurality, 88; social, 166; and social models, 213; and social value, 196; within texts, 32, 44, 58, 77, 85, 162, 185–86, 191, 193, 201, 222, 234, 270, 284

Yāfit (Japheth), 4, 13, 53, 59

Yemen, 50, 206, 233, 245, 255, 265, 279–81, 309, 317; and Abyssinia, 229; and ʿAntara b. Shaddād, 6; and Jewish communities, 255n81; and Sayf b. Dhī Yazan, 23, 195; and *Sīrat Sayf b. Dhī Yazan*, 229; and Yemenis, 73

Zaydān, Jurjī, 180

Zuhayr, 62–63, 80

Zuṭṭ, 16, 198